P9-CSA-129

SPEECH

Communication Matters

Second Edition

SPEECH

Communication Matters

Second Edition

Randall McCutcheon

James Schaffer

Joseph R. Wycoff

National Textbook Company
a division of NTC/Contemporary Publishing Group
Lincolnwood, Illinois USA

Cover Photos: AP Wide World Photos, PhotoDisc

Intext photo credits following index.

ISBN 0-658-01335-1

Published by National Textbook Company, a division of NTC/Contemporary Publishing Group, Inc.
4255 West Touhy Avenue, Lincolnwood (Chicago), Illinois 60646-1975 U.S.A.

4 5 6 7 8 9 10 11 12 (058 / 055) 09 08 07 06 05 04 03

Contents in Brief

Table of Contents

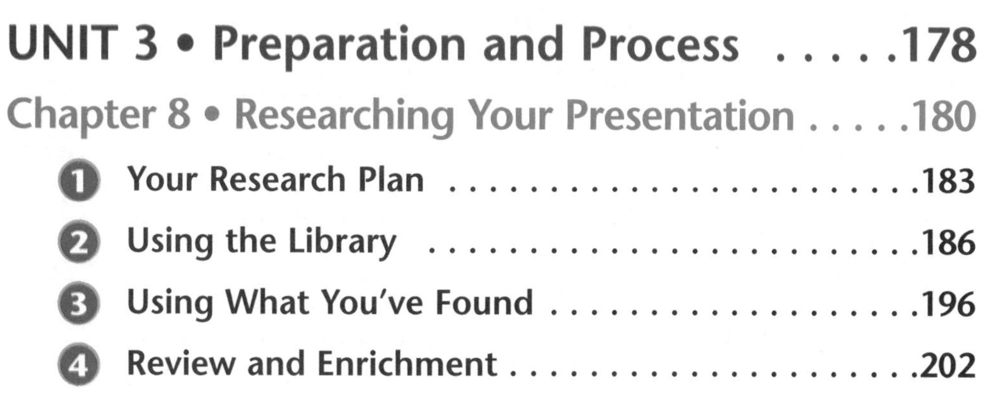

Table of Contents

Table of Contents

COMMUNICATION Breakdown

COMMUNICATION Breakdown

COMMUNICATION Breakthrough

COMMUNICATION Breakthrough

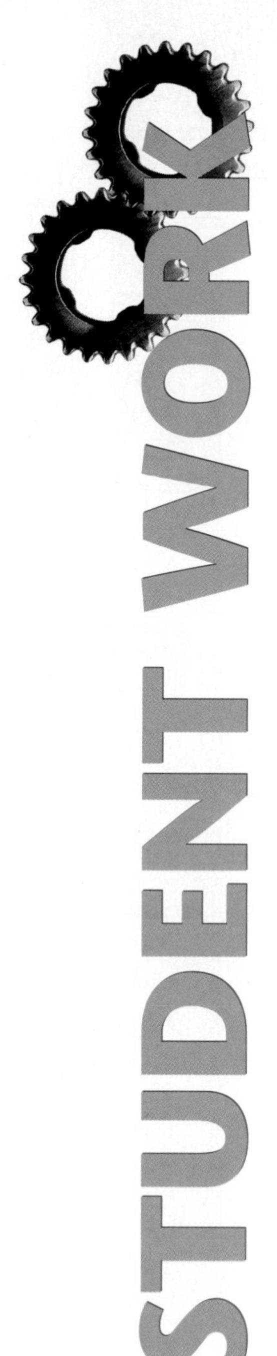

STUDENT WORK

WORDS FROM THE WORKPLACE

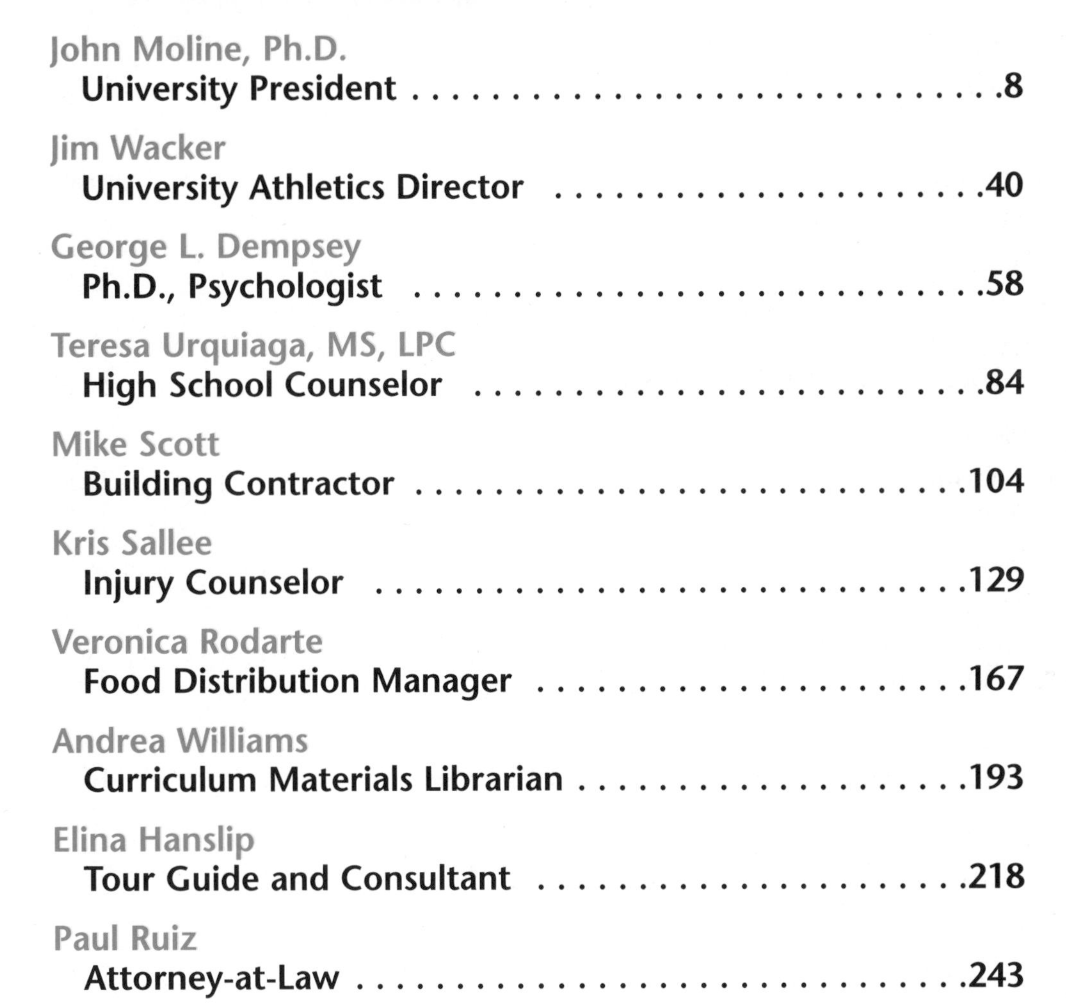

Special Features

WORDS FROM THE WORKPLACE

WORDS FROM THE WORKPLACE

INSTANT IMPACT

INSTANT IMPACT

INSTANT IMPACT

INSTANT IMPACT

Dedications and Acknowledgements

Dedications

to my grandmother
—Randall McCutcheon

to Mary Lynn for her unwavering love and support, and to Suzanne, Sarah, and Stephen, who make it all worthwhile.
—James Schaffer

to Babe and Ralph; Jeff, Jon, and Joe; Erin, Erica, and Asher; and Pam: Words have the power to show love, admiration, and appreciation—and so I've written these for you. And to teachers everywhere: Keep in mind that for at least one child in your classroom—*you're* the reason that he or she gets out of bed every morning. . . and comes to school!
—Joseph R. Wycoff

Acknowledgements

Randall McCutcheon would like to thank the following individuals for their assistance: Jane Durso—my assistant—for her immeasurable contributions to my creativity and correctness; Tim Averill, Art Chu, Katie Johnson, Sally McAfee—for their invaluable input on chapter rough drafts; David Abaire, Kim Atura, Maryagnes Barbieri, Brittany Bentz, Robert Bovinette, Sarah Bynum, Emily Clauss, Tessamarie Crump, Preston Dell, Shaun Gallegos, Austan Goolsbee, Miranda Gray, Sue Ann Gunn, Andy Howe, Taja Jewel, Alisa Lasater, Bryan Leblanc, Tessa Lecuyer, James Mallios, Jeremy Mallory, Chris Marianetti, Diana Marianetti, Sharahn McClung, Dr. Michael McElroy, Melanie Morgan, Holly Mounce, Bruce Musgrave, Lanny Naegelin, John Nielsen, Carleyna Nunes, Michael Overton, Carolyn Peltier, Flora Soto-Endicott, Nancy Van Devender, Rani Waterman, Mathilde Walker, Colleen Youngdahl—for their assistance and generosity.

James Schaffer wishes to gratefully acknowledge the generous contributions of Mary Lynn Schaffer, who edited the seemingly endless rough drafts; Rachel Pokora, Jane Holt, Jon Erricson, and Dutch Fichthorn for their technical expertise.

Joseph Wycoff would like to thank the following people for their assistance: his wife, Pamela Campbell Cady Wycoff; the student speakers from Apple Valley High School (Minnesota) and Chesterton High School (Indiana) for their example speeches; the Apple Valley library staff; and the National Forensic League (Ripon, Wisconsin).

About the Authors

Randall McCutcheon, Director of Forensics, Albuquerque Academy, Albuquerque, New Mexico, has over twenty-five years of experience teaching speech. He has authored three other books: *Journalism Matters*, an introductory high school journalism textbook; *Can You Find It?*, a guide to teaching research skills to high school students (it received the Ben Franklin Award for best self-help book of the year in 1990); and *Get Off My Brain*, a survival guide for students who hate to study (it was selected by the New York Public Library as one of 1998's Best Books for Teenagers).

Nationally recognized by the U.S. Department of Education for innovation in curriculum, Mr. McCutcheon was selected Nebraska Teacher of the Year, 1979, and the National Forensic League's Coach of the Year, 1987. He holds membership in the Speech Communication Association, the National Forensic League, and the Catholic Forensic League. He completed his undergraduate work at the University of Nebraska with emphasis in speech and theater. His graduate level work was in the study of rhetoric, persuasion, and interpersonal communication. After nearly a decade of working in radio and television, he has taught in public and private schools in Nebraska, Iowa, Massachusetts, and New Mexico, and coached his speech teams to twenty-three state and five national championships (NFL and CFL).

James Schaffer, an associate professor and publications advisor at Nebraska Wesleyan University, earned a Ph.D. in English from the University of Virginia.

A strong interest in the space program led Schaffer to apply for the Teacher in Space contest. He became a national semi-finalist and was named State Aerospace Educator of the Year. He also won a Christa McAuliffe Fellowship from the U.S. Department of Education that enabled him to give over 400 programs on space travel to school and community groups.

As a high school teacher for 15 years at Lincoln East High School, he advised award-winning publications, including a newspaper, magazine, and yearbook. He and his wife Mary Lynn, also an educator, have three children—Suzanne, Sarah, and Stephen—who all love to speak.

Joseph R. Wycoff teaches English/Language Arts at Apple Valley High School in Apple Valley, Minnesota, where he is actively involved with the Speech and Debate Program. Before moving to Minnesota, Mr. Wycoff taught at Chesterton High School (Indiana) for thirty-one years. At Chesterton, he taught English and was the Coach/Director of Speech and Debate for twenty years. During that time, his teams won fifteen Indiana State Speech championships and three consecutive National Forensic League titles (1989, 1990, and 1991). He is a member of the Indiana Coaching Hall of Fame, and in 1992 he was inducted into the National Forensic League National Hall of Fame—the youngest member ever so honored. As an educator and as a coach, he has won numerous awards. In teaching, he has been named Teacher of the Year by his students, Professional of the Year by the faculty, and Educator of the Year by the administration. He was an Indiana Teacher of the Year finalist, and in 1989 he received a Creative Endowment Grant from the Eli Lilly Grant Foundation. He received his Masters of Arts from Valparaiso University (Indiana).

Mr. Wycoff has traveled to over thirty-five states, giving over one hundred instructional/motivational seminars to both students and adults on "burnout," leadership, ethics in competition, and effective communication; and has taught summer speech sessions at Bradley University (Illinois), Longwood College (Virginia), and the University of Iowa. Mr. Wycoff has three adult sons—Jeff, Jon, and Joe. His wife, Pam Campbell Cady Wycoff, is the current Director of Speech and Debate at Apple Valley High School.

Speech: Communication Matters, Second Edition, is an introductory speech communication textbook. As with the first edition, it focuses on the theme of ethics and responsibility as the basis for all effective oral communication. The first two chapters—*Building Responsibility* and *Building Confidence*—expand on the themes expressed in the first edition, showing students that the foundation of all successful communication consists of working to be a good person, communicating constructively, and caring about your audience. These key ideas are at the core of successful communication and are reinforced throughout the text.

Quintilian, the Roman rhetoric teacher speaking centuries ago, argued, "The perfect orator is a good man speaking well." Although Quintilian would have said a "good person" today, the truth in his observation is inescapable. It is not the gift of gab, carefully rehearsed gestures, emotional appeals, nor a booming voice that get you to the top. Instead, the winning combination in basic communication is a positive, honest message; hard work; and caring for your audience—in short, being a good person speaking well.

A speaker, a communicator, should be ethical. The authors of *Speech: Communication Matters* recognize that it is not enough to bemoan the fact that we are failing to sufficiently discuss ethics and social responsibility in our teaching of communication skills. We must teach these ideals. Therefore, this textbook focuses on developing in each student what Aristotle described as good character, intelligence, and good will.

Your students will find *Speech: Communication Matters, Second Edition* interesting to read. The authors, being high school teachers and speech coaches themselves, know the importance of getting and holding the attention of teens. The authors have also added numerous cartoons and quotes for humor and meaning, and written the text in a personal, friendly style that students will find engaging. If high school students can enjoy reading any textbook, *Speech: Communications Matters* is that text. It is a "doing" text, with countless suggestions for activities that reinforce the content. Every chapter is divided into several sections, each of which concludes with a review consisting of *Recalling the Facts, Thinking Critically,* and *Taking Charge* activities.

Each chapter begins with a carefully chosen quotation appropriate to its subject followed by succinctly stated *Learning Objectives,* the *Chapter Outline, New Speech Terms,* and *General Vocabulary Terms.* The *Looking Ahead* section at the start of each chapter is designed to pique student interest in the chapter subject matter.

Other chapter features include:

- *Communication Breakthroughs* and *Communication Breakdowns*—stories providing meaningful examples for students to analyze, including discussion questions.

- *Instant Impacts*—smaller, boxed, features containing quotes, anecdotes, and other bits of information that students will find entertaining and informative.
- *Words from the Workplace*—interviews spotlighting real people who use communication in their occupations.
- *Student Works*—speeches, most of which are competition winners, providing both inspiration and models for discussion.

Concluding each chapter is the *Chapter Review and Enrichment* crafted to not only test the students' grasp of, but also reinforce their use of, the materials presented in the chapter. *Suggested Speech Topics* at the end of the review provide another springboard for implementing skills learned.

Speech: Communication Matters, Second Edition will teach your students the value of proper speech. One things it is not, however, is a heavy-going communications theory text. Rather, it is informative, involving, and invigorating.

Reviewers

The authors would like to thank the following high school teachers for their comments and suggestions during the development of the text.

Joni Anker
Eagan High School
Eagan, Minnesota

Antonette Aragon
Thompson Valley High School
Loveland, Colorado

Cindy Bomboske
Monacan High School
Richmond, Virginia

Barbara J. Evans
Mayo High School
Rochester, Minnesota

Kim Falco
Franklin High School
El Paso, Texas

Karen S. Finch
Blacksburg High School
Blacksburg, Virginia

Tommy Lindsay, Jr.
James Logan High School
Union City, California

Lou Ann Mahlandt
Lafayette High School
St. Joseph, Missouri

Connie McKee
Amarillo High School
Amarillo, Texas

Debbie Nicholas
Woodrow Wilson High School
Dallas, Texas

Jane Saunders
Travis High School
Austin, Texas

Patricia Smith
Connally High School
Austin, Texas

Michael Tile
John F. Kennedy High School
Silver Spring, Maryland

Bryan Waltz
North High School
Evansville, Indiana

John Weddendorf
Westland High School
Galloway, Ohio

The Person

UNIT CONTENTS

CHAPTER 1

BUILDING RESPONSIBILITY

"Few things can help an individual more than to place responsibility on him, and to let him know that you trust him."

—Booker T. Washington

Learning Objectives

After completing this chapter, you will be able to do the following.

- Identify and analyze the ethical and social responsibilities of communicators.
- Identify the components of the communication process and their functions.
- Explain the importance of effective communication skills in personal, professional, and social contexts.
- Recognize your audience as an important element in building responsible communication skills.
- Realize the importance and impact of both verbal and nonverbal communication.

Chapter Outline

Following are the main sections in this chapter.

1. What Is Communication?
2. Laying the Proper Foundation
3. Building the Proper Motivation

New Speech Terms

In this chapter, you will learn the meanings of the speech terms listed below.

ethics
communication
sender
message
receiver
feedback
communication barrier
written communication
oral (or verbal) communication
nonverbal communication
symbol
intrapersonal communication
interpersonal communication
oratory/rhetoric
orator
logical appeal
emotional appeal
ethical (personal) appeal
dialogue
motivation
stereotyping

General Vocabulary

Expanding your general vocabulary will help you become a more effective communicator. Listed below are some words appearing in this chapter that you should make part of your everyday vocabulary.

responsible
epitomize
credibility
mesmerized
flippant
reciprocal

Looking Ahead

Francis Horn, a past president of the University of Rhode Island, said, "Never before has it been so essential to learn to separate the true from the false. We have come to put great emphasis on education in science and engineering. But speech, rather than science or engineering, may actually hold the key to the future of the world."

Horn is telling us that before we turn to test tubes and computers for all of the world's solutions, we had better get in touch with each other. Very simply, we need to master the art of talk and meaningful communication. There is a world of difference between random, meaningless talk—and responsible talk.

In this chapter, you will learn what communication is and, more specifically, what speech communication is. Next, you will learn the role that responsibility plays in the communication process. Finally, you will learn that effective speech communication can be better accomplished when the building of character comes before the building of speech content and skillful delivery.

Introduction

Unit 1 of this book deals with "The Person" and Chapter 1 with "Building Responsibility." To understand how these two titles are connected, let's examine a few of the key words.

Ethics can be a dangerous word to use because it can mean different things to different people. However, few would disagree with the observation that ethics refers to a person's sense of right and wrong. If you are an ethical person, you work to do what's right. You have a sense of conscience and a personalized code of conduct that you feel is important in the building of character. An ethical judge strives to be totally impartial when hearing a case in court. An ethical police officer follows the law and values the safety of citizens. Likewise, an ethical communicator puts a high premium on using his or her words constructively and promoting what's right.

Responsibility goes hand in hand with ethics, but what does it mean to be *responsible*? Quite simply, being responsible means that you will be answerable and accountable for your actions and that you will get done what you say you will. If you are responsible, people can count on you—your word means something. Responsible citizens vote, responsible drivers wear seat belts, and responsible speakers pay attention to the words that they use and the way that they use them.

When you combine ethical with responsible, you take the first step in building successful oral communication.

Before dealing with ethics or responsibility in any more detail, though, let's examine exactly what communication means and how the speech communication process works.

One way you can be responsible is to volunteer for projects that help improve and renovate blighted areas in your city.

SECTION 1 What Is Communication?

When the author Robert Louis Stevenson said, "There can be no fairer ambition than to excel in talk," he was speaking about the art of effective oral communication. **Communication** is the process of sending and receiving messages, and it occurs whenever we express ourselves in a manner that is clearly understood.

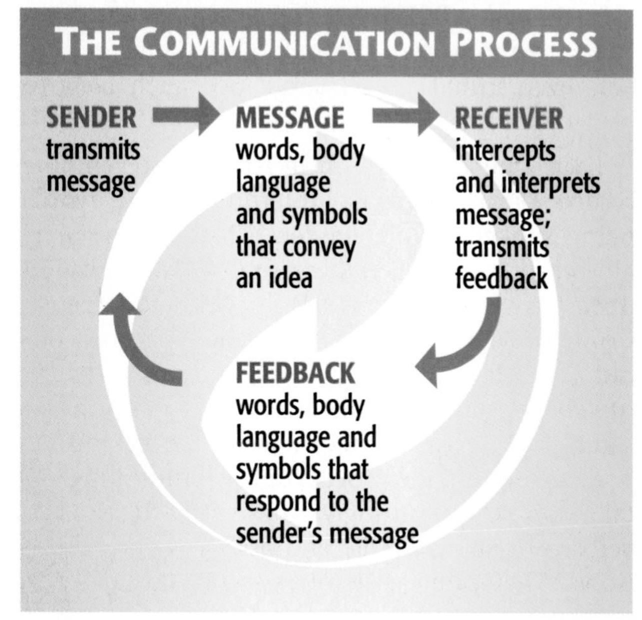

THE COMMUNICATION PROCESS
SENDER
transmits message
MESSAGE
words, body language and symbols that convey an idea
RECEIVER
intercepts and interprets message; transmits feedback
FEEDBACK
words, body language and symbols that respond to the sender's message

The Communication Process

Sam and Lynette are discussing basketball. Sam believes that David Robinson and Tim Duncan of the San Antonio Spurs are the best two players in the National Basketball Association. He points to the facts that San Antonio has won an NBA championship under the leadership of Robinson and that Duncan has been named Most Valuable Player in the playoffs. Lynette, on the other hand, favors John Stockton and Karl Malone of the Utah Jazz. She lists that team's record over the recent years and the numerous awards that both Stockton and Malone have won. Both Sam and Lynette are communicating a message, listening to what the other has to say, and then responding. Consequently, they are actively involved in the communication process, which consists of the sender, the receiver, the message, and feedback.

The **sender** is the one who transmits the **message:** that which is sent or said. The sender starts the communication process by using words. Words are the symbols you use to convey your ideas. Your words must clearly communicate to your listener the exact message you are trying to convey. The **receiver** is the person who intercepts the message and then decodes, or interprets, it. **Feedback** includes the reactions that the receiver gives to the message offered by the sender.

Every day, when you talk on the telephone, write letters or tend to your e-mail, or watch television, you are either sending messages or receiving them. Teachers communicate with students when they give clear directions for taking an exam. Students communicate when they accurately explain the assignment to a classmate who has been absent. Parents communicate when they leave specific instructions for the baby-sitter. When words are clearly put together, they build a solid communication system intended to communicate a specific message.

In a perfect world, meaningful communication would always occur. The sender would send a clear message that would be accurately picked up by the receiver—who would then provide positive feedback that the words have been understood. However, sometimes problems arise. The message is blocked by certain communication barriers. A **communication barrier** is any obstacle that gets in the way of effective communication. These obstacles might be . . .

- Attitudinal—("I really don't *like* what we're talking about here!")
- Social—("This person is *not* one of my friends!")
- Educational—("I'm far too *smart* to listen to this stuff!")
- Cultural—("This person's *heritage* isn't like mine at all!")
- Environmental—("I'm too *hot* in this room to even think!" or "There's too much *noise* to concentrate!")

Each one of these obstacles can prevent the receiver from correctly interpreting the words being spoken by the sender. What's the answer? How can we remove these oral communication obstacles? The answer is simple, yet sound: focus! Communication experts advise us to get rid of our distractions and try to find a common field of experience—or a realistic way to be "on the same page" with the person who is speaking. They tell us that the process of communicating takes work. Accordingly, they offer three verbs, or action words, as possible solutions. Their advice involves both the sender and the receiver.

To the sender:

1. THINK before you speak. ("What is the real message that I want to send?")
2. ARTICULATE your words. ("Am I enunciating each syllable, or am I slurring my words together?")
3. WATCH the receiver of your words to make sure that you are getting the correct nonverbal signals. ("She isn't responding correctly. I had better say this a different way.")

To the receiver:

1. ASK questions; make polite requests. ("Could the heat be a little lower, please? It is hampering my ability to concentrate.")
2. LEARN more about issues and people. They can both make you smarter. (Say to yourself, "I need to listen here. It's good to hear an opinion or voice other than my own.")
3. RELATE to the background and experiences of those speaking. They're saying what they're saying for a reason. It's worth your time to listen and then to try to understand their world. ("I should try to understand what they've gone through—and what message they're trying to convey to me.")

The above advice applies to both the social and the professional worlds. You shouldn't tune out possible friends, nor should you tune

Facial expressions and body language communicate nonverbal messages.

LUANN reprinted by permission of United Feature Syndicate, Inc.

SECTION 1 What Is Communication?

When the author Robert Louis Stevenson said, "There can be no fairer ambition than to excel in talk," he was speaking about the art of effective oral communication. **Communication** is the process of sending and receiving messages, and it occurs whenever we express ourselves in a manner that is clearly understood.

The Communication Process

Sam and Lynette are discussing basketball. Sam believes that David Robinson and Tim Duncan of the San Antonio Spurs are the best two players in the National Basketball Association. He points to the facts that San Antonio has won an NBA championship under the leadership of Robinson and that Duncan has been named Most Valuable Player in the playoffs. Lynette, on the other hand, favors John Stockton and Karl Malone of the Utah Jazz. She lists that team's record over the recent years and the numerous awards that both Stockton and Malone have won. Both Sam and Lynette are communicating a message, listening to what the other has to say, and then responding. Consequently, they are actively involved in the communication process, which consists of the sender, the receiver, the message, and feedback.

The **sender** is the one who transmits the **message:** that which is sent or said. The sender starts the communication process by using words. Words are the symbols you use to convey your ideas. Your words must clearly communicate to your listener the exact message you are trying to convey. The **receiver** is the person who intercepts the message and then decodes, or interprets, it. **Feedback** includes the reactions that the receiver gives to the message offered by the sender.

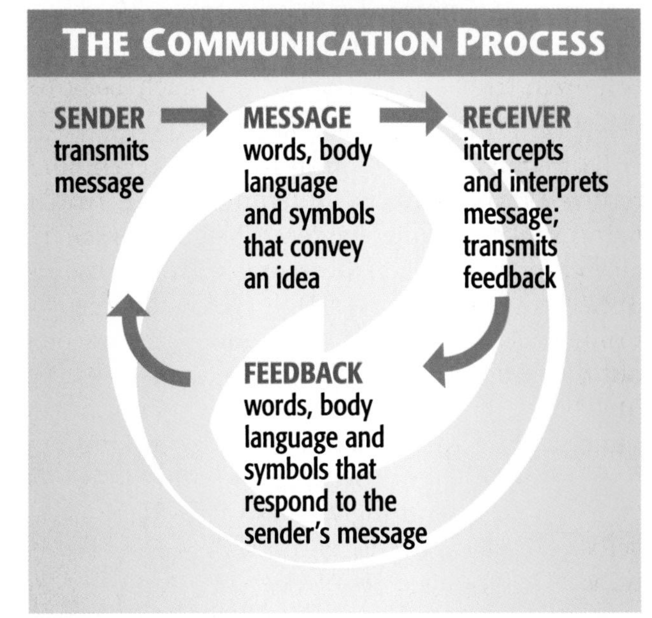
THE COMMUNICATION PROCESS
SENDER transmits message
MESSAGE words, body language and symbols that convey an idea
RECEIVER intercepts and interprets message; transmits feedback
FEEDBACK words, body language and symbols that respond to the sender's message

Every day, when you talk on the telephone, write letters or tend to your e-mail, or watch television, you are either sending messages or receiving them. Teachers communicate with students when they give clear directions for taking an exam. Students communicate when they accurately explain the assignment to a classmate who has been absent. Parents communicate when they leave specific instructions for the baby-sitter. When words are clearly put together, they build a solid communication system intended to communicate a specific message.

In a perfect world, meaningful communication would always occur. The sender would send a clear message that would be accurately picked up by the receiver—who would then provide positive feedback that the words have been understood. However, sometimes problems arise. The message is blocked by certain communication barriers. A **communication barrier** is any obstacle that gets in the way of effective communication. These obstacles might be . . .

- Attitudinal—("I really don't *like* what we're talking about here!")
- Social—("This person is *not* one of my friends!")
- Educational—("I'm far too *smart* to listen to this stuff!")
- Cultural—("This person's *heritage* isn't like mine at all!")
- Environmental—("I'm too *hot* in this room to even think!" or "There's too much *noise* to concentrate!")

Each one of these obstacles can prevent the receiver from correctly interpreting the words being spoken by the sender. What's the answer? How can we remove these oral communication obstacles? The answer is simple, yet sound: focus! Communication experts advise us to get rid of our distractions and try to find a common field of experience—or a realistic way to be "on the same page" with the person who is speaking. They tell us that the process of communicating takes work. Accordingly, they offer three verbs, or action words, as possible solutions. Their advice involves both the sender and the receiver.

To the sender:

1. THINK before you speak. ("What is the real message that I want to send?")
2. ARTICULATE your words. ("Am I enunciating each syllable, or am I slurring my words together?")
3. WATCH the receiver of your words to make sure that you are getting the correct nonverbal signals. ("She isn't responding correctly. I had better say this a different way.")

To the receiver:

1. ASK questions; make polite requests. ("Could the heat be a little lower, please? It is hampering my ability to concentrate.")
2. LEARN more about issues and people. They can both make you smarter. (Say to yourself, "I need to listen here. It's good to hear an opinion or voice other than my own.")
3. RELATE to the background and experiences of those speaking. They're saying what they're saying for a reason. It's worth your time to listen and then to try to understand their world. ("I should try to understand what they've gone through—and what message they're trying to convey to me.")

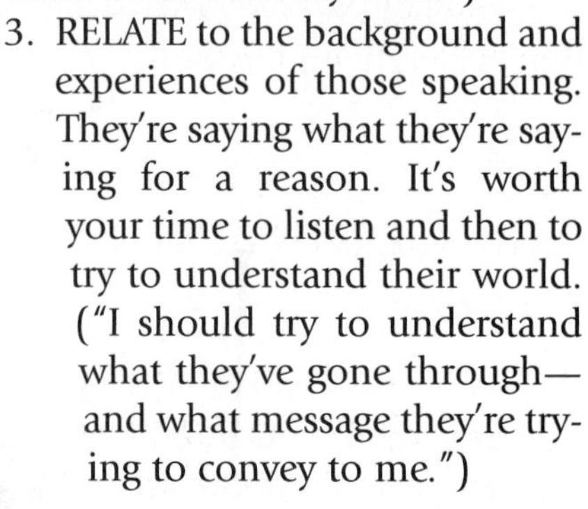

Facial expressions and body language communicate nonverbal messages.

The above advice applies to both the social and the professional worlds. You shouldn't tune out possible friends, nor should you tune

LUANN reprinted by permission of United Feature Syndicate, Inc.

The best way to converse with a person in a wheelchair is eye-to-eye.

out your boss, your colleagues at work, or customers. Apply some CPR, or Communication for Positive Results, by allowing the communication process to help you build relationships. Participate actively in the communication process.

Any communication that must be read is called **written communication**. When the communication is spoken, it's often called **oral** or **verbal communication.** Your ability to put words together effectively, either in written or verbal form, will help determine your impact as a communicator. In this book, you will be learning specifically how to become a more effective oral communicator, a more persuasive speaker.

Let's now take a look at nonverbal communication and symbols. Both are important elements in communication and are further discussed in later chapters, where they can be seen in action.

Nonverbal Communication

While the verbal message involves the actual words being spoken, the nonverbal message might be relayed through facial expressions or body movements. Thus, **nonverbal communication** expresses your attitudes or moods about a person, situation, or idea. The person who is cheerful and sitting up straight communicates through "body language" one sort of message. The person who frowns and slouches communicates another sort.

Nonverbal signals may mean different things to different people. For instance, giving someone the thumbs-up sign is a compliment in America but is considered rude and offensive in Australia. In the United States, nodding the head means "yes," but in Greece it means "no." The book *Do's and Taboos*

INSTANT IMPACT

WHEN YOU MEET SOMEONE WITH A DISABILITY

The communication process isn't just a colorful metaphor with little reference to the real world. The sender, the receiver, the message, and feedback are all vital elements for building communication bridges.

Being introduced to a person in a wheelchair or someone who's blind may catch you off guard. Some of us are unsure of how to act and are afraid of saying or doing the wrong thing. The American Association of Retired Persons (AARP) offers a few suggestions.

If the person . . .

. . . is visually impaired: Never pet or play with a guide dog; you'll distract the animal from its job.

. . . has a speech impediment: Be patient, listen attentively, and resist the temptation to finish his sentences or speak for him.

. . . is in a wheelchair: Sit down, if possible, so you chat eye to eye. Don't touch the wheelchair because it's considered within the boundaries of an individual's personal space.

. . . has a hearing loss: Always speak directly to the person, not to her interpreter or assistant. If you raise your voice, it becomes distorted and even more difficult to understand. Speak clearly and slowly, facing her. Deaf people depend on facial expressions and gestures for communication cues.

The AARP adds that you should never assume someone needs or wants help—but don't be afraid to inquire politely.

Source: *Good Housekeeping,* January 1999.

WORDS FROM THE WORKPLACE

John Moline, Ph.D.
University President

Q. *What advice can you give to students to show them the importance of communication skills in the world of work?*

A. Communication is 90% of what I do, so the skills needed to do it effectively are absolutely essential in my job as president. Both oral and written communication are essential. Communication is a two-way street. I take communication to include not just speaking and writing, but listening, reading, and reading between the lines carefully. Listening requires not jumping to conclusions or trying to think of an answer before you have heard what the other person is really trying to say.

Q. *How important are communication skills when you hire administrators or staff?*

A. Effective communication skills are usually the main difference between the people I hire and the people I don't hire. People who lack effective communication skills can't get the job done without unnecessarily offending people that they have to get along with. Effective communication skills are rooted in a person's attitude. The attitude I look for is a desire to love one's neighbor—warts and all—as oneself. An increasing number of psychologists and business writers have identified a whole array of traits that I think go with this love. They call it emotional intelligence, or EQ.

Q. *What are some suggestions for students who want to communicate wisely in the next millennium?*

A. Communication skills aren't like motor skills, the ability to ride a bicycle, for example. Effective communication turns as much on WHY you are saying or doing something as on WHAT you are saying or doing. If you make the "why" something that promotes the good of your listeners or readers, and let this show, you will be well on your way to communicating effectively. This means doing the things that feed a good attitude in yourself, and avoiding the things that damage it.

around the World goes on to add that waving the entire hand means "goodbye" in America, but in Europe, where only the fingers are used to say farewell, it means "no." The book's editor, Roger Axtell, suggests that we all need to realize the impact that nonverbal communication can have on the receiver.

Symbols

Another way people communicate is through symbols. A **symbol** is anything that stands for an idea and is used for communication. Since symbols represent something else by association, they include both nonverbal and verbal communication.

In a nonverbal manner, the "peace" sign calls for nonviolence. Tangible objects such

COMMUNICATION

Break down

What Symbols Can Say

Symbols can often communicate the same as words. Michael B. Green, a former member of the Crips, one of the nation's most notorious youth gangs, provided this street's-eye view of gangs and what sports apparel can symbolize.

"I used to wear British Knights tennis shoes. To us the BK on the side of the shoe stood for Blood Killer. I heard somebody might come out with a new shoe called Christian Knights, so the Bloods (the Crips' rival) will wear them. The CK would stand for Crip Killer. If kids had these shoes, went into the wrong neighborhood and were seen by a rival gang, they could get killed. Now I'm seeing it's stupid, but back then, I didn't care.

"The shoes, the jackets and the hats are just symbols; everybody's got a symbol. I can drive down the street and point out a gang member just by the way he or she dresses. Say we go somewhere. We see a guy in some dress slacks, a nice sweater, loafers. You couldn't convince me that he's a gang member. But then you show me a guy, say, in Levi's jeans, or, say, a Cowboy jacket or a Raider hat, or shoes, he's a gang member. You can tell, just by a dress code.

"I've been locked up 2½ years, and I've already lost five friends out on the street. The answers? Well, if the parents can't avoid being separated, they should spend time with their kids individually and teach them things. What does your daughter like? Ballet? Put her on those programs. Does your son like baseball? Spend time teaching him. The only way [the gangs] will stop is if parents take their five-, six-, seven-year-old kids under their wings.

"This environment [prison] will make you realize that you were doing wrong out there. One of my best friends in here is a Blood. I knew him on the street. Five years ago I would have killed him. It was like brainwashing. It's programmed into your brain that the Bloods are the enemy. Every time you see a red rag, you shoot."

Michael Green served a 63-month sentence in prison, beginning in 1990.

(Adapted from a *Sports Illustrated* article entitled "Senseless," by Rick Telonder.)

Questions

1. What is the real tragedy of this story?
2. How can symbols destroy the possibility of effective communication? How can they also be used for good?
3. What has Michael realized? What do his words prove?

as the flag can stand for freedom, and the bald eagle can stand for America. A letter jacket can represent your school. In the award-winning play *A Raisin in the Sun* by Lorraine Hansberry, the small plant signifies the hopes and determination of the family. Nonverbal symbols are powerful, for they speak in pictures and appeal to people's imaginations and emotions.

Words—verbal symbols—can also be powerful. Advertisers often use key words that symbolize desirable qualities, hoping that you will associate the word with their product. Words such as trust, honesty, heritage, family, and America might be spoken to arouse your sense of community. Words can even *epitomize* the spirit of an entire nation. When Martin Luther King, Jr., said, "I have a dream," his dream eloquently stood for the hope that someday all Americans would stand together with dignity.

As a sender of messages to receivers, you must pay attention to the nonverbal communication and the symbols that you use if you wish to be taken seriously as a conscientious communicator.

THE "V" SIGN IN HISTORY

In the 1940s, British Prime Minister Winston Churchill used the "V" sign to rally the British against German aggression.

In the 1960s, the "V" sign stood for peace and nonviolence.

In 1999, the "V" sign symbolized victory for Bernard Williams at the Pan American Games.

SECTION 1 REVIEW

Recalling the Facts ...

1. The four major parts of the communication process are the ____________, the __________, the __________, and ____________.
2. A responsible communicator works to eliminate communication barriers. One communication barrier is attitudinal. Name the other four, as given in your reading.
3. Another name for oral communication is ____________ communication.

Thinking Critically ...

1. Nonverbal communication often refers to the attitude you give off to others. What are five positive nonverbal characteristics? Five negative nonverbal characteristics? Write out your lists. (Example: alert eye contact versus a "Get real!" look while someone is talking.) For each of your ten total items, be ready to say what each communicates. What nonverbal characteristics might help you in school? List them.

Taking Charge ...

1. Bring in an item from home, school, the community, or work that symbolizes something special. Be prepared to share with the class what your symbol means and what it should communicate to others who see it. Could it send different messages to different people? Explain.

SECTION 2 Laying the Proper Foundation

People building a house don't begin by putting up the walls or decorating the rooms. They begin by establishing a solid foundation that will anchor the rest of the structure. Similarly, you build the ethics of communication and responsibility when you anchor your oral communication to a solid value structure. Command of language, posture, eye contact, gestures, and other speech basics are certainly important and will be covered later in the book, but the "pouring" of your "value structure foundation" must come first. It consists of three essential elements: (1) working to be a good person, (2) communicating constructively, and (3) caring about your audience. Let's look at each separately.

Like a house, your communication skills need a strong foundation.

Working to Be a Good Person

The nineteenth-century statesman and orator Daniel Webster said that if all of his talents and abilities except one were taken away, he would ask to keep his ability to speak. "With the ability to speak," he added, "I could regain all that I had lost." Here Webster is telling people of the vital role that speaking can play in their lives. However, he would also likely say that being a polished speaker isn't enough. He would promote the idea that those who speak should work to make the world a better place.

Some prominent speakers have worked to advance humankind. Some have worked to harm humankind. All of us would agree that Adolf Hitler was a powerful speaker, yet his words led to the deaths of millions of people during World War II. The minister and cult figure Jim Jones *mesmerized* his followers in Guyana, South America, in the late 1970s; hundreds died when he commanded them to commit suicide by drinking cyanide-laced Kool-Aid. Unfortunately, we don't have to look far to see what's wrong in our twenty-first-century world. The news is full of people who use their power of speech to dupe the public and take advantage of unsuspecting victims. However, the authors of this text believe that while it would be foolish to ignore people whose words have exhibited a less than desirable value structure, it would be educationally negligent not to be optimistic and promote positive examples and role models.

For instance, contrast the previous two examples with the words of the Polish freedom fighter Lech Walesa, who said to the U.S. Congress in 1989:

> The world remembers the wonderful principle of the American democracy: "government of the people, by the people, for the people." I too remember these words; I, a shipyard worker from Gdansk, who has devoted his entire life . . . to the service of this idea: "government of the people, by the people, for the people." Against privilege and monopoly, against contempt and injustice . . . I do what I must do.

Here, Walesa is telling the world that he is driven by his sense of conscience, his sense of right and wrong—and his words still ring true today.

Sometimes the most important speaking you do is the speaking you do with yourself. This ability to conduct an inner dialogue with yourself and to assess your thoughts, feelings, and reactions is known as **intrapersonal communication.** Many of our actions begin with these silent conversations. You must be honest and positive in your self-communication. Peggy Noonan, ex-presidential speechwriter and key political consultant, stated that every speaker must go through some personal "leveling," where he or she has an individual heart-to-heart talk to decide exactly what message the spoken words should convey. It is this type of personal "grounding," she adds, that makes a speaker's ideas real and believable.

For instance, when you have done something right, compliment yourself; when there is room for improvement, silently note what you can do better the next time. Negative intrapersonal communication occurs when you cloud your thoughts with self-doubt. Saying to yourself, "I can't do this. I'm too stupid!" or "I'm not popular enough for anyone to listen to me!" is counterproductive and doesn't give your talents a chance to work. Be honest but be positive and give yourself the benefit of the doubt.

Michael Jordan, the ex-basketball star, says that he loves to be a positive role model for children because "it's the right thing to do." Perhaps his belief is a result of intrapersonal communication.

INSTANT IMPACT

THE "RIGHT" STUFF

Being a responsible communicator and using your words well is certainly a goal shared by many. Country singers George Strait and Clint Black have said that their music is dedicated to their audiences. They feel that the words to their songs should be meaningful and, most of all, honest. Nationally recognized news anchor Dan Rather of CBS also wants his words to represent honesty. In an interview with *People* magazine, Rather said that even though he makes nearly $6 million a year, he would like to be remembered by the American people for performing responsible journalism and for using his words to tell the American people "the truth." He adds that working "just as a journalist" is fine with him. "Sensationalism," he adds, "is for the tabloids."

Michael Jordan provides students with a positive role model during the Principal for a Day program at a Chicago high school.

Because this type of communication affects the kind of person you are, what you communicate to yourself should exhibit a solid work ethic, a sense of integrity, compassion for others, and personal honesty. Most would agree that these are some of the qualities that make up a good person.

You should give a priority to being a good person, then; but the second element of our value structure foundation is also important.

Communicating Constructively

Besides being able to talk to yourself (intrapersonal communication), you need to be able to talk effectively to others. This form of one-on-one communication is called **interpersonal communication.** This type of communication, which is specifically discussed in Chapter 5, takes place any time messages are transmitted between two or more people. Interpersonal communication is not limited to formal speaking situations. Your conversations in the hallway with other students, after class with teachers, at the dinner table with your family, or on the job with fellow workers are all examples of interpersonal communication. You have an opportunity to build good feelings and trust between and among people. Your job in communicating in this way is to realize that the spoken word should build, inspire, and motivate others, never belittle or deceive them. Thus, when comedians use words to insult, when politicians use words to distort, when teachers use words to condemn, when businesspeople use words to justify ruining the environment, or when students spread rumors about other students, they are doing an injustice to what speech should do.

Ryan White died of AIDS at the age of 18 after spending the last years of his life speaking at schools to educate others about the disease.

Oratory, or **rhetoric,** is the art or study of public speaking. An **orator** is a person who delivers oratory and uses words effectively. The Roman teacher Quintilian called the perfect orator "a good person speaking well." The young AIDS victim Ryan White was certainly a Quintilian-type orator when he spent the final years of his life speaking at schools to educate others about facts and myths regarding

..SO WHAT WE'RE TALKING ABOUT HERE IS EMPOWERMENT THROUGH INNER DIALOGUE HOPEFULLY LEADING TO LIFE ENHANCEMENT..
SCHULZ

PEANUTS reprinted by permission of United Feature Syndicate, Inc.

SPEAKING OUT FOR HISPANICS

INSTANT IMPACT

According to the U.S. Bureau of Labor Statistics, during the next decade 58 percent of the incoming labor force will consist of minorities. With this in mind, several companies around the nation have taken a leadership role in working with many of these minorities. *Hispanic Magazine* compiled a list called the Hispanic 100 that named the top 100 companies providing job opportunities and educational training for Hispanics. Among the companies listed were Ford, General Motors, Chrysler, Hughes Aircraft, Rockwell International, Apple Computer, American Airlines, Coca-Cola, and Dow Chemical.

The companies in the Hispanic 100 contribute not only jobs and training programs, but also their voices. As their corporate officials travel around the nation (and the globe), many of them speak to audiences on the positive contributions the Hispanic community can make to the corporate world. The Hispanic 100 are not only training the workforce for the twenty-first century, they are also building the reputation and esteem of an important segment of America's population.

AIDS. Also, after his mother was diagnosed with breast cancer, Jon Wagner-Holz, 17, of California, created a national hot line for children whose parents have cancer. He wanted to use his experience both to help others and to allow other young people to have a communication outlet for their words and feelings. These examples should remind us that people have special talents that need to be voiced.

How do you use your words? You must be willing to build up others if you wish to become the effective communicator that this book promotes. This idea carries through to the third and final element that makes up the foundation of your value structure: a genuine concern for the audience.

Caring About Your Audience

The noted actor and director Sir Laurence Olivier once said that performers can bring creative life to a play only if they respect the audience enough to think that the audience will understand the play. This lesson can also be applied to speaking. The speaker must respect the members of an audience and show a genuine concern for their thoughts and feelings.

Before speaking, consider questions such as these:

- Is this material appropriate for this group?
- How would I feel if I were asked that question?
- Am I giving my audience new information?
- Is my material too difficult or too easy for my audience?

Also, pay attention to audience feedback and then adapt. You might be doing something wrong. Keep in mind that if you are *flippant* in your presentation, you might nonverbally convey the attitude that your audience isn't very important to you. Or, if you are speaking in a dull monotone, you might convey the attitude that you are bored with your audience.

As Olivier implied, the most effective communi-

Actor/director Sir Laurence Olivier drew his audiences into his performances by respecting them.

cation occurs when there is *reciprocal* respect between the performer and the audience—or the sender and the receiver.

One way that you can show audience members you care about them is by paying attention to the ideas of the Greek scientist and philosopher Aristotle. Aristotle said that there are three major methods for appealing to an audience: logical, emotional, and ethical. (These methods will also be discussed in Chapter 14, "Speeches to Persuade.")

The Greek philosopher Aristotle (right) stated three methods for appealing to audiences—logical, emotional, and personal.

- You offer a **logical appeal** when you provide your audience both with sequence and analysis in your organization and factual evidence to prove your point.
- You offer an **emotional appeal** when you "strike a chord" in your audience and appeal to their sense of patriotism, family, justice, or the like.
- You offer an **ethical** (or **personal**) **appeal** when you show your audience that you have a natural honesty about you, a strong constitution regarding right and wrong, and a no-compromise approach to values.

Remember, **dialogue,** or conversation, that doesn't begin with each person respecting the other often ends in hurt feelings and fractured communication. Taking the time to lay the proper foundation should help alleviate this problem.

SECTION 2 REVIEW

Recalling the Facts ...

1. This section talked about the value structure foundation. What are the three essential elements that make up this foundation?
2. What type of communication involves your having a conversation with yourself? What type is a "one-on-one" with someone else?
3. What is the name given to "the art or study of public speaking"?
4. Which of Artistotle's appeals draws an audience because of sound logic and reasoning?

Thinking Critically ...

1. University of Minnesota Professor James Norwood wants to teach his theater survey course by e-mail. However, university officials frown on his plans, saying that students need to be taught by a "live" instructor giving "live" instruction. What might be the harm of teaching by e-mail? What part of the communication process is lost when teaching is totally technological?
2. Audiences can often make things tough for a speaker. How is it that an audience can often make or break a person's ability to be a responsible speaker? What can you do (as the speaker) to get off to a good start with your audience?

Taking Charge ...

1. Where in school or at work can we all be better listeners and audience members? Why is this important? How can an audience make a speaker feel more at ease? Make a chart with headings for school, home, and work at the top. For each heading, list how and where you can become a better listener or audience member.
2. Tell of a time when you were in an audience that didn't listen well. Describe the results.

SECTION 3 Building the Proper Motivation

To this point, we have examined what communication is and how a solid value structure is the speaker's foundation. Now we need to take a look at what should be the driving force behind the speaker's words—the motivation.

Motivation is something, such as a need or a desire, that causes a person to act. Two internal forces should be responsible for motivating words: (1) the desire to treat both people and situations fairly and to avoid stereotyping others and (2) the desire to set a good example for others.

Stereotypes

Stereotyping means labeling every person in a group based on a preconceived idea as to what that group represents. To believe that all football players lack intelligence or that all straight-*A* students are "nerds" is unfair. Even though many people lack confidence in those responsible for leading and representing them, don't fall into the "stereotype trap" and say, for example, that all politicians or lawyers are dishonest or are only out for themselves.

When you look at the photos on this page, do you automatically fall into a "stereotype trap"?

It is possible to form very broad stereotypes—not only about people but about situations, too. For example, the ideas that all people are dishonest and that nothing is right are stereotypes. You must realize that forming an awareness of your world means seeing more than "doom and gloom." Keep in mind that every individual must be evaluated on his or her own merit and that every instance must be evaluated for its own impact.

However, because so many leaders and heroes have been disappointing and so many con artists and angle players have lied to the public, many people have become skeptical about trusting anyone. For example, look at this article from a prominent Midwestern newspaper:

> A company that said its pills could "blast away" pounds off customers without any exercise or dieting must pay more than $48 million in penalties, the Federal Trade Commission said recently. The FTC charged *Slim America* with deceptive advertising. The SuperFormula diet product was billed as the "New Triple Medical Breakthrough." It claimed that you could lose 49 pounds in just 29 days.

It is difficult to become motivated to communicate effectively when we hear how often words can work to tear down or deceive. Too often, words are empty and promises are broken. So where do you go? Where is the answer? Where is your motivation?

The answers to all of these questions can be found in you. Much of your motivation to use the spoken word correctly must come from a desire to provide solutions that will make the world a better place. You can do this by working to set a positive example for others.

COMMUNICATION **Break through**

A Worthwhile Conversation

Caleb Ray Lopes, of Rohnert Park, California, wrote the following brief essay when he was 19. Please read his story carefully. Can you see how his story is an example of effective communication leading to real understanding?

"I wish I could have talked to my teachers about what their lives are like. I went through my senior year always bad-mouthing and playing games with this one English teacher. I only thought about myself and how I felt. I knew nothing about this woman and her private life. The very last day of school, I went to ask this teacher for my final grade and she dropped everything just to talk to me for an hour and a half about our differences throughout the year and to answer some of the questions I had always had about her. I still think about this moment and wonder why she concerned herself with a student who had given her so much trouble. She taught me more in that conversation that day than I had learned all year. I wish I could have learned it before."

Excerpted from *Parade.*

Questions

1. How do you think that both Caleb and the teacher learned a valuable lesson?
2. What role did intrapersonal communication play in this story?
3. What role did interpersonal communication play in the story?
4. How might stereotypes have been a factor in the relationship between Caleb and his teacher? Please explain.

Setting an Example

Every day you may communicate with your parents, with your brothers and sisters, with the bus driver, with your friends and neighbors, with your teachers and community.

You are making an impression. You have the opportunity to prove that speaking is power and that your words can work to promote what is good in both ideas and people. Set a positive example for others to follow. Walk what you talk.

John F. Kennedy, Jr., shown with his wife Carolyn Bessette-Kennedy, communicated through speech *and* actions.

Using your "voice" is not only what you say. Your voice can also be heard by what you "build" by your actions. For example, America mourned the tragic death of John F. Kennedy, Jr., in the summer of 1999 when he was killed in a plane crash, along with his wife and her sister. Kennedy believed in the word responsibility, and he communicated this by both his speech and his actions. He used his words to initiate Reaching Up, a program designed to assist health care workers who work with the mentally handicapped. In addition, he formed the Robin Hood Foundation, which offers help to those in need living in the inner city. In the truest sense of Quintilian's quote, he was a "good person speaking well."

Recording their last studio album, the classic rock group Led Zeppelin produced the famed album *In Through the Out Door.* It had six different covers. The albums were wrapped in brown paper so that buyers wouldn't know which cover they were getting until they bought the album, took it home, and unwrapped it. For Led Zeppelin, this marketing tactic was OK.

However, as an effective oral communicator, you should do better than this. You must work to be a "known quantity," a speaker and a person worthy of respect, a role model for others to follow.

Teacher and astronaut Christa McAuliffe set a positive example for others.

The job isn't easy, but the teacher and astronaut Christa McAuliffe was such a person. Even though she died in the tragic explosion of the space shuttle *Challenger,* a poem she took with her on that final flight should serve as inspiration to everyone. It said: "Move over sun and give me some sky. / I've got some wings and I'm ready to fly. / World, / You're going to hear from me!"

Isn't it time that the rest of the world hears from you? Remember: When people believe in you, they will believe what you have to say.

SECTION 3 REVIEW

Recalling the Facts ...

1. What is the word that means "the desire that causes a person to act"?
2. When you label people without first getting to know them, you are unfairly __________ing them.
3. In the Communication Breakdown section, Michael B. Green learned that "a red rag," or a __________, had nothing to do with the internal makeup of the person who was wearing it.

Thinking Critically ...

Roy P. Benavidez was an Army Special Forces sergeant whose deeds in Vietnam combat in 1968 earned him the Medal of Honor. He saved the lives of eight comrades, even though he suffered more than 30 bullet and bayonet wounds. After the war, he dedicated his life to speaking to school and community groups. Benavidez talked about the value of hard work, sacrifice, dedication to a cause, and life. He told kids to stay in school and take care of each other. Although he died in 1998, his words live on for the countless number of people to whom he spoke. Roy P. Benavidez was, truly, a responsible speaker who used the spoken word to build relationships.

1. What do you think motivated him to want to talk to school kids and community groups? Was he a "good person speaking well"? Explain.
2. A number of customers from around the country have bought car phones that don't hook up to anything. They are purchased as "show." Also, at a busy street corner in a major midwestern city, people can rent briefcases by the day for that special "power" look. Do you see any societal problem with these examples, or are they harmless? Explain.

Taking Charge ...

1. Stereotyping is a problem that affects all of society. Make a poster, and through both words and pictures, indicate how people can unfairly stereotype others. What is the answer to the problem of stereotyping? Include the answer on your poster.

STUDENT WORK

"Phantom" *by Catharine Dommer*

Catharine Dommer presented the following award-winning oration both in local and state competition at a National Forensic League National Speech and Debate Tournament in Glenbrook, Illinois. She delivered this speech when she was a sophomore in high school. Now a classroom teacher of English and speech, Dommer says that she teaches and motivates her students by using many of the lessons provided in this textbook. She particularly values this first unit: "The Person."

Breathing lies;
Leering satyrs,
Peering eyes.

So

Run and hide but a face will still pursue;
Look around—there's another mask behind you!

The Phantom of the Opera! Even sounds mysterious, doesn't it? Andrew Lloyd Webber's hit musical based on the novel features these bizarre lyrics that illustrate the chaotic art of deception. I think that Michael Walsh described the plot well in *Time* magazine: "Ugly guy who hangs out in basement of Paris Opera gets crush on cute chorister . . . goes berserk when boyfriend comes on scene . . . gets ditched by the girl and crawls into a hole to die." Not exactly your typical tale of boy meets girl, boy gets girl, boy loses girl! The Phantom lived in isolation and hid behind a mask to hide his profoundly disfigured face. He *needed* his mask to woo the woman he loved and protect her from the harsh reality.

Unfortunately, the masks that we wear aren't nearly as noble. We've become the land of the Great American Masquerade.

Now, we're all familiar with that classic tale of back-stabbing romance that tells of how Miles Standish lost the love of his fair Priscilla. He trusted his not-so-faithful friend John Alden to "fix them up." Well, when Alden tried, Priscilla said, "Speak for yourself, Johnny" and in the end it was John who got the girl. But, as Shakespeare once said, "Most friendship is feigning; most loving mere folly." Miles should have studied up on his Shakespeare and done the job himself—because his buddy butchered him!

The *mask* of friendship is all around us, as some phantoms want to win our trust and then betray the friendship. The deceptive masks they wear can victimize those under their spell by victimizing their bodies, taking their money, and destroying their trust.

Take, for instance, Jane Fonda. She makes her exercise videos to prove to women in their fifties that they can still be beautiful. Thus, she has emerged as "a friend of the common woman's body." Columnist Barbara Drakis said that she's made $7 million from selling her videos to loyal fans who are willing to *pay* for a body like Jane's with their own sweat, blood, and tears! These Fonda disciples probably wouldn't be as faithful if they knew that "Robo-Fonda" has had facial surgery, a breast lift, tummy tuck, and liposuction. Granted, I'm sure that exercise is a great asset to the beautiful bodies over 50, but the only thing that Fonda has *proven* is that it's a lot easier to be beautiful when you can afford reconstructive surgery. Yet she still got her $7 million.

Many of today's swindlers are comparable to the old-time quack doctors who sold phony remedies. Only today's "quacks" don't need to travel by horse and buggy—they can use today's technology to simply "reach out and touch someone." The National Consumers League said that "small investors lose an estimated $40 billion a year to con men and swindlers," and "much of it over the phone." The most popular scams involve familiar offers like credit repair, penny stocks, travel deals, and precious metals. Beware of those who wear the mask of "the friend of the consumer," and remember that when an offer sounds too good to be true, it probably is.

So now we have people wearing the mask of friendship on exercise videos and on the telephone. This may sound like nothing to sweat over, but what if I were to tell you that this same masquerade is also being played at hospitals?

The article "Profiting from Pain" from a recent *Time* magazine told of a South Carolina drug ring that got its goods in a macabre way: from cancer victims who were terminal. Ring leaders posed as good Samaritans who stole pain pills and morphine while visiting patients, and later sold them on the streets. Meanwhile, the cancer patients had only aspirin to ease their pain.

The masquerade as "friends of the suffering" enabled the drug dealers to appear unsuspicious. It seems as if we always have to be on our guard for the twentieth-century Phantom who tells you to "close your eyes . . . open your mind . . . and trust me." And note that one thing that all of these masqueraders have in common is that they wore the mask of friendship for the money. Benjamin Franklin once wrote, "He that is of the opinion that money will do everything may well be suspected of doing everything for money."

Even our government is suspect, especially when it comes to the environment. The article "Pollution Control and Indulgences" by Eugene J. McCarthy elaborated on the government's Clean Air Act. This act attempts to combat pollution by giving industries the freedom to pollute a limited amount. However, if an industry does not pollute as much as its quota permits, it can then *sell* the excess pollution rights. We can now buy the right to pollute! Maybe we're seeing the mask of the environmental protector . . . or are we simply the victims of environmental fraud?

Song lyrics from *Phantom of the Opera* proclaim, "A nation waits, and how it hates to be cheated!" But it seems as if *this* nation has adopted cheating as a survival tactic. We're taught that we have to be tough to be successful, even if toughness isn't in our personality. Now "who is who?" really becomes a complicated game—how can we tell, when everyone is busy trying to be someone else?

But the game becomes serious when the children see their role models freely mixing fact with fiction. They watch *The Wizard of Oz* and learn that "the man behind the curtain" is really not a wizard at all—just an ordinary man that used machines to be powerful—and he was the good guy! Children need to be able to figure out what is real and what is not. If they're confused children, they may become confused adults who never know what they want from life. The book *Married Without Masks* by Nancy Groom says, "Many couples go for years feeling unfulfilled in marriage" because "being *that close* to another person means vulnerability, and most of us deal with vulnerability by hiding behind self-protective masks."

Remember that "Many people spend their lives climbing the ladder of success only to find, when they get to the top, the ladder is leaning against the wrong building!" *Power of Myth* by Joseph Campbell states, "People say that what we're seeking is a meaning for life . . . I think that what we're seeking is an experience of *being* alive . . . So that we actually feel the *rapture* of *being alive* . . . !" I don't know about you, but when I'm old and gray I want to be able to remember the *better* experiences of life, like sunsets on the lake and roasting marshmallows over a campfire, Christmases with family, Fourth of July fireworks, old friends, and new babies. Next to all of that, a life of illusions and disguises sounds very cold—and very lonely.

Whether masks are worn for money, power, or security, we need to be able to find the *real* people behind them. Even the Phantom asked his love to "find the man behind the monster," behind the mask. Once we overcome the fear of being ourselves, maybe then we can be *ourselves* with *each other.*

We might feel as assured as the Phantom of the Opera when he heard, "God give me strength to show you that you are not alone!"

Then, as if at a New Year's masquerade when the clock strikes midnight, we will *all* take off the masks, and see each other as we *really* are.

CHAPTER 1 Review and Enrichment...

Looking Back

Listed below are the major ideas discussed in this chapter.

- A good speaker is aware that she or he has an ethical obligation to use the spoken word responsibly.
- The four parts of the communication process are the sender, the receiver, the message, and feedback.
- A good speaker is aware of communication barriers and works to eliminate them.
- Effective communication can be built through writing or the spoken word.
- A key component in communication is nonverbal communication.
- Symbols can project a meaningful message.
- The foundation for effective oral communication must be firmly laid before any content or delivery work is done.
- The foundation for effective oral communication consists of working to be a good person, using communication constructively, and valuing the audience.
- Aristotle said that a speaker could use logical, emotional, and ethical appeals.
- Intrapersonal communication involves the talking that you do with yourself.
- Interpersonal communication is one-to-one or one-to-many communication.
- You should work to avoid stereotypes and to set a good example for others.

Speech Vocabulary

For each speech vocabulary word, state the definition as given in the text.

ethics
communication
sender
message
receiver
feedback
communication barrier
written communication
oral (or verbal) communication
nonverbal communication
symbol
intrapersonal communication
interpersonal communication
oratory
rhetoric
orator
logical appeal
emotional appeal
ethical (personal) appeal
dialogue
motivation
stereotyping

General Vocabulary

Define each general vocabulary word by using the dictionary. Include the definition as used in the chapter and an original sentence of your own.

responsible
epitomize
credibility
mesmerized
flippant
reciprocal

CHAPTER 1 Review and Enrichment...

To Remember

Answer the following based on your reading of the chapter.

1. The sender can send the message to the receiver. However, without ____________, the sender doesn't know if the message was truly understood.
2. Some advice for eliminating communication barriers was given to the "sender." What are the three verbs, or action words, for eliminating communication barriers?
3. What are the three verbs suggested to the "receiver"?
4. Another word for body language is ____________ communication.
5. What are the three essential elements of a value structure foundation?
6. Professional speechwriter and political consultant Peggy Noonan gave us some advice for what type of oral communication?
7. What is one-to-one communication called?
8. Aristotle said that an audience is influenced by someone with ____________ appeal.

To Do

1. Interview a teacher, a professional club member, or someone in business and find out why communication is important to this person. What qualities does he or she try to promote when speaking?
2. Find an article in the newspaper that exhibits "a good person speaking (or doing) well." Now find an article that shows the opposite. Be ready to share your thoughts with the class.

To Talk About

1. It has been said that "nice guys finish last." What evidence can you find to prove or disprove this statement? What conclusions can you draw? Why do we need ethical and responsible people in society?
2. Some 53 percent of Americans questioned in a survey sponsored by the First Amendment Center at Vanderbilt University said that the press has too much freedom. This number has increased more than 15 percent since the middle of the 1990s. The survey identified free speech as one of the most cherished constitutional rights, followed by freedom of religion and the Second Amendment right to bear arms. In addition, in 1997, nearly 80 percent said that newspapers should be able to publish freely without government approval. In 1999, that number dropped to 65 percent.

   However, isn't it ironic that when asked to name any of the rights guaranteed by the First Amendment, nearly 50 percent of those surveyed couldn't name even one?

   - Why is it *not* responsible to value the First Amendment but not know exactly what it says?
   - Why do you believe that many Americans feel that the press has "too much freedom"? Can you give any examples?
   - Regardless, why is freedom of the press essential in a democracy?
3. Language is often used to manipulate. In advertisements language is used to influence

people to buy particular items. Sometimes advertisements promise things they can't deliver. Sometimes the ads aren't ethical. Bring some newspaper or magazine ads to class. Work in a group to analyze the ads. Discuss the following questions.

- What type of language is used to convince the reader that he or she needs the product being advertised?
- Do you think the ad is ethical? Why or why not?
- Does it make claims that the product can't fulfill?
- Would you buy the product advertised based on the advertisement? Why or why not?

To Write About

1. Write a brief biography of one or more of the people discussed in this chapter. What contribution to speaking or society did each make? Was the contribution for good or ill?
2. A popular movie of the late 1980s, directed by Spike Lee, was titled *Do the Right Thing.* Why is doing the right thing sometimes so difficult? Give at least two reasons, and provide a documented or personal example for each.
3. Certain individuals in your school are leaders. What makes people follow others? A poll taken stated that the trait students valued most in a friend was honesty. Why do you believe this to be true?

Related Speech Topics

Find research to prove that people are taking positive stands regarding the following issues:

The environment
Education (local and national)
The homeless
Child abuse
Equal rights
Farmers/agriculture
School programs (academic, athletic, and social)
Sexual harassment in the workplace
Consumer protection
Entertainment/the media
Politics
The family
Sports and academics

CHAPTER 2

BUILDING CONFIDENCE

"Public speaking is no more difficult than breathing, using chopsticks, or tying a bow tie. The mysterious becomes simple . . . once you know how to do it."

–Charles Osgood,
news commentator and author, in his article "Speaking Easy"

Learning Objectives

After completing this chapter, you will be able to do the following.

- Discuss what confidence means and how it is a vital element in effective speaking.
- Recognize the realities of stage fright and how you can appropriately deal with the problem.
- Realize the value of perception as it applies to confidence in your speaking.
- Implement the planks of confidence in your speaking.

Chapter Outline

Following are the main sections in this chapter.

1. Understanding Stage Fright
2. Establishing an Accurate Perception
3. Examining the Planks of Confidence

New Speech Terms

In this chapter, you will learn the meanings of the speech terms listed below.

confidence
stage fright
fear
phobia
performance anxiety
perception
self-esteem
content
organization
notes
friendliness
impression
dedication
empathy
common ground
newness
conviction
enthusiasm

General Vocabulary

Expanding your general vocabulary will help you become a more effective communicator. Listed below are some words appearing in this chapter that you should make part of your everyday vocabulary.

irrational
eulogy
synonymous
innovation
allegory
assertion
prioritizing
mannequin

Looking AHEAD

It doesn't matter what you do in life—your chances of succeeding are improved when you are confident in yourself and in your abilities. This is particularly important when it comes to oral communication. It's tough to be confident as a speaker when you believe that you have little to offer.

Having confidence in speaking is closely related to having confidence about anything that you do in life. It has been said that you're confident when you feel that you're good at something. A construction contractor doesn't worry about a difficult job because he knows that he has the correct equipment and the intellectual know-how to do the job well. A computer programmer faced with a heavy workload and a detailed technical assignment doesn't quit because she knows that her training will prepare her to face any task.

Military strategists often say that "forewarned is forearmed." In other words, if you know what's coming, then you can adequately prepare for the challenge. For our purposes, the challenge is effective speaking. With this message in mind, the purpose of this chapter is to warn you of some apparent obstacles that speakers face, and then to arm you with the necessary tools that it takes for a "confidence victory." In Chapter 2 we will examine what the word *confidence* means, how fear is a real-world enemy, how perception plays a key role in speaking success, and why the "planks of confidence" are a necessary first line of defense against stage fright.

Introduction

Confidence is not a trait that you're born with. It is, however, a trait that anyone can develop. The same confidence that great athletes like Ricky Williams or Michelle Kwan depend on to help them perform their best is the same attribute that will help you to succeed. So, if you're not born with confidence, then how do you get it? You begin by understanding exactly what it means to have confidence.

What does confidence mean? Simply put, **confidence** is the feeling you have when you believe that you are capable of handling a situation successfully. This attitude is a result of ongoing preparation and practice. The more times that you try something, the more likely you are to improve and to gauge what it takes to be successful in a given situation.

You may be asking, "How does this apply to oral communication? To the job world? To my social life?" Let's return to the example started in Chapter 1 stating that the construction of a house begins with the pouring of a solid foundation and that a solid value structure is the foundation that anchors the spoken word.

Now, what's the next step? Carpenters next build the shell of the house by bolting the outside framework to the foundation. This skeletal framework is essential. It provides stability. Similarly, confidence is the internal skeletal framework of effective oral communication. Anchored to a solid value system, it gives stability to the speaker and makes her or his message believable. Thus, confidence is the attitude of assurance that causes an audience to take a speaker seriously.

Confidence leads to success.

But not everyone can speak with confidence, even if they understand its importance. Why? It's because of stage fright.

SECTION 1

Understanding Stage Fright

Stage fright, also referred to as *communication apprehension,* means, very simply, that we're afraid to speak. This is generally true in public situations. Surveys indicate that 80 to 90 percent of Americans admit feeling extremely uncomfortable about any form of public speaking. Before we examine the "fear of speaking," however, let's take a look at the nature of fear itself.

What Is Fear?

According to Dr. William Guys, professor of speech communication at Western Michigan University, **fear** is a "biological process by which animals, including humans, secure the necessary energy to do a job that really matters—one that might potentially result in physical and/or psychological injury." Therefore, keep in mind that fear is normal! It's designed to protect us from harm. Fear activates our emergency energy system so that we can cope with danger.

We have two sources of energy in our bodies. The "regular" energy system is based on the food we eat, the air we breathe, and the sleep we get. All of this contributes to our ability to function on a basic level. However, when we're confronted with danger, our "emergency" energy system kicks in. This source of energy is mainly in the form of adrenaline. Think about it. When you're alone and you hear a mysterious noise in the house, your heart may immediately begin to beat faster. This is because your body is preparing to deal with the potential danger.

Comedian Jerry Seinfeld has a rather amusing perspective on the fear of speaking.

Understanding the nature of fear can help you in any situation. For some, the fear may be in the form of test anxiety; for others, it might be standing on the free-throw line with all eyes on them; and for many of us, it's the possibility of messing up the "big interview." Yet, in every situation, we have a choice of dealing with it—or running from it. Biologists call this the "fight or flight syndrome." Keep in mind that to "fight" does not mean literally to punch out an opponent, but rather it means to confront a problem situation head-on. Granted, there are times when "flight" is the smart thing to do. When the train is coming and you're standing on the tracks, move! However, too many times, we think that the upcoming speech is as dangerous as the oncoming train. When our concern reaches this level, it becomes what is known as a **phobia**—or a persistent, *irrational* fear. When it comes to speaking, we need to remember that it's to our benefit to confront our fears—and *fight* to make our ideas known.

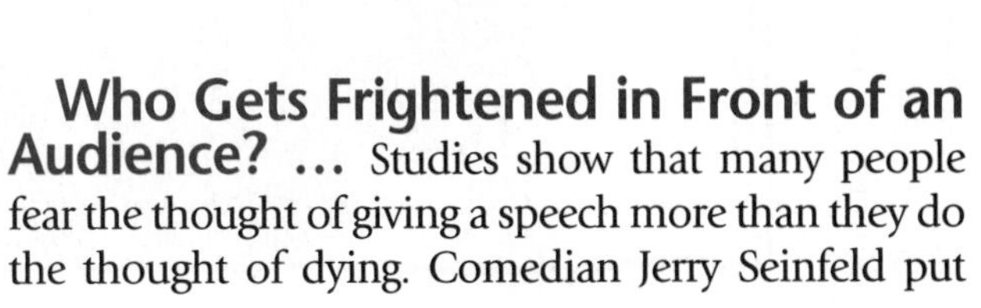

Who Gets Frightened in Front of an Audience? ... Studies show that many people fear the thought of giving a speech more than they do the thought of dying. Comedian Jerry Seinfeld put

this in perspective when he stated, "What this means is that if we are at a funeral, we would rather be the person in the casket—rather than be the one who is supposed to deliver the *eulogy!*" Yes, the fear of speaking is universal and can affect anyone, regardless of background or professional training. Barbara Tannenbaum is a senior lecturer in the Theater, Speech, and Dance Department at Brown University, who also teaches the "art of public speaking" and is a popular communications consultant. She notes that some of her most timid, shy, and apprehensive clients include doctors, bankers, judges, business executives, and politicians. She adds that the one trait they all have in common is that they're "frozen in terror" when it comes to speaking in front of others. So, keep in mind that if you're "scared stiff" about speaking, you're in good company. It doesn't matter whether you are

- interviewing for a job,
- meeting people for the first time,
- answering a question in class,
- speaking at a community function,
- explaining a task to coworkers.

If a receiver of your message is present, you may suffer varying degrees of stage fright.

Even Bill Gates experiences speaker's anxiety.

What Are the Symptoms? ... A popular radio and television commercial for a motel chain ended with a very down-home-style voice offering the memorable line, "We'll leave the light on for ya." Did you know that the speaker was so nervous while taping the original commercial that he forgot some of the words and was left with some time to fill? The result was that he adlibbed this now-famous ending. However, forgetting the words isn't the only symptom that accompanies our fear of speaking.

Have you ever experienced an upset stomach, a flushed face, dizziness, a fast heartbeat, shortness of breath, excessive perspiration, or wobbly legs either before or during a speech? If so, you're quite normal. These are common physical signs of communication apprehension, and they usually occur right before we speak and during the first 30 seconds or so after we have actually opened our mouths.

THEY SAY PUBLIC SPEAKING IS MOST PEOPLES NUMBER ONE FEAR !.. BUT THIS HAS TO BE RIGHT UP THERE !
JOE MARTIN
8-15

COMMUNICATION

Break*down*

Even Those on Stage Get Stage Fright

In an article titled "Stage Fright? Don't Collapse—Confront It," columnist Frank James gives a humorous account of his first major communication disaster. He notes that while a seventh grader in the Bronx, he tried to impress Janet Bing, a girl he had a crush on. When he finally mustered up the courage to talk to her face to face, his courage suddenly left him. So, he thought he would go to his second plan of action and impress her by athletically running down the stairs two at a time. He adds, "I tripped and wound up taking at least a dozen steps at once, head first. My body escaped unhurt, but my ego didn't."

He goes on to add that his stage fright put him in very good company. He writes that when British Prime Minister Winston Churchill was a young politician, he became so frightened while delivering a memorized speech to Parliament that he totally blanked. From that point on, Churchill always had a copy of his speech with him and refused to speak publicly without it.

Entertainers, public officials, and media personalities can also be victimized by their **performance anxiety,** or an extreme fear of audiences. This is also known as stage fright. Singer Carly Simon had millions of people listen to her records and tapes during the 1970s and 1980s, but later she virtually disappeared from the music scene because of her fear of performing in front of live audiences. In California, a 44-year-old San Diego municipal judge was placed on permanent disability because he couldn't face a courtroom where all eyes were on him constantly when he spoke. Finally, in the early 1980s, one of the most popular TV weathermen in the country, Willard Scott, developed stage fright and hyperventilated in front of millions.

Questions

1. Sometimes in social situations we try too hard to be impressive. In the first paragraph, what were two ways that seventh grader Frank James tried too hard? What were the negative consequences?
2. Communication apprehension can really be a problem when it involves our jobs. Statesman Winston Churchill found a way to solve his stage fright. He used detailed, accurate notes when he spoke. But what about the singer, the judge, and the weatherman? How did stage fright affect their careers? Analyze why it's ironic that *they* would suffer this condition.

But why? Why do we get these symptoms? The first reason is that our bodies are being flooded with energy. This is because they're preparing for what they perceive to be an emergency situation. Another reason, though, is that most of us don't like to be evaluated or judged. We dislike the thought of opening up to an audience or of having others examine us or our thoughts too closely. The truth of the matter is that often we don't think our ideas are worth listening to, we doubt we can say our ideas well, or we fear the audience won't like us while we are speaking. Because we simply don't feel prepared to face all of these potential obstacles, we're certain that the worst will happen!

Socrates said that we must move ourselves before we try to move the world.

Well, maybe it's time that we step back and see things a little differently. The Greek philosopher Socrates said that before we can move the world, we first have to move ourselves. But where do we get the confidence to start moving? How can we make our "internal skeletal frameworks" talked about earlier solid enough to withstand the strong winds and powerful rains of stage fright? Let's start by making sure that we have an accurate perception of our audience, of our speech, and of ourselves.

SECTION 1 REVIEW

Recalling the Facts ...

1. Define the term *stage fright*.
2. As discussed in this section, what word means "the feeling you have when you believe that you're capable of handling a situation successfully"?
3. As has been explained, what is the definition of the word *fear*?
4. Many people experience physical symptoms when they know that they are going to speak. What are the two reasons given that explain the reasons *why* these symptoms occur?

Thinking Critically ...

1. Many people find that they lose much of their speaking fear as the speech progresses. Why do you think that this might happen? Give at least two reasons and offer your thinking for each. Write your answers.
2. Sometimes an individual is called a "people person." This means that he or she is relaxed and friendly around others. How could this type of person be a real benefit at the workplace or at a social activity? What prevents some of us from becoming a "people person"? Discuss your responses with a partner or in a small group.

Taking Charge ...

1. Take a class inventory (of at least ten other students) and find out what they consider the most outstanding traits of a confident person (intelligence, an outgoing personality, and so on). Why is being confident important in the business world? Can confidence ever be taken too far? Analyze how confidence can be a positive factor when used the right way, but a negative factor when used the wrong way. Be ready to discuss your answers with the class.
2. Regardless of your job, you will have to be confident in your abilities and in your oral communication skills. Talk to someone who is employed and ask him or her why exhibiting confidence is important in what he or she does—and how confidence is an important factor in the impact that he or she might have on others.

SECTION 2 Establishing an Accurate Perception

As we will use the term here, **perception** refers to how you see things. To perceive means to gain an awareness and understanding of a person, an idea, or a situation. Obviously, an accurate perception is a tool that helps us learn more about ourselves, our objectives, and other people. In contrast, an inaccurate perception can cause us to blow things out of proportion, make a problem greater than it really is, and become our own worst enemies.

Nervousness can cause us to blow things out of proportion.

In constructing a house, carpenters often use a main support beam. This beam runs from one side of a room to another and works to make the internal structure stable. Establishing an accurate, realistic perception is the "main support beam" in building speaking confidence. It is this internal mind-set that allows you to say with a confident attitude, "I see things as they are, not as my fears might lead me to see them."

INSTANT IMPACT

THE "DEER" THEORY OF STAGE FRIGHT

Charles Osgood, who offered the quotation that we used to begin this chapter, has an interesting theory on stage fright. He says, "Have you ever been driving at night and come upon a deer frozen in the beam of your headlights? Here's my theory. The deer thinks the lights are spotlights, and what has it paralyzed is stage fright. It imagines the worst: It has to give a speech."

COMMUNICATION Breakthrough

To Be Confident, Be Prepared

Ross and Patty Pangere are an American success story. The owners of RossCo, a multimillion-dollar construction-contracting business in the Midwest, this husband and wife team has experienced communication apprehension. For example, even though Ross had given hundreds of presentations to current and potential clients, he never felt totally at ease.

Being a perfectionist, Ross Pangere took charge of his oral communication: he sought a confidence boost. He attended speech workshops, brought in communication consultants, and listened to audiotapes on effective speaking. He learned the value of "being yourself," of having a clear message, and of developing a simple yet substance-oriented organizational plan. But the greatest lesson that he learned, he summed up in one word: *practice!* Ross became "confident" when he knew that he was so absolutely in charge of his material that he could speak effectively regardless of the situation. He concludes by saying, "In today's world, those who can't confidently communicate and speak with poise simply can't compete."

Patty Pangere also built her confidence in business dealings when she took the time to sharpen her technological skills. In charge of a complicated computer system, she states that after she became "technologically prepared," her apprehension decreased. Like Ross, because she thoroughly understood her subject matter, she could talk confidently with anyone.

Ross and Patty Pangere would like for students to learn from their experiences. Whether it's successful speaking or a successful life, you'll feel more "in charge" if you'll take the time to "do your homework." And if they can do it, then you can, too. Together, Ross and Patty understand that confidence and competence are directly linked, and because of this, they accomplished an oral *communication breakthrough.*

Questions

1. Do you think this lesson about confidence and being prepared applies only to business owners, or could it also apply to any worker?
2. Ross Pangere, who has been legally blind for over 20 years, and his wife have built a thriving business. What challenges in oral communication has he had to overcome that the rest of us might not ever face?

Your Perception of the Audience

People too often think that giving a speech is a life-or-death situation. They can visualize passing out or feeling sick. They might think, "I know the audience sees my legs shaking" or "Everyone in the room is staring at the bead of sweat that's running down my forehead."

However, research proves that many speaking fears are simply unwarranted. Michael T. Motley, writing for *Psychology Today,* stated:

> Studies on how well an audience perceives anxiety should comfort nervous speakers. Researchers have found that most report noticing little or no anxiety in a speaker. Even when individuals are trained to detect anxiety cues and are instructed to look for them, there is little correlation between their evaluations and how anxious speakers actually felt.

Studies show that audiences often cannot perceive nervousness in speakers.

This encouraging quote shows that audiences are often unaware of a speaker's nervousness. Remember, your audience will ignore or forgive any type of mistake or awkwardness if audience members feel that you are genuinely interested in them and that you are genuinely trying to share with them.

Your Perception of the Speech

Part of the problem with giving a speech is the perception of what exactly the word *speech* should mean.

You should see speaking as an opportunity to share something you consider valuable—your message—with your audience. Thus, the word *speech* should not be viewed as being *synonymous* with performance. Instead, a speech should be viewed as a chance that you've been given to say something meaningful to others.

Speaking is not putting on a show. Too many times people seem to think of a speaking assignment as a Hollywood screen test. When this happens, they make the assignment more difficult than it needs to be. All of a sudden, they believe that their words and actions have to be extraordinary. Don't fall into this trap!

If you remember that a speech should be seen as a tremendous opportunity to share, an opportunity to enjoy a meaningful moment, an opportunity to communicate verbally with people you care about (your audience), then you can reduce your feelings of stage fright.

The speech is an extension of you. It is an extension of your personality and of your feelings, likes, and dislikes. Have confidence, and see your speech as a potential beacon to guide others, not as a performance that your audience will judge by holding up score cards as judges do in the Olympics.

Your speech will not be judged like a sporting event. It will be judged as an extension of you.

THE AUDIENCE ISN'T A MONSTER

INSTANT IMPACT

Antonio Louw is founder and chairman of Louw's Management Corp. in New Jersey. His company helps both executives and key employees to improve their communication and business skills.

He has worked with companies around the world and notes that Americans are the most petrified about speaking. One of the major reasons for our fears, he believes, is that in our minds, we turn our audiences into monsters that are ready to pounce on our imperfections. "There's this fear of making a mistake or making a fool of yourself," he says. "I teach people to remember that the purpose of a public speech is to entertain, inform, or persuade. It's certainly not to avoid making a mistake!"

He gives an example of a young Chicago woman, an advertising executive, who was terrified of public speaking and audiences. She was intelligent and insightful, but she suffered stage fright. Louw took her out to the streets of Chicago during rush hour. He directed her to go up to strangers on the street and ask them the time. He states, "She was afraid at first, but after she repeated this act and actually confronted people, she realized that she could do it!" He concludes by saying that audiences are simply people, and that most people are supportive and *want* speakers to succeed.

Steve Bair proves this point nicely. He was competing in Tulsa, Oklahoma, in the final round of the Original Oratory category of the National Forensic League championship. Only 6 contestants remained out of the over 180 contestants that had started in his category. Thousands of people in the audience had come to see the most talented high school speakers in the United States. Three microphones were on the stage, and there were television cameras and spotlights visible.

Suddenly, it was Steve Bair's turn to speak. Even though he had spoken hundreds of times before, his legs began to shake. He became warm, and his mouth felt like cotton.

He was suffering stage fright.

Steve started talking to himself (remember the discussion of intrapersonal communication in Chapter 1). He said, "Hey, I'm not performing for these people. I'm sharing. I'm just a person who cares about people, and I also care about this speech. I care what it has to say. I'm happy that I now have the chance to say it in front of so many people!"

Steve Bair went on to win the national championship.

This true account ought to teach you something: Your speech is not some alien creature to be feared or an enemy that you should run from. Your perception of the speech should include an awareness of how powerful words can be and a vision of how your words can make that power a reality.

Your Perception of Yourself

It is sometimes difficult for people to accept who they are. The media have created so many "beautiful people" that, in comparison, the rest of us may feel we stand little chance. The rock singer Madonna urged people to "strike a pose," and tennis star Andre Agassi once revealed in a popular commercial that "image is everything."

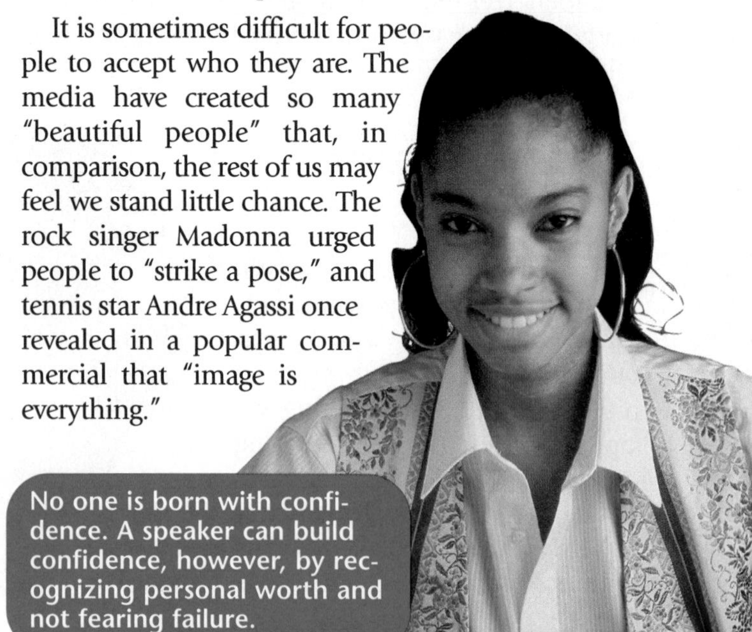

No one is born with confidence. A speaker can build confidence, however, by recognizing personal worth and not fearing failure.

Consequently, it is easy for us to perceive ourselves as not being pretty enough, handsome enough, intelligent enough, or witty enough. The book *One Hundred Percent American* by Daniel E. Weiss states that 99 percent of all women in the nation would change at least one thing about their looks. If you lack confidence in yourself, doesn't it stand to reason that you will also lack confidence in your spoken words?

Of course, in speaking, you should strive for excellence; but you should not think that you always have to be perfect. Don't equate making a mistake with being a total failure. If you do, you might want to give up and not even allow your oral communication the opportunity to succeed. How do you change this sort of negative perception of yourself?

First of all, recognize your own individual worth and like who you are. Consider the following story:

> Once upon a time, an unhappy horse wished for longer, thinner legs, a neck like a swan, and a saddle that would grow on his back as part of his body. He thought all of these things would bring him great happiness, because they would make him more beautiful. Well, it so happened that the horse's wishes were granted and he was given all the things he wished for. But when the horse went to a reflecting pond to admire his improved image, he was horrified. The things that had seemed so desirable individually had become totally undesirable collectively—he had been changed into a camel!
>
> Moral of the story: It is better to improve what you have than to wish for the things you don't have.

This moral also applies to perception and confidence in speaking. First, if you see yourself as an individual and unique rather than being different or inadequate, then you can start to build a confidence that stresses your uniqueness and emphasizes your own personal potential.

Second, don't fear being human. Don't be afraid to acknowledge the fact that you don't do everything perfectly. Politicians, company executives, movie stars—everyone makes mistakes. While it is true that you can make errors and sometimes fail, set out to learn from those failures.

Did you know that a professor at the University of Houston developed a course that became known as "Failure 101"? The object of the course was to convince students that failure should be seen as an opportunity for *innovation* instead of immediate defeat. His students loved the class. It showed them that not always being right the first time can, ironically, lead to discovery. For example, the inventor Thomas Edison faced many failures before he discovered the electric light.

The psychologist John Rosemond adds that confidence, or **self-esteem,** is often the result of this discovery process. He says that no one is born with confidence. On the contrary, confidence is built. When you can face your fears, your frustrations, and

Don't Be Afraid to Fail

You've failed many times, although you may not remember.

You fell down the first time you tried to walk.

You almost drowned the first time you tried to swim, didn't you?

Did you hit the ball the first time you swung a bat?

Heavy hitters, the ones who hit the most home runs, also strike out a lot.

R. H. Macy failed seven times before his store in New York caught on.

English novelist John Creasey got 753 rejection slips before he published 564 books.

Babe Ruth struck out 1,330 times, but he also hit 714 home runs.

Don't worry about failure.

Worry about the chances you miss when you don't *even try.*

A message as published in the *Wall Street Journal.*

even your failures—and still come out standing on your own two feet—then confidence is being nurtured. Remember, you gain confidence every time that you face adversity and come out on top.

How does this apply to communication?

Very simply, it means that you shouldn't be afraid to fail. Don't worry that you are going to "mess up" in your speech. Suppose you make a mistake and realize

- that your notes are shaking uncontrollably in your hands,
- that your eye contact is only with the back wall,
- that your knees are shaking,
- that you're opening your mouth but no words are coming out,
- that you are sweating.

Don't panic! Remember that this isn't brain surgery. It's sharing a truth and delivering a message. So smile . . . remember that you're human . . . take a deep breath . . . and think about how you're going to correct these problems when you speak the next time. And there will be a next time.

Sometimes the greatest therapy for stage fright is to laugh at your own mistakes in your speech. Your audience will probably laugh with you because they, like you, are simply human.

What Have You Learned about Perception?

One of the main points that you have learned about perception is that it is a key element in building confidence in speaking. Why? Because an accurate perception of things can help you to overcome stage fright. It will allow you to deal with what is real as opposed to what you might imagine to be real.

Plato's allegory of the cave shows that perception is not always reality.

To illustrate, let's examine a story from the philosophical past. In *The Republic,* written in the fifth century B.C.E., Plato offers the famous allegory of the cave. This *allegory* describes people as prisoners in a cave, facing away from the opening of the cave and thus away from the light. Unable to see themselves or anyone else because they are shackled, they see only the shadows on the wall in front of them. Since they are never allowed to turn around and see the light, their perception is that the shadows are what is real.

What's the connection of this allegory to speaking? The answer is this: If you believe that

- your audience is aware of everything that you do wrong in your speech,
- your speech is a performance rather than a sharing, or that
- you have little to offer as either a person or a speaker . . .

then you are being victimized by the "shadows" of stage fright and fear. Isn't it time that you "see the light"? The truth is that

- your audience doesn't see everything that you do wrong,
- your speech is a worthwhile sharing of good ideas and information, and that
- you have a lot to offer.

Let your perception work for you. Firmly implant the "main support beam"—an accurate perception—that is essential in the overall construction of building confidence.

Next, let's examine some of the specific planks that make up the confidence framework.

Don't let the shadows of stage fright victimize you!

SECTION 2 REVIEW

Recalling the Facts ...

1. How you see things is known as ______________.
2. A speech should not be viewed as a performance. Instead, how would you define a speech?
3. Psychologist John Rosemond states that confidence is often the result of a discovery process. Another term for *confidence,* he notes, is self-______________.

Thinking Critically ...

1. This section mentions that the media have created the "beautiful people"—or those people who seem to look perfect and lead perfect lives. However, this perception is not always true. Many "superstars," representing different professions, have had their own share of problems. List some of those people. After you have made your list, analyze why we perceive their lives to be great. Finally, after describing the positive aspects of these people's lives, discuss the problems that they have had to face.
2. Socially, why is it sometimes difficult for us just to "be ourselves"?

Taking Charge ...

1. It's important for us to make the "right" impression on other people. With this in mind, interview a teacher, a coach, or an employer—and ask the following question: "Based on your perception, what qualities does a good student, a good performer, or a good employee possess?" Keep a list of the responses and be prepared to share this list with the class.

SECTION 3 Examining the Planks of Confidence

Once again, think of a house. When you see the shell of a house being put up, you can't help but notice the individual pieces of wood, usually two-by-fours of varying lengths, that make up the walls and the roof. These individual pieces of wood might be referred to as planks.

Let's now take the word confidence and use each letter in the word as a figurative "plank." In the process, you will "nail down" some of the major ingredients of confidence. These are ten components that can help you build self-confidence.

Content	Dedication
Organization	Empathy
Notes	Newness
Friendliness	Conviction
Impression	Enthusiasm

As you read about each plank, keep in mind that your confidence level will grow with each one you develop.

Content

Content ... *Have something worthwhile to say.* You can't be confident as a speaker if you are not confident in your content. It is a good feeling to know that you have researched your topic and have done your homework.

High school students are often unfairly portrayed as having little academic promise or real-world awareness, caught up in music videos and skateboards. Don't allow this stereotype to stand. Show that intellectually you have credibility and deserve attention. Audiences respect a person who shares a message that contains facts and pertinent evidence. Build a relevant message with solid content by going to the library or surfing the Internet, reading newspapers or current magazines, interviewing someone who knows something related to your topic, or watching the news or educational television.

Remember, don't base your speaking on *assertions* or emotional appeals only. Spend time building an evidence file that shows appropriate documentation and obvious "legwork" on your part.

Organization

Organization ... *Have some type of an outline that is easy for both you and your audience to follow.* It is a reassuring feeling to know that you are operating from a format that is logical. Every speech needs **organization,** and must have a main idea or main point being addressed, clear areas of analysis, and supporting evidence that fits. Also

This Connecticut student has so much CONFIDENCE that he is lobbying the state's legislators in support of a bill that would let the two student members of the state board of education have voting rights.

important are an introduction that leads to the thesis statement and a conclusion that summarizes the areas of analysis and provides some ending emotional appeal.

Mark McCormack, a businessman and author, states that he gains confidence in his business dealings by dividing part of his day into five one-hour blocks. Each block has a specific purpose. For instance, one of his one-hour blocks involves *prioritizing* his phone calls and determining exactly how much time, on the average, he can spend on each. He says that this approach gives sequence to his business day and helps the day make sense.

This message can also apply to confidence in speaking. Don't be scatterbrained—don't always rely on "the spontaneity of the moment." Offer clarity and sequence to your audience. Your audience members will appreciate your guiding them, and you will feel more confident that your audience is getting your point.

Notes ... *Jot down your ideas in a brief, directed (preferably outlined) form.* A notecard can be a comforting "security net" in case you fear losing your place in the speech. However, be sure to avoid the two greatest problems regarding **notes:** (1) having too many words on a single notecard and (2) having too many notecards.

Referring to key words or phrases on notecards can help a speaker stay confidently on track.

Notes are not supposed to be a substitute for preparation. They are not for you to read to your audience. Instead, notes should provide you with a memory springboard. Seeing a key word or phrase should remind you of where you are and where you should be going in your speech. Used correctly, notes can be your friend. They can be the training wheels of oral communication, keeping you confidently on course and, most importantly, on topic.

Friendliness ... *Be congenial.* You can gain confidence if you express **friendliness** and see that your audience is giving you positive feedback. This positive feedback is often the result of your conveying a warm, friendly attitude. Writing for *Management Digest,* Roger Ailes, a noted author and communication consultant, says that being likable is the "magic bullet" in speaking. He writes, "With [friendliness], your audience will forgive just about everything else you do wrong. Without it, you can hit every bull's-eye in the room and no one will be impressed."

LETTERMAN GETS SERIOUS

INSTANT IMPACT

Late-night talk show host David Letterman gave the following statements to *GQ* reporter Jennet Conant about his Indianapolis, Indiana, high school speech experience:

"There was a period in high school when you had to figure out who you were. I thought that I wasn't fitting in with 'this group' or 'that group,' and so I started to examine my own personal inventory. I thought, 'Is there anything I can do that is going to make me desirable or different?' Then I took a public speaking class. For the first time, I felt *confident*. It came easily to me—at least it was easier than algebra. So it was clear to me that this course was something to take *seriously.*"

WORDS FROM THE WORKPLACE

Jim Wacker
University Athletic Director

Q. *How does good communication play a role in your day-to-day activities?*

A. In my role as Athletic Director at Southwest Texas State University, it is imperative that I am able to communicate effectively with large, diverse, and varied groups, as well as with individuals.

Q. *What advice, suggestions, or tips can you give to students to show them the importance of communication skills, either verbal or nonverbal, in your world of work?*

A. I am always reminding the coaches, staff, and other administrators how important it is to have excellent communication skills as well as the ability to know when to smile and say nothing at all. Body language is critically important. Positive communication always depends on having a positive outlook on life. Count your blessings and not your curses, and remember the saying: "Any fool can criticize, condemn, and complain, and most fools do." A few specific behaviors that I believe will promote the improvement of your communication skills are:

- Spend more time reading than watching TV—so what you say will be informative and realistic.
- Genuinely care about the people you communicate with and build them up more than you tear them down.
- Positive reinforcement is essential—we all have to hear those beautiful words, "you done good" as often as possible.

So don't be afraid to smile and to talk to individuals in the room. Don't view your audience as a collective mass of faceless people. Let both your words and your nonverbal communication work for you. Remember, an audience that likes you is more likely to be receptive to your message.

Impression ... *Getting off to a good start is essential in building confidence.* How your audience perceives you right from the beginning is very important. Do you, for instance, convey a positive attitude on your way to the front of the room? This text has already referred to the study that showed that 55 percent of what others think of you is determined before you ever open your mouth. If this is true, you should telegraph to your audience the feeling, "I'm really glad to be here today," before you begin to speak. This, in turn, should raise your confidence level.

Impression also refers to the way you are dressed and groomed. The issue here isn't money. The issue involves common sense and appropriate judgment. If it is your objective to be taken seriously as a speaker, then never allow your clothing, hair, makeup, or jewelry to get in the way of your message. These things should not draw attention away from your main purpose: effective communication. While it is true that "clothes don't make the person," it is certainly also true that they can help. Showing the audience members that you took the time to look good for them means that you respect them. Isn't respect what all of us are after? Build confidence by setting a good example and offering a solid first impression.

Like a musician, a speaker needs to practice, practice, practice to feel confident when delivering her speech.

Dedication ...

Practice. Practice. Practice. Too many times a student adequately researches a speech and prepares a catchy introduction and a dynamic conclusion, only to forget a basic part of speech presentation—orally practicing the actual delivery of the speech. Confidence does not come about as a result of going over the material mentally in the corner of your room while listening to music through your headphones; it requires **dedication.** You must get used to the sound of your own voice and speak as often as you can. You must try as much as possible to simulate the real thing.

Professionals in both sports and entertainment speak of the countless number of hours that they spend on basics: a simple exercise on the piano, covering first base on a bunt, a basic tennis stroke, or a routine dance step. These professional women and men know the value of practice.

Speaking is no different. Take the time to actually say the words you've worked so hard to create on paper. Gain command of your information. Practice looking at people while speaking. Practice your gestures. Practice moving to see how your body feels while taking a step. Be dedicated so that when the time comes to speak before an audience, you won't be caught helpless. Instead, you will feel more confident because you will already have been there!

C	O	N	F	I	D	E	N	C	E
CONTENT	ORGANIZATION	NOTES	FRIENDLINESS	IMPRESSION	DEDICATION	EMPATHY	NEWNESS	CONVICTION	ENTHUSIASM
Value Structure Foundation									

Empathy ...

Know how it feels to feel that way. The term **empathy** means a sincere understanding of the feelings, thoughts, and motives of others. You shouldn't assume that you are the only person with problems during your day. Other people face these same difficulties.

In the novel *To Kill a Mockingbird* by Harper Lee, one of the characters, Atticus Finch, tells his daughter, Scout, that you never truly understand a man until you "climb into his skin and walk around in it."

As speakers, learn from this advice. You can feel much more at ease if you will take a few minutes to get to know how your audience members are feeling. What are they thinking? What's on their minds? Have you made an attempt to "climb into their skins"? Could it be that they are facing problems at home? With their boyfriends or girlfriends? Once you empathize, not only will you understand your audience better, you will understand feedback better. For instance, keep in mind that when audience members are looking out the window, slouching in their seats, or not paying attention, it might simply mean that they are having a bad day.

Have you ever had a bad day? If so, then you will understand and refuse to take things personally. Keep speaking and working for **common ground.** When you establish common ground with your audience, you are saying with both verbal and nonverbal communication, "We're *all* in this together, and together we will work to solve what might be on our minds." The consequence might be that you will become a more confident speaker.

Guides need to rediscover their stories every time they tell them to keep them fresh for each group.

Newness ... *Apply some originality.*

We often feel confident if we have something new and original to say. **Newness** could mean taking a different slant or approaching your topic in your own unique way. A clever anecdote that you've read might make an original way to start your speech. A meaningful quotation that you've discovered could add an original punch to your conclusion. What about charts, graphs, or artwork to accompany your words? If appropriate and well done, they can offer an innovative means of uniquely reinforcing your point.

One of the best ways to put some originality in your speech is to tell a personal story. In his article "We Must Rediscover Our Stories," Richard Louv says that Americans have lost sight of the impact that their personal stories can have. Somehow people assume that if a story isn't at the video store or on a television soap opera, it must be worthless. However, Louv notes that personal stories—family stories—are "real gold."

So tell your story! No one has one quite like yours. Your originality can show your audience that you are a creative, intelligent speaker. It can also help to establish the necessary common ground spoken of earlier and, in the process, add to your confidence in speaking.

Conviction ... *Believe in what you say.*

Mahatma Gandhi, the Hindu spiritual leader, once said, "One needs to be slow to form convictions, but once formed they must be defended against the heaviest of odds." Even though most of our lives are not as dramatic as this quotation, the message is clear: Know what your principles are, and have the courage to stand up and voice those principles. Confidence can be greatly magnified when you have a strong belief in what your spoken words are conveying.

Some speech topics can be boring unless you add your own special dimension of personal **conviction.** For example, giving a speech on "My Summer Vacation" can come across as lifeless and monotonous. But what if on your summer vacation you saw a work by Michelangelo, the sixteenth-century painter and sculptor, that made you realize something about people or art that you passionately wish to share?

Similarly, talking about "My Job" or "My Friends" can be tedious. But what if your job pro-

Mahatma Gandhi personified conviction.

motes hard work, and you believe that hard work and a strong work ethic are important for success? And what if your friends are the elderly couple down the street, and you have seen firsthand the value of kindness, touch, a smile, and compassion?

Suddenly, each of these "ordinary" topics takes on a new, more vital meaning that you can relate directly to your audience. Your conviction will tell your audience that you take your topic seriously. Your audience will, in turn, take you and your speech more seriously.

Conviction can also allow you to take your mind off your fears, gestures, and facial expressions and let you focus on your speech content.

The main point about conviction is this: If you are confident about the importance of your message, then your audience is more likely to be persuaded.

Conviction that you are doing a worthwhile activity lets you focus your speech.

Enthusiasm ... *Get fired up!* The character Spock of *Star Trek* fame is well known for relying on logic and reason and for exhibiting little emotional involvement. This might work with the audience of science fiction, but it probably won't work with your audience. No one wants to listen to an unemotional *mannequin,* standing lifelessly at the front of the room. You need energy. You need **enthusiasm.** You need to inspire your audience by showing them that you are fired up in two ways that work hand in hand: intellectually, so that your mind is sharp and alert, and also physically, so that your body is actively involved.

The most ordinary speech can become entertaining and delightful if you share your enthusiasm with your audience. Enthusiasm is directed energy. So if you feel energized, others in the room will feel that same electricity.

In addition, enthusiasm is often a convenient outlet for much of the nervous energy that public speaking might bring. However, nervous energy must be controlled. When you are about to make a speech, take a few deep breaths. Let yourself relax. Have your body release some of the nervous tension that might develop right before you speak.

Many of the great thinkers have given us advice on the value of enthusiasm. Ralph Waldo Emerson, the American essayist and poet of the mid-nineteenth century, said that nothing great was ever achieved without it. One of the best pieces of advice came from the motivational speaker and businessman William McFee, who declared that the world belongs to the enthusiast who can "keep his cool." As a speaker, if you can keep your cool, yet show your audience members that you are excited about being with them and sharing your message, then you are sure to become a more confident communicator.

So where does this bring us?

Abraham Lincoln was once asked how he would cut down a tree if he were given eight hours to complete the job. He responded by saying that he would sharpen the blade on his axe for seven hours—so that he could easily cut down the tree in one hour. In other words, he would spend most of his time preparing so that his job would be easier.

Lincoln was a powerful and believable speaker because he fully prepared for every speech.

Chapter 2 (as well as Chapter 1) has worked to teach you the same type of lesson regarding directed preparation, a lesson that will be extended in later chapters. Remember, a speech is built in much the same way a house is built—from the foundation up. You are ensuring success with your spoken words when you build a solid confidence framework that exhibits a responsible, ethical approach to communication.

SECTION 3 REVIEW

Recalling the Facts ...

1. Which of the ten planks of confidence might be a convenient outlet for much of the nervous energy that your body might feel prior to and during your speech?
2. A notecard can be a comforting "security net" for a speech. What are the two greatest problems regarding notes?
3. Businessman and author Mark McCormack outlines his day by dividing it into how many blocks of time? How long is each? What procedure does he use to organize his phone calls?

Thinking Critically ...

1. This chapter listed ten planks of confidence. Can you think of at least two other traits that might be commonly viewed as "confidence" but may actually be negative qualities? What is your reasoning behind each choice? Write your responses.
2. Why is practice essential for success at any undertaking? What problems might develop without it? How could failing to practice particular skills hurt you at work? Could this also damage your confidence? Be ready to give specifics out loud.

Taking Charge ...

1. Conviction is certainly an important plank of confidence. Name two issues that you feel very strongly about. They may be personal, school, community, national, or world issues. What points would you stress about each if you had to give a speech? Share your views in small groups.
2. Item 1 above deals with your conviction about an issue. However, you need to have evidence (facts) to be smart about your position. Interview an adult who is knowledgeable on one of your issues and give his or her information to your group. In addition, bring in one article from a magazine or newspaper (the school paper is fine, too) that proves your point. Be prepared to summarize the article for your small group.

STUDENT WORK

"It's the G.I. Joe Thing To Do" *By Tony W. Garcia*

Junior Tony W. Garcia is a student from the Midwest who believes that confidence comes from within. An honor student, he wishes to attend one of the military schools, such as West Point or the Air Force Academy. He says, "I believe in what the military teaches: discipline and teamwork. I think that when you have self-discipline and a firm values framework that drives you, you have confidence in yourself and in those around you."

Tony wrote this speech during his junior year in high school, and he delivered it for both state and national competition in Original Oratory.

I remember when I was just a little guy that my favorite intellectual weekend activity was "snuggling up" with a bowl of Frosted Flakes and watching Saturday morning cartoons, Scooby-Doo, Speedy Gonzalez, and the immortal Droopy the Dog. I should have been an interpreter. But, hey, we're in Original Oratory, and oratories are supposed to be creative, cognitive constructions that are both didactic and aximoatic. In other words, they're supposed to make a point. They're supposed to teach a lesson. Well, that being the criterion, my favorite cartoon character is definitely oratory material. In fact, he was founded on the lesson that boys shouldn't play with Barbie. See, in the 1960s, a toymaker named Stanley Weston was irritated at the fact that too many young males were taking the "hands-on" approach when it came to their sisters' dolls. So, in the place of hormones and sex, he gave them a more wholesome American value: violence—and the Ultimate Toy Warrior, G.I. Joe, the Real American Hero. I don't think the reason I was so entranced by Joe was because of the action figures or his ultra-soft bedsheets—I haven't used mine in over about a month. No, the reason I liked Joe so much was because of what he stood for: self-control. Discipline. Unfortunately, I can't say America stands for the same thing. For, too often, America lacks the G.I. Joe mentality—too often, America lacks discipline. Author Philip K. Howard states that the same lethargic spirit that toppled great nations of the past might be America's undoing, for he believes the absence of discipline, order, and personal toughness is a cancer that Americans must face quickly. This condition stems from two current attitudes that seem to contradict G.I. Joe's sage-like mentality: first, there's no real need to follow orders; and second, why go through the rigors of "basic training"?

G.I. Joe gave out many orders, and Snake-Eyes and Flint always took them. "Yo Joe!" But, it's not quite so simple in America, is it? I guess we just aren't as disciplined. Take doctors' orders for example. Doctors preach for us to cut the calories, exercise—just be smart. This is certainly sound advice since we are the country that consumes 90 acres of pizza and 200 million M&M's daily. So, it's not hard to imagine why the American Medical Association claims that over half of this country's population is overweight. A simple solution, you say, is to exercise, right? Well, since 87 percent of all Americans who own running shoes—don't run, exercise isn't a very realistic possibility. We just seem to have a problem following orders—even if they're for our own good. I had my own bout with this problem in the third grade. Contrary to orders I had received, I decided to stick a paper clip into an electrical socket. I should have followed my orders. I think Wilie Coyote said it best: "Oww!" Yes, I had an obedience problem, but so did Edith Sweetwine's students. After twenty-five years in the Detroit school system, she quit her job after growing tired of the disrespect, lack of discipline, and the cursing from her *first grade* students. And she's not alone. A 1999 survey of teachers in the Midwest found that one of the major reasons why teachers quit teaching is a lack of discipline in the schools. Even the young 'uns won't follow orders.

Now, G.I. Joe was a military man; you might even say a "macho macho" military man. And he believed in the hard, tough, disciplined training

that it took to win the battle. But America doesn't really buy into all of that hard work stuff. Which bring us to our second point: "Why go through the rigors of basic training?" Why bother being disciplined enough to learn the "basics"? American students might not be getting the education they need—or maybe they're just not learning it. Studies show that over one-third of incoming college freshmen are having to take at least one remedial course. In addition, former White House counsel C. Boyden Grey says standardized test score standards have been loosened to "camouflage lower student achievement." But, so what if we lose a few points here, gain a few there? After all, it's not a matter of life and death. But it can be. In 1996 a company's gross lack of discipline and employees' lack of "basic" training meant that Valujet Flight 592 would crash in the Florida Everglades. Now, we're not talking some numbers on a page or circles on a national standardized test. Now we're talking about over one hundred lost lives—in a tragedy that federal documents now show was completely preventable.

Ladies and gentlemen, we are a nation that lacks discipline. Now, the word discipline implies self-control, and through self-control one attains order. And order gives structure. And without structure our lives become chaotic. We don't pay our bills, we stay out too late, we don't get enough sleep, we're tardy to class, we don't get papers in on time, we don't get papers graded on time, we talk too much, we yell too quickly, we make lists too long—which is why I had better stop. Being a military man, G.I. Joe was always structured—and G.I. Joe always won. So what's our problem? We seem to have taken Burger King's "Have It Your Way," and made it an American maxim. Well, we have it our way—and maybe that's the problem. We're spoiled. Author of *A Nation of Victims*, Charles J. Sykes, says that the "inner child" America is obsessed with is actually a "bawling, squalling creature who wants everything right now, from sexual gratification to consumer goods." Nowadays, almost everyone seems to feel entitled to all sorts of successes, without having to make the sacrifices or practice the self-discipline that it takes to get them.

Is there any hope? Sure—we all have someone in our lives or in our families we can look to for a little disciplined guidance. Me? I look to my great great grandfather, who, after immigrating to America at the turn of the century, spent his first Minnesota winter in a cave along the Mississippi, worked and saved up enough money to start a farm, have a family, establish a town, and build a church. Now, that would take some discipline. And he taught me a valuable lesson about hard work and self-control. So, now I know. And as G.I. Joe would say at the end of every episode: "Now you know, and knowing is half the battle." What about the other half? Let's go to what I call the three B's: Brains, Butt, and Backbone. First, brains. Think! Sometimes you can't trust your instincts—think things through, and formulate a plan. Next, butt: get off of it! Implement that plan. And finally, backbone: make a stand. Stand up for what you think is right. Be disciplined. It's the G.I. Joe thing to do.

Looking Back

Listed below are the major ideas discussed in this chapter.

- Confidence is the feeling that you have when you know that you can accomplish a certain task successfully.
- Confidence in speaking is the internal skeletal framework that is anchored to the solid value foundation described in Chapter 1.
- Confidence is the motivating factor behind the power and believability of your words and is an essential element in your being taken seriously by an audience.
- Stage fright often threatens a speaker's confidence. We can think of it as a strong wind that works to blow down a confidence structure.
- Fear is a biological process that allows you to deal with potentially dangerous situations.
- People are often victimized by phobias, or fears, that get out of hand.
- Everyone is potentially susceptible to performance anxiety (or stage fright), even professionals. The symptoms range from a rapid heartbeat to excessive perspiration to an upset stomach.
- One way to overcome this fear is to establish an accurate perception of your audience, your speech, and yourself.
- Perception is the main support beam of confidence. It challenges you to see things as they really are, not as your fears might lead you to believe they are.
- A second way to deal with performance anxiety and build your speaking confidence is by examining the ten planks of confidence: content, organization, notes, friendliness, impression, dedication, empathy, newness, conviction, and enthusiasm.
- Confidence is a consequence of preparation and hard work and is the driving force behind speaking effectiveness.

Speech Vocabulary

1. For each speech vocabulary word, give the definition as it appears in the text. Underline the word. Make sure that you can spell each word.

   confidence
   phobia
   fear
   performance anxiety
   stage fright
   perception
   self-esteem
   content
   organization
   notes
   friendliness
   impression
   dedication
   empathy
   common ground
   newness
   conviction
   enthusiasm

2. For each of the ten planks of confidence, copy the phrase or sentence from the chapter discussion that best describes what the plank is promoting. Do this in addition to writing down the short descriptive phrase that is given immediately beside each plank.

CHAPTER 2 Review and Enrichment...

General Vocabulary

1. Define each general vocabulary term by using a dictionary. Include the part of speech, the definition of the word as it is used in the chapter, and an original sentence of your own. Make sure that you can spell each word.

   irrational
   eulogy
   synonymous
   innovation
   allegory
   assertion
   prioritizing
   mannequin

2. Write an original story about "The Day I Overcame My Fear" or "The Day It Was My Turn to Perform!" Use at least 12 words from the combined speech and general vocabulary lists. Underline and number each word.
3. Are there any other words in Chapter 2 that you aren't familiar with? That you don't know how to spell? Find at least three, and add them to your lists.

To Remember

Answer the following questions based on your reading of the chapter.

1. Confidence is the feeling you have when you know that you can get the job done well. Confidence is the ______________ of effective oral communication.
2. What is the name of the major type of energy that is released by the body in fear situations?
3. A persistent, irrational fear can be referred to as a ______________.
4. Another name for performance anxiety is ______________.
5. Perception refers to how we see things. Perception is the ______________ in building speaking confidence.
6. What percentage of American women would change at least one thing about their looks?
7. A university course known as ______________ works to prove the value of effort. The course shows people that they can learn from their mistakes.
8. Roger Ailes calls what word the "magic bullet" in speaking?
9. Richard Louv states that our real impact in speaking can come from our personal ______________, which he refers to as "real gold."
10. When you establish ______________ ______________ with your audience, you are forming a bond that says, "We're all in this together."

To Do

1. Wilma Rudolph was a world-class runner who captured three gold medals for the United States at the 1960 Olympics. However, it is a wonder she could even walk. A series of childhood illnesses had so crippled her that she was unable to walk until she was eight years old. It was through sheer determination and commitment that she overcame the odds. Research a figure from history who also had the confidence to overcome the odds. Show how something great was accomplished by this person. Also, inter-

view someone in your family or community who has exhibited the confidence to do something admirable in the face of adversity.

2. Compile a self-improvement chart. On it, list the things about you that you can't change. In another column, list the things about you that you *can* change and that you would like to improve. For each item that you can change, jot down how you are going to improve. Be sure to include areas of speaking in which you know that you can improve.

To Talk About

1. The science fiction writer Ray Bradbury recently said that Americans, particularly young people, should never watch the evening news. He believes that the news too often erodes our sense of confidence in the future. Is he right? What problems might arise if we don't watch the news? How does what we see on the news affect our personal confidence?
2. It has been said that some people "die with potential." This means that some people never work hard enough to actualize all of their talents or abilities. Why is this such a catastrophe? How can each of us prevent this from happening in our lives?

To Write About

1. The things that might give us stage fright as a child are different from the things we could be frightened by later. Explain the stage fright that a child could feel. What about a teenager? A parent? An employer? An elderly person? How can you help others when you know that they are experiencing stage fright?
2. Denice Barsich, whose good-Samaritan action resulted in the loss of her right leg, hasn't lost her zest for life. She was hit by a car while helping a fellow motorist out of a snow-filled ditch. She says that one of her goals is to "dance at my husband's Christmas party." Denice Barsich has one other objective: not to be bitter and to teach her children about the sanctity of life. What does she teach us by her words? Do we often take things for granted?
3. Organization is always an important element in clear communication. Make a list titled "Three Things I Must Get Done in School." Describe not only what your three objectives are but also how, where, and when you plan to accomplish each. Make another list titled "Three Things I Must Accomplish at Home or at Work." Do the same with these.

Related Speech Topics

MADD (Mothers Against Drunk Driving)
Apartheid (racial discrimination in South Africa)
Sexual harassment
Censorship
Left brain/right brain research
Phobias
Cooperative learning in education
Cheating in the United States
Firefighters
Peer pressure
Creativity
The work ethic
Law enforcement
Advancements in technology

Person to Person

UNIT CONTENTS

CHAPTER 3

LISTENING

"Nobody ever listened himself out of a job."

—President Calvin Coolidge

Learning Objectives

After completing this chapter, you will be able to do the following.

- Explain the difference between hearing and listening.
- Identify the components of the listening process.
- Describe four different kinds of listening.
- Explain why good listening habits are important.

Chapter Outline

Following are the main sections in this chapter.

1. Listening Is More Than Hearing
2. Roadblocks to Good Listening
3. Effective Listening Strategies

New Speech Terms

In this chapter, you will learn the meanings of the speech terms listed below.

passive listening
active listening
listening spare time
appreciative listening
discriminative listening
empathic listening
critical listening
filter
testimonial
false comparison
jump on the bandwagon
stack the deck
name calling
paraphrase
summarize

General Vocabulary

Expanding your general vocabulary will help you become a more effective communicator. Listed below are some words appearing in this chapter that you should make part of your everyday vocabulary.

excursion
disintegration
sounding board
vulnerable
gluttony
avarice
sloth
peripheral
bias
propaganda
rhetorical
retention
acronym

Looking AHEAD

In one of Shakespeare's most famous lines, Mark Antony calls on his fellow Romans to "lend me your ears." In this chapter, we will ask you to lend us your ears for some retooling.

Most of us, it seems, are poor listeners—an unfortunate situation that can often lead to mistakes, misunderstandings, and even disaster. Yet listening is a skill that you can master if you are willing to adopt the right attitude and practice a few simple techniques. If we succeed as good listeners, we not only help ourselves in the quest for knowledge and success, but we also help the talker, who is encouraged by our attention and gains confidence from our interest.

In a sense, the message of this chapter is, "What you get out of listening depends on what you put into it." Here you will learn how to evaluate yourself as a listener and how to recognize communication barriers that keep us from listening. You will also learn how to develop good listening habits such as paraphrasing, summarizing, and note-taking.

Introduction

You don't know how it happened. You think you were paying attention when your friend started to tell you about an argument she had with her father. But somewhere along the way, your eyes glazed over, and her voice became a dull hum in the background of your mind. When you finally shook yourself out of your trance, she was asking, "So what should I do?" Once again, poor listening has you in hot water.

As listeners, we tend to think that the responsibility for successful communication lies with the person doing the talking. This attitude causes us to become lazy or **passive listeners.** We let the talker do all the work while we go along for the ride. We tolerate distractions—putting up with a noise in the hall, for instance, instead of getting up to shut the door. We pay more attention to how someone looks or talks than to what she or he has to say. And we generally fail to respond to the talker's message by asking questions or remembering things that were said.

Effective listeners, by contrast, play an active role by guiding the talker toward common interests. **Active listening** is a valuable skill. *Fortune* magazine rates listening as the top management skill needed for success in business. Employers constantly say that what they want most are employees who listen, understand, and follow directions.

Listening is also critical to success in family life and among friends. Good listeners do well in school—they follow directions better and don't waste time wondering what the assignment was. Put another way, good listening helps you keep things in perspective: "Nature has given us one tongue, but two ears," wrote the Greek philosopher Epictetus, "that we may hear twice as much as we speak."

Effective listeners are active listeners.

SECTION 1 Listening Is More Than Hearing

Listening is the "receiving" part of the communication process, but simply sensing what was said is just the beginning. We receive a message from someone talking when sound waves set off vibrations in our ears. Hearing, however, is only an automatic reaction of the senses and nervous system. By contrast, listening is the vastly more complicated process of understanding what was said.

When you listen, according to Webster's *New World Dictionary,* you "make a conscious effort to hear." Clearly, listening takes effort—it's a voluntary act in which we use our higher mental processes.

Some people think listening is not a skill at all, but something we do naturally. Unfortunately, we're not doing it very well. Studies show that we remember only about 25 percent of what we hear; in other words, we forget, ignore, distort, or misunderstand the great majority of incoming messages. Are we hard of hearing or hard of listening?

The cost of poor listening is high. Poor listening may keep you from doing well on an exam, but it can cost all of us much more. One researcher put it this way: "If each of America's more than 100 million workers prevented just one $10 mistake by better listening, their organizations would save $1 billion."

Do workers make many $10 mistakes? You bet. A $10 mistake is as simple as missing a meeting (you weren't listening when the boss mentioned the time), putting an item of stock in the wrong place (you were daydreaming), or having to retype a letter (you were thinking about the weekend).

Have you ever heard people say they don't have time for something—taking a walk, visiting a sick friend, writing someone a note? Not true. We all have the same 24 hours each day; what they mean is that something isn't important enough to make time for.

The same is true for listening. We will be poor listeners until we make up our minds to change. Listening keeps you informed, up to date, and out of trouble. It increases your impact when you do speak. It gives you an edge, power, and influence. It makes other people like or even love you. But while hearing is easy, listening is hard. You have to train yourself to listen.

THE BUCKETS reprinted by permission of United Feature Syndicate, Inc.

Listening with Time to Spare

One reason listening can be troublesome is that our minds and mouths work at different rates of speed. Although most people speak about 120–180 words per minute, we can listen about six times as fast. Our brains simply work faster than our mouths. This "rate gap" helps explain why our minds sometimes start to wander while we listen. This fact is both a curse and a blessing for listeners.

At the rate a speaker normally talks, you can sandwich many thoughts between her words, and still not miss a thing. In other words, most of us find ourselves with a little **listening spare time** on our hands.

Stray thoughts may take you away from the speaker briefly, but they don't keep you from grasping her meaning. So you continue jumping back and forth, tuning in, tuning out, tuning in as you think some of your own thoughts and then turning back to the speaker—a bit like the way a computer can do multitasking.

These private *excursions* away from the speaker can, however, be dangerous. Let's imagine that you are speaking with one of your teachers and the teacher happens to mention your best friend. For just a moment, you start thinking about what you and your friend are planning to do on the weekend. You follow that thought for a while, longer than you intended, and then suddenly remember the teacher. "Whoops! What was that he just said?"

Unfortunately, you discover you've stayed away too long and missed a critical part of the message. The *disintegration* of your listening has begun. Eventually you give up; it's simply too hard to catch up. You nod your head occasionally for the sake of courtesy, but this is not listening. You've switched over to cruise control.

Fortunately, this extra time can also be a listener's best friend. We can train ourselves to use it to improve our listening skills. Think of yourself as the rabbit in the fable of the tortoise and the hare. The tortoise represents the speaker, who moves down a path at a steady pace without ever speeding up, stopping, or taking a detour. The hare represents you, the listener, who can dash ahead, stop awhile, fall behind, and then catch up again.

The hare loses the race, but you'll be a winner if you can capitalize on your thought-speed to make the most of listening opportunities. In a later section, we'll show you how to do just that.

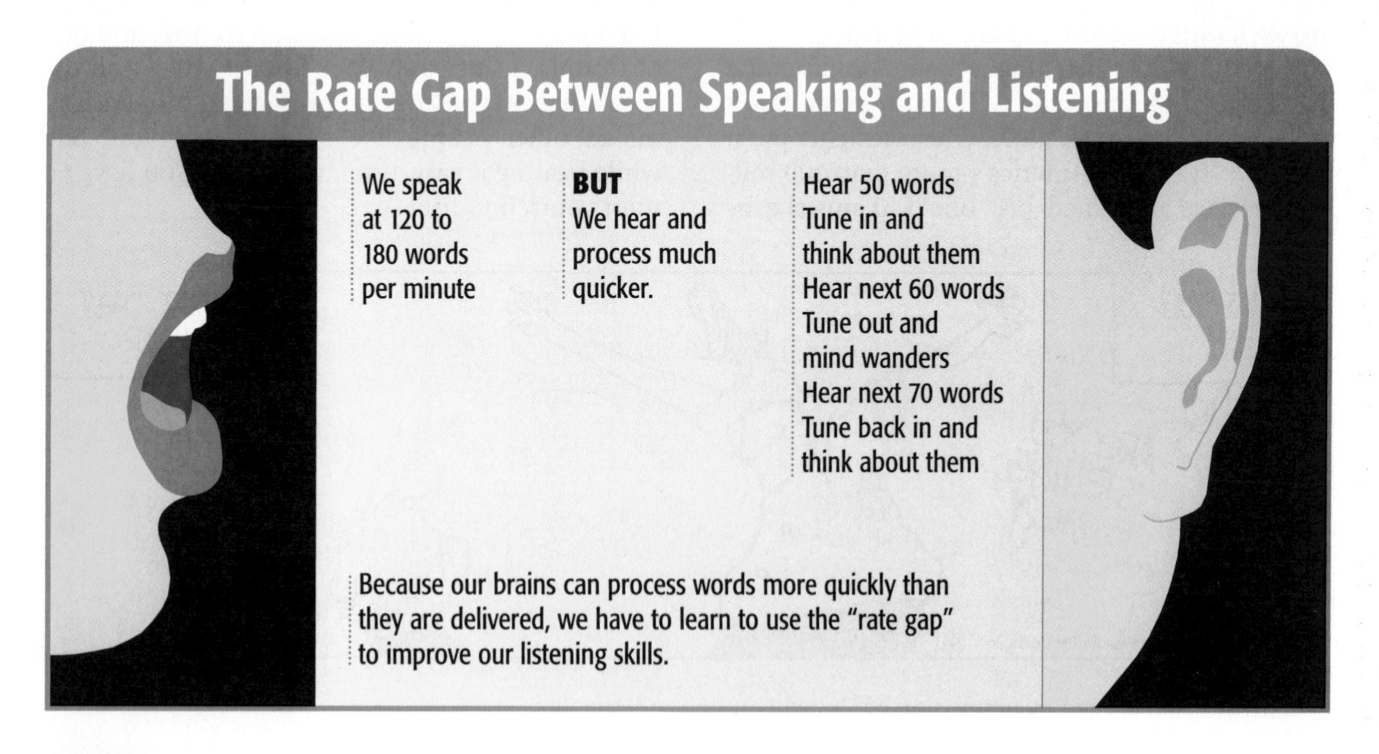

The Rate Gap Between Speaking and Listening
We speak at 120 to 180 words per minute
BUT We hear and process much quicker.
Hear 50 words
Tune in and think about them
Hear next 60 words
Tune out and mind wanders
Hear next 70 words
Tune back in and think about them
Because our brains can process words more quickly than they are delivered, we have to learn to use the "rate gap" to improve our listening skills.

Four Ways to Listen ... An air-traffic controller straining to hear a "Mayday" call from a plane in trouble isn't listening the way you are when your Aunt Bessie calls from Des Moines to chat. We listen most carefully to what we feel is important to us.

We say we're "all ears" when the coach announces the starting lineup or the music teacher names soloists for the big performance, but somehow our ears jam up when Mom or Dad wants to talk about household chores. The fact is, we have different listening styles for different occasions. How successful we are as listeners may depend in part on choosing the right listening style for the situation.

Appreciative Listening

Perhaps the most basic listening style is **appreciative listening.** We listen appreciatively when we enjoy music, a bird's song, or the murmur of a brook. We need a different style, one called **discriminative listening,** when we want to single out one particular sound from a noisy environment. You discriminate, for example, when you listen for a friend's voice in a crowded room.

The third listening style is more complex. **Empathic listening,** the style practiced by counselors, psychiatrists, and good friends, encourages people to talk freely without fear of embarrassment. Friends act as our *sounding boards* when we just want someone to listen. The empathic listener in conversation with a troubled friend accepts what is said, tries hard to understand, and, above all, makes no judgments. He listens without offering any solutions.

The fourth style, **critical listening,** is the one we will examine most closely. Critical listeners evaluate what they hear and decide if another person's

THE SHIP THAT COULDN'T BE SUNK

INSTANT IMPACT

One of the greatest tragedies in the history of sea travel occurred on the night of April 12, 1912, when the crew of the *Titanic* refused to listen to repeated warnings of icebergs. The crew had been led to believe that this brand-new passenger liner was "unsinkable," and few doubted that boastful claim. Even after the ship struck an iceberg and was slowly sinking, some of the passengers ignored the captain's orders to get into the lifeboats.

When the ship finally began tilting dangerously, it was too late. There weren't enough lifeboats for all the passengers and, worse still, the *Californian,* the only other ship in the area (about ten miles away), made no attempt to reach the wreck. Her radio operator had gone off duty. As a result, more than a thousand people needlessly lost their lives.

WORDS FROM THE WORKPLACE

George L. Dempsey, Ph.D.

Psychologist

Q. *How do your listening skills contribute to good communication with your patients?*

A. My listening skills give me the ability to see the world through THEIR eyes. Seeing through their eyes allows me to understand the emotions by understanding their perceptions. This also enables me to form a close and honest relationship with my patients, which promotes trust. Ultimately, trust between patient and doctor is what enhances good communication.

Q. *What are some of the skills you use in listening to your patients?*

A. One of the skills I use is paraphrasing what I hear, which is a way of reacting to what I hear. Another technique is to listen for my patients' feelings and ignore the content. I also find that ASKING THEM what would be helpful is beneficial.

Q. *What tips can you give to students to show them the importance of communication skills in the world of your work?*

A. Anyone trying to communicate in my profession must really, really like people. Second, they really need to like creative thinking and logic systems. "Helping" people involves the ability to see things the way THEY do in order to help them see the flaws with their perception. Third, I would tell people that they need not to require immediate gratification. Fourth, I would tell them that they need to possess highly polished interpersonal skills along with a high degree of integrity and personal dignity. Lastly, make sure you have spent time resolving your own issues.

message is logical, is worthwhile, or has value. We need to be critical listeners when someone wants us to buy something, vote a certain way, or support a particular idea. We also need to be critical listeners in school, where *listening* and *thinking* are closely linked.

Why Listening Matters ... The good listener is popular everywhere. You will make more friends by listening than by speaking. Good listeners encourage speakers to do their best. Listening is a way of saying to the talker, "You are important, and I am interested in what you have to say." And after a while, good listeners actually get to know something.

Effective listening involves not only tuning in to others, but tuning in to ourselves as well. Listening carefully to what we say and how we say it can teach us an immense amount about ourselves.

Statements we make often reflect our own self-concepts. If, for example, you heard yourself making the following statements, what would you conclude?

- "I can't handle angry people."
- "Someday I'm going to get organized."
- "I'd like to tell my boss how I feel, but I can't."

Listening is, in the final analysis, a thinking skill, because it requires us to be selective with our attention, to classify and categorize information, and to sort out important principles and concepts from a stream of facts, jokes, and stories.

Good listening skills are especially important in a society that grants freedom of speech to all people, whatever their views or causes. In the remainder of this chapter, we will focus on how to get rid of bad listening habits and how to acquire good ones.

Empathic Listening

SECTION 1 REVIEW

Recalling the Facts ...

1. What is the difference between active and passive listening?
2. Name and briefly identify four listening styles.

Thinking Critically ...

1. Read descriptions of well-known people—perhaps people you are studying in other classes—and have your classmates guess their names.
2. Consider the empathic role of listening. Why would nonjudgmental listening be so valuable? Why is it that we can sometimes share our feelings freely with a stranger (someone we sit next to on the bus, for instance) but have difficulty being open with close friends or family?

Taking Charge ...

1. Record a portion of a radio talk show or call-in program. Play back what you have recorded several times so that you know it well, and make a list of specific questions about the information presented. Then play the segment for your classmates and ask your list of questions to check for understanding. Next, ask your classmates what feelings they remember being expressed in the segment. Have they listened better for facts or feelings? What do feelings sound like?
2. How many times have you heard a student ask a question and then the next student with her or his hand raised asks the very same question? To help your classmates listen to each other more attentively, stage a class discussion on some controversial topic. Each speaker must restate the previous speaker's point (to that speaker's satisfaction) before giving his or her own opinion. For example, you might say, "I understand you believe that watching TV can be a good way to learn about history. Let me explain why I disagree."

SECTION 2

Roadblocks to Good Listening

Even Shakespeare, whose words have been heard by millions all over the globe, regretted poor listening. He had one of his characters lament, "It is the disease of not listening . . . that I am troubled withal." Part of the reason listening is difficult is that we spend so little time working on it. Most of the communication instruction we get in school is geared toward reading, despite the fact that we listen about three times as much as we read. Consciously, we seem to pay more attention to what reaches our eyes than to what reaches our ears.

A Small Price to Pay

Good listening costs us something. To really listen we must *pay* attention. Small wonder that we use the word "pay," which implies exchanging one thing for another. In listening, we pay out our most personal assets—our time, interest, and effort—to receive something in return: information, entertainment, and perhaps even comfort. Listening is hard work, which is why we do not give our attention easily.

1. TUNE OUT DULL TOPICS.
2. FAKE ATTENTION.
3. YIELD TO DISTRACTIONS.
4. CRITICIZE DELIVERY OR PHYSICAL APPEARANCE.
5. JUMP TO CONCLUSIONS.
6. OVERREACT TO EMOTIONAL WORDS.
7. INTERRUPT.

But while we are paying attention, we must also exercise judgment; as listeners, we risk being deceived. The spoken word seems to affect us much more powerfully than the written word. Researchers say that many of our most deeply held convictions come from things we hear, not things we read. A committee of the National Council on the Teaching of English concluded that students' "political ideals and ethical standards are influenced, if not largely determined, by their listening."

Unfortunately, professional persuaders such as politicians, advertisers, and con artists of every kind know this too. They have learned that people are most *vulnerable* when they are listening. Remember that while you should be willing to listen to almost anything, you must not give up your ability to think for yourself.

Why Is Listening Difficult?

Among the biggest hurdles to good listening is the very human desire to speak. Most of the time when someone is speaking to us, we're thinking of what we want to say next, not listening at all. We prefer speaking to listening. Good listeners must learn to let go of their egos. Train yourself not to worry about what you want to say until the other person has finished talking.

Our very busy lives (not to mention MTV, surfing the 'Net, and video games) have also caused us to develop extremely short attention spans. Our tiny attention spans and impatience sometimes lead us to assume we know what someone will say next. This is an especially poor habit because you're likely to shape what you do hear to fit what you expect. You will only hear, in other words, what you want to hear.

Bad Habits Make for Bad Company

During the Middle Ages, people worried about committing the seven deadly sins—*gluttony*, anger, greed, lechery, envy, *avarice*, and *sloth*. Today we should worry about committing the seven deadly habits of bad listening. Any one of them will keep you from becoming an effective listener.

1. *Tuning out dull topics*
   Many listeners decide early on that a topic is simply not interesting—"Class, let's review our procedures for a fire drill." This decision rapidly leads to the MEGO syndrome ("My Eyes Glaze Over").

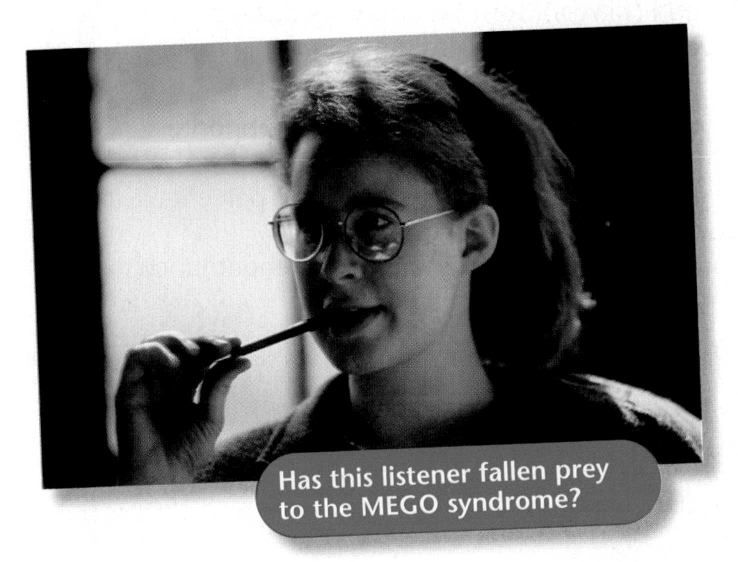

Has this listener fallen prey to the MEGO syndrome?

   Don't let yourself become a lazy listener if what you are listening to doesn't seem appealing. Instead, listen for something you can use yourself—an idea, a quote, a story, or even a joke. An energetic listener can nearly always find something of value in what another person is saying.

2. *Faking attention*
   It's no sin to be courteous, but sometimes we take good manners to an unfortunate extreme. When we find someone's conversation boring but are too polite (or too afraid) to risk offending him, we pretend to pay attention, though all the while our minds are a thousand miles away. Don't assume that all a speaker really wants from us is that we *look* as if we're listening.

   To help yourself stay on track, create a mental paraphrase of what the speaker is saying—that is, translate the speaker's thoughts into your own words. And repeat key points to

GENDER TALK

INSTANT IMPACT

Do you get irritated when people interrupt? Or are you the one doing most of the interrupting? Studies show that there may be significant differences between the sexes when it comes to stopping a speaker in midsentence.

When a man and a woman are talking, for example, the man makes about 96 percent of the interruptions.

Men appear to have a few other gender-specific habits regarding speech. Some researchers say that men have been taught since childhood to become problem solvers. As a result, men tend to enter a conversation too quickly, and usually with a ready answer. They fail to draw out the speaker with questions or to listen for more information before jumping to a conclusion.

Deborah Tannen, author of a popular book on conversational styles called *You Just Don't Understand,* argues that most women use "rapport talk" as a way of establishing connections and relationships. From childhood, she writes, women tend to listen for things they have in common with others.

Men, on the other hand, use "report talk" to preserve their independence and maintain status. They do this primarily by showing knowledge and skill, and by holding center stage through storytelling or joking. From childhood, men learn to use talking as a way to get and keep attention. Consequently, they have a harder time learning to be good listeners.

Source: Deborah Tannen, *You Just Don't Understand* (New York: Ballantine Books, 1990).

COMMUNICATION Breakdown

The College Lecture

College students may look as if they're listening to the day's lecture, but their minds may be elsewhere, says Paul Cameron, an assistant professor of psychology at Wayne State University. To prove his point, Cameron fired a gun (blanks) from time to time during a lecture and then asked students what they were thinking when they heard the shot. He found that

- About 20 percent of the students were thinking about someone of the opposite sex.
- Another 20 percent were thinking of a memory.
- Only 20 percent were actually paying attention to the lecturer (just 12 percent described themselves as active listeners).
- Of the rest, some were worrying, some daydreaming, some thinking about lunch, and 8 percent were thinking about religion.

Cameron obtained these results in a nine-week course in introductory psychology for college sophomores. The gun was fired 21 times at random intervals, usually when Cameron, who was himself the lecturer, was in the middle of a sentence. We would guess no one speaks out of turn in his class!

Source: San Francisco *Sunday Examiner and Chronicle.*

Questions

1. How well do you listen to classroom instructions or lectures?
2. What other things do you think about while you're listening?
3. What could you do to help focus your listening skills during class time?

yourself periodically throughout the conversation. Both steps will help you maintain an attitude of genuine interest.

3. ***Yielding to distractions***
Peripheral noises or movements often can affect our concentration. A window drops shut, someone sneezes, a book falls to the floor. All too often, we give our attention to the hubbub around us instead of to the speaker. How often have you let your parents' words fall on deaf ears while you were busy with a video game? The truth is that we can block out almost any distraction when we concentrate.

4. ***Criticizing delivery or physical appearance***
Many people abandon their good listening habits when they become preoccupied with a speaker's physical appearance ("He must have found that shirt in his dad's closet") or delivery ("Let's count how many times she says 'like'"). Regardless of who the speaker is, the content of his message is what counts. Don't use poor physical appearance or speaking style as an alibi for not listening. And don't let yourself be put off by someone's manner, accent, or clothing. Be generous enough to overlook lisps, slurs, and mumbles.

5. ***Jumping to conclusions***
   Be patient. Occasionally, personal *biases* against a speaker's background or position ("Does this old man really know anything about a song by Lauryn Hill?") interfere with listening. Such biases may cause a listener to ask too many questions, interrupt too often, or try to pick an argument. Again, withhold judgment until you're sure you know the speaker's position.
6. ***Overreacting to emotional words***
   We all react from time to time to certain words or phrases that push our "hot buttons." If a speaker says, for example, "liberal," "abortion," or, even worse, "grade point average," you might experience a strong emotional reaction, one that can either block out or perk up your ability to listen. In such cases, you need to make an extra effort to remain objective. Your memory of key facts or arguments may be wiped out by the first rush of hot blood.

   Our emotions have a lot to do with our ability to listen. At times, they act as filters to screen out things we don't want to hear. If we hear something that attacks our deepest feelings or convictions, for example, our ears go temporarily deaf. Instead of listening, we lay plans to trap the speaker or try to think of a question that will embarrass her. Perhaps we simply turn to thoughts that support our own feelings and tune the speaker out.

   In any event, listening comes to a screeching halt. When you feel your emotional barriers begin to rise, stay calm. Wait until the speaker has finished. Then, and only then, review the speaker's main ideas and make up your mind how to respond.
7. ***Interrupting***
   "We never listen when we are eager to speak." wrote the French philosopher La Rochefoucauld. Try to find out if you spend most of your listening time thinking about what you want to say. The natural result of this habit is for you to interrupt—an almost certain sign that you don't know or care about what the other person is saying. We risk becoming first-class bores when we interrupt.

Filters That Distort

Information goes through many **filters** when it passes from speaker to listener. Listeners filter what they hear based on their backgrounds and personalities. Just as sunlight becomes weaker as it passes through a tinted window, communication can become distorted when it passes through personal filters. When you tell your father that you totaled the car, his reaction will be affected by whether he

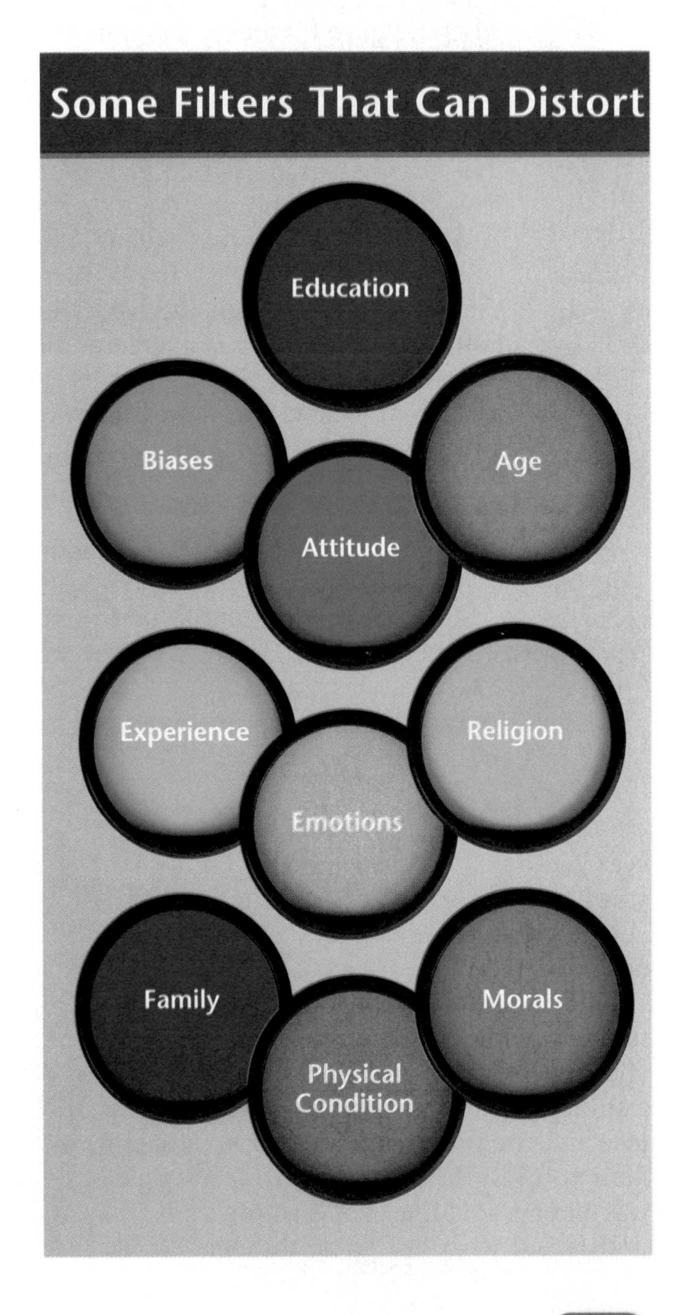

COMMUNICATION **Break through**

Keep Emotions in Check

Specialists say that strong emotions can be powerful obstacles to good listening. When we become too emotionally involved in a situation, we tend to hear what we *want* to hear—not what is actually being said. Our emotions keep us from focusing on the real message.

Race horse trainer Phil Johnson discovered how much of a problem emotions can be when he gave his jockey last-minute instructions before the start of an important race at New York's Belmont Park. Johnson told the rider to hang back at the beginning of the race and then make a run for the front in the home stretch. But as he talked, he noticed that the jockey wasn't looking at him. Instead, the jockey kept staring at one of the other horses in the paddock, a horse the jockey had ridden in a previous race. "I have to beat that horse," the rider said, interrupting Johnson.

When the starting gate sprang open, Johnson quickly learned that his message had fallen on deaf ears. Much to his disappointment, he watched as his jockey dashed to the front, running neck and neck with the horse the jockey had ridden before. Eventually Johnson's horse tired and finished well back in the field.

Three weeks later Johnson entered the same horse in another race but this time with a different jockey. This jockey followed Johnson's instructions carefully and won, earning a nice reward for less than two minutes of listening.

Questions

1. Can you think of a situation where your emotions might keep you from listening attentively to someone?
2. Why is it important to try to remain objective and open-minded when listening to people with whom you think you may disagree?

ever had a bad accident himself. Or, when you listen to a coworker's decision to quit, your own attitudes about work will influence your reaction.

Filters become a problem when they interfere with good listening habits. As a young person, for example, you may have trouble listening to older people. You may lose patience with their style of speech or perhaps you just think to yourself, "This person was young so long ago, she can't possibly understand what I'm going through." In this case your age acts as a filter to prevent genuine communication from taking place.

Improving your ability to listen is largely a matter of mental conditioning. Anytime you feel your emotional barriers or filters start to rise, make a conscious effort to:

- Refrain from judging or evaluating the speaker.
- Focus your attention on the message (make the problem under discussion the enemy; that way you and the speaker are on the same side).
- Search for areas where you agree.

- Keep an open mind. (If someone says something that bothers you, write it on a slip of paper. You can ask a question about it later when the speaker finishes—because it's safely stored, you don't have to think about it anymore.)

People from different ethnic backgrounds or people whose first language is not English can also bump up against your filters, and you can bump up against theirs. Again, special care must be taken to be a responsible listener. When this happens, you should:

- Be patient.
- Pay closer attention to body language.
- Hold your temper when you disagree.
- Try hard to put yourself in the speaker's position.

Always keep an open mind as you listen.

To become successful in life and work, you need to learn as much as you can about your own filters. The more you recognize them, the more you will be able to listen extra hard when you hear something that you might ordinarily ignore. But no matter how much your filters affect your listening, you should always show respect for the other person's point of view.

SECTION 2 REVIEW

Recalling the Facts ...

1. List two reasons why listening is difficult.
2. Name and briefly describe five bad listening habits.

Thinking Critically ...

1. Poor listening is a failure that many people accept. "I can sit and look at a person and never hear a word he says," they say with little or no embarrassment. Could part of the reason be that we never practice? Stephen Covey, author of *The Seven Habits of Highly Effective People,* notes that "we spend years learning how to read, write, and speak, but we hardly get any training in listening." Where and how could we train people to listen well?
2. Make a list of all the different kinds of distractions—both internal and external—that can interfere with good listening. What strategies can you suggest to overcome these distractions?

Taking Charge ...

1. Try an experiment with distractions. Arrange with your teacher to have several distractions occur sometime during a class presentation—have a classmate deliver a pass from the office, "plant" a classmate who will drop a book, and so on. Ask another classmate to monitor what happens to the class's attention during each distraction. Discuss how these distractions affected attentiveness.

SECTION 3 Effective Listening Strategies

You can learn to be a good listener. Studies have shown that a little bit of knowledge and a lot of practice can lead to improved listening. To practice well, however, takes the right attitude—the attitude that you will make the effort to become a better listener.

To become a good listener, you must stay alert on several fronts at once, working with ears, eyes, and your whole being. Total body listening means, for starters, adopting the right posture for listening: Face the speaker, establish eye contact, and block out distractions. Lean forward and nod occasionally. Good listening requires all of our senses and plenty of mental energy.

Good listeners use not only their ears but also their other senses.

Listening to a Speech

Just as there are times to bear down and times to ease up, you should listen more carefully at some times than others. Your attention may lag in driver's education class, for example, as the teacher explains a formula for converting the safe following distance from seconds to feet. When it comes time to listen for directions on your driver's test, though, you will summon your most intense concentration.

Listening to speeches and presentations works the same way. Knowing how speeches are usually organized, for example, can make us smarter listeners because we will be sure to listen most intently when it matters the most. The following discussion illustrates how to listen during each of the three major parts of a speech. (A thorough discussion of how to organize a speech appears in Chapter 9.)

The Beginning ... Many people with good intentions try to listen hardest at the beginning of a speech. Actually, this is not such a great strategy. The beginning may be the most entertaining part of the speech—because the speaker is doing her utmost to gain your attention—but it is usually not the most important. Often, listeners get so caught up in the speaker's jokes, stories, and examples that they forget to be alert for the key idea.

Somewhere shortly after the beginning of a speech, the speaker will state the main idea of her talk. Once you find the main idea, your listening job becomes much easier. Now you will recognize the facts and details in the rest of the speech as strengthening or reinforcing the main idea. If you miss the main idea, these facts and details will send you spinning in all directions as you keep asking yourself, "Now how does this connect to what was said before?"

Rather than hanging on every word as a speech begins, you should think about the title of the speech and make a few guesses about what direction the speaker might take. This is a key to good listening—constantly trying to figure out what the speaker's main point is and testing hypotheses . . . until, bingo! You pounce on the main idea when it pops up. Notice how this approach differs from that of someone who assumes he knows what the speaker will say and, on that assumption, stops listening.

The Middle ... Be a critical listener during the body of the speech. Your main goal, of course, is to understand what the speaker has to say. But this is also the time to test the strength of the speaker's message. Question the support that the speaker uses to defend assertions. How recent are the speaker's examples? How relevant are his quotes? What is the source for his statistics—or has he even given a source? In other words, this is the time to evaluate the accuracy and fairness of what you hear.

The End ... During the last part of a speech, the listener must be on guard for emotional appeals and *propaganda,* material designed to distort the truth or deceive the audience. You can tell that a speech is nearly over when the speaker repeats the main idea, summarizes her most important support, or says "in conclusion" or words to that effect. Speakers often end their speeches by trying to appeal to the listener's feelings. Your job as a listener is to recognize whether the speaker is trying to mislead you.

This is the time to be most alert for *rhetorical* devices, that is, tricks of language. Such tricks might include **testimonials** ("You should agree with me because many famous celebrities do"), **false comparisons** (comparing unlike things such as apples with oranges), or suggestions to **jump on the bandwagon** ("Everyone is aboard—don't be left out"). As a speaker ends her speech, ask yourself whether she has earned whatever acceptance or support she is asking you to give.

Use Your Listening "Spare Time" to Advantage

As mentioned earlier, you can listen much faster than anyone can speak. This means that during a speech you can easily fall victim to what listening expert Sally Scobey calls the "meandering mind menace." As our minds race ahead of the speaker, we may begin to daydream—fretting over old worries or mulling over pet projects. But we can train ourselves to use this extra time more usefully. For example, here are four ways to keep your mind fully engaged.

Explore ... One way to use your spare listening time is to explore what lies ahead in the speech by asking, "What does this person want me to believe?" If you guess correctly, your understanding and *retention* will be strengthened. If you guess wrong, you can quickly compare the point you expected with the one the speaker actually made, and then consider why the speech surprised you. Bad listeners guess what the speaker is going to say and stop paying attention; good listeners guess too, but they listen intently to find out if their guess was correct.

Analyze ... Another way to spend your listening spare time is to analyze the speaker's message. As the speaker makes arguments and defends assertions, ask yourself, "Are these reasons, examples, and facts

Exploring, analyzing, reviewing, and searching allow you to use your listening "spare time" effectively.

convincing? Are things exactly as he says they are? Does this information match what I already know? Is he leaving anything out?"

Many clever speakers may try to mislead you with deceptive reasoning. They may **stack the deck** against a particular person or idea by giving only one side of the story. They may use **name calling** (giving someone a negative label without any evidence) or many other unbalanced arguments to convince you. But a good listener is a hard sell.

INSTANT IMPACT

THE SILENT LISTENER

Once when President Calvin Coolidge was in the White House, he had a visitor from his home state of Massachusetts. The visitor, Channing Cox, had succeeded Coolidge as governor and had come to ask him a question about the business of government. Cox asked Coolidge how he had been able to see so many visitors each day as governor.

"I've heard you always left the office at 5 P.M.," Cox said. "I never leave that early, and often I'm there 'til 9. Why the difference?"

Coolidge thought for a moment and then replied in his usual abrupt manner: "You talk back."

Review ... Every so often you should review what you have heard. Speakers usually allow time for listeners to catch their breath. They may pause, for example, to make a transition: "Now let me talk about . . . " These moments give you a perfect opportunity to review.

Review

Mentally run over the points already made, stopping a split second to examine each. Reviewing helps you remember. Tell yourself that you will have to give a report on this speech sometime, and begin mentally preparing your report while the speech is still going. Planning to share what you have heard with others is a great way to motivate yourself to remember.

Search for Hidden Meanings ... Throughout a speech, lecture, or presentation you should "listen between the lines" in search of hidden meanings. Are there failures or shortcomings the speaker should admit but doesn't? Does the speaker's silence on something indicate it might be a sore point? A speaker's body language and nonverbal behavior can offer big clues to what he is really thinking. (We will take a close look at body language in Chapter 4.) Often what a person doesn't say may be as important as what she does say.

Here is a handy *acronym* that might help you remember these suggestions. Think EARS:

- **E for explore.** Think ahead of the speaker.
- **A for analyze.** Consider carefully what's being said; look at it from several angles.
- **R for review.** Take advantage of your spare listening time to review.
- **S for search.** Be alert for hidden meanings.

Ask for Explanations

In many situations, you will find you need more information. When you ask for an explanation, you help the speaker make his message more understandable. To get additional information, you might say something like, "Would you please clarify that?" Other useful comments include

- "Would you say that again?"
- "I don't understand what you mean."
- "Excuse me, but could you be more specific?"

People are usually delighted to help, but if you suggest that they *need* help, they may get angry. When you are confused, be sure to say something like "Maybe I misunderstood," and not "You aren't being very clear."

By asking for explanations or paraphrasing, you can be sure you understand what your manager wants you to do.

Paraphrase the Message

You can also help others by trying to **paraphrase** a message, or repeat in your own words what you think you heard. Your boss, for example, may give you detailed instructions on how to close the store for the evening or describe several errands you must run. In either case, paraphrasing goes a step beyond just asking for a further explanation.

Paraphrases often begin like this:

- "What I hear you saying is . . ."
- "Correct me if I'm wrong, but . . ."
- "In other words, your view is . . ."

When you paraphrase, you restate the speaker's message as a way of checking its accuracy. When you paraphrase someone, try to capture only the essence or main points of the message. Be selective rather than exhaustive. Try, too, to focus on the content of what was said rather than any feelings expressed. This can help defuse a potentially emotional situation.

A good listener will do the following:

1. Provide encouragement.
2. Ask for explanations.
3. Paraphase the message.
4. Summarize the message.
5. Put it down on paper.

Summarize the Message

You can go one step beyond a paraphrase by trying to **summarize** what you see as the main idea in a speech or conversation. Summaries are especially important when you need to relay a message from one person to another. The manager may ask you, for example, to convey her instructions to your coworkers.

When you summarize something, you condense the important points into a brief comment. Some typical summary statements might begin this way:

- "What the manager said so far is . . ."
- "Your key ideas, as I understand them, are . . ."
- "Recapping what you have been saying . . ."

Summaries are useful anytime a speaker becomes especially long-winded or confusing. Suppose a customer of long standing has come to complain about your company's service. This is what he says:

"Two out of the last six shipments have arrived at least a week overdue. I hope you realize that

How Well Do You Listen?

Think about your responses to the following statements about your listening skills.

1.	I often interrupt people to interject what I need to say.	Y	N
2.	I anticipate what someone is about to say and finish the statement.	Y	N
3.	During a conversation, I am easily distracted by what is happening around me.	Y	N
4.	I feel uncomfortable when I look directly at a speaker for more than a few seconds.	Y	N
5.	I "tune out" speakers I don't agree with.	Y	N
6.	I like to focus on a speaker's clothes and hair instead of what is being said.	Y	N
7.	I am turned off by a speaker who uses words I don't know.	Y	N
8.	Sometimes I daydream while people are talking to me.	Y	N
9.	During conversations, while the other person is speaking, I like to plan what I want to say.	Y	N
10.	I often pretend to be interested in what a speaker is saying even when I'm not.	Y	N

How did you do? If you answered "no" to each statement, you are an excellent listener. If you answered "yes" one to three times, your listening skills could stand a little improvement. If you answered "yes" to more than three statements, you need to work hard on developing better listening habits for greater success at school, at work, or with your friends and family.

costs us $1,000 a day. The last time we ordered parts from you, they were late too—and that's never happened before. The agents I've spoken with have been rude. What's happening around here?"

You summarize this conversation to your coworkers and manager as follows:

"Mr. Brown feels that we are letting him down all around—shipments, parts, and now service. He wants an explanation."

Summarizing is especially useful in situations involving conflicts or complaints or when some kind of problem solving is needed. Summarizing is also helpful at the close of a telephone conversation, especially when a variety of points have been discussed or one of the parties is expected to do something.

Don't depend on your memory alone. Write it down.

Put It Down on Paper

Memory alone can't guarantee that we will remember an important conversation a week or even a few days later. That's why note-taking is usually considered a listening skill. It seems that just making the effort to take notes will almost always help improve our listening. Those who take notes understand more and remember more.

For one thing, taking notes improves our attentiveness. "It helps you focus on the highlights of what is being said," notes Germaine Knapp, a communications consultant. Note-taking also increases the chances that you will review what has been said.

From time to time, a good note-taker looks back on his notes to see if they are complete. Such review is crucial to good listening. And, surprisingly, note-taking often helps the speaker. Speakers feel flattered when people write down things they say. They usually try to be as accurate as possible if they know someone is keeping track.

Keep these tips in mind when you take notes on important meetings or conversations:

- Be prepared. Try to carry a small notepad and pen with you whenever you think you might need to take notes.
- Get it down. Don't take the time to be neat. You can always recopy your notes later. The important thing is to work quickly—writing just clearly enough so that you can remember what you wrote and why.
- Don't try to write everything. Avoid complete sentences. Draw lines to connect ideas; omit vowels. Develop your own system of shorthand using symbols, pictures, punctuation, and abbreviations. For example, this note:

  Glenna, lnch w/HP client, FRI 11:30 @ Macaroni's

  means that you and Glenna Douglas (a colleague) have a lunch meeting scheduled with a Hewlett-Packard client on Friday at 11:30 A.M. at Macaroni's restaurant.

SECTION 3 REVIEW

Recalling the Facts ...

1. When are the most important times to listen carefully during a speech?
2. How can you use your listening "spare time" to best advantage?
3. Explain the difference between asking for an explanation, paraphrasing a message, and summarizing a message.

Thinking Critically ...

1. The average person spends 9 percent of his daily communication time writing, 16 percent reading, 30 percent speaking, and a whopping 45 percent listening. Students spend even more time listening—up to 60 percent during school hours, according to some studies. Do these percentages seem accurate? Which classes require the most listening? Which the least?

Taking Charge ...

1. As a way to increase your listening awareness, list all the sounds you hear in the next five minutes. Do this two or three times a day in different environments, to sharpen your listening skills.
2. Watch one of the courtroom shows on television. Arrange to tape-record the judge's decision and comments, but don't listen. Instead, draw your own conclusions about the case based on what you've heard during the trial. Then compare your ruling with the judge's.

STUDENT WORK

"It's Time to Listen to Teens" *By Merry Hayes*

Merry Hayes, a student at Lincoln East High School in Nebraska, wrote the following editorial for the school newspaper. Her editorial was chosen by the Columbia Scholastic Press Association as the best in the nation. She argues that parents can help their teens cope with stress by listening to them.

These are the best years of our lives.

So we are told.

Correction.

These are the stress years of our lives.

A major problem facing today's teenager is stress. Stress caused by parents, peers, and even society as a whole.

From the very moment of birth, our parents have planned our dreams, hopes, goals, and future—leaving no room for dissent, no room for freedom, no room for failure.

The sons and daughters of the world feel a stifling pressure from their parents to succeed. They fear that not living up to their parents' expectations or up to the image of big brother the football star, or big sister the Harvard graduate, will result in the hideous social disease called failure.

Even our peers, those who are closest to us, those who provide security, and those who understand our problems, put pressure on us.

No one wants to be seen wearing outdated clothes or get caught saying an "in" word that was "out" a long time ago.

Thus, the wheels go round and round. Where will it stop? Nobody knows. This merry-go-round spins so fast for some that they can't get off. They paid for their ticket, and many will keep on paying for it, with their lives.

These pressures can lead to alcohol, drugs, and even death. Some years ago in Plano, Texas, six students of a suburban high school committed suicide because they thought it was the "in" thing to do. This rash of suicides started when two very popular students killed themselves. In the eyes of their friends, they were the modern-day Romeo and Juliet.

Society has formed the ideal that success is everything and pressure must be applied to achieve it. People have a right to make their own decisions and their own mistakes without being pushed into it by an outsider. Pressuring someone into using drugs or alcohol is very destructive to that person. Likewise, pushing someone into college who is unprepared or unwilling can be equally ruinous.

However, some stress is good for a person. We all need a little motivation now and then or else nothing would ever get done. But there is only so much a person can take. Teenagers have enough problems as it is without being the rope in a tug of war between parents and peers.

These teenage years should be the best of times, but they will be the worst of times if something is not done to ease the pressure.

Parents and peers should reduce their demands on these young adults and, instead, accept them as they are and encourage them to be what they want, and only what they want. They can start by listening.

Questions

1. What problems can unrealistic expectations cause?
2. What problems could be solved if both parents and teens listened better?

CHAPTER 3 Review and Enrichment...

Looking Back

Listed below are the major ideas discussed in this chapter.

- Hearing is an automatic reaction of the senses and nervous system to sound. Listening, on the other hand, is a voluntary act.
- Poor listening costs us millions of dollars in lost business, mismanaged time, and waste. In places such as construction sites, poor listening could cause accidents or deaths.
- Because we can listen faster than anyone can speak, we have some "spare time" to use to our advantage. We can use this time to explore, analyze, review, and search for hidden meanings.
- Success in listening depends on choosing the right listening style for the situation.
- The seven deadly habits of poor listening are tuning out dull topics, faking attention, yielding to distractions, criticizing a speaker's delivery, jumping to conclusions, overreacting to emotional words, and interrupting.
- Strong emotions can sometimes prevent us from being good listeners.
- Knowledge of how a typical speech is organized can be helpful to listeners, because different sections of a speech call for different kinds of listening.
- Note-taking can help improve our listening habits.

Speech Vocabulary

Fill in the blank with the correct term from the list below.

passive listening
active listening
listening spare time
appreciative listening
discriminative listening
empathic listening
critical listening
false comparison
jump on the bandwagon
paraphrase
summarize
filter
testimonials
stack the deck
name calling

1. We use ______________ when we listen to someone relate her problems, hopes, or dreams, especially when the person doesn't want our approval or advice.
2. We can use our ______________ to explore, analyze, and review a speaker's message.
3. When we recognize sounds, we are only hearing. If we pay little attention to those sounds, we are using ______________. But if we try energetically to make sense of those sounds, we are using ______________.
4. If you buy a music CD to enjoy, you use ______________; but if you intend to write a review of the CD for the school newspaper, you use ______________.
5. ______________ is the kind of listening that enables you to hear a friend across a crowded room.
6. Some of the propaganda techniques that professional persuaders use are ______________ (using the name of a celebrity), ______________ (holding up one candidate against a much older one), ______________ ("Don't be left out!"), ______________ (presenting only favorable evidence), and ______________ (mudslinging).
7. Our personal biases may cause us to ______________ out certain messages.

CHAPTER 3 Review and Enrichment...

General Vocabulary

Match each of the following terms on the left with a definition on the right that helps explain its meaning.

____ A. excursion
____ B. disintegration
____ C. sounding board
____ D. vulnerable
____ E. peripheral
____ F. rhetorical
____ G. retention
____ H. acronym
____ I. bias
____ J. gluttony
____ K. avarice
____ L. propaganda
____ M. sloth

1. ability to remember
2. extreme desire to gain wealth
3. excessive eating or drinking
4. on the outside
5. fall into fragments
6. a person who gives feedback
7. laziness
8. tricks of language
9. trip or journey
10. unprotected
11. word formed from the initial letters of several words
12. words designed to distort the truth
13. a settled or prejudiced outlook

To Remember

Answer the following based on your reading of the chapter.

1. What is the difference between hearing and listening?
2. What are the four basic listening styles?
3. What are three reasons why listening is difficult?
4. Name the seven deadly habits of bad listening.
5. What should your listening strategy be when you feel strongly moved by what a speaker says?
6. What does a good listener look like? In other words, what is the right posture and bearing for a person who wants to listen well?
7. At what point in a formal speech is it important to listen most intently?
8. Give an example of a situation where paraphrasing would be useful. Do the same for summarizing.

To Do

1. To find out how well or poorly you listen, try this simple exercise. The next time someone begins a conversation, ask yourself, "Am I really listening or am I just waiting my turn to talk?" Pay attention to your own mental processes. Are you:
   - Easily distracted?
   - Faking attention?
   - Interrupting frequently?
   - Daydreaming?
   - Jumping to conclusions?
   - Finding fault with the speaker?
   - Thinking of what you want to say?

   If your answer is yes to any of the items on this list, you have committed at least one of the seven deadly habits of bad listening. What remedies can you suggest?
2. Make a list of listening skills and habits, both good and bad. For example, "Do I listen attentively without interrupting?" "Do I listen carefully for main ideas and supporting

points?" or "Do I keep my emotions under control?" Then grade yourself on a recent conversation, discussion, or lecture.

3. How well do students listen to each other? Appoint an observer. After a student has given a speech to the class, ask the observer to rate the class on its listening skills. What was the typical posture? How attentive were the listeners? What encouragement did they give?
4. Ask several students to prepare short talks. Tell them that they may have to speak under very difficult circumstances but that they should continue no matter what happens. Ask the speakers to leave the room and then instruct to class to listen very carefully to what each speaker says until a secret signal is given. At that point the students are to stop paying attention, perhaps by reading books or looking out the window. Call the student speakers back, one at a time, and ask them to give their talks. When they are finished, ask them to discuss how they felt when the class withdrew its attention and what changes they made in their speeches as a result.

To Talk About

1. What role does listening play in our everyday lives?
2. Certain people seem to naturally command our attention. Researchers say we listen quite willingly to those who have status (celebrities), those with seniority (parents and teachers), those who can do something for us, and members of the opposite sex. Do you agree with this conclusion? Are there other categories of people to whom you pay special attention? Is that attention warranted?
3. How well do we listen in different settings—for instance, at a family meal, in class, at a party, or on the job? Discuss the differences you notice in listening styles.

To Write About

1. Compile a list of occupations where listening is vital. Examples might include psychologist, counselor, and social worker. Interview someone in your community who works at one of those careers and write a report based on that person's definition of "professional" listening.
2. Examine what topics might cause you to "hear only what you want to hear." Examples might include either side of an issue like abortion or gun control. What ideas do you have about getting someone to listen to the other side of an issue?
3. Write about the teacher whose lectures you find easiest to understand. Explain what techniques that teacher uses to be successful.

Related Speech Topics

Silence is (or is not) golden.

Poor listening habits can lead to major problems in business and many other areas of life.

If we spend 60 percent of every school day listening, why aren't we learning more?

We are vulnerable to professional persuaders such as politicians and advertisers.

"Dangling conversations" might describe most of our interactions, because we like to talk more than we wish to listen.

Females are better listeners than males (or vice versa).

It's not what we say but what we *don't* say that counts.

How to take notes well.

CHAPTER 4

NONVERBAL COMMUNICATION

"Watch out for the man whose stomach doesn't move when he laughs."

–Chinese proverb

Learning Objectives

After completing this chapter, you will be able to do the following.

- Distinguish between verbal and nonverbal communication.
- Use body language to reinforce your verbal message.
- Recognize when someone is not telling the truth.
- Explain how the same gesture can have different meanings in different cultures.

Chapter Outline

Following are the main sections in this chapter.

1. Body Basics
2. Interpreting Nonverbal Messages
3. Multicultural Messages

New Speech Terms

In this chapter, you will learn the meanings of the speech terms listed below.

nonverbal message
body language
eye contact
tone of voice
gesture
personal space
intimate distance
personal distance
social distance
public distance

General Vocabulary

Expanding your general vocabulary will help you become a more effective communicator. Listed below are some words appearing in this chapter that you should make part of your everyday vocabulary.

sympathetic
diverse
distal
proximal
timbre
suppress
anthropologist
comparative
intimacy
stoic

Looking AHEAD

We speak only with our mouths, but we communicate with our whole bodies. In fact, experts say that more than half of all communication is nonverbal. To truly understand other people, then, you must learn how to read their body language as well as interpret their words. You must learn what their facial expressions, hand gestures, and other signals mean. Even people's body temperature can be significant, as it reveals itself in the color of their faces or the moisture in their palms.

In this chapter, you will learn how to interpret body language, how body language varies from culture to culture, and how to use body language to make your own communication more effective and convincing.

Introduction

You can communicate even when you don't say a word. In 1990, a photographer for *National Geographic* magazine lined up the members of the U.S. Supreme Court for their official photograph. Justice Sandra Day O'Connor found herself standing directly behind Justice Byron White. According to news reports, O'Connor quietly formed a V with her fingers and held them just above White's head, making the old "rabbit ears" sign.

O'Connor was sending a **nonverbal message** to everyone who saw the picture—a message that says, "We don't take ourselves quite as seriously as it looks." Nonverbal messages play an enormous and often unappreciated role in all our communication.

"You *see,*" said the detective Sherlock Holmes to his somewhat dim-witted assistant Dr. Watson, "but you do not *observe.*" What Holmes meant was that the best way to understand people was to watch them—to notice what they do as well as what they say.

Albert Mehrabian, a professor of psychology at UCLA, claims that talking is the least important way we communicate. What counts most, he says, are our nonverbal messages. These messages include the way we sit or stand, how we tilt our heads, our facial expressions, our gestures, and our tone of voice.

Nonverbal messages often say as much or more than the words spoken.

SECTION 1 Body Basics

Understanding nonverbal communication is vital in many ways. It helps us understand, for example, how others react to us and to our ideas. If someone you are speaking to crosses his arms or legs, you may suspect that he feels threatened by what you are saying or disagrees with you. If your listener opens his hands toward you, you may expect agreement or at least a *sympathetic* ear.

Silent language says these three are friends.

People from different cultures may attach different meanings to the same gestures. For example, consider the "Hook 'em Horns" sign, made famous by fans of the University of Texas football team. To make the sign, hold up your index and pinky fingers. In Texas, it signifies support for the team, but beware—in Italy, this sign is an insult. In Brazil, it means good luck; and among Hindus, it means a cow. Being sensitive to the way different people interpret nonverbal messages can help you communicate more effectively wherever you are.

Knowing something about nonverbal communication can also be helpful when you send messages. Your physical actions can either reinforce or contradict what you say. If you feel nervous about speaking to a group, for instance, you may avoid looking at your listeners, lean on the podium, or drop your voice to a low mumble.

With a little practice, however, you can master a different set of nonverbal habits—mannerisms that will convey confidence and authority. Eventually, by learning to look confident, you begin to feel confident.

Body Language

Also called the "silent language," **body language** is the way we use our bodies to send messages. A speaker for Toastmasters International once found an effective way to demonstrate to an audience how body language works. He asked his listeners to place their thumbs and forefingers together (as in the OK sign) and then told them to place their hands on their chins. But while he was saying this, he did something different—he placed his own thumb and forefinger on his cheek.

Typically, 90 percent of his listeners followed his *actions,* not his words. Despite his instructions, they put their hands on their cheeks just as he did. "In business," notes Susan Bixler, president of Professional Image, "body language always wins out over verbal communication."

Why is body language important? First, because people usually remember more of what they see than what they hear, and second, because we have learned it helps us recognize the truth. When a person's words and body language are consistent, we believe that person. When their words and body language say different things, we tend to believe the body language and doubt the words.

WALK THE WALK

INSTANT IMPACT

One of the most interesting body movements is the walk. Some have called the way we walk a "second signature," because each person's walk is distinct. Part of the way we walk is a result of body structure, of course, but pace and length of stride seem to change with our emotions. If you are happy, you move more quickly and seem lighter on your feet. If you're unhappy, your shoulders droop, and you walk as though your shoes were made of lead.

Studies show that people tend to like men and women who have a bounce to their walk, swing their arms, and take long, strong strides. In fact, some psychologists say a long stride is such a positive body movement that you can improve your disposition—and make yourself happier—just by taking longer steps.

Often complicated feelings spill out in the form of body language. If a speaker is having difficulty controlling her anger, for example, she might raise her voice or turn away. "No mortal can keep a secret," noted Sigmund Freud. "If his lips are silent, he chatters with his fingertips." Even though people can control their words, and sometimes their facial expressions, there is often a "leakage" of feelings, perhaps in a gesture, a shift of position, or a tone of voice. Any one of these nonverbal signals may help you to interpret the messages you receive.

Body language is also remarkably *diverse.* Mario Pei, a communications expert, once estimated that humans produce up to 700,000 different physical signs. The face alone is capable of 250,000 different expressions. Other researchers have identified some 5,000 separate hand gestures and 1,000 kinds of postures. Clearly, we send messages by a dizzying array of nonverbal means. These messages are fun to watch and challenging to interpret. And unlike verbal communication, which is intermittent, body language is constant.

Learning to Read Body Language ...

Recognizing body language is an inexact art, so you must be careful about how you interpret it. A certain movement or facial expression may be quite meaningful, or it may mean nothing at all. As a starting point, the lists below provide you with some common body language terms and their generally accepted meanings.

Positive Body Language Certain physical cues can be quite reliable as indicators of positive feelings. Here are some things you can do, for example, to signal interest in another person during a conversation:

- *Relaxed posture.* Sit comfortably and breathe in a relaxed manner. Avoid abrupt movements.
- *Arms relaxed.* Uncross your arms and hold your hands palms up as a sign of openness.
- *Good eye contact.* Look the other person in the eye, particularly when she or he is speaking. Look away occasionally to avoid staring.
- *Nod agreement.* When you nod your head at something the other person has said, you indicate that you agree or understand. But don't overdo it. Continuous head bobbing usually means that the listener has tuned out.

- *Smile at humor.* This signals a warm personal relationship.
- *Lean closer.* Reducing the distance between you and a partner, particularly when the other person is speaking, indicates interest is up and barriers are down.
- *Use gestures.* Talking with your hands indicates involvement in the conversation and openness to the other person.

For all of these positive behaviors, moderation is the key. When these movements are exaggerated, they can become more negative than positive.

Negative Body Language Most positive gestures are *distal;* that is, they are directed toward others. Most negative gestures, on the other hand, are *proximal*—they are directed toward your own body. Negative body language is somewhat less reliable as a method for reading another person's mood, because actions that are generally considered negative may just be a sign of nervousness. Still, be on the lookout for these behaviors:

- *Body tension.* A wrinkled brow, jerky body motions, or hands clasped in front can all indicate discomfort with the topic or the other person.
- *Arms folded.* This creates a barrier and can indicate resistance to what is being said.
- *Speaking hand to mouth.* Putting your hands near your mouth, scratching your cheek or eyebrow—these are things that say, "Don't listen to me, I'm not sure of what I am saying."
- *Fidgeting.* If you move around a lot, play with things, or drum with your fingers, you send signals of boredom, nervousness, or impatience.
- *Yawning.* This often happens if the other person is talking too much or in too much technical detail.

Using Body Language Effectively ...

We normally think of body language as a reflection of what a person is feeling, and it is. But it is also true that if you change your body language, your feelings will begin to change as well. That's why, when you feel yourself dragging in the middle of the afternoon, a quick walk around the block can rejuvenate you. You also tend to feel better when

PEANUTS reprinted by permission of United Feature Syndicate, Inc.

you put on fresh clothes, or if you just smile.

This principle has two practical applications: (1) You can make yourself look and feel better by using more positive body language. The famous football coach Vince Lombardi used to tell his players before an away game, "You've got to look good getting off the bus." In other words, if you look and act like a winner, you are more likely to be one. (2) Body language is contagious. If person X uses neutral body language, and person Y uses positive body language, person X will gradually begin to mirror Y's behavior. Thus, your positive body language can gradually affect the behavior of those around you.

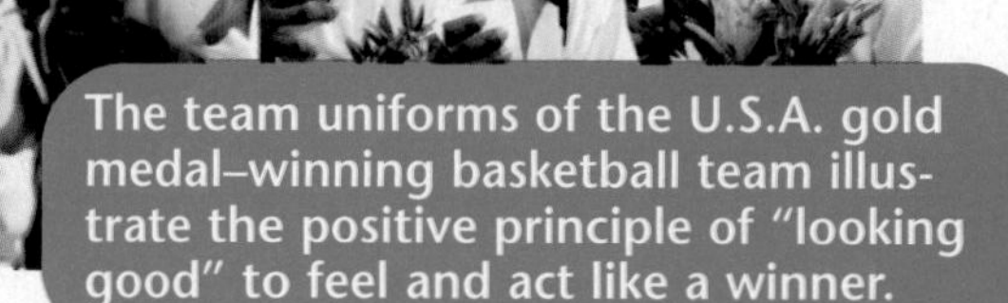

The team uniforms of the U.S.A. gold medal–winning basketball team illustrate the positive principle of "looking good" to feel and act like a winner.

SECTION 1 REVIEW

Recalling the Facts ...

Try this quick quiz to see how well you can interpret nonverbal messages. Match the action in the left-hand column with the message in the right-hand column:

Action	Message
1. Slapping your forehead with the heel of your hand	a. "I'm angry."
2. Wrinkling your forehead and frowning	b. "I forgot something."
3. Tapping your fingers on a desk or table	c. "I'm getting impatient."
4. Slamming a book down on a desk or table	d. "I don't understand."
5. Wrinkling your nose	e. "I don't like that."

Thinking Critically ...

1. Why do actions speak louder than words?
2. To learn more about body language, try a mirroring exercise. Find a partner and stand facing each other. One of you now becomes the mirror image for the other by trying to copy your partner's body movements. Try holding a conversation. After a while reverse roles and repeat the activity. What are each person's characteristic gestures?

Taking Charge ...

1. To observe body language in action, try an experiment the next time you ride a crowded elevator. When you board the elevator, don't turn around and face the door. Instead, stand facing the other people. If you want to create even more tension, grin. Very likely, the other passengers will glare back, surprised and upset. The reason? You have broken the (unspoken) rules.

   Discuss with your classmates what you discover. Brainstorm other situations where breaking the nonverbal rules might affect others.
2. Pair off with a partner and try to communicate the following feelings nonverbally: frustration, tension, joy, friendliness, anger, hate, and happiness. Think of a few others, and see if your partner can guess what emotion you are trying to communicate.

SECTION 2 Interpreting Nonverbal Messages

Learning to read body language is complicated by the fact that people often express different and even contradictory messages in their verbal and nonverbal behaviors. Are you nodding your head "yes" while you're saying "no"?

A common example of this double message is the experience we've all had of hearing someone with a red face and bulging veins yell, "Angry? No, *I'm not angry!*" Like this person, you may sometimes try to put on a false front. You try to keep a straight face, for example, when laughing might hurt someone's feelings, or you try to act calm when you don't want someone to worry about you.

We all try to "massage our message" from time to time. In other words, we attempt to use our bodies to disguise our real feelings. For example, we may pretend not to be hurt even though our hearts are breaking.

We have learned how to "behave" ourselves, how to hide our true feelings. We choose roles and act our parts. But rarely, if ever, do we turn in a perfect performance. Thus, who we really are and what we really mean often slips out into our behavior, into what we say, the way we say it, and the way our bodies act.

Here are some tips for reading the *true* meaning of nonverbal communication:

- Don't just look, but *see.*
- Consider the person's normal physical and verbal behavior patterns, and be alert for variations from that norm.
- Remember that one signal alone means nothing; what you're looking for are clusters of signals.

Facial Expressions

Because of their visibility, we pay a great deal of attention to other people's faces. Babies, for example, take special interest in the huge faces they see peering over their cribs. Although the face is capable of making hundreds of distinct movements and communicating many emotional states, six emotions seem to be the foundation of most expressions—surprise, fear, anger, disgust, happiness, and sadness. Blends of these primary emotions account for nearly all of our facial expressions.

No one area of the face best reveals emotions, but for any given emotion, certain features may be most important. For example, the nose-cheek-

mouth area is most important for disgust. For fear, it is the eyes and eyelids. Sadness shows itself best in the brows and forehead, while happiness can be found in the cheeks and mouth.

If you watch a person's face in slow motion (on film or videotape), you discover that people change expressions rapidly. Some expressions last only a few hundredths of a second—in fact, they are so fleeting that they are rarely noticed in everyday conversation.

Some of these fleeting expressions reveal a person's true feelings, but they are quickly replaced by deliberate expressions the person feels are more socially appropriate. You can disguise your face more easily than almost any other part of your body. That means that despite our natural tendency to search faces for meaning, they are not necessarily the best place to look.

WORDS FROM THE WORKPLACE

Teresa Urquiaga, MS, LPC

High School Counselor

Q. *How does nonverbal communication play a role in your day-to-day professional activities?*

A. As a high school counselor, nonverbal communication plays an important role in helping me to determine if a student is being honest with me and with himself. For example, if a student tells me that he is not angry, but he is speaking to me in a loud, belligerent tone, sitting with his arms crossed (closed body language), and scowling, I am able to determine that this student still has some anger that needs to be diffused. Developmentally, adolescents are seeking to establish their social and emotional independence, and they often retreat within themselves and feel hesitant to share their true thoughts and feelings with adults. Thus, parents, teachers, and counselors must rely on an adolescent's nonverbal communication to get a more accurate picture of what an adolescent is truly thinking or feeling. In addition, nonverbal communication can also help me to determine if I am making a connection with a student. For example, if I help a student to feel accepted and understood, that student's face might light up, he might lean towards me a bit, and his voice might sound excited (Yes! That is exactly how I feel!).

Q. *What advice can you give to students to show them the importance of nonverbal communication in the world of your work?*

A. I pay attention to the nonverbal cues that my students are sending. Body language, facial expression, tone of voice, and general appearance speak volumes. In addition, I pay attention to my own body language; I try to notice if I am nonverbally reacting to a student in a negative way so that I can deal with my own thoughts and emotions. I want to communicate a presence of openness, unconditional acceptance, and warmth, so I try to keep my body language open, my voice calm, and my facial expressions appropriate to what is being said.

Tone of Voice

By contrast, **tone of voice** offers a valuable clue to a speaker's feelings. The pitch and *timbre* (distinctive tone) of a person's voice, her pauses and rhythm, have something to say, over and above the words themselves. Rollo May, a famous psychotherapist, asked himself, "What does the voice say when I stop listening to the words?"

The simple word "oh," for example, says very little as you see it printed here. But in spoken form, "oh" can have many different meanings. According to the way it is spoken, "oh" can mean:

- "You surprised me."
- "I made a mistake."
- "You're a pain in the neck."
- "You make me so happy."
- "I'm bored."
- "I'm fascinated."
- "I understand."
- "I don't understand."

The rate of speech also tells us something about the speaker's feelings. People talk fast when they are excited or anxious. People often speak faster, too, when they are trying to persuade us or sell us something. On the other hand, people tend to talk more slowly when they are depressed, disgusted, or simply tired.

John Hull learned to be especially sensitive to tone of voice when he became blind at age 48. "With the people I know very well," he said, "I find that all of the emotion that would normally be expressed in the face is there in the voice: the tiredness, the anxiety, the excitement. My impressions based on the voice seem to be just as accurate as those of sighted people. The capacity of the voice to reveal the self is truly amazing. These are the things that matter to me now."

How to Tell When Someone Is Lying

According to Desmond Morris, author of *The Naked Ape,* we control some parts of our bodies better than others. The easiest parts to control are those whose actions we are most aware of. Smiles and frowns are easy to control. So facial expressions are a poor test of someone's sincerity.

How to Tell If Someone Is Lying

Increased face touching can indicate that someone is not telling the truth. Watch for the following behaviors.

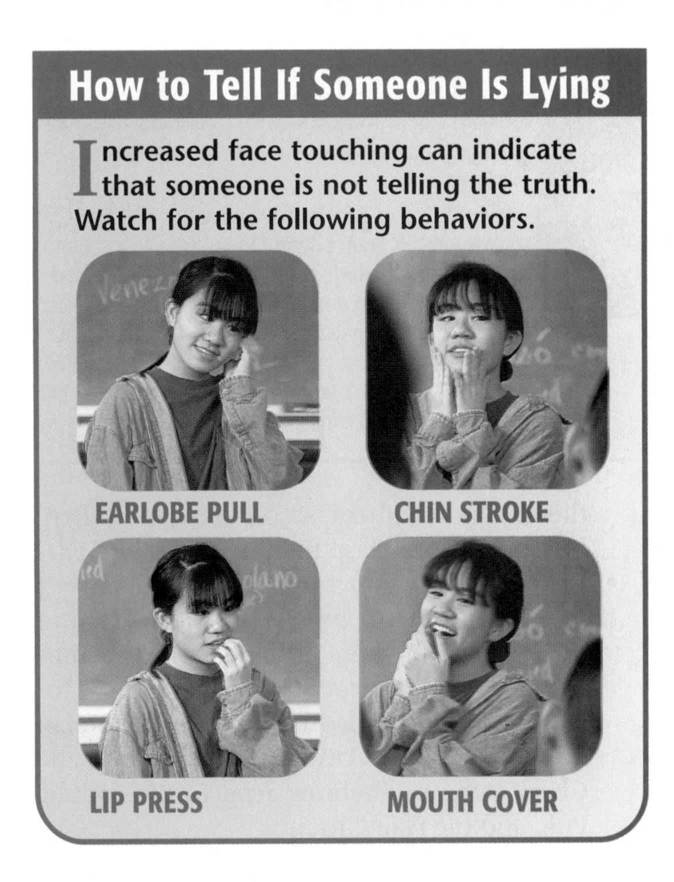

General body postures, on the other hand, can be very revealing because we are not fully conscious of them—we don't usually know, for example, whether we are slumping or standing tall. Legs and feet are the parts of the body where we have the least awareness.

Then what can we do to discover a person's true thoughts? Are there specific body messages we can look for? Morris conducted a series of experiments to provide some answers. He asked a group of nurses to lie about a movie they had seen. He then assembled a set of behaviors that seem to persist during moments of deception. They are:

- **Decreased hand activity.** The hand gestures the nurses would normally use were reduced. The reason may be that hand actions, which illustrate what we say, are not entirely under our conscious control. Unconsciously, when you are not being truthful, you may sense that your hands will give you away, so you *suppress*

How can you tell if a smile is genuine?

Smiles are much more complicated than most people realize. Paul Ekman, a researcher at the University of California at San Francisco, has identified 18 distinctive smiles–most of them phony. One of the most common is the "qualifer" smile, which superiors often use when rejecting an idea or criticizing an employee. In such a smile, the corners of the lips are usually tightened, with the bottom lip pushed up slightly. But Ekman says most people can identify the real thing. Look at the upper half of a person's face. Genuine or "felt" smiles involve the muscles that make the eyes crinkle with pleasure.

them. You hide them, sit on them, stuff them into pockets, or clasp them together.

- **Increased face touching.** We all touch our faces from time to time when we speak, but the frequency of these simple actions rises during moments of stress, such as lying. Hand-to-face favorites include the Chin Stroke, the Lip Press, the Mouth Cover, the Nose Touch, the Cheek Rub, the Eyebrow Scratch, the Earlobe Pull, and the Hair Groom.

Why these actions might indicate lying can be explained with the Mouth Cover. According to Morris, as false words emerge from the speaker's mouth, one part of his brain becomes uncomfortable and sends a message to his hand to "cover up" what the lips are doing. The other part of his brain, however, cannot permit this cover-up to work. The result is a halfhearted motion, with the hand-to-mouth gesture ending up as a slight brush.

- **Stiff and rigid posture.** "Most people move less when they're lying," says psychologist Albert Mehrabian. "Their movements and body positions become less fluid." However, some people move more when they feel conflicted, as the next point shows.
- **Increased body shifting.** Most of us can remember squirming as children when we were being interrogated by our parents. Our squirms were symptoms of an almost overpowering desire to escape. As adults, we learn to suppress these actions, but they do not disappear entirely. If you know a person well, you may be able to spot times when he seems unusually restless. That body language may be an indication that the person is uncomfortable about something he is saying.

SECTION 2 REVIEW

Recalling the Facts ...

1. Because we all try to disguise our real feelings from time to time, reading body language can be difficult. Describe some ways we can use body language to distinguish genuine feelings from false ones.
2. How can you tell a real smile from a phony one?

Thinking Critically ...

1. Ask a partner to tell you two stories—one true and one false. Your partner should try to make the false story sound reasonable so that wild exaggerations don't give the story away. Listen to both stories, carefully observing your partner's body language. Can you guess which story is true? After you have tried to guess, reverse roles and tell two stories to your partner.

Taking Charge ...

1. Watch a film, videotape, or, even better, a cartoon with the sound off, and try to guess what is being expressed by body language alone. Then play the film or tape again with the volume up. How well did you do with your guesses? Reverse this procedure so that you listen but do not look. How much do you feel you lose by relying only on verbal messages?

SECTION 3 Multicultural Messages

While practiced everywhere, body language is not a universal language. The familiar "thumbs up" gesture that means "everything's OK" or "good going," especially when used by a pilot or an astronaut, has other meanings in other places. North Americans recognize the thumbs up gesture as a sign that you are hitchhiking, but don't use it to get a ride in Nigeria—there, it's a rude insult.

Roger Axtell, who traveled the world for 30 years as an executive with the Parker Pen Company, wrote a guide for business travelers—*Do's and Taboos Around the World*—that he hoped would help head off international incidents.

"In Buenos Aires," Axtell writes, "a manager met me with his arms outstretched. I realized, 'That man's going to hug me.' I'm from Wisconsin. We don't do things like that. And by the way, there's an art to the social hug. You have to turn your head a bit. We ended up smashing noses. It wasn't a very auspicious beginning."

Most Americans reserve hugs for their families and close friends, but other cultures may hug when greeting strangers.

Cultural Differences

Generally, we expect to communicate better face to face than indirectly, say, on the telephone. Nonverbal information, such as one's appearance, tone of voice, facial expression, and body language, all provide extra information that enriches understanding. However, when cultural differences are involved, more nonverbal information is not always better.

For one thing, when you are not in good command of a foreign language, you tend to lose some control over your nonverbal expressions. So, English spoken with a foreign accent not only is hard to understand, but can also lead to a poorly controlled tone of voice or awkward facial expressions. Sometimes it is hard not to judge a person based on such behaviors, and it takes some patience to move beyond first impressions.

Gestures Around the World

If humans can produce 5,000 different **gestures,** why is it that we use the same ones over and over? Probably because they are the ones we need for everyday situations: when we greet each other, beckon to one another, and especially when we touch one another.

Nodding your head up and down means yes—unless, of course, you live in Bulgaria or parts of Greece, Turkey, and Iran, where it means just the opposite. Tapping your head with your forefinger can have two meanings. Sometimes it means "that person is very intelligent!" and sometimes "that person is crazy!" It all depends on the facial expression that goes with the gesture.

COMMUNICATION Breakthrough

The Ultimate Gesture

If you feel bewildered by the seemingly infinite number of gestures used around the world, perhaps you would do well to remember the "ultimate gesture." Researchers call it that because it carries more positive characteristics than any other single gesture.

First, this "ultimate gesture" is known everywhere in the world. It is absolutely universal.

Second, it is rarely, if ever, misunderstood. Primitive tribes and world leaders alike know this gesture. They—like you, no doubt—recognize it in others and use it themselves.

Third, scientists believe this particular gesture releases chemicals called endorphins into your system, creating a feeling of mild euphoria—a sense of great happiness or well-being.

Fourth, as you travel around the world, this gesture may help you slip out of the prickliest of situations.

What is this singular signal, this miracle, this giant of all gestures?

It is, quite simply, the smile.

Source: Adapted from *Gestures: The Do's and Taboos of Body Language Around the World* by Roger E. Axtell (John Wiley & Sons, 1997).

Question

What other universal gestures or expressions can you suggest?

All over the world, scratching your head seems to mean "I am confused." Apparently, everyone gets confused. In an Italian study, psychologists filmed people in telephone booths. One clip showed a man holding the receiver in his left hand and gesturing vigorously with his right. As the conversation became more agitated, he tucked the receiver under his chin in order to free both hands for gesturing, beating the air with his fists.

This man probably couldn't talk at all if we tied his hands behind his back. Let's take a closer look at what other gestures can mean in different cultures.

Signs of Greeting . . . Some *anthropologists,* scientists who study human cultural development, believe the use of an outstretched hand as a form of greeting goes far back in history. Citizens of the Roman Empire greeted each other with a hand-and-forearm clasp, mainly to show that neither party was carrying a weapon. Some believe the hug or embrace (a form of greeting common in Mediterranean countries) had a similar purpose. The hug gave you physical assurance that no weapons were hiding beneath anyone's robe.

Worldwide, many other forms of greeting are used. In the Middle East, some citizens can still be seen giving the salaam. To give the salaam, you sweep your right hand upward, first touching the heart, then the forehead, and finally up and outward, perhaps with a slight nod of the head. At the same time you say, *Salaam alaykum,* meaning "Peace be with you."

Eskimos greet by slapping their hands on each other's head or shoulders. Polynesians welcome strangers by embracing them and then rubbing their backs. The Maori people in New Zealand rub noses, and some East Africans spit at each other's feet. Americans traveling to Tibet should be culturally alert. People there are said to greet one another by sticking out their tongues.

Handshakes Handshakes seem to come in three styles: gentle, firm, and Texan. England's Prince Charles, who travels widely and must be something of an expert on international greetings, has complained about the finger-crunching grip of Americans, "especially Texans."

Kisses The French like handshakes but they don't stop there. Close friendships require warmer greetings. Men kiss each other, squeeze each other's shoulders, slap backs, punch kidneys, and pinch cheeks. When men greet women or women greet other women, a kiss on each cheek is expected.

How Countries Feel about Touching

Here is a rough comparison of how countries around the globe feel about touching:

Enjoy Touching

Middle Eastern countries
Latin countries
Italy and Greece
Russia

Middle Ground

France
China
Ireland
India

Don't Touch

Japan
United States and Canada
England
Australia

In Japan, a bow from the waist is the preferred greeting.

Bows The most polite greeting of all is the bow. In many Asian countries—especially Japan, where style and courtesy are highly valued—a bow from the waist is the preferred way to greet someone. A bow indicates respect and humility, and often reflects social status. To the Japanese, bowing is indispensable because it allows them to greet one another without invading each other's personal space.

Who bows first? In Japanese society, rank is very important. In business, for example, a middle-level manager in a large company outranks a department head. Therefore, the person of lower rank (in this case, the department head) bows first and lower. Normally, American travelers are not expected to make a full bow to their Japanese companions, but they might make a slight bow to indicate that they respect Japanese customs.

Even being culturally sensitive, however, won't keep you from awkward situations. Many Japanese people, especially those who travel abroad, have adopted Western ways. As a result, you may find yourself bowing in a Japanese person's direction just as he reaches out to shake your hand. When cultures collide, we often meet each other somewhere in the middle.

A GOOD SOLE

INSTANT IMPACT

The Swedish actress Liv Ullman once learned that touching is not always welcome. When she toured a famine-stricken area in Bangladesh on behalf of UNICEF, she had an especially warm visit with a woman about her own age. After the conversation was over, Ullman gave the woman a hug, but she felt her suddenly pull away. Through her interpreter, Ullman asked why.

"In my country," the woman said, "we kiss feet when we say good-bye." Ullman didn't hesitate—she bent down and kissed the woman's feet. Then they hugged, each woman thus exchanging the ritual of her own world.

Touching Customs

We live in a world of extremes—some cultures enjoy lots of body contact; others avoid it completely. One psychologist measured this desire to touch by watching how people behave in busy downtown coffee shops. He found that couples in San Juan, Puerto Rico, touched each other about 180 times per hour, while couples in Paris touched about 110 times per hour. The *comparative* numbers for the United States and Northern Europe were dramatically different. Couples in Gainesville, Florida, for example, touched each other just twice an hour, and couples in London never touched at all.

Art from *DO's and TABOOs of Hosting International Visitors,* by Roger Axtell.

Touching is the language of physical *intimacy.* Because of this, touch can be the most powerful of all the communication channels. In May 1985, Brigitte Gerney was trapped for six hours beneath the wreckage of a collapsed construction crane in New York City. Throughout her ordeal, she held the hand of a rescue worker, who stayed by her side as heavy machinery removed the tons of twisted steel from her crushed legs. A stranger's touch gave her hope and the will to live.

Touch appears to affect the sexes differently. Women sometimes react much more favorably to touch than men. In an interesting study, psychologists asked a group of nurses to lightly touch a patient once or twice shortly before the patient underwent surgery. The touching produced a strongly positive reaction—but only among women. It appeared to lower their blood pressure and anxiety levels both before and after surgery.

You can't avoid personal contact at rush hour. Sometimes you have no "personal space."

For men, however, the touching proved to be very upsetting. Their blood pressure and anxiety levels both rose. The psychologists suspect that because men are taught to be more *stoic,* that is, to hide their feelings and to ignore their fears, the touching rattled them by reminding them that life is fragile.

How do you feel about touching and being touched? Salespeople *think* they know—research shows that it is harder to say no to someone who touches you when making a request—but not everyone is happy about being touched by a stranger. Think about your own comfort level when you find yourself in a crowd. Are you relaxed and loose, or does physical contact make you feel awkward and tense?

In some situations, we can't help touching each other. Take a crowded elevator, for instance. Normally, people stand shoulder to shoulder and arm to arm, accepting such close contact without complaint. The rule seems to be "Touch only from

Types of Space

INTIMATE

under 18 inches

This distance is primarily for confidential exchanges and is almost always reserved for close friends.

PERSONAL

1 1/2 to 4 feet

This distance is comfortable for conversation between friends.

SOCIAL

4 to 12 feet

This is the ordinary distance people maintain from one another for most social and business exchanges.

PUBLIC

over 12 feet

At this distance, perhaps in a shopping mall or on the street, people barely acknowledge each other's presence. At most they give a nod or a shake of the head.

shoulder to elbow, but nowhere else." Even though the Japanese are regarded as a nontouching society, their crowded cities force them to be jammed into subways and trains. Edward T. Hall, an anthropologist, says the Japanese handle their uneasiness about being packed into public places by avoiding eye contact and drawing within themselves emotionally, thus "touching without feeling."

Watch My Space

Sometimes we speak of "keeping our distance" from someone we dislike or "getting close" to someone we like. Anthropologists say that we all live inside a bubble of **personal space.** The bubble represents our personal territory, and we resent it when someone invades our space.

Americans like to stand about 24 to 30 inches from one another. This just happens to be an arm's length away. "When two Americans stand facing one another in any normal social or business situation," says George Renwick, "one could stretch out his arm and put his thumb in the other person's ear." Asian people stand farther apart when talking. Latin Americans and Middle Easterners, on the other hand, stand much closer, literally toe to toe. They also like to touch their partner's arm or elbow when conversing.

SECTION 3 REVIEW

Recalling the Facts ...

1. Give a few examples of how greetings differ from one country to another.
2. How does touch affect men and women differently?

Thinking Critically ...

1. Touching customs that vary from culture to culture can have unfortunate consequences. When a customer makes a purchase and receives change, Koreans, for example, typically place the money on the counter to avoid any physical contact. "They won't touch my hand," one New York customer complained. The Korean merchant explained that in his homeland, people are taught to avoid all physical contact with strangers, especially direct eye contact. Can you suggest a way that Korean merchants could be consistent with their cultural customs but still make their customers feel welcome?
2. How important is it to be familiar with the body language customs of other cultures? Would it be better if all cultures had the same body language? Why or why not?

Taking Charge ...

1. Invite several recent immigrants to class and ask them to discuss the differences they notice in nonverbal language between the United States and their homelands.

COMMUNICATION

Breakdown

When a Woman Acts Like a Man

In *You Just Don't Understand,* linguist Deborah Tannen argues that men and women speak different languages. What she doesn't say, however, is that the sexes also use different body languages. That idea is what caused journalist Sheila Feeney to try an unusual experiment. What if, she asked, she walked like a man? Eventually, after doing some interviews with experts, she compiled a top-five list of classic male moves:

- **The land grab.** Any woman who has ever battled for an armrest in a movie theater or bugged her boyfriend to take his legs off the couch won't be surprised to learn that men take up more space than women do. Lillian Glass, a communications specialist, advises women executives to spread their papers around a meeting table and use sweeping arm gestures to help establish their authority.
- **He touched me.** Despite what you might think, men are more likely to touch women than vice versa. And where they touch is critical: Gals restrict themselves to the forearms and hands, while guys go for anywhere on the upper body—hence all that back-slapping, shoulder-shaking, and arm-pumping. When's the last time you saw one female give a jab to the bicep of another female friend?
- **The stare master.** Unlike women, men often look at people without softening their appraising stare, says Dr. Glass. She says women are more conditioned to seek and give approval. Feeney decided to stare at a few men on the street. Some broke into smiles, some even said hello, but the overwhelming majority of strangers and acquaintances she picked as victims became distinctly uncomfortable.
- **The chest butt.** "If you really want to try something, orient your body directly at another person," says Dr. David Givens, an expert in nonverbal communication. Unless they're about to shout someone down or punch him in the nose, men instinctively turn from each other when talking. Standing face to face is something men will only do when they're *mad.*
- **Look away, look away.** Women complain that men don't always seem to pay attention to what they're saying. Their eyes wander to their watches, to the television, to the newspaper. Yet the power move of avoiding someone's gaze while he's talking proved to be tough for Feeney. She said she felt unforgivably mean each time she glanced away while someone was speaking to her.

Source: Deborah Tannen, *You Just Don't Understand* (New York: Ballantine Books, 1990).

Question:

What other kinds of gender-specific body language can you identify?

STUDENT WORK

"Appreciating the Difference" *By Charlie Paul*

In the following speech a student makes the case that different groups have different body languages. Paying closer attention to body language and nonverbal communication might help us overcome some cultural misunderstandings.

Facial expressions, hand gestures, and body language all say as much as voices, but they mean different things to different people—depending on where your ancestors immigrated from and where you live.

In the last political presidential campaign, I began to notice that I had never actually seen a television clip or picture where Bill Clinton was not smiling. It took me a great deal of time before I realized that Clinton's smile actually represented a regional difference in body language—a kind of Southern accent of the face. Each culture has a set of unwritten rules regarding the situations in which smiling is or is not expected, and people in the South habitually smile a great deal. In fact, a person from Arkansas who seldom smiled would probably be asked what was wrong.

No one is actually taught when to smile and when not to. As children grow up, they simply emulate the behavior of the people around them; they absorb a kind of nonverbal code as they learn the spoken language. A German, for instance, gestures in a manner that is as distinctively German as his speech.

In the United States, body language can be very complicated. We are a nation of immigrants and descendants of immigrants—all of whom came with their own language and ethnic differences. Spoken accents tend to disappear long before body dialects, so second-generation Hispanic-Americans, for example, often look Hispanic in the way that they move and gesture though they don't sound Hispanic at all. . . .

It would be an oversimplification to say that a person was expressive or inexpressive entirely on the basis of ethnic background. Personality enters into the picture, and of course, ethnic differences can also be crosscut by regional and religious ones. What is more interesting to note is that what is learned can be unlearned. Dr. Robert Sheckley, a New York psychiatrist, stated that "American women generally have much more animated facial expressions than men, but in recent years professional women in the workforce have learned to be less expressive." Sheckley went on to say that regardless of the occupation, women are often expected to conceal their emotions.

Body language is a very complicated subject, and the differences between the sexes and people of different origins can often lead to problems or misunderstandings. Not long ago, for example, I was in a friend's kitchen when suddenly I realized I literally had my body pressed up against a wall—even though we had started the conversation in the middle of the room. I thought about what had happened. I tend to keep my distance from people during conversation, but my friend obviously feels more at ease in situations of close proximity. So as she moved forward, I moved back to maintain the distance that was comfortable for me and we gradually inched across the room. If I hadn't stopped and thought about the situation, I might have concluded that she was being very aggressive and pushy—just as she might have thought that I was standoffish and aloof. . . .

Opinions differ as to how important body languages are, but researchers all agree that they do exist—and they don't have to create problems.

One way to help prevent misunderstanding is for everyone to realize that we really don't all speak the same body language. Beyond that, maybe we need to learn to appreciate our differences, rather than keep trying to overlook them, so that we can open ourselves up to the fascinating variations in people. To quote my Irish granddad, "May the gentle rain and wind fade all your problems."

CHAPTER 4 Review and Enrichment...

Looking Back

Listed below are the major ideas discussed in this chapter.

- Nonverbal messages are a vital part of face-to-face communication.
- Nonverbal messages frequently overpower verbal messages.
- Although body language is used worldwide, it is not a universal language.
- Some cultures are much more comfortable with touching than others.
- The distance you keep between yourself and others (your "personal space") helps define the kind of communication that is taking place.
- We tend to look for nonverbal messages in other people's faces, but the face is the part of the body that can be most easily controlled and therefore disguised.
- We can learn to spot someone who is lying by studying body language. People who are lying tend to use fewer hand gestures, to touch their faces more often, and to shift position more frequently.
- You should assess your own body language from time to time, especially to see whether it contributes to a professional demeanor.

Speech Vocabulary

Match the vocabulary term on the left with the correct definition on the right.

1. nonverbal message
2. body language
3. gesture
4. tone of voice
5. personal space
6. intimate distance
7. personal distance
8. social distance
9. public distance
10. eye contact

a. all our physical movements
b. the distance for a conversation among friends
c. looking directly at your communication partner
d. any means of communication other than words
e. the distance we keep between ourselves and strangers
f. style or manner of expression
g. the distance for normal business conversations
h. the distance for personal conversations
i. our "personal territory"
j. hand or arm movement

CHAPTER 4 Review and Enrichment...

General Vocabulary

Match the vocabulary term on the left with the correct definition on the right.

1. sympathetic
2. diverse
3. distal
4. proximal
5. timbre
6. suppress
7. anthropologist
8. comparative
9. intimacy
10. stoic

a. someone who studies human cultures
b. relative
c. located away from
d. unlike, widely varied
e. being close or familiar
f. subdue or crush
g. in agreement with or inclined to
h. indifferent to grief or joy
i. distinctive tone of voice
j. located close by or moving nearer

To Remember

Answer the following based on your reading of the chapter.

1. Approximately how many different gestures can human beings produce?
2. The handshake and other forms of greeting go far back in time. What purpose do anthropologists think these gestures originally served?
3. Name two countries where touching among friends is common and two where it is not.
4. How far apart would two close friends ordinarily stand or sit during a friendly conversation? What about two strangers?
5. What might a tendency to touch his or her face suggest about a speaker?

To Do

1. Challenge your classmates to do short pantomimes of professions. Ask them to nonverbally present an ER room in a hospital, a nursery school, or an amusement park.
2. Try a game of charades with your friends. Act out movie titles or current events to see how well you can communicate without words.
3. Watch a film or videotape of the great mime Marcel Marceau. What could a mime teach you about using more expressive body language? Try pantomiming the action of throwing a ball. Have the ball change in weight and size. Have it become sticky, muddy, hot, wet, or cold.
4. Bring some home videos to class. After reading the discussion of facial expressions on pages 83–84, watch the available videos, focusing on the facial expressions. When faces are prominently displayed on the screen, stop the video and take turns with your classmates commenting on what you think that particular expression "says." How would you assess your skill at reading expressions? Do some of your classmates seem more skilled than others at interpreting facial expressions?
5. Take turns telling about one of the following with your hands held behind your back.

- How to shave
- How to mix a cake
- How to serve a tennis ball
- How to shake a rug
- How to apply makeup
- How to pass a football
- How to use a curling iron

6. When you want to express confidence, you try to look bigger. You stretch yourself up to your full height—head back, chest out, nose up. We call this "walking tall." When you're sad or discouraged, you make yourself look smaller by bending over, tucking your head in, and looking down. Practice trying these different kinds of walks at school. What kinds of reactions does each style elicit?

To Talk About

1. How important is nonverbal communication in everyday life? In school? On the job?
2. How big is your bubble? How much room do you need around yourself to be comfortable? Does that change with different social situations or different people?
3. How do you know when someone is not telling the truth? What clues do you look for? Read the discussion "How to Tell When Someone Is Lying" on pages 85–86. Which of the different types of body language mentioned do you think are the best indicators that someone might be lying? Do you think reading this information will make you more apt to recognize when someone is lying to you?
4. The "Instant Impact" on page 80 discusses the distinct way that each individual has of walking. The feature even refers to a person's walk as his or her "second signature." Have you noticed the way that a particular person walks? Do you agree with the idea that everyone has a dinstinct walk? How would you describe your walk?

To Write About

1. Keep a log of your personal space for one day. Each time you have a conversation, make a note of how close to you the person stood or sat. Observe how the spatial distance between you and others varies according to the following factors: their status or authority, gender, age, and social or cultural background. Compare your log with those of classmates.
2. Write a description of how to do one of these things:
   - Shoot a free throw.
   - Wash your dog.

   Next, write a speech explaining the same process, and plan to use hand gestures and facial expressions to illustrate it. How many words did body language save you? What parts of the explanation became easier?

Related Speech Topics

How to speak body language
You're in my space!
The sure-fire liar detector plan
Read a person like a book
Gestures around the world
Eye contact—Don't forget it!
Smiles—the universal language
Fear, anxiety, and the body
Talking without hands: Can you do it?
Clothes make the man, true or false?

CHAPTER 5

INTERPERSONAL COMMUNICATION

"*Gossip is the art of saying nothing in a way that leaves practically nothing unsaid.*"

–Walter Winchell

Learning Objectives

After completing this chapter, you will be able to do the following.

- Understand the value of effective interpersonal communication.
- Understand the importance of assertiveness, courtesy, and tact when dealing with people.
- Implement effective strategies for successful one-to-one communication.
- Use communication to build positive professional and social interpersonal relationships.

Chapter Outline

Following are the main sections in this chapter.

1. Appropriate Tone
2. People Skills

New Speech Terms

In this chapter, you will learn the meanings of the speech terms listed below.

interpersonal communication
social communication
professional communication
courtesy
tact
tone
aggressive tone
nonassertive tone
assertive tone
people skills
dialogue

General Vocabulary

Expanding your general vocabulary will help you become a more effective communicator. Listed below are some words appearing in this chapter that you should make part of your everyday vocabulary.

prospective
etiquette
brash
manipulating
criticism
reprimanded

Looking Ahead

Each year, *Fortune Magazine* releases its list of "America's Most Admired Companies." *Fortune* polls over 13,000 executives to determine what specific factors make a company successful. Two major factors remain constant: (1) successful companies have solid reputations with the public, and (2) they put a high priority on communication. In a similar manner, if we wish to be admired in our social and professional lives, we need to pay attention to how we associate and communicate with others.

This might be easier said than done. Effective communication takes into consideration the people involved, the nature of the message, and the circumstances. Let's face it, we don't always act and talk the same way with everyone—and we shouldn't. You have words and behaviors that you use when you are alone with your friends. These same words and behaviors might not be suitable, however, if you are talking with your family or if you are with a potential employer. Regardless of the situation, if you don't take the time to *think* before you communicate, your words and actions might lead to serious problems.

Therefore, the purpose of this chapter is to show you the power of **interpersonal communication**, or the art of getting along with and communicating effectively with other people—especially in a one-on-one setting. So, regardless of the situation, let's examine some of the "building blocks" that it takes to become an effective communicator when you are working "face-to-face" with another person.

Introduction

"Interpersonal communication" is not a term that is easily handled in one chapter. The authors of this book believe that your ability to deliver different messages to different individuals is the result of learning a number of skills that are dealt with in various chapters. For example, you must have *confidence* (Chapter 2) if you want to convince your boss that your idea for a new procedure is a good one. In addition, you must exhibit the power of *organization* (Chapter 9) if you want to present your ideas in a logical, systematic order that your friends and classmates can follow. In other words, to be effective at "interpersonal communication," you must look at the "big picture" and consider all of the ingredients that go into what it takes to be a good communicator.

Indeed, your ability to get along and communicate with another person is a complex process. However, the "big picture" of communication would be incomplete if we didn't deal with the specifics of "interpersonal communication" —particularly when the term involves certain rules that are *appropriate* in both social and professional situations.

It doesn't matter whether you're playing a game of Monopoly or basketball, you must know the rules. If you don't know what's allowed and what's not, then you have no chance of winning—because you are constantly playing "in the dark." **Social communication** is communication that occurs in your personal and your community life, while **professional communication** is communication that takes place on the job or is related to your career. Both of these types of communication are similar to board games and

Appropriate and respectful communication will help you get ahead in whatever career you choose.

sporting contests in one respect: there are certain rules that should be followed. Yes, even though they are often unspoken or unwritten, there are certain rules or procedures that apply if you want to get ahead in your social life and in your professional career. Knowing what to do when is the sign of a person who is smart and who wishes to be in charge of a situation.

Studies indicate that over 70 percent of our day is spent working and interacting with other people. Thus, remember that appropriate interpersonal communication is respectful communication. For example,

- When you speak to a person, you make direct eye contact.
- When you meet your *prospective* boss, you offer a firm handshake.
- When you bring a friend into your house, you introduce her or him to your family.
- When the teacher is ready to begin, you end your personal conversation.

The importance of knowing how to act or behave in a given situation is not a new concept. History notes that our country's first president, George Washington, often referred to a book on *etiquette,* or social appropriateness, to help him in the political arena and in society. Even one of America's great statesmen, Benjamin Franklin, wrote in the 1700s, "Use no hurtful deceit. Think innocently and justly; and, if you speak, speak accordingly." Both Washington and Franklin were showing the value of two key words that, regardless of the time period, are pivotal for interpersonal communication success: courtesy and tact. And what was true then is still true today in the twenty-first century!

The word **courtesy** refers to the way that you treat people. It means politeness. When you are courteous, you exhibit respectful consideration for others; in addition, you show good manners. The word **tact** is slightly different in that it refers to the way that you deal with people. To be tactful in a situation means that you are being diplomatic. You try to say or do what is most fitting, based on the occasion.

Benjamin Franklin's protocol advice is as valuable today as it was three hundred years ago.

In this chapter we will examine the ways that courtesy and tact work together with the "art of appropriateness." Specifically, we will look closely at how tone, "people skills," and respecting differences can contribute to your interpersonal communication skills.

SECTION 1

Appropriate Tone

When communicating with other people, it is important that you use the correct **tone,** or the mood that you verbally—and nonverbally—create. In addition to the words that you use, your tone is the "attitude" that you give to others. Do you have an angry tone? Is your tone positive and upbeat?

You may have heard the phrases, "It's not what you say but the way that you say it!" or, "Don't use that tone of voice with me!" These statements probably mean that your tone is rude or discourteous.

Courteous, tactful, respectful communicators are aware of what to do and what *not* to do when it comes to creating the correct "communication mood." Let's take a look at three different approaches that your tone might take.

No one likes to be manipulated.

An Aggressive Tone

Most people think an **aggressive tone** or communication approach is often pushy and *brash.* In a similar manner, an aggressive person considers only one point of view: his or hers. This method of communication cares little about the feelings of others; it is a "my-way-or-the-highway" attitude—with little or no room for compromise or meaningful discussion. The aggressive approach wants to win at all costs, even if that means intimidating, *manipulating,* or belittling others in the process.

Analysis: This is not an appropriate interpersonal communication tone to set in either a social or a professional setting. Chances are that in the long run you won't get what you're after. Studies have shown that when you use your words to bully or steamroll others, you discourage their creativity and their enthusiasm. Your friends might not be friends for long! And your colleagues will probably turn away from you—or simply turn you off. So don't come on too strong for too long!

A Nonassertive Tone

You could characterize a **nonassertive tone** or communication approach as one that shows a lack of action and energy. A nonassertive person rarely speaks and often appears disinterested or uninvolved to the point that others don't know how to "read" him or her. This particular tone communicates to everyone, "I lack self-confidence, don't believe that my ideas are any good, or just don't care about what is going on."

Analysis: This interpersonal communication approach can be particularly inappropriate at work. While some of your friends may take the time to get to know "the real you," employers and coworkers might interpret your silence and lack of involvement as boredom or low self-esteem. Others might think that you are simply rude. So get involved. Make your voice heard. Speak up and show others that you can vocally and attitudinally be an energetic, vibrant part of what is happening.

An Assertive Tone

What you're after is an assertive tone. The middle ground between aggressive and nonassertive, the **assertive tone** or communication approach is direct, yet tactful. Assertive communicators know when to talk, when to keep quiet, and how to give their opinions in a manner that is courteous and respectful. They create an overall mood of harmony because they always consider these specifics before acting or speaking:

- Location—Is this the right place to talk?
- Timing—Is this the right time to talk?
- Intensity—What can I do to keep calm and not come off as overbearing?
- Relationships—How well do I know the person to whom I'm about to speak? Also, how does each person's role and responsibility affect this situation?

Analysis: You are sure to be a winner if you use an assertive tone in your interpersonal dealings with people. Whether in social or professional situations, the assertive communicator has a warm, friendly voice; uses respectful words; has a calm, relaxed appearance; sends positive nonverbal signals to others; and makes direct, yet nonthreatening eye contact.

Using an assertive tone will help you solve problems and avoid shouting matches, because your "communication attitude" will set the stage for brains and cool heads to prevail. So be assertive. It's the appropriate thing to do!

The assertive speaker is direct yet tactful—a winning combination.

INSTANT IMPACT

BEWARE OF GOSSIP

Those people who like to talk about others should take notice. Research shows that workplace gossip, those "juicy stories" that people love to spread around, will come back to haunt them. A 1998 article titled "A Crash Course in Conflict Resolution" suggested that employees view those who spread gossip as "busters"—or those people who get in the way or "bust up" a positive, happy workplace environment.

Rumor-spreaders, or those who act as if they are "in the know," are not seen as true friends and, overall, are not trusted. Studies at both Purdue University and Ohio State University confirm that when a person makes a positive *or* a negative comment about someone else, listeners associate those qualities with the speaker as well.

Researchers end with one piece of advice: at work, if you don't have something nice to say about someone, keep quiet. Otherwise, you could end up being the real loser!

Using the Telephone Effectively

You just read about the importance of using correct tone when communicating both verbally and nonverbally. In the next section, you will learn the value of people skills. Let's take a look at how these two topics play a role in using the telephone. Perhaps we can dramatize telephone etiquette by eavesdropping on a phone conversation. Imagine that a young man is calling to ask about a job he has seen advertised in the newspaper. This is how the conversation might go:

Operator: Hello, this is Poppa Lock Company. How may I help you?
Kevin: Uh, yeah. I'd like to speak to someone in charge.
Operator: In charge of what?
Kevin: Well, I'm kinda looking for a job.
Operator: That would be Ms. Hansen. Just a moment, please. I'll connect you.
Assistant: Hello, this is Renee Jones.
Kevin: I'm trying to reach Ms. Hansen.
Renee: May I ask in reference to what?
Kevin: Yeah, I'm calling about a job. So, could you put her on?
Renee: What job is that, sir?
Kevin: Well, the one where you drive around and help people who are locked out of their cars.
Renee: Do you mean one of our customer assistants?
Kevin: (a little annoyed) I suppose.
Renee: What are your qualifications for this job?
Kevin: I don't know. I never had a job like this before.
Renee: (clears her throat) Have you graduated from high school yet?
Kevin: Not quite, but can I talk to Ms. Hansen now?
Renee: (coldly) Unfortunately, Ms. Hansen is not available, but if you give me your phone number, I'll have her call you if she wants any more information.
Kevin: 424-6223.
Renee: Thank you. (Hangs up)

After Ms. Hansen reads a summary of this conversation, do you suppose she will call Kevin back? It seems unlikely—Kevin probably lost the chance to get the job because of the mistakes he made. For example, Kevin gave the impression that he really didn't care about the job. Phrases such as "So, could you put her on?" indicate a lack of respect and courtesy.

Some of Kevin's other mistakes—those that might have been overlooked, had his attitude been better—were:

- He didn't give his name to Ms. Hansen's assistant or use the word "please." His lack of politeness got the conversation off to a bad start.
- He didn't state his purpose for calling until he was asked.
- He didn't mention that he had seen an ad for the job in the newspaper.
- He failed to mention any qualifications.

What could Kevin have said and done during this telephone conversation to help him make a good impression? Certainly he should have patiently and politely repeated his name and reason for calling to each person he spoke to. He should have answered the question about qualifications by mentioning things that would show that he could

(continued)

do a good job. For example, he might have said, "I had a good attendance record at school. I know how to keep accurate records, and I know how to follow directions."

Kevin should have avoided using slang—such as "yeah" (use your best English in professional situations). He should also have used the name of the person he was speaking to ("May I speak to Ms. Hansen" rather than "So, could you put her on?"). Calling a person by name is polite and makes a good impression. He might have asked for information about the job such as the hours and the type of work.

Finally, he should have found out if he could have an interview. Unfortunately, Ms. Hansen's assistant cut him off long before the conversation reached that point. She probably decided that Kevin was not the kind of person the company wanted to hire.

Tips for Success ... Here's what the conversation with Ms. Hansen's assistant might have been like if Kevin had handled it better.

Assistant: Hello, this is Renee Jones.

Kevin: Hello, Ms. Jones. My name is Kevin Lee. I'm calling in regard to your ad in Sunday's *Omaha World-Herald* for a customer assistant.

Renee: Just one minute; I'll put you through to Ms. Hansen.

Ms. Hansen: This is Jane Hansen.

Kevin: Ms. Hansen, my name is Kevin Lee. I'm calling in regard to your ad in Sunday's *Omaha World-Herald* for a customer assistant.

Ms. Hansen: Fine, Mr. Lee. What are your qualifications for the job?

Kevin: Well, Ms. Hansen, I'm pretty responsible. In fact, I was a stock clerk in a grocery store last summer. I also got good grades in math, and I have a good attendance record.

Ms. Hansen: Did you graduate from high school?

Kevin: Not yet, Ms. Hansen, but I hope to next June. Can you tell me something about the job? What would I be doing?

Ms. Hansen: You would be on call for anyone who's locked out of their car. You drive to the location they give you and then, using one of our special devices, help the customer into their car.

Kevin: That sounds like something I could do.

Ms. Hansen: You sound like someone we might be interested in, Kevin. Why don't you come over to my office for an interview tomorrow at 10:00 A.M.?

Kevin: Certainly. Where should I come for the interview?

Ms. Hansen: My office is Suite 105 in the Agoura Hills Building at 7th and Maple.

Kevin: (reading his notes) That's Suite 105 in the Agoura Hills Building, 7th and Maple, at 10 o'clock tomorrow morning.

Ms. Hansen: That's right.

Kevin: Thank you, Ms. Hansen. I'll be there. Good-bye.

Notice that Kevin made a good impression on the assistant because he was prepared. That is probably why she put him through immediately to Ms. Hansen.

WORDS FROM THE WORKPLACE

Mike Scott
Building Contractor

Q. *Mr. Scott, how does communication play a role in your day-to-day world of home construction?*

A. I deal with subcontractors and suppliers, homeowners, bankers, and attorneys. Each day I get up early to begin calling to confirm the scheduling of the day's activities. I speak with individuals who speak very little or no English, technical construction lingo, or very legal terms. Since I am on the phone, I cannot use nonverbal language or point to a picture. I must make sure that everyone completely understands me.

Q. *What suggestions can you give to students to show them the importance of communication skills?*

A. There have been times when I assumed that the person I was talking with understood what I was saying, only to find out later that that person did not understand at all. I now ask them to explain what I just told them.

Many times a homeowner will use a technical term incorrectly. Often I will ask them to be more specific in describing what they want me to do, and in so doing, I discover that what I thought I heard them say was not what they meant to say.

Finally, when I deal with bankers and attorneys I attempt to communicate with them on their level, by using legal terms with which they are familiar. I also make certain that I am very specific in my choice of words. A mistake here can be costly in time and money.

SECTION 1 REVIEW

Recalling the Facts ...

1. Approximately how much time is spent daily interacting with other people?
2. List the three types of "tones" discussed, and tell which of the three is the most desirable for effective social and professional communication.

Thinking Critically ...

1. In January of 2000, sports journalist John Feinstein delivered a speech titled "Sports in the New Millennium." He stressed that professional athletes had a "social obligation" to stay in school before they turned pro and also, Feinstein said, that they needed to be effective speakers. Do you agree? Explain.

Taking Charge ...

1. People often react to your words by the "way" that you speak. Say each of the following statements in different tones. After each, analyze the potential effect that your statement might have.
   a. "I plan to do my homework right after dinner!"
   b. "Does someone else have an idea to share with the group?"
   c. "Would you go to a movie with me?"

SECTION 2 People Skills

Before you take the time to know language, you should get to know people. What do they like? What upsets them? What makes them comfortable or uncomfortable? You may have heard the phrase, "That person has 'people skills.' " When you have **people skills,** you exhibit the ability to work well with others because you take the time to make them feel at ease. Those possessing such skills know and then apply certain polite communication procedures that are appropriate just about anywhere.

How would you rate your people skills? If need be, you can improve.

If you have people skills, friends and coworkers like to be around you and enjoy your company. You and your words create a friendly, productive environment. When you and others show such interpersonal communication skills, not only are spirits high, but also work gets done. Those with people skills know the value and appropriateness of (1) making introductions, (2) participating effectively in conversations, (3) offering and receiving criticism, and (4) giving clear and accurate directions.

Making Introductions

If you want to help make people at ease and feel a part of the group, then make sure that they know each other. Find out people's names. Take the time to introduce each other. For example, if you are with a friend and others join you, social and business "appropriateness" demands that you know how to introduce people. Here are a few suggestions:

Stop what you are doing.
Be friendly.
Address everyone by name. "John, Maria—I would like you to meet my coworker, Constance."

INSTEAD OF TRYING TO COME UP WITH ALL OF THESE CLEVER THINGS TO SAY TO BECKY...
WONDER WOMAN

WHY DON'T YOU JUST BE YOURSELF AND TALK TO HER LIKE A NORMAL PERSON?
KOMIX KORNER
X-MEN
BATIUK
4-22

LOOK, MONROE ... IF YOU'RE NOT GOING TO BE SERIOUS ABOUT THIS, THEN I DON'T WANT TO TALK ABOUT IT AT ALL!

FUNKY WINKERBEAN reprinted by special permission of North American Syndicate.

State what you are doing. "She and I have been working on that inventory report that is due on Monday."

Introduce the others. "Constance, this is John, who works in the Production Department; and this is Maria, who works in Advertising."

Ask a question or make a comment to get the others talking. "John, I think that you and Constance are from the same part of the country. Didn't you say that you were from Texas?"

Work to make everyone feel included in the conversation.

A firm but relaxed grip insures offering "the hand of friendship" in American social and professional situations.

If the relationship or meeting is more formal, the terms "Mr." or "Ms." might be used. Also, even though some may think that the practice has fallen out of favor, introducing women or elders first is often a sign of appropriateness and respect—and it can help you and your introduction make a lasting impression.

Another way that you can make a positive impression is through a handshake. Usually you shake hands with another person not when you are introducing others, but when you are the one being introduced. In job interviews, when you are meeting adults, or in more structured occasions (banquets, weddings, or graduation), it is a good idea to shake hands with the person you are meeting, particularly if it is the first time that you two have met. When making the handshake, keep these ideas in mind:

- First, make friendly eye contact.
- Next, don't be afraid to extend your hand first.
- Finally, offer a firm but relaxed grip on the other person's hand.

Socially and professionally, the "hand of friendship" is appropriate and is seen as a sign of "interpersonal" respect.

Participating Effectively in Conversations

Developing your people skills means knowing how to properly participate in a conversation. Conversation, or **dialogue,** is the oral exchange of thoughts and feelings involving two or more people. You may have heard the saying that "It takes two to tango." Well, just as it takes two people to dance the tango, it takes two to talk in a conversation. Avoid falling victim, however, to three "conversation killers"—talking too much, talking too little, or interrupting others.

- **Talking too much.** Nobody likes a "motormouth" or a "know-it-all." Dominating a conversation and talking too much (particularly about yourself!) irritates people and makes them feel left out. It focuses all the attention on you. Instead, let other people talk. Find out what they think. How do they feel about certain subjects? What's new and exciting in their lives? You can't build positive relationships if other people feel that the conversation is one-sided. Respect other people's ideas, and give them the time to express those ideas. Use some interpersonal communication sense and share the "talk time."

Don't be a "buttinski"! Let others talk.

- **Talking too little.** By contrast, talking too little in a conversation can end the conversation quickly. Those long "dead spots" of silence make everyone uncomfortable. Talking too little can cause others to think that they are uninteresting or boring—or, even worse, that you are bored or not interested in what they have to say. Don't give this impression. If you are going to make "people skills" inroads, then you must be an active participant in the conversation. Be congenial, enjoy people, talk! And don't think that you have to talk a lot. Sometimes the person who talks occasionally, but who talks at the right time (saying the right things), is the one who is admired and remembered.
- **Interrupting others.** The quickest way to break up a conversation is to cut people off when they start to speak or to interrupt them while they are speaking. In the social world, it doesn't take people long to size you up and decide what kind of a person you are. Authors Camille Lavington and Stephanie Losee, in the article "You've Only Got Three Seconds," say that at work, it takes your coworkers about three seconds after meeting you to decide how you are going to fit in. So don't interrupt when others are talking. Allow other people to finish their thoughts. Not only will it help the conversation, it will also help your image—as a person who is familiar with "interpersonal" appropriateness.

Offering and Receiving Criticism

The word *criticism* means "an evaluation or a judgment." We usually hear this word used in a negative context, where someone or something is being corrected or *reprimanded.* Appropriate people skills, however, teach that giving or receiving criticism doesn't have to be a negative, miserable experience. There's a right way and a wrong way to do most things, and the way that we offer and receive criticism is no exception.

Offering Criticism. We should view offering criticism as a way of encouraging someone to improve. Earlier, you read about the assertive, the aggressive, and the nonassertive tones, or the communication "attitude" or mood that you create. When you are talking to your friend about a problem that has come up between you two, the worst thing you can do is to start condemning the other person. At work, don't criticize a fellow worker to the extent that you break off a relationship. Use an assertive tone, not an aggressive one. Also, don't criticize someone with "the silent treatment." It just causes friction.

Constructive criticism is tactful and positive. It builds upon what is good.

Instead, convey a constructive interpersonal communication attitude. Don't hurt people's feelings or make them feel silly. Make people feel as if they belong. Giving criticism should be viewed as a way of encouraging someone to improve. Therefore, use language that shows tact and politeness. Remember: criticism should work to build up, not tear down, a relationship.

Constructive Language	*Destructive Language*
"I'd like for you to . . .	
. . . show more incentive."	"You're lazy!"
. . . pay greater attention to detail."	"You're so careless and sloppy!"
. . . value punctuality more."	"You're late too often!"
. . . work to improve your skills."	"You make far too many mistakes!"

Don't make the person you are criticizing feel as if you are "off on an emotional rant" or are verbally abusing him or her. If you find that you are angry, it might be a good idea to wait to address the problem. Cool off! When you criticize someone, your comments should focus on the quality of the work or the specific behavioral act—not on the person. Create a communication situation where everyone can win.

Your language should be friendly, your nonverbal communication congenial, and your overall message informative and instructive. Don't just criticize; offer possible solutions as well. Let the other person know exactly what might be done to correct the problem. Finally, offer good news! You can bet that this positive interpersonal communication approach will be appreciated.

Receiving Criticism. There is also a proper way to respond when receiving criticism. It is often difficult for us to hear that we are doing things wrong or that our work is not up to par. Maybe this is just part of human nature. But we must remember that sometimes paying close attention to constructive criticism is the way that we learn how to get better, both as a friend and as a worker. Here are some steps to follow:

a. *Maintain your composure.* Don't fly off the handle and become defensive.
b. *Allow others to finish what they have to say.* Let your friend, family member, coworker, or boss say all that they want to say.
c. *Don't interrupt.* Maybe your question or comment will be handled later in the discussion.
d. *Be a good listener.* What you are hearing could be "right on the money" for an action that really does need to be improved.
e. *Ask questions (courteously).* The answers might help clear up a point that you were unsure about.
f. *Thank the person for her or his thoughts and observations,* and ask for a "follow-up" meeting to see if any changes have been noted.

Communication consultants Peter and Susan Glaser believe that the best interpersonal communication occurs when simple language is honestly presented face-to-face. Whether you are criticizing someone else or are the one being criticized, remember that you are intent on solving problems—not creating them. Show others that you have both verbal and nonverbal people sense, and handle criticism in a way that is both respectful and appropriate.

DILBERT reprinted by permission of United Feature Syndicate, Inc.

COMMUNICATION

Break through

Classes Help the "New Workforce" Learn the Rules

- Show up on time.
- Don't send someone in your place if you can't come to work.
- Reason with your bosses instead of losing your temper.

We can no longer assume that everyone entering the world of work knows common business rules such as those listed above. Those who make up the "New Workforce" are often unacquainted with what's proper at the workplace. The "New Workforce" is made up of people who want to work, and work hard, but who come from countries or cultures that have work ethics and work habits that are different from the traditional workplace customs.

"That's why 'soft skill' classes are becoming as necessary as résumé writing at some social service agencies," says Jennifer Walter, an instructor for the St. Paul Rehabilitation Center (SPRC) in Minneapolis, Minnesota. She adds that in some countries, it's not OK to talk directly to your supervisor.

Funded by grants and government money, SPRC offers many classes that teach appropriate "interpersonal" skills and workplace etiquette. Some businesses have requested the classes, and have helped with the expenses. The "New Workforce" is taught to understand what many employers assume is obvious. Of course you set the alarm an hour early if you have to drop your child at school before you go to work. Of course you wear dress shoes and dress socks, not white athletic socks, to an interview. Of course you look people in the eye when addressing them.

"People who are taking these classes may not have a stable work history," says JoAnn Brown, who teaches a week-long workshop on preparing for an interview. "They just need to be given opportunities. Most people really do want to work!"

Source: Amy Gage, staff columnist, *On Balance* (section), *St. Paul Pioneer Press*, March 11, 1999.

Questions

1. Obviously, this story shows a "communication breakthrough" in business, but how could these types of classes, particularly as they relate to interpersonal communication skills, offer a *social* breakthrough, as well, for the "New Workforce"?
2. Examine your own background. Were you raised to value education? How can a person's background be a factor in getting a good job?

Giving Clear and Accurate Directions

Have you ever been told the wrong directions to someone's house? Have you ever been given an assignment or a task to do at home, in school, or at work—but not given all the information? If so, then you know the confusion and irritation that poorly given directions can cause. When directions are unclear, then the people involved are themselves unclear on how to complete a task or get from point A to point B in an effective, efficient manner.

But how do you give directions? If you are working with a group of your friends on a class project, is everyone "on the same page" as to who is responsible for what at what time? If having interpersonal "people skills" means that you work well with others, are a real team player, and promote group harmony, then you realize the importance of giving clear and accurate directions. When the directions are clear, people feel more organized and confident. Why? Because they know where they are going and what is expected of them.

But what is the "appropriate" way to give directions? Socially and professionally, remember the four ABCs when it comes to pointing people in the right direction:

If this policeman has followed his ABCs, the driver will find her way.

- Always *Be* Clear
- Always *Be* Complete
- Always *Be* Concise
- Always *Be* Considerate

Always Be Clear. Use words that leave no room for interpretation or possible confusion. If you are giving someone directions to a location and you say to turn "south" at the stoplight, you might want to follow that up with the word "left." If pages 1–4 in the Worker's Manual are to be read, does that mean pages—1, 2, 3, and 4—or just pages 1 and 4? Be clear. Also, in terms of clarity, try to present ideas logically and in an organized manner.

Think before you speak.
Go slowly.
List your directions in sequential order.
Use transition words (such as *first of all, next,* or *finally*).
Stress key words, such as action verbs (*turn, copy,* or *print*) or concrete nouns (*red light, computer, folder,* or *time sheet*).
Eliminate unnecessary words and steps.
Watch for nonverbal signs of confusion.
Ask for the directions to be repeated back to you when you've finished.

Always Be Complete. Be thorough. Don't stop short with your words and leave out important information. Give the whole story so that your audience isn't guessing. Don't assume that people can fill in the blanks or that they "know" what you are saying. To be positive that you have been complete, when you are finished giving your directions, restate your point and summarize important information.

Always Be Concise. Shakespeare said that "Brevity is the soul of wit." So be brief with your directions. Get to the point. Use your words convincingly and conversationally, but use them sparingly. Your directions can be better followed if you don't surround them with unnecessary words and irrelevant ideas.

Always Be Considerate. If directions are to be given clearly, or if they are to be totally understood, then they must be provided in the proper environment. Consider, for example, the appropriateness of the

- Location—Ask yourself, "Is this area too noisy for these directions to be heard?"
- Timing—"Is this the right time to give these directions? It's just about noon; I guess I'll wait until after lunch instead."
- Tone—"I can't be

Watch for signs of confusion.

COMMUNICATION Break

NASA Needs Better *Eye-to-Eye* Communication!

Evidence shows that the year 1999 had both good and bad news for the National Aeronautic and Space Administration, better known as NASA. The *Los Angeles Times* reported that while images from the Hubble Space Telescope continue to aid our understanding of the universe, several space ventures failed.

For example, the most publicized event involved the Mars Climate Orbiter. This $125 million craft would have studied the climate of the "Red Planet." However, the orbiter was lost on September 23, 1999. The reason? There was a "navigational error" that occurred when the people in charge used different measurements in converting English to metric units. The result was that the Orbiter got too close to Mars and burned up in its atmosphere.

The March 14, 2000, article by the *Times* states that there was definitely a "communication breakdown" because different branches of NASA *never* clearly communicated with each other. There were too many assumptions, the article notes, and not enough one-on-one communication that used clear language that everyone understood.

In this instance, poor interpersonal communication skills at NASA led to the loss of millions of dollars and a scientific letdown because everyone involved was not "on the same page."

Question

Miscommunication can occur at any level of government—local, state, or federal. Cite a recent instance of government miscommunication that resulted in the loss of tax dollars, as was the case for NASA, or in public embarrassment for the officials involved.

aggressive in the way that I give these directions. I had better relax so that I don't make everyone nervous and on edge."

Before you ask someone a question, make a request, or give directions, ask yourself these three questions: "Is this the appropriate place to talk?", "Is this the appropriate time to talk?", and "Is this the appropriate way to talk?" Answering "yes" to these questions before you speak can help you avoid interpersonal communication breakdowns and show others that your people skills are hard at work.

Is this the right place to be asking directions?

Building Relationships

At the 1998 Group of Seven meeting, which was held in Denver, the heads of the world's seven leading industrialized nations had a very full agenda. The Colorado State International Business Protocol Office issued "guidebooks" to representatives from all attending countries so that no international incident would get in the way of business. Some of the advice was:

- Do not mimic Italians' hand gestures.
- Arrive on time for business meetings with Germans.
- Keep your suit jacket on when dining with the French.
- Be reserved about touching or demonstrating other displays of affection with the British.
- Try to bow at a 15-degree angle when meeting Japanese delegates.
- Make eye contact when you shake hands with Americans.
- Do not shake hands or exchange greetings with the Russians in doorways, as they believe that it may bring bad luck.

The organizers knew that the countries involved had different customs and ways of doing things. These different customs had to be treated with both dignity and respect if the meeting was going to be successful.

Is the international community really that much different from your own? The fact of the matter is that knowing the appropriate "rules" of communication—specifically interpersonal communication—when dealing with a diverse group of people not only makes you more appealing, it also allows you to be a more effective communicator with all types of audiences.

More than 200 years ago, Hector St. John DeCrèvecœur called America the great "melting pot"—a divine mixture of nationalities, customs, and traditions. Today, in a world that is so interconnected, where the media or the Internet can transport us to another continent in a matter of seconds, doesn't it make sense that we all should work hard to understand each other and get along?

SECTION 2 REVIEW

Recalling the Facts ...

1. Some of the areas that contribute to getting along with others and communicating appropriately include (1) making __________, (2) participating effectively in ________, (3) offering and receiving ________, and (4) giving clear and accurate ________.
2. What are the three "conversation killers"?
3. List the four ABCs for giving directions.

Thinking Critically ...

1. Willis Johnson is the president of Classic Cinemas, based in Downers Grove, Illinois. Johnson has 13 theaters with 41 screens. He says, "Everyone is entitled to enjoyment of a film without distraction." He adds that even though people can sit at home and talk to their TV sets, it's not appropriate to sit in a theater and "talk to the screen or to each other." Do you agree? What are some other places, events, or occasions where talking might be considered inappropriate? When is it OK to talk at a public gathering? Give some examples.

Taking Charge ...

1. Giving clear and accurate directions takes time and thought. For example, how do you explain to someone how to use a copy machine? How do you fix a copy machine that is jammed? You must explain the process in the correct order and use clear language. Select one of the following and clearly explain the "process." Be prepared to speak in small groups or before the class.
   a. yesterday's homework assignment
   b. your school's attendance rules
   c. your school's substance abuse policy
   d. a favorite recipe
   e. changing a tire
   f. a favorite game (chess, Monopoly, or hockey, for example)

   If you have another process idea, check with your teacher for approval.

STUDENT WORK

"Peer Mediation" *By Apple Valley High School*

When you are working with others, communication problems can arise. Sometimes, talking or getting along with your friends or colleagues at school, at work, or in social settings can be difficult. Knowing this, a group of students, along with faculty advisors, put together a Peer Mediation brochure.

This brochure explains some terms, tells students how to go about solving their problems with other people, and instructs them on where to go for direction and advice. It is constructive communication, because it has "students talking to students" in an assertive, nonthreatening, confidential way.

Peer Mediation

Read what this brochure from a suburban Minneapolis school says about conflict, resolution, and the value of effective communication. Remember that this program was put together primarily by students who cared about other students.

PEER MEDIATION

No Insults
No Fighting
No Judgments

NO PROBLEM

CON-FLICT

a: disagreement
b: emotional tension resulting from incompatible inner needs or drives

WHAT IS MEDIATION?

Mediation gives you, the student, the opportunity to solve your own conflicts before they escalate, in a safe and confidential environment. You are given the chance to talk through your conflict with other students as mediators to guide you.

This process has helped many of your peers work out friendships, clear up misunderstandings and avoid the trouble that comes when conflicts get out of hand.

QUESTIONS?

- Stop in guidance office.
- This program is for the students so your feedback is important.

STUDENT WORK

ROLE OF THE MEDIATOR:

Be neutral—a mediator does not take sides.

Confidentiality—what is said in a mediation stays in the room.

Enforce the rules—a mediator keeps the mediation positive and safe by enforcing the rules.

To facilitate the process—a mediator does not try to solve the problem; mediators help students work through their conflicts.

CONSTRUCTIVE CONFLICT CAN:

- Bind people together.
- Bring a balance of power to a relationship.
- Create and bring about new growth and new ideas.

Any student can participate in mediation. Just fill out the form on the back of this sheet and drop it in a referral box.

Mediations can take place at any time throughout the day. They are usually set up one day in advance.

Mediations take place in quiet spaces such as conference rooms and vacant classrooms to help students focus on working through the conflict.

In order for mediation to work for everyone, you must follow these simple rules:

- Agree to try to solve the problem.
- No put-downs or threats.
- No interrupting.
- Be honest.

BENEFITS OF PEER MEDIATION:

- Empowers students to resolve their own conflicts.
- Creates a more positive school climate.
- Teaches students valuable skills to better solve conflicts.
- Prevents many disputes from escalating.
- Enables students to resolve conflicts without adult intervention.

REFERRAL FORM

Date ______________________

Name of person making referral:

____

People involved in conflict:

______________ gr. ________

______________ gr. ________

Briefly describe the conflict:

____

____

You've made a positive choice!

Return this form to one of the mediation referral boxes (located in the library, counselor's area or by room 114).

CHAPTER 5 Review and Enrichment...

Looking Back

Listed below are the major ideas discussed in this chapter.

- Effective interpersonal communication skills are important, particularly in social and professional settings.
- Smart interpersonal communicators always choose what is "appropriate" for the occasion and the audience.
- The communication tone that you use will telegraph to others your mood or attitude; avoid being aggressive or nonassertive, but practice your assertiveness.
- Whether you are at work or out in public, it is important to use courtesy and tact. Your verbal and nonverbal communication should be polite and exhibit "people diplomacy."
- "People skills," such as introducing a friend, shaking hands, or making a request or asking a question, are examples of appropriate communication.
- Positive communication can help you not only "get along," but also "get ahead" in the world.

Speech Vocabulary

Match the speech vocabulary term on the left with the correct definition on the right.

1. interpersonal communication
2. social communication
3. professional communication
4. courtesy
5. dialogue

a. conversation
b. being polite
c. language spoken at work
d. communicating constructively with others
e. language spoken with your friends

1. tact
2. tone
3. aggressive tone
4. nonassertive tone
5. assertive tone
6. people skills

a. apathetic, univolved
b. diplomatic in your approach
c. pushy or bossy
d. your mood or attitude
e. confident, yet respectful
f. your words create a warm, productive environment, and others like to be around you

General Vocabulary

To become a better social and professional communicator, you need a solid vocabulary. These "General Vocabulary" words can help you build your language arsenal. Look up each word in the dictionary, and copy the most appropriate definition. Next, use each in a sentence. Feel free to use another form of the word if it feels more natural to you ("manipulate" instead of "manipulating," for example).

1. prospective
2. etiquette
3. brash
4. manipulating
5. criticism
6. reprimanded

CHAPTER 5 Review and Enrichment...

To Remember

Answer the following based on your reading of the chapter.

1. According to *Fortune Magazine,* what two factors determine a company's success?
2. What is the difference between an aggressive tone and an assertive tone?
3. What does the phrase "That person has 'people skills' " mean?
4. What three things should you keep in mind when you shake hands with another person?
5. When should the terms "Mr." or "Ms." be used when making introductions?
6. What were the three errors that a person might make when participating in a conversation?
7. What does the word "criticism" mean?
8. What are the four ABCs for giving clear and accurate directions?
9. What kind of information was included in the "guidebooks" issued at the 1998 Group of Seven Meeting?
10. What is meant by the great American "melting pot"?

To Do

1. Find out the number of students or the percentage of different nationalities in your school. How many females are there compared to how many males? What is the age range? Do this by class (grades 9, 10, 11, 12). Talk to your guidance counselors or to your administrators. Your classroom teacher might be able to assist. Give your findings orally to the class or to a small group.
2. Talk to a business professional about appropriate dress. Ask questions about how particular outfits might be appropriate or inappropriate, depending on the job or the situation. Also, if hired, what do different professions *expect* the high school graduate to know regarding language, behavior, and appropriate interpersonal communication skills? Write the responses.
3. Ask a businessperson about the importance of the specific people skills listed in the chapter. Can he or she add any others? Be prepared to report your findings to the class.
4. Work with a group to role play assertiveness in the following situations.
   - Someone cuts in front of the lunch line.
   - Someone walks into the room and changes the TV channel while you're already watching something.
   - A friend who has stayed overnight pulled out almost all of your CDs from their cases and is about to leave without having put any of them back.

   After each of the above, discuss the advantages of assertive behavior versus aggressive or nonassertive behavior.

To Talk About

1. We often live in a world of "in your face" interpersonal communication, where being big, bold, and brash seems to be effective. While this approach might work in championship wrestling or on talk shows such as Jerry Springer's, why is this approach not necessarily a good one in business? How can being "in your face" prove to be a negative communication tool

in your social dealings, as well? How is the entertainment business often different from the "real world"—when it comes to effective communication and what it takes to convince or motivate people?

2. Most everyone would agree that "casual talk" is the language of the streets. However, how could this language be inappropriate in certain jobs or professions? Give examples. What about social occasions? Which ones would be casual, and which ones might be more formal? List them and explain how our language might differ depending on where we are and who is in the audience.
3. Work with a group to define assertive, passive, and aggressive communication. Now come up with examples of the difference between assertive and aggressive communication. Read the following situations and discuss how an aggressive person and then an assertive person would communicate.
   - A fellow worker is not doing his fair share of the work.
   - A classmate is disrupting class, making it hard for others to concentrate.
   - A brother or sister is spending too much time listening to your radio in your room.

To Write About

1. Students often argue that college is not the answer when it comes to wages and income. However, an article from a recent issue of *Business Week* says differently. The article notes that from 1979 to 1995, the average difference between the earnings of high school and college graduates went from 33 percent to 50 percent. It also said that now nearly 25 percent of America's workforce consists of college graduates. What does this say to you about staying in school and trying to improve on your education? How can school help your abilities to communicate with others effectively? Write your answers.
2. Technical training is often as valuable as a college degree. What are some "technical" professions or "skilled trades" that are highly valued in the American market? What type of schooling do you need? Where do you get it? What is the cost? What are the opportunities? Why are strong interpersonal communication skills important in these areas? Do some research and then write about your answers.

Related Speech Topics

This chapter has shown how the best speaking occurs when we demonstrate tact, courtesy, and respect. With that in mind, examine these possible speaking topics.

Illegal immigrants contribute significantly to the U.S. economy.

Age should not matter when it comes to hiring or firing.

Having bilingual skills can be an advantage in many professions.

Harassment can be stopped if different groups get tough and make a stand.

Friends play a greater role in the language that you use than do your parents or other adults.

Regardless of the organization, teamwork is critical for success.

We are often a nation that lacks self-discipline, particularly when it comes to school, work, or personal relationships.

CHAPTER 6

INTERVIEWING

"An interview is frequently the course you chart between what you came in knowing and what you're finding out as it's happening."

–Terry Gross, host of *Fresh Air,* National Public Radio

Learning Objectives

After completing this chapter, you will be able to do the following.

- Use interviews to gather material for your speeches.
- Schedule an interview at a time and place that will increase its chances for success.
- Create open-ended questions to draw out the best possible answers.
- Dress appropriately and present yourself in a professional manner.

Chapter Outline

Following are the main sections in this chapter.

1. Using Interviews to Gather Information
2. Preparing for an Interview
3. Conducting an Ethical Interview
4. Interviewing for a Job or Scholarship

New Speech Terms

In this chapter, you will learn the meanings of the speech terms listed below.

interviewer
subject
rapport
verbatim
open-ended question
follow-up question
yes-no question
leading question
portfolio
puff ball
pause
bridge
sparkler
sound bite

General Vocabulary

Expanding your general vocabulary will help you become a more effective communicator. Listed below are some words appearing in this chapter that you should make part of your everyday vocabulary.

pollster
proxy
vicariously
grovel
chauffeur
embalm
unobtrusive
canned

Looking AHEAD

Interviewing plays a vital role in how we communicate with each other. In this chapter, you will learn to use interviews to gather firsthand information. This information will add credibility and authenticity to your speeches. It can also provide the "punch" or the personal anecdote that makes your speech memorable.

As you study this chapter, you will learn that interviewing others is a challenging but rewarding exercise. Careful preparation and sound strategy, however, will help you get the most out of every interview. Sometimes it will be your turn to be interviewed. This chapter will show you how to prepare for an interview and how to maximize your chances of success. The chapter will also give you tips for answering tough questions and knowing the right etiquette for handling yourself after an interview.

Introduction

Interviews are among the best ways to find out something new. Most of the informative reports and speeches you give in school are based either on library research or on firsthand interviews. Talking with an expert can often be more helpful than reading an article or book, and it's almost certain to be more fun. You can spice up any speech with a few well-chosen quotes and stories from a lively interview.

An interview is a conversation controlled but not dominated by one person who asks questions of another person. In other words, an interview is a conversation with a special purpose. That purpose might be to learn what people think or to gather information about a new idea or discovery. It might also be to find out more about someone who has applied for a job or admission to college.

Rosie O'Donnell (right) has become an expert at interviewing others. Here she celebrates her 500th episode with guests Wynonna Judd, Katie Couric, and co-host for the day Bette Midler.

SECTION 1 Using Interviews to Gather Information

Interview comes from a French word, *entrevoir,* which means "to see one another." Interviewing, you might say, is a contact sport—eye contact, that is. A good interview grows out of a personal relationship between people. Don't think of it as Ping-Pong; think of it as a handshake.

Learning good interviewing skills is one of the smartest investments you can make in your future. People in many different careers do interviews. A book editor interviews prospective authors; an insurance agent interviews clients about their homes, cars, or possessions; a teacher interviews students about their academic problems. A financial adviser, a lawyer, an architect—all these professionals use interviews in their jobs.

We focus this chapter on how to be an **interviewer** (the person who asks the questions), because you will frequently use interviews to gather material for your speeches. We believe that if you can learn how to conduct a good interview, you will also have a better chance of being a good **subject** (the person who answers the questions). When your turn comes to be interviewed—for a job, for instance—you will be better prepared by being a good interviewer yourself.

A good interviewer asks questions she or he knows the audience wants answered.

Consider Your Audience

The number of interviews that take place is staggering. Opinion *pollsters* alone conduct an estimated 20 million interviews each year. Add to that figure the enormous number of job application and college admission interviews. We read about interviews every day—when we check the sports page, for example, to see how an Olympic athlete felt about winning a gold medal—and we watch countless interviews on television. In fact, your ideas about interviewing may have been formed by watching television news shows like *60 Minutes, 20/20,* and *48 Hours.*

A professional interviewer has one specific purpose: to act as a *proxy* for the audience. We can't all sit down for a chat with Adam Sandler, for instance, or Jennifer Lopez, but we are grateful that someone else can do it for us. Thus, we depend heavily on interviewers to act as our stand-ins.

Interviewers head into locker rooms for postgame reports, climb on board *Air Force One* to interview the president, and travel with troops heading into battle. Popular talk shows like those hosted by Oprah Winfrey and Larry King give audiences the chance to ask questions of celebrities and guest experts. We listen in on these shows hoping that the interviewer asks the questions we'd like to ask, so that we can *vicariously* take part in the interview ourselves.

Your task as an interviewer, then, is to keep the interests of your potential audience in mind. Who will ultimately hear the information you are gathering? The teacher? Your classmates? The general public? Try to ask your subject what those people would like to know. The ability to anticipate what listeners want to know is part of what has made Barbara Walters television's most celebrated interviewer. It's an ability that gives Mike Wallace and his *60 Minutes* crew the courage to leap over barriers and smash down doors in pursuit of a good story.

Be Curious

The quality you need most to become a good interviewer is curiosity. Do you want to know about people's thoughts, words, and deeds? The best interviewers bring a passionate curiosity to the job. They have a burning desire to know. They get the answers people want to hear about fascinating characters and about those caught up in interesting events. Great interviewers are brave enough to ask the natural questions, even at the risk of making themselves seem foolish.

While you may be more eager to interview a star basketball player or a world-class model than to interview your algebra teacher, you must always make an effort to generate some curiosity about whatever person you choose to interview. Everyone has an interesting story to tell, and you can find it if you ask the right questions. Who would suspect, for instance, that your physical education teacher once shot baskets with Michael Jordan or that your math teacher was in a movie as a child?

MSNBC's "Hardball" host Chris Matthews typifies the passion and curiosity that are qualities of all successful interviewers. Here he interviews Donald Trump.

A lack of curiosity, on the other hand, leads to lazy thinking. If you're not genuinely interested in what your subject has to say, you may find yourself behaving in the following ways:

- I make up a list of questions and go through them from beginning to end—no matter what the person I'm interviewing wants to talk about.
- I don't listen much to the answer. I just worry about the next question.

"I WON THE JACKPOT, YOU KNOW"

INSTANT IMPACT

It was a beautiful day in Beverly Hills, but then things went sour. Retired Air Force Col. Barney Oldfield was listening to his favorite radio show when he became annoyed with the phrase "you know."

Oldfield decided to keep track of the "you knows" for his own amusement. He was stunned when the total reached 117 during the 60-minute broadcast.

"It was an oral abomination," said the 1933 University of Nebraska journalism graduate who now lives in California.

Oldfield created an annual "You Know" contest, and a recent winner was high school senior Jessica Reinsch, who uttered the phrase "you know" 61 times during a 15-minute radio interview.

"I had been conscious of it, but it didn't ever connect that it was that annoying," she said. "Now I hear it all the time. I catch myself now. It seems weird."

As you prepare for an interview, take special note of the "quickie" words that we all tend to use in everyday speech. Words like "gonna," "yeah," "y'know," "like," and "kinda" are job-killers. They can make you sound uneducated and coarse, and possibly cost you a job offer.

- If an answer confuses me or the subject mentions something I haven't heard about, I don't like to let on. I just go on to the next question.
- I'm so edgy about what the person thinks of me that I can never get comfortable. All my energy in the interview goes into playing the role.

Would you be self-conscious if you had the chance to interview Michael Jordan? Famous people often help interviewers to relax.

Having a great interest in the person you're interviewing helps you overcome self-consciousness. It also drives nervousness away and gives you the courage to interview someone you respect or admire.

Keep in mind that most people like to talk about themselves, their work, and their opinions. The slightest hint that you're interested is often all the invitation they need to start talking. Curiosity might make you seem naive at times, but a true desire to know is the only proven way to bring an interview to life. If you have the right attitude, you may hear yourself making these enthusiastic comments during an interview:

- "That's fascinating. Tell me more."
- "I had no idea—whatever made them do that?"
- "How did you feel when that happened?"

SECTION 1 REVIEW

Recalling the Facts ...

1. Curiosity may have killed the cat, but it will help you be a good interviewer. What role does curiosity play in an interview?
2. Provide three short comments you could make during an interview that would encourage your subject to continue talking.

Thinking Critically ...

1. Watch a televised interview program such as *Larry King Live* or *Nightline*. What research do you think was involved in preparing the questions? How did the interviewer react to vague or unsatisfactory answers? Did the interviewer offer any personal information or "open up" to help the subjects talk?

Taking Charge ...

1. Conduct a "kid in the hall" poll. Think of an interesting, timely question that can be answered quickly (yes or no, agree or disagree). The question could relate to school policies or community issues. A possible question, for example, is "Should we limit all elected officials to two terms?" Ask the question of 20 people in your school. Record their responses and report your findings back to the class. You might even offer your information to the school newspaper as a "roving reporter."
2. Conduct an opinion survey. Work in a small group to develop a questionnaire on some subject of interest. Write or type a list of eight to ten questions on a single sheet of paper and reproduce enough so that you can hand out 100 copies. Ask if you can pass out the survey in some of your other classes or at lunch. Collect the surveys, tabulate the results, and report the outcome.

COMMUNICATION

Presidential Announcements

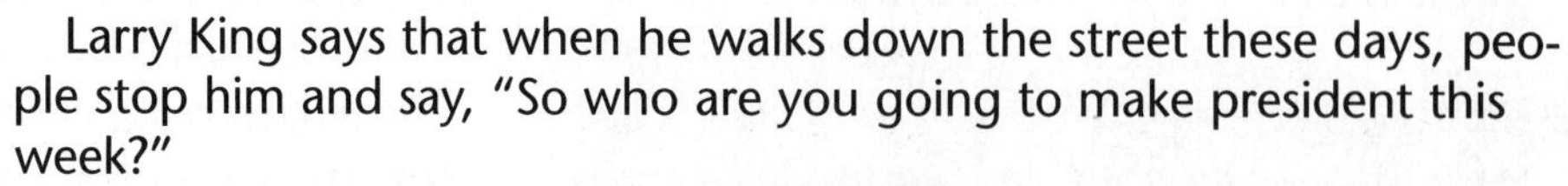

Larry King says that when he walks down the street these days, people stop him and say, "So who are you going to make president this week?"

King, the host of a daily three-hour radio talk program and a nightly television interview program, made history in 1992 when he nudged a reluctant candidate, Ross Perot, into announcing a bid for the presidency. Before the presidential campaign was over, King's program had become a frequent stop for the other major candidates.

Part of King's success lies in his skill as a listener. "I like questions that begin with 'why' and 'how,' " he says, "and I listen to the answers, which lead to more questions."

Although King doesn't consider himself a journalist, he says that asking questions comes easily: "My earliest memory is of asking questions. 'What did you do that for? Why did you do it?' "

King grew up in Brooklyn as the son of Russian Jewish immigrants. At age 22, he took a bus to Miami, changed his name (from Larry Zeiger), and got a job as a deejay on WIOD. Before long he had his own sports show and was soon interviewing local celebrities.

Eventually, after a roller-coaster career littered with bankruptcy, 6 failed marriages, and an arrest for larceny, King found a home in Washington with *The Larry King Show.* This program of guest interviews and an open phone line can now be heard on over 300 stations nationwide.

One of King's personal rules is not to prepare too much. "I never drive to work thinking of questions," he says, "but good things follow from what I do."

King says that this method enables him to ask the kind of questions the people in his audience would ask. Rather than try to draw out facts from his guests, King focuses on their feelings, emotions, and motives.

Today, with his trademark slicked-back hair, glasses, and suspenders, King comes as close to being a kingmaker as anyone in the media. Over 4 million people tune in each day to find out who and what he's going to listen to next.

Question

1. What role do talk shows and interview programs play in the American political process?
2. What is your opinion of Larry King's interviewing skills? Listen to one or two programs, then discuss in class his original questions, his ability to ask effective follow-up questions, and his overall skill in obtaining information from the interviewee.

SECTION 2 Preparing for an Interview

"Bend and *grovel* if you must," suggests John Brady, founder of a communications consulting firm, "but get the interview. This may turn you into a wimplike creature, but do it. You ain't got nothing 'til you've got that person sitting down to give you a couple of hours of his or her time."

Brady overstates the case, but his point is clear: Without a person to talk to, you have no interview. Carefully choosing a person to interview and arranging a time and place suitable for the interview are problems you must solve before you can ask the first question.

Getting an Interview

John Brady is not above taking his own advice. To get an interview with a famous author, Jessica Mitford, he once volunteered to be a *chauffeur.* Mitford was visiting a college near where Brady lived, but her schedule was packed. College officials had arranged for a student to drive Mitford from campus to the airport when her visit was over, a distance of about 75 miles. Brady persuaded the student to let him drive Mitford instead. The student didn't mind ("I really don't know what to talk with her about," he said), so Brady picked Mitford up, turned on his tape recorder, and got a terrific interview.

Finding the right person to interview given your topic is the first important step to a successful interview.

Most interview situations, of course, aren't that difficult. You will probably find that most of the people you want to talk with are agreeable and cooperative. At times, however, it may take some persistence on your part to get a few of them to agree to speak. And then there are those who are just too busy or stubborn. Let them alone and find someone more willing to talk.

Select a Subject Carefully ... No matter how skillful you are, an interview won't work if you haven't chosen the right person. Suppose you decide to do a speech on dreams. You discover a sleep research lab in town by thumbing through the yellow pages of the phone directory. A few calls later, you have scheduled an interview with the lab's director to discuss the current state of research on dreams. By interviewing that expert, you are sure to learn more and gain better information than you would have by asking a few friends about their dreams.

By the way, it's probably easier than you think to interview public officials. They know speaking about their jobs is one of their most important responsibilities. (Most politicians like the attention, too.) Public officials also have access to up-to-date information, and though you may get put on hold, you generally won't be turned down.

Before you call Christina Aguilera for a soul-searching interview, however, you should realize that a casual fan doesn't have much pull in

Hollywood. Large organizations with enormous numbers of readers, like *USA Today*, can get interviews where you cannot. But don't be discouraged—even a high school paper carries some weight. If you are having trouble setting up an interview, volunteer to write a story about your subject for the school paper. The added prestige (and exposure) may persuade your subject to grant you an interview after all.

"HELLO, I'M BARBARA WALTERS"

INSTANT IMPACT

Barbara Walters's ground-breaking exclusive interviews with world figures and her enterprising reporting have made her one of the most highly acclaimed journalists on television.

Walters began proving herself to a nationwide audience on December 14, 1976, when the first *Barbara Walters Special* aired. On the inaugural show, Walters visited the Plains, Georgia, home of President-elect Jimmy Carter and his wife, Rosalynn. Later in the same program, through the miracle of television we got to see Barbara as she went to the Malibu ranch of Barbra Streisand.

Throughout the show, Walters showed her talent for asking the kinds of questions her viewers wanted answered. She asked Streisand how she felt performing for thousands. She insisted that Carter choose between *Gone with the Wind's* Melanie and Scarlett. It was unlike anything viewers had seen, and they loved it.

Source: Adapted from *Entertainment Weekly.*

Choose When and Where ... The best setting for an interview is a place where you won't be disturbed. You want to have your subject's undivided attention. Many people like to be interviewed where they work—in their offices, for example. That may be convenient for them, but it can create problems for you. The telephone is sure to ring, and coworkers will stop by to chat. Any interruptions during the interview will distract your subject, break the **rapport**—the feeling of trust and cooperation—you have developed, and stretch out the time the whole interview takes. Getting your subject off somewhere private can do your interview a world of good.

Be sure, too, that you don't cheat yourself on the amount of time you request. Beginners often worry that they will take too much of the subject's time. Consequently, they ask for too little and quit too early. Ask for an hour of your subject's time. You can probably get a good interview in less time than that, but you run the risk of not getting the information you need if you ask for less.

You can always leave an interview early, but it's rude to take more time than you requested. By asking for an hour, you also tell your subject that you have plenty of questions and that you feel he or she has valuable and worthwhile answers. If your subject is so busy that only a few moments can be spared, consider interviewing someone else.

A quiet place where you have your subject's undivided attention is the best place to conduct an interview.

WORDS FROM THE WORKPLACE

Kris Sallee
Injury Counselor

Q. *What advice can you give to students to show them the importance of communication in the workplace?*

A. Communication is the end all, and be all, of almost all types of business. I would suggest that students take the time to remember that everyone wants his or her situation to be treated with special care, and you must listen to people's needs, wants, or desires in order to successfully complete the business transaction. Try to find a "center" point to begin the dialogue and build your relationship as appropriate from there.

Q. *How does communication play a role in the day-to-day activities of your work?*

A. We speak to injured employees every day by telephone. By using good telephone and communication skills we are able to help many employees reach a successful resolution to the problems they face with worker's compensation. I am able to help them by using active listening skills to really hear what they are saying. I communicate their responsibilities to them clearly and make sure they understand. I must be able to gather information in order to provide each individual with the resources that will be most helpful to that person.

Q. *Do you have any stories that might illustrate how good communication skills helped you in a business situation?*

A. Many times during the interview process, the people I speak to are somewhat hesitant to truly communicate their needs and wants. By developing a common bond with the person, we are able to find a basis from which to begin. A gentleman that I was working with recently became very defensive when I called to discuss his injury. He was in pain and mad that he had been hurt and wanted to pass blame. My first responsibility was to listen and to really hear what he was saying. By doing this I was able to tell him whom to contact to get the situation rectified so it would not happen to him again.

If I had not taken the time to listen and respond, several other employees might have been injured, just as he was.

Doing Your Homework

Having arranged an interview, you next need to learn all you can about your subject. "You should read every single thing that you can possibly get on the person you're about to interview," advises longtime talk show host Phil Donahue. "It keeps you out of trapdoors and keeps you from looking foolish."

The preparation you do before an interview helps you create good questions. If you wanted to interview a new teacher at your school, for example, you could find out beforehand where the teacher had previously taught, his area of expertise, and where he went to college. Once you have the basic biographical facts taken care of, you will be free to concentrate on more imaginative questions—the kind that produce the most interesting answers.

Make a distinction between a simple question and a foolish one. You can ask the principal about open campus policies in a sensible way, but if you ask how long the lunch period is, you are asking the principal to do your legwork for you—that's a question you can answer for yourself. Nothing will irritate a subject more, especially one who has been interviewed many times, than being asked a question whose answer you could easily have found in many other ways. Asking a subject such questions shows you haven't done your homework. They waste that person's time and undermine his or her opinion of you.

Collect as much background information about your subject as you can before your interview. Newspapers, libraries, and the Internet are useful resources.

Dress for Success ... Students often wonder what they should wear to an interview. Even though you may prefer to dress casually, you should wear whatever you think will bring the best response from the person you are interviewing. Good school clothes (avoid T-shirts and the latest fashion statement) should work well, but an interview with the governor or some other VIP (very important person) is going to require more formal clothing. Your credibility is at stake.

If the governor is used to people who wear suits, you must wear an outfit that he or she will take seriously. You don't have to overdo it, of course—especially if you're going to conduct your interview while leaning on a tractor tire—but you want your subjects to know that you're serious and that their comments will be treated with respect.

Which style of dress is more appropriate for an interview?

Take What You Need ... Be sure you take the right equipment with you to an interview. You should always have a small notebook and pen, even if you plan to use a tape recorder. The notebook shows your subject that you mean business, and it encourages talking.

Many interviewers use tape recorders to help them remember an interview. For one thing, tape recorders are the only way to be absolutely accurate. With a recorder, you can always be sure of getting information **verbatim** (word-for-word). For another, no matter how good you are at taking notes, you may miss something important. With a tape recording, you can go back and find what you left out of your notes. In many situations, a portable cassette recorder is well worth the bother, especially if the interview is likely to be unusually long.

Given all that a tape recorder can do, you might be surprised to learn that some professional interviewers prefer not to use one. Some interviewers say they carry only a pen and notepad because a tape recorder can make a subject ill at ease. Tape recordings don't protect you against mistakes, either. "You misquoted me," a subject might say. "I know that was what I said, but it wasn't what I meant."

Asking Effective Questions

Once you've contacted a subject, arranged a time and place to talk, and done a background check, you're ready for the last step before the interview itself: preparing a list of questions. Your goal is to guide the conversation where you want it to go. You want your subject to relax and to talk freely, but you also have an agenda with questions that need answering. The way you phrase these questions and the order in which you present them will determine, to a great degree, the success of your interview.

It is absolutely critical to prepare a list of questions in advance. Doing so will force you to think through the entire interview and plan the best order for your questions. Ideally, the answer to one question will lead naturally into the next. "You start a question, and it's like rolling a stone," said the writer Robert Louis Stevenson. "You sit quietly on the top of a hill; and away the stone goes, starting others." Preparing questions ahead of time is also the best way to make sure each minute of your interview counts.

You can organize an interview and make efficient use of the time allotted for it by preparing a list of questions in advance.

SAY WHAT?

INSTANT IMPACT

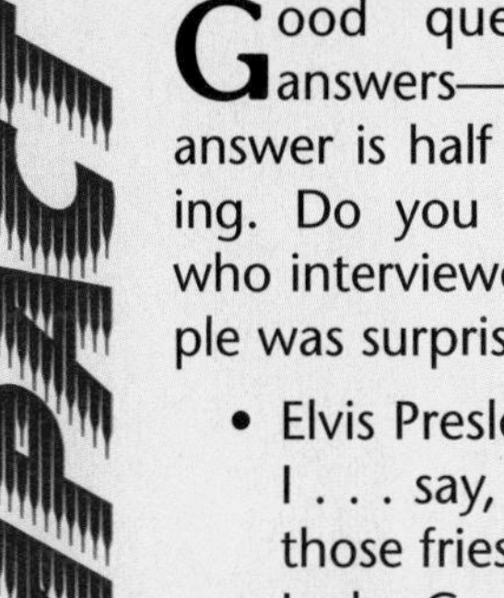

Good questions elicit good answers—and anticipating the answer is half the fun of interviewing. Do you suppose the person who interviewed the following people was surprised by their answers?

- Elvis Presley: "My last boss and I . . . say, are you going to eat those fries?"
- Lady Godiva: "What do you *mean* this isn't business casual?"
- Macbeth: "Would I go after my boss's job? Do I look like the kind of guy who would knock off his boss for a promotion?"
- Julius Caesar: "My first job involved a lot of office politics and back stabbing. I'd like to get away from that."
- Pandora: "I can bring a lot to your company. I like discovering new things, and I've got a *boxful* of ideas."
- Jesse James: "I can list among my experience and skills: leadership, extensive travel, event planning, intimate understanding of firearms, and a knowledge of security measures at numerous banks."

Keep Your Questions Brief ... Make your questions brief and to the point. Avoid those complicated two- or three-part questions you may have seen television reporters use during press conferences: "Mr. President, can you tell us what you know about plans to export more wheat, and where those shipments will be going, and when they'll start?"

You would be wiser to give the person you're interviewing one manageable question at a time. Keep your questions simple and direct. If the subject has trouble interpreting your question, rephrase it. For example, suppose you ask the question: "Did the school board drop its laundry program for athletics in the interest of economy or was it bowing to community pressure?" If this question is too much for your subject, try this: "Why do athletes have to wash their own towels this year?"

Reporters like CNN's Bernard Shaw and his co-hosts are sure to use the five Ws and H as the basis for their interviews.

Use a Variety of Questions ... Build your most important questions on the famous five Ws and an H (*who, what, why, when, where,* and *how*). Imagine, for instance, that the parents of one of your classmates have opened a new pet cemetery in your town. You want to give a speech on how people handle the death of a pet and decide to interview the parents. By using the five Ws and the H, you develop this list of questions:

- WHO brings their pets to your cemetery? Can you tell me about your customers?
- WHAT kind of burial or funeral arrangements do they request?
- WHY do you think people spend so much money on their pets?
- WHEN did you first decide to start a pet cemetery?
- WHERE are other pet cemeteries in our region located?
- HOW do you *embalm* a pet?
- HOW do you restore the appearance of pets who have been killed in car accidents?

Open-Ended Questions. Strive as much as possible to develop **open-ended questions.** These are similar to the essay questions on a written test. Instead of asking for a narrow response (yes-no, true-false), the question allows the subject to decide how best to answer.

Your goal is to use short questions to produce long answers. For example, instead of asking "Did you really fall into a vat of chocolate?" ask "What was it like to fall into a vat of chocolate?" In the

HOW WAS YOUR DAY TODAY?
FINE.

Communicating With Your Teenager
Parents frustrated with one-word answers must learn to ask more complex questions.
A-L
JERRY SCOTT AND JIM BORGMAN 7-23

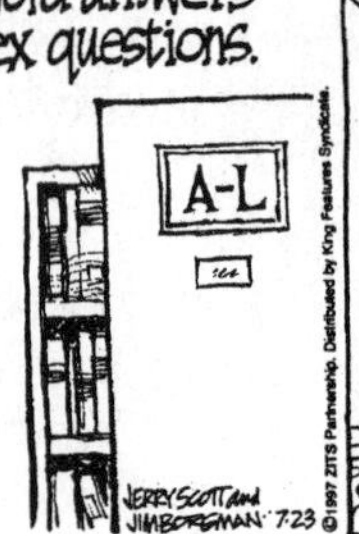

SO, JEREMY, WHAT DID YOU ACCOMPLISH TODAY?
STUFF.

following interview, notice how a student interviewer uses open-ended questions to draw out Martha Quinn, one of Music Television's original veejays.

> **Q: MTV seems now to be a part of American culture. What's it like knowing you were a factor in that?**
>
> A: I'm thrilled that I've been a part of it. A factor? I don't know. I feel like a little piece of plankton in a tidal wave. I don't really know that I had that much to do with it; I just got swept along in it. But it was a wonderful time to be around in the music business, you know, when new things are coming out.
>
> **Q: MTV's future seems fairly certain, but what about Martha Quinn's future? What does your future hold?**
>
> A: You know, more than anything, I wish I was one of those people who has a plan. "Oh, I know exactly what I'm going to be doing." You know, like Dolly Parton. I once read somewhere that she has her whole career planned. I hope in my best possible life that I'd have some sort of fun TV work, whether it be a sitcom or fun variety show or something like that.

Open-ended questions leave room for the subject to maneuver. While such questions may cause you to lose some control over the interview, what you gain is worth it. You may hear the subject tell you something that takes your breath away.

Follow-Up Questions. Inexperienced interviewers tend to look for safety in long lists of prepared questions. Of course, as noted, you must plan what to ask. But a long "must ask" list can drain the life from an interview, turning it into a tedious trip from Question A to Question Z. Along the way, you can miss a lot of good conversation in your concern to cover "everything on my list."

What's the solution? Prepare your list of questions, but stay flexible—be ready to react to the twists and turns of conversation. Listen for intriguing statements, and when you hear one, ask a **follow-up question.** Such questions help you pursue topics that pop up unexpectedly. One of the best questions is simply "Why?" Chase good ideas, even if it means letting some of your prepared questions slide.

To use follow-up questions well, you must think on your feet. Recall for a moment the interview with Martha Quinn. By listening attentively, this interviewer was able to recognize that Quinn's first audition with MTV was something special, an experience that deserved to be explored at length:

Interview Follow-Up

Dear

We appreciate your willingness to be interviewed for a future newspaper story and would like your responses to the following questions. They will help us evaluate our reporters and improve their skills. Feel free to make any comments you feel are appropriate.

1. **Was the Interviewer courteous, prepared, and alert?**
2. **Were the questions thoughtful and to the point?**
3. **Did the Interviewer double-check the spelling of names, important facts, and significant quotes?**

Please read the attached story and also answer the following questions:

1. **Does the story seem fair and accurate?**
2. **Do you feel you were misquoted or misrepresented?**
3. **Use camera metaphors for how the writer handles the subject. Where does he move in close, where fade back? Where is the story sharp or fuzzy?**
4. **Any other comments, pro or con?**

Thank you. Please return this sheet to the journalism room or put it in Mr. Schaffer's mailbox in the office as soon as possible.

Q: How did you get on MTV to begin with?

A: I was a college intern at WNBC in New York, and I had gotten myself through college doing television commercials. And when MTV came out, someone said, "Hey, Martha, that'd be perfect for you." Just a casual comment, and next thing I knew, I was kind of moseying down to the studio to audition for this wacky, weird thing.

Q: Were you nervous?

A: It was not a big deal to me, because I was auditioning every day of my life for, you know, Twix or Clearasil or something. And I was like, "Oh, OK, this is kind of weird, but I'll go check it out."

Q: How did you feel after the audition?

A: When I walked out of the audition, I thought, "Wow, that is the perfect job for me."

Q: And how did you feel later?

A: By the time I went to sleep that night, my life was to be changed for the next *ten years.* Can you imagine? I would like to go back and read my horoscope for that day. Seriously.

Sometimes people tell you things that are so interesting, unusual, or meaningful that they deserve your complete attention, regardless of whatever other question you were poised to ask. Follow your instincts. If someone tells you something of exceptional interest or importance, ditch your old questions and follow this new topic for all it's worth.

Questions to Avoid ... Some kinds of questions work better in an interview than others. **Yes-no questions,** for example, should be avoided. For one thing, they allow your subject to answer the question without telling you anything. They also give the subject an excuse to stop talking.

Suppose that during an interview with Barbara Walters, you said: "Several years ago you caused a sensation by signing a $5 million contract with ABC. Are you worth that much money?" If Walters answers yes, she has only told you what you already know—she accepted the contract. If she says no, you think she's just being modest. Either way, you won't have learned anything, and you'll have nothing new to tell anybody else.

But what if you had asked the question this way: "Miss Walters, what do you think of the public reaction to your $5 million contract with ABC?" Now, Walters will be free to talk about how she has earned respect in a male-dominated profession. She might tell you about how she studied

Alan Hunter, Martha Quinn, John Goodman, Nina Blackwood, and J. J. Jackson were the first VJs on MTV in the mid-eighties.

camera work and editing or about the thousands of letters she sent and phone calls she made to set up interviews.

If your questions are superficial and limited, the answers will be, too. Reword your yes-no questions into open-ended ones. In most cases, your reworded questions will lead to more interesting and useful replies.

You should also avoid **leading questions,** because they influence the answers you receive. For example, instead of asking, "Was the UFO shaped like a saucer or like a cigar?" say, "What was the UFO shaped like?" Let your subjects choose their own words.

Thalia DaCosta won MTV's nationwide second annual "Wanna Be a VJ?" search. Will she be as successful as Martha Quinn?

SECTION 2 REVIEW

Recalling the Facts ...

1. What are two kinds of questions that you should *avoid* during an interview?
2. Describe three kinds of questions that you should try to use during an interview.

Thinking Critically ...

1. Discuss the places in your school where you could conduct an interview. Which are the best? Which are the worst? Try conducting an interview with a classmate in one of the best places, and then move to the worst and continue the interview. Report back to the class on how the different environments affected your interview.
2. Think of a famous person you would like to interview. Write a list of ten questions you would ask that person if you had the chance. (Don't hesitate to do a little research.)

Taking Charge ...

1. Rewrite these yes-no questions to make them open-ended (assume your subject is Will Smith):
   - Did you like working on television?
   - Is it important that TV shows have characters who can be good role models for young people?
   - Will you be on television again in the future?

SECTION 3 Conducting an Ethical Interview

The most important thing you can do while conducting an interview may be obvious, but it's still important: Listen well. (See Chapter 3.) Good listening keeps you attentive and encourages your subject to speak. She or he is much more likely to talk openly if it's clear that you are listening carefully. Maintain a polite but professional distance, neither arguing nor agreeing. A head nod from time to time encourages the subject but does not necessarily mean that you agree—it just means you understand.

CNN's Judy Woodruff is a respected professional interviewer often assigned to question international dignitaries such as China's Premier Zhu.

Try to remember that each time you do an interview, you influence the future. If you treat your subject fairly and honestly, that person is likely to be cooperative the next time someone asks for an interview. On the other hand, if you bungle the job, the subject may swear off interviews forever.

It's not unusual for someone who has had a bad experience to refuse to talk again—several major league baseball players, for example, have taken this position and refuse to talk to reporters. Give your subjects respectful attention no matter what their ideas might be. The people who march to a different drummer often make the best interviews.

Getting Off on the Right Foot

When you arrive for the interview, remind your subject who you are and why you want the interview. You can say, for example, "I'm gathering information for a speech I'm giving to my class." In any case, the subject needs to know how you plan to use the information that he or she will provide.

Beginning an Interview

The first part of your interview should include several routine, get-acquainted questions that the subject will have no difficulty answering. These nonthreatening, factual questions get the conversational ball rolling. They also give you a chance to show some interest and enthusiasm about the person you're interviewing. Don't be a phony, though; find something that genuinely interests you in what the person is saying.

If possible, use each answer as a springboard for the next question. By carefully drawing on what the person has just said, you can lead him or her smoothly toward the next question. For example, "You say you enjoy rock concerts? Which one was your favorite?" Or, "I'm an oldest child, too, and I always liked being the oldest. How do you feel about it?" Questions like these allow you to "warm up" the subject before you get into the heart of the interview.

Take Quick Notes and Look Up Often ... If you're gathering information for a speech, you will certainly want to take notes during the interview. Taking notes gives you a record of what was said and helps you to be a better listener. Note-taking also gives you a convenient and *unobtrusive* way to check off the questions you wanted to ask as you move along.

Most professional interviewers have developed their own brand of speed-writing for taking notes. Some note-takers omit vowels and word endings; others use abbreviations. You may already have a few of your own shortcuts. Develop a personal system or study a manual on speed-writing. But whatever route you take, remember that what matters most in an interview is that you can listen, think, and write all at the same time.

Although you do need to take notes, don't let yourself get buried in your notebook. Look up from time to time. It will help your subject know that you're still holding up your half of the conversation. Many beginners have tried to write down every answer in longhand and then panicked when they forgot a word or didn't hear an important phrase because they were too busy writing. The more effort you spend on recording the conversation, the less energy you have to keep up with it. Thus, take quick, brief notes and maintain good eye contact.

It probably took many interviews before Oprah Winfrey felt as relaxed as she appears here interviewing country music star Garth Brooks.

Handling Sensitive Questions with Care

Some of your questions are bound to hit a nerve. If you sense that the subject is touchy about something, but still think you must ask about that topic, watch for an opening. Wait until your subject happens to mention the sensitive area, and then gracefully follow up. Make it seem as if the subject brought it up herself. For instance, you might say, "Really. Now who would accuse you of anything like that? Tell me about it."

If the person doesn't mention the sensitive area on her own, wait until the end of the interview to ask about it. That way you and your subject have had an opportunity to establish some trust. Ask your tough question matter-of-factly, in the same tone of voice as your other questions; don't broadcast that the "bomb" is coming, and try not to react when you hear something big. The subject will freeze up if she thinks she said something that shocked you.

Be Persistent ... What should you do if your subject doesn't answer your question? This happens occasionally to every interviewer. The fact that someone talks in response to your question does *not* mean that the question has been answered.

Sometimes, the interviewee may misunderstand your question. In that case, restate or rephrase it. Don't be afraid to ask a question twice. Doing so won't make you look dumb or hard of hearing; most people, in fact, will be impressed that you know what you want.

Of course, sometimes people will ignore your question and try to answer a different one, one they would prefer answering. Here you need some tact, but you also need some determination. Ask the question again if you aren't satisfied with the answer. If you sense the subject is reluctant to talk about that particular question, try being silent for a moment. Many times, an uncomfortable silence tells the subject that you want to hear more.

In fact, silence is one of the best ways to get another person to talk. Be patient if you think your subject is dredging up some long-lost memory. Remembering can take time. Let your subject break the silence. If you are quiet, the subject realizes that you are waiting for what you hope will be the rest of the answer.

Concluding the Interview

When you have finished all your questions, give your subject one last chance. Say, "Is there something

COMMUNICATION **Break***down*

Jenny Jones under Fire

Sometimes interviews can go sour, and that can be a big problem if the interview happens to be in the national spotlight.

The producers of the *Jenny Jones Show* found this out the hard way when they were sued for $50 million by the family of Scott Amedure. Amedure revealed on the show that he had a crush on his neighbor, Jonathan Schmitz, who also appeared on the show. Stunned by the revelation, Schmitz later shot and killed Amedure.

Amedure's family claimed that the program purposely misled Schmitz and encouraged outrageous fantasies to create "good television." (The show was only taped and never actually shown to the viewing public.) Jones's producers, however, say the show had nothing to do with the murder.

Amedure's attorney, Geoffrey Fieger, angrily indicted the talk show host Jenny Jones and the entire culture of talk TV. "Audience ratings drive everything they do," he claimed. "It's improper to use human beings for the vicarious pleasure of others. These shows are undermining our culture."

Karen Campbell, the show's producer, said that Schmitz did not appear upset after the taping, and nothing indicated that he would harm anyone. He did say, however, that he was nervous about appearing on the show.

"This is going to be in front of millions of people," he told her. "It could be embarrassing."

Questions

1. Why do you think people agree to appear on TV talk shows such as *The Jerry Springer Show,* knowing that they might be embarrassed?
2. Where would you draw a line between appropriate and inappropriate questions for TV talk shows?

else you would like to tell me?" Usually, there is. After that, thank the person and take your leave. A thank-you note or E-mail message a day or two later adds a classy touch to your interview.

Write up your notes as soon as possible after the interview, while the subject's words are still fresh in your mind. Your notes make much more sense to you at that point than they will a few hours later. In fact, if you wait several days to read over your notes, you may find that they no longer make sense at all. Don't hesitate to check a fact if you're in doubt. Was the figure she gave you $1 million or $1 billion? A mistake makes both you and your subject look bad.

Conducting Interviews over the Phone

An interview is probably best done face-to-face, but sometimes that just isn't possible. As an alternative, you may wish to interview someone over the telephone. A phone interview forces you to really concentrate on what your subject is saying. When you're conducting a phone interview, close your eyes and just listen. Listen to each answer for fresh and interesting thoughts.

Keep in mind, though, that it's all too easy to let your mind wander when you don't have your subject right in front of you. Eventually, you doodle, thumb through a paperback, or think about an assignment for another class. When you check your notes later, you notice ideas you should have pursued and ideas that don't make sense. Finally, you find that you don't have what you need. When you do a phone interview, therefore, keep distractions to a minimum.

While conducting a telephone interview, remember to keep distractions to a minimum and listen carefully to each answer.

SECTION 3 REVIEW

Recalling the Facts ...

1. What is the best way to begin an interview?
2. What question should you use to end an interview?

Thinking Critically ...

1. Arrange with your teacher to have a public official visit your class for a group interview. Have each member of the class prepare three questions ahead of time. Then, during the visit, notice whether any questions are repeated. Are class members listening well and creating follow-up questions, or are they simply sticking to the questions they have prepared?

Taking Charge ...

1. Pair off with a classmate and interview one another. Imagine that your classmate is new to the school and you will soon give a short speech introducing him to the rest of the class. Prepare a list of at least ten questions and find out something fascinating.
2. Conduct a practice interview in front of the class, and then ask the class to critique your effort. For a twist, ask your subject (perhaps a teacher or administrator) to be as obstinate or tight-lipped as possible. How can an interviewer deal with a potentially hostile subject?

SECTION 4 Interviewing for a Job or Scholarship

Interviews are certainly vital to your future success. Many colleges are relying less on standardized test scores (the ACT and SAT, for instance) as criteria for admission and giving greater emphasis to personal interviews. Consequently, how well you do in an interview can determine whether you are accepted by the college of your choice.

Sooner or later, too, you will interview for a job. How you conduct yourself in interview situations will be a great test of both your speaking and listening skills. Remember, though, that the employer must satisfy you too. Richard Nelson Boles, author of *What Color Is Your Parachute?*, describes this sizing-up process as the "dating game." You have to like each other before you can "go steady"—that is, get the job.

Use Communication Skills to Your Advantage

Remember that prospective employers are not out to embarrass you or trip you up; they only want to gain an accurate impression of you and your abilities. In particular, they want to know how you communicate with other people. Of course they are interested in your qualifications, but they can find that information on your résumé. When they call you in for a personal interview, they mainly want to hear you talk and see how well you can communicate.

Do you "fit" the organization? Employers say they are always looking for certain traits no matter what the job: confidence, enthusiasm, and dependability. Employers want someone who can communicate effectively with customers and with other employees.

Remember that during an interview, it's important to be an attentive and active listener.

"Your personality and how you conduct yourself during the interview have the greatest impact on your chances of landing the job," says Guyla Armstrong, assistant professor of business at the University of Nebraska–Kearney. She warns that most people "will blow some questions." Many students, in particular, perform poorly in their first interviews because they don't prepare, don't dress right, and don't know what to expect. You should realize, she says, that the person interviewing you will probably be about 20 years older and will expect you to show poise and maturity.

The advice that follows is intended to give you an idea of what to expect during an interview. Some people believe that just being themselves is enough, but you may well find yourself in a highly competitive selection process. You need to know how to effectively communicate your skills and experience, as well as how to portray your personality as one that will fit in with the business.

Be Alert and Energetic . . . During the interview, try to show energy and enthusiasm. Sit on the edge of your chair and lean slightly forward. If you're female, be sure to cross your legs at the ankles. When you make gestures (and it's helpful to do so if they come naturally), get your hands about chest high. Using gestures burns off tension and looks good—it makes you animated.

Keep eye contact with the person interviewing you. Don't become so wrapped up in answering questions that you forget to connect on a personal level with your interviewer.

Pay Attention ... Pay attention to the interviewer's name and use her name occasionally in your answers. That helps the interviewer know that you notice people and remember their names. As much as possible, turn the conversation toward things you know and keep it away from unfamiliar topics.

During the interview, remember to be an active listener and show respect to the interviewer.

If you must be late, call ahead to alert the interviewer of your predicament. This shows that you are conscientious and professional.

Professional interview adviser Susan Bixler recommends that if the interviewer doesn't extend his or her hand at the end of the interview, you should wait one moment, and then extend your own hand. This shows a high level of confidence and business awareness.

Get There on Time ... A day or two before the interview, call to confirm the time and place. Ask how long you should allow for the interview and if there's anything you should bring. Sometimes, for example, employers like applicants to bring their **portfolios** along. A portfolio contains a sample of your best school assignments or examples of other work you have done.

Plan to arrive about 15 minutes early. If you are unfamiliar with the route, ask for directions and do a practice drive. You don't know what traffic problems you'll encounter or if you'll get lost. And if you drive, you'll have to find a parking place.

Check in with the interviewer or an assistant about five to ten minutes before your appointment. By the way, go to the interview by yourself. It shows confidence. Many teens want to take along a friend for moral support—don't do it; it's not perceived as professional behavior.

ARE YOU MISSING AN EARRING?

INSTANT IMPACT

Susan Bixler, author of *The Professional Image,* recommends that job candidates conduct a 30-second check in front of a mirror prior to any interview. The check provides the reassurance needed to concentrate on people and matters at hand. You don't want to worry about a broken zipper, crumbs from lunch on your shirt, or a run in your stocking.

To perform the check, start at the top of your body and work down. Check your hair, teeth, makeup, and earrings. Straighten your tie; check for stains or open buttons. Then check your belt, zipper, stockings, and shoes. Those shoes are shined, aren't they?

After the Interview

Consider every interview a learning experience. As soon as possible after the interview, jot down some notes on how you would like to improve. Replay the highs and the lows. What went well? What could you have done better?

Always follow an interview with a thank-you letter. Begin by thanking the interviewer for taking the time to meet with you. Then restate your interest in the position.

You might also keep in touch with the business. After a week or two, call to find out if the job has been filled. If you accept another offer in the meantime, be sure to notify the interviewer that you're no longer a candidate. You never know when you might be applying to that business again.

Finally, if you do not get the job, you may want to ask the interviewer for some constructive criticism or recommendations for future interviews.

Try to anticipate questions and plan your answers so you can be an active participant in your interview.

Anticipate the Questions

Good planning means that you try to guess, as best you can, the questions you may be asked in an interview and give some thought to how you might answer them. For example, the interviewer will almost certainly ask you to describe yourself. Other potential questions may be more difficult.

The interviewer may want to know, for example, why you've never held a job for very long. You should guess that a question like this will be coming and have a reasonable answer in mind—"I've had many responsibilities at home, looking after my younger brothers and sisters, but they're all in school now."

Most interviews boil down to why you are applying, what kind of person you are, and what you can do. Know the answers to those questions like you know your own name.

Here are some possible questions you might face:

General

- Why do you want to work for us?
- What are your strengths and weaknesses?
- What would you like to be doing five years from now?

Educational

- What is your grade point average?
- What have been your favorite and least favorite courses?
- Were your extracurricular activities worth the time you put into them?

Job-related

- Why should I hire you?
- How long a commitment do you plan to give me?

Personal

- Tell me something about yourself.
- What accomplishment in your life has made you the proudest?
- What is the last book you read?

Think about how you would answer those questions, so that you don't stumble for words when they do come up. Some students even memorize their answers, but be careful that you don't have your responses down so well that they seem *canned*. You don't want to sound like a robot. Instead, your goal is to be so well prepared you can relax and be completely spontaneous.

Make Positive Points

Answering questions may make you feel as if you're playing defense. That's only natural, but you also need to have an offense planned for your interview. Prepare a short list of positive points you wish to make about yourself.

Perhaps you want to be sure your future employer knows about your volunteer experience, how well you're doing in school, or your plans for the future. Whatever the case, prepare a list of points you want to be sure to bring up during the interview—whether the interviewer asks you about them or not.

How can you get your positive points across? Be alert for situations where you can bring them into the conversation. Here are a few possibilities:

If you offer a story about yourself while using a bridge, be sure that story is true.

1. **Puff balls.** Puff balls are easy questions lobbed in your direction. A typical puff ball might be: "Tell me about yourself." Use a question like this as a springboard to tell the interviewer something you have planned to say.

   Puff ball questions give you the perfect chance to put your best foot forward. But beware: if you haven't practiced ahead of time, a question like this may leave you at a loss for words.

2. **Pauses.** Inevitably, you will feel a lull in the conversation. Every interview has some "down time." Perhaps the interviewer has looked down at her notes, scratched her shoulder, or taken a sip of coffee.

   In any event, a pause gives you another chance to use some initiative. Remember, you're not a witness in a murder trial; you don't have to wait to be cross-examined. While the interviewer is momentarily distracted, jump in and offer to talk about a subject you know will show your skills and abilities to best advantage.

   You might say, for example, "By the way, Mr. Youssefi, may I tell you a little about the Habitat for Humanity project our school did last year?"

3. **Bridges.** A bridge is a transition from one answer to another. Suppose the interviewer asks, "Have you ever been late for work?" Obviously, the interviewer expects a one-word answer —yes or no—but you can do more. You first answer her question—"Yes"—and then, by cleverly using a bridge, you turn the original question toward something else you wanted to talk about. "I was late once," you say, "but it was because I stopped to help a child who had fallen off a bike." (Be sure, of course, that any story you tell about yourself is true.) This bridge gives you a chance to show how responsible you are—so responsible,

in fact, that you realize some things are even more important than being on time.

Positive points aren't effective, however, if they sound like propaganda. So add a **sparkler**—something that makes the point come alive: an analogy, a story, an anecdote, or a quote. Creating a picture in the interviewer's head helps activate both sides of his or her brain. For example, you could say, "When my government class was doing a unit on Congress, I invited our representative to speak to us. He was in the middle of a reelection campaign, and his visit made the evening news."

You can help make your positive point stand out by being brief. Think of your interview as if it were being televised and keep your answer to the length of a **sound bite.** Sound bites are those short cuttings from interviews that we hear on television and radio broadcasts.

Sound bites last, as a rule, no more than 30 seconds, and they fit the needs of most interviewers who frequently have many other people to interview. Plan to answer each question in 30 seconds. You might also have a 2-minute answer prepared (if time permits), or even a 5-minute answer, depending on the circumstances.

Always emphasize the full range of your computer skills in an interview.

Interview Checklist

As a final check before you go to a job interview, ask yourself these questions:

1. **Do I have copies of my résumé?**
2. **Do I have a list of three references with addresses and telephone numbers?**
3. **Have I made sure I will be on time?**
4. **Have I dressed neatly and appropriately?**
5. **Even if I feel tired, can I remember to sit up and look alert?**
6. **Can I remember not to criticize others, especially past employers?**
7. **Can I make good eye contact with the interviewer?**
8. **Can I remember the interviewer's name and use it during the interview?**
9. **Can I remember to thank the interviewer at the close of the interview?**
10. **Have I turned off any electronic devices (beepers, cell phones, etc.)?**

Rehearse Tough Questions ... What questions do you dread being asked in an interview? Some of the more common anxiety-inducing questions include: "Where do you see yourself in five years?," "Why should I hire you?," and "Why do you want to work here?" When you think about it, they are all legitimate questions, and each presents you with an opportunity to sell yourself.

- "Where do you see yourself in five years?"

The interviewer probably wants to know if you are ambitious. If you find it hard to look five years down the road, try this: "Five years seems like a long time. I can see myself going to college and studying for a degree in sports management, but I might take a year off first when I finish high school."

- "Why should I hire you?"

Here's where the firm finds out how well you understand its needs. How about a response like this: "I think you should hire me because I have the skills you need in this position. My computer courses at school have taught me how to use your software, and my communication skills are strong as a result of my student government experience."

During a job interview, be alert for opportunities to introduce.

- "Why do you want to work here?"

This is where the employer finds out how much you know about its organization. You want to convey your interest in contributing to its mission. For example: "Some of my older friends have worked here in the past and they said they liked their jobs and were treated fairly."

If the interviewer asks why you are lacking in a particular area (be it grades, work experience, or extracurricular activities), you need to stay positive. In response to a question about a low GPA, for example, you might say something like this—"I had not yet learned how to say no. I was on the soccer team, the speech team, and Student Council. There just weren't enough hours in the day and my grades began to slip. But I learned my lesson and now know how to prioritize."

SECTION 4 REVIEW

Recalling the Facts ...

1. Why is it wise to arrive 10 to 15 minutes early to an interview?
2. How can you make a positive point even if you aren't directly asked about it?

Thinking Critically ...

1. What are some of the ways interviews can be misused? Could a company, for instance, use job interviews to find out what people think of competing companies?

Taking Charge ...

1. Ask a counselor to conduct some sample job interviews among your classmates or invite the manager of a local fast-food restaurant to class to conduct mock interviews.

STUDENT WORK

"Backpack Ban Sparks Debate" *By Amanda Hergert*

The following story, written by Amanda Hergert for the Lincoln Southeast High School newspaper, the *Clarion,* shows how skillfully a student can blend the results of several interviews into a compelling article. Notice that Amanda spoke to students in two different schools.

Imagine walking down the hall, minding your own business, when suddenly a student near you turns sharply and you are knocked to the ground by a lethal backpack. Such is the fear of Hastings Senior High School officials.

Beginning with the next school year, Hastings students will not be allowed to carry backpacks around the halls of school. Officials say backpacks pose health and safety risks to students, including posture and back problems. Backpacks can easily conceal drugs, alcohol, and weapons.

Students argue they need their backpacks in order to get to class on time with the books and supplies. Many of them don't use their lockers because they are out of the way and too hard to get to during passing time.

Hastings senior Braden Grams finds the ban very extreme. "We don't have enough lockers for everyone to have their own and some people don't trust their locker partner. Also, so many people wear backpacks that the freshmen just do it to fit in," Grams said.

"With a big cut in state aid, administrators have better things to worry about than backpacks cluttering classrooms," Grams said. "It's really about contraband, which we don't have a huge problem with, except for tobacco and occasionally alcohol. It is rarely brought to school with an intent to consume while on school property."

Southeast students have mixed reactions to the idea in general.

"If there's a gun or violence problem [in Hastings], it isn't a bad idea. As far as [banning them] in Lincoln [is concerned], I don't see it because there hasn't been a problem," Jake Cammack said.

Cammack admits that he has experienced back problems due to his heavy backpack. "When I take it off, I'm sore. I'm probably stunting my growth," he said. He also admits that his backpack has been something of a safety hazard. When Cammack sees someone he knows walking down the hall, he turns so that his backpack will stop them. But, "Sometimes they don't see me and run into it," he said.

"You get attached to your backpack really quick," Cammack said. "If they ever ban backpacks, I'm dropping out of school."

According to sophomore April Eisenhauer, "LSE is a really big school, and some people have inconvenient lockers. [If you carry a backpack] you have more time to socialize between classes and it's easier to carry around your books. It's also a change from middle school, when you weren't allowed to wear them."

"I think if the ban was at LSE, I would protest, and so would others," Eisenhauer said.

Looking Back

Listed below are the major ideas discussed in this chapter.

- Interviews play an important role in our efforts to gather information.
- The best place for an interview is a location where you can have your subject's complete attention.
- Learn as much as possible about the person you wish to interview before speaking with him or her.
- Dress appropriately for an interview. Wear whatever you think will bring the best response from the person you are interviewing.
- You must be on time for an interview, and bring a pen and notebook. Some interviewers also like to use a tape recorder.
- It may be best to begin an interview with several get-acquainted questions, ones that will put your subject at ease.
- Questions should be brief and to the point.
- Open-ended questions allow the subject great flexibility in answering. Such questions can sometimes lead to new and surprising pieces of information.
- Follow-up questions help you pursue statements that need clarifying.
- Yes-no questions and questions that require a one-word answer should, for the most part, be avoided.
- Keep eye contact with your subject. Don't become so wrapped up in note-taking that you forget to hold up your end of the conversation.
- Gestures are useful during an interview to burn off tension, add life to your voice, and help you seem animated and energetic.
- Stress a few positive points about yourself when opportunity permits.

Speech Vocabulary

Match the speech vocabulary term on the left with the correct definition on the right.

1. interviewer
2. subject
3. verbatim
4. portfolio
5. rapport
6. open-ended question
7. follow-up question
8. yes-no question
9. leading question
10. puff ball
11. pause
12. bridge
13. sparkler
14. sound bite

a. a "soft" question
b. a transition from a question to a positive point
c. quoting someone word-for-word
d. a sample of school assignments and other work
e. a short cut for an interview designed for broadcast
f. supporting material—an anecdote, for example
g. the person who asks the questions
h. lull in the conversation
i. the person you wish to interview
j. a sense of trust between two people
k. question that requires a one-word answer
l. question that leaves room for answers
m. question that hints at the answer
n. question that follows a train of thought

CHAPTER 6 Review and Enrichment...

General Vocabulary

Match each of the following terms with the correct definition in the right-hand column.

1. pollster
2. proxy
3. vicariously
4. grovel
5. chauffeur
6. embalm
7. unobtrusive
8. canned

a. to treat a corpse with preservatives
b. overly rehearsed or memorized
c. to cringe or humble oneself
d. someone who drives a car for someone else
e. not easily noticed
f. acting in place of someone else
g. experienced through imagination
h. a person who takes opinion surveys

To Remember

1. What do the interviewer and an interview subject want from an interview?
2. If, as an interviewer, you find yourself overly concerned with your next question or whether your subject likes you, you may lack an important quality. What is it?
3. Why would the principal be a better source of information than a teacher for some interviews? For what interviews would a teacher or a student be the best source?
4. What are some reasons why a subject's office, though convenient, is not the best place to conduct an interview?
5. Name several sources of information you could use to find out about the person you wish to interview.
6. Why is it important to dress appropriately and professionally for an interview?
7. What are some of the reasons you might want to use a tape recorder during an interview?
8. What are the advantages of writing out your questions before the interview?
9. Why should you avoid asking yes-no questions?
10. The best strategy for an interviewer to take is to pretend to agree with everything the subject says. True or false? Why?
11. Name three opportunities that may present themselves during an interview, opportunities for you to talk about your own positive points.

To Do

1. Attend a local press conference. They are called frequently by state and local officials. Prepare a few questions ahead of time. Ask the officials if you can ask questions; if not, compare your questions with those asked by professional reporters. Evaluate the quality of the questions asked and the responses given.
2. Check up on yourself. Send a follow-up sheet to a person you have recently interviewed. Ask that person about how he or she thought the interview went. Were you courteous, well-prepared, and alert? Were your questions thoughtful and to the point? Use the evaluation to improve future interviews.
3. Have two students interview the same person. Have one person stay outside while the other interview is going on. Discuss the differences in both questions and responses.

4. Assume you have been assigned to interview the president of your student council. What research should you do to prepare for the interview? What questions would you ask?
5. As you learned in this chapter, curiosity is one of the most important qualities of a successful interviewer. What are you curious about?
6. Make a list of twenty or thirty things that you would like to know. Then for each item on your list, think of at least two sources of information on that topic. Pick the two topics you think you would most enjoy researching, and find the answer to the question that you were originally curious about.

To Talk About

1. What problems are caused by the need to take notes at an interview?
2. What are some of the ways you might deal with a situation in which a subject is reluctant to give out any information?
3. Can you think of any situations in which a phone interview might be preferable to a face-to-face interview?
4. Discuss who the best subjects would be for a variety of speeches. Have half the class think of the speeches and the other half think of the best people to interview. For example, who would be the best subject on the history of homecoming at your school? The first basketball team? The growth of women's athletics?
5. Interview a family member. This should be a non-threatening interview—a good one to begin developing your interview skills. Do not, however, take this interview lightly just because the subject will be someone close to you. Pick an interesting topic and ask probing questions. Try to find out something you don't already know.

To Write About

1. Oral history has become a popular way to learn about the past. Draft a proposal for an oral history of your school, an institution in your community, or a major national event. Examples of such events could include the explosion of the space shuttle *Challenger,* a major hurricane, or the impeachment trial of President Clinton. Include possible interview subjects and sample question lists.
2. Compare your note-taking techniques with those of classmates. Do you use an outline form? If not, do you use some combination of letters, numbers, indentions, underlining, stars, or some other system for separating major points from minor ones? What can you do to improve your system for taking notes?

Related Speech Topics

Barbara Walters
Larry King
TV talk shows
The ethics of "sound-bite" news reporting
An individual's right to privacy versus the public's right to know
The most interesting person I have ever met

CHAPTER 7

GROUP DISCUSSION

"**N**othing is interesting if you're not interested."

—Helen MacInness

Learning Objectives

After completing this chapter, you will be able to do the following.

- Explain why cooperative attitudes are necessary for group discussions.
- Describe the major kinds of group discussions.
- Discuss the factors that determine the success of group discussions.
- Identify the steps of the problem-solving process.
- Develop a list of questions you could use to direct a group discussion.

Chapter Outline

Following are the main sections in this chapter.

1. Working Together Makes Sense
2. Group Problem Solving
3. How to Contribute to a Discussion

New Speech Terms

In this chapter, you will learn the meanings of the speech terms listed below.

discussion
cooperative
competitive
panel
forum
round table
symposium
town hall meeting
cohesion
criteria
brainstorming
constructive conflict
disruptive conflict
moderator
questions of fact
questions of interpretation
questions of evaluation
consensus
groupthink

General Vocabulary

Expanding your general vocabulary will help you become a more effective communicator. Listed below are some words appearing in this chapter that you should make part of your everyday vocabulary.

sequential
scenario
bombard
mediation
status quo
polarizing
apathetic
monopolize
paraphrase

Looking Ahead

We are all born into a group—our families—and spend much of our lives interacting with groups. Groups are important because they have more power than any one person, and their decisions usually carry great weight.

In this chapter, you will learn how to help shape group decisions by participating in discussions. A good group discussion is a spirited exchange of lively thoughts, clever remarks, and interesting stories. You will learn here how to make valuable contributions to the discussion as well as how to appreciate different points of view.

Introduction

You know how it goes. José gets an idea and sketches it out on a piece of paper with a few doodles. Then along comes Mary, who says, "Hey, wait a minute—that makes me think of something. . . ." Soon Fred comes over and says, "But look, if we change this or add that, we can probably make your idea better." Before long, a group of people working together has surpassed what any one person could have accomplished working alone.

We do some things better by ourselves—reading, for example, or riding a unicycle—but we do many things better in groups.

Group work helps us learn the skills we need to cooperate in an increasingly interdependent society. A strong group goal can help us overcome our reluctance to ask for help or perhaps to offer help to another student. Group work also helps us overcome some of the misunderstandings we have because of our different racial or ethnic backgrounds. When we have a stake in each other's success, we have a strong motivation to cooperate.

Groups can start with a simple idea and brainstorm together until the result is an exceptional plan.

SECTION 1 Working Together Makes Sense

We all think of ourselves as individuals, but we actually gain much of our identity from participation in groups. You may discover how grown-up you are, for example, in family discussions about who gets to use the car, or how persuasive you can be in a student council meeting on where to hold the prom. Group discussions help us learn something different about ourselves from what we learn in unplanned and spontaneous conversations. Group discussion has a goal.

We can define **discussion** as a cooperative exchange of information, opinions, and ideas. In practical terms, discussion is one of the best methods we have for solving problems. In a discussion, group members help bring all sides of a problem to the surface for consideration. We tend to talk each other out of biases and preconceived ideas. More important, we are usually willing to support solutions if we have played a part in developing them ourselves.

"What's this about your refusing to attend another meeting today because you want to *get some work done?*"

BERRY'S WORLD reprinted by permission of United Feature Syndicate, Inc.

The Right Attitude for Group Work

An ideal group member is open-minded, someone who can interact with fellow group members in a **cooperative**—rather than **competitive**—atmosphere. A discussion, for example, is not a debate—you don't have to defend a particular point of view. All discussion is dynamic; people are welcome, even encouraged, to change their minds as they hear other ideas and gain more information.

Discussion does require patience. Compared with conversation, discussion can seem somewhat slow because every member has a chance to speak, and some people who aren't listening may repeat what's already been said. Many of us complain, too, that meetings waste time. The people who do most of the talking seem to have the least to say. You may sometimes feel you must give in to work with a group. You may not agree with the group's decision, for instance, but you don't want to make everyone upset with you by being difficult.

Just because group discussion isn't perfect, however, doesn't mean it isn't valuable. Like everything else, group discussion works when we make it work. The best discussions give each of us a chance to be heard and, more important, a chance to make good decisions.

In many ways, discussion is the basis of our democratic system. We face conflict every day—rubbing shoulders with each other—but we can find ways to resolve our differences. Through sharing information, ideas, and feelings in discussion, we can find solutions that help all of us become wiser and more understanding people.

If you prefer just to let things happen and go with the flow, you will not do well at discussion. Discussion is purposeful talk by people who are committed to working together. A discussion is truly effective only when each member takes his or her share of the responsibility. Too often, discussions are held back by people who avoid that responsibility. Whenever one group member decides to let others do the work, that person weakens the discussion. All members must be committed to listen, to think, and to reason with one another.

BUSINESSES FIND TEAMWORK PRODUCTIVE

INSTANT IMPACT

Schools are becoming more cooperative, and so are American businesses. Many companies have already discovered that teamwork means higher morale and greater productivity. Jerry Junkins, president of Texas Instruments, says, "No matter what your business, teams are the wave of the future." Consider these success stories:

- At a General Mills cereal plant in Lodi, California, teams of workers schedule, operate, and maintain machinery so effectively that the factory runs without any managers during the night shift.
- A team of Federal Express clerks spotted and eventually solved a billing problem that was costing the company over $2 million a year.
- Teams of workers in Sheboygan, Wisconsin, helped Johnsville Foods decide to go ahead with a major expansion. The workers convinced top executives that they could produce more sausage if allowed to streamline the process. Since then, production is up 50 percent.

These teams have proven that groups can be more effective than the old boss-worker arrangement at getting the job done.

Discussion Formats

Group discussions take many forms. You may be most familiar with classroom discussions that focus on interpreting literature or analyzing historical events. You may also be familiar with group or club meetings that use parliamentary procedure. (See Chapter 20 for a description of those rules.) There are, however, other kinds of discussions, including the panel, the symposium, and the town hall meeting. Let's take a closer look at each.

Panel Discussion . . . The **panel** is a relatively informal discussion that takes place before an audience. Panel members, often three or four in number, sit facing the audience. Most of the time panelists talk directly to each other, but each may make a short introductory speech.

Panel discussions help audiences become better informed on public issues. A school might set up a panel discussion on teen smoking, for example, and use teenagers, parents, a school counselor, and a representative from the local cancer society as panel members.

Michael J. Fox (right) moderates a panel discussion to answer the question, "Why are Canadians so funny?"

An open **forum** may follow the panel discussion. During the forum, panel members invite questions and comments from the audience. Often a discussion leader will field the questions and restate them if they are unclear or could not be heard by everyone. The leader then directs the questions to specific panel members or to the panel as a whole.

A special kind of panel discussion called a **round table** is commonly used in business and industry. As the name suggests, a small group of participants, usually three to eight, talks about a topic of common concern while sitting around a table. If a number of accidents have occurred in a manufacturing plant, for example, the company supervisors might be asked to discuss their suggestions for new safety procedures. Presidential cabinet meetings are another good example of round table discussions, as are many Sunday morning television news programs.

Can you watch your local town hall meetings on cable TV?

Symposium ... A more formal kind of discussion is the **symposium.** The usual purpose of a symposium is to present opposing points of view. During a symposium, invited experts deliver short speeches on a particular subject.

A discussion leader usually introduces each speaker and may give a brief statement at the end of each presentation to link together the entire discussion. Each speaker stands and faces the audience, and after all the speeches have been heard, the audience may ask questions or make comments.

A school might schedule a symposium, for example, if it is planning to build a new gymnasium. Symposium speakers might include an architect, an athletic director, a city planner, and a concerned taxpayer worried about the potential cost.

Town Hall Meeting ... Another kind of discussion is the **town hall meeting,** a form that dates back to the early American colonies. In those days, colonists would assemble in a large hall to discuss their problems. A vote would usually be taken after the discussion to settle the issue. Today, technology enables people all over the country to take part in town hall meetings on television or via the Internet.

Television anchorperson Ted Koppel hosted a famous town hall meeting in which American citizens asked questions of two major foreign leaders—Mikhail Gorbachev and Boris Yeltsin. Ross Perot, who ran for president as an independent candidate, accurately predicted the future when he promised "electronic town hall meetings" where citizens from all over the country could speak their minds to the president via telephone and television hookups.

Factors for Success

Some discussions work better than others. We can improve a discussion's chances for success by paying attention to two physical factors—the size of the group and how group members are seated. We should also consider one psychological factor—group cohesion.

Group Size ... Face-to-face communication helps make a group a group. Clearly, the size of a group affects how comfortable people are in sharing their ideas.

Some researchers say five to seven members is the best size for a group, because people participate better in small, informal settings. Even the least talkative person, research has shown, will talk in a small group. Groups of four or fewer, however, are probably too small because they lack the diversity needed to give the discussion some spark.

Groups of more than seven people are often too big. In these groups, quiet persons rarely talk and then only to people with high status. (People gain status in a group by virtue of their age, expertise, experience, or personality.) In groups of more than ten, a few people do most of the talking while the rest listen.

Circle discussions allow all participants to be face-to-face.

As a group gets bigger, of course, each person has fewer opportunities to speak. Consequently, large groups can alienate some members. Thus, many large groups delegate most of the work to small groups called committees.

Seating Arrangements ... The way people are seated in a discussion can have a good deal to do with its success or failure. If someone in the group takes a central position—at the head of a U-shaped group of chairs, for example, or in front of a row of desks—talk appears to flow through him or her. That person then dominates the discussion.

On the other hand, if the group sits in a circle, all participants can easily look at one another, and talk tends to flow from member to member or from a member to the entire group without being channeled through one person.

Class discussions sometimes fail to come to life because of their unfortunate physical arrangements. If the teacher stands at the front of the classroom and all comments are directed toward him or her, there is little student-to-student interaction.

Studies show that people who participate in groups with circular seating feel more satisfied with their contributions, more pleased with the group's work, and more confident that they have done well in solving problems than those who participate in leader-oriented groups. People in groups also need breathing space. Studies of rats, monkeys, and humans show that close confinement produces high levels of stress.

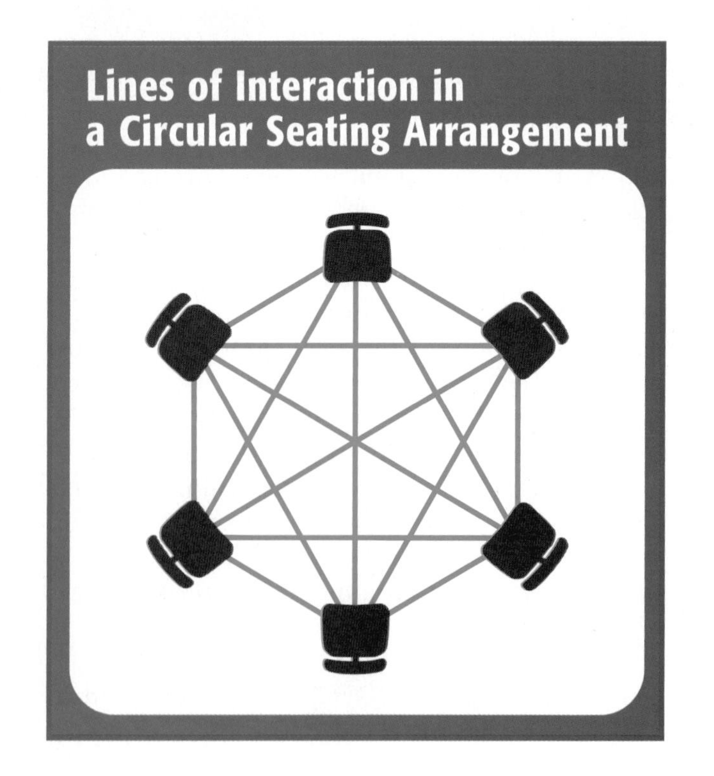

Cramped quarters seem to increase conflict and aggression. If the members of your group don't know each other well, have them sit several feet apart. As they get to know each other, they will probably move closer together.

Cohesion ... The success of a group discussion also depends on an intangible quality called **cohesion.** When members have respect for each other, share some of the same values, and look to each other for support, they may be called cohesive.

Generally, cohesive groups are those in which people are pulling in the same direction. In contrast, members in a noncohesive group seem to care less about what the group does than about their own personal goals.

Cohesive groups tend to pull in the same direction.

If belonging to the group is important, members will become more cohesive. Belonging to groups matters to many people because it gives them a chance to socialize and feel a sense of purpose. When a group has a good track record—when it has a history of solving problems, for example—its members will more likely remain loyal. On the other hand, if a group fails to meet its objectives, members may lose interest in belonging and show little enthusiasm for finding new members. Thus, success in group discussions often leads to more success because it helps build cohesion.

SECTION 1 REVIEW

Recalling the Facts ...

1. How is a discussion different from a conversation?
2. Explain the differences between a panel discussion, a symposium, and a town hall meeting.

Thinking Critically ...

1. Imagine the school board is planning to adopt a school dress code. How would you organize a discussion in your school on the topic? Whom would you invite to participate? What are some of the issues that should be addressed?

Taking Charge ...

1. Conduct a self-critique by asking yourself these questions: How well do I participate in discussions? How often do I speak? Do I see myself as a regular or occasional contributor? Is there something I can do that isn't being done well by anyone else in the group?
2. Watch a televised discussion (a news program like *Face the Nation* or *Inside Washington* would work well) and analyze the discussion in terms of the size of the group, the seating arrangement, and what the group accomplished or failed to accomplish. How did each individual member's knowledge of the topic influence the discussion?

SECTION 2 Group Problem Solving

We form groups to do a variety of tasks. Sometimes the purpose of the group is to gather information (you might join a study group, for example, to help you pass that chemistry exam) and sometimes to make decisions (should our Spirit Week theme be *Tarzan* or *Buffy the Vampire Slayer*?). But groups are never so important as when they are formed to solve problems.

Stick to the Pattern

Unlike conversations, which flow from topic to topic on a whim, discussions generally follow a logical, *sequential* pattern. This allows everyone to know what progress is being made. By relying on an established pattern, groups can complete their work more quickly and with less wasted effort.

Defining the problem is the first step in solving it.

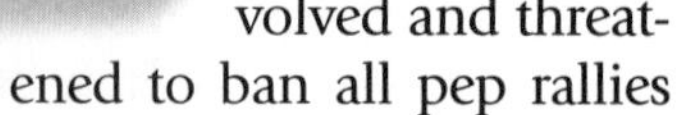

Many discussion groups follow a pattern developed by an American educator and philosopher named John Dewey. Dewey said that discussion members need to cultivate what he called the "vital habits of democracy." Members need to "follow an argument, grasp the point of view of another, expand the boundaries of understanding, and debate the alternative purposes that might be pursued."

The following six steps are a modern update of Dewey's system. If you stick to them in problem-solving discussions, you should have a good chance for success.

1. Define the Problem ...

The first step in solving a problem is to make sure you understand it. This may require the group to consider how the problem came about and why it needs to be solved. The group should also establish what problems it does not want to consider. In other words, a group tries to limit its objective so that it can focus on finding a specific solution to a specific problem.

To see how this step might work in real life, consider the following *scenario.* The story is based on an incident that really happened (the names and places have been changed).

A recent pep rally at Centerville High School has everyone upset. The principal interrupted the rally during one of the skits because he found it offensive and in poor taste. He has suspended the nine students who were involved and threatened to ban all pep rallies for the rest of the school year.

Now a group of student leaders, including members of the student council, the captains of the athletic teams, the editors of the newspaper and the yearbook, and several cheerleaders, has gotten together to see what can be done. Let's listen in on their discussion.

"I think the principal is completely out of bounds on this one," says Fred Jones, captain of the football team.

"I do, too," replies Nancy Beeler, a cheerleader. "But let's face it. We aren't going to make him change his mind about the suspensions. Those students and their parents are going to have to fight that one."

"Nancy's right," comments Bobby Vasquez, student council president. "But maybe we can do something about his ban on pep rallies. I think we can make a big enough stink that he'll let us have some more pep rallies, especially if we can prove that responsible people will be in charge."

These students have identified their problem—a possible ban on pep rallies—and have begun to define that problem by limiting it. The students are upset with the principal for suspending nine of their classmates, but they're not going to let that issue sidetrack them from their real goal—namely, to get pep rallies reinstated for the rest of the year.

By the way, this is a good place to warn you that many groups start a discussion without recording what happens. Later on, when they want to remember what someone said, they discover that nobody was keeping track. Most groups would be wise to select a recorder who will be responsible for writing down the minutes—a summary of the important ideas and major decisions.

2. Establish Criteria for a Workable Solution ...

After defining the problem, the group should decide on **criteria,** or a set of standards, that its solution must meet. By establishing these standards at the beginning of a discussion, much unnecessary arguing can be avoided. It would do no good, for example, if a new club planned a fund-raising dance and then found out the school calendar was already full. If the group had first determined that open dates were available, its members could then have discussed the kind of dance they wished to have.

The students in our pep rally group have agreed, after considerable debate, on the following criteria:

TAKING CRITICISM

INSTANT IMPACT

None of us likes to be criticized—it hurts. But to be successful, we need to be open to any advice that will help us become better people and better workers. To receive criticism effectively, try these techniques:

- **Put your shield up.** When someone says something to you with a critical tone, immediately picture a protective shield surrounding you. This buys you a few seconds to examine your critic's intentions. Should you accept the criticism as a way to grow personally or professionally? Or should you dismiss it as only a hurtful message?
- **Act like a coffee filter.** If you explore the criticism further, you need to strain out the emotional grounds—the critic's fear or anger—from the facts. This allows you to respond only to the useful information and not the critic's emotions.
- **Pretend you're Sherlock Holmes.** Don't rest until you get all the pieces of the mystery. Ask for specifics. For example, "When you said the report was incomplete, exactly what did you mean?"
- **Say, "You're right."** It's a lot easier to say than "I'm wrong." And these few words pour water on the potential blaze of a heated discussion.

Source: Mel Ann Coley, Coley Training and Development.

By establishing your criteria for a workable solution, you can reduce group conflict.

1. Pep rallies should continue to be part of the regular school schedule.
2. The pep rallies will continue to be planned and organized by students, but the students must have faculty supervision.
3. No students should be suspended or disciplined for participating in pep rallies, provided the faculty sponsor has been involved in planning the skits.
4. The pep rallies will not use vulgar jokes or offensive language, although school officials should recognize that rallies are meant to be fun.

The students have everything they want in this list—a guarantee that rallies will be run and organized by students and a promise that the administration will not punish students who participate in pep rallies. But they also believe that the list contains a few things important to the principal—faculty supervision and a promise to keep the rallies free of the kinds of jokes that caused the problem in the first place.

Once the group has established its criteria for an acceptable solution, it can get more specific about what exactly must be done. In our example, the students know they want at least a minimum number of rallies, with a maximum of student input. They know, in other words, what a possible solution might look like.

3. Analyze the Problem ... The next step in a discussion is to analyze the problem. The object is to break the problem down into small pieces for closer inspection. Some groups call this fact-finding.

When a doctor analyzes a patient's condition, for example, she begins with a thorough examination. She takes an inventory of the patient's current condition (pulse, blood pressure, temperature, and so on), and she examines the patient's medical history, looking for possible clues as to what has caused the patient to become sick. Similarly, groups gather as much information as they can to throw light on a particular problem.

Our pep rally students spent some time talking about other school problems that might have caused the principal to be so sensitive:

> "Hey, do you remember that swimsuit issue in the school paper last month?" says Bobby.
>
> "I sure do," responds Tammy Swanson, the newspaper editor. "The principal was really upset with us—at least that's what our advisor said."
>
> "And he wasn't too happy about all the publicity we've had lately about teen mothers," comments

Modern Update of John Dewey's System for Discussion

1. **Define the problem.**
2. **Establish criteria for a workable solution.**
3. **Analyze the problem.**
4. **Suggest possible solutions.**
5. **Evaluate each solution and select the best one.**
6. **Suggest ways for testing or carrying out the solution.**

Marisa Ruiz, another cheerleader. "I know he got quite a few phone calls from angry parents."

"I guess maybe he has good reason to be a little touchy right now," says Bobby.

"That might be right," replies Nancy, "but I still think he overreacted. Maybe we can change his mind if we can prove to him that we have a responsible plan."

We tend to forget that problems don't happen overnight. Most usually have long histories. Learning the background of a problem can often help us gain insights into why people react to the problem the way they do. It never hurts to see the situation from another person's point of view.

You probably brainstorm every day. Brainstorming allows everyone's creativity a chance to shine.

4. Suggest Possible Solutions . . . The fourth step in the problem-solving process is to propose as many solutions as possible. One of the best ways to create solutions is called **brainstorming.** In brainstorming, a group tries to *bombard* the problem with fresh ideas. Every idea is welcome; none are laughed at or rejected.

Group members offer their ideas as quickly as possible, not bothering to decide whether the solutions are practical. "Everyone is creative," says James Ferry, president of an idea development company in Boston. "It's just a matter of making them believe it." The theory behind brainstorming is that the more ideas a group can produce, the more likely it will be to find one that works.

Alice Salmon, editor of the school yearbook in our pep rally case, shows her creative thinking when she suggests that pep rallies be scheduled at the beginning of each athletic season, rather than once a month as they have been in the past.

"I think one pep rally for each sports season is enough," she says. "That way we can have a more positive purpose. We can focus on wishing our teams well instead of focusing on the opponent. I hate those rallies where all we do is chant 'Kill the Bulldogs' or 'Throttle the Meadowlarks.'"

Another student, Miguel Fuentes of the cross-country team, reminds everyone that good rallies take lots of effort.

"Alice has a point. It's hard work to make a good skit," he says. "We've got to make sure the principal understands that."

"I have an idea," offers Tina McIntire of the volleyball team. "If the principal won't let us have any more pep rallies, let's boycott all the games. Let's all stay away from the football field this Friday night."

Once the group has generated a large number of ideas (including some like Tina's that will be rejected in the end), it may discover that the obvious solution is not the best. Too often, a group reaches this phase only to have someone say, "Well, it appears pretty obvious what the solution ought to be," or "I guess we're pretty much in agreement." Comments like these undermine discussion because they stop any further thinking.

No solution should be accepted until several have been proposed, examined, and compared. Accepting a solution without considering the alternatives is like playing the lottery: It gives the group only one chance, and a feeble one at that.

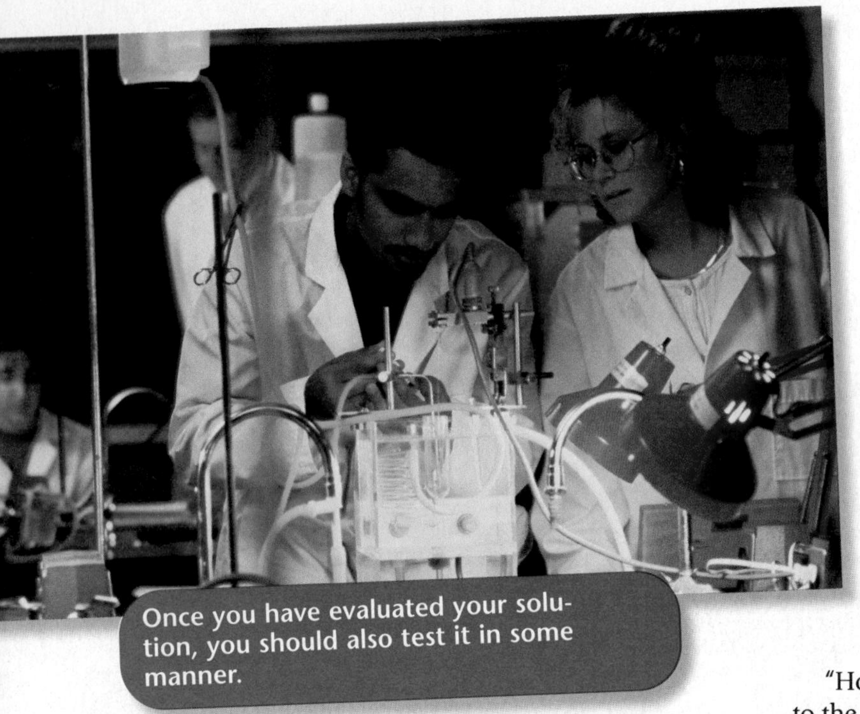

Once you have evaluated your solution, you should also test it in some manner.

5. Evaluate Each Solution and Select the Best One ... The next step is to consider your options. If two or three solutions seem equally good, the group members should turn back to their criteria and make a careful comparison. Does each solution meet the standards they agreed on in the second step of this process? If not, that solution should be changed or eliminated. The best solution is the one that most clearly fits the criteria.

In the case of our pep rally students, they have decided to support Alice's idea about one pep rally per season.

"I really like Alice's idea," says Marisa. "I think it will show the principal that we're acting in good faith if we're willing to give up some of the pep rallies we've had in the past."

"I agree," says Tammy, "but if the principal is going to buy our idea, we've got to convince him our rallies will be in good taste."

"Let's don't go overboard here," comments Bobby. "I want to remind him that pep rallies are supposed to be fun. Can't we be outrageous without being offensive? He was a teenager once—where's his sense of humor?"

"How about this," offers Fred. "Let's take Alice's idea, urge the principal to trust the faculty sponsors, and keep Plan B as a backup."

"Plan B? What's Plan B?" asks Tammy.

"If the principal won't let us schedule pep rallies during the regular school day, maybe he'll let us have them before or after school."

6. Suggest Ways for Testing or Carrying Out the Solution ... Discussing how to carry out a solution is the final step in the problem-solving process. Group members must make sure that their solution is practical. If possible, the group might give its idea a brief test. That's what our pep rally students decided to do.

"How about this?" says Alice. "Let's take our idea to the pep club sponsor and several of the coaches first. They might have some suggestions for us."

"Why not?" says Miguel. "And if they like the idea, they might tell the principal they're supporting us."

"Sounds good to me," responds Tammy. "I'd like to have all the backing I can get when we take this to the principal."

Managing Conflict

A good discussion will inevitably cause conflict. "Where all men think alike," said the columnist Walter Lippmann, "no one thinks very much." Differences of opinion—over ideas and issues—are the very heart of discussion. Problems that appear simple at first become more complex as you discover what other group members have to say on the subject.

Discussion can cause disagreements between members over facts, interpretations, and solutions. And such conflict will surely produce stress. We all find it difficult, for instance, not to take attacks on our ideas personally. Yet, only when we entertain conflicting ideas can we understand how complex most problems really are. Conflict, when effectively and sensitively managed, can be extremely valuable in our efforts to reach the best solution.

COMMUNICATION

Peer Solutions: Mediators Help Fellow Students Talk Through Problems

Just as a small rain cloud can build into a thunderstorm, a petty squabble at school can grow into a full-fledged fight. It might start with a nasty rumor: She said that he said that she was a liar. Eventually it degenerates to "I'm gonna beat you to a pulp."

But it doesn't have to be that way. Students in many schools are learning a better way to resolve their conflicts, rationally and peacefully, through *mediation.*

In a calm, methodical way, student mediators help their peers talk through their problems. The mediators themselves don't solve the problems; they are simply guides helping the disputing parties navigate their way through conflict to a reasonable solution.

"We're just here to facilitate the conversation," said Lisa Ballard, a Highland High School senior in Albuquerque. If mediators tried to impose their own solutions, she said, the people involved would just say, "Why do I have to do what *you* tell me to?"

Few disputes involve strangers. Often, problems arise between couples or best friends, said mediator Sheila Orozco. "Most of the time it's people that know each other," she said. "Sometimes they'll just want to talk."

According to peer mediator Sarah Schaffer, many disputes revolve around rumors—"You said this about me and you weren't supposed to tell anyone. Now they're mad at me." Pretty soon the parties get caught up in emotions. Mediation provides time and space to step back from the argument for a few moments.

The mediation process itself begins with a statement of ground rules. Each of the disputants, for example, must agree to try to solve the problem. Then they move into fact-finding ("state what happened") and a great deal of restatement. At each step, the disputants must restate what each other said, to show that they understand that person's point of view.

The mediation process takes students seriously and allows them to express themselves. "It almost honors the conflict. It acknowledges that it's something real," said Sara Keeney, director of school mediation at the New Mexico Center for Dispute Resolution. "You're allowed to have your feelings. You're allowed to be angry."

Often, that's enough. "They don't all end happy," said Angelic Martinez of the mediations. Sometimes, the parties "just agree to leave each other alone." That may not be a Hollywood ending, but at least they've talked out the problem and perhaps heard the other side of the story for the first time.

Source: *Albuquerque Journal.*

Questions

1. Does your school have a program to deal with conflict among students?
2. What steps could you take to initiate some type of peer mediation to solve conflict?

Conflict as a Positive Force . . . As Mark Twain said, "A difference of opinion is what makes a good horse race." Discussion is not worth the trouble unless a genuine problem is at stake and people have real differences about how it should be solved. Peter Drucker, a well-known management consultant, says that disagreements are valuable because they provide alternative ways of looking at a problem. Alternatives, he says, are necessary if a group is going to do more than simply approve the first idea that comes along.

Constructive conflict develops when members use their differences to discover the best ideas and not to score points against one another. Group members should especially seek out ideas that are contrary to the prevailing opinions. Find a few "off-the-wall" ideas, solutions that seem far-fetched at first. By analyzing these ideas, the group will become less committed to the *status quo* and more willing to try something new.

Does this look like positive or disruptive conflict?

Disruptive Conflict . . . Some conflict, however, can be disruptive. **Disruptive conflict** can destroy a group by *polarizing* the members (dividing them into competing sides that refuse to compromise) and by turning the discussion into a debate where personal victory is more important than a successful group decision. If "getting my way" is more important to you than helping the group, you have lost that cooperative attitude so essential to good discussion. If the captain of the football team in the pep rally example, for instance, had insisted on having a rally before each home game, his stubbornness might have made it impossible for the group to go ahead with its plan.

Almost every group has a few people who become nuisances—people who seem to fight the discussion process every step of the way. Often, these people can learn to be productive; they're simply acting like nuisances temporarily because they are bored or distracted. The health of the group, however, depends on dealing with them head-on. Look for the following behaviors in your next meeting and take steps to turn these negatives into positives.

Nitpickers want everything spelled out and will quibble until they get what they want. "If it weren't for me," such people seem to be thinking, "this group would be in trouble." Nitpickers need to have a say, but not get their way. Be sure these group members get opportunities to speak, but insist that they keep their comments brief.

Eager beavers want to offer a solution whether or not they have given it any thought. In their eagerness, they may distract the group's attention from

PEANUTS reprinted by permission of United Feature Syndicate, Inc.

ideas that have been more carefully considered. If the group can help funnel their enthusiasm, eager beavers can turn into valuable members.

Fence sitters don't dare take a position until they're sure what the "key people" will say. If the group can make it clear, however, that their opinions really matter, they may slowly gather courage and begin to say what they think, not what they think they should say.

Wisecrackers are the group clowns, people who seek attention in any way possible. Wisecrackers appear more often in groups where members are bored and looking for a diversion. In a more serious group, members quickly become impatient with such antics. If you find a wisecracker or two in your group, pick up the pace of the discussion—your group may have too much time on its hands.

Superior beings look down their noses at the whole business. Perhaps they didn't want to be part of the group in the first place. The group's best course with these members is to make them feel needed. The group must show it values their opinions, regardless of how superior and indifferent these people appear.

Dominators don't know when to quit talking. Once aware that they're preventing others from contributing, however, they can become top members. Making such persons recorders or evaluators (members who must be quiet during the meeting) is one way to help them become more aware of who's talking and who isn't during the group process. Once they know this, they may be more receptive to other people's ideas.

SECTION 2 REVIEW

Recalling the Facts ...

1. List the six steps of John Dewey's system for discussion.
2. Explain the difference between constructive conflict and disruptive conflict. Give an example of each.

Thinking Critically ...

1. John Dewey claims that his system for organizing a discussion would help develop the essential skills needed for a democratic society. In what ways does his system promote democracy? Are there any elements of his system that could be considered undemocratic?

Taking Charge ...

1. Observe a discussion from start to finish (you might watch a city council, school board, or legislative meeting). Can you state the problem or issue the group attempted to resolve? How many of the members actually took part in the discussion? Did the discussion follow the steps outlined in Dewey's problem-solving process? When the group got off course, did any members make an effort to steer the discussion back to the main point? If possible, speak with one of the participants after the discussion and compare your impressions with hers.
2. Learn to deal with annoying group members. Plan a topic of discussion for a group and label six cards ahead of time with the words "nitpicker," "eager beaver," "fence sitter," "wisecracker," "superior being," and "dominator." Secretly give one card to each of six persons in the group. Ask each person with a card to play that role as well as possible (refer to the chapter text for a description of each role). As the discussion develops, observe how other students react to the six card-holders. Notice what kind of leadership develops and what kinds of frustrations occur. After the discussion, ask the students what they thought each of the six card-holders was doing.

SECTION 3 How to Contribute to a Discussion

Groups need participation from every member because people are more likely to support decisions that they play a role in shaping. On the other hand, group members become *apathetic* or even hostile toward ideas that are handed to them from on high.

During World War II, government officials tried to convince people to use less popular meats, such as kidneys and sweetbreads, as a conservation measure. A follow-up study showed that while only 3 percent of those who heard lectures on the subject used these meats, 32 percent (ten times as many) of those who discussed the idea in group meetings were persuaded to do so.

Contributing as a Participant

We can't all be leaders, at least not all of the time. But everyone in a discussion has an important role to play. Indeed, the group can only be as effective as its weakest member. Remember, the objective of a group is to blend the knowledge, information, and reasoning of every member into a decision that represents its best collective thinking.

As a member of a group discussion, you have a number of responsibilities. Some of them involve the way you present what you have to say.

1. Be clear and simple. Reinforce what you say with looks and gestures.
2. Encourage members to react to your ideas. Questions like "Was I clear?" "What do you think about what I just said?" and "Do you have any questions?" indicate that you want feedback.
3. Be interesting. Although most of us dislike performing, it doesn't cost much to speak with vitality and enthusiasm.
4. Offer reasons for what you say. Make sure you take into account what other people are thinking. "The fool tells me his reasons," Aristotle said; "the wise man persuades me with my own."
5. Think before speaking, but don't think so long about what you want to say that an opportunity slips by. When your comment matters, seize the moment.

Expressions and gestures help to reinforce your ideas and keep the interest of your listeners.

Active Listening ... Everyone who participates in a discussion must also be an active listener. That means that even if you don't have anything to say at a particular time, you aren't free to loaf. You need to examine ideas as they are presented and figure out whether you understand them. Then, when it's your turn to contribute, you can make a meaningful comment.

As you listen to what others say, try to be impartial. Free yourself from preconceived ideas. Don't be like the person who says, "My mind is made up. Don't confuse me with facts." This sort of person comes to a discussion unwilling to accept any opinions different from his own. If left unchallenged, such a person can wreck the whole discussion.

Most important, be attentive and courteous. If you find yourself asking people to repeat themselves or to go back over ground they have already covered, you are slowing the process down and making the meeting dull for everyone. Avoid making silly or irrelevant comments. Contributions to the discussion are meaningful only when they connect with what has just been said.

Preparing for Discussion ... It's a fact of life that you often come to a discussion with your head full of other thoughts and interests. You probably have not reviewed your notes or even tried to decide what you think about the issues that will come up in the meeting. But taking a little

WORDS FROM THE WORKPLACE

Veronica Rodarte

Food Distribution Manager

Q: *How does communication play a role in your day-to-day work activities?*

A: Communication plays an essential role in my job. Not only is good communication beneficial to my customers, it's also an asset when I do business with buyers, suppliers, and other fellow associates.

Q: *Do you have any stories that might illustrate how good communication skills helped in a business situation, how poor communication skills hurt a situation by losing a customer or sale for the company?*

A: Several months ago, a customer approached my sales counter and quickly told me he was not interested in buying anything and was only browsing. I offered him my help, if he needed it, and gave him his space to scan my counter. Without making him feel pressured or obligated, I offered the customer a couple of samples and suggested other products that would complement these products. I noticed the customer felt more at ease and started asking me questions pertaining to other products. The customer didn't purchase anything that day, but I still thanked him, reminded him of other services we offer, and wished him good day. Needless to say, that very same customer has returned time and time again and has now purchased hundreds of dollars' worth of my company's products. I think this example shows how companies can succeed or fail based on the way the employees communicate with their customers.

Q: *What suggestions for improving their communication skills can you give students?*

A: They should realize the importance of using their communication skills to demonstrate concern for the customer. They should learn to use verbal acknowledgement, a smile, good eye contact, and a sincere thank-you to make the customer feel important and recognized. Once you have established that contact with the customer, you can apply your tools of suggestive selling. Even the most hesitant customer will remember your congenial attitude and will more than likely return for future business.

MANAGING DIFFICULT GROUP MEMBERS

INSTANT IMPACT

Certain kinds of behavior can quickly sidetrack a discussion. Here are a few tips you can use to handle some familiar types of difficult people.

- **Monopolizers.** They interrupt, ramble, and repeat because they enjoy hearing themselves talk. Don't argue with them; instead, confront them. Wait for them to come up for air and interrupt them by name. Agree that they've made their point and immediately invite someone else to comment on the topic.
- **Distractors.** They seek attention, and to get it, they'll often bring up irrelevant topics that waste time. To halt distracters, restate the meeting's purpose and ask them to answer a specific question, forcing them to focus on the main topic.
- **Skeptics.** They find fault with everything you or others say. Have a friendly talk with them *before* the meeting and explain what behavior you expect. If that fails, cut them off by repeating that you want solutions, not criticism. Then ask them to contribute.
- **Snipers.** They resort to stage whispers and snide comments to challenge your authority. Shine the spotlight on them and bluntly ask them to share their comment with everyone. Most will be so embarrassed that they'll decline.

Source: Don Gabor, *Talking with Confidence for the Painfully Shy* (New York: Crown Publishing, 1997).

time to prepare can pay big dividends, both for you and for the group.

Preparation is largely a matter of looking ahead. By thinking out what questions and objections might be raised about your position ahead of time, you will be better able to cope with the give-and-take of the discussion process.

It's also a good idea to know how you work under pressure. Some people love the hubbub of discussion and enjoy each conflict that arises. Others find arguments and clashes over ideas very stressful. Understanding who you are will help you define your role in a group. Try experimenting with varying degrees of participation to find your comfort level.

No matter what, always keep in mind that you have skills and talents to offer the group. You may take good notes or be able to make a joke at a tense moment. Try to find out what the group needs from you. Be aware, though, that if you start out as a silent member, people will expect you to be silent the next time. They may try to encourage you to talk at first, but if you don't respond, they may come to ignore you. So don't wait for the second meeting to make a contribution; take the plunge right away.

Contributing as a Leader ... Although some groups can function well for a while without a leader, there are clearly times when every group needs one. A certain nudge of guidance seems to be necessary for a group to function smoothly.

For that reason, it may be unwise for a group to wait for a leader to emerge naturally. Instead, the group should designate a leader, at least for a particular meeting or a particular goal. With a designated leader, the members of the group know who is responsible for settling disputes and main-

Someone must take the lead in any group.

COMMUNICATION **Break down**

Let's Stop Wasteful Meetings

Many companies waste time and reduce productivity by holding ineffective meetings. This conclusion was underscored in a story in the *Wall Street Journal,* which reported that CEOs throughout the country felt that meetings account for the largest share of unproductive time on the job.

A study by the Wharton Center for Applied Research found that managers spend from 10 to 23 hours a week in meetings. The study also concluded that nearly one-third of those meetings could be handled better through face-to-face talks, by phone, by memo, or by e-mail.

Here are some suggestions to make your meetings more effective:

- Before deciding to hold a meeting, ask yourself whether the meeting is *really* necessary—or could whatever needs to be done be handled some other way?
- If you hold regularly scheduled meetings, ask yourself whether you could skip one of the meetings from time to time when nothing urgent is pending.
- Make sure that the people who are needed to make decisions attend the meeting. Don't invite those who aren't needed; you'll only waste their time.
- Develop an agenda and distribute it a day or so before the meeting. Insist that people come prepared to discuss the items on the agenda. Putting your goals in writing will help sharpen your focus.
- Don't pass out material at the beginning of a meeting. People will read it instead of listen to you.
- Start and end every meeting on time.
- Be sure that everyone knows who's responsible for doing what as a result of the meeting. Put this in writing promptly to help prevent misunderstandings.

taining an atmosphere where everyone's comments are welcome and appreciated. Without such a person, groups can break into cliques, become chaotic, or just waste time.

Leadership may change hands as the attitudes of the group or the areas of discussion change. Members may want the leadership of one person on one topic and turn for leadership to someone else at another time. The group decides not only whom it will follow but also how much authority it will give to the leader and how long it will accept that person's leadership. Fortunately, any interested member can learn to be an effective leader.

What a Leader Should Know ... Any group member should be willing and prepared to become a leader if asked. We can summarize a discussion leader's responsibilities this way:

1. A good leader should know how to run a meeting.
2. A good leader should know the people in the group.

3. A good leader should know the issues the group will discuss.

A discussion leader should pay her greatest attention to matters of procedure. She should know how to run a meeting, partly by virtue of experience and partly by a solid understanding of parliamentary procedure (see Chapter 20). This allows her to remain impartial. She becomes a neutral mediator to whom the participants in a discussion can turn when disagreements threaten to get out of control.

A shrewd leader should know the people in her group. That way she can plan to calm down those who talk too much and encourage those who talk too little. She should know who can be relied on to speak and who needs to be prodded.

A leader should also have a full grasp of the issues the group will discuss. This does not mean that the leader has to know more than anyone else. In fact, a competent leader may know very little about specific details. She must, nonetheless, understand the nature of the problem and the most productive way to analyze it.

Like a conductor, a good leader directs the discussion toward harmony.

Getting a Meeting Started ... The leader of a group is first and foremost a **moderator.** A moderator must get the discussion started, keep it moving, and bring it to a close. Getting a discussion started can be a major challenge, especially for an inexperienced leader.

Most groups need to be led into useful discussion. Imagine a situation where your leader, after finishing his introduction (which might be a brief welcome and a reminder of why the meeting has been called), simply says, "Well, who wants to begin?" This tactic is almost certain to fail. Groups need greater direction, especially in the beginning.

A useful method for starting a discussion is to pose a question. This opening question should be directed to the group as a whole and not to any one individual. It would be unwise to put someone on the spot this early in the discussion.

Most discussion questions can be grouped into three categories: fact, interpretation, and evaluation. **Questions of fact** ask group members to recall information that touches on the business at hand. **Questions of interpretation** ask them to give their opinions on what the information means. **Questions of evaluation** ask members to agree or disagree with possible solutions and to make value judgments.

A leader should use interpretive questions at the beginning of a discussion and, if possible, write them out ahead of time. Suppose you are preparing to lead a group discussion. The best interpretive questions are those that you have no ready answers for but that you believe can be answered. Prepare a question for the group and then ask yourself whether the group has enough information to deal effectively with the question. If not, throw that question out and find another.

Good interpretive questions are questions you care about, ones that really matter. You can never be sure, of course, that everyone in the group will share your enthusiasm for a particular question, but if you are eager to get an answer, chances are that others will be, too. If you don't care, why should anyone else?

We can summarize the qualities of good interpretive questions like this:

1. They contain doubt.
2. They can be answered.
3. They are likely to interest the group.

Think back for a moment to the students who were worried about their pep rallies being canceled. During their discussion, they asked several interpretive questions: "What will students think about having fewer pep rallies?" "How will the principal react to our idea about faculty supervision?" "How important are pep rallies, anyway?" They also asked at least one question of fact: "Have we ever had problems with pep rallies before?" and one evaluative question: "Is this plan good for our school?"

Keep the Discussion Going ... Once underway, a well-informed group will usually move along without much prodding from the leader. Good leaders strive for balanced participation. More often than not, groups have at least one person who talks too much and one who talks too little.

Make eye contact with group members. It gives important nonverbal support.

Leaders should work to see that everyone participates and that no one *monopolizes* the group's time. If several speakers try to speak at once, preference should be given to the one who has spoken less. Sometimes real diplomacy is needed to keep the discussion from becoming one-sided. Leaders must rely on tact and good humor to see that everyone talks but that no one talks too much.

Leaders must be especially careful with members who are reluctant to speak. For example, leaders should resist the temptation to ask a timid person a direct question. This tactic can backfire because if the person is taken by surprise, he will be even less likely to speak thereafter. It may be safe, however, to ask for a comment on an idea already being considered, as in "Sean, what do you think of Samantha's idea?"

Leaders should provide occasional *paraphrases* of what someone has said. They may sometimes need to repeat in their own words what a member has said, especially if the person has been talking for a long time. Leaders should also provide occasional summaries of what the group has accomplished so far. Summaries help the group avoid repetition and spotlight areas of agreement or disagreement. Both paraphrases and summaries help everyone know where the group is in the discussion.

Set an Example ... A leader can increase the members' desire to participate by recognizing and praising (when appropriate) their contributions. Leaders give such recognition with statements like "That's an important point. Thank you for bringing it to our attention," as well as nonverbal support like good eye contact and head nodding. Carefully timed praise also encourages group loyalty.

Finally, leaders should avoid sending negative nonverbal signals. For example, the leader shouldn't yawn when someone else is talking. Nothing will turn a group off more quickly than an inattentive leader.

Close the Discussion ... At some point, the leader will move to end the discussion. A leader should be alert for signs that the group is ready to quit, or at least ready to be done with the question at hand. The group may begin to repeat itself, to take up minor points, or to wander away from the question. When this happens, the group members have probably gone as far as they can with the issue. The leader must also be aware of any time limits (the bell is about to ring, for instance) that mean the discussion must stop. In either case, it is time to settle the question.

The ideal conclusion of a group discussion is for the group to reach a **consensus.** Consensus means a *nearly* unanimous agreement among the group's members about a particular solution. It happens most often when members unselfishly seek common ground. But it doesn't happen all the time, and it never happens without a great deal of effort.

Group consensus can only happen through hard work.

As desirable as consensus is, you should be on guard against giving up an argument or a position too easily just to go along with the group. In its most extreme form, this desire to go along with the group causes people to abandon their own personal beliefs. People sometimes call this very human desire to get along **groupthink** because it's an instance of letting a group do our thinking for us.

If you let your friends talk you into doing something, you have become a victim of groupthink. Thinking for yourself within a group can be tough, but no group can profit when its members give up their own individuality.

SECTION 3 REVIEW

Recalling the Facts ...

1. Name at least three of the responsibilities each person accepts by joining a group discussion.
2. What are the three most important things a group leader should know?

Thinking Critically ...

1. What should a group do if no one wishes to be the leader? What are some possible methods for choosing a group leader, no matter how reluctant he or she might be?

Taking Charge ...

1. Make a list of interpretive questions for a discussion on one of the following topics:
   - What qualities should a good presidential candidate possess?
   - Is year-round school a good idea?
   - Should term limits be imposed on all elected officials?

   Once you have selected a topic and written a list of interpretive questions, write five factual questions and three evaluation questions for the discussion.
2. Find an article in the newspaper that explains how two groups disagree on an issue. Analyze how each group would respond to these questions:
   - How does our side see the problem?
   - What solution can we suggest?
   - What are the advantages of our solution?
   - What are the disadvantages of our solution?

   Can you suggest a way these two groups could resolve their differences and settle on a compromise solution? Must one group give in, or can both groups find a middle ground?

STUDENT WORK

"Living on the Fringe"

Talking out our problems is one of the best ways we have to solve them. Often we discover that other people have the same dilemmas and simply knowing that they share our feelings helps. In the following discussion (adapted from a newspaper article) notice how group members flip back and forth between task and maintenance messages. Task messages help move the discussion forward (by giving information, for example), while maintenance messages help keep the group harmonious ("I know just how you feel").

Wherever you go in schools, it seems, everyone has a place. *Their* table in the lunchroom. *Their* spot on the hill. Senior Hall.

They give themselves names: punk rockers, jocks, preps, G's, cowboys, thugs, wannabes, nerds. They divide themselves into sects, groups, and cliques. "We all just kind of avoid each other and stick with our own kind," says a sophomore.

Sometimes the divisions hurt. "I'm considered a loner or a traveler," says a ninth-grade girl. "Everyone fits somewhere or else they're a floater like me."

"I was just strange to other people," says a junior. "They automatically decide they're really cool and I'm the geek."

High school can be a hard place for outcasts. Let's eavesdrop on a discussion among students who have felt at least sometimes that they were outcasts.

Josh: They make fun of you for the way you are?

John: Yeah, you?

Josh: Yeah.

John: I tried to fit in as much as I could but I never really did. It started in my grade school. Maybe I had the wrong shoes. Maybe the wrong socks. Maybe the wrong hair style. Did I say the wrong things on the playground? I was never sure.

Josh: Do you regret anything about that time?

John: No. Everything happens for a reason, for knowledge or to show us who we are, show us our faults.

Josh: What happened when you got to high school?

John: My old friends wrote me off. They got it in their minds that I wasn't acceptable. Most of them were into sports and I wasn't.

Nicole: I've never fit in anywhere I've gone. About as long as I can remember I got teased for being different. I'm an Air Force brat and we've moved everywhere—California, Germany. Kids knew that but they still picked on me. I never figured out what I did that was so bad.

Jennifer: I don't think there's anybody that doesn't have somebody. Everybody has somebody. You just have to find out who that is.

Justin: I think one of the things I especially like about our school is the diversity here. You just walk in the halls and see all sorts of different people.

Mike: I've heard a lot of talk about the Gothic-type kids. You know, I've heard some people say that they freak them out or whatever. But I used to dress like that so I don't really understand that viewpoint or how you can be frightened of them. Most of them I've seen are really nice and I think for some people the fear just grows from the misunderstanding.

Elizabeth: I think people who are quiet . . . those are some of the strongest people because they don't rely on people around them to hold them up.

Brieanna: I think everyone feels like they're not accepted at some time.

Joe: When I see people making fun of people in high school, I think it has to do with people feeling insecure about themselves, feeling as if . . . they don't have as much integrity as other people, so they have to put others down so they can seem like they're better persons.

Josh: They'd call me names. Fatso, Stupid. I hit back sometimes.

Hilary: In middle school you start to get more freedom. Your body is changing. You can hang out with whoever you want. But you are confused about who you are.

Tanner: I felt like I was completely alone. There wasn't anybody that I knew very well—and I'm a really shy person so it was hard for me to make friends. They called me names, made fun of me and my appearance, whispered about me, teased me, made jokes of me. And every day I sat there, didn't say a word to any one of them, and just took it. Now when I look back, I regret my silence.

Emily: Even in the beginning of high school, I did feel like I was made fun of a lot . . . I think it was more just like I cared so much about fitting in—I wanted so bad to be in a certain group. Now it doesn't bother me that much. I know who my friends are and I know who is important to me and that's all that matters. I don't have to be accepted by everyone.

Mike: I had a conflict recently with some of my punk rocker friends and some of my G friends. And it's just that, you know, the clothes that they wear and everything and they instantly make this assumption that this person's going to act this way and then they meet each other and they're playing off the stereotypes and both groups are looking at each other like "that's not me." It's hard for groups to get along.

Jennifer: They're just friends that I hang out with that would not get along . . . You do different activities with different people.

Mike: Really, if you just find something that you like to do and try to get with another group of people who have that same interest, then you start to fit in with them more and you don't worry about the "cool" kids so much. Once you feel that you're part of that group, you kind of feel like you're OK and you're accepted, you don't really care about being popular or anything any more. You are happy with what you're doing.

(Adapted from the *Lincoln Journal Star.*)

Looking Back

Listed below are the major ideas discussed in this chapter.

- Group discussion is a cooperative process in which participants exchange information, discuss ideas, and solve problems.
- Group discussion is especially valuable because people are more likely to support decisions they have had a share in making.
- Public forms of discussion are the panel, the symposium, and the town hall meeting.
- The ideal group size is five to seven people.
- Many groups use a standard problem-solving process based on John Dewey's six steps.
- Differences of opinion within a group should be encouraged as a way of exploring alternatives.
- Disruptive conflict can occur when individuals put greater importance on getting their way than supporting a group decision.
- Good participants use active listening skills and watch for the right moment to speak.
- Although some groups can function without a leader, most groups profit from having one because the leader can make the group function more smoothly and effectively.
- A leader can begin a discussion by asking an interpretive question, which requires members to provide evidence and reasoning to support their opinions.
- The leader can also help the group by providing occasional summaries of what has gone on and paraphrases of what members have said.
- Groups must strive for consensus but be alert for groupthink, where personal beliefs are overcome by the pressure to conform.

Speech Vocabulary

Match the speech term on the left with the correct definition on the right.

1. discussion
2. cooperative
3. competitive
4. panel
5. forum
6. round table
7. symposium
8. town hall meeting
9. cohesion
10. criteria
11. brainstorming
12. constructive conflict
13. disruptive conflict
14. moderator
15. question of fact
16. question of interpretation
17. question of evaluation
18. consensus
19. groupthink

a. difference of opinion that leads to creative alternatives
b. set of standards for evaluation
c. creative process for coming up with ideas
d. discussion format typical of cabinet meetings
e. helpful and unselfish
f. informal discussion before an audience
g. independent and self-oriented
h. discussion format in which a few experts give short speeches
i. nearly unanimous agreement
j. social "glue" that holds a group together
k. exchange of information and ideas among a group
l. tendency to conform to group opinion
m. opportunity for audience members to ask questions
n. discussion format involving an entire community
o. disagreement that prevents a group from making a decision
p. a question about opinions
q. a question about value judgments
r. a question about information
s. impartial person who organizes a discussion

CHAPTER 7 Review and Enrichment...

General Vocabulary

Match the term with the correct definition.

1. sequential
2. scenario
3. bombard
4. status quo
5. polarizing
6. apathetic
7. monopolize
8. paraphrase

a. express something in other words
b. dominate to the exclusion of others
c. to attack vigorously or persistently
d. showing little feeling or interest
e dividing into two opposing sides
f. plot outline
g. having a logical, step-by-step pattern
h. the existing state of affairs

To Remember

Answer the following based on your reading of the chapter.

1. Give three reasons why discussion is one of the best methods for solving problems.
2. Why is a group of five more likely to have a successful discussion than a group of three or a group of twelve?
3. What are the six steps of the problem-solving process?
4. What is brainstorming?
5. What are the major duties of a group discussion leader?
6. Explain the difference between questions of fact, questions of interpretation, and questions of evaluation.
7. Why should a leader occasionally summarize what the group has done?
8. What is a consensus?
9. How can you prepare for a discussion?

To Do

1. Make a participation diagram of the next discussion you attend. On a sheet of paper, arrange a group of circles to represent the group members and where they are seated. Put each person's initials in his or her circle. Next, draw lines to connect each circle with every other circle.

   Each time someone says something to someone else, put a slash mark through the line connecting the two people's circles. If an individual makes a comment to the entire group and not to anyone in particular, place a mark inside that person's circle. At the end of the discussion, you can analyze the group's interaction. Who spoke the most? The least? Where were most of the comments directed?
2. Ask your teacher to choose two groups of five students each. The remainder of the class will form one large group. Ask each group to discuss the same question, perhaps "Should school lunches be catered by fast-food chains like McDonald's or Burger King?" Have an observer in each group report back to the class on how many people participated and how much they said. Are there noticeable differences between the participation levels in larger and smaller groups? Were the decisions the same in each group?

To Talk About

1. What would you do if the following occurred in a group discussion?
   - One person who obviously has not done any research on the topic criticizes many valid remarks made by other members.
   - Two members sit and whisper while other members talk about the topic.
   - One member insists on dominating the discussion. The fact that this person has many notes shows that he or she has done plenty of research.
   - The discussion leader shows signs of being hopelessly disorganized. The group is drifting and beginning to repeat itself.
2. Why is equal participation from all members a good goal for group discussion?
3. How important is it to achieve consensus in a group discussion?
4. How can you tell whether conflict in a group discussion is creative and constructive or self-centered and disruptive?

To Write About

1. Write a letter to a leader in your community. Ask that person for a definition of leadership and a few examples of how good leadership has made a difference. Share the reply with your classmates.
2. Suppose your class wanted to plan a school assembly to better inform students about the dangers of driving while intoxicated. Would it be better to have a panel discussion, symposium, round table, or town hall meeting? Why? Explain your answer in a one-page paper.

Related Speech Topics

Groups make better decisions
Things my parents taught me
Things I wish my parents had taught me
Leadership styles of famous people
A friend is someone you can talk to
Making decisions for dinner
How to choose a leader
How to be a good group leader
How to be a good group member

Preparation and Process

UNIT CONTENTS

CHAPTER 8

RESEARCHING YOUR PRESENTATION

"If truth is beauty, then why don't more people get their hair done at the library?"

–Lily Tomlin

Learning Objectives

After completing this chapter, you will be able to do the following.

- Discuss the impact of the Information Age on your future.
- Develop a plan that will help you focus your research efforts.
- Identify four shortcuts that will reduce the time you spend researching.
- Use the library resources to find material for your speeches.
- Distinguish between plagiarism and intellectual honesty.

Chapter Outline

Following are the main sections in this chapter.

1. Your Research Plan
2. Using the Library
3. Using What You've Found

New Speech Terms

In this chapter, you will learn the meanings of the speech terms listed below.

audience analysis
interlibrary loan
database
online
card catalog
author card
title card
subject card
table of contents
index
plagiarism
paraphrasing
ghostwriter

General Vocabulary

Expanding your general vocabulary will help you become a more effective communicator. Listed below are some words appearing in this chapter that you should make part of your everyday vocabulary.

prerequisite
entrepreneur
alienate
haven
nuclear family
microcosm
panacea
crooned
serendipity
compendium
ubiquitous
attribution

Looking AHEAD

How can you find your way out of the library bewilderness? Shortcuts can help you better use your research time effectively as you acquire the necessary information to prepare a successful speech. Furthermore, access to the Internet has made possible access to a wealth of information. Note-taking is essential to any research effort—but how do you decide what to write down? What is plagiarism, and how can you avoid intellectual dishonesty? These questions and others arise as you research any topic for an upcoming presentation. Developing the ability to find the answers to such questions is a necessary *prerequisite* for anyone who wants to survive in this Information Age. This chapter is one step in your journey toward this goal.

Introduction

We live in the Information Age. More than 50,000 books are published each year in the United States. Our store of knowledge and information is doubling every five years. Potential for additional growth on the World Wide Web is mind-boggling. The author Richard Saul Wurman points out that "a weekday edition of the *New York Times* contains more information than the average person was likely to come across in a lifetime in seventeenth-century England." It is not surprising, then, that the enormous amount of available information can be overwhelming to the student researcher in need of evidence for an upcoming speech.

At the same time, students are becoming increasingly aware that information skills are essential to survival in the world today. Whether you're a college student studying the latest advances in organ transplants or a young *entrepreneur* starting an auto repair shop, you need to know how to find the right answers. This crucial concern was addressed by the members of the U.S. National Commission on Libraries and Information Science. They said that "a basic objective of education is for each student to learn how to identify needed information, locate and organize it, and present it in a clear and persuasive manner."

Clearly, the process of researching supporting materials for each of your assigned speeches challenges you to become a more effective problem solver. As a problem solver, you will soon experience the thrill of the hunt and the joy of finding that juicy—but effectively hidden, until now—bit of information. The trick, of course, is to have a plan.

One of your biggest research assignments will be to investigate the college or university you want to attend.

SECTION 1 Your Research Plan

Let's assume you have just chosen a speech topic. Chances are that you know something about the topic. Fortunately, one of the best ways to begin organizing your thoughts is to assess what you already know. You will soon realize, though, that with most topics you need assistance. Successful speeches require supporting information. Supporting information requires specific research. Specific research provides sources to quote—people who know more about a given topic than you. The ancient Greeks referred to this process of accumulating information as building a "storehouse of knowledge."

Have you ever been stopped at the mall or in front of a store to answer a researcher's questions?

Playing the Research Game

Before you start accumulating information, you should have a carefully thought out plan. If you are like most beginning researchers, though, you don't yet know how to plan—how to play the research game. Although you can gather supporting materials from such methods as interviewing or surveying, most of the research game is played in the library. Entering a library, though, you may feel as if you are trapped inside some gigantic alien pinball machine—the flippers frozen, the tilt beyond your control. Thus, the time you spend "playing library" is largely wasted.

Gathering Information

So how do you avoid wasting time? Speakers disagree as to the best method. Some begin with a rough outline of the speech and then find evidence to support the subpoints. Others do some preliminary research and then create an outline that incorporates the facts that they have gathered. In choosing one of these approaches, perhaps the most important factor is how much you know about the topic before you begin. If you are speaking on the topic "We must reduce unemployment" and you are not well

KNOWING IT ALL

INSTANT IMPACT

Dr. Michael B. McElroy, Chair of the Department of Earth and Planetary Sciences at Harvard University, has concluded the following.

The libraries of Harvard University alone contain over 11 million volumes. Assuming that each volume has about 150 pages, with about 400 words per page, we may calculate the store of wisdom at Harvard to run to approximately 660 billion words. If we assume that the accomplished reader can process about 50 words per minute, it is easy, for a skilled arithmetician at least, to estimate how long it would take to survey the material at Harvard. The answer is a staggering 25,000 years, and that does not allow time for sleep or other distraction.

Source: Randall McCutcheon, *Can You Find It?*, Free Spirit Publishing (Minneapolis, Minn.): 1989, p. 1.

informed about economic theory, then you should probably do some preliminary reading before making any decisions about how to organize your speech. If, on the other hand, you are speaking on the topic "The student council should play a more active role in the school," you might want to start by jotting down a rough outline of your views on the topic.

To save more time, consider finding an expert to give focus to your research. A phone call to a government official, a college professor, or an author can save you hours of wading through books and articles that are not relevant to your search. Experts can suggest the best sources on a particular topic, and they often can provide quotable statements to work into your speeches. You can even become your own expert by undertaking opinion polls on controversial topics or by conducting a series of interviews with representatives on both sides of a specific issue.

As you gather information for your speech, remember to adapt to the audience that will hear your presentation. For example, a speech before your classmates during second period may require less formality than a commencement address before members of the community. In any speaking situation, keep in mind that the audience may not have the same interests as you do. Skateboarding, for example, may occupy your every waking thought but be of little consequence to most members of your audience. Therefore, you have to plan your speech—no matter what the topic—by first considering the needs and expectations of those people who will be listening to you. This process, **audience analysis,** involves asking yourself the following questions:

- What do the listeners already know about my topic?
- How do I capture their interest?
- How formal should my language be?
- What should I avoid saying that might *alienate* some audience members?
- What can I say to change the minds of people who might disagree with my positions?

You should make it clear that you care about your audience and that you want to share the information in your speech with them.

CAZENOVIA

NFL quarterback Doug Flutie, a public speaker for raising awareness about autism, received an honorary Doctor of Human Letters when he addressed Cazenovia College's 1999 graduates.

COMMUNICATION

Library Business Booms in Hard Times

Libraries become *havens* for the unemployed during hard economic times. Patricia Glass Schuman, past president of the Chicago-based American Library Association, says that people use libraries not only to look for jobs but also for entertainment. They turn to the library for a video or a book when they can't afford to go to the movies.

Jobless patrons, according to the Associated Press, "empty shelves of career-guide books and raid newspaper bins for help-wanted ads." Some libraries expand their services to meet the needs of the unemployed by offering a job-listing telephone service.

The Skokie Public Library in suburban Chicago has turned one room into an Employment Resource Center. Once a week, the library places job listings and other career information there. People who need to prepare résumés can get help from the reference librarian. To guide people in planning job-information searches, the reference librarian conducts 30-minute interviews.

Clearly, the thousands of libraries in this country are an immense resource, providing not only volumes and volumes of books but also the expert skills of professional librarians who care.

Question

What other services do you think libraries could provide for the unemployed?

SECTION  REVIEW

Recalling the Facts ...

1. How do you avoid wasting time when preparing a presentation?

Thinking Critically ...

1. World War III is about to take place. You are responsible for selecting and saving three books that can have an impact on future generations. One must be a children's book, one a book that made a significant impact on your life, and one a reference book. You have three minutes to explain why these three books would be an important contribution.

Taking Charge ...

1. Now it's your turn. Choose a potential topic for a speech and call a local expert. Make certain that you first identify yourself and the nature of your inquiry. Then ask the expert for possible ways to find the best information on the topic you have selected. Finally, be sure to thank your expert.

SECTION 2

Using the Library

"You know what scares me," the author Stephen King once said, "are people who don't use the library." King was suggesting that a trip to the library is a crucial step in preparing any piece of writing—your next speech, for example. You can significantly increase your credibility as a speaker (what the Greek rhetorician Aristotle called your *ethos*) by quoting authoritative sources. A medical doctor, for instance, is likely to know more about the causes of sports injuries than you, so quote a doctor when speaking about sports injuries.

The library is your most complete source for researching any topic.

You need to supplement your personal knowledge with solid research. Unfortunately, as suggested earlier, the mushrooming store of information makes it difficult to know where to begin and how to conduct a successful search for supporting material. Most students feel lost in the beginning, "deskperadoes" fenced in by inexperience. But hang in there. Do not be intimidated by the library. Your frustration, your initial wild goose chases, will soon end as you become more efficient, more productive.

How do you get the most out of a library? To help you use the library, this section describes some useful shortcuts and then tells you how to find books and periodicals. It also discusses other sources of information found in the library.

Four Shortcuts

You can use your research time effectively by employing four shortcuts:

1. Whether you use your school library or another nearby library, make certain to take advantage of the reference librarian's knowledge. Reference librarians are trained to answer your questions and to give you guidance in your research efforts. They can save you hours of disappointment. They know things that many teenagers do not. And they actually enjoy helping you find the right information, so don't be afraid to ask.
2. A public library's reference department will usually give you assistance over the phone. The librarians working in these departments will find facts for you—for free. If you need to know, for example, the Supreme Court's most recent ruling on capital punishment, or how to get financial aid for college, then "reach out and touch" the "someone" with answers: the reference librarian. It pays to plan ahead.
3. If your library does not have the book you want and you can wait for a few weeks, try interlibrary loan. **Interlibrary loan** is a cooperative system by which libraries lend specific books to one another on order. In other words, a library in Amarillo, Texas, may mail to your library that hard-to-find work on the

finer points of fly fishing for the mere cost of postage and an insurance fee.

4. Although the computer has no intelligence of its own, it offers certain advantages over traditional approaches to finding information. The timeliness, speed, and scope of data available make the computer an invaluable research tool.

To find information by computer, you must search online databases. A **database** is simply a collection of related information. **Online** services provide rapid access to many computer databases containing information on many topics. More and more libraries are subscribing to one or more specialized online database services. Often, there is a charge for requesting a database search. Check with your librarian about costs before you start a search.

Note that a search through databases is limited by what a particular database includes and by how well you choose "key words," those words that best describe the desired information. For example, in researching a speech on the disintegration of the *nuclear family,* you might begin a subject search by typing the key word *divorce* into the computer. Some other key words you might try include *single parents* and *child care.*

Regardless of what search method you use, you're most likely going to end up in the reference section of your library.

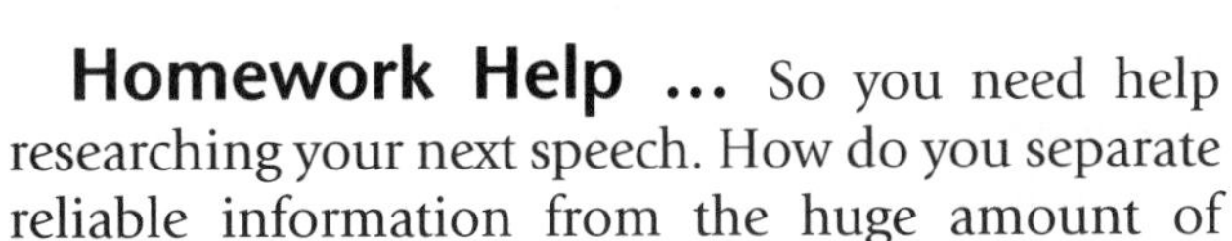

Homework Help ... So you need help researching your next speech. How do you separate reliable information from the huge amount of junk that passes for fact on the Internet? According to Don Oldenburg of the *Washington Post,* the information highway is littered with "the truth" as defined by those with an ax to grind. You might try, therefore, some of the following more trustworthy sites. Please note that some web sites may have changed their addresses.

- Schoolwork.org
  www.schoolwork.org
  Sponsored by New York state librarians, this site offers a host of solid research resources and several online newspapers.

INSTANT IMPACT

AMERICANS CHECK IT OUT

According to *Sunday Morning,* a news program on CBS, the libraries in cities play an important role in our lives. For one thing, they frequently double as informal daycare centers. Adult immigrants turn to the public libraries to learn to write English in adult literacy programs. Senior citizens leaf through magazines, and students research topics at reference tables. In fact, libraries are used by all ages, races, and economic classes. More than 60 percent of U.S. citizens visit the library at least once each year, and 40 percent use it every month. "A trip to the library," says the *Utne Reader,* "offers a pulsing *microcosm* of American life."

- My Virtual Reference Desk
  www.refdesk.com
  This site links to dictionaries, encyclopedias, reference/research materials.
- **www.libraryspot.com**
  This site links to over 300 libraries, including the Library of Congress.
- Ask Jeeves
  www.Ask.com
  Jeeves will take you to an Internet site that answers your question.

Unweaving the Tangled Web

The comedian Dennis Miller suggests that the Internet is a communication tool bringing the whole world together. Miller explains: "I mean, you sit down to log on to America Online in your hometown, and it's just staggering to think that at the same moment, halfway around the world in China, someone you've never met is sitting at his computer, hearing the exact same busy signal you're hearing."

When you do connect, though, virtually any topic imaginable is at your fingertips. For example, a pin drops in New Delhi and there's an article about it on CNN Interactive. In the article, you'll find pictures, sounds, video clips, quotes from those who saw the pin drop, and links to related pin-dropping sites. And if the event you're researching is significant, chances are there's even a feature section on it that contains more information on pins dropping.

CNN Interactive (**www.cnn.com**) is updated 24 hours a day, 7 days a week. Suppose that you are delivering a speech on pins dropping in various locations. That night, you can get up-to-the-second information on the pin drop in question—so current that your speech is much more pertinent than those of your fellow students. Knowing how to find the most recent information on a topic can make the difference someday when you are trying to earn a promotion in the workplace or building your own business.

Can't find what you're looking for at the CNN site? Then it's time to move on to a search engine. Numerous search engines are out there, but why try one when you can try them all? Go to

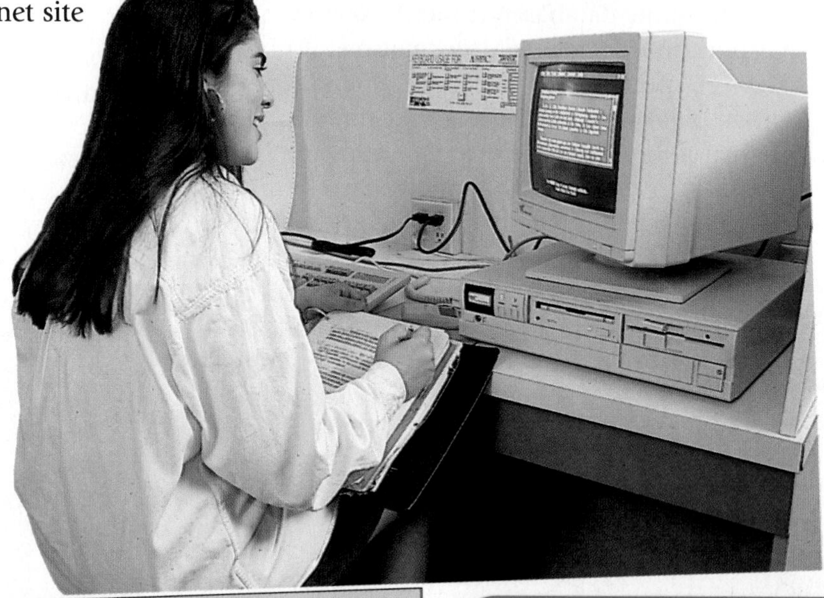

Finding exactly what you're looking for isn't always easy. There are numerous search engines out there. The biggest one is search.com.

Search.com (**www.search.com**), the Grand Central Station of search engines. A few clicks of your mouse button and you can board a multitude of engines and databases. Remember that you can find numerous newspapers and magazines on the web. Of course, some of the sources charge a fee for downloading information.

The Internet, however, is not a *panacea* for researchers. Consider some of the pitfalls of relying too heavily on the information superhighway:

- Anyone can publish on the Internet. The reliability and quality of information is therefore often in question. A gym teacher, for example, can dribble on and on in cyberspace—and you have no defense, no way to handcheck his credentials.

- Much of the good stuff you find lacks either context or historical perspective.
- You can get distracted by all of the useless junk that litters the information superhighway.
- Relying on the web simply because of its speed and convenience may cause you to overlook a more appropriate print source.

Therefore, don't confuse "easy to use" with "easy to learn." If you practice, though, you will become more proficient in finding what you need on the Internet. And you can have—to paraphrase reporter Joshua Quittner—your magic cookie and eat it, too.

DOT-COMS ARE BUGGING YOU

INSTANT IMPACT

Most Web users are aware that online ads have small files called "cookies" to identify you and show you personalized content. Did you know, though, that even when no ad is in sight, many commercial sites are peppered with these tiny bugs? In other words, the web is bugged. According to *USA Today,* these bugs hide behind one-by-one pixel dots, about the size of a pinpoint, the smallest image you can put on a screen. Reporter Elizabeth Weise says that the only way to tell they're there is to call up the site's underlying computer code and look for them, line by line.

David Medine, associate director for financial practices at the Federal Trade Commission, raises an important issue: "There's a tension developing between maximizing ad revenues and protecting consumers' privacy." Ask yourself, how much do you want corporations to know about you? Should some marketing person know the music you like or the games you play? Is it anyone else's business if you buy mouth wash? Should they bug you about it?

Evaluating Web Sites

It is becoming increasingly important to evaluate the quality of the information that you find on the Internet. The question has become: Who is providing the information, the content? *Boston Globe* columnist Ellen Goodman has argued that "everybody is talking about 'content' as if there were a spigot somewhere to fill up the electronic jar."

Goodman has a point. Students often assume that because the information comes from the Internet, then it must be correct and current. Unfortunately, these students don't realize that good content gathering takes time. The lazy gatherer makes mistakes at the speed of cyberspace.

Jim Kapoun, a reference librarian at Southwest State University in Marshall, Minnesota, has developed five criteria for web evaluation (see the chart). Kapoun's method has merit because he evaluates web sites the same way he would evaluate print items for inclusion into a library collection. The five criteria for print evaluation include accuracy, authority, objectivity, currency, and coverage.

You, as a student researcher, must remember that technology can speed up the distribution of thoughts, but you are responsible for the painstaking process of thinking about what they mean. In a sense, you are an investigative journalist who sifts through the facts and reports only what is true. As Goodman says, "A journalist is to a content provider as a farmer is to a waiter. They're both in the food biz. But the farmer is the one to count on."

Finding Books with the Card Catalog

When Kermit the Frog *crooned,* "It's not easy being green," he might well have been describing the challenge awaiting you in the **card catalog.** The inexperienced, or "green," researcher, though,

5 Criteria for Evaluating Web Pages

Evaluation of Web Documents	How to Interpret the Basics
1. Accuracy of Web Documents • Who wrote the page and can you contact him or her? • What is the purpose of the document and why was it produced? • Is this person qualified to write this document?	**Accuracy** • Make sure author provides an e-mail address or a contact address/phone number. • Know the distinction between author and webmaster.
2. Authority of Web Documents • Who published the document and is it separate from the "webmaster"? • Check the domain of the document. What institution publishes this document? • Does the publisher list his or her qualifications?	**Authority** • What credentials are listed for the author(s)? • Where is the document published? Check URL domain.
3. Objectivity of Web Documents • What goals/objectives does this page meet? • How detailed is the information? • What opinions (if any) are expressed by the author?	**Objectivity** • Determine if page is a mask for advertising; if so information might be biased. • View any web page as you would an infomercial on television. Ask yourself why this was written and for whom.
4. Currentness of Web Documents • When was it produced? • When was it updated? • How up-to-date are the links (if any)?	**Currentness** • How many dead links are on the page? • Are the links current or updated regularly? • Is the information on the page outdated?
5. Coverage of the Web Documents • Are the links (if any) evaluated and do they complement the document's theme? • Is it all images or a balance of text and images? • Is the information presented cited correctly?	**Coverage** • If page requires special software to view the information, how much are you missing if you don't have the software? • Is it free, or is there a fee to obtain the information? • Is there an option for text only, or frames, or a suggested browser for better viewing?

Putting It All Together

- Accuracy. If your page lists the author and institution that published the page and provides a way of contacting him/her, and . . .
- Authority. If your page lists the author credentials and its domain is preferred (.edu, .gov, .org, or .net), and . . .
- Objectivity. If your page provides accurate information with limited advertising and it is objective in presenting the information, and . . .
- Currentness. If your page is current and updated regularly (as stated on the page) and the links (if any) are also up-to-date, and . . .
- Coverage. If you can view the information properly—not limited to fees, browser technology, or software requirement, then:

You may have a high-quality web page that could be of value to your research!

Source: *College and Research Libraries News,* July/August 1998 / 523 soon discovers the value of understanding this library resource. Although many libraries are scrapping the card catalog in favor of the more accessible online system, the card catalog remains an invaluable part of some high school research efforts. The card catalog tells you what books the library has and where you can find them. The catalog includes three kinds of cards: the **author card,** the **title card,** and the **subject card.** When you don't have specific books in mind, then you should examine the subject cards available on your topic choice. If you know the author or title of a particular work you need, you can begin your search by examining one of those cards. Today, since many libraries have computerized their catalogs, you can do title, author, and subject searches with the computerized catalog, too. If you've used one card catalog, you know how to use them all.

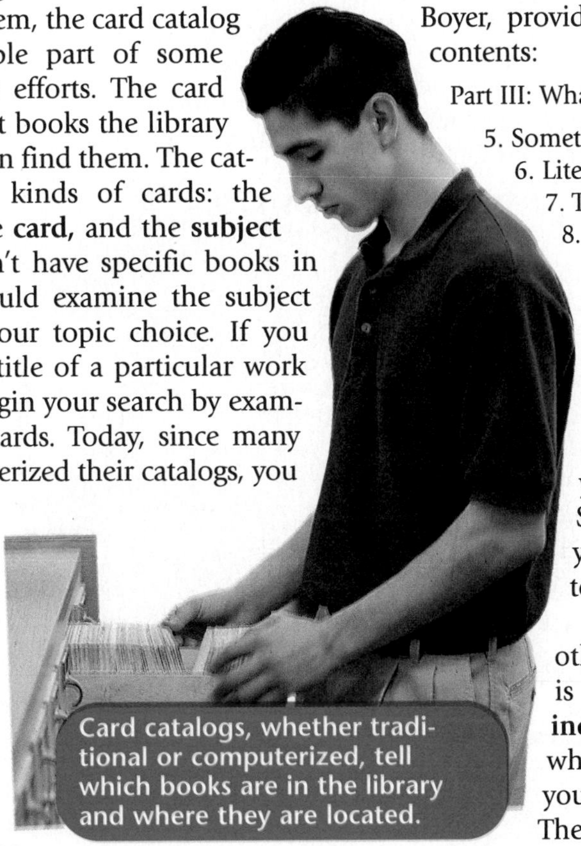

Card catalogs, whether traditional or computerized, tell which books are in the library and where they are located.

When you find an entry on a book you want, record the call number shown on the screen so that you can locate the book on the library shelves. (A tip: When you find the book you are seeking, examine the nearby books for related information. Books are grouped by subject matter, and you might accidentally discover other material that you can use in your speech. Making pleasant discoveries by accident in this way is known as *serendipity.*)

Finding Information in Books

Now that you've found that book, you should become familiar with two sections that are found in most works: the table of contents and the index.

The **table of contents** outlines for you the general plan of the work. A table of contents may include the page number where a chapter begins, a summary of the content of each chapter, and a breakdown of each chapter into its major sections. For example, in the book *High School: A Report on Secondary Education in America,* the author, Ernest Boyer, provides this information in the table of contents:

Part III: What Every Student Should Learn

5. Something for Everyone 71
6. Literacy: The Essential Tool 85
7. The Curriculum Has a Core 94
8. Transition: To Work and Learning 118
9. Instruction: A Time to Learn 141

If you are preparing a speech on the value of literacy, then the table of contents makes it clear that you should turn to page 85. If, however, you are preparing a speech on the Scholastic Assessment Test (SAT), then you might be stumped if you turned to the table of contents.

The index to Boyer's book, on the other hand, informs you that the SAT is discussed on pages 132–134. The **index** (a Latin word meaning "one who points out") tells exactly where you may find particular information. The key to using an index effectively is to look up the right term. In Boyer's book, for example, you must look up the information you seek under *Scholastic* and not under the more commonly used acronym *SAT.*

Finding Periodicals

The computerized catalog is the best starting place in searching for books, but it is not the best place to look for articles in journals, magazines, newspapers, or other periodical publications. For these articles, you will need to look in various indexes.

You might, for instance, try the Newsbank Electronic Index, a computer service that accesses more than 2 million newspaper articles. This reference resource contains information on virtually every newsworthy issue in the United States. In addition, newspapers like the *New York Times* have their own indexes.

For journals and magazines, you should use a periodical index. The listings in a periodical index are usually arranged by subject and author. Perhaps the best-known general index of this type is the *Reader's Guide to Periodical Literature.* The *Reader's Guide* is an index to the articles in some 300 familiar and generally popular magazines. Certain libraries also subscribe to the ProQuest computer system, which holds information on articles from more than 700 different popular and scholarly publications. ProQuest searches a CD periodical index for references to any word or word combination you use to activate the system. Unlike the *Reader's Guide*, ProQuest includes abstracts, or summaries, of the articles so that you can tell whether they are pertinent to your topic.

Once you've used a search system like ProQuest, you'll need to examine and take notes on the best articles.

Other Sources of Information

Libraries contain other sources of information, such as almanacs, atlases, biographies, encyclopedias, and collections of quotations.

Almanacs . . . An almanac is an annual publication that provides you with a storehouse of statistics and general facts. The *World Almanac and Book of Facts,* one of the most popular almanacs, describes itself as a "*compendium* of universal knowledge." This knowledge includes everything from offbeat stories about the world's dumbest robbers to the sports records of your favorite college and professional teams. You will find an almanac useful for learning the order in which the events of a particular year happened, as well as discovering facts about countries and their governments. The *Facts on File Yearbook* and the *Information Please Almanac* are also available in most libraries.

Atlases . . . Maps are collected in atlases—in essence, they are graphic illustrations of many of the facts found in almanacs. *Rand McNally Goode's World Atlas,* for example, may give you geographical information for your speeches. In addition to maps of climate, rainfall, and time zones, the atlas contains tables and indexes concerning water resources, demographics, income, education, life expectancy, population change, labor structure, and westward expansion. A special feature is the pronunciation index. The *Times Atlas of the World,* too, is noted for its coverage and accuracy. Atlases fall out of date as country borders shift or nations change names, however.

Biographies . . . If your speech topic includes discussing a well-known individual, you should consult a biographical reference work. *Biography Index,* published since 1949, is a quarterly, cumulative index to biographical material in both books and magazines.

You should know in researching biographical material that few biographical collections bother to verify facts. Generally, the people who are written about fill out questionnaires. Sometimes they lie. Consider the case of one hoaxer who managed to get a fictitious biography of his dog into *Who's Who in America.*

Unlike *Who's Who, Current Biography* details both positive and negative information about the

WORDS FROM THE WORKPLACE

Andrea Williams
Curriculum Materials Librarian

Q. *What is the biggest problem you face in helping students research topics?*

A. Generally, students are not focused on what they want to talk about. Their topics are usually too broad. They have too much information, and they don't know how to use the information they have. I try to help them narrow their topics or options.

Q. *What important communication skills are students lacking that would help them become better researchers?*

A. They don't seem to be comfortable or skilled at analyzing material and breaking it down into parts. When they come to the reference desk for help, they need to be able to talk with the librarian. They shouldn't be bashful about asking questions because the librarian doesn't know what they really want unless they speak up. I think many students are intimidated by the library. That's why it's so important for librarians to have good oral communication skills.

Q. *Do you feel that computerized research systems make it easier or harder for students to find what they are looking for?*

A. It's a lot easier today for students to get their hands on material. The problem now is that students are inundated with *too much* information, which is not always a good thing. They need to be able to sort through all the information they get from databases, the Internet, etc., and learn how to separate the information.

Q. *Do you have any techniques that you use to point students in the right direction?*

A. I ask them to explain to me in their own words exactly what the instructor expects from the assignment. If they can't tell me in a way that I can understand what they are to do, then they probably don't understand the assignment in the first place. That's a real problem.

biographees. *Current Biography,* issued monthly and then published annually as a combined volume, contains "brief, objective, accurate, and well-documented biographical articles about living leaders in all fields of human accomplishment the world over."

The multivolume *Dictionary of American Biography* (DAB) is known for its scholarly articles and objectivity. The prose in the DAB is a bit more stuffy than that in *Current Biography,* but its thoroughness and reliability make it worth checking.

Encyclopedias ... The American Library Association hails the *Academic American Encyclopedia* (AAE) as "the most current and up-to-date encyclopedia in the English language for high school, college, and adult readers." The AAE has entered the computer age—it is available in three electronic formats as well as the printed version. In coverage and style, though, the new *Encyclopedia Britannica* is reputed to be the most scholarly. No matter which encyclopedia you choose, make certain that you read the introductory material in the first volume. The editors will clue you in on how to find the out-of-the-ordinary material in that particular reference work.

Specialized encyclopedias can help you research some speech topics. For a speech on genetic engineering, for example, you might want to use the *McGraw-Hill Encyclopedia of Science and Technology.* The *International Encyclopedia of Social Sciences* covers topics in fields such as anthropology, history, political science, and sociology.

© The New Yorker Collection 1977, Dana Fradon from cartoonbank.com. All rights reserved.

Quotation Collections . . . Books of quotations are important tools for speakers. You can add spice—a colorful phrase, a clear example, a humorous insight—to almost any speech with a well-chosen quotation. *Bartlett's Familiar Quotations* is probably the most familiar collection and the most widely available. Bartlett's is now even available on CD-ROM for your home computer. You may want to turn to *Peter's Quotations,* though, for the thoughts of more current individuals. If you were preparing a speech on the topic of work satisfaction, you might use the following quotations from the *Oxford Dictionary of Modern Quotations* to suggest that we all approach work differently.

> "One machine can do the work of fifty ordinary men. No machine can do the work of one extraordinary man." (Elbert Hubbard)

> "I do most of my work sitting down; that's where I shine." (Robert Benchley)

THE WEIRD WIDE WEB

INSTANT IMPACT

Erfert Fenton and David Pogue have collected what they believe to be the "weirdest" sites on the Internet. In their book *The Weird Wide Web,* they guide you through UFO lore, vile experiments with Hostess Twinkies, poems about Spam, and sound clips of William "Captain Kirk" Shatner "singing" "Lucy in the Sky with Diamonds."

In the section of the book about food, they speculate on why there are so many web pages devoted to Spam. They wonder: "Is Hormel's canned meat product perhaps a metaphor for the Internet itself—made up of diverse elements, *ubiquitous,* and virtually indestructible?" They advise any serious Spamophile to start with Bob Gorman's Page O' Spam (**www.semantic.rsi.com/spam**), which is the quintessential Spam site—the Spam de la Spam.

The authors admit that the sites they recommend are often here today and gone tomorrow. They suggest, therefore, that you seek out weird sites on your own. Two excellent resources are Yahoo's Useless Pages Index (**www.yahoo.com/Entertainment/Useless_Pages**) and the Centre for the Easily Amused (**www.amused.com**).

Gwendolyn S. Ball, Erfert's mom, comments: "This book is much funnier than Erfert's other computer books."

"If A is a success in life, then A equals X plus Y plus Z. Work is X; Y is play; and Z is keeping your mouth shut." (Albert Einstein)

Albert Einstein was one of the greatest thinkers of our time. How might you use his quotation in a speech?

SECTION 2 REVIEW

Recalling the Facts ...

1. Name the cooperative system by which libraries lend specific books to one another on order.
2. What information do you find in a book's table of contents?

Thinking Critically ...

1. This section introduces the Internet as an important research tool. For some, surfing the 'Net is an addictive pastime. What problems do you see growing out of this addiction?

Taking Charge ...

1. Choosing key words is vital in conducting computer searches. If you wanted to write a speech on the subject of crime, you would first need to narrow the topic. For example, you might narrow it to computer crimes. You can choose key words to create other possible approaches to the general subject of crime. To keep the topic of your speech from being too broad, you might consider typing into the computer some of these key words:

   Alcoholism and crime
   Crimes without victims
   Education and crime
   Hate crimes
   Juvenile delinquency
   Organized crime
   Rural crime
   Violent crime

   For other key words on the topic of crime, consult *Subject Headings,* a reference work published by the Library of Congress.

   Now it's your turn. Share with your classmates the key words that you might use for a subject search on the following topics: drug use, football, the environment, nutrition, military spending, or some other topic that you intend to use for a speech.

SECTION 3 Using What You've Found

Once you've located books or articles on your speech topic, how do you use them effectively? Which information do you include? What about quotations from your sources? This section discusses taking notes and quoting material. Finally, it describes how one student successfully carried out a research plan.

Before you leave the library, take more notes than you think you'll ever need.

Taking Notes

Whenever you investigate a written source of information or interview an expert, you should take notes. A rule of thumb is to record more notes than you think you will ever need because a return trip to the library is inefficient and calling an expert for a second interview is impolite. Still, don't record everything. Select information that makes you think, "Wow, that's important" or "Gee whiz, that sure would sound great to my audience."

Your notes should be organized so that you can easily incorporate them into your speeches. You may find it useful to write your notes on three-by-five or four-by-six cards. If you place only one item of information on each card, then it is a simple matter to shuffle the cards until you're satisfied that you have the subtopics arranged in a logical order.

Each notecard should have a general heading at the top and a complete source citation at the bottom. Use quotation marks if you are copying the text verbatim.

Commitment to Liberty:

"Let every nation know, whether it wishes us well or ill, that we shall pay any price, bear any burden, meet any hardship, support any friend, oppose any foe, in order to assure the survival and success of liberty."

John F. Kennedy from his inaugural address, delivered Friday, January 20, 1961.

Quoting Material: Avoid Heavy Lifting

Plagiarism is copying or imitating the language, ideas, or thoughts of another and passing them off as your original work. In discussing plagiarism, it is important to draw some distinctions. Material considered "common knowledge" is traditionally (by agreement among those in the scholarly community) handled differently than material protected by copyright. That means you do not need to quote a source if you are reciting a fact that is available from many sources (for example, that George Washington had wooden dentures).

The general rule is this: If you're in doubt, name your source. As Mark Twain advised, "When in doubt, tell the truth." If you give credit, of course, then you are not plagiarizing. This brief excerpt from a student speech on the need for preparing for high-stakes tests shows one way to name the quoted source: "Daniel McGinn, in the September 6, 1999, issue of *Newsweek,* advises that 'a good vocabulary is essential for passing most standardized tests, so read to your children early and often.'"

Be careful of web sites that offer to write your papers or speeches for you. Nor should you simply copy and paste information into your speech and call it your own; to do so is plagiarism.

Paraphrasing another's unique ideas is not an acceptable way of avoiding *attribution.* **Paraphrasing,** or simply rewording the original passage, is still taking someone else's ideas. Excessive paraphrasing made Senator Joseph Biden of Delaware the most famous political plagiarist of our time. On September 12, 1987, the *New York Times* reported that Biden, then a presidential candidate, had "borrowed" crucial passages of a campaign speech he gave in Iowa from a speech that Neil Kinnock, a Labour party leader, had delivered during his election campaign in Britain. Compare the following passages from the two speeches.

> Kinnock: "Why am I the first Kinnock in a thousand generations to be able to get to university? . . . Was it because our predecessors were thick? . . . Was it because they were weak, those people who could work eight hours underground and then come up and play football, weak? It was because there was no platform upon which they could stand."

> Biden: "Why is it that Joe Biden is the first in his family ever to go to a university? . . . Is it because our fathers and mothers were not bright? . . . Is it because they didn't work hard, my ancestors who worked in the coal mines of Northeast Pennsylvania and would come up after 12 hours and play football for 4 hours? . . . It's because they didn't have a platform on which to stand."

Biden eventually withdrew from the presidential race.

Author Thomas Mallon highlights the irony in this case: "Nearly all 'original' political speeches are, after all, plagiarized—composed by paid **ghostwriters** before delivery in the first person by the candidate himself: a universally accepted form of mutual back-scratching."

Students find themselves tempted to plagiarize for many reasons: low self-esteem and the pressure to get good grades are often cited as causes. If you feel that you must have that A or that your own ideas are of little worth, plagiarism is not the answer. The consequences of stealing another's work are high. Some students have failed courses, and others have been expelled from school. People have lost their jobs.

For example, in July of 1991, H. Joachim Maitre, dean of the College of Communication at Boston University, resigned after having

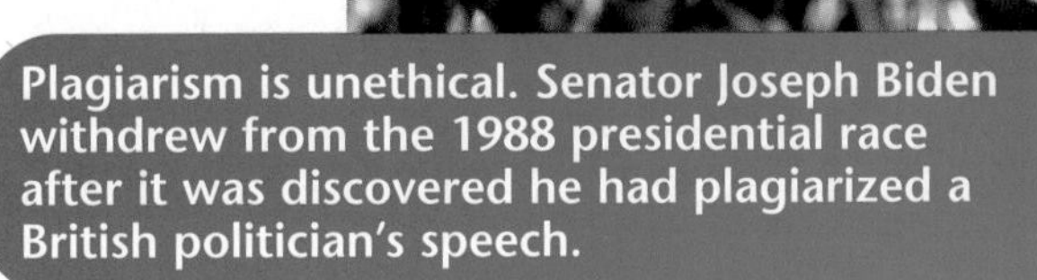

Plagiarism is unethical. Senator Joseph Biden withdrew from the 1988 presidential race after it was discovered he had plagiarized a British politician's speech.

been accused of plagiarism. In Maitre's commencement speech, several passages were identical or nearly identical to an article written by Michael Medved, a PBS film critic. Following the accusation, Maitre said he "must have slipped into a black hole." You can avoid that same black hole by simply doing your own work.

The subjects you discuss with friends at lunch could provide speech topics.

Putting Your Research Together

Ideas for your speeches can come from almost anywhere, but your research should follow a plan. The student speech at the end of this chapter was inspired by a conversation among some high school friends sharing lunch in the cafeteria. One student based his next speech on their discussion of the Internet. His research plan followed the ten steps listed below:

10 Research Techniques for Uncommon Sense

1. **Incorporating Real Life:** I searched my memory for a personal example to use as the introduction and to set up the transition into the thesis statement.
2. **Surfing the 'Net:** I went to the web site used by my friend to become a minister. The specific information found there provided additional concrete details.
3. **Reading Books:** I studied Jim Hightower's book *There's Nothing in the Road but Yellow Stripes and Dead Armadillos.*
4. **Finding Reviews:** I turned to the reference work *Book Review Digest* to discover what the critics were saying about the books I consulted.

I DIDN'T KNOW YOU FELT SO STRONGLY ABOUT FREE SPEECH, SENATOR!
FREE SPEECH IS MY TOP PRIORITY AS A U.S. SENATOR.
MACNELLY

ESPECIALLY THESE DAYS.

©95 Tribune Media Services, Inc. All Rights Reserved
DO YOU HAVE ANY IDEA WHAT THESE SPEECH-WRITER CLOWNS CHARGE?
9/20

Putting Your Research Together

- Incorporating Real Life
- Surfing the Net
- Reading Books
- Finding Reviews
- Poring over Periodicals
- Checking Out Columnists
- Finding Quotes
- Interviewing Sources
- Creating Structure
- Following the Rule of Three

5. **Poring over Periodicals:** I collected popular periodicals like *Time* and *Newsweek,* searching for examples of uncommon sense.
6. **Checking Out Columnists:** The editorial page of my local newspaper was a gold mine of information. Columnists John Leo and Meg Greenfield offered invaluable insights.
7. **Finding Quotes:** I used Microsoft Bookshelf (a software application) for the John Calvin quote. This quote both explained my thesis and provided a transition into the Calvin and Hobbes cartoon.
8. **Interviewing Sources:** I discussed with my math teacher the importance of attending class.
9. **Creating Structure:** I searched through my collection of Calvin and Hobbes cartoon strips for a humorous idea. Fortunately, I was able to tailor three arguments and a conclusion to the four frames of one of the cartoons.
10. **Following the Rule of Three:** Three is the magic number in this speech. I revealed three ways in which we have uncommon sense. Three Calvin quotes. Three reasons why common sense isn't all it's cracked up to be. Three ways in which we pass the blame. Three . . . I think you get the point. I think you get the point. I think you get the point.

SECTION 3 REVIEW

Recalling the Facts ...

1. What is plagiarism?
2. How many ideas should you record on a single notecard?

Thinking Critically ...

1. Most politicians have ghostwriters. Imagine a future in which politicians were required to offer sound ideas instead of sound bites. Would different candidates be elected to office? Why or why not?

Taking Charge ...

1. Study the research plan of the student who wrote the speech on uncommon sense. Choose a topic for a speech that you would like to present. After coming up with at least five steps you would take in researching this topic, share your ideas with the rest of the class.

STUDENT WORK

"Uncommon Sense" *By Chris Marianetti*

This speech by Chris Marianetti, originally written for class, was adapted to use in forensic competition. He delivered it in the national finals of oratory in 1998.

One day at lunch—tater tot Tuesday I believe—I sallied over to my assigned table, actually Sally was nowhere to be seen. I noticed that my classmate and general-good-fellow Chris Noble, surrounded by a group of disciples, was preaching to everyone that he was now an ordained minister. "Doth my ears deceive me?—I thought to myself . . . in an English accent—"Chris Noble an ordained minister? Impossible?" It turns out that Chris was telling the truth. He had become an ordained minister . . . for the Universal Life Church. Chris then informed me of how divinely simple it was; just go on the World Wide Web and click on "become an ordained minister." Furthermore, Chris claimed, now that he had the whole web in his hands, he could even ordain me—against my will. It seems you merely have to fill out an electronic form, and you can, as Chris pontificates, marry people in 48 states and perform services for the Universal Life Church. Chris's teachers are not at all amused—perhaps because he now puts "Reverend Noble" on all his papers. I did have an epiphany, however: not all knowledge is good.

But this speech is not an attack on the Net. It is, instead, an attack on conventional wisdom, an attack on common sense. "Are you listening, Reverend Noble?" Common sense is the knowledge a person attains based on society's conventional wisdom. But as pundit Jim Hightower, author of *There's Nothing in the Road but Yellow Stripes and Dead Armadillos,* points out, "Conventional wisdom is to wisdom what near beer is to beer—only not as close." Too often common sense serves as a sort of thoughtless mastery, and that is not an oxymoron. We master a body of information, but learning facts is not understanding understanding. For example, my calculus teacher tells me it's just common sense that I should never miss a class—end of discussion. But if I listened to Mr. Epler, then I wouldn't be here today, would I? Common sense isn't all it's cracked up to be. My friends tell me if I want to be popular, I have to play soccer. My minister tells me to stop and smell the roses—but I have a chronic sinus condition. And my parents' dream is that someday, if I work real hard, I can be a White House intern. So much for common sense. So it appears what we need today is not common sense, but Uncommon Sense. We need to accept responsibility for our transgressions into the land of blind faith. Just because everybody's doing it or believes it, doesn't make it right . . . even if it is common sense. We need Uncommon Sense and, as the famous theologian John Calvin once stated, "bring the guilty to defend themselves."

Now, I believe that Calvin, the eloquent, effulgent, erudite, six-year-old from the highly popular comic strip "Calvin and Hobbes" explains it even better. So let us examine a cartoon strip frame by frame to see what we can learn about Uncommon Sense. The FIRST FRAME of one of my favorite Bill Watterson cartoons presents the usual rambling, intelligent, and beloved Calvin proclaiming, "Nothing I do is my fault." But, unfortunately, for our society, many have now accepted this no-fault ideology. I mean, truthfully, it's been around since Adam and Eve—who better to demonstrate, right? You see, prior to the apple incident, they had not formally signed a contract with God specifying the details of the Eden contract. Or they could, as Meg Greenfield states in her article "The Apple Looked Good," "claim temptation itself as an extenuating circumstance." Greenfield, in her column in *Newsweek,* "The Last Word," often evaluates society's obsession with laying of the blame. In the July 1997 issue she examines exactly how politicians have done this. And the last new wisdom to pop out of the politician's bag of dodging tricks is that of complication. The press has certainly helped here.

When things appear to become too complex, the press asks, "This is getting too complicated; where are the dancing bears?"

In the SECOND FRAME of this cartoon Calvin now complains, "My family is dysfunctional and my parents won't empower me; consequently, I'm not self-actualized." His no-fault ideology has progressed one step further. He now needs something to blame his problems on. In other words, he's allowed to do these things because his parents won't empower him. And our non-toon society has also found a loophole to allow them not to take responsibility. While a six-year-old cites his parents for allowing him to misbehave, we cite our rights—it's only common sense, right? In fact, in an article entitled "A Man's Got a Right to Rights," syndicated columnist John Leo examines some of our new-founded rights. He complains that, "freshly minted rights are so common these days, they even pop out of cereal boxes." So let us examine some of these cereal box rights. Take, for example, the Fundamental Right of Freedom . . . for trees and rocks. Women's right to use a men's restroom. A prisoner's right to procreate before being executed. And, finally, my personal favorite: the right to steal or burn bundles of newspapers so that others can't read them. While these examples might be amusing they are symptomatic of a much more insidious consequence. It seems we can no longer blame others for their actions either, even if these actions include killing another human being. Recently, the *Chronicle of Higher Education* reported that students have been unable to oppose such moral wrongdoings like slavery, human sacrifice, and even the Holocaust because they feel they are in no position to judge the morality of others. They ask, "Who am I to judge?" And this view, known as nonjudgmentalism, is sweeping across our nation, and, according to professor Robert Simon of Hamilton College, is apparent in 10 to 20 percent of his students. Clearly, our moral compass has lost direction.

In the THIRD FRAME of this cartoon Calvin now rationalizes that, "my behavior is addictive, functioning in a diseased process of toxic codependency. I need holistic healing and wellness before I'll accept any responsibility for my actions." It seems that Calvin, like many in America, finds it easier to blame his problems on a disease or disorder than to accept responsibility for them. Take, for example, an automobile driver. Let's say he is tailing your car, honks rudely from behind you, swerves viciously into the next lane, cuts you off, flips you off, and yells obscenities in his loudest voice. Well, we can no longer refer to these individuals as irate swine. No, according to the American Psychiatric Association, these individuals appear to be suffering from a severe case of—road rage: an official mental disorder about to be certified and appropriately added to the *Diagnostic and Statistical Manual of Mental Disorders.* In an article in the *Washington Post* arguing that mental disorders have now become a growth industry, we learn of some of our new disorders. Like caffeine-induced anxiety disorder, inhalant abuse, or even telephone scatologia—that's those of you who are addicted to making heavy-breathing sexual phone calls . . . you know who you are. Perhaps they will invent a disease for us orators—how about "oratorical apprehension disorder"? It's only common sense. The *New York Times* reported last year that if only half the number of growing disorders are paid for, like the real ones, the cost will be roughly $75 billion. It's no wonder why we invent a disease or disorder for everything under and over the rainbow—everybody's doing it, doing it, doing it—after all it's only common sense.

In the FOURTH and final FRAME of this cartoon Calvin now admits, "I love the culture of victimhood." And what is the lovable tiger Hobbes's response? "I think one of us needs to stick his head in a bucket of ice water." Now, granted, ice water is a solution, but probably not the one we are looking for. Life is not a cartoon, and uncommon sense is still uncommon. But, in a society threatened by a no-fault ideology, cereal box rights, and mental disorders becoming a growth industry, there are no easy answers. Uncommon sense begins with each uncommon person. So, each of us has to decide: I will no longer be limited by the common sense of others; I will think for myself. And although the Reverend Noble is not among us, let us pray.

CHAPTER 8 Review and Enrichment...

Looking Back

Listed below are the major ideas discussed in this chapter.

- Before you start accumulating information, you should have a research plan.
- Thorough research will increase your credibility as a speaker.
- Consulting with a reference librarian can save you valuable time.
- A database stores related information.
- The card catalog or computerized catalog is your way to know what books the library has and where to find them.
- The Internet is a communication tool but it is not always a panacea for researchers.
- The table of contents outlines the general plan of a book.
- The index helps you locate particular information in a book.
- The best-known periodical index is the *Reader's Guide to Periodical Literature.*
- Notes should be organized so that you can easily incorporate them into your speeches.
- When taking notes, you should place only one item of information on each notecard.
- Plagiarism is intellectually dishonest.

Speech Vocabulary

Match the speech term on the left with the definition on the right.

1. database
2. online
3. index
4. table of contents
5. interlibrary loan
6. paraphrasing
7. plagiarism
8. ghostwriter

a. a cooperative system among libraries
b. accessible via the Internet
c. a collection of related information
d. restating in your own words
e. using another person's ideas as your own
f. someone who writes for another person
g. the general plan of a work
h. from the Latin for "one who points out"

General Vocabulary

Define the following terms and use each in a sentence.

prerequisite	microcosm	nuclear family	compendium
entrepreneur	panacea	ubiquitous	attribution
alienate	haven	crooned	serendipity

CHAPTER 8 Review and Enrichment...

To Remember

Answer the following questions based on your reading of the chapter.

1. The ancient Greeks referred to the process of accumulating information as building a ______________.
2. Libraries in cities frequently double as informal ______________.
3. The ______________ is an index to the articles in over 300 popular magazines.
4. ______________ is a Latin word meaning "one who points out."
5. ______________ is copying or imitating the language, ideas, or thoughts of another and passing them off as your own.

To Do

1. With the help of a reference librarian, find articles that discuss plagiarism. Discuss your findings in class.
2. Ask a librarian to help you devise a scavenger hunt in the reference section. The hunt should acquaint you with some of the most important reference works, including a dictionary of word and phrase origins.

To Talk About

1. What is wrong with excessive paraphrasing if you give credit to the original source?
2. To support their positions on controversial issues, politicians often quote opinion polls. What issues in your school would lend themselves to opinion polling?

To Write About

1. Write an essay about plagiarism. A possible topic: Why intellectual honesty matters.
2. Write an essay in which you examine censorship as it affects what books are on the shelves of a school library.
3. According to author Richard Saul Wurman, "Information anxiety is produced by the ever-widening gap between what we understand and what we think we should understand. It is the black hole between data and knowledge." Write a creative essay or a play describing a typical day in the life of someone terrified by the information explosion.

Related Speech Topics

Ghostwriting: the invisible touch
To quote or not to quote, that is the question
Information skills: a survival course
The school librarian: a friend in deed
Censorship: how far is too far?
Information anxiety
The Internet: How valid is the information?

CHAPTER 9

ORGANIZING YOUR SPEECH

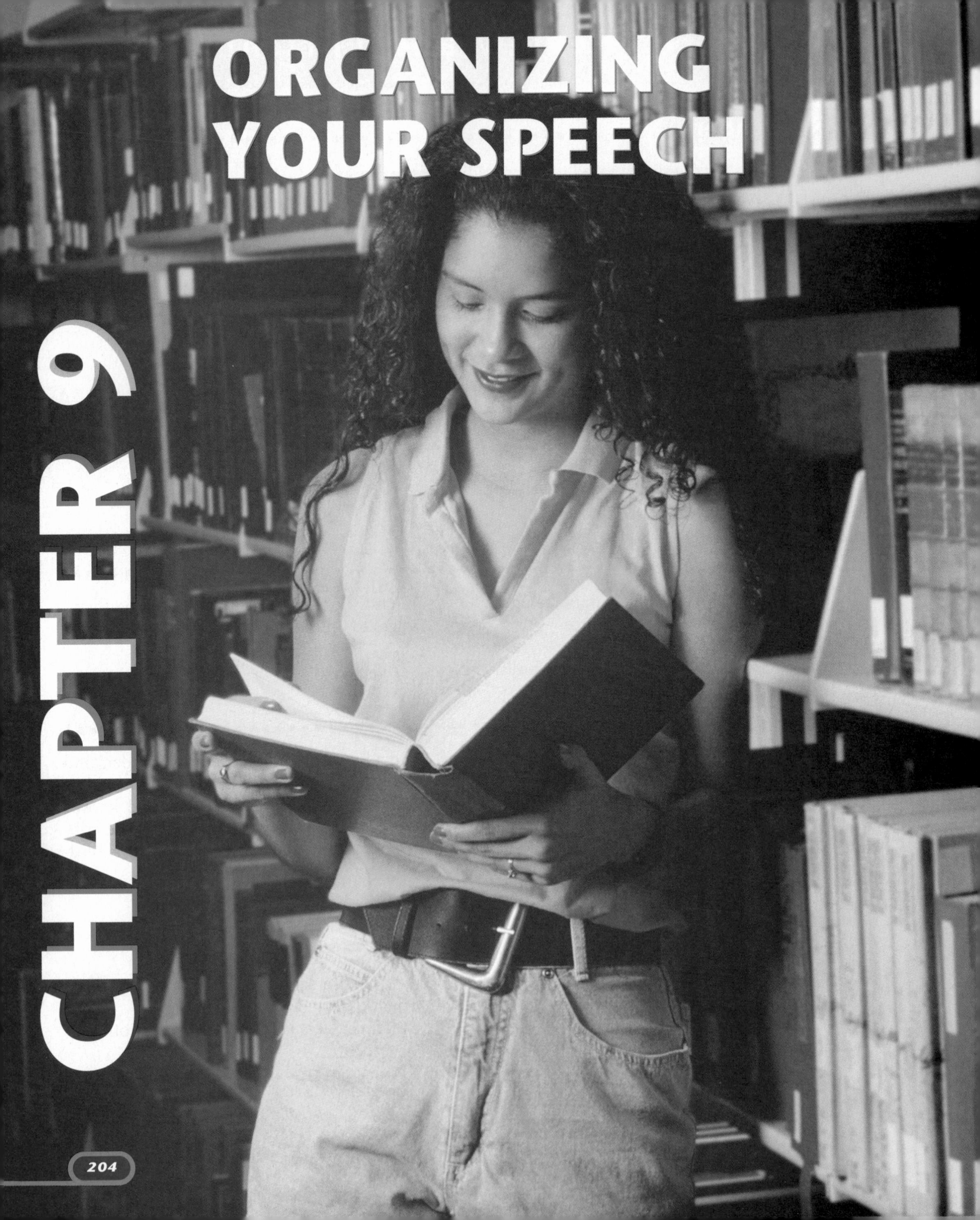

"To me, things are organized when all of the piles of clothes in my room are stacked to the same height!"

–Lucille Ball,
American comedienne, star of *I Love Lucy*

Learning Objectives

After completing this chapter, you will be able to do the following.

- Use effective strategies to organize and to outline presentations.
- Use effective verbal strategies in presentations.
- Apply effective organization to aspects of your life.
- Develop appropriate introductions and conclusions for your speeches that will give positive first and final impressions.
- Develop a meaningful body for your speech that shows clarity and logical progression.
- Identify and use the various patterns of organization for speeches.

Chapter Outline

Following are the main sections in this chapter.

1. The Introduction
2. The Body
3. The Conclusion

New Speech Terms

In this chapter, you will learn the meanings of the speech terms listed below.

introduction
rhetorical questions
quotation
narrative
link
thesis statement
preview statement
body
outline
purpose statement
subordination
main heading
supporting materials
transition
chronological pattern
climactic pattern
spatial pattern
cause-effect pattern
problem-solution pattern

General Vocabulary

Expanding your general vocabulary will help you become a more effective communicator. Listed below are some words appearing in this chapter that you should make part of your everyday vocabulary.

equilibrium
vested
gigantic
fiasco
jeopardy
enhanced
haphazardly
intensification
indented
inhibition

Looking AHEAD

You don't have to read reams of paper to realize what it means not to be organized. Homework doesn't get finished, phone calls don't get made, jobs don't get accomplished, invitations don't get sent out, the car doesn't get washed, and the alarm clock doesn't go off in the morning. Whether at the library or at work, without proper organization, you waste much time and energy in your frantic rush to find what you are after or to meet deadlines.

In addition to sacrificing time and energy, you might also lose out educationally if you lack organizational skills. A study done at UCLA's Higher Education Research Institute found that over 30 percent of all students who entered a four-year college or university had to take special courses designed to strengthen their study and organizational skills.

Organization offers you a sense of balance and personal *equilibrium.* Organization helps you take the loose ends of your life, put them in order, and, in the process, keep sane! When eighteenth-century English statesman and orator Edmund Burke said, "Good order is the foundation of all good things," he was implying that through structure and organization, both individuals and societies have the potential to progress.

Thus, in this chapter, you will learn about organization and about how directed planning can often be beneficial in your personal life, your life at work, and your speaking. In addition, you will work with the three parts of the speech—the introduction, the body, and the conclusion—and examine the individual components that make up each. You will learn about outlining and then examine five types of organizational patterns that can help you develop your thoughts. You will also recognize how important it is for the introduction, the body, and the conclusion to work together for maximum speaking effectiveness.

Introduction

In the ancient Babylonian culture (2700–538 B.C.), a home builder had to "bet his life"—literally—that his house would hold up. According to the Babylonians' Code of Hammurabi, if a builder made a house that collapsed and caused the death of the house's owner, the builder was also put to death. Needless to say, the builder had a profoundly *vested* interest in constructing a house that was guaranteed to be strong and reliable.

Blueprints and outlines will keep you organized.

The consequences of a poorly presented speech aren't nearly so dramatic or life threatening. The "death of an idea," however, might be the result when a speech fails to communicate because it hasn't been built with care. One way that you as an effective speaker can provide this care is to present your message with clear organization.

Do the following statements sound familiar?

- "How could I forget to do that?"
- "We should have done this step first!"
- "I have no idea how I'm going to get this job done!"

If so, there is a good chance that you need a lesson in effective organization. Effective organization is a systematic plan that makes sense and helps you to get things done. Generally speaking, organization is the logical grouping and ordering of "like" parts. This systematic grouping and logical arrangement allow you to keep a handle on what is happening.

SECTION 1 The Introduction

Thomas Boyden, an executive for Shell Oil, says that when he was interviewing top collegiate applicants for prospective management positions, he would give each applicant approximately 15 minutes. During that 15-minute evaluation, he would observe three different things: (1) the confidence and congeniality that the applicant showed at first, (2) the sense of logic, organization, and self-discipline that the applicant could exhibit "under fire" during the interview, and (3) the poise that the applicant showed when leaving the interview. In other words, the interview would be divided into three distinct parts, and each part was important in making the whole interview a success.

What is true in the business world is also true in the oral communication world. Just like Boyden's interview, your speech should be organized into three distinct parts that, when presented effectively, can make a positive impression. We now examine these three parts, starting here with the introduction.

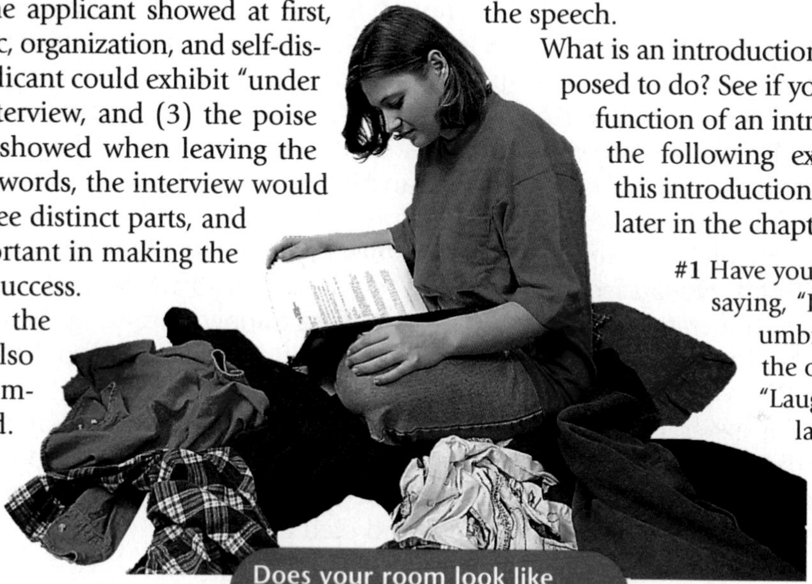

Does your room look like this? Does this show whether or not you are organized?

A secondary teacher once said that he was confident that his students would always give speeches that had an introduction, a body, and a conclusion—but not necessarily in that order! It is your job to make sure that your speeches are organized so that you put things in the correct order. That means you should begin with a well-thought-out **introduction.**

Whatever you are doing, isn't it important to get off to a good start? Doing so often supplies you with the momentum and confidence that you need to complete your task. Many speakers say that, psychologically, the toughest part of a speech is the beginning, or the introduction. It is during your introduction that you find out whether your audience accepts you. Consequently, a good introduction can "make or break" you because it sets the tone—at least in your head—for the remainder of the speech.

What is an introduction, and what is it supposed to do? See if you can determine the function of an introduction by reading the following example. (Remember this introduction. It will be referred to later in the chapter.)

> **#1** Have you ever heard the saying, "Let a smile be your umbrella"? What about the observation, "Laugh and the world laughs with you"? Both of these statements deal with how a positive attitude and a sense of humor can make a bad situation a little bit better for both you and the people around you. **#2** However, did you know that your ability to laugh can mean a great deal more than a pleasant smile or momentary delight? As a matter of fact, laughter can be very beneficial in many ways. **#3** Consequently, I would like to discuss the various areas in your lives where laughter can play a significantly positive role. **#4** Let's take a look at how laughter can help you on the job, with your friends and family, and with your health.

Do you see how the interesting information in the beginning (indicated by #1) might encourage an audience to listen? Next, do you see how there is a clear connection made between the introductory

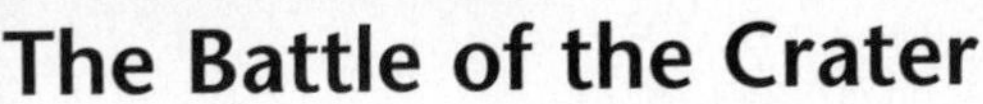

COMMUNICATION Breakdown

The Battle of the Crater

One of the most famous battles of the Civil War took place at Petersburg, Virginia, in 1864. Under the leadership of General Ambrose Everett Burnside, federal forces had undertaken the monumental engineering task of burrowing below the enemy and forming a shaft 500 feet in length that stretched under the Confederate lines. The shaft was then filled with four tons of dynamite. When the dynamite was ignited, the explosion blew more than 250 rebel soldiers high into the air and created a *gigantic* hole that measured over 150 feet long, 50 feet wide, and 30 feet deep! The blast was so powerful that both sides stood in awe at its effect, but it didn't take long for the Southern troops, shocked and stunned, to hurry for cover.

The problem for the North was that no clear plan had been developed for a follow-through. General Burnside, as historians tell it, was so shaken by the sight of the blast that he stood at the back of his troops and drank rum. He gave no verbal command. As a result, the Battle of the Crater turned into a *fiasco.*

Acting mainly on instinct, Northern soldiers charged *into* the crater, not to the left or the right of it. No ladders were taken in the unorganized attack, and the men reached the end of the crater only to find that they were trapped. Realizing the plight of the North, the Southern troops regrouped and picked off the federal soldiers like "fish in a barrel."

Civil War experts agree that the absence of effective organization and leadership by the North not only prevented a glorious victory at Petersburg but also cost hundreds of Northern soldiers their lives! To this day, the crater remains in Petersburg, Virginia, as a monument to the soldiers who fought and died there.

Questions

1. What should Northern leaders have done prior to setting off the explosion?
2. Who do you feel is specifically at fault for this tragedy?

material and the speech topic (indicated by #2)? Also, do you see exactly what the speech will be about (indicated by #3)? Finally, do you see a clear statement of the areas that will be discussed in the speech (indicated by #4)?

Basically, an introduction does four things:

1. It gets the attention of the audience.
2. It provides a clear link from your attention-getter to your speech topic, or thesis statement.
3. It gives your specific thesis statement.
4. It presents a preview of the major areas that will be discussed.

Attention-Getters

The first words that you say to an audience must make them want to listen to you. You must "grab" your audience's attention. You have probably heard that telling a joke is a good way to start your speech. No one will deny that humor is refreshing and that everyone likes to laugh. You must ask yourself, however, what type of humor works for you. Is a humorous opening appropriate for your speech topic? What happens if nobody laughs? A humorous approach can backfire.

While it is true that a light, funny attention-getter can be a tremendous boost to your confidence, you do not have to use humor or a funny story to get off to a solid start. Examine your personality and then realistically answer the following questions: "What works for me, and what do I feel comfortable presenting?" With this in mind, let's examine five types of attention-getters that can help you to get your speech off to a smooth start.

A humorous opening worked for this speech; but use humor cautiously.

1. Asking Questions ... One of the best methods of gaining an audience's attention is to get audience members directly involved in what you are saying. Immediately asking them a question or a series of questions not only fires up their curiosity about your topic, it also makes them active participants in your speech.

If you were doing a speech called "The Power of Word Building," you might begin by asking your audience this:

> How many of you know the meaning of the word *verisimilitude*? Do you know what *veracity* means? What about the word *verity*? Well, all three of these words have something to do with the word *truth*, and I wouldn't be telling you the truth if I didn't confess that I had to look these words up in a dictionary. However, building vocabulary is a challenge that each of us should accept if . . .

How about these questions for a speech on shifting blame:

> Have you ever heard someone say, "The devil made me do it"? Have you ever heard the expression "Don't blame me. It's not my fault"? If you answered yes to one or both of these questions, then you would probably agree with me that many people in today's society find it easy to make excuses and blame someone or something else for their problems. I would like to talk about . . .

ORGANIZING YOUR SPEECH—AND YOUR LIFE!

INSTANT IMPACT

Mary Sue Alley Crommelin, past president of the Virginia Association of Speech Coaches, offered these words regarding her interpretation of the word *organization:*

"The organization of a speech begins with an abundance of examples. It is then our job to analyze, to evaluate, and then to put them in a logical sequence. How do they relate? How do they apply? What conclusions can we draw? How does each advance the purpose of the thesis?

The writing of a speech is much like life. Each involves choices. Each involves 'evidence' that has to be sorted. We have to sift through all that comes our way, and, in short, throw some choices away as quickly as we would toss aside some pieces of evidence for a speech. Why? Because some choices simply don't fit!

The choices that we make in life—as in a speech—will logically and predictably lead to certain results. We'd better know how to organize and sequence life's events into something meaningful . . . both for ourselves and for humanity."

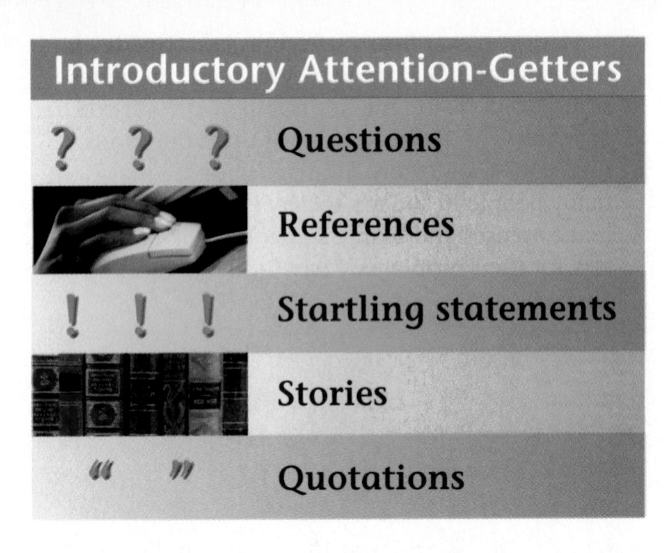

Do you see how questions can provide the attention-getting spark you want to begin your speech? Sometimes you might ask audience members to respond to your questions by actually raising their hands or speaking out loud. But beware! While this technique can sometimes promote spirited audience involvement, it can also lead to chaos and loss of concentration if the responses to your questions don't turn out as you expected. Are you prepared to handle such a situation? Is it worth the risk?

Often, it is best to use rhetorical questions. **Rhetorical questions,** like the ones given in the examples, don't really demand a verbal response. Instead, they ask the members of your audience to answer silently in their heads. Rhetorical questions are also "safe" questions because they often answer themselves: "Do any of you like to get your feelings hurt?" "Do any of us in this room want our friends or families to join the thousands who die each year because of people who drink and drive?" Such questions don't demand a response, but they do challenge your audience to think. This type of mental stimulation offers you the potential for immediate attention-getting success.

Your audience may enjoy answering questions in your speech. If you use questions, however, you need to be ready for any answer.

2. Making References ... Like asking questions, making references can allow you to work well with your audience. You might refer to people in the audience, your physical surroundings, other speakers who are on the program, or the significance of the occasion. This approach allows you to be comfortable, congenial, and conversational with your audience by including it in your opening remarks. Audiences like to be included, and including them provides a type of speaker-audience unity that says, "You and I are in this speech together!" For instance, you might say this:

> I see that John and Ina are in the audience. When we first started this class project over two months ago, they were the ones who provided the leadership and enthusiasm that the rest of us needed at that time. The word *leadership* is exactly what I wish to talk about tonight because . . .

Or you might say this:

> For some reason, every time that we are in this auditorium, the air-conditioning is out. Maybe we should all bring our own fans next time. However, the temperature might not be the only thing that is "sticky" tonight. My topic, "Why AIDS Needs to Be Talked about in Schools," could also make some people warm and uncomfortable. I have confidence, nevertheless, that if we work together . . .

As usual, of course, you must use good taste and common sense. For example, it might be risky to make a casual reference to someone in the audience whom you barely know. Making references should get you off to a positive start with your listeners, not put your speech in *jeopardy.* In general, though, audiences appreciate a speaker who shows that he or she is aware of and in tune with what is happening.

3. Making a Startling Statement ...

Sometimes your best attention-getter is one that jolts your audience into paying attention.

One student spoke to a high school about the problems associated with violence in society. While she spoke, she comfortably moved her right hand as if she were "keeping the beat" to a song that only she heard. Her first words were these:

> I love music. I love dancing. I love how men and women, young and old, rich or poor, can move and smile and laugh and keep the rhythm to their favorite songs. However, today I'm not here to talk about music—because, ironically, every time that my hand comes down to "keep the beat," a young child is physically or sexually abused in this country. And the violence is real . . .

Picture yourself in this audience. Wouldn't you be immediately drawn in by the speaker and to the tremendous power of her message?

Startling statements can jolt your audience into listening.

You may also choose to use startling statistics to grab the attention of the audience. While conducting your research, notice any data or studies that might surprise the listeners and make them even more interested in the topic. For example, if your research indicated that one in ten families will be the victims of a drunk driving accident, or that one in five people will be the victim of a violent crime, you may be able to shock your audience into the reality of these social problems. Use the numbers to quantify the extent of the issue in our lives and to grab the audience's attention.

As impressive as this technique might appear, it has its drawbacks. Too many speakers have tried to startle their audiences, only to find that their attention-getters offended people instead. Don't be foolish. An audience will forgive an honest mistake, but it will rarely forgive bad taste! Yes, the startling statement can work for you, but you must use sound judgment and take the time to know your audience.

4. Giving a Quotation ...

You deliver a **quotation** each time you repeat the exact words that someone else has said. Giving a quotation is a popular attention-getter. For one thing, quotations can add a degree of style and sophistication to speech presentations. For another, quotations are abundant and fairly easy to find, so you can surely find one that fits your needs.

Choose quotations that are clear and appropriate for your speech topic and select authors who are reliable and can be trusted. Although some famous people need no introduction, it is a good practice while delivering your attention-getter to give your audience some idea of who your author is and what he or she has done that is noteworthy. Why is this the case? Generally speaking, audiences are likely to be impressed if the sources that you are quoting are impressive.

Here's how one student started his speech on "What Has Happened to Friendship?"

> "First in war—first in peace—and first in the hearts of his countrymen." These are the words that began Revolutionary War General Henry Lee's famous funeral oration for George Washington. The quotation shows us a man of conscience and a man who cared for his fellow man. However, do we care for our fellow man today the same as Washington did in his day? I would like to take a look at . . .

The quotation immediately gives the speech an academic and historical flavor. Henry Lee's words say to the audience, "Take this speech seriously and give it your attention, please!" Another student, speaking on "Americans—Why Are We So Gullible?" began with a similar historical quotation:

> "You can fool all of the people some of the time and you can fool some of the people all of the time, but you can't fool *all* of the people *all* of the time." Abraham Lincoln, the author of this quotation, might have added the words "*except* in America," because Americans are often easy prey for those wishing to make a fast buck. Let's examine why Americans are so gullible and take a look . . .

Don't think that your quotation must be serious or must have been delivered by someone who lived centuries ago. On the contrary, some of the most effective quotations are lighter and have been given by people who are alive right now. Take the time to search through your resources so that you can find the quotation that will be the perfect attention-getter for your speech.

5. Telling a Story . . . One of the most popular attention-getters is the **narrative**—the telling of a story. Everyone loves a story, especially one that is told well. Illustrations and personal accounts can quickly give you an "in" with your audience because these stories give your personality a chance to work and are so much in demand. Americans are storytellers (and story *listeners*) at heart.

Keep in mind that your story should be short and to the point. Don't get so caught up in your account that you lose sight of the purpose of your speech. The best stories are the ones that hold the interest of the audience yet lead clearly into your speech topic.

Have you had an experience that you would call special? Have you gone through some heart-stopping ordeal that you would like to share? Such experiences can make good stories. Here is an example:

> A few weeks ago, my mom and dad had gone out for the evening and I was alone at home. About 2 A.M. I heard a noise by the downstairs window. Even though I hoped that the sounds would go away, they didn't. As a matter of fact, they got louder. It sounded as if someone were struggling to reach the latch of the window. I was petrified, but somehow I managed to go downstairs. Slowly, I moved the curtain to see what was outside. You can imagine my fear when I saw two eyes looking right back at me! It was a *raccoon*. The good news is that, in this instance, I was able to deal with my fear. The bad news is that I almost collapsed in the process. What does *fear* mean and how can we . . .

Remember how much you loved stories when you were young? Everyone loves stories!

Stories can be insightful, and they can also be fun for you to deliver and your audience to hear. And stories don't have to be personal. They can be interesting accounts about other people, places, events, and so on. Any story can be an effective attention-getter if it sets the mood that you are after and creates an effective picture in the minds of your listeners that relates to your speech thesis.

Let's move on to the next aspect of the introduction, the link.

The Link

Probably the section of the introduction that students most often overlook when preparing their speeches is the **link.** It serves two purposes. First, the link is the statement that comes between the attention-getter and the thesis statement and logically connects the two. It does you little good to have a clever attention-getter if the audience sees no relation between it and the focus of your speech. Second, the link should develop a "bridge" between the audience and the topic. Here, your objective is to connect with audience members so that they are motivated to listen to your topic. Much like with the attention-getter, you are continuing to draw in their interest by helping them to understand the value of the topic. This helps the audience to feel that listening is worthwhile. The motivation may stem from showing your audience how your speech has common ground—or relevance to their lives. You could also motivate them by showing them how your topic has real significance, or why it might be "a big deal" in their lives.

Read the following introduction, which was prepared and delivered by a high school student, Carmella Hise. Pay particular attention to the role of the link sentences (italicized): The link to the topic is labeled A. The link to the audience is labeled B.

> "I'm going to let you in on a secret that will change your lives. Girls, for just $10, you can learn what makes a guy fall in love and how to make him want you! The right way to flirt! If you act now, we'll rush you our best-seller, *Secrets of Kissing*. You see, it's all part of the 'Get Him System,' G.H.—a no-fail love guide that tells you the truth. No more old-fashioned advice that you already know."
>
> Believe it or not, this is more than a mere attention-getter for my speech. This is taken from an actual ad found in the February edition of *Young Miss* magazine. (A) *My speech for today will deal with one of the words in the last sentence of the ad,* old-fashioned; *for it is my opinion that, contrary to what is stated in the* Get Him *ad, maybe a sense of old-fashioned tradition is exactly what we need in today's society.* (B) *According to William Bennett, former Secretary of Education and noted author, "Increasingly, Americans are lacking a solid grounding in traditional values."* Therefore, I would specifically like to examine some traditional American values . . .

In addition to clearly explaining her attention-getter, Carmella logically linked the ad in the magazine, and specifically the word *old-fashioned,* to her speech thesis. She then took it a step further and pointed out that her topic had significance because, more and more, Americans are not receiving an adquate background in "values education." She chose to use a noted authority who agreed with her position. This helped her to gain credibility. It also showed the importance of her topic. Therefore, her link established that her topic is one that we need to learn more about—so that we can have a better ethical foundation.

What does Carmella Hise think about the values portrayed in the type of teen magazine these girls are reading?

Do you see how Carmella's link took her where she wanted to be—ready to state her speech thesis?

Even though the link can be more than one sentence long, usually one sentence can do the job. The effectiveness and impact of both your attention-getter and your speech thesis are *enhanced* when your link statement connects as it should. In addition, you stand a better chance of "connecting" with your audience.

The Thesis Statement

The third part of the introduction is the sentence that will tell your audience exactly what you will be speaking about. This sentence, which will be discussed further in Chapter 13, "Speeches to Inform," is called the **thesis statement.**

If you have a catchy attention-getter and a smooth link to a thesis statement that is vague, your speech may be unclear. The reason that you wanted to get the audience's attention is that you had something worthwhile to say. That something is your thesis statement, or the focus of what your speech is going to address. Your audience must never wonder, "What exactly is this speech about?" A brief, to-the-point thesis statement can help you avoid such a problem.

One way to make sure that your audience knows that you are introducing your thesis is to say it. Don't permit your audience to take an organizational "detour." Saying something like "This leads me to my thesis, which is . . . " can be a smart way to make sure that you and your audience are both following the same communication road map.

Generally, a thesis should both clarify the overall goal of your speech (to inform, to persuade, or to entertain) and state your specific topic. Be sure to let your audience know the particular focus of your topic.

For example, if you are going to inform the audience, use words in the thesis such as

Today, I will *inform* you about . . .
My goal is to *explain* . . .
With this information, I hope you will better *understand* . . .

If the goal is to persuade, use words or phrases such as

I want to *persuade* you that . . .
My goal is to *convince* you that . . .
It is my belief that each of you *should* . . .

In addition to stating the goal of your speech, the thesis should also clarify the angle or slant of your topic. To simply say you are going to talk about "music" is too vague. Tell the audience the specific focus of your topic. Perhaps you want to specifically inform the audience about the different types of summer music programs offered by your community. Or, perhaps you want to convince students that there are distinct benefits to joining the school's marching band. Both speeches deal with music, but their goals and slants are different. Your audience deserves to know the exact point of your speech. It will also help you to keep your speech focused and your information on target.

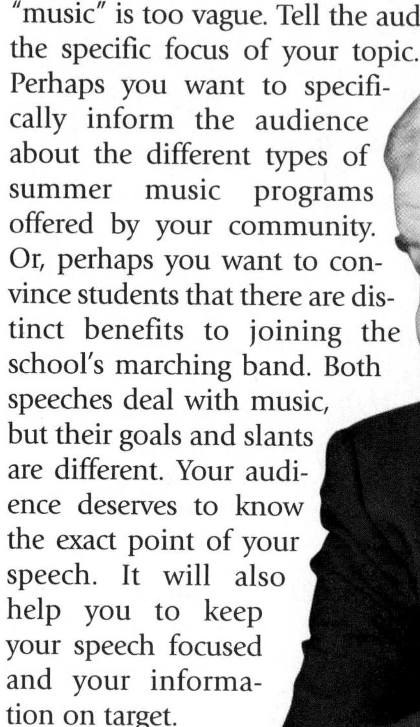

Speakers often use gestures to emphasize their thesis statements.

The Preview Statement

If you have gone to the movies or watched television, you have no doubt seen previews of upcoming films or television episodes. These brief "snapshots" usually focus on the high points of what you will be seeing later. Similarly, speeches include previews in the form of preview statements.

The **preview statement** is usually one sentence at the end of the introduction that gives the audience an overview of the major areas that will be discussed in the body of the speech. For instance, if you were giving a speech on the negative effects of alcohol, your preview might mention alcohol's physical, mental, and societal effects. A speech on success stories in the Olympics could include a preview statement on physical and mental preparation.

Of course, the major areas mentioned in your preview statement will be repeated later in the body of your speech with specific examples added for support. Often, the examples and evidence you have collected will determine what your areas of discussion will be and, thus, what your preview statement should include. Although not all speeches have a preview statement, it is often wise to provide one for your audience. Audience members can't catch everything the first time. They might miss your main points when said within the body of your speech. A preview statement tells your audience where your speech will be heading and, as a result, makes the body of your speech easier for your listeners to follow.

A speech on Olympic athlete Jesse Owens could include that he was honored with a commemorative stamp.

SECTION 1 REVIEW

Recalling the Facts ...

1. What is the name for the part of the introduction that students most often overlook when preparing their speeches?
2. You want your audience to listen to you because you have something worthwhile to say. What do you call that something, or the statement in the introduction that is the focus of your speech?
3. What is the last part of the introduction that gives the audience snapshots of the areas that you will cover in your speech?
4. There are various types of attention-getters that you could use in your introduction. One very popular type is the narrative. What does the word *narrative* mean?

Thinking Critically ...

1. Nineteenth-century British writer Baron Lytton once said, "Every great person exhibits the talent of organization—whether it be in a poem, a philosophical system, a policy, or a strategy." In other words, being organized is an attribute shared by most successful people. Analyze and evaluate how organization can be important when you are (a) trying to get a job, (b) on the job, (c) having a party, or (d) trying to solve a problem that you have with a friend.

Taking Charge ...

1. Select one of the attention-getting devices from the chapter and use it as a means of introducing a person in your class to the rest of the class. Be sure to explain your attention-getter, link it to the fact that you are introducing someone, introduce the person, and then mention two areas in which the person is interested. Have some fun, but stay focused on your objective—providing an introduction that will make your friend glad that you are the one doing the introduction. Write out what you are going to say before you do the introducing.

SECTION 2 The Body

The **body** of the speech is the heart, the brain, even the nerve center of the entire presentation. It is the place where you exhibit in an organized manner your powers of persuasion and reasoning. Audiences need to be convinced. They need to be informed. They need to be shown. After your audience hears your introduction and knows your speech thesis, you need to show or prove your point. You do this in the body of the speech.

Let's take a look at two important ways to make the body of your speech clear and convincing: outlining and using organizational patterns.

Outlining Your Speech

Have you ever taken a trip that involved driving a long distance? If so, someone in your family probably used a map to study various routes and then mark the selected route for the drive.

Your outline is your road map.

An **outline** is the speaker's map. It is the way that you give form and direction to your organization. An outline allows you to know not only where you are going but also where you are and where you have been. An outline keeps you on track.

The author Victor Hugo is credited with the quote, "No army can withstand the strength of an idea whose time has come." However, few will support an idea that they can't understand. Similarly, few people can follow a speech that appears to be *haphazardly* thrown together or that is difficult to comprehend because of poor organization.

You have probably heard the story about the driver who is miserably lost. Miles off the main highway, he stops to ask a farmer for directions, only to be told, "Sorry, I know where you're goin', but you can't get there from here." It should be comforting for you to know that by following your outline, you can always "get there from here" because you have stayed on your planned speaking course.

How do you actually make an outline? Even though you outline your entire speech, most of your outlining will deal with the body. Therefore, let's use the body of the speech to examine outlining. First, look below at the components of a speaking outline and how they look on the page:

Purpose Statement

I. Main heading (Roman numeral)
  A. Supporting material (capital letter)
    1. Detail (number)

Now let's examine in simple language exactly how a speaking outline works. You will usually begin by establishing the central idea of your speech, or the purpose statement.

Purpose Statement ...

The **purpose statement** is closely associated with the thesis given at the end of your introduction. It is placed near the top of your paper (without Roman numerals, letters, or numbers) and states both your selected speech topic and your specific purpose in speaking. Here are some examples:

Write your own purpose statement about preserving your local natural habitat.

The purpose of this speech is to inform the audience about the pros and cons of midyear high school graduation for seniors.

The purpose of this speech is to explain to the audience the steps that a person must go through to become certified in lifesaving.

The purpose of this speech is to persuade the group that immediate action must be taken if we wish to save our local environment.

In your actual speech, you might not *say* your purpose statement exactly as you have written it. You will probably reword your ideas when you formulate your thesis. However, the purpose statement needs to be written out at the top of your outline to serve as a primary reminder of what your speech is going to be about.

Outlining follows the process of **subordination**, or ranking in terms of importance. Your purpose statement, written at the top of the page, is the most important part of your speech. Everything else spoken—whether in the introduction, the body, or the conclusion—will fall under its direction.

Main Headings ... After you have determined your purpose statement, you need to decide what your main headings will be. **Main headings** are the major divisions, areas, or arguments of your purpose statement. They represent the main ideas that you wish to analyze. Main headings are indicated by the use of Roman numerals. For instance, suppose your purpose statement is this:

> The purpose of this speech is to show my audience the serious harms related to smoking.

The main headings in the body of your speech might read as follows:

MUST FOLLOWERS HAVE FOCUS?

INSTANT IMPACT

We live in a world where it is desirable to be in charge. Many people who wish to be in charge realize the value of effective organization and seek out what the experts say. They don't have to look far. The bookshelves are loaded with books and pamphlets on such topics as *Management and the Mind* and *Organization and the Power Person.* However, a valuable bit of information was released from the Carnegie Mellon Graduate School of Industrial Administration about followers.

According to the Carnegie Mellon report, two of the most important traits of a good follower are self-management and a sense of focus. The report stated that for any group to function cohesively and efficiently, followers must have a sense of organization regarding how they manage their time, how they prioritize issues, and how they zero in on what matters and what doesn't. Without skilled followers, the study said, society can become filled with robots—people who are easily manipulated. The study concluded that great leaders are often the result of great followers who see, adhere to, and carry out a definite plan of action.

What's the point? Whether you are in the spotlight or on the sidelines, it takes everyone to make a solution work.

WORDS FROM THE WORKPLACE

Elina Hanslip

Tour Guide and Consultant

Q. *Ms. Hanslip, how valuable are organizational skills in your role as a tour guide and consultant?*

A. The success of any tour is very dependent on all the work I do prior to the trip. Every aspect of the trip must be well thought out. All the arrangements for eating, tour sites, transportation, overnight accommodations, and all the information packets and brochures must be made well in advance of our departure. The actual trip is the easiest part of my job. It is all of the preparation, or organization, if you will, that really determines the success of the trip.

Q. *What kind of communication problems do you encounter in the tour guide business?*

A. I speak six different languages, and I often have trouble communicating the same information to groups that speak two or three different languages within the tour. I like to tell jokes to help people feel a little more relaxed, but I must always remember that humor does not always translate into different languages very well. What may sound like a funny story in German may not be as funny in French, for example. Getting some background information on the tour participants is helpful. It allows me to prepare my speeches and my very specific instructions on times, dates, and directions, so that my messages can be as clear as possible in all situations.

Q. *What advice can you offer to students who are interested in preparing to be effective communicators in a line of work similar to yours?*

A. Gather all the information you can get about the destination of the trip or tour. Keep accurate, up-to-date files about hotels, sites, places to dine, festivals, or anything that may be interesting to your clients. Then prepare your plan well in advance and practice your instructions. It is a favorite habit of mine to use small note cards to keep me on track. Organization and practice are very important, but you can't forget to be interesting and excited about what you are doing. Your attitude can communicate more than what you say.

I. Smoking can lead to significant *health problems for the smoker.*
II. Smoking can even affect the *health of others* innocently in the vicinity of the smoker.
III. Smoking can contribute to *economic problems.*

Notice by what is italicized that each main heading is a clear division of exactly what is going to be addressed in the speech.

Supporting Material ... The **supporting materials** you gather provide *intensification* and reinforcement for the main headings. They are listed under the main headings; each main heading has its own supporting statements. Supporting materials make up the "Now I would like to get more specific" sections of the speech. It is in these sections that you present the examples, personal stories, and pertinent observations that all audiences need to hear if they are going to believe you.

It is important to remember that your supporting material must be logically narrower and more specific than your main headings. Furthermore, if your organization is accurate, your supporting materials not only will support each main head but will also link back to support the purpose statement. Keep in mind that while the main headings logically divide and prove the purpose statement, the supporting material extends what has been suggested by the main headings.

Supporting materials are identified in your outline by capital letters. They don't have to be written out in great detail. Most of the time, a key word or phrase should be enough to jog your memory and allow your speaking talents and your preparation to take over. An outline is not supposed to be a substitute for memory. Ultimately, it is up to you, based on your familiarity with your material, to remember what you want to say.

Here are some examples of supporting materials you might use in the previously mentioned speech on the harms of smoking:

The purpose of this speech is to show my audience the serious harms related to smoking.

I. Smoking can lead to significant health problems for the smoker.
   A. Lung disease often results.
   B. Thousands die each year.
   C. Members of my family are among the victims.

Details ... Many speakers go one step deeper into the outline and give details. Details narrow the outline even further, providing information that breaks down the supporting material to pinpoint accuracy. When you get to the detail part of your outline, you will almost always be able to include exact names, dates, events, numbers, or personal accounts that will impress your listeners and solidify your point. Note how details, which are indicated by numbers in the outline, can give real impact to the working outline on the harms of smoking.

The purpose of this speech is to show my audience the serious harms related to smoking.

I. Smoking can lead to significant health problems for the smoker.
   A. Lung disease often results.
      1. Men are at 40 percent greater risk than women.
      2. Smoking causes over 60 percent of all lung problems.
   B. Thousands die each year.
      1. 390,000 die annually.
      2. Over 100,000 are under the age of 50.
      3. 20 percent are teenagers.
   C. Members of my family are among the victims.
      1. My grandfather died from lung disease caused by smoking.
      2. My father has to take oxygen twice a week.

Details can give life to your speech. They can add dimensions of personality, humanness, and intellectual stimulation to the coldest of topics. As a result, they will help draw your audience members in and make them feel a part of your speech, which is one of your goals.

Simple organization and good details will make your speech meaningful. Here a young reporter gets the details from Minnesota Lynx player Kristin Folkl.

It is possible to go still further and subdivide the details of your outline, but this isn't generally a good idea. Remember, not only do *you* have to keep track of where you are in your speech, but so does your *audience*.

And your audience doesn't have a script of your speech handy. Make things meaningful, but keep your organization simple and easy to follow. You'll be happier with the results.

Proper Outlining Form ... As you write your speech outline, you'll want to follow some standard guidelines. For example, notice how the various parts of the outline (the purpose statement, the main headings, the supporting material, and the details) are *indented* differently. The indentions indicate the subordination of ideas. Also notice the use of periods after each Roman numeral, letter, and number.

It is important to remember that each part of an outline should contain at least two items. First, you must have at least two main headings. You can have more than two, and usually you will, but you *must* have at least two. After that, you aren't required to have further subordinate parts, but in each case, if you have one, you must have at least one more. Thus, if you have an A, you should at least have a B. If you have a 1, you should have a 2, and so on. The reason for this is that you can't divide anything into one part.

Proper outlining insures that your whole speech is strong.

A few students might sometimes perceive the indenting, Roman numerals, letters, and numbers as "busy work." Keep in mind, however, that outlining means order, order means effective organization, and effective organization means you'll be in charge. What the bones are to the body, the outline is to the speech. If you take the time to think of a significant purpose statement, group your ideas logically into main headings, and create valid supporting materials and details, you will be on your way to building a speech that will be ordered, structurally sound, and—unlike some homes in ancient Babylon—certain not to crumble.

Do you remember the example introduction given earlier in the chapter? The thesis was, "I would like to discuss the various areas in your lives where laughter can play a significantly positive role." The first main heading might deal with how laughter can help on the job. Let's hear how this main idea might sound if it were used to start out the body of the speech. This speech in its entirety is outlined on page 229.

> First of all, laughter can help you on the job. Did you know that a sense of humor can help make you a more productive worker? For instance, the pamphlet *Smart Management Skills* states that employees and bosses who will take the time to laugh at their shortcomings are more likely to turn out more work of higher quality. The reason? The pamphlet explains that giving in to your "funny bone" relieves stress and allows you to see the occupational "big picture" better. The consequence, says author John C. Smith, is that "you actually work faster and more accurately if you will laugh and 'not take yourself too seriously.'" Next, laughter can help you cut down on absenteeism from work. A study done at Walker University showed that workers who frequently told jokes and laughed with fellow workers missed 20 percent fewer days a year than workers who were serious most of the time. One worker even added, "The laughing and having a good time makes me want to come to work. I don't like to miss."

Do you see the main heading? Can you pick out the supporting materials? What about the details?

Sample Outline

Purpose statement: The purpose of this speech is to inform the audience of the positive role that laughter can play in their lives.

INTRODUCTION

I. Have you ever heard the sayings "Let a smile be your umbrella" and "Laugh and the world laughs with you"?
   A. Both of these sayings show how a positive attitude and laughter can work to your advantage.
   B. Laughter can do more than provide a pleasant smile.

II. I would like to discuss the various areas in your lives where laughter can play a significantly positive role.
   A. Laughter can help you on the job.
   B. Laughter can help you with family and friends.
   C. Laughter can help your health.

BODY

I. Laughter can help you on the job.
   A. Laughter can make you a more productive worker.
      1. Mention pamphlet on employees and bosses.
      2. Giving in to your "funny bone" relieves stress and lets you see the occupational "big picture."
   B. Laughter helps you cut down on absenteeism.
      1. Walker University study gives the 20 percent fewer days missed statistic.
      2. Worker who laughs wants to come to work.

II. Laughter can help you with family and friends.
   A. Family problems can be handled better.
      1. Northwestern University reports that most family disputes can be "defused" by a well-timed joke or a laugh that the family is involved in together.
      2. Trust often results from taking the time to laugh with one another.
   B. People are often drawn to laughter and a sense of humor.
      1. Friends believe that your ability to laugh with them is a sign that you accept them.
      2. Psychological study: people are attracted to those who laugh heartily because they see those people as potential leaders.

III. Laughter can also benefit your health.
   A. Laughter can help people with serious illnesses.
      1. My aunt who had cancer found that watching cartoons and laughing gave her a positive attitude about her condition.
      2. Terminally ill patients in Chicago lived two to four years longer.
   B. Laughter can help with common ailments.
      1. Doctors state that the energy that it takes to laugh is actually a form of exercise that helps the body fight aches and pains.
      2. They add that laughing keeps the throat and vocal cords loose and active and helps ward off serious sore throats and colds.

CONCLUSION

I. Thus, laughter can make you a better worker, a more sensitive family member and friend, and a healthier person.
   A. It takes no special talent.
   B. It costs nothing.

II. So "Let a smile be your umbrella" is certainly good advice.

Next, look for the words and phrases that signal where the discussion is going. These expressions—such as *first of all, for instance,* and *next*—are termed **transitions.** They will appear throughout your speech, but they are especially helpful in the body of the speech. At a minimum, be sure to have a clear transition at the beginning of the body of your speech—and between each main point within the body of the speech. Also, use a transition to indicate the conclusion of the speech so that the audience is prepared for the ending. These are the "road signs" for the speech. Transitions allow both you and your audience to know exactly where you are in your speech and how all of the parts of your outline fit together.

See the figure below for some transitions that you might use.

Organizational Patterns

Let's now take a look at some of the ways that you can organize the body of your speech. Think once again of the trip that you might take in the family car. You could probably use a number of routes to reach your destination. After looking at the various options, you would probably choose the one that best satisfied your needs in terms of time, scenery, road conditions, points of interest, or the like. You need to make this same type of study when deciding how to organize the body of your speech.

Just as there are often several roads that lead to a specific location, there are several organizational patterns from which you can choose. Let's take a look at the five patterns of organization that

Relationship Intended Between Parts of Your Speech	Possible Transitional Words and Phrases
To add ideas	beyond that, in addition, besides, likewise, moreover, also, futhermore, next, finally
To illustrate or demonstrate	for example, in other words, even though, for instance, that is, to illustrate, specifically, as proof, a case in point
To yield a point	granted, of course, since this is so, although true
To show contrast	conversely, however, nevertheless, on the contrary, on the other hand, while this may be true
To emphasize a point	above all, indeed, more important, in fact, surely, without a doubt
To compare	at the same time, in the same way, likewise, similarly
To show order	first, second, in the second place, finally, in conclusion, last, next
To repeat or restate	in other words, that is to say, in short, in any case
To summarize	for these reasons, in conclusion, all in all, overall
To show relationships in space	close by, nearby, next to, in front of, behind
To show relationships in time	before, afterward, formerly, later, meanwhile, next, presently, previously, subsequently, ultimately, soon after

speech teachers from across the country say they find most appropriate for student speeches. As you are reading, keep in mind that these organizational patterns can sometimes be combined for greater effect.

1. Chronological Pattern ...

The **chronological pattern** of organization puts things in a time sequence, or in the order in which they happened. Chronological order is an excellent choice if you want your audience to see the parts of your speech building into a complete picture from beginning to end. Here are some examples:

The Role of the Political Cartoon in Shaping Public Views
- I. Colonial times
- II. Revolutionary days
- III. Current happenings

The Evolution of Batman as a Heroic Figure
- I. Initial comic book portrayal
- II. 1950s and 1960s TV show portrayal
- III. 1990s movie portrayal

2. Climactic Pattern ...

You will often want to save your most important point for last. In the **climactic pattern** of organization, you organize your main headings in order of importance. This type of organization can give your speech dramatic impact because it allows the speech to build in significance.

Types of Crime in America
- I. Shoplifting
- II. White-collar crime
- III. Violent crime

It is also possible to have a chronological pattern of organization that advances in a climactic manner.

The death of John F. Kennedy, Jr., his wife, and her sister
- I. Plane dives in sea off Martha's Vineyard
- II. Millions mourn
- III. Conclusion that crash probably caused by inexperience

3. Spatial Pattern ...

When you use the **spatial pattern** of organization, you are dividing up your topic on the basis of space relationships. The advantage of this arrangement is that your audience can see how the body of your speech fits together by the spatial layout picture that you create for them.

Introducing the Modern School
- I. Library is the central hub.
- II. Classrooms radiate from library.
- III. Offices are extensions.

ADVICE FROM A FORMER FIRST LADY

INSTANT IMPACT

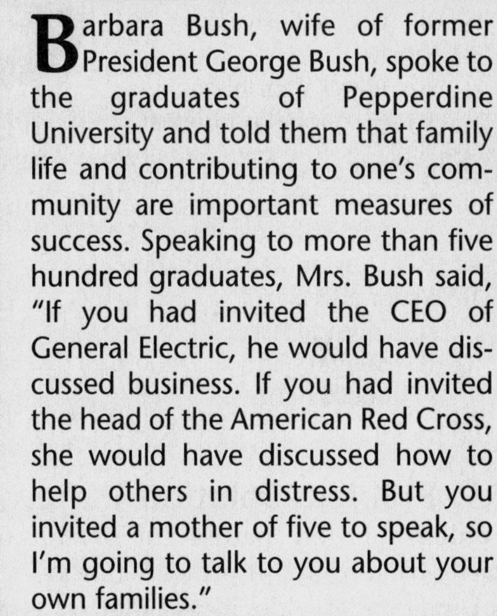

Barbara Bush, wife of former President George Bush, spoke to the graduates of Pepperdine University and told them that family life and contributing to one's community are important measures of success. Speaking to more than five hundred graduates, Mrs. Bush said, "If you had invited the CEO of General Electric, he would have discussed business. If you had invited the head of the American Red Cross, she would have discussed how to help others in distress. But you invited a mother of five to speak, so I'm going to talk to you about your own families."

She went on to add that the graduates would probably never regret missing a certain test or a specific meeting. She noted, however, that they would most certainly miss the times in their lives that they hadn't spent with their husbands, wives, children, or community. The answer, she suggested, was for them to organize their lives so that the important things came first.

Source: Associated Press.

The World of Drugs

I. North American involvement

II. Central American involvement

III. Asian involvement

4. Cause-Effect Pattern ... In the **cause-effect pattern** of organization, you are saying to your listeners, "because of *that, this* happened." In other words, the one area (the cause) leads directly to the other area (the effect). Often, the main headings in a cause-effect outline will be the words *cause* and *effect,* and the supporting material will supply an analysis. Here are examples:

Anorexia

I. Causes
   A. Media influences
   B. Low self-esteem

II. Effects
   A. Physical problems
   B. Emotional problems

Child Abuse

I. Major causes
   A. Cycle of violence
   B. Drug and alcohol abuse

II. Major effects
   A. Physical harm
   B. Mental harm
   C. Social harm

5. Problem-Solution Pattern ... The **problem-solution pattern** of organization does exactly what it says: It presents a problem and then provides ideas about how the problem can be solved. Much like the cause-effect pattern, this method is very logical and gives you an opportunity to show some insightful analysis in areas that are easy for your audience to follow.

There Is a Need to Recycle

I. Problems
   A. Lack of knowledge
   B. Economics
   C. Lack of incentive

II. Solutions
   A. Education in schools and the media
   B. Government encouragement
   C. Personal commitment

Keep in mind that not all speeches must include profound solutions. Sometimes the best solutions are those that are simple, practical, and easy to understand. Overall, solutions and action steps usually fall into three categories: policy, attitudinal, and awareness.

Policy Solutions A *policy solution* asks your audience to write the president or a congressperson, to start a petition drive for signatures in favor of a local candidate, or to rally as a group for a local march to the capital. Policy solutions usually demand some form of physical action on your audience's part. In addition, policy solutions actively challenge an existing institution or problem.

Attitudinal Solutions An *attitudinal solution* deals more with attitudes, opinions, and moods. It asks your audience to change or strengthen their mental state regarding an issue. For example, an attitudinal solution could ask your listeners to become more open-minded about people or to change their perspective about what the word *success* really means.

Awareness Solutions The *awareness solution* reminds your audience to be conscious of what they have heard and possibly implement what has been talked about in their own lives. The awareness solution is especially appropriate for informative speeches or demonstration speeches, in which the speaker is not offering the solution to a problem. The awareness solution can remind the audience that a wealth of information has been shared—that, for instance, "cross-country skiing can be fun if you will just try to apply the steps that we've looked at today."

Of course, the type of solution you use depends on the type of speech that you are delivering. You do

have some choices, though. If your speech deals with the problems of the inner city, you can suggest that audience members write to their state representatives to find out what assistance plans for the inner city are in the works—a policy solution. Or you can challenge audience members to examine their sense of justice and fair play and urge them to open their hearts to the less fortunate—an attitudinal solution. Audiences want to hear something that is within the realm of possibility.

Beverly Hubbs, a one-time guidance counselor and spokesperson for the Positive Life Program at a large Midwestern high school, tells both students and parents that many different roads lead to feelings of personal success. She says, "All people aren't the same. There is usually a right answer out there for all of us if we will take the time to hunt."

This is also good advice for you to follow as you organize your speech. Different topics call for different organizations. You have been presented with five organizational patterns that are tried and true. Combine your content with your originality and choose wisely. Remember, the body of your speech is the majority of your speaking "trip." Organize your speech so that your audience enjoys the journey. Let's now move to the final part of the speech, the conclusion.

SECTION 2 REVIEW

Recalling the Facts ...

1. An _____ is the speaker's map. It is the way that you give form and direction to your organization.
2. The major divisions or areas that you are going to use in the body of your speech are called ___ ___.
3. What is the name of the organizational pattern that puts things in a time sequence?
4. The attitudinal solution is part of which organizational pattern?

Thinking Critically ...

1. Look at the chapter quotation on page 205. Analyze and evaluate it. Do you agree with it? How does it apply to organization and speech writing? If you don't take the time to outline your speech, will it be like the clothes piled around the room—almost organized but not finished?
2. Outlining and being organized is critical when explaining something to someone. For example, analyze what would happen if a teacher tried to explain a lesson without a plan. What would be the results? At work, what if your boss tried to explain your job to you but didn't have any verbal organization? Why do you think that the "body" is the most important part of what is said?

Taking Charge ...

1. You have seen how outlining and subordination work, moving from general to specific. Using this knowledge, arrange each of the following in the correct outline sequence. Your outline should take the following form (be sure to make indentions):

   Topic
   I.
   A.
   1.

   - Baseball, sports, Chicago Cubs, recreation
   - Female authors, literature, Harper Lee, fiction
   - Bill Clinton, politics, executive branch, president of the United States
   - Corvette, transportation, Chevrolet, automobile
   - High school, English, education, American literature

COMMUNICATION

Breakthrough

How to Win Friends and Influence People

It has been called "calculatedly corny and cunningly folksy," but the Dale Carnegie course on public speaking and public relations has influenced millions of graduates from all walks of life. The main word that the Carnegie course stresses is *positivism*—looking at what can go right rather than what can go wrong in a person's life and career. Author of the book *How to Win Friends and Influence People,* Dale Carnegie started to advise individuals and businesses on public speaking in 1912. Since that time, more than seventy countries have adopted the principles of the course. In the United States, more than 150,000 students enroll each year.

Much of the Carnegie success is gained through businesses that pay for their employees to take the 14-session course, which costs around $1,000. Carnegie administrators say that 400 of the Fortune 500 companies, the most prestigious companies in the nation, send people to take the course.

The course tries to stamp out the *inhibitions* and insecurities that people have about themselves. It is organized around the following principles:

1. Become genuinely interested in other people.
2. Smile!
3. Remember that people want to be called by name.
4. Be a good listener.
5. Talk in terms of the other person's interest.
6. Make the other person feel important—and do it sincerely.

With converts from around the globe, the Dale Carnegie approach to feeling good about yourself, about your future, and about other people is a speech communication breakthrough. It allows people to work with real issues and come up with real answers. Millions of people can't be wrong.

Questions

1. Why do you think that the Dale Carnegie course on public speaking is still popular after all these years?
2. How could the six listed principles (above) help you to "win friends and influence people"?
3. Which of the six is the most important to you?

SECTION 3 The Conclusion

It has been said that if you want to deliver a good speech to your audience, you should "tell 'em what you're gonna tell 'em, tell 'em, and then tell 'em what you told 'em." This statement not only is amusing but also contains a great deal of truth. What is the lesson? First of all, your speech needs an introduction that previews for your audience your specific purpose in speaking. Next, your speech needs a body that proves your point. Finally, your speech needs a conclusion in which you wrap up what you have to say in a neat communication package.

Read the following conclusion for the speech on the positive role that laughter can play. Parts of the speech were used as examples earlier in the chapter. As in the introduction, pay attention to the numbers.

> **#1** In conclusion, you have seen how laughter can make you a more productive and effective worker, a more sensitive friend and family member, and even a healthier person. I think that after hearing that laughter can actually help us overcome serious illness and can help terminally ill patients live two to four years longer, we should all start to smile. So, let's establish and maintain a "laughing attitude." We can all do it—and it costs nothing. **#2** Therefore, the words that you heard at the beginning of this speech, "Let a smile be your umbrella," might be sound advice. Go ahead and laugh. Hopefully, the world will laugh with you!

The conclusion effectively summarizes the major points of the speech and restates the thesis (indicated by #1). It also offers a final clincher section, or a final impression (indicated by #2). Let's examine the role of each.

The Summary ... The first part of your conclusion is usually the summary. (You might go back and see how the word *summarize* was used in Chapter 3, "Listening.") The summary should remind your audience of the main headings, or major areas of analysis, that you covered in your speech. Sometimes your summary might even include a particularly memorable or hard-hitting detail. (However, the summary should not become so repetitive that your audience is left saying, "Wait a minute! Didn't you tell me all of that already?") In addition, repeat your speech thesis in the summary. This approach is sound because it guarantees that your audience will remember the point you were

THE WIZARD OF ID — Brant parker and Johnny hart

trying to make. Remember that a summary is a quick wrap-up. Get to the point and then move on.

The Final Clincher or Final Impression

If you started with a quotation, you might want your final clincher to be one as well.

Just as it is important to make a good first impression, it is important to make a solid final impression. Your final statement ends your speech, clinches your argument, and makes a memorable final impression. While some speakers may hold to the idea that you should always "leave 'em laughin'," this isn't necessarily true. The tone and nature of your speech should determine your final clincher.

If you go back to the types of attention-getters discussed earlier, you will see some methods that can be effective for your final lines as well. For instance, asking a question, making a startling statement, giving a quotation, telling a story, or making references can work for you at the end of your speech as well as at the beginning. You might also consider ending the speech the same way that you started it. In other words, if you begin your speech with a quiz, you might end your speech by answering those questions for your audience in a creative, insightful manner. Did you begin with a quotation? Why not end with a quotation that makes a similar point or one that accentuates what your speech has promoted? Just keep this in mind about the words that you choose to end your speech:

- They must fit the mood of your speech.
- They must make sense.
- They should bring some finality to your speech so that your audience realizes that you have finished.

SECTION 3 REVIEW

Recalling the Facts ...

1. What is the name given to what is usually the first part of the conclusion?
2. In addition to quickly repeating your main headings, reminding the audience of your ________ is also a smart idea.
3. What is the name given to that part of the conclusion that challenges, inspires, or motivates your audience?

Thinking Critically ...

1. Good managers in business, as well as good teachers, always conclude the meeting (or the class) with a quick wrap-up of what has gone on. They have found that *not* providing a solid summary can lead to communication problems. One executive even believed that her final words to the group might be her most important words. Evaluate this statement. Do you agree? Disagree? Regardless, analyze what communication problems might result if some type of conclusion or quick, accurate summary is not given to the group.

Taking Charge ...

1. Pretend that you are being given one opportunity to convince your teacher that you deserve an A in the class. Give your reasons, supply evidence, and then end with a quick summary. However, tell a story or give a personal example that would be an entertaining final clincher or final impression. Your teacher will ask you either to outline your conclusion or to write it out word for word. Be creative. Be logical. Have fun.

STUDENT WORK

"A Boring Outline" *By Michael Gotch*

The following speech received special recognition in National Forensic League district competition. It was written by Michael Gotch, who went on to become the National Forensic League national champion in original oratory in 1989. (Note: *All* of the words below, even the parts of the outline, were given out loud to the audience.)

Introduction

I. *Attention-getter* definition: dramatic example, pertinent quote, or startling statement to gain the attention of the audience.
   A. All of you are going to die!
   B. I'm going to die, too!
   C. We are not happy about this, are we?

II. Link to thesis

III. Thesis statement: style over substance

Now, even though this is certainly not the best beginning of a speech that you have probably heard, you have to admit that it is generic. And although what I described may sound like something off a black and white box at the local supermarket, it was simply oratory brought down to its most basic form—*the outline.* Now, if I were to give my entire speech like this, totally void of all entertainment, glamour, or gimmick, about half of you would probably be asleep within a short while. Why? Because in a world like ours, if you are not entertaining, pack it up! The way to the top these days lies with the "glitz." However, lately, in our quest for ultimate entertainment, we have forgotten to look beyond the gimmick to see if what lies behind is truly worth supporting. As we examine the situation, three major areas seem apparent. So let's really go out on a limb and call these areas Roman numerals I, II, and III, and look at each a little more closely.

Body of the Speech

Roman numeral I. The entertainment industry. What better place to start than with our world of film and television. The "movers and shakers." But what has happened to the creativity? Which television shows are the most popular today? The answer: *The Cosby Show, Family Ties,* and *Growing Pains.* Bill Moyers seems to have the answer to their success. He stated in a recent interview with *Newsweek,* "These shows are light, enjoyable, and easy to watch," and although a few do work to strengthen some basic family values, most, according to Moyers, "demand nothing more than our attention." They must not demand much from their creators, either, seeing that the "family sitcom" makes up one-third of the programming on television today. Each one seems molded from its predecessor with only minor differences. A night of fun and relaxation isn't bad, but do we ever judge a show on its intellectual value? Now, I'm not saying that we should all go home and watch *Gandhi* and a PBS special on mating flies. However, we do need to think before we decide because lately, entertainment has influenced the way that we make important decisions—decisions about people. This leads me to my second point.

Roman numeral II. Leaders. The simple truth is that today we are no longer looking beyond the "glitz" to examine the person. We are beginning to choose our leaders, political or otherwise, on the basis of their entertainment value. Their style. Before Roy Romer became governor of Colorado, he was a short, pasty-faced man with horn-rimmed glasses. Today, little (if anything) remains the same, thanks to Jo Farell of J. F. Images Modeling Agency. He's now handsomer, thanks to the "gorgeous gray" found by Farell's hairstylist; he also looks healthier due to Elonzo skin care treatments. And he seems friendlier, thanks to a new suit from Brooks Brothers. The reason for this change is not difficult to understand. To win, Romer needed a sharper image. Robert Feeter, president of Marketing Opinion Research of Detroit, states, "If you have the visual right, you have the communication right. It almost doesn't matter what you say." In other

words, the *image,* not the *intellect,* controls. This brings me to my final point.

Roman numeral III. Education. Today, we don't want to learn about people or things unless they are fun, exciting, and once again, entertaining. In 1968, *Sesame Street* was hailed as a breakthrough. Learning would be fun. However, studies by Dr. Neil Postman now show that *Sesame Street* doesn't teach children to love school. It teaches them to love school *only* if school is like *Sesame Street.* What's so surprising is that many schools today try to be! On October 30, 1986, it was a day like any other at Dominguez High School in Southern California. Classes began at 8 A.M. But along with the usual stream of morning announcements came one *not* so usual. It was an announcement that the United States and the Soviet Union had begun World War III. A state of shock and utter disbelief settled over the school, causing students and teachers alike to flee the classrooms. Of course, this was just a prank—set up by the *principal* of the school. According to one spokesman for the school district, this was just another one of the many ways that the principal tried to "jazz up" the school day.

You see, the harm in focusing on style instead of substance goes much deeper and is much more significant than merely choosing the wrong movie or reading the wrong book. One harm is that we no longer tell the truth—unless the truth sells. Television news programs once thought of as informative and engaging are now becoming little more than video versions of *People* magazine. As a result, we paint ourselves a distorted picture of society, sadly leaving out some important factors, simply because they aren't entertaining. We begin to hear only what we want to hear and flatter our world instead of examine it.

Conclusion

Have we really become such a cold, cruel, unfeeling society? Fortunately, there is a solution, and that brings me to my conclusion. Every good speech has a conclusion, doesn't it? Maybe the answer lies in the word *boredom.* When you ask most people why they constantly need entertainment, a popular response is, "Well, I certainly don't want to be bored!" Did you ever stop to think that when we are *alone,* we can create our own entertainment because we can now exercise our brains and allow *our own imaginations* to work! We can think freely without interruption. There's also a simplicity in boredom that gives us time to organize our priorities responsibly without being swayed or conned. Boredom gives us time to examine and review the day objectively and intelligently—time to give importance to events that deserve it, and time to forget the ones that don't. When you and I can learn to treasure our quiet moments alone, then *we will have beaten the system!*

How's that for an outline with a final impression?

Looking Back

Listed below are the major ideas discussed in this chapter.

- Organization is the plan that you develop to get things done. Whether for a speech, for your job, or for school, organization brings order and direction to the task at hand.
- The introduction is the beginning of your speech and usually consists of four parts: the attention-getter, the link, the thesis statement, and the preview statement.
- The body of your speech is the "meat" of your presentation and must be organized so that the audience can clearly follow what you are saying.
- Subordinating ideas—ordering them by importance—allows you to effectively outline your speech.
- The thesis statement is the most critical sentence in your speech because everything else in the speech revolves around it.
- Main headings (indicated by Roman numerals) are the major subdivisions of your purpose statement or thesis.
- Supporting materials (indicated by capital letters) divide the main headings into more specific categories and present more detailed information.
- Details (indicated by numbers) are subdivisions of the supporting materials and often are specific names, dates, statistics, and the like.
- Transitions are the links that take you from area to area throughout your presentation and keep the audience informed as to where you are in your speech.
- Different patterns can be used to organize the body of a speech; the pattern to use is the one that will work best with the thesis.
- The conclusion is the final part of the speech and consists of the summary and the final clincher or final impression.

Speech Vocabulary

introduction
rhetorical questions
quotation
narrative
link
thesis statement
preview statement
body
outline
purpose statement
subordination
main heading
supporting materials
transition
chronological pattern
climactic pattern
spatial pattern
cause-effect pattern
problem-solution pattern

1. For each new speech term, find and then write down the definition given in the text. List the number of the page on which each word appears. Now write an original sentence showing each vocabulary word "in action."
2. Make flash cards. On one side of each card, print a new speech term. On the other side, write the definition. Keep track of the words that give you problems and eliminate the words that you can handle. This will prepare you for a vocabulary exam.

CHAPTER 9 Review and Enrichment...

General Vocabulary

equilibrium
vested
gigantic
fiasco
jeopardy
enhanced
haphazardly
intensification
indented
inhibition

1. Use the dictionary to define the general vocabulary terms. Dictate each of the words to a classmate to work on the spelling. Next, read the definitions out loud, and have the classmate tell you the word that matches each definition. Try mixing up the order of the words.
2. Write an original sentence using each general vocabulary word. After you are finished, try to write a short essay, titled "What Might Happen If I Don't Organize My Life," using at least five of the words. Make your story make sense!

To Remember

Answer the following questions based on your reading of the chapter.

1. What type of question does not really ask for a response from the audience?
2. The part of the introduction that combines your introduction with your speech topic is called the ____________.
3. The ____________ states exactly what your speech is going to do and reminds you what you must accomplish with your audience.
4. The organizational pattern that saves your most important point for last is called the ____________ pattern.
5. The words or short phrases that link ideas together are called ____________.
6. Name the three types of solutions: ____________, ____________, and ____________.
7. Quotations, stories, and questions are all types of ____________ that can be used in the introduction.
8. The organizational pattern that uses space as a factor is called what?

To Do

1. Using as topics the school extracurricular activities "Sports," "Music," "Academics," and "Other," find all the information that you can and outline your findings. For "Sports," what are the teams? What are their records? Who are the key players? The coaches? An outline for "Sports" might begin like this:

   I. Baseball
      A. 1999 record, 18–3
      B. Strengths
         1. Hitting
         2. Bench strength
   II. Basketball

2. Organize *tomorrow.* Begin with the hour that you get out of bed. Keep a running record of at least two or three objectives that you would like to accomplish during each hour up to the time that you go to bed. For school, you can list what you would like to accomplish in each class. For leisure time at home, be specific in exactly how you want that time to be spent. Give honest, constructive answers that might actually improve your overall sense of personal organization.

CHAPTER 9 Review and Enrichment...

To Talk About

1. A person speaking about stress management said to her audience: "In this life, where grabbing for the gusto may mean one more demand on an already overflowing life calendar, it's important to decide what's really important." She was referring to the ability to prioritize, or rank things in their order of importance. How do you think that prioritizing could help cut down on stress in your life?
2. Why is it important to use details when you are trying to defend a particular position? Why isn't your opinion enough? What would be the value of organization if you were trying to convince someone to do something?
3. Which types of introductions and final appeal techniques do you find most impressive? Give your reasoning. Which do you find least desirable? Why?
4. Do some problem-solution brainstorming. What are some school problems? What are a few possible solutions? What are some societal problems? Solutions? Be practical! Also, for each of the following, discuss how a cause-effect relationship could exist: drugs and crime, alcohol and suicide, preparation and success, trust and friendship, education and employment opportunities.

To Write About

1. The report "Voices from the Classroom" (conducted by Sylvan Learning Centers) is based on a survey of nearly 1,500 eleventh and twelfth graders from 20 different high schools around the country. Believe it or not, nine out of ten students said that it is important for parents to help students with homework and to set definite study rules and guidelines! The students said that parents need to start this procedure when children are young. Write an organized paper giving reasons why you agree or disagree with this finding.
2. Write a one-page paper detailing the plan that you would have if you could map out your future. Before you write, make an outline. Be sure to include main headings, supporting materials, and details. What about transitions? Think through your reasoning and create a credible plan. Be sure to include your specific job choice.

Related Speech Topics

There should be equal pay for equal work.
The school day should be shorter.
Only juniors and seniors should be able to attend the school prom.
Volunteer work should be mandatory for high school graduation.
Students should have to pay if they wish to be involved in extracurricular activities.
Competition has serious drawbacks.
A politician convicted of a crime should be immediately removed from office.
A student's discipline in class should be a significant factor in the student's grade in that class.

CHAPTER 10

LOGIC AND REASONING

"'Contrariwise,' continued Tweedledee, 'if it was so, it might be; and if it were so, it would be; but as it isn't, it ain't. That's logic'."

— Lewis Carroll, *Alice in Wonderland*

Learning Objectives

After completing this chapter, you will be able to do the following.

- Distinguish among several different types of reasoning and recognize faulty or misleading types.
- Better adapt your use of logic to a specific audience.
- Analyze your own logic to determine if your conclusions are valid.

Chapter Outline

Following are the main sections in this chapter.

New Speech Terms

In this chapter, you will learn the meanings of the speech terms listed below.

evidence
reasoning
logic
induction
case study
sign
analogy
deduction
premise
syllogism
fallacy
hasty generalization
false premise
circumstantial evidence
causality
correlation
false analogy
ignoring the question
begging the question

General Vocabulary

Expanding your general vocabulary will help you become a more effective communicator. Listed below are some words appearing in this chapter that you should make part of your everyday vocabulary.

integrate
systematic
internship
segregation
degraded
incorrigible
manipulate
distortion
rigorous
rebuffed
rife
expedient

Looking AHEAD

Although sound reasoning is an essential component of communication, speakers often spew forth illogical statements that show little understanding of a speaker's responsibility to the audience and to the truth. In this chapter, you will learn the fundamental rules of logical reasoning and how to apply these rules effectively in your speaking. You will also explore how to *integrate* evidence into a speech and how to recognize the faulty logic that often is used. In short, you will take an important step toward becoming more logical and therefore more effective as a communicator.

Introduction

If you want to be an effective speaker, you should support your ideas with sufficient evidence and valid reasoning. **Evidence** is anything that establishes a fact or gives us reasons to believe something. **Reasoning** is the process of thinking and drawing conclusions about that evidence. You apply the process of reasoning in choosing and developing arguments. **Logic,** the science of reasoning, uses a system of rules to help you think correctly during the process.

As you construct arguments, remember that an argument is not the same thing as a fully developed, persuasive speech. You should use several arguments to make a complete presentation. Think of writing your speech as if you were building a bridge. Each argument becomes a girder that holds up your bridge. One weak or misplaced girder and the entire bridge may come crashing down.

Supporting your ideas with evidence, reasoning, and logic assures that your last argument will connect the ends of the bridge.

SECTION 1 Evaluating Ideas: Methods of Reasoning

To become more logical, you must learn about the types of reasoning. Understanding them can make your thinking clearer and more *systematic.*

Inductive Reasoning

In mathematics, a technique exists for proving theorems in which the mathematician uses certain specific cases to help prove a general truth. This process is called inductive reasoning, or **induction.** Induction, though, isn't used only by mathematicians. Anyone who argues from specific instances to a generalization is using inductive reasoning.

Suppose, for example, that you are preparing a speech about the importance of learning to read. You want to determine whether students who begin reading at a younger age earn better grades in school. You find five studies that link early reading with better performance in history but poorer performance in science. Based on inductive reasoning, you can conclude that starting to read at a younger age does not necessarily mean earning better grades.

If this young reporter just saw Kobe Bryant make two spectacular dunks and concluded that he was the "next Michael Jordan," she would be using what kind of reasoning?

As another example, think about the local politician who argues in favor of year-round school because students in countries that have such a system score better on international math, science, and geography tests than students in American schools. This politician is reasoning inductively.

A special type of inductive reasoning with which you should be familiar is the **case study.** A case study allows you to analyze a "typical" example in great detail so that you can draw general conclusions. For example, to learn more about the life of a journalist, you might undertake a monthlong *internship* with the local newspaper and then apply your observations in a speech on the field of journalism as a whole.

Suppose you want to argue in your speech that journalists work long hours. You could record the daily schedules of four different journalists whom you meet during your internship. If you find that these four journalists work long shifts, you might argue that it is likely that *all* journalists work long hours. In making this argument, you are using inductive reasoning.

Reasoning by Sign ... A special type of inductive reasoning is reasoning by **sign,** in which we draw conclusions about a given situation based on physical evidence. Perhaps the most familiar example of reasoning by sign is the work of

Young children are more apt to use inductive than deductive reasoning.

NAVAJO CODE TALKERS

INSTANT IMPACT

During World War II, the United States Marines relied on the unique logic of the Navajo Code Talkers. Established in September of 1942, the Navajos created the first and only code that was never broken by the Japanese.

As the war began, the American forces were having trouble preventing the Japanese from anticipating every move they made. The Japanese had been intercepting their radio transmissions and eventually had broken every code the Americans tried.

One Navajo, Phillip Johnston, learned of the difficulties and went to Washington with the idea to use his native language. The marines were skeptical but gave Johnston permission to try. Once other Navajos understood the intent, many were eager to help. By the end of the war there were 450 Code Talkers. Since Navajo is not a written language and a Code Talker was never captured, the Japanese were never able to decipher the logic of this unique communication.

Consider these examples from the Navajo Code provided by Arlene Hirshfelder and Martha Kreipe in the Native American Almanac:

A	Wol-la-chee	Ant
B	Shush	Bear
C	Mosai	Cat

Sherlock Holmes, the fictional sleuth. Holmes seemingly could solve the most complicated mysteries by simply studying the dust balls under the sofa. Reasoning by sign can be persuasive. For example, in Sir Arthur Conan Doyle's novel *The Hound of the Baskervilles,* Holmes explains to his associate, Dr. Watson, that it is "elementary" to determine the breed of a dog by observing the dog's teeth marks on a stick.

"Being a heavy stick, the dog held it tightly by the middle, and the marks of his teeth are plainly visible. The dog's jaw, as shown in the space between these marks, is too broad in my opinion for a terrier and not broad enough for a mastiff. It may have been—yes, by Jove, it is a curly-haired spaniel."

He had risen and paced the room as he spoke. Now he halted in the recess of the window. There was such a ring of conviction in his voice that I glanced up in surprise.

"My dear fellow, how can you be so sure of that?"

"For the very simple reason that I see the dog himself on our very door-step, and there is the ring of its owner."

COMMUNICATION

Breakthrough

Separate but Unequal

In 1951, Oliver Brown, an African American railroad worker from Topeka, Kansas, sued the city of Topeka for preventing his daughter from attending a local all-white school. Eight-year-old Linda Brown was forced to ride a bus for five miles when there was a school only four blocks from her home. The case, which went all the way to the Supreme Court (*Brown v. Board of Education*), challenged the constitutionality of an 1896 ruling, *Plessy v. Ferguson.* In *Plessy,* the court had decided that *segregation* was permissible as long as blacks and whites had access to "separate but equal" facilities. Thurgood Marshall and his team of lawyers, though, presented evidence demonstrating that "separate but equal" was a logical impossibility. There could be no such thing as "separate but equal" facilities when society was arranged unequally.

In a 9–0 landmark decision, the Supreme Court ruled that segregated facilities *degraded* minorities and prevented them from having equal educational opportunities. As Chief Justice Earl Warren wrote, "separate educational facilities are inherently unequal." *Plessy* was overturned. Although the *Brown* decision applied only to education, it inspired minorities to seek rights in other fields, and it became a turning point in the civil rights movement.

Questions

1. Do you believe that minorities have equal educational opportunities today? Why or why not?
2. What can be done to improve educational opportunities for everyone?

Reasoning by Analogy ... Another common method of inductive reasoning is the use of analogy. An **analogy** is an illustration in which the characteristics of a familiar object or event are used to explain or describe the characteristics of a less familiar object or event. Analogies are used by the creators of standardized tests to measure intelligence. For example, "Hand is to person as (a) tree is to sky, (b) dirty is to laundry, (c) foot is to powder, (d) paw is to dog." The point of those tests is not to make you blind from filling in thousands of tiny bubbles with No. 2 pencils but to see if you can pick out similarities.

Be careful when using analogies.

When you reason by analogy, you demonstrate similarities as you develop an argument. Suppose that a particular food is found to cause cancer in white rats. You might then reason by analogy that there is some risk to humans as well. Because no two sets of conditions are exactly alike, though, the perfect analogy doesn't exist. (White rats rarely guzzle soda as they gorge themselves on tortilla chips.) Therefore, you should not rely entirely on an analogy to prove your position in any speech and should always supplement your arguments with other forms of proof.

A SIGN OF THE TIMES

INSTANT IMPACT

To reach a verdict, juries often depend on witnesses who reason by sign. This method of reasoning, though, is not foolproof. Take the case of Meir Kahane, who was shot to death in a crowded hall in a Manhattan hotel on November 5, 1990. The prosecution called 51 witnesses to support its charge of murder.

"Many witnesses," reported the *Washington Post,* "testified that they were standing only a few feet away when they heard the shots and turned to see El Sayyid Nosair cradling a .357 revolver and crouching near Kahane." According to one columnist, Charles Krauthammer, one witness saw Nosair pointing the gun at Kahane. Furthermore, as Nosair attempted to escape, he shot two people.

The jury returned its verdict on December 21, 1991: not guilty. The judge denounced the verdict as "devoid of common sense and logic" and "against the overwhelming weight of evidence."

Only four months later, the Rodney King jury, too, seemed to go against the weight of evidence in that highly publicized trial. Millions of citizens had witnessed the beating of King on videotape. Many of these citizens—reasoning by sign—believed that the four policemen should be found guilty. The jury disagreed. For three days following the verdict, the world watched on television as Los Angeles experienced terrible urban violence.

People were exposed to the Rodney King beating (top photo) for months on the nightly news—a form of physical evidence. Most reasoned by sign that the four officers were guilty. A surprising "not guilty" verdict triggered widespread rioting in Los Angeles (bottom photo).

Deductive Reasoning

A counterpart to inductive reasoning is deductive reasoning, or **deduction.** Inductive reasoning moves from specific instances to a generalization; deductive reasoning moves from generalizations, or **premises,** to a specific instance. Premises are the statements on which reasoning is based.

Consider this simple example of deductive reasoning. It consists of two premises and a conclusion, and it is called a **syllogism:**

1. All students go to school.
2. You are a student.
3. Therefore, you go to school.

Deductive reasoning is not always this straightforward. For example, let's look at the role of justices on the U.S. Supreme Court. Their task is to try to apply a set of widely accepted principles (premises)—the Constitution—to specific cases. However, it is often difficult to tell whether the principles actually apply. Therefore, the justices must reason from the general principles to the specific cases to decide if the cases are valid.

Suppose that you are preparing a speech in which you plan to argue that flag burning should be allowed. By using deductive reasoning, you can develop an argument based on the First Amendment to the U.S. Constitution. The First Amendment is a general principle that is supposed to protect free expression, but does burning the flag count as "expression"? If it does, then you could invoke the First Amendment and, by deduction, conclude that flag burning is legal, as follows:

1. The First Amendment says to allow all types of expression.
2. Flag burning is a type of expression.
3. Therefore, flag burning should be allowed.

Should people be allowed to burn the American flag under their First Amendment rights?

Of course, the premise that states that flag burning is a form of expression must be true if listeners are to accept the argument in your speech.

SECTION 1 REVIEW

Recalling the Facts ...

1. What is the difference between inductive and deductive reasoning?
2. Why is there no such thing as a perfect analogy?

Thinking Critically ...

1. The phone book has been described as the ultimate example of unbiased writing—no opinions involved, just a list. Often, our biases interfere with our ability to present logical speeches. How can we balance the need for truth with our desire to persuade people to agree with our opinions?

Taking Charge ...

1. Now it's your turn. Using three of the forms of reasoning discussed in this chapter, develop three arguments for a topic of your choosing. For example, if you were trying to persuade the members of your audience that they should all attend college, you might offer these arguments:

Inductive reasoning—You interviewed ten people who graduated from college, and they all agreed that a college education was a good idea for them.

Deductive reasoning—College-educated people get the better-paying jobs. You want a better-paying job. Therefore, you should get a college education.

Reasoning by sign—The last time you visited a college campus, you saw a group of students having fun at a dormitory party. If you attend college, you will have fun at parties, too.

SECTION 2

Fallacies

The arguments just presented to support college attendance for everyone are not without their flaws. In this section, we examine common forms of flawed arguments, or fallacies. **Fallacies** are errors in reasoning or mistaken beliefs. They are the do-not's of logic.

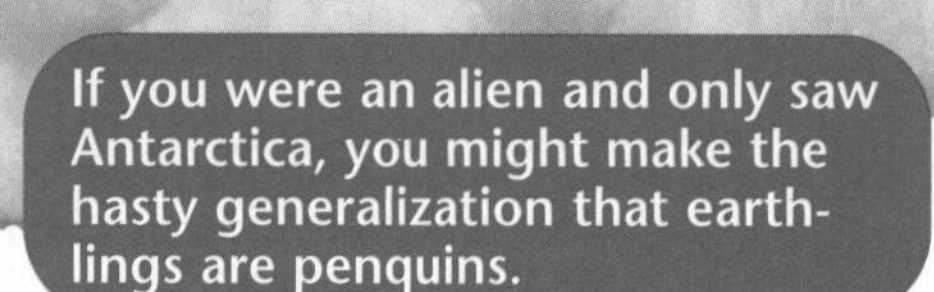

If you were an alien and only saw Antarctica, you might make the hasty generalization that earthlings are penquins.

Because fallacies weaken your credibility as a speaker, it is important to learn to understand, recognize, and avoid them. Some of the more common fallacies include hasty generalizations, false premises, circumstantial evidence, mistaken causality, misuse of numbers, false analogy, ignoring the question, and begging the question.

Hasty Generalization

A **hasty generalization** is a faulty argument that occurs because the sample chosen is too small or is in some way not representative. Therefore, the conclusion drawn based on this information is flawed. For example, you flip through three television channels with your remote control, and all you see are commercials. Your conclusion that the only thing on television is commercials is a hasty generalization—wrong but, unfortunately, not by much. Or suppose that you are an alien from another planet who saw Antarctica on your first visit to Earth. You might conclude that the only inhabitants of this planet were fish and penguins and the only landscapes were glaciers. Your sample size is large—there are plenty of glaciers, fish, and penguins in Antarctica—but your conclusion is still wrong because the sample is not representative of the whole.

False Premise

A **false premise** is an error in deduction. For example, parents like to tell their children, "All teenagers are irresponsible. You are a teenager. Therefore, you are not responsible enough to leave the house tonight." Now study the example to find the premise based on a hasty generalization.

All cats have four legs.
I have four legs.
Therefore, I am a cat.

Although it may be true that you are an *incorrigible* slacker, the premise that all teenagers are irresponsible is false. Of course, if you choose to argue the fine points of logic with your parents, they might choose to restrict your opportunity to watch all of those commercials on television.

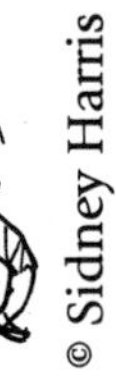

WORDS FROM THE WORKPLACE

Paul Ruiz
Attorney-at-Law

Q: *How does communication play a role in the day-to-day activities of your work?*

A: My job is all about communication. Whether it is communication with a client to understand what he needs, and what I can do for him; communication with fellow attorneys regarding legal research and legal issues; or, communication with a judge or a regulator to help my client, I must be able to use language properly in order to do my job. One cannot imagine a more unfortunate situation than having as your representative in court, before a judge, and sometimes a jury, a lawyer who is unable to get his or her point across effectively. Especially in cases where the stakes are high—such as a criminal case or a case where a company is being sued for millions of dollars—a lawyer absolutely must be able to communicate effectively in order to represent the client to the best of his or her abilities.

Q: *What advice can you give to students to show them how important communication skills are in the world of work?*

A: Two words—*listen* and *read.* I say *listen* because it is a skill too few people take the time to master. When people talk to you, listen to what they are saying. Don't interrupt. Are they clear about what they want? Are they precise in the words they use? Listen to the news, listen to sportscasters, listen to talk shows. Be aware of how language is used (and sometimes misused) in everyday life. Think about how you would improve on the words and phrases you hear.

I say *read* because, in today's hurry-up world, few people take the time to read the newspaper, a magazine, or a book, but those are the best places to discover the proper use of the English language. Vocabulary is key to good communication skills and, unless we challenge ourselves with new and unfamiliar words, we will not be able to truly express ourselves to the best of our ability.

Circumstantial Evidence

People like to draw conclusions based on **circumstantial evidence**—the evidence at hand. If they rely too much on circumstantial evidence, though, they commit an error in reasoning by sign. For example, it might seem perfectly "logical" to assume that the person holding the smoking gun at the scene of the murder was the one who committed the crime—but is it? What if it turned out that the person holding the smoking gun was trying to defend the person who got murdered, while the actual murderer ran away? The point is that circumstantial evidence only suggests a conclusion; it does not prove it.

Mistaken Causality

To say two events are **causally** related is to claim that one event brings about the other. For example, one billiard ball strikes another and causes the second ball to bounce off the cushion at an angle. There is a causal relationship because the first ball caused the action of the second ball. To say that two events are **correlated,** however, is to claim only that the two events are related in some way. The relationship may not be causal. For example, a bus passes a church every day at twelve o'clock, and the clock in the church rings 12 times. The bus doesn't make the bell ring; the two events just happen at the same time.

The toppling dominos illustrate a *real* case of cause and effect.

One of the most common errors in causal reasoning involves assuming that one event causes another simply because it happens before the other. This error usually goes by a Latin name: *post hoc, ergo propter hoc* ("after this, therefore, because of this"). Suppose you pass a major math test after going out to the movies the night before. If you then count on the cinema instead of careful preparation each time you face an exam, you are guilty of a *post hoc* fallacy.

Playing with Numbers

Many speakers *manipulate* statistics to misrepresent facts. They numb you with numbers in an attempt to persuade you to agree with their cause. Statistics, however, are subject to built-in biases, insufficient samples, and other forms of *distortion*. A classic example of playing with numbers comes from Mark Twain. In *Life on the Mississippi*, Twain, writing in 1874, observed that the lower part of the Mississippi River had been shortened 242 miles during the past 176 years—a little more than a mile and a third each year. Twain concluded, "any calm person who is not blind or idiotic can see that in the Old Oolitic Silurian Period, just a million years ago next November, the Lower Mississippi River was upward of one million three hundred thousand miles long. . . . And by the same token any person can see that seven hundred and forty-two years from now the Lower Mississippi will be only a mile and three-quarters long."

Although Twain admitted he couldn't afford to tell the whole truth because he had a family to support, not everyone is so honest. You should watch out for speakers who spout statistics to sound impressive. Be especially wary of politicians who use statistics to predict the future. Darrell Huff, in his book *How to Lie with Statistics,* points out that "the future trend represents no more than an educated guess."

Mark Twain manipulated numbers for comic effect in *Life on the Mississippi.*

False Analogy

As mentioned, no two sets of conditions are exactly alike, so no analogies are perfect. A **false analogy** compares two things that are not really the same.

Analogies are often misapplied. Let's suppose for a minute that you are arguing that students ought to be able to use notes and textbooks during examinations. After all, lawyers don't have to memorize every law, and physicians don't have to remember entire medical journal articles by heart. Rather, in a courtroom or a hospital, they are allowed to look up facts as needed. Similarly, students should be able to use their textbooks during an examination. At first, this argument seems plausible. Isn't the purpose of education to prepare students for the "real world"?

The analogy is flawed, however, because the situations are not really the same. The purpose of a trial or an operation is not to test whether the lawyer or doctor has learned law or medicine, whereas the purpose of a test in school *is* to see how much students have learned. The situations are fundamentally different.

Ignoring the Question

Speakers often attempt to divert the attention of the audience from the matter at hand. When they do so, they are **ignoring the question.** They may focus on personal attacks or appeal to popular prejudice. Political speeches by politicians from both major parties are *rife* with this strategy. In the 1988 presidential campaign, some campaigners linked Massachusetts Governor Michael Dukakis with the early parole in his state of a convicted murderer, Willie Horton. The perception that Dukakis was "soft" on crime—a conclusion not supported by the facts—could not be shaken, and he lost the election.

GOOD MILES PER GALLEON

INSTANT IMPACT

"Columbus's calculations were illogical," says Samuel Eliot Morison, "but his mind never followed rules of logic. He knew he could make it, and had to put the mileage low in order to attract support." To the everlasting glory of Spain, Ferdinand and Isabella had perhaps less *rigorous* mathematicians than those of the princes who had *rebuffed* Columbus. The strength of his convictions aside, it is still a lucky thing that in the midst of his 10,000-mile journey, America got in the way.

Sources: Samuel Eliot Morison, *Admiral of the Ocean Sea,* Little, Brown (1943), and *The European Discovery of America,* Oxford (1974), from Tad Tuleja, *Fabulous Fallacies,* Harmony Books (New York: 1982).

FUNKY WINKERBEAN reprinted by special permission of North American Syndicate.

The success of mudslinging (as personal attacks are sometimes called in politics) in recent campaigns makes this strategy a significant threat to the democratic process. As a speaker, you have the responsibility not to mislead. Emotional appeals that resort to the passion of the moment rather than reinforce the truth should be avoided. As Adlai Stevenson once said, "He who slings mud generally loses ground."

Begging the Question

When your argument assumes that whatever you are trying to prove is true, you are **begging the question.** Circular reasoning is a common form of this fallacy. A circular argument assumes that a premise is true, draws a conclusion from the unsupported premise, and then uses this conclusion to prove the premise: "Students will devote more time to studying if they have more study halls. We should decrease the number of classes a student takes and increase the number of study halls if we want students to study more."

A word or phrase may beg the question, as when your grandmother asks, "How do you like my delicious apple pie?"

Would your grandmother beg the question if she asked you how you liked her apple pie?

SECTION 2 REVIEW

Recalling the Facts ...

1. What type of fallacy occurs when you rely on a sample that is too small or is not representative of the whole?
2. Explain mistaken causality.

Thinking Critically ...

1. In attempting to give her client the best possible defense, how far should an attorney go in persuading the jury? Can she justify omitting facts that might damage her client's case, even though that information might better serve the truth?

Taking Charge ...

1. To assure that you recognize the fallacies discussed in this chapter, create three of your own. For example, if you were writing a speech as a candidate for president of the student council, you might include these fallacious statements:

- In a recent survey, 100 percent of those students polled preferred me for the presidency (playing with numbers—you asked only four friends).
- Whenever my opponent speaks at a pep rally, we lose the next game. Therefore, if we want to win, he should be forbidden from speaking (causality—an example of the *post hoc* fallacy).
- Furthermore, my opponent shouldn't be allowed to run for office because he, himself, is a loser, a zero, a nothing (ignoring the question—this strategy involves attacking your opponent before he has had a chance to speak).

Now it's your turn. Create three fallacies for one of the following situations:

a. Trying to persuade a teacher that you should have to attend class only when you want
b. Discussing with your parents the need for you to have a car of your own
c. Asking your boss for a raise

SECTION 3 The Ethics of Audience Adaptation

Logic and reasoning are often sacrificed when the speaker says to the audience only what it wants to hear. To vary your convictions and beliefs simply to please the audience may be *expedient,* but it is unethical. Of course, that depends on "what the definition of is, is." As you know, President Clinton learned many painful lessons about expedience. Clinton, however, was not the first leader to play fast and loose with logic. Take the politician who promises no new taxes and then, after being elected, raises taxes by calling those increases "revenue enhancements."

Our best and most successful leaders do not say whatever is most expedient; they say what they truly believe.

"I'd like to take a moment to define what I mean by 'defining moment.' "

Former President Ronald Reagan pledged during his 1980 campaign that any tax increase would have to come over his dead body. Later, Reagan approved House Bill 4961, the "Tax Equality and Fiscal Responsibility Act of 1982." This bill generated $99 billion in tax revenues, and somehow the president survived. Republican leaders referred to the legislation not as a tax bill but as a "reform bill" because they knew what the voters wanted to hear.

As a citizen in a democracy, you have an obligation to be highly skilled in the use of logical reasoning. You must recognize half-truths and untruths so that those who misuse the power of speech can't use speech against you. Furthermore, you have the responsibility to communicate what you know to be the truth.

An ethical speaker should try to give the audience the information that it most needs. If audience members are prejudiced, the ethical speaker should be the objective voice of reason. A speaker who believes in equal rights for everyone must challenge any practice that is discriminatory.

Furthermore, you should never present false evidence. Never appeal to the emotions of your listeners at the expense of logical reasoning. Never pretend to be an authority on a subject if you are not. In short, the responsible speaker must always be ethical. The Roman historian Sallust made the role of the responsible speaker clear: "Prefer to *be* rather than to *seem* good."

An ethical speaker should always take the high road and never pass along false information.

SECTION 3 REVIEW

Recalling the Facts ...

1. Why is political expedience unethical?
2. Why is logic important to a citizen in a democracy?

Thinking Critically ...

1. Political speechwriter Peggy Noonan argues it's not the flowery words or flourishes that matter but the logic behind your case. She contends that logic "shows respect for the brains of the listeners." Do you think politicians show this respect? Explain.
2. Politicians often come to mind when the topic is ethical speaking. However, ethical speaking is also an issue in other areas of our daily lives. Make a list of topics, such as advertisements, where ethical speaking plays an important role.

Taking Charge ...

1. Now it's your turn. Read the excerpt from Shulman's short story, "Love Is a Fallacy" on page 249. Incorporating your knowledge of contemporary attitudes, write your version of what would happen between Dobie and Polly if they were dating today.

COMMUNICATION

Break*down*

Characters (l. to r.) Maynard G. Krebs, Dobie Gillis, and Zelda Gilroy from the Dobie Gillis T.V. show.

Love Is a Fallacy

In his humorous short story "Love Is a Fallacy," Max Shulman describes the blossoming relationship between Dobie Gillis, a law student, and Polly Espy, the young woman of his dreams. Dobie, something of a sexist, feels that he must teach Polly to think so that she might be a suitable wife for a successful young attorney. (The story was written in 1951. Attitudes have changed since then.)

As the story opens, Polly is dating Dobie's roommate, Petey Bellows. "Cool . . . and logical" Dobie comes up with a plan. Petey has "nothing upstairs" and wants a raccoon coat; Dobie has a raccoon coat and wants Polly. A deal is struck.

On their first date, Polly responds to dinner with "Gee, that was a delish dinner!" and to a movie with "Gee, that was a marvy movie!" On the drive home, she says, "Gee, I had a sensaysh time!" Dobie determines that she must learn the rules of logic as soon as possible. Polly finds the lessons difficult at first but more fun than "dancing." After five grueling nights of study, Dobie tires of logic and decides to turn to matters more romantic.

> "Polly, tonight we will not discuss fallacies."
>
> "Aw, gee."
>
> "My dear, we have now spent five evenings together. We have gotten along splendidly. It is clear that we are well matched."
>
> "Hasty generalization," says Polly. "How can you say that we are well matched on the basis of only five dates?"
>
> "My dear, five dates is plenty. After all, you don't have to eat a whole cake to know it's good."
>
> "False analogy. I'm not a cake. I'm a girl."
>
> Dobie has taught Polly well—for when he finally asks her to go steady, she replies that she has already promised herself to Petey Bellows. Outraged, Dobie asks, "Can you give me one logical reason why you should go steady with Petey Bellows?" Replies Polly, "I certainly can. He's got a raccoon coat."

Questions

1. How important is it to use "cool" language with your friends? Why?
2. How important is it to be "logical"? Why?

STUDENT WORK

"Logic and Reasoning" *by Holly Mounce*

Holly Mounce, a tenth grader, answers the question: Are we born smart or do we get smart? Notice how, in the excerpt from her speech that follows, she applies logical reasoning to build an argument supporting her answer. Her reasons explain her answer (the thesis) and are supported by evidence.

Several days ago, while immersed in the living heck of final exams, I plopped my limp, exhausted, malnourished body onto the couch. I then began to moan about the sheer agony that finals inevitably bring. My groans were interrupted by a friend's casual remark, "Don't worry, you don't have to study. You'll do fine." And here's the kicker: "You're smart." I kind of blew it off at that point, but reflecting on this too-frequently repeated occurrence, I realized how many students believe that "if you're smart, you'll do well," and even worse, "you have to be smart to do well." I always believed that I succeeded in school because I deprived myself of excessive amounts of sleep and sacrificed a social life.

These reflections led me to consider the crisis in the American school system. According to Jim Stigler, author of *The Learning Gap*—after comparing the math test scores from over 75 Asian and American schools—"the scores of fifth graders in the best performing American schools were lower than their counterparts in the worst performing Asian school." Therefore, we must ask ourselves the crucially important question, "Are we born smart or do we get smart?"

The answer to this question is that we get smart for two significant reasons: first, the way in which persistence affects our ability to improve, and second, how a positive attitude leads us to success.

But how does our level of persistence make a difference? Well, there really are two factors that we need to consider and the first is that hard work pays off. Students in Asian schools are challenged to make connections on their own, and then later are reinforced by the teacher and their peers. Most American schools depend on handing students hard facts rather than teaching them how to think for themselves. Stigler points out that in Asian schools, "Children of varied abilities have the same learning opportunity, and the result is that a large number of Japanese advance farther in math."

But there is a second, more important factor, and that is the dedication of the students. In a University of Michigan study, the researchers learned "if the Japanese kids were uninterrupted, they seemed willing to plow on indefinitely"—even when confronted by an impossible math problem. The Japanese children assumed that if they kept working, they'd eventually get it.

Persistence is only part of the story, though. The rest of the story is developing positive attitudes in the children. Here again there are two factors. The first is what happens to the student's perspective. Columbia University psychologist Carol Dweck conducted a study in which she asked 229 seventh-grade students whether people are "born smart" or "get smart" by working hard. She found that "the scores of kids with the 'get smart' beliefs stayed high or improved, and those kids subscribing to the 'born smart' assumption stayed low or declined."

The second factor is the effect of parents, teachers, and peers on a student's self-esteem. Jeff Howard, president of the Institute, noted that "Most kids respond immediately to their teachers' changed expectations." To prove this he cites achievement-test scores of 137 third-grade students from six Detroit public schools who were enrolled in the Efficacy Institute program. The students' scores rose 2.4 grade levels in one year, compared with a control group of peers whose scores went up by less than half a grade level.

So in the final analysis, in answering the question, "Are we born smart or do we get smart?", I must again say we get smart. Persistence and a positive perspective pay off. After all, isn't it time that we heed the advice of that favorite blue train of American literature, " I *think* I can . . ."

CHAPTER 10 Review and Enrichment...

Looking Back

Listed below are the major ideas discussed in this chapter.

- Speakers should support their ideas with valid evidence and correct reasoning.
- Reasoning is the process of thinking and drawing conclusions about evidence.
- Inductive reasoning uses specific cases to prove a general truth.
- Reasoning by sign is drawing conclusions about a given situation based on physical evidence.
- An analogy attempts to describe a fact or set of data in terms of its similarity to another fact or set of data.
- Deductive reasoning moves from generalizations, or premises, to a specific instance.
- Common fallacies include the hasty generalization, the false premise, circumstantial evidence, confusing correlation with causality, playing with numbers, the false analogy, ignoring the question, and begging the question.
- Logic and reasoning are often sacrificed when the speaker says to the audience only what it wants to hear.

Speech Vocabulary

Using the speech terms listed below, fill in the blanks of the sentences in this exercise.

induction
deduction
case study
sign
causally
correlated
circumstantial evidence
begging the question
hasty generalization
false analogy
ignoring the question

1. The federal government has recently declared that it wants to learn more about how states spend their budgets. It is planning to conduct a ______________ of Arkansas's budget plans over the past five years.
2. You study drunk driving laws in 20 states and conclude that harsher driving penalties could benefit every state in the nation. This process is an example of reasoning by ______________. However, 20 states might not be a large enough sample to justify changing the laws in all states. The conclusion, if false, might turn out to be a ______________.
3. "The fact that my client was present at the scene of the crime does not mean that she is guilty," argued the attorney. "Her presence is merely ______________."
4. "Ninety-five percent of serial killers have milk in their refrigerators. Therefore, milk has a 95 percent chance of causing one to become a serial killer." This flawed reasoning is an example of two things that have ______________ but not ______________.
5. If a highway patrol officer observes a car weaving from lane to lane and deduces that the driver of the swerving car may be drunk, he is reasoning by ______________.
6. When you reason from general premises to specific cases, you are using the process of ______.
7. If the authors of this book asked you, "How do you like this great quiz so far?" they would be ______________.

General Vocabulary

Define the following terms and use each in a sentence.

integrate	degraded	rigorous
systematic	incorrigible	rebuffed
internship	manipulate	rife
segregation	distortion	expedient

To Remember

Answer the following based on your reading of the chapter.

1. What is the difference between inductive and deductive reasoning?
2. A case study allows you to examine a ______________ example in great detail in order to draw more general conclusions.
3. Sherlock Holmes was known for his ability to examine physical evidence and reason by ______________.
4. Because no two sets of conditions are alike, the perfect ______________ doesn't exist.
5. The fallacy of ______________ often occurs when you rely on a sample that is too small or is not representative of the whole.
6. Assuming that one event causes another because it happens before the other is committing an error in reasoning known as the ______________ fallacy.
7. When Mark Twain predicted that the Mississippi River would someday be only a mile and three-quarters long, he was guilty of ______________.
8. Circular reasoning is a common form of the fallacy known as ______________.
9. When Dobie Gillis informs Polly Espy that you don't have to eat a whole cake to know it's good, she replies that his assumption is a ______________.
10. Speakers who attempt to divert the attention of the audience from the matter at hand are guilty of ______________.

To Do

1. Attend a public discussion or political rally on a current "hot" issue (or watch a speech on television). List the fallacies you hear. Try to decide whether the speaker is advancing the truth or a personal cause.
2. Pick a topic that a friend and you disagree about. Construct arguments for both sides that are free from fallacious reasoning.
3. Research the use of logic and reasoning in TV or radio advertising. Discuss with your classmates how advertising claims violate the principles of logic.

To Talk About

1. You learned earlier that we live in an information age. Do you think that this abundance of information has helped us become more logical, or do you think that all of the facts and figures allow us to more easily "play with numbers"?
2. Why is it important for a citizen in a democracy to understand the process of reasoning?
3. What careers rely heavily on the use of logic and reasoning?
4. Work in a small group to gather information and obtain evidence about the relationship between city services and crime rates. Groups should present their conclusions using deductive reasoning.
5. Conduct a brief poll with fellow students. Ask at least five students (one at a time) if they would like shorter class periods. (It's likely that all five students will say "yes.") From these results, what does inductive reasoning suggest?
6. Work with a group to gather several newspaper articles on the same topic. Use inductive reasoning to develop a group opinion about the content of the articles.

To Write About

1. Create a fictional character that is the "evil twin" of *Star Trek*'s Mr. Spock. Every statement made by this character is illogical. Write a brief monologue in which this flawed reasoning is evident.
2. Write an essay about a school rule that you believe is wrong. Try to provide a logical alternative to this rule.
3. Construct an imaginary conversation between two friends in which one person is always logical and the other is not (reread the Max Shulman story for inspiration).
4. Work with a partner to examine an editorial from your local paper. Apply inductive reasoning to determine whether the conclusions are correct. Then describe in a brief written summary what editing changes you would make in the editorials.
5. Create a list of your own examples of hasty generalizations. Remember that most stereotypes are really examples of this fallacy. For example, all football players are dumb. What other hasty generalizations can you list?
6. Write out a step-by-step process you follow at work or at home when doing chores. Beside each step of the process, write an explanation of the reasoning behind the step. (For example, if you pile dishes on the left side of the sink before washing them, explain that it is because the garbage disposal is on the left.)

Related Speech Topics

Aristotle and logos
Mudslinging in politics
Sound bites: does logic bite the dust?
Mother does not always know best
Doublespeak
The reasoning of our Founding Fathers
The logic of humor
Advertising claims
Hasty generalizations I have known
The fallacies in hate speech
The logic of analogies
Business ethics
Statistics you can trust
Causal relationships
Correlated relationships
Reasoning by deduction
Reasoning by induction
Signs I should have recognized

CHAPTER 11

EFFECTIVE LANGUAGE

"*I know that you believe that you understand what you think I said, but I'm not sure that you realize that what you heard is not what I meant.*"

—Richard Milhous Nixon, thirty-seventh president of the United States

Learning Objectives

After completing this chapter, you will be able to do the following.

- Show how the spoken word differs from the written word.
- Know the value of language that creates word pictures.
- Explain why using effective oral language is important in professional and social settings.
- Use effective strategies in presentations.
- Understand the musical language created through the use of sound devices.
- Recognize language that can prevent effective communication.
- Evaluate language effectiveness of speeches.

Chapter Outline

Following are the main sections in this chapter.

1. The Spoken Word versus the Written Word
2. Creating Word Pictures: Figures of Speech
3. Making Music with Words: Sound Devices
4. Language to Avoid

New Speech Terms

In this chapter, you will learn the meanings of the speech terms listed below.

concrete word
abstract word
denotation
connotation
imagery
metaphor
simile
allusion
antithesis
oxymoron
irony
hyperbole
understatement
euphemism
personification
repetition
alliteration
assonance
consonance
parallelism
jargon
slang

General Vocabulary

Expanding your general vocabulary will help you become a more effective communicator. Listed below are some words appearing in this chapter that you should make part of your everyday vocabulary.

tangible
conscience
picturesque
crystallize
exaggerate
compression
pervasiveness
cadence
emancipation
demeaning
braille

Looking AHEAD

Mark Twain told us that the difference between the right word and the *almost*-right word is the difference between lightning and the lightning bug. Indeed, there is a world of difference between the word or phrase that will say exactly what you mean and the word or phrase that is simply "in the ballpark." For example, here are a few automobile accident reports that have been filed by people insured by the Omaha Property and Casualty Insurance Company and State Farm Insurance, Bloomington, Illinois:

- I pulled away from the side of the road, glanced at my mother-in-law, and headed over the embankment.
- An invisible car came out of nowhere, struck my vehicle, and vanished.
- I was on my way to the doctor with rear end trouble when my universal joint gave way, causing me to have an accident.*

Even though you might laugh at these reports, they prove a significant point: selecting the wrong word or using unclear phrasing can lead to communication that is not only confusing but embarrassing.

No one is exempt. Even as brilliant an orator as John F. Kennedy, former president of the United States, can make an error. A popular story involves the conclusion of Kennedy's powerful speech at the Berlin Wall in 1963. Kennedy wished to say, "Ich bin Berliner!"—meaning, "I am a Berliner!" However, what he said was, "Ich bin *ein* Berliner!" In German, words for nationalities are not preceded by articles (*ein* is an article meaning "a" or "an"). It happens, though, that *Berliner* is also the name of a pastry. Thus, what Kennedy really told the German people was, "I am a jelly doughnut!" Even the best communicators can make mistakes if they are not careful.

This means you! At school, in the community, or at work, the language that you use around others is tremendously important. To many, your language is parallel to your intelligence and your dependability. Thererefore, in this chapter, you will learn that effective oral communication depends, in part, on accuracy and economy of language. You will examine the figures of speech used to create the language of effective imagery. In addition, you will be introduced to the sound devices that help to produce the "music" heard in language. Finally, you will be warned about specific types of language that should be avoided because they can create communication barriers between you and your audience.

*Excerpted from Richard Lederer's *Anguished English* (Bantam Doubleday Dell Publishing Group, 1989).

Introduction

Imagine that you are in the circus. As an acrobat you perform high above the ground without a net, and the path you must follow from point A to point B is merely a tightrope. Your steps must be measured and exact. One false step and your career, as well as your life, could be over. You know that your movement must be absolutely precise. Simply being "close" to the tightrope would likely result in your becoming a memory in the circus world.

How successful this speaker is in communicating his ideas will depend to a large extent on his ability to choose exactly the right words.

What do you do? You touch, you feel, and you don't move until you know that the next step is exactly right.

This chapter isn't about the circus world, but it *is* about exactness—the exactness of language. Like the tightrope walker, you must painstakingly search—only this time it is for the most effective words and phrases to communicate your ideas. In the job world, as well as in social settings, using effective language when you speak can make a sensational impression on your audience.

In earlier chapters, the building of a successful speech was compared to the building of a well-constructed house. We can extend that comparison by saying the successful builder of a speech knows that effective language, along with an effective delivery, is what covers the planks of confidence that were discussed in Chapter 2. Your listeners can't "see" your words, but they can certainly hear them. And language that is appropriate, informative, and colorful will establish a communication "open house" that is sure to draw an audience, whether it be at work or with friends.

We now take a look at some areas of effective delivery that can help you brighten up your house of oral communication.

Being an effective communicator is like walking a tightrope. To be successful, you must work very hard at being exact and precise.

SECTION 1 The Spoken Word versus the Written Word

You probably have a favorite author. If you don't have a favorite yet, you will someday. Perhaps there is a good book that you like to read over again, an editorial that says exactly what you believe, or a song that contains words that you never grow tired of reexamining. One of the fantastic things about the written word is that you can *see* it—as often as you like.

The written word has a distinct advantage over the spoken word: It offers language that you are given time to consider, and with time often comes understanding. Think about how often you didn't understand a reading assignment in school until you had gone over the assignment a second, a third, or even a fourth time.

Studies show, however, that over 90 percent of all communication is not written but spoken. Indeed, the word language comes from the Latin word *lingua*, which means "tongue." The language of speech must be different from written language if it is to communicate effectively. The audience must "get it" the first time. With the spoken word, you rarely have a second chance to make an impact on your audience.

What must the good speaker keep in mind regarding language if he or she wants to make the right impression? The good speaker knows the value of two key words: accuracy and economy.

Accuracy of Language

The average person has a vocabulary of approximately 10,000 words. You might use a certain part of your vocabulary only with your friends, and another, rather different part only with your parents or other adults. Why? Because you realize that certain language is appropriate in some situations but not in others. Even with this realization, however, we may use words that are confusing to those listening because those words don't accurately communicate what we think that we are saying. We may be speaking about one thing while our audience is hearing something totally different.

If you want to be an effective speaker, regardless of the situation—with your friends at the mall, with your teachers, with colleagues at work, then you need to understand the importance of language accuracy. Accuracy means using words that say exactly what you mean. How can you develop accuracy in your verbal expression? Let's start by taking a look at concrete words as opposed to abstract ones.

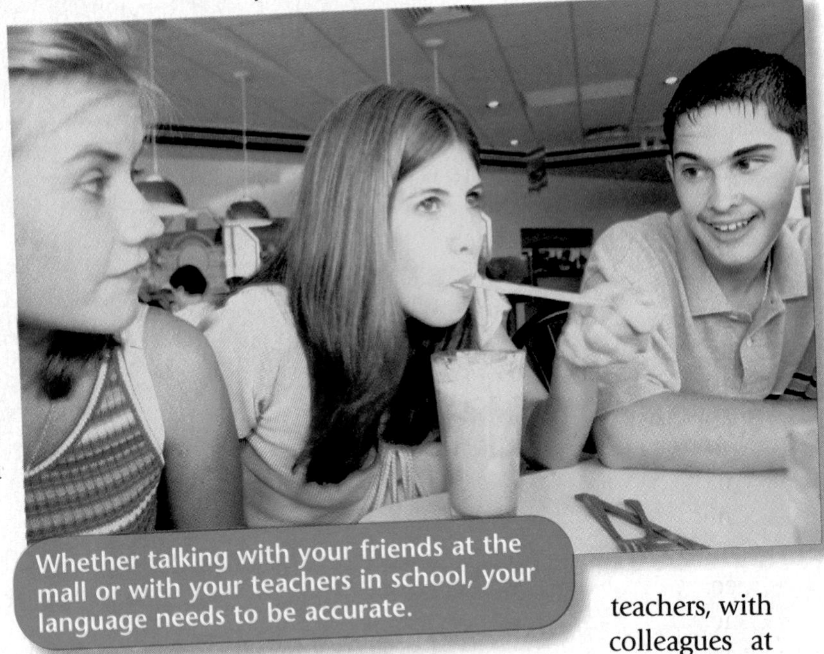

Whether talking with your friends at the mall or with your teachers in school, your language needs to be accurate.

Concrete and Abstract Words ...

Concrete words name things that we can perceive

through sight, hearing, touch, taste, or smell. **Abstract words,** on the other hand, don't deal with the senses but are names for qualities, attributes, concepts, and the like. For example, words such as baseball, car, and radio are concrete words. They name things we can see and hear and touch. Compare this list with the words recreation, transportation, and media. These words are much more general. As a result, they are open to personalized interpretation.

Look at a few lines of a song that you've probably heard several times:

> Take me out to the ball game
> Take me out with the crowd
> Buy me some peanuts and Crackerjack
> I don't care if we never get back

Can you identify the concrete words that are used to help create the atmosphere of a baseball game? Can you almost "taste" the peanuts and Crackerjack? These *tangible* objects are being used to communicate a message. It is often highly effective to use concrete words that say clearly what we want our audience to hear. In contrast, using abstract words without clearly defining them means taking the risk of not communicating accurately with the audience. When this happens, your language is not working for you. It might even be undermining your intent. Sometimes the most effective language is created when the speaker uses concrete and abstract words together, clearly and accurately.

Which of these two pictures comes to mind when you hear the word *mother*? What other pictures does the word *mother* connote for you?

Denotation and Connotation ...

Closely associated with the terms concrete and abstract are the terms denotation and connotation. **Denotation** refers to the basic meaning of a word, which can easily be found in the dictionary. **Connotation** refers to the meaning of a word that goes beyond the dictionary definition; it is the meaning we associate with the word.

What about the word mother? Mother can be defined as "a woman who bears a child," but many of us would also associate mother with ideas such as love, friendship, and family. Suppose you were going to speak on the idea that women ought to have the same opportunities as men in the job market. It would probably be unwise to say, "I think that women can make excellent contributions to any job and should be paid the same as men. Women shouldn't be limited to simply being mothers!" Because of connotations associated with the word mother, this statement might imply to some people in your audience that you see mothers as lower in status, that you are antifamily, or that raising children is easy.

It is desirable to use words that clearly denote a certain meaning. You must think through the different connotations that a word might have before you use it in your speech. For example, the words rebel, loner, eccentric, and mediocre might mean one thing to you but something entirely different to your audience.

Abstract words may have many different connotations. For example, consider the words success, failure, family, patriotism, and justice. How might these words be interpreted differently by different people? For example, is "success" in your eyes the same as it might be in someone else's?

Don't think that you must always avoid abstract words because of this difficulty. Abstract words can be powerful. They can inspire us and appeal to our emotions. We must, however, use them with care.

Economy of Language

Just as you must be accurate in the words that you select for your speech, you must also be economical in the number of words that you use. Keep in mind that the members of your audience, contrary to what they must do when reading the written word, must remember all that you say. Economy means "careful or thrifty use." Thus, economy of language suggests carefully managing the quantity of words you use to communicate verbally.

The famous essay "Civil Disobedience" by Henry David Thoreau was originally delivered as a lecture in 1848 under the title "Resistance to Civil Government." It dealt with the role of individual *conscience* versus the role of state authority. Here is a portion of that speech:

> Must the citizen ever for a moment, or in the least degree, resign his conscience to the legislator? Why has every man a conscience, then? I think that we should be men first, and subjects afterward. If I devote myself to other pursuits and contemplations, I must first see, at least, that I do not pursue them sitting upon another man's shoulders. I must get off him first, that he may pursue his contemplations too. . . . There will never be a really free and enlightened State, until the State comes to recognize the individual as a higher power.

This material given as a speech had little impact. It wasn't until later, as an essay, that it gained prominence. Can you see why it would be difficult to digest as a speech?

This speech offers a great deal of intellectual content to absorb at one time. In addition, notice the number of words that it takes for Thoreau to say what he thinks. As an essay to be read at one's leisure, "Civil Disobedience" is a masterpiece because readers can take the time to study the words and ideas in print. As a speech, it would probably be difficult to listen to. Why? If spoken language becomes long and involved, the listener can get lost.

How can we prevent this? It is Thoreau himself who offers us sound advice when he states in his masterpiece *Walden*, "Simplify, simplify." Apply his advice to both your spoken words and the organization of your ideas if you wish the audience to "march to your drum beat."

How? First of all, pay attention to the number of words that it takes for you to say something. For instance, look how each of these statements might be shortened.

> *Original Statement:* At the beginning of the day before I have my breakfast, I always work to keep my blood circulating and my body fit.
>
> *Shortened Statement:* I like to exercise first thing in the morning.
>
> *Original Statement:* Because of the way you look and because we have always had so much fun together, you and I might not find it a bad thing to talk and do stuff together.
>
> *Shortened Statement:* I'd like to spend some time with you.
>
> *Original Statement:* The way that my math teacher evaluates me in school shows that there are areas in which I can do a lot better.
>
> *Shortened Statement:* I'm failing algebra.

INSTANT IMPACT

I DIDN'T MEAN TO SAY *THAT!*

Earlier in the chapter, you read how John F. Kennedy meant to say one thing but said something else to the German people. Translation problems are quite common. Someone at the United Nations once entered a common English saying into a translating computer. The machine was asked to translate into Russian and then back into English the saying, "The spirit is willing, but the flesh is weak." The result was, "The wine is good, but the meat is spoiled." When Pepsi-Cola invaded the Chinese market, the product's slogan, "Come alive with the Pepsi generation," was translated as, "Pepsi brings back your dead ancestors!" Language "details" like these can make the difference between saying exactly what you mean and missing the mark.

Source: Richard Lederer, *Anguished English* (New York: Bantam Doubleday Dell Publishing Group, 1989).

Notice how words can get in the way and clutter up your message. This "clutter" can sometimes confuse your audience. Remember to avoid unnecessary prepositional phrases ("In the beginning of the story at the top of the page"). Avoid using too many clauses run together in one sentence ("The main character, who is in his midtwenties, knows that the sister who is hiding in the closet is innocent because she wasn't at the scene of the crime that had taken place earlier"). Avoid repeating the same idea with different wording ("The main character was an excellent student, had received As on her report card, and had always done very well in school").

One effective way to be simple and direct is by using rhetorical questions. As discussed in Chapter 9, rhetorical questions are questions that you ask the audience but that you don't really intend the audience to answer out loud. For example, "What do all of these statistics mean?" and "Where is the solution to this problem?" are rhetorical questions. Each could allow you to say with one question what it might have taken you two or three sentences to explain otherwise.

The twentieth-century Irish poet and playwright William Butler Yeats once said, "Think like a wise [person], but communicate in the language of the people." If you give priority to accuracy and economy when choosing your language, then you might achieve with your spoken words the spirit of what Yeats is saying. Let's look at how figures of speech can make your language memorable.

SECTION 1 REVIEW

Recalling the Facts ...

1. Based on findings, each person has an average vocabulary of how many words?
2. Words that we can understand through the "senses" are called ____________ words, while those words that involve "qualities and attributes" are called ____________ words.
3. Two terms used in this section are *denotation* and *connotation.* Which one is the "dictionary definition" of a word?
4. This section talked about the economy of language. Henry David Thoreau's *Walden* reinforced this point by stressing the word "____________"—when it came to keeping a person's life in order.

Thinking Critically ...

1. At the beginning of this chapter, you saw a statement by Richard Nixon. Here is a statement by another past president of the United States, Dwight David Eisenhower: "How can we appraise a proposal if the terms hurled at our ears can mean anything or nothing. . . . If our attitudes are muddled, our language is often to blame." What was Eisenhower saying? He was speaking specifically about the government in this quote. Can you think of any examples in which the "language of government" seems to take on different meanings? Can you find any instances in which governmental language is muddled and confusing? What about the language of sports? The language used in your home? The language used in certain professions?

Taking Charge ...

1. This section discussed abstract words and gave some specific examples. Write out your own personalized definitions (don't use the dictionary) for the abstract words *honesty, patriotism,* and *friendship.* Talk with a classmate to see what your definitions have in common. What are the differences? Be ready to discuss your findings in class.

SECTION 2 Creating Word Pictures: Figures of Speech

You have probably heard stories about how ancient royalty, without the advantages of the printing press or modern postal service, used messengers to communicate from kingdom to kingdom. (You have probably also heard that some of these messengers were put to death for being "bearers of ill tidings.") The messengers, similar to the deliverers of our twentieth-century "singing telegrams," would often sing the words of the messages using rhyme and colorful, descriptive language. The use of *picturesque* language, presented in a musical manner, undoubtedly made the message easier to remember. It also made a pleasing sound to the ears of those listening. Spoken language is most effective when it creates music for the ear and pictures for the imagination.

Like singing telegrams, a speech is most effective when it has a musical quality.

Language that creates pictures in our minds and excites our senses is called **imagery.** Figures of speech are specific types of imagery. Here, we classify and describe figures of speech in terms of three working categories: comparison, contrast, and exaggeration. Understanding figures of speech and then using them effectively will make your speeches more descriptive.

Comparison Imagery

From each pair of statements, which one has more impact?

Education is important.
Education is the key that unlocks many of life's opportunities.

You have to work hard to make a marriage work.
Marriage is like a plant: If you care for it and give it time and attention, it will grow and prosper.

You are not always nice to me.
Why must you always act as if you're Napoleon whenever we're together!

The second example in each pair is more dynamic and presents a more exact picture. The first example in each pair isn't necessarily wrong; it is simply not as lively.

The second example in each of the pairs uses comparison imagery. Comparison involves showing similarities. As mentioned, imagery refers to word pictures. Consequently, to use comparison imagery means to show similarities through the use of picturesque language. Let's take a look at the three most common forms of comparison imagery: metaphor, simile, and allusion.

Metaphor and Simile . . . A **metaphor** is a figure of speech, not using the word *like* or *as,* that compares two usually unrelated things. A **simile** is the same as a metaphor, except that it uses *like* or *as* to make the comparison.

For example, if you were talking to your classmates on the value of a high school education and employment, you could say,

> A high school diploma is important for the job choices that you will have later in your life.

Or, you could say,

> A high school diploma is the key that will give you the potential to unlock many occupational doors later in life.

The second example is a metaphor. It compares a diploma to a key that can open doors to a successful future. The comparison shows that, even though diplomas and keys are basically different, they are similar because each is of definite worth. Do you see how a metaphor can help to liven up your language?

If you wanted to stress that our government is spending large amounts of money each day, you could say:

> Every day, our government spends extremely large sums of money.

A MEANINGFUL METAPHOR

Robert W. Goodman is the father of Andrew Goodman, one of three civil rights workers who were murdered in 1964 in Mississippi. In response to his son's death, Goodman said, "Our grief, though personal, belongs to the nation. The values that our son expressed in his simple action of going to Mississippi are still the bonds that bind this nation together—its Constitution, its law, its Bill of Rights."

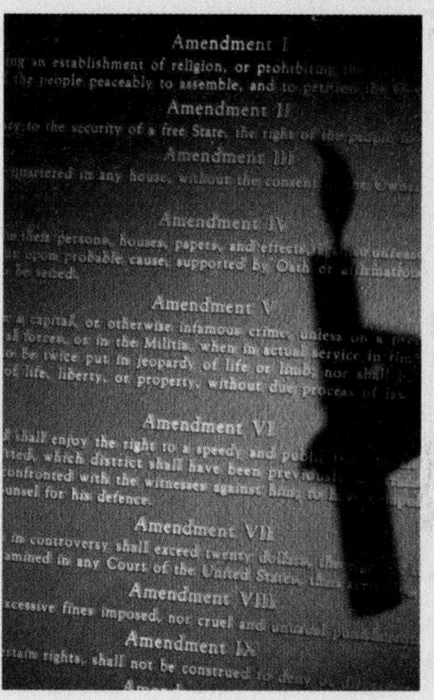

Alternatively, you could say:

> Every day, our government spends money as fast as McDonald's sells hamburgers!

The second sentence is a simile, indicating that Washington is like the fast-food industry when it comes to handing out billions of dollars (rather than millions of hamburgers) each day.

If you used the fast-food image throughout your speech, you would be creating an analogy, which was discussed in Chapter 10. An analogy, which can also take the form of a story, is the extended use of a metaphor or a simile.

A high school diploma is the "key" to success. Can you think of other metaphors that emphasize the value of education?

Figure of Speech	What it Does
Metaphor	Compares two usually unrelated things, without using *like* or *as*.
Simile	Compares two usually unrelated things, using *like* or *as*.
Allusion	Refers to a well-known person, place, thing, or idea.
Antithesis	Balances or contrasts a term against its opposite.
Oxymoron	Places opposite terms side by side.
Irony	Implies the opposite of what seems to be said on the surface.
Hyperbole	Makes more of something.
Understatement	Makes less of something.
Personification	Gives human characteristics to nonhuman things.

Allusion . . . Another way to create an effective word picture is through the use of allusion. An **allusion** is a reference to a well-known person, place, thing, or idea.

Earlier, a reference was made to Napoleon, showing how someone was comparing a friend to a dictator, implying that the friend was acting very bossy. Obviously not a comparison to be taken literally, the Napoleon allusion made the point that one person was not happy with the other's "I'm in charge" attitude.

What would it mean if you referred to a community member as Scrooge? A classmate as Bart Simpson? A school athlete as Brandi Chastain? The pencil drawing on a desk as a Picasso? Allusions such as these can give the listener an immediate mental "snapshot" of what you are saying.

Be sure, however, that your audience knows what the reference means. Remember, the most effective allusions are commonly recognized by just about everyone. It does little good to use an allusion if it leaves your audience wondering what you are talking about.

Use good judgment. Effective language involves creative comparisons that stick with your audience. If the comparisons don't stick, the language wasn't effective.

Contrast Imagery

At the conclusion of John F. Kennedy's 1961 inaugural address are the famous words, "Ask not what your country can do for you: Ask what you can do for your country." Kennedy contrasts the ideas of country and you. Contrast imagery is the general term used to describe language that sets up opposition for effect. Contrast imagery often takes the form of antithesis, oxymoron, and irony.

THAT OTHER TEAM IS TRASH-TALKING US, CHARLIE BROWN..

I GOT EVEN WITH THEM, THOUGH...
6-21

I SAID, "YOU GUYS THINK YOU'RE SO GREAT..MOZART WAS WRITING SYMPHONIES WHEN HE WAS YOUR AGE!"

THAT REALLY SHUT 'EM UP..
I'LL BET IT DID..
SCHULZ

Antithesis ...

One type of imagery, **antithesis,** is the specific balancing or contrasting of one term against another, which is its opposite. For instance, look at these pairs of words: *hot-cold, young-old, dry-wet, up-down, small-large, success-failure, love-hate, leader-follower, temporary-permanent.* These are a few examples of antithesis. A fair question right now would be, "How can I *use* antithesis in my speech to make the impression I want?"

Speaking at a meeting at which you are encouraging citizens to join a community-service club, you could begin your presentation by saying, "It doesn't matter whether you are young or old, experienced or inexperienced, rich or poor, you can make a difference in this organization." Whether you are attempting to inform, persuade, or motivate your audience, this use of "opposites" in language can be effective.

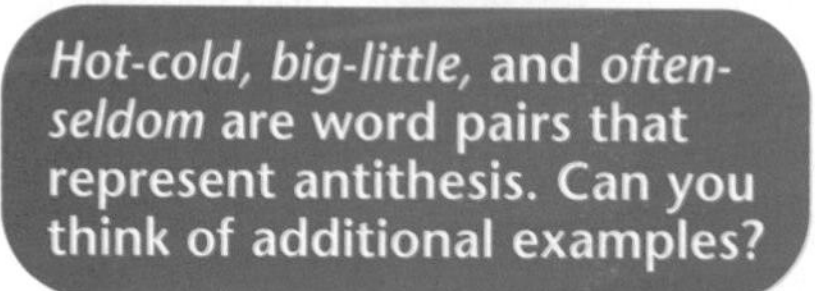

Hot-cold, big-little, and *often-seldom* are word pairs that represent antithesis. Can you think of additional examples?

Oxymoron ...

Another type of contrast imagery places words that are in opposition directly side by side. This apparent word contradiction is called an **oxymoron.** The oxymoron forms a contrast image that often jolts listeners and demands that they think and pay attention. Note the following examples:

> She is the *momentary love-of-my-life.*
>
> My parents want me to have such *boring fun.*
>
> Because I always fall gracefully, friends say I have *athletic clumsiness.*
>
> Parents of teenagers often exhibit *smiling insecurity.*
>
> Why must our society have so many instances of *selective equality?*

An oxymoron can create not only a quick, clever image for your audience to envision but also some impressive intellectual pictures that you can proudly display.

In his epic poem the *Iliad* (which was based on stories passed down orally from generation to generation), the ancient Greek poet Homer used an oxymoron in the phrase "the delicate feasting of dogs." The obvious contrasting of the words *delicate* and *feasting* (since dogs do not feast delicately) formed the image Homer wanted. He was able to *crystallize* a scene and a message by carefully selecting two words.

Irony ...

Another type of comparison imagery, **irony** is a figure of speech using words that imply the opposite of what they seem to say on the surface. When you use irony, you are using contrast because you say one thing but mean something entirely different.

Here is a story that shows how irony can be used in "picture making." You wake up Monday morning to find that your alarm clock hasn't gone off and that you are going to be late for school. Because you are in a hurry, you pour orange juice on your cereal instead of milk. The bowl

What figure of speech would this man be using if he said, "How lucky I am that my car broke down. Now I don't have to wash the car this afternoon"?

HAGAR THE HORRIBLE reprinted by special permission of King Features Syndicate.

spills and runs onto your Spanish homework. Your mother lets you off at the front door of the school, and you notice that you have two different-colored socks on. As you rush in the door, a friend in the hallway says hello to you and asks how your morning is going.

Your response: "Fine! Great! I'm having a *tremendous* morning."

What you really mean is, "This is a terrible morning. I wish I had stayed in bed!" It's obvious here that your words don't say what you really mean.

Here's another example. A television news commentator was giving an account of how a rock music fan filed a lawsuit in 1992 against the rock group Motley Crüe, claiming that the intense volume of the group's music at a sold-out concert he attended damaged his hearing. Said the news commentator, "Yes, you certainly wouldn't go to a rock concert thinking that there was going to be loud music, now, would you?"

Did he actually mean those words? Of course not. What he was saying to his television audience was, "How in the world could someone go to a rock concert and not expect loud music? Loud music and rock concerts go together."

Of course, the speaker's delivery and body language helped to show everyone watching that he didn't mean what he was actually saying. The creative power of contrast allowed his real message to come through to his audience. Irony is most effective when your words and your delivery work together.

Exaggeration Imagery

Our third and final category of figures of speech is exaggeration imagery. To *exaggerate* means to make something greater than it actually is. Francis Bacon, a seventeenth-century English philosopher, essayist, and statesman, once said that the only people who should be forgiven for exaggeration are those in love. In addition to "those in love," Bacon might have included "those speaking." While exaggeration in some situations—exaggeration of evidence in the courtroom, for example—might not be a wise idea, exaggeration of imagery in front of an audience can do wonders to accentuate the words we speak. Three types of exaggeration imagery are hyperbole, understatement, and personification.

Hyperbole ... Mark Twain gave us Tom Sawyer. William Shakespeare gave us Falstaff. Both of these famous authors gave us likable literary characters who exaggerated the truth. Tom Sawyer made too much of adventure, and Falstaff made too much of himself. Both humorously overstated their accomplishments. This overstatement is called **hyperbole,** and for speakers it is a method of saying more than what is true for the sake of emphasis.

Have you ever heard statements like these?

> I *called you a million times* last night, and the line was always busy!

Would it be hyperbole for this man to say, "I couldn't find anything decent to wear today"?

> I have *worked my fingers to the bone* cleaning this house!
>
> Mom, I *don't have a single thread of clothing* to wear to school!
>
> I *laughed my head off!*

No one actually called a million times, had bare bones for fingers, was totally without clothes, or had his head come off. Hyperbole is a form of imagery that blows a picture out of proportion and stretches audiences' imaginations.

It can also add a refreshing touch of humor. For example, a basketball team had lost 17 consecutive games when it finally won one. In its next game, it won again on a last-second shot. The student announcer, who was broadcasting from his school radio station, chanted wildly over the air, "The *streak* is still alive! The *streak* is still alive!"

Exaggeration imagery can intensify your message tremendously. You should not, however, exaggerate to the point that no one believes or trusts what you have to say. Use exaggeration to enhance your speech, but be sure to convey your message in unambiguous language.

Understatement ... Whereas hyperbole makes *more* of something, **understatement** makes *less* of something. Even though understatement doesn't exaggerate, it can logically be included in this section because it is the antonym, or opposite, of hyperbole. Understatement uses language that "draws the listener in" because it cleverly "distorts" in its own way and makes us see an absurdity more clearly. Here are some examples of understatement:

> Families out of work and without a paycheck can experience some economic *discomfort.*
>
> The winner of the basketball Slam Dunk competition can jump *a little.*

Clearly, a family without a paycheck could experience major financial problems, not mere discomfort; and a Slam Dunk champion would probably soar, not jump a little.

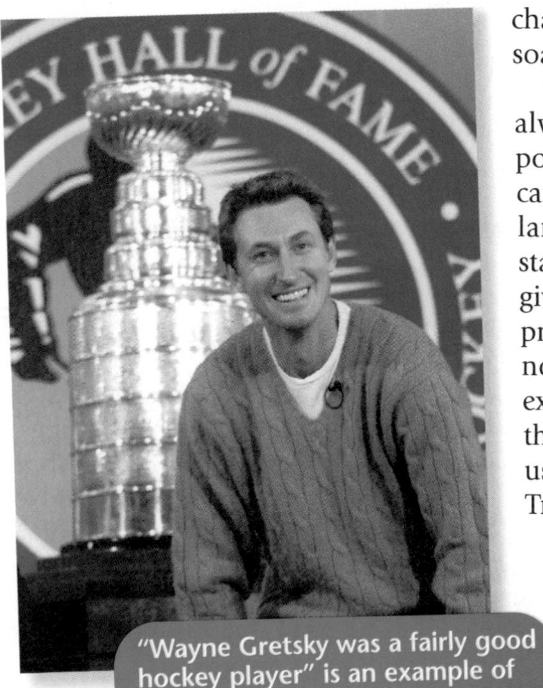

"Wayne Gretsky was a fairly good hockey player" is an example of what figure of speech?

Understatement doesn't always have the shock power of hyperbole, but it can work as an effective language tool. For instance, a student who was giving a speech on the problems of modern technology offered as an example the radar gun that state troopers often use to catch speeders. Trying to show that the devices aren't always accurate and that motorists can sometimes be unfairly victimized, he produced evidence

COMMUNICATION

Dealing with "Doublespeak"

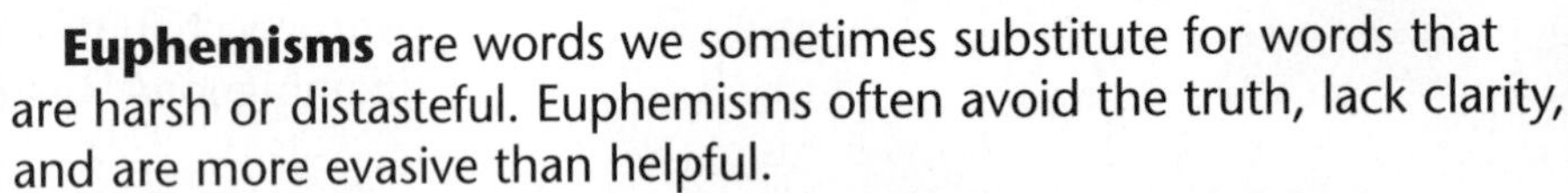

Euphemisms are words we sometimes substitute for words that are harsh or distasteful. Euphemisms often avoid the truth, lack clarity, and are more evasive than helpful.

Pentagon officials often win the Doublespeak Award, which is given yearly to the individuals or groups that have done the most outstanding job of using language meant to "bamboozle and befuddle." Once, in the 1990s, the National Council of Teachers of English presented the award to the Pentagon (U.S. Defense Department) for giving us an "armed situation"—not a war—in the Persian Gulf.

War is tough on words, according to the English teachers. The Gulf War was rich in euphemisms, says William Lutz, a Rutgers University professor and chairman of the organization's Committee on Public Doublespeak.

For instance, bombing attacks against Iraq were "efforts," and warplanes were "weapons systems." When pilots were on missions, they were "visiting a site." Buildings were "hard targets," and people were "soft" ones. Bombs didn't kill. They "degraded, neutralized, cleansed, or sanitized." Killing the enemy was termed "servicing the target."

The allies were also guilty as charged by the teachers. The government of Saudi Arabia, unable to accept U.S. female soldiers, called them "males with female features."

Source: Adapted from a Gary (Indiana) *Post-Tribune* wire service report.

Questions

1. How could euphemisms or "doublespeak" potentially lead to a communication breakdown?
2. Does the business world use any doublespeak ("downsizing" for "you're fired," for example)?

showing that a radar gun once mistakenly clocked a tree going over 30 miles an hour!

He followed this example by saying, "Now isn't it obvious that the radar gun might show a slight difference in what it registers as your speed and the speed that you're actually traveling?" The words *slight difference* were obviously understating what he actually meant (the difference between zero and 30 miles per hour is more than slight). Nevertheless, they created the impact that he was after. The image was powerfully made through "reverse exaggeration," or understatement.

Personification ... The final type of exaggeration imagery is personification. **Personification** is giving human characteristics to nonhuman things. Walt Disney, the cartoonist and movie maker, thrilled millions of people by making animals and other parts of nature act like humans. People of all ages are fascinated when teapots can talk, when sea creatures can fall in love, or when jungle animals can dance and sing. All of a sudden, these things seem like human beings.

Personification communicates a message through language and pictures that people can easily understand. Personification can be as effective in speaking as it is in animation, for it allows the listeners to visualize in human terms. Look at these examples:

> The *eyes* of profit can be deceiving.
>
> Don't allow dishonesty to *sneak up* on you!
>
> Crime can *dress up* in a number of different disguises when you are at work.

Profit doesn't have eyes, dishonesty can't physically sneak up, and crime can't dress up. Each example takes something abstract (profit, dishonesty, and crime) and adds a human dimension for increased emphasis.

Using exaggeration imagery can add color and style to your speaking presentations. Try it. Hyperbole, understatement, and personification can mean the world to your speech content—and to your speaking confidence!

Cartoon characters typify exaggeration imagery.

SECTION 2 REVIEW

Recalling the Facts ...

1. In this section, when a person says one thing but means something entirely different, she or he is using ______________.
2. The use of opposites such as "hot and cold" and "success and failure" is known as ______________.
3. A speech reference to a well-known person or historical event that is intended to create a mental picture is termed an ______________.
4. Using word opposites that are side by side ("In the workplace, *friendly hostility* does little to promote a positive work environment") is called ______________.

Thinking Critically ...

1. The Hindu leader Jawaharlal Nehru once said, "A language is something infinitely greater than grammar and philology [scholarship]. It is the poetic testament of the genius of a race and culture, and the living embodiment of the thoughts and fancies that have molded them." Analyze what this quotation means. What does Nehru mean by "poetic testament"? Is language greater when it comes from the head? From the heart? From both? Evaluate, and then explain your response.

Taking Charge ...

1. You have two tasks:
   a. Create your own metaphor or simile for the following: your report card, music, pizza, and money. (Example—simile: My best friend, Thuy, is like a compass. She always gives me a sense of direction as to where I'm going with my life.)
   b. Make a list of at least three television or radio advertisements for products or services that use imagery as a sales tactic. Be ready to say what specific figure of speech is being used (simile, antithesis, and so on) for each and why the advertisement is effective.

COMMUNICATION **Break** ***through***

The Gettysburg Address

The Gettysburg Address was delivered by President Abraham Lincoln on November 19, 1863, in Gettysburg, Pennsylvania. It was delivered on the field where four months earlier the Battle of Gettysburg had been fought. Lincoln's speech was intended to dedicate the site as a graveyard, a memorial for those Civil War soldiers who had died in the battle.

Although it received little attention at the time, the speech is an acknowledged masterpiece of *compression.* Its simplicity (the speech lasted less than three minutes) contrasted greatly with the two-hour speech of the accomplished orator Edward Everett, who had spoken earlier that same day.

The Gettysburg Address was a Communication Breakthrough because it eloquently put into words the belief that, even for a country torn by civil strife, there was hope for the survival of democracy and of the nation.

> Four score and seven years ago our fathers brought forth on this continent, a new nation, conceived in Liberty, and dedicated to the proposition that all men are created equal.
>
> Now we are engaged in a great civil war; testing whether that nation, or any nation so conceived and so dedicated, can long endure. We are met on a great battlefield of that war. We have come to dedicate a portion of that field, as a final resting place for those who here gave their lives that that nation might live. It is altogether fitting and proper that we should do this.
>
> But, in a larger sense, we can not dedicate—we can not consecrate—we can not hallow—this ground. The brave men, living and dead, who struggled here, have consecrated it, far above our poor power to add or detract. The world will little note, nor long remember what we say here, but it can never forget what they did here. It is for us the living, rather, to be dedicated here to the unfinished work which they who fought here have thus far so nobly advanced. It is rather for us to be here dedicated to the great task remaining before us—that from these honored dead we take increased devotion to that cause for which they gave the last full measure of devotion—that we here highly resolve that these dead shall not have died in vain—that this nation, under God, shall have a new birth of freedom—and that government of the people, by the people, and for the people, shall not perish from the earth.

We will examine the Gettysburg Address later in this chapter.

Question

1. What words or phrases make Lincoln's address so poignant and memorable?

SECTION 3 Making Music with Words: Sound Devices

We have discussed the importance of figures of speech and have shown how language can "come alive" when speakers use imagery to excite the imaginations of the audience. Now, what about the *sound* of the language when spoken?

The music of words can combine with the imagery of words to make communication even more effective. Maybe this is the reason why over 20 million greeting cards are sold every day in the United States. Greeting cards, for the most part, are written in language that speaks in pictures and sounds pleasing to the ear. Most of us are attracted to language like this.

The twentieth-century English playwright Christopher Fry once said: "The pleasure and excitement of words is that they are living and generating things." Much of the living and generating that Fry speaks of is the result of well-chosen sound devices that we can cleverly incorporate into our speaking. Most of the music of language is derived from some form of **repetition,** the act or process of repeating. We can use repetition to make music with words by repeating individual sounds and by repeating words or groups of words.

Repeating Individual Sounds

We can repeat individual sounds in three ways: through alliteration, assonance, and consonance.

Alliteration ... Say each of the following sentences out loud:

> A *c*orporation must *c*are about the *c*onsumer.
>
> *P*arents *p*rovide their children with the *p*ower to succeed.
>
> The *w*ill to *w*in is the combination of a *w*ork ethic plus the *w*illingness to dedicate yourself to a *w*orthwhile cause.

As you can see, in each sentence, a sound is noticeably repeated—in the first sentence, the *c* sound; in the second sentence, the *p* sound; and in the third sentence, the *w* sound. All of these sentences exhibit the sound device known as alliteration. **Alliteration** is the repetition of the initial sound of two or more words that are close together.

All you have to do to see the *pervasiveness* of alliteration is to watch television or to read the tabloids at the supermarket checkout counter. Weather forecasters might say, "Yes, folks, the *w*inter *w*inds *w*hipped through the *w*indy city of Chicago today," stressing the first *w* sound in the

*W*inter *w*inds *w*hip through the *w*indy city as *w*alkers *w*ear their *w*raps.

WORDS FROM THE WORKPLACE

Dolores Gamboa

High School English Teacher

Q. *How does communication play a role in the day-to-day activities of your work?*

A. Effective communication is so necessary to successfully express a complete thought, feeling, or desire to another individual or group. I must have the ability to explain concepts so students can comprehend the material being presented. If communication is not effective, then students are left confused, and the educator has wasted the students' time.

I once thought that in order to communicate effectively, one would have to have the ability to use correct grammar. Becoming an educator and participating in parent conferences, I realized that some parents felt uncomfortable with their communication skills. Often parents felt uncomfortable about their lack of good grammar skills. I made it my responsibility to assure them that they were doing fine and that I understood them. Today, I feel that if broken English or even a combination of Spanish/English can convey a person's thoughts or ideas, then the communication has been effective, perfect grammar or not.

Q. *As a teacher, what advice would you give to students regarding the importance of becoming effective communicators as they enter the world of work?*

A. In our society, people judge you by your ability to express yourself. Students must understand that when they enter the workforce, employers and fellow employees will evaluate them on how effective they are in their communication skills, both oral or written. It's important to be able to communicate effectively through language in order to move up the ladder of success. I can still remember Ms. Halton, my eighth grade English teacher, telling us to project our voices, to use correct grammar, to think before we spoke, and to *never* say things like "You know." My father had a favorite saying: "Successful people know how to communicate." Today, whenever I speak to children, students, or parents, I keep those words of wisdom in mind.

words winter, winds, whipped, and windy to make their forecast stand out and make people take notice. Similarly, a tabloid headline could read, "My Mother Married a Martian."

Do you see why alliteration works? It gives special significance to the specific language you choose to speak. In the following passage, the American patriot Benjamin Franklin used alliteration as a key sound ingredient to enhance the impact of his statements regarding the newly formed Constitution of 1787. Read this speech out loud so that you can better hear the language at work.

> Mr. President,
>
> I doubt . . . whether any other convention . . . may be able to make a better constitution; for, you assemble a number of men, [with] all their prejudices, their passions, their errors of opinion. . . . From such an assembly can a perfect production be expected? It therefore astonishes me, Sir, to find this system approaching so near to perfection as it does.

He went on to add:

> Thus I consent, Sir, to this Constitution, because I expect no better, and because I am not sure that it is not the best.

The repetition of initial *m, p,* and *b* sounds in nearby words draws attention to Franklin's statements. Can you hear the musical element that alliteration offers when you say the words aloud?

Ben Franklin was a masterful writer who perfected the use of many literary devices, including alliteration and assonance.

Assonance ... Read Franklin's speech again. What about the words *may, able,* and *make* at the beginning of the speech? Notice the long *a* sound in each word. The repetition of vowel sounds is known as **assonance.** The vowel sounds can occur anywhere in the words. Thus, the sentence, "We believe that peace means a chance for all of the oppressed people of the world," plays on the long e sound in five words for effect.

Consonance ... In the sentence just used above, examine the words *peace, oppressed,* and *people.* Notice that the *p* sound is repeated not only at the beginning of *peace* and *people* but also near the middle of *oppressed* and *people.* The sound device used here is known as consonance. Whereas assonance deals with repeated vowel sounds, **consonance** is the repetition of consonant sounds anywhere in words.

Let's look at another example of each way to repeat individual sounds, so that all three will be clear:

- I love to leap in the air and to land in the lake. (*l* sound, alliteration)
- I love to hike high in the mountains and see the sunrise. (long *i* sound, assonance)
- In dealing with hardships at work, I depend on my friends and family for direction. (*d* sound, consonance)

Rereading Franklin's speech should show you that all three of these devices can be used simultaneously. Go through the speech again and point out places where alliteration, assonance, and consonance work together to form the melodious "beat" or rhythm that gives the message its music and makes the language more memorable.

Repeating Words or Groups of Words: Parallel Structure

A student in a high school speech class was talking about his commitment to automobiles. He said, "If you want to be knowledgeable about a car engine, you have to work, work, work!" He later mentioned that he worked on cars "before school in my garage, during school in automotive class, and after school at a friend's house." He finally said, "Treat your car with respect. Your car will take care of you only when you take care of your car."

Parallel structure will help convey your message accurately.

Whether he knew it or not, the student was using parallel structure to help convey his message. Using parallel structure, also known as **parallelism,** means using the same grammatical form to express ideas that should, logically, be treated equally. Often, parallelism involves repeating words or phrases.

Look at what the student speaker said. Notice how he repeated the word *work* three times for emphasis. He also repeated the word *school* in three successive phrases that are grammatically and logically related. He concluded by stating, *"Your car will take care of you* only when *you take care of your car."* Notice how the two parts of the sentence use the same form and almost the same words. Parallel structure reinforces an idea or a series of ideas. It also creates a musical effect for the audience, which helps a speaker get the message across more convincingly.

Historians believe this photo may be the only one taken when Lincoln made his three-minute Gettysburg address. Lincoln is circled in the enlargement shown above.

Let's go back to the Gettysburg Address (Communication Breakthrough, page 270) and analyze three specific instances in which Abraham Lincoln brilliantly implemented the technique of parallel structure:

1. At the beginning of the third paragraph, Lincoln declares, "But, in a larger sense, *we can not dedicate—we can not consecrate—we can not hallow*—this ground." Music, a driving *cadence,* results from the repetition of the word arrangement introduced by *we can not.*
2. Two sentences later, Lincoln states, *"The world will little note . . . what we say here,* but *it can never forget what they did here."* Even though only a few of the words are repeated, the structure of the two parts of this sentence is the same.
3. Finally, Lincoln concludes by declaring "that this nation, under God, shall have a new birth of freedom—and that government *of the people, by the people,* and *for the people,* shall not perish from the earth." The parallel structure of the three prepositional phrases offers a climactic ending to one of the most monumental speeches ever delivered in American history. In addition, "this nation . . . shall have a new birth of freedom" and "that government . . . shall not perish from the earth" are strikingly similar in construction.

Frederick Douglass

We conclude this section by examining how another speaker of Lincoln's time, Frederick Douglass, used parallel structure. Douglass was born a slave in Maryland around 1817 and became a prominent voice in the antislavery movement. A well-educated man, Douglass saw that *emancipation* was a necessary step in the struggle of blacks for independence. During the Civil War, he helped organize regiments of African-American soldiers for the Union Army, and later in his life he held numerous government positions. Note that Douglass delivered the following speech in 1865 at the annual meeting of the Massachusetts Anti-Slavery Society, two years after Lincoln's Gettysburg Address. (Be sure to read the speech out loud.)

"What the Black Man Wants"

> Everybody has asked the question . . . "What shall we do with the Negro?" I have had but one answer from the beginning. Do nothing with us! Your doing with us has already played mischief with us. Do nothing with us! If the apples will not remain on the tree of their own strength, if they are worm-eaten at the core, if they are early ripe and disposed to fall, let them fall! I am not for tying or fastening them on the tree in any way, except by nature's plan, and if they will not stay there, let them fall. And if the Negro can not stand on his own legs, let him fall also. All I ask is, give him a chance to stand on his own legs! Let him alone! If you see him on his way to school, let him alone,—don't disturb him. If you see him going to the dinner table at a hotel, let him go! If you see him going to the ballot-box, let him alone,—don't disturb him! . . . Let him fall if he can not stand alone! If you will only untie his hands, and give him a chance, I think he will live.

By now, it should be clear that your speaking effectiveness is often only as good as your language effectiveness. But part of language effectiveness involves avoiding certain language pitfalls that can cause both you and your audience to take a "communication tumble."

SECTION  REVIEW

Recalling the Facts ...

Match each of the numbered examples with the letter choices below:

a. parallel structure b. alliteration c. assonance d. consonance

1. The *b*oss was *b*usy *b*uying merchandise for the display.
2. The product was successful, the workers were confident, and the management was happy. (Analyze the sentence in its entirety.)
3. Ap*p*lying for the *p*erfect job takes exce*p*tional *p*lanning.
4. A compl*e*te sp*ee*ch will *e*ncourage your audience to bel*ie*ve your message.

Thinking Critically ...

1. Reread the speeches by Lincoln and Douglass. Both speeches seem to deal with aspects of (a) life, (b) death, and (c) hope. Analyze each speech and then provide examples of where each (a, b, and c) is addressed. Evaluate how each speaker seems to deal with these three a little differently. Point out examples.

Taking Charge ...

1. In newspaper and magazine headlines, find two examples of effective sound devices (alliteration, assonance, consonance, or parallel structure). Next, apply what you have learned. Find an ordinary headline and rewrite it, creating your own original headline. You might want to write a serious headline, and then create a more humorous one.

SECTION 4 Language to Avoid

The quotation spoken by President Nixon on the first page of this chapter is an excellent example of how *not* to communicate. Even though you may be able to figure out what the quotation means eventually, who wants to wait? Besides, audiences don't have time to stop and figure out a confusing statement when a speech is being delivered. The next idea is on its way.

You have already seen one communication problem, euphemisms, in the Communication Breakdown (page 268). Euphemisms cloud clear communication by offering language that is puzzling and distorted. Unfortunately, the losers are usually the listeners.

Here, we take a look at three other language areas that you should avoid in your speaking: jargon, sexist language, and shocking or obscene language.

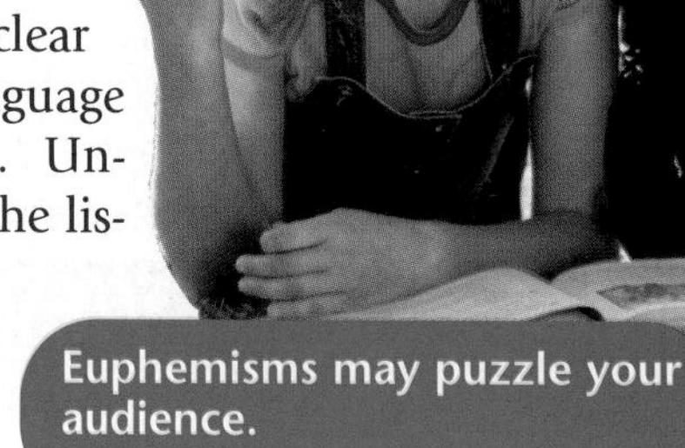

Euphemisms may puzzle your audience.

nical" terms. How effective would the communication be if you used the following terms, devised in high-tech circles?

> *batmobiling*—putting up emotional shields (from the retracting armor that covers the batmobile, as in "She started talking marriage and he started batmobiling.")
>
> *generica*—fast-food joints, strip malls, subdivisions, as in "We were so lost in generica that I couldn't remember what city it was."
>
> *irritainment*—annoying but you can't stop watching, e.g., the president's impeachment trial
>
> **Source:** *Funny Times,* June 1998.

You can see how jargon can be colorfully expressive, yet it is language to avoid when speaking in certain formal professional contexts.

Avoid Jargon

Jargon usually refers to the specialized vocabulary of those in the same line of work, such as doctors or computer programmers. Because only a small group of people understand what the language means, it is often unintelligible to most of the general public. In this sense, it is similar to **slang,** nonstandard words that may also be associated with certain groups, such as teenagers.

Like euphemisms, jargon is often heard in government circles, but it can pop up in any discussion.

Suppose you are giving an oral presentation about your job working at a computer company and your audience was unaware of certain "tech-

Every occupation has its jargon. These computer technologists would need to carefully monitor their language if giving an address to a general audience.

Avoid Sexist Language

Sexist language is language that unfairly groups women, and some would argue men, too, into stereotyped categories. Such stereotyping can be *demeaning*. Schools, textbooks, speakers, and even dictionaries are now recognizing the importance of fair play regarding the language used for men and women.

Society has traditionally associated girl babies with pink blankets and boy babies with blue blankets, girls with dolls and boys with trucks. Similarly, society often seems inclined to stereotype males as tough, take-charge, dominant leaders and females as weak, passive, subservient followers. Is this fair? Your spoken language must show that you believe that both sexes possess and can demonstrate equal abilities and talents and that gender has no relevance to a person's worth.

What sexist stereotype does this photo put to rest?

Look at these pairs of words: *man*kind-humankind, *father*land-homeland, spokes*man*-spokesperson, congress*man*-representative, *man*-hours-working hours, and *man*made-synthetic. Do you see how the second word in each pair avoids the sexist connotation that the first word presents?

Don't think that sexist language applies only to women. How fair is it, for example, to use the term *housewives*, when nowadays it is not uncommon for men to stay at home and contribute to house duties? Why not use the term *homemaker*, instead, in your speech? Remember, be vigilant to avoid any language that unfairly stereotypes men and women. Always keep in mind that the words you speak should promote the idea that all people have dignity.

Avoid Shocking or Obscene Language

Speakers often try to appeal to their audiences by speaking casually or by using "street language." Street language, however, can be shocking to an audience not expecting it. Use good judgment. While shocking language might draw your audience's attention, it can also quickly turn off most people.

Obscene language is any language that offends by going against common standards of decency. Since what is considered obscene may vary from area to area, speakers must avoid any possibility that their words might be construed as indecent. Recently a canoeist battling a rough river swore loudly and repeatedly about his troubles and was later convicted of using obscene language within earshot of children.

While a startling fact or statistic can work to your communication advantage, using an off-color story or a derogatory term will not. A student once started his speech by walking to the front and saying, "Hello, morons!" To him, this was clever. Granted, some of the students in the audience laughed (some perhaps out of shock), but many were offended by his introduction and tuned out what he said next.

If you find yourself about to include shocking or obscene language in a speech, ask yourself the following questions. Is a curse word worth the price? Is vulgarity ever worth the sacrifice of effective verbal communication? The answer to each question is no. Your audience deserves more.

Consider the story of Helen Keller, which attests to the power of language. Keller was born in Alabama in 1880. She was diagnosed early in life (at 18 months) as being unable to see, hear, or speak. Doctors early on said that she was mentally retarded and that she would never be able to function as a normal human being. However, when Keller was eight years old, Anne Sullivan, from the Perkins Institution and Massachusetts School for the Blind, began working with her. The two were to be close companions for nearly half a century.

Helen Keller learned from Sullivan what words meant. Sullivan spelled into the palm of Keller's hand the names of such familiar things as doll and puppy. At first slowly, but later rapidly, Keller learned the names of objects. Within a few years, she was reading and writing *braille* fluently.

When she was ten, Keller pleaded to be taught how to speak. Sullivan discovered that her student could learn by placing her fingers on the larynx of her teacher's throat and sensing the vibrations.

The story is told of how Keller was once asked which she would choose if she had the choice, seeing or hearing. She said that she would choose hearing. If she could hear the language used effectively, she said, the speaker could create for her all those things that her eyes could not see. In other words, spoken language would allow her to "see" in her imagination, and she would have the best of both worlds.

SECTION 4 REVIEW

Recalling the Facts ...

1. What is the term mentioned in this section that means a specialized vocabulary understood only by a special few?
2. One of the most moving stories in American culture is that of Helen Keller. She once said that if she had to choose, she would choose being able to hear over being able to see. What was her reason? (Give the exact words from the page.)
3. Teenagers are often said "to have a language of their own." These nonstandard words are called ______________, and should be avoided when speaking to a varied audience.

Thinking Critically ...

1. In Australia, teenagers have a language of their own. The statement, "She was given *the elbow* by her boyfriend," for example, means that she was "dumped" by him. When do you think that it is appropriate to use slang? When is using slang a bad idea? Can slang ever be a problem for your audience? For an audience of professional people? What can you do to make sure that this isn't a problem for *you?*

Taking Charge ...

1. Interview a friend, a parent or relative, a teacher, or a community member who works at a job that has a specialized vocabulary. Have the person name and then define for you at least five terms that could be categorized as jargon. Finally, ask the person to explain how jargon can sometimes be beneficial at the workplace. Write down the responses and be prepared to offer a short speech to the class.

STUDENT WORK

"The Real Thing" *By Kelly Slater*

Kelly Slater finished fourth in the United States in oratory at the 1990 National Forensic League National Speech and Debate Tournament, held in San Jose, California. Her speech, entitled "The Real Thing," dealt with a contemporary society that often values what appears to be real over what is actually authentic. Notice the vivid language and the word pictures that her words create.

The arena is set.
The multitudes are hushed in anticipation,
crammed into a coliseum filled with
the stench of sweat,
waiting for the combatants to appear.
Suddenly, without warning,
they emerge, cutting through the
dense humidity in
regal attire, robes of rich hues
and majestic style. As the mighty
enemies slowly lumber toward the center,
their stage and battlefield, the throng
falls into a rhythmic cadence of cheering,
booming voices proclaiming their
allegiance to either side.
Older generations prepare to shelter their young,
for they know
blood will soon be shed.
Achilles and Hector?
No.

Power Women of Wrestling!

Yes, it's Queen Kong and Lady Godiva, folks, known for her "pretzel hold" of death. You know, it's always been my dream to live a day in the life of Lady Godiva. However, for many, this dream can become reality with the help of Larry Sharpe and his New Jersey wrestling academy, "The Monster Factory." For just $3,000 and four to six months of training, Sharpe turns out new meat-hungry monsters left and right, instilling in them three basic techniques: (1) make the matches look real, (2) fake the injuries, and (3) mold the outcome, so that the audience buys it. However, the tactics of Sharpe's Monsters and the Power Women of Wrestling have unfortunately worked their way beyond the ropes of the ring and into the arena of the real world. As a result, we've reached the point where if it looks real, we'll take it. Whether it is or not is of little priority because we'd just as soon make it, fake it, or mold it.

It's been said that sometimes truth is stranger than fiction. Ironically, sometimes they're the same thing. Have you ever taken a road trip with your family and just couldn't seem to keep the kids occupied? Well, there's a hot new game out in Nebraska called "Fun with Roadkill." However, with this game you will not only be relieved of thinking of a new game to play, but relieved of taking a vacation at all, because "Fun with Roadkill" is a videocassette. You can just pop this video-vacation into the VCR at your convenience and not have to worry about stopping for "potty breaks." What could be better?

We can stage vacation; we can stage roadkill; we can even stage war. Did you know that between 1984 and 1987, CBS aired four different accounts of what it claimed to be the war in Afghanistan. However, it was recently revealed that the scenes were not real, but a mixture of recreations—scenes of training camps and not actual combat. It makes you wonder if what you're seeing on the news is real anymore. Perhaps the greatest irony lies in the fact that this particular footage won the most prestigious award in broadcast journalism. Just what are we rewarding? Perhaps this use of deception to get the prepackaged product that is quick, easy, and ready to use is as far as we'll go, but unfortunately it isn't. We'll go past the point of merely making things look real to actually faking it, when we flat out lie. And that's our second area.

Finley Peter Dunne once said, "A lie with a purpose is one of the worst kind, and the most profitable." Artist Mark Kostabi certainly agrees, and he's

proud of it. Four years ago, Mr. Kostabi decided that making deals and sustaining an image were more important than his original work. As a result, he now pays other artists between $4.50 and $10.50 an hour to imitate his art and forge his signature. In 1988, he earned over $1 million doing this. Well, he didn't exactly earn it. Mark Kostabi may be a liar, but at least he admits it. In fact, I'd expect that from someone with those values. However, I was surprised when I read that all of Bill Cosby's books were written by two other men. Do you recognize the name Peggy Noonan? You should, because when we hear the president give a speech, it is sometimes her words that we hear. Now, I'm not indicting the president [Reagan or Bush], but I am wondering what ever happened to the days of the seven Lincoln-Douglas debates, void of TelePrompTers, speech writers, panels of consultants, and reporters—without the glitz, the glamour, without the blatant deceptions and the fake product. Today, anything can be fake. We have fake food, fake fur, fake jewelry, and fake art. Would you believe that due to recent animal rights protesters, we're now trying to make real fur look like cloth? Ironically, the real product is being made to look like the imitation. Perhaps columnist Marilyn Gardner sums it up when she said, "If life is a true-false test depending on clear distinctions between real and counterfeit, then the 1980s may have flunked the final exam." Have we reached the point where we don't know what's real and what's not?

Now, granted, most of us do know that the world of the Power Women of Wrestling is one of orchestrated battles and pseudo-catastrophes. However, when our own world becomes one of "make it" and "fake it," we end up "molding" things that weren't meant to be molded, and we can begin with the entire concept of excellence. Three years ago, my high school adopted a statewide honors diploma. After its first year, parents complained that not enough kids received it. As a result, the school broadened the standards and lowered the criteria. Now the exclusiveness is gone. When the rules and criteria become putty in our hands, we're molding new standards and broadening our scope to the point of cheating. Just what is excellence anymore? You see, if we don't know what is real, we don't know what or who is good. The result is that the terms *excellence* and *champion* can be neutered, and originality lost in the process. Bill Laimbeer, of the world championship basketball team the Detroit Pistons, recently received his world championship ring. However, after he learned that over 21,000 replicas were given out to fans, he said, "I felt cheated. I worked nine years for this. There shouldn't be any copies."

You see, some things just weren't meant to be faked or copied—the sound of a baby's first laugh, the first day of school, a first kiss, a real Monet, a live performance of Beethoven's Fifth Symphony, a grandparent holding his grandchild for the first time, the wondrous moment of birth. For, in oneness there is beauty, and in beauty we just might find the truth.

Paul Slansky, in his book *The Clothes Have No Emperor: A Chronicle of the American 80s,* describes America as a "stage set with fake money, fake art on the walls and a clumsy supporting cast that holds no one accountable." However, the 1980s are over, and I'm convinced that we can make the 90s more than a mere carbon copy of the past decade. If we (1) hold fast to our standards, and (2) reward and recognize the original, then we just might make it.

The arena awaits once again.
Centered in an amphitheater void of sound
the lights are dim
the clothes drab
but the eyes of the enemies—
exploding with the lust for battle.
This time there will be a winner.
This time not the Power Women of Wrestling
but the Power of Wisdom
and the Promise of What's Real . . .
The arena is ours.

CHAPTER 11 Review and Enrichment...

Looking Back

Listed below are the major ideas discussed in this chapter.

- Choosing the correct words is like walking a tightrope—it must be done with care.
- The spoken word must communicate immediately with the audience, while the written word offers the reader the luxury of time.
- Accuracy of language and economy of language are two qualities that help create a positive speaking impression.
- Concrete words name things that you can perceive through your senses. Abstract words deal with concepts that are more intangible.
- Denotation refers to the dictionary definition of a word; connotation goes much further and involves all of the possible meanings that a word might suggest.
- Using figures of speech, or word pictures, makes your speaking come alive.
- Comparison imagery stresses similarities and includes metaphors, similes, and allusions.
- Contrast imagery takes the form of antithesis, oxymoron, and irony.
- Exaggeration imagery includes hyperbole, understatement, and personification.
- In addition to imagery, sound devices—or the "music" found in words—are also important.
- Most of the "music" of speech is a result of the repetition of sounds and the repetition of the same or similar words or groups of words.
- Certain language should be avoided: jargon, sexist language, and shocking language, which might be viewed as obscene or vulgar.

Speech Vocabulary

concrete word
abstract word
denotation
connotation
imagery
metaphor
simile
allusion
antithesis
oxymoron
irony
hyperbole
understatement
euphemism
personification
repetition
alliteration
assonance
consonance
parallelism
jargon
slang

1. For each word in the speech vocabulary list, give the definition as found in the chapter. Feel free to use the dictionary or the glossary. Prepare a quiz by listing any ten vocabulary words and numbering them from 1 to 10. Give these orally to another student to work on the spelling. Mix up the definitions and letter them from a to j. Have the definitions on a sheet of paper, and instruct the student to write the letter of the correct definition beside each vocabulary word.
2. Create ten original sentences using a total of at least ten different vocabulary words (you may use more) from the speech vocabulary list. Your sentences must be divided into the following groups: two sentences with alliteration, two sentences with assonance, two sentences with consonance, two sentences with personification, and two sentences with hyperbole. Have some fun and make your sentences enjoyable and entertaining. Also, be sure that they make sense. Be prepared to give your sentences out loud to the rest of the class.

CHAPTER 11 Review and Enrichment...

General Vocabulary

tangible
conscience
picturesque
crystallize
exaggerate
compression
pervasiveness
cadence
emancipation
demeaning
braille

1. For each general vocabulary word, write the definition as given in the dictionary. In addition, find the page on which each word appears and copy the sentence out of the book so that you can see how the word is used.
2. Write an original sentence for at least five of the general vocabulary words.

To Remember

Answer the following questions based on your reading of the chapter.

1. The term ______________ differs from the term *denotation* in that it refers to the meaning of a word that goes beyond the dictionary definition.
2. A metaphor compares two unrelated things without using *like* or *as*, while a ______________ makes a comparison that uses *like* or *as*.
3. Hyperbole exaggerates for effect and says more than what is true, while its opposite, ______________, makes less of something to get a desired response.
4. The repetition of the sounds at the beginnings of two or more words that are close together is called ______________.
5. A question that really doesn't call for a response from the audience is a ______________ question.
6. Language that unfairly stereotypes males or females is called ______________.
7. Referring to something or someone well known in order to make a creative comparison is called making an ______________.
8. Giving human characteristics to nonhuman things is called ______________.

To Do

1. Go to your school or public library and find a speech. You can find speeches in books or in periodicals such as *Vital Speeches*. Analyze your speech by listing the concrete words and the abstract words, the imagery, and the key sound devices used. What is effective to you, and what is unclear or lacks impact? Be specific. In addition, be sure that you can give a complete explanation of your entire speech.
2. Find someone in your school or community who is familiar with sign language or the world of the deaf. Interview the person and discover how the language works.
3. Think of a pleasant experience that you have had. Using a tape recorder, close your eyes and record your memories. Use vivid imagery and descriptive phrasing. Next, play back the recording. Did your language work for you? If not, go back and repeat the task—this time choosing a different experience.
4. Keep a notebook listing the jargon that you hear around school, at your job, at a parent's place of employment, and so on. Include definitions of the terms. Over time, does the language seem to change? Why?

CHAPTER 11 Review and Enrichment...

To Talk About

1. In Oregon, a newspaper put readers on notice that it will not print news about or recognize any sports teams that have mascots degrading the American Indian. Thus, team names like the Braves and the Redskins will not be mentioned. What is your opinion about this issue? What about a professional women's basketball team called the Missies or the Babes? What is your reaction? Are such names sexist? Why or why not? Where should we draw the line as to what language is offensive and what language is not? Be logical and give evidence whenever possible.
2. Find a copy of Benjamin Franklin's "The Way to Wealth." Notice how this collection of maxims (sayings) not only teaches a lesson but also communicates through effective language. Give your favorite maxims from the work and explain what image or sound devices they use.
3. Are commercials fair in their language? One television advertisement spoke of the need for romance and the personal touch in listeners' lives. For those interested, a phone number was given. When people called, however, a recording talked to them. When is the advertiser at fault in such situations? When are *we* at fault? What language should we especially look out for?

To Write About

1. Forming oxymorons can be fun and challenging. (An example is "cold war.") Write five of your own. Also, create some euphemisms for these jobs: dog catcher, window washer, custodian, elementary school teacher, chaperone to a dance, and person who cuts lawns. (An example is a short person might be called "vertically challenged.") Have fun, but make them make sense.
2. Write an introduction for a friend in class as if you were going to introduce him or her to your friends at work. Fill your introduction with job jargon. Now rewrite the introduction and replace all of the jargon with standard language. Be prepared to read your introductions out loud.
3. Write a description of how your day has gone so far. Stress in your language the following: personification, parallel structure, and simile or metaphor. Describe not only what is happening on the outside but also what is happening in your "inside world."
4. Write about a favorite song of yours. Why are the words to the song important to you? What do they mean? What are your favorite images in the song? What pictures does the song bring to mind? Be specific and give examples.

Related Speech Topics

What goes on in my first-hour class
A day at my job
The magic of bicycling
The best thing about a school dance
"Rush hour" at my house before school
Why I enjoy the beach
If I had only 24 hours to live, I'd . . .
Why Valentine's Day is special
The excitement of a sports event
My first day driving
The day I had to perform for an audience
Left-brain versus right-brain research (creativity versus cognition)
Sales and public relations
"Equal opportunity" in the professional world
Slang
Euphemisms
Sexism
Racism
The physically challenged

CHAPTER 12

EFFECTIVE DELIVERY

"As a vessel is known by the sound whether it be cracked or not, so [people] are proved by their speeches whether they be wise or foolish."

— Demosthenes, ancient Greek orator and statesman

Learning Objectives

After completing this chapter, you will be able to do the following.

- Explain the components of an effective delivery.
- Understand what delivery means and how it applies to oral communication.
- Identify types of nonverbal communication and their effects.
- Use appropriate delivery techniques to gain command of your information.
- Use effective verbal and nonverbal strategies in speech presentations.
- Evaluate the effectiveness of your own and others' presentations.

Chapter Outline

Following are the main sections in this chapter.

1. Types of Delivery
2. Using Your Voice
3. Using Your Body
4. Using Your Face

New Speech Terms

In this chapter, you will learn the meanings of the speech terms listed below.

delivery
manuscript method
memorized method
extemporaneous method
impromptu method
vocalized pause
power source
vocal process
phonation
oral cavity
rate
pitch
monotone
inflection
volume
articulation
pronunciation
platform movement
proxemics
posture

General Vocabulary

Expanding your general vocabulary will help you become a more effective communicator. Listed below are some words appearing in this chapter that you should make part of your everyday vocabulary.

regurgitating
methodically
syllable
alienated
superficial

Looking Ahead

The U.S. Postal Service has a very simple advertising slogan, "We deliver." This statement is saying that you can count on the post office and mail carriers to get your mail to you in a timely fashion. In a similar manner, as a good speaker, you must "deliver" your spoken words so that the audience gets the message. Your words are the "mail," and, thus, must be delivered accurately and effectively.

Your speech delivery is made up of two elements: verbal and nonverbal communication. Both are vital to making the right impression—because now the audience *hears* what you have to say and *sees* (through body language) how you say it. Do not underestimate your delivery. A current book titled *Emotional Contagion* says, to put it simply, that moods and language patterns are contagious. Studies reveal that if your words are delivered in a slow, boring manner, your audience will give off a bored response. On the other hand, a congenial, uplifting speaker can light up a group. If our words and emotions can potentially impact the moods and communication of others, shouldn't our vocal messages be constructive and helpful?

This chapter will help you understand and apply specific delivery skills. First, you will learn that your delivery is the actual "selling" of your verbal message. Next, you will look at various methods that you can select to deliver your speech. Finally, you will analyze the specific components of delivery—your voice, your body, and your face—and see how your speech can be a "special delivery" when these three work in harmony.

Introduction

Once, while talking to a group of college students, the great jazz musician Miles Davis was asked, "What specific musical philosophy do you give credit for making your trumpet style what it is?" Davis looked calmly at the student and said, "The only way that I ever started to get any type of 'style' was when I picked up my trumpet and blew!"

Similarly, you have no real speaking style until you actually speak. The manner in which you speak is called your **delivery.** Delivery refers to the mode or manner you use to transmit messages to your audience. When we discuss delivery, we're not talking about "what you say" but about "how you say it." It might be said that your

Miles Davis

delivery is your style of presentation, your personalized means of giving life and significance to your words. If we put this in a mathematical format, it might look like this:

Messages + Communication = Delivery

All good speakers know the value of delivery. The first two chapters of this book discussed how the speaker begins to build a good speech by

- constructing a solid foundation made up of values, and
- attaching the planks of confidence.

But, regardless of how solid the foundation of a house might be, few people would buy the house if the outside were in poor condition. Appearance, of course, is an important selling point, and most houses are spruced up and painted before being put on the market. Delivery is the "outside selling point" of a speech.

Well-written words that are poorly delivered will likely have little impact on an audience. Poorly written words delivered with great style will also probably fail to affect the audience. However, well-written words delivered with purpose and conviction will prove to be convincing.

Real estate agents have a term to describe something certain people do when they try to sell their homes. It's called dynamizing. This means that the owners will take time and special care to enhance the appearance of their homes to make a dynamic first impression. You need to give this same type of care and effort to dynamizing your speech delivery. Let's start by examining the different types of delivery you might choose. Like Miles Davis, let's now "pick up the trumpet and start to blow."

Just as you work hard to get your house ready to sell, you must also take the same care to dynamize and sell your speech.

SECTION 1 Types of Delivery

A number of singers can deliver the same piece of music, yet each singer will probably sound different from the others when the notes come out of his or her mouth. The country style of Garth Brooks, for example, doesn't sound the same as the rock style of Alanis Morrisette or Elton John. Different people have different approaches based on what sound works and what sound doesn't work for them. The same is true for speakers.

What works for you? What type of delivery will be effective, depending on your audience, the speaking occasion, and your specific speech purpose? Examining the pros and cons of four different types of delivery might help us answer this question. The four types are

the *manuscript* method,
the *memorized* method,
the *extemporaneous* method, and
the *impromptu* method.

The Manuscript Method

First is the **manuscript method.** In this type of delivery, you write out your material word for word and then deliver your speech from a lectern, or a stand used to hold your papers. You primarily read your material. The manuscript method is often used when speaking to very large groups. Political figures and elected officials often use the manuscript method of delivery (via an unseen TelePrompTer and a set of monitors) because they want to be absolutely sure of their words and the phrasing of their ideas. Business leaders speaking at their annual stockholders meeting usually hold a manuscript because they want accurate money figures (and the right spin on them) for their investors. Sports figures often use the manuscript method to give a prepared statement about retiring.

A good thing about the manuscript method is that when you use it, you are unlikely to make an error in the content of your speech. The words are right on the paper in front of you. Also, most likely, you will have had ample time to plan exactly what you want to say. Often, the manuscript method is an excellent way for new speakers to practice getting up in front of people. The manuscript functions as a "security blanket" and allows speakers to be more comfortable with their audience.

Potential problems arise with this method, however. You might lose touch with your audience because you are concentrating on your papers. While you are looking at your speech, you can't be looking at the people in the room. Remember, if the members of your audience do not feel that you are involved with them, they will very quickly "turn you off," and you will lose credibility as a speaker. People don't believe someone who won't look at them. In short, the manuscript method has real advantages, but be sure not to allow the words on your paper to take priority over the eyes of your audience.

"Special Delivery" Tip: When your speech is written out word for word, make sure that your writing is easy to read, that your words are large enough, and that you have key words highlighted or underlined. Typing or printing your words is a smart choice. Be sure the actual manuscript appears professional to the audience.

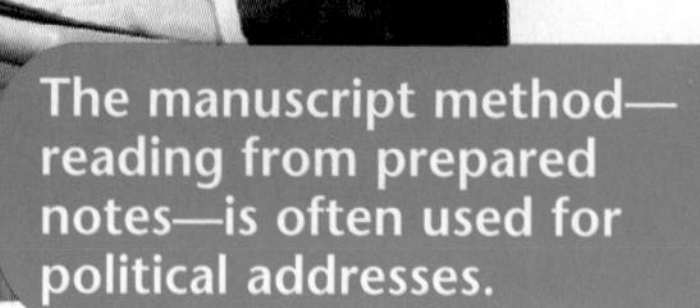
The manuscript method—reading from prepared notes—is often used for political addresses.

Do you think the speaker has lost touch with her audience? Is she making eye contact?

Writing should only be on one side and the paper should never be wrinkled or torn.

The Memorized Method

The second type of delivery is the **memorized method.** In this type of delivery, you commit every word of your speech to memory. You use no notes and have no papers to place on the lectern.

The memorized method has many of the same advantages as the manuscript method. You know each word of your speech by heart. Each idea has been thoroughly examined beforehand and each word carefully put into place. You can even have a good idea of where appropriate gestures, facial expressions, and movement will fit.

Orators memorize their speeches.

Here, too, difficulties present themselves, however. Even though it might seem that memorizing your speech would make you more relaxed and confident in your delivery, that is not always the case. As a matter of fact, you might become even more tense the second you realize that you have forgotten a word in your speech.

How many times have you seen someone responsible for introducing a speaker memorize the material and then forget his or her place? Have you ever seen students running for student government, class office, or offices in school clubs who have memorized their speeches, only to go absolutely blank the first time their eyes met the eyes of the audience?

The main problem with the memorized method, especially with beginners, is that you usually end up spending so much time thinking of the words in your head that you forget to share your message honestly. Like the manuscript method, the memorized method of delivery puts the words in charge! Remember, you must be in charge. Audiences don't want to see a robot in front of them simply *regurgitating* words from a memorized speech. Audiences want to listen to people who will talk to them person to person, openly and honestly. As with the manuscript method of delivery, then, be careful. Always give your utmost attention to the eyes of your audience.

"Special Delivery" Tip: Memorize in small sections. Practice your memorization out loud. The more times you say the words, the more likely you are to deliver them as planned. The most important parts of your speech to memorize are the first lines and the final lines. This way, you can be confident about the beginning and the ending of your speech. Finally, always have a "safety valve" in case you forget where you are. This could be a relevant personal story, a reference to someone in the audience, or a series of important statistics that relate to your topic. By buying some time you might remember where you were in the speech, and then continue right on.

The Extemporaneous Method

The third type of delivery, and perhaps the best, is the extemporaneous method. With the **extemporaneous method,** you don't write out your speech word for word, nor do you commit the words to memory. You may use an outline to keep your carefully prepared ideas in order, but you are free to choose on the spot the words that you will use to voice those ideas. You have some verbal latitude.

A three-by-five or four-by-six notecard is often used for the extemporaneous speech. For example, you might want to jot down each of the major transitions (discussed in detail in Chapter 9) or some words or phrases that make your speech flow from one section to another (*in the first place, next, last,* and so on). You could include key words related to major divisions to make sure that your main points are clear ("The economy is my next area of concern"). But you are also free to do some thinking on your feet.

Extemporaneous speaking occurs with friends every day.

The greatest advantage of the extemporaneous method is that you can be natural; you can be yourself. You can look at your audience and know where you are going in your speech and how your audience is reacting to what you're saying. The extemporaneous form of delivery allows you to pay attention to audience feedback and, if needed, to do some immediate adjusting.

Another good thing about the extemporaneous method of delivery is that your body is allowed to become a part of the communication process.

It is no secret that the extemporaneous style is the most believable. This is because it allows you to be you. It lets you and your audience connect logically and emotionally. There is some danger that when you use the extemporaneous method you may flub up your fluency or forget something you wanted to say. In the long run, though, this is the type of delivery that can dynamize an audience.

"Special Delivery" Tip: Get control of your notecards! Chapter 2 on "Building Confidence" offered some sound advice: even though notes can give you a sense of security, they are not supposed to be a substitute for memory. Don't have too many notecards. No more than a few should do the trick in most instances. Put down key words and phrases, and outline. Outlines highlight the key points and are easy for your eyes to follow. Finally, practice with the actual notecards before the presentation so that you are comfortable holding them.

The Impromptu Method

Finally, consider the **impromptu method.** Impromptu means "not rehearsed." This type of delivery involves speaking spontaneously or "off the cuff," usually for a relatively short time. With the impromptu method, you have little time for preparation. The impromptu method calls for a quick mind and instant audience analysis.

The impromptu type of delivery, like the extemporaneous type, allows you to be yourself. You don't have time to be phony with your audience or to appear artificial or contrived. Many of the good points that characterize the extemporaneous method of delivery also apply to impromptu speaking.

An effective impromptu speaker can come across as witty and intelligent. The point is that a quick impromptu style of delivery can be impressive if you have the talent, organizational skills, and confidence to pull it off.

As you might expect, the impromptu method of delivery has drawbacks as well. With no notes, you might lose your train of thought and appear disorganized. Or you might be at a loss for the right word and come across as lacking an adequate vocabulary. Probably the greatest problem with impromptu speaking is the potential for "dead space," those seconds in which you don't know what to say. This is where **vocalized pauses,** such as "and a," "you know," "like," and "uh," are often used as filler. If used too often, vocalized pauses can become extremely distracting to an audience because they prevent a fluent presentation of your ideas. Usually, when our fluency goes downhill, so does our confidence. It's no wonder that impromptu speaking is the most frightening of all of the delivery options.

In spite of its drawbacks, impromptu speaking is probably the type of speaking you will most often be called on to do in your life. Don't run from it. At home, at school, at community functions, on the job, or with friends, impromptu speaking is a necessity. Think about it. Have you ever been asked to give your reasoning for an answer in class or to state your opinion on an issue? Have you ever been asked to say how you feel emotionally? To explain why you think your idea might work? To describe a problem that you perceive? To solve a community concern?

You can do it! Think in simple terms, prepare a list of organizational words that you can frequently use, be clear, and be brief. Remember the value of reading and being informed. You must recognize that the impromptu method of delivery is a real-world necessity. If you practice it, you can master it.

"Special Delivery" Tip: Don't get caught off guard. The impromptu method of speaking means that you have both the brain and the word power to communicate instantly. Whether in a social or business situation, you will probably have an idea of what's coming. Be prepared.

Know who is in attendance.
Know the feeling of your audience.
Know what makes your audience laugh.
Do your homework.

Show your audience that you are a "thinker" and that your words show both emotional and intellectual conviction.

Comparing Delivery Methods

So which type of delivery is best? The answer is that you are best off when you incorporate parts of all four types in your speaking. There will be times when you will want to read a section of your material to your audience, such as when you have a list of facts or a long quotation that you don't want to misquote. Also, you may find that memorizing your introduction and your conclusion will help you feel more confident and establish rapport with your listeners. In addition, having a working outline that allows you to extemporaneously speak on your feet is a good way to gain credibility with your audience. Finally, the impromptu method of delivery makes you believable and up to the minute, because you are responding without preparation, on the spot, much as a CNN reporter does at the scene of a major news happening.

Whichever method of delivery you use, remember that you are showing your audience how you choose to say your words. Say them with thought, say them with feeling, and, most of all, say them well.

Next, take a look at how you can use your voice to make your delivery come alive.

SECTION 1 REVIEW

Recalling the Facts ...

1. There are four delivery types. Which one allows almost no time for preparation? Which one is read from a script?
2. Which delivery type uses notecards but is not intended to be read?
3. When using notecards, what are two pitfalls that you should avoid?
4. Give an instance where the memorized type of delivery might be appropriate.

Thinking Critically ...

1. It has been said that the ultimate compliment in speaking is when the audience believes you. In other words, regardless of the delivery type, you are effective if your listeners feel that you are being honest and fair. With this in mind, do you think that a person who uses notecards when speaking is *more* or *less* believable, or does it depend on the speaking situation? Explain what you mean. How can using notecards sometimes add to a speaker's credibility? Give a speaking circumstance where notes might not be a smart choice.
2. A national poll conducted in the 1990s asked people to identify the brightest, most intelligent people. The top five vote-getters (in order) were Carl Sagan, astronomer and author; Norman Schwarzkopf, retired U.S. Army general, who led the Allied forces against Iraq in the Gulf War; William F. Buckley, Jr., host of the television show *Firing Line*; Bill Moyers, writer and PBS television host; and George Bush, former president. Discuss the backgrounds of these people with your teacher. What has each delivered to American society? What do these five seem to you to have in common? Do you see any major differences? Finally, why were there no entertainers, sports figures, or Nobel prize winners on the list? Be specific.

Taking Charge ...

1. Practice three of the four methods of delivery using the student speech by Joseph Wycoff at the end of this chapter. First, find a paragraph that you enjoy and deliver it to a classmate or to the class by reading from a script. Next, try to commit that same paragraph (or most of it) to memory and deliver it. Finally, using a three-by-five or four-by-six notecard, deliver that same paragraph and look down at your notecard only when you need to be reminded of key words or phrases. Which method is the most effective for you? Why? Be ready to discuss your answers with the class.

SECTION 2 Using Your Voice

It doesn't matter whether you are a weightlifter, a sports car driver, or a scientist; you need a power source. A **power source** is the energy that makes things go. The power source for the weightlifter is muscle. The power source for the automobile is the engine. A scientist uses brain power. For speakers, the power source is the entire **vocal process.**

Martin Luther King, Jr., was a powerful and persuasive speaker who used his voice to fullest advantage.

The power source used to produce the voice is also used to help us breathe, chew, and swallow. However, in the vocal process, it is specifically our breathing system that provides the power for voice production, or **phonation.** The breathing system consists of the lungs, the rib cage, and all of the associated muscles. Let's examine how all of this works.

First, think about your lungs. From the lungs, we get the air necessary to produce sound. However, the lungs have no muscles; they are just two sacks, like balloons, waiting to be filled with air. We fill them when we breathe in. The muscles of the chest can help in this filling process, but the real power source for breathing is the diaphragm.

The diaphragm is a muscle that separates the chest from the abdominal area. It reaches from the front of the ribs to the spine. Breathing from the diaphragm, not the throat, produces an effective voice and helps produce a resonant voice, or a full, rich voice that is easily heard and pleasant to the ear.

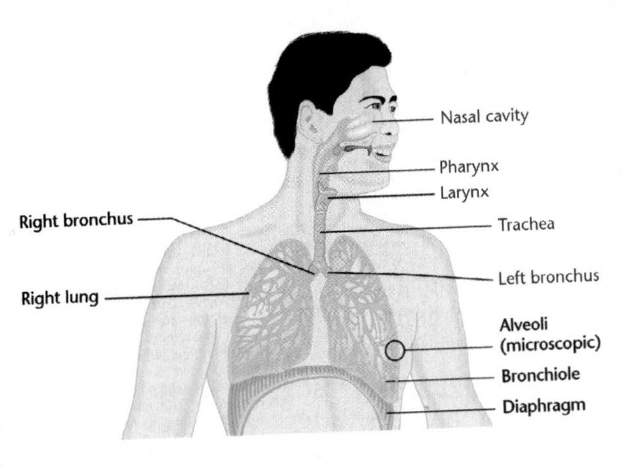

The Respiratory System

Bette Ambrosio, a former speech teacher at Highland Park High School in Dallas, has a method of teaching diaphragmatic breathing. First, she has her speech students lie down on the floor and put both of their hands on the diaphragm area, fingertips touching. If they are breathing correctly, the fingertips will part at each breath. "If the fingertips don't," she says, "students are chest breathers. Chest breathers are short of breath and weak in volume." Put her exercise to good use and breathe correctly from your diaphragm.

Where does the air go after it leaves the lungs? From each lung, it travels through a tube called a bronchus. The bronchi meet and form the trachea, or windpipe. The windpipe leads upward to the larynx (pronounced *lar-inks*), also known as the voice box, which is the voice-producing organ. The vocal cords are located in the larynx. From the larynx, air moves on to the pharynx, which is the cavity in the back of the mouth and nose, otherwise known as the **oral cavity.** The pharynx is connected to the outside air.

This overall power system performs two major functions for the speaker:

- It delivers the air needed to speak.
- It regulates the amount of air specifically needed to speak.

While it is true that the product of your power source is only air, it is also only air that goes into a tire. Just as tires without air don't roll, voices without a sufficient amount of air don't communicate well. You must "pump up" your lungs to give your words a smoother ride.

Specific features of voice must also be taken into account. These are rate, pitch, volume, articulation, and pronunciation.

Rate

The speed at which we speak is the **rate.** The average rate of speaking is approximately 120 to 180 words per minute. Sometimes people speak too quickly, and sometimes they speak too slowly. Most of the time, if you have a problem with rate, it will be that you are speaking too fast. People often speak more rapidly than they realize. Furthermore, when people are in any way frightened (as when they have stage fright), they tend to speed up.

Demosthenes is said to have overcome his speech difficulties by shouting into the wind.

When speakers talk too rapidly, audiences don't have time to understand fully what is being said. The words are difficult to understand, and the meaning is unclear. Of course, it is possible to speak too slowly, but most of the time, this is better than speaking too fast. Your audience can adjust to a rate that is very deliberate but has difficulty trying to digest a ton of information in a hurry.

Another problem occurs with speaking very fast. When you speak too rapidly, you run out of breath. This makes you swallow at awkward times, start to sweat, or think that you are going to pass out. Thus, a fast rate makes everything go wrong.

How can you avoid speaking too fast? Take a deep breath (as basketball players do at the free throw line), give each word its due, and speak deliberately and with feeling. Your audience will not only understand your message better, but also will have the time to actually feel as you do. With a slower rate, you can think on your feet. In addition, you can read audience feedback and tell how you are doing. Think about watching your favorite video while fast-forwarding the entire time. All of the film might be shown, but the video will not be fully enjoyed because the words won't be heard or understood. Don't play your speech at the wrong speed.

History can teach us a lesson. Demosthenes, who gave us the introductory quotation on this chapter's cover page, is credited by scholars as being the greatest of the orators in ancient Greece. His teachings represent the highest achievement in Greek rhetoric. As a small child, he apparently stammered or had a speech defect. To overcome this, he placed pebbles in his mouth and stood beside the sea, shouting into the wind, so that he would be forced to speak slowly and deliberately. Believe it or not, this method made him slow down his rate of speech. This slower rate allowed him to pronounce words accurately and enunciate distinctly.

We have emphasized one important point about rate: Speak slowly enough. It is also important to vary your rate somewhat, as you will see in the next section.

Pitch

Your **pitch** is the vocal notes that you hit while speaking—the highs and lows of your voice. Think of a musical scale played on the piano. At one end is a low note, and at the other end is a high note. Of course, many notes work between.

You can't easily sell a house whose exterior is dull and lifeless; likewise, you can't "sell" a speech delivered in a very narrow vocal range—you will bore everyone to death. In other words, you must avoid monotone. You speak in a **monotone** when you deliver all of your words *methodically* at almost the same rate and pitch.

Rate and pitch work hand in hand, as illustrated in the diagram shown here.

PITCH

RATE

Dead Zone

If you vary your speed of speaking and the notes that your voice hits, then you will be on your way to using your voice well for an effective delivery. Imagine a bouncing ball moving all around the two words shown here. As the ball is bouncing, your rate and pitch are showing variety and are working well together. However, if the bouncing ball stops bouncing and just stays in one spot, you are in trouble. You are hitting a very small vocal range at the same speed. You are in "the dead zone," and what is dying is your speech (and maybe your listeners as well!).

How many times have you complained about a teacher who always spoke the same way at the same speed? You probably said, "That teacher just about puts me to sleep every time she lectures! Why can't she liven things up a little?" The same is true for you.

Of course, you can't liven things up by simply hitting different notes at random. You can, however, use pitch to give the most important word or words in a sentence more emphasis. By giving a particular word more emphasis, you make the audience aware that some of your words are more important than others. Altering your vocal tone or your pitch is called voice **inflection,** and it is often used to help create emphasis.

Repeat the following sentence, each time emphasizing a different word for a different effect.

- *I* think that you are the best.
- I *think* that you are the best.
- I think that *you* are the best.
- I think that you *are* the best.
- I think that you are *the* best.
- I think that you are the *best.*

Analyze how emphasizing a different word each time changes the meaning of the sentence. Now repeat each sentence again and make it a question. Do you see the impact that your voice can have? Changing the inflection of a word or a specific phrase can help you use your information effectively. It can also help you support and emphasize your point.

In addition to emphasizing your words through the variation of rate and pitch, you can, of course, emphasize words or ideas through volume, which is the next area of analysis.

Volume

It does little good for you to have an outstanding speech if no one can hear you. On the other hand, people don't want to hear your words shouted at them. You must thus learn to control your speaking volume. **Volume** is the loudness or softness of your voice.

Picture yourself in these situations:

- seated next to a friend at a rock concert,
- seated next to a friend before the morning announcements at school,

Would a student rock concert be a good place to try out your most outstanding speech on a friend next to you?

- seated next to a friend in the library, or
- seated in a small conference room for an employees' meeting.

How would your volume be different in each situation?

These examples might be obvious, but you will need to vary your volume for other situations as well. For instance, the volume you use at the family dinner table will be quite different from the volume you use to give a speech in English class. The volume for a round-table discussion in science greatly differs from the volume for addressing a crowded room at a community function. Your volume is adequate when everyone in the room can comfortably hear you.

This means that you have to be alert to physical problems that might arise. What do you do if you are speaking in a small room and the air conditioner is blasting? What if the windows are open and the sound of automobiles and machinery outside is loud and distracting?

Of course, you could walk over and turn off the air conditioner or shut the windows. But this might be unwise if the weather is hot and muggy. Your audience might revolt. Thus, it is wise always to be ready to speak over any problem by adjusting your volume level. If the audience is saying to itself while you are speaking, "Turn it up, please!" they will probably soon tune you out. Don't let this happen. Give your words a chance to be heard.

How can you accomplish this? By practicing taking deep breaths and using the power source described earlier, you can have adequate volume in any speaking situation. Breathe from your diaphragm, open your mouth, and drop your lower jaw. Allow the natural amount of air moving through the oral cavity to create the volume you desire. Take deep breaths in through your nose, or inhale, and slowly release the air through your mouth as you form your words, or exhale.

INSTANT IMPACT

A KINGLY VOICE?

Charlemagne (742–814) was an early king of France. He was considered one of the greatest warriors of his time. He stood nearly six feet five inches tall and weighed just short of 300 pounds. Charlemagne had particularly strong legs and powerful arms. It was said that he was among the finest hunters and riders in his court and that he could kill a man with a single blow of his fist. However, he was often the object of ridicule (behind his back, of course) because he spoke in a high and squeaky voice. His contemporaries compared his voice to the voice of a 12-year-old child.

Articulation and Pronunciation

In the hit musical *My Fair Lady,* Professor Henry Higgins worked to turn the lowly flower peddler Eliza Doolittle into a lady. He tried to rid her of her accent by having her repeat such classic lines as, "The rain in Spain falls mainly on the plain." She was to speak slowly, clearly, and distinctly, making sure to pronounce the long *a* sound in the words *rain* and *Spain.* Higgins was working with the way Eliza used her voice. Specifically, he was working with her articulation and pronunciation.

Articulation refers to the crispness, the distinctness, with which we say the *syllables* in a word. The jaw, the lips, and the tongue are known as the main articulators.

Do you say your words clearly, or do you sometimes have the "mushmouth syndrome," in which syllables in words are run together or omitted entirely? Most of us are aware that the word *probably* has three syllables, for example, but we often leave out the middle syllable and say *probly.* Can you think of similar examples?

Middle *t* sounds (water, matter, better, for example) are particularly troublesome. You might have a tendency to articulate a *d* sound instead of the *t.* Another problem is the *ing* sound at the ends of words (coming, going, swimming). Don't drop the final *g* sound so that the word becomes *swimmin'.*

Poor articulation is most evident in the way people say entire sentences. Have you ever heard these?

"Whataya gonna do d'night?"	(What are you going to do tonight?)
"Didja see'm doot?"	(Did you see him do it?)
"Doya wanna talk ter onaphone?"	(Do you want to talk to her on the phone?)

Articulation problems most often occur when people speak too fast, fail to open their mouths when they speak, or fail to use their tongues adequately to produce specific sounds. To avoid these problems, don't be lazy with your voice.

The actor James Earl Jones, the original voice of Darth Vader in *Star Wars,* has a deep, booming voice and superb articulation. You can clearly hear every syllable of every word he says in his plays and movies. Did you know that as a child he stammered so badly that he was forced to write notes to his friends and teachers if he wanted to communicate?

How did he overcome this speaking problem? He went through speech therapy. He also joined his high school speech and debate team. In other words, he was aware of his speaking problems and actively worked to overcome them. Follow this example of James Earl Jones and practice to make your articulation the best that it can be. It will show your audience that you are serious not only about your verbal message, but also about your individual words and sentences—their crispness, their clarity, their sharpness.

Eliza Doolittle learns articulation and pronunciation from Professor Henry Higgins in the musical *My Fair Lady.*

Pronunciation refers to saying the sounds of a word properly and stressing the correct syllable. Nothing can destroy a good speech more quickly than a mispronounced word. It shows the audience

COMMUNICATION

Meaningful Conversation?

Many experts agree that too often American children are unfairly stereotyped as being rude and uncaring. To hear some people speak, all young people have these faults. Obviously, this type of labeling is unfair. However, few would disagree with the statement that there are too many instances of dishonesty, materialism, and violence.

But who is to blame?

It has been stated that the schools are partly to blame. Vietnam, the sexual revolution, and all forms of civil disobedience have left educators fearful of promoting to students the concepts of right and wrong because "who's to say what's right?" Education is still dealing with this values dilemma.

What about the family? In the last 25 years, the divorce rate has quadrupled. Today, more than half the children in the United States will spend part of their childhoods in single-parent homes. A Rutgers University sociologist believes that children are becoming less and less important in their parents' lives. He says, "Fading is the fundamental assumption that children are to be loved at the highest level of priority."

What about parent-child communication?

In 1965, the average parent spent roughly 30 waking hours a week with his or her children, according to the Family Research Council in Washington, D.C. Today, it's 17 hours. Of that time, "meaningful conversation" takes up a grand total of four and one-half minutes, reported Richard Louv in his book *Childhood's Future.* Another interesting note: The average child watches more than 20 hours of television a week.

Source: Carole Carlson, Gary (Indiana) *Post-Tribune,* December, 1991.

Questions

1. Can you think of reasons why parents and their children are spending less time together now than they did years ago?
2. What problems might result from children watching television so much more than they talk with their parents?

that you haven't done your homework in preparation for your speech. Two excellent ways to improve your pronunciation are to use the dictionary whenever in doubt and to listen to how intelligent people around you are using the word.

There are several areas in which you should be especially careful. Be sure that you have learned how to pronounce a business associate's name, the name of a country, or the name of a special group before you speak. Be especially careful in pronouncing foreign names and scientific terms. Right or wrong, people often associate how smart you are with how you articulate and pronounce your words. Make the correct impression on the job by not only polishing your shoes, but also "polishing up" your voice skills.

SECTION 2 REVIEW

Recalling the Facts ...

1. "In the vocal process, it is our breathing system that provides the power for voice production, or ______________."
2. In the hit musical *My Fair Lady,* Professor Higgins wanted Eliza Doolitle to speak slowly, clearly, and distinctly. Specifically, they were working on her ____________ and her ______________.
3. Altering your vocal tone or your pitch is called voice ______________, and it is often used to help create emphasis.
4. What do you call it when you deliver all of your words methodically at almost the same rate and pitch?

Thinking Critically ...

1. You have read about the value of delivery in oral communication. There is no question that the method of delivering your words is of paramount importance if you wish to influence or inspire your audience. With this is mind, consider the following quote from Chuang-tzu, a Chinese philosopher of the 3rd century B.C.E.: "Great wisdom is generous, petty wisdom is contentious. Great speech is impassioned, small speech cantankerous." What do you think that Chuang-tzu meant by this statement?
2. Name the television personality or celebrity whose delivery you believe is best at selling a product. Name the person in your school or community whose delivery you believe is best at selling an idea. In your opinion, what makes these people the best at delivering a message?

Taking Charge ...

1. As a class and then in small groups, say the tongue twisters below out loud. With each, start slowly and repeat, trying to pick up speed. If you are slurring, you need to stop and go back to a more controllable rate. You—and your mouth—must be in charge.

   a. Pat's pop shop
   b. Chrysanthemum/geranium
   c. Aluminum/linoleum
   d. Unique New York
   e. Red leather/yellow leather
   f. Toy boat
   g. Sister Susie's sewing shirts for soldiers

Now, try these tougher ones.

   h. Peter Piper picked a peck of pickled peppers. If Peter Piper picked a peck of pickled peppers, where's the peck of pickled peppers Peter Piper picked?
   i. Theophilus Thistle the thistle sifter sifted a sieve of unsifted thistles. If Theophilus Thistle the thistle sifter sifted a sieve of unsifted thistles, where is the sieve of unsifted thistles that Theophilus Thistle the thistle sifter sifted?
   j. Betty Botter bought some butter. "But," she said, "this butter's bitter. If I put it in my batter it will make my batter bitter. But a bit of better butter will but make my batter better." So, she bought a bit of butter, better than the bitter butter, that made her bitter batter better. So, 'twas better that Betty Botter bought a bit of better butter.

SECTION 3 Using Your Body

In the novel *The Scarlet Letter,* by Nathaniel Hawthorne, many of the seventeenth-century Puritan characters show one face to the public but are very different on the inside. While this "two-sidedness" might be an excellent literary device for character and thematic analysis, using it in your speaking isn't smart. Your body, like your voice, must be a positive extension of your message. You can't allow your speech to say one thing while your body is saying something entirely different.

What message is this man telegraphing?

You have already read about the impact of nonverbal communication. Such communication does not actually deliver your words, but it does deliver your attitude about those words.

You read about body language in other chapters, specifically Chapter 4. When you deliver a speech, many things you do with your body—standing with one leg bent, tilting your head back, slouching, lowering your chin, keeping your arms in extremely close to your body, leaning toward your audience, scratching your head, standing with your entire body rigid, or standing relaxed with your hands comfortably at your side—convey nonverbal messages to your audience. If you are speaking on the value of a product that you are selling, but your body telegraphs to the audience that you are bored or uneasy, who in the world would want to buy your product?

Your body language, then, is a key contributor to nonverbal communication. So is your face; we will deal with that later in the chapter. Let's now take a look at two other aspects of using your body and their effects: platform movement and gestures. Both are important in promoting an effective delivery.

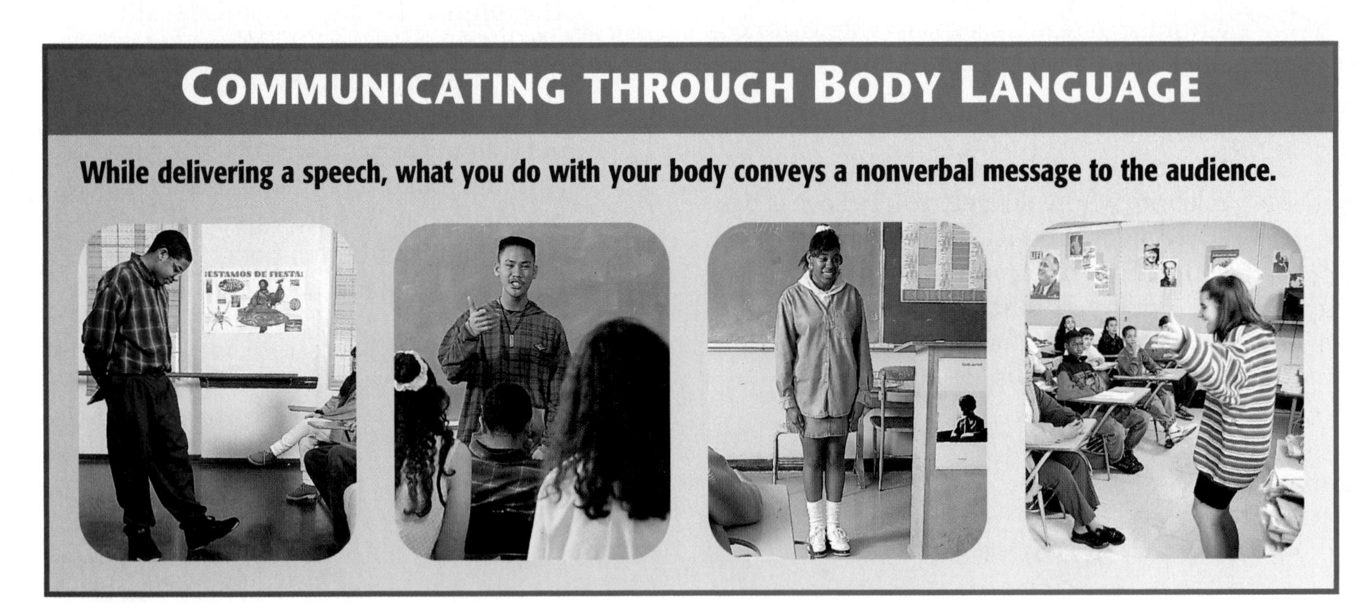

COMMUNICATING THROUGH BODY LANGUAGE
While delivering a speech, what you do with your body conveys a nonverbal message to the audience.
¡ESTAMOS DE FIESTA!

COMMUNICATION Breakthrough

Hearing Your Favorite Book

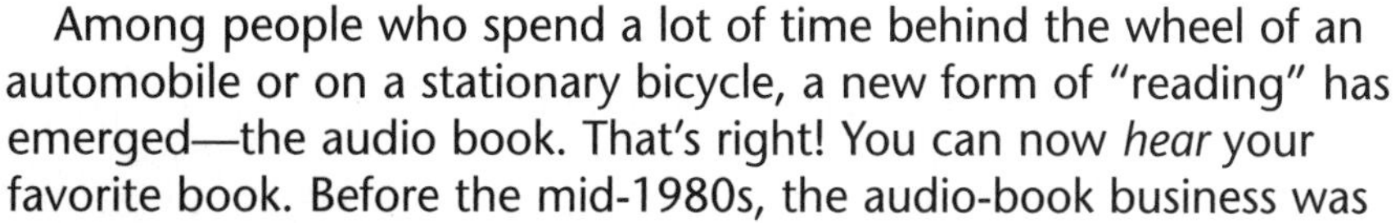

Among people who spend a lot of time behind the wheel of an automobile or on a stationary bicycle, a new form of "reading" has emerged—the audio book. That's right! You can now *hear* your favorite book. Before the mid-1980s, the audio-book business was nonexistent, but in today's market it has annual sales of over $1 billion. Anyone with an automobile tape deck or a portable cassette or CD player is fair game.

"What we find," says Leslie Nadell of Random House Audio Publishing, "is that once people have listened to one audio book they become instant converts."

Even though many literary purists might be bothered by the abridged versions of the works, audio books have gained praise from authors themselves. All authors must approve the material before it is put on the market. People who listen to the tapes have been impressed by the excellent voices and the vibrant, exciting delivery that many of the speakers present on tape. Many of the best readers are the authors themselves. Glowing reports have been turned in for John le Carré and Eudora Welty, as well as E. B. White *(Charlotte's Web)*. The worst reader so far: Norman Mailer. Of the actors, John Lithgow sounds as excellent on tape as he does in the theater. By the way, the largest customers for the audiocassettes are public libraries.

Adapted from: Katrine Ames, "The New Oral Tradition," *Newsweek.*

Questions

1. Some people might argue that an audio book takes away from the reader's imagination; however, what possible advantages could the audio book offer?
2. Can you think of specific instances where the audio book would be a practical asset?
3. Why do you think that libraries are the largest customers of audio books?

Platform Movement

A good speaker is similar to a good dancer in that both must have a sense of rhythm. In the speaker, all body movement should have a rhythmic flow that is fluid and natural and fits with the words being spoken. This rhythm should be apparent in the speaker's platform movement.

Very simply, **platform movement** means walking or stepping in a purposeful manner from one spot to another while speaking. Obviously, it need not involve a real platform. While you may at times be on stage (introducing a guest speaker for a meeting or an awards program, for example), you are usually simply standing at the front of your classroom or some other room when you deliver your speech.

Most of your speeches will be delivered in the front of your classroom.

Before discussing what you should do, let's take a look at what you shouldn't do regarding platform movement.

- Don't pace back and forth as if you are a duck at a shooting gallery.
- Don't wander, or take strolls from spot to spot with no purpose.
- Don't avoid movement because you are afraid you will look silly.

Movement should accentuate and reinforce your speaking. It should be logical and make sense to your audience. Platform movement not only shows your audience that you are literally moving from one part of your speech to another, but it also gives the audience a break from staring at you in one spot the entire time. It provides a type of "eye relief." This makes you a little more dynamic and exciting if you do it correctly.

"But how do I move, and when are the right times to move?" you may ask. There are three situations that allow for effective platform movement.

Platform movement is effective when going from one section of a speech to another, for changing emotional appeal, or when it feels natural.

First, it is logical to move when you are going from one section of your speech to another. For instance, after you have delivered your introduction, you might want to move a bit, to set up and draw attention to your thesis or topic sentence. In addition, many speakers like to use movements between their main points and again before their conclusion. These movements add variety and give special importance to specific sections of their speeches. Always begin your speech by "squaring up," or centering yourself with your audience, not with the room. You should also end your speech near the middle of your audience. This adds a touch of cohesion, courtesy, and completeness to your speech.

Second, movement is often effective when you are changing your emotional appeal. Suppose you are describing the problems that teenagers face in society today. You might be speaking at a fairly even rate and emotional level. However, when you start listing the startling statistics related to teenage suicide, your emotional level might rise. You might start speaking more quickly and becoming more emotionally intense. At this point, a platform movement might be logical to show that your body is as involved as your words in what you are communicating. Similarly, if you were speaking on the problems of stereotyping teenagers, and then began to report on the great things that teenagers have done for others, such as working with disabled children and supporting community projects, a change in emotional level and movement might be appropriate. When your emotions are in action, often so are your feet! Allow your movement the chance to help set the speaking mood you want.

Finally, platform movement is often appropriate when it just feels right to you. Don't let rules always direct what you do in speaking. Sometimes it is appropriate to simply allow yourself to be yourself. After you have worked and practiced your speech, trust your communication instincts.

You might have an urge to move while delivering an example or while giving your conclusion. Go ahead and give it a try. Your audience (and your teacher) will let you know after you are finished if your movement was distracting or ill timed, and then you can make adjustments for the *next* time you speak.

Platform movement should be done so naturally that your audience isn't even aware of it. You should not have to be told how to move or at what speed. You simply move while delivering your speech as you would move anywhere else. When

Your movement on stage should appear as natural as your movement in your school hallway.

you are walking in the hallway at school, no one has to tell your legs and feet what to do. You move and walk instinctively. Let your legs and your body work together so that your movement is believable, parallels the tone of your speech, and, most of all, is you.

Nevertheless, there are a few specific points to remember about how to move.

- Always move in a comfortable, relaxed manner by leading with the leg in the direction you are moving. If you are walking to the right, for example, move the right leg first. There are two good reasons to do this. The first is that it keeps your body "open" to the audience. If you are crossing your legs over as you move, you might turn almost sideways and present a profile to your audience. When this happens, your audience members lose part of your face and potentially part of your words. They can't hear what you might be delivering to the walls. The second reason is that it keeps you, believe it or not, from tripping over your own feet.
- Move toward your audience. When you are moving in your speech, your walking should be directed toward some portion of the audience or even a specific listener. You should be moving as if to say, "Here's a point that I particularly want you to hear." In other words, you are moving because you are sharing your words with your listeners. Vary the direction of your movement. This is a good way to make sure that no portion of your audience feels neglected or ignored.

Of course, you shouldn't make the angle of your movement too extreme, and you shouldn't move so close to an audience member that he or she might feel uncomfortable. Be aware of **proxemics,** or how much physical space you

INSTANT IMPACT

"DELIVERY" HAS ITS DAY IN COURT

Creators of a play about the rock legend Janis Joplin once won a key court ruling. Heirs of the blues/rock-and-roll singer, who died in 1970, had sued the authors of a play titled *Janis,* claiming that they had exclusive rights to Joplin's performance style. The heirs claimed that they owned the rights to her "voice, delivery, mannerisms, appearance, dress, and actions (gestures included) accompanying her performance."

The judge disagreed, saying that even though Janis Joplin's style was indeed unique, people have too many similarities in delivery for one person to claim them exclusively. If the heirs' position were upheld, the judge questioned, how could comedians or satirists ever imitate a celebrity without facing a possible lawsuit?

leave between you and your audience. Use your common sense in determining your distance from the audience. Know the speaking area, and always make sure that you can comfortably move back to the center of the room, leaving an appropriate amount of space between you and your audience.

- Know exactly the number of steps that you are going to take. You can usually be comfortable with taking one step forward (toward your audience), or using a three-step or a five-step method.

The three-step method is fairly easy to master. You simply take your first step (moving the correct leg, of course), cross over with the second step, and then move the first leg forward so that you are once again standing firmly on both feet. This method is appropriate for moving in smaller areas, but it is recommended in any setting because it is easy to control. Control is what you are after.

The five-step method works exactly the same way as the three-step method except that, obviously, you take two more steps. This method can be used in larger speaking areas. The danger with the five-step method is that you might forget what you are doing and start to roam around the front of the room.

Even though an experienced speaker might not need to plan exactly how many steps to take (that is, three steps or five steps), a beginner should. So keep your movement centralized and be sure to avoid situations in which you might lose control of your movements and walk right out the door (as tempting as it might be).

Gestures

Even though they are nonverbal, gestures definitely communicate. Gestures, as explained in Chapter 4, are actions in which the body or parts of the body move to express an idea or emotion. We might think of **posture** as referring to the position of the body when it is still (like when your teacher tells you, "Stand up straight. Stop slouching. Don't lean on that desk. Get your hands out of your pockets."). Gestures, however, refer to the body in motion.

Talk show host Jay Leno accentuates his point with arms, hands, shoulders, and head as he talks with actress Kelly Preston.

Let's take a look at how gestures specifically relate to delivery. Like platform movement, gestures should be natural and fit what you are saying. Gestures should not be contrived or artificial. Body gestures are usually associated with the arms, the hands, the shoulders, and the head. Like a good jazz band, a good corporation, or a smoothly running engine, gestures work best when all of the parts work together. A good speaker does not allow an individual part of the body to work in isolation.

If you want to know how to gesture effectively, then watch people (especially professional communicators, such as talk show hosts) when they talk. Watch what the shoulders do when the hands are in motion. Notice how the head can accentuate a point.

Probably the single greatest problem that you might have will involve this question: What do I do with my hands?

Eighteenth-century American clergyman John Witherspoon once said, "Never rise to speak till you have something to say; and when you have said it, cease." In other words, he was advising all speakers not to overdo it with their words. This same principle can be applied to gestures. Make your gestures clear, but don't overdo them. There is nothing wrong with having your arms and hands comfortably at your sides, at your "base." This relays to your audience that you are relaxed and in control.

If you are holding notecards in your hands, you may hold them with one hand or with both hands. Either way, your notes should be comfortably held at your waist, and they should not be a distraction.

Even though some instructors permit students not using notes to put their hands behind them or folded in front of them, it is best to start practicing as soon as possible bringing your hands back to your sides.

When you do gesture with your hands, bring your gestures up and out. Remember, again, that these gestures aren't supposed to be the center of attention or sell popcorn. They are supposed to supplement your content.

Here are three tips that can help you become more comfortable with your hands.

1. Learn the Gesture Zone ... It is important that you develop a sense of control with your hands. Too often, our hands will take off, almost as if they have minds of their own, and do things that we aren't aware of. One method that will help you control your hands is to learn your gesture zone.

The gesture zone is an imaginary box in front of you, similar to a television screen. To find your gesture zone, start by placing your arms in front of you with your palms up and your elbows fairly close to your body. Your arms should be near waist level. Now draw the *bottom* of the gesture zone by moving your hands together. Repeat this to get a feel for how your hands can move near your waist and be effective.

Next, put your hands back in the original position—arms in front of you with both palms facing up (don't get your arms too far apart). Turn your hands so that your palms are at right angles to the floor (parallel to your body). Move your hands up and down, but be sure never to go higher than your shoulder area. (From the audience's point of

This man's gesture is within the ideal gesture zone.

DEFINING YOUR GESTURE ZONE

BOTTOM

SIDES

TOP

view, if you gestured higher than the shoulder area, your face would be partially covered by your gestures, and this should never happen—because many listeners watch your lip movements to help them "hear" your words.) You are now drawing the *sides* of the gesture zone.

Finally, after you have found the sides of your gesture zone, draw in the *top* by repeating the procedure you used to find the bottom, only now turn your palms down so that they are facing the floor.

Now, draw the entire gesture zone. Do it again. Notice how your box ranges from your waist to just below your shoulders. Practice gesturing inside of this imaginary control zone. Certain gestures will call for you to gesture outside of the zone, but don't get fancy until you know what you are doing. Pay particular attention to gestures that are too sweeping or wide. The idea is to keep the audience focused on your face.

2. Learn to "Lift and Lay" Your Hands ... Gestures can be a distraction if you don't work at doing them correctly. Three common errors in gesturing are the following:

- the "flyaway" gesture, in which your hands simply shoot out from your sides like missiles and appear directionless;
- the "judo-chop" gesture, in which you appear to mercilessly and repeatedly hatchet your message into the minds of your audience; and
- the "penguin-wave" gesture, in which you have your hands down at your side and then attempt to gesture by simply flicking your wrists or fingers as a penguin might flick its wings while walking on land.

In contrast, when you "lift and lay," you lift your arms and hands so that they move comfortably up and out, and then lay your hands at the end of a gesture as if you were laying them on an imaginary ledge or a table. Of course, this too takes place in the gesture zone. In a sense, you are also laying your ideas on the table to be considered. Just as you can give finality to your gesture, you can also give added importance to your words. Even though the distance traveled isn't great, this technique gives a sense of control and finality to your gesture.

3. Practice the "String" Idea ... As mentioned, taking the time to watch and analyze people while they are speaking is a good idea. It teaches you about what happens during both verbal and nonverbal communication. It also teaches you what makes sense and what doesn't. For instance, have you ever seen anyone gesture without moving a portion of his or her upper body—the shoulders, the neck, or the head? Unless you are watching a science fiction movie, the answer is no.

When you speak informally you don't think about your body. However, you *should* think about it. If you are upset about a test score and throw your hands up in despair, what do you do with your shoulders? Your head? Do they move, also? If you are questioning a group about its position on a controversial issue, and you use your hand and fingers emphatically to make your point, what do you do with your head? Does it move? Of course.

The "string" idea—that one part of the body moves when another does—certainly shows in this athlete's posture.

What does all this have to do with the "string" idea?

Imagine that you have a long piece of string. Hold one end with one hand and the other end with the other hand. Now, tie the two ends together. Place the string around your neck. Pretend to place one arm (or both) through the other end of the loop, as if it were a sling. What happens when you extend that arm? Doesn't the string force your head to move, too? It is as though your body is connected by a series of strings (or rubber bands) that react to one another.

This brother and sister didn't get to be black belts in karate without practice, practice, and more practice.

What is the point of this exercise? The "string" idea is simply a good way to remind yourself to keep the upper portion of your body actively involved when gesturing.

After a while, you will begin to do some things that are more natural for you. At first, though, paying attention to these three tips—the gesture zone, the "lift and lay," and the "string" idea—will give you a good start on gesturing properly and making your hands believable.

You may feel uncomfortable practicing gestures. Remember, though, that it makes little sense to spend a great deal of time writing out speeches but hardly any time working at the exercises needed to become a good speaker. All good musicians and all great athletes pay their dues by doing drills. The drill work may be monotonous, but in the long run, the basics are invaluable. Performing nonverbal "gesture drills" is a good way to give precision to your body movement.

SECTION 3 REVIEW

Recalling the Facts ...

1. The term given for taking steps and moving from one spot to another is __________ __________.
2. You can control your hands when you are gesturing by being aware of the __________ __________.
3. You should involve your entire body when you gesture. The "__________ test" is a method of showing you how your head and shoulders should be an active extension of arm gestures.

Thinking Critically ...

1. Nineteenth-century Irish politician Daniel O'Connell said, "A good speech is a good thing, but the *verdict* is the thing." This means that the audience has to determine whether you have delivered or not. Analyze or evaluate three people, famous or not, whom you consider to have delivered in some fashion. They might have developed an idea, performed an amazing feat, or excelled during a time of crisis. Explain what they did, how they did it (the steps involved), and the impact that their delivery had.

Taking Charge ...

1. List at least five types of hand and arm gestures that people use and the emotions or attitudes that go along with them. Create a sentence to go with each emotion or attitude and gesture. Be prepared to demonstrate.

SECTION 4 Using Your Face

A genuine smile is your best sales tool.

Probably the most important nonverbal element in an effective delivery is your face. Studies have shown that more than the words spoken or even the body language, the face determines whether someone is believed or not. The expressions on your face while you talk can show your listeners how you feel about them, how you feel about your material, and how you feel about yourself as a speaker.

You have already read about the role of nonverbal communication; however, this text can't emphasize enough the importance of your unspoken attitude. Quite frankly, if your face doesn't "sell it," your audience doesn't "buy it." If you are speaking on the value of teamwork where you work, but you convey to fellow employees that they are beneath you in intelligence—not by your words but by your facial gestures—how can you expect them to ardently support your position? You will only have *alienated* them.

If you are speaking about drug abuse or about how street people are being victimized, but your face gives off an expression that says you are disinterested, bored, or disgusted, what will your audience think about your attitude toward your subject matter? What if you are discussing a serious topic and a broad smile appears on your face? Why are you smiling? Your face just doesn't match the mood or tone of the speech.

One of the most common errors in speaking is to present a well-thought-out speech, only to have its impact ruined by an absolutely petrified facial expression. If you seem frightened, you lose credibility. If you appear to lack confidence in yourself, your audience will lack confidence in both you and what you are saying.

"A picture is worth a thousand words," and your face while you are speaking is that picture. What part of the face is the most important?

The Eyes

"The eyes are the windows to the soul." This famous quotation is vital for the good speaker to understand. It is through your eyes that the people in your audience will primarily judge you: your overall honesty, your conviction about your message, and your genuine concern for them.

An effective delivery depends on your ability to look at the people in your audience and make meaningful eye contact with them. Forget about the myths you might have heard about looking at the tops of heads or imagining your audience sitting in their seats dressed in just their underwear. These are simply foolish shortcuts intended to

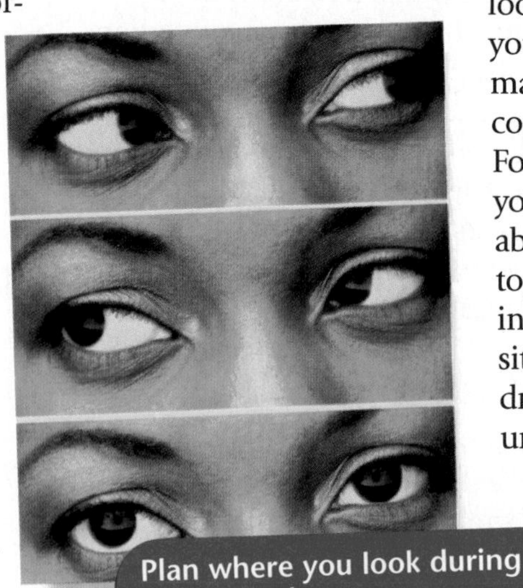

Plan where you look during your speech.

WORDS FROM THE WORKPLACE

Carmen Mathe
Artistic Director

Q. *Ms. Mathe, you have to deal with artists from all over the world. What is your greatest communication challenge?*

A. Our dancers come, literally, from all points of the globe geographically. We have some dancers from China, Russia, South America, and of course, the United States. When dealing with people of such a diverse cultural background, one has to understand that there is cultural significance behind each word spoken. Even gestures have different meanings. One must, therefore, be aware of what the student thinks I mean by the word I have used. I know what I mean, but does the student?

Effective delivery has to do with reaching the student and having that student respond. Effective delivery is actually the effective sharing of one's personality and ability in such a way as to produce a given, desired result. It is *not* giving a flowery speech. It is sharing one's life and skills.

Q. *How important are communication skills in your role as artistic director?*

A. Communication occurs on several levels. When we communicate, it may be by the movement of the dance, which is often a greater form of communication. I must be able to give them a picture of the dance, a picture that appears in their minds, which allows them to translate it to movement. In the final analysis, oral communication is of fundamental importance to the teacher. I must be able to explain to the student exactly what it is that I want them to achieve in their performance. The responsibility is mine as director to get them to understand what it is they should be doing and feeling.

make you seem to have eye contact when you are actually avoiding your audience's eyes.

Are you nervous? Are you a little intimidated by the speaking assignment? If the answer is "Yes, I definitely am!" then you do not need the *superficial* quick fix of pretending to have good eye contact. You need to face the problem and learn the value of eyes.

Keep these eye "strategies" in mind:

- Look at each person for a number of seconds before moving on to a different person in the audience. This is referred to as sustained eye contact. Deliver a sentence or two, ensuring that you are not making the audience member nervous or paranoid. You don't want to have a "stare-down" contest or stand too close. Your intent is to make the people in your audience realize that you are interested in each and every one of them. Remember, you are not looking at each person simply because you think that you're supposed to do so. You are offering sustained eye contact because you care about what each member of your audience thinks. Think of your speech as a gold mine and share its wealth with your audience through eye contact.

- Don't forget to make eye contact with people at the far sides of the audience. Some speakers forget about the people at the extremes of the room, the far left and the far right, both in the front and in the back of the room. Beware of having tunnel vision and speaking only to those seated immediately in front of you or those directly in the center of the room. It only makes sense that the more people you look at, the more people you have the potential to influence. Look to the corners.
- Make eye contact with people, not things. Your goal is to make a positive impression on your audience. Consequently, you shouldn't talk to the back wall, the parking lot outside, the window, or empty desks. Of course, you can look up or off once in a while if you are in thought. For the most part, though, your eyes should go to the eyes of your audience. Remember, if you avoid eye contact, you probably won't be trusted. Don't negate all of your hard work by delivering some of your best material to the floor. Give people priority!

Don't have tunnel vision. Make eye contact with everyone in the room.

Audience Feedback

One of the best reasons for you to have good eye contact with the members of your audience is that it allows you to see how they are reacting to what you are saying. You can read the feedback. Are people fidgeting in their chairs? Do they appear irritated? Are they smiling and nodding their heads? Are they leaning toward you, or leaning away from you and avoiding eye contact? Do they look confused?

You need to pay attention to feedback so that you can make the necessary adjustments. For instance, you might see that some people in the back of the room are straining to hear you. This should direct you to move closer to them or to raise your volume level. You might notice that some people are wrinkling their brows as if they don't totally understand your point. Stop and explain. Audience feedback is your communication effectiveness yardstick. Take the time to look at your audience and see how you are measuring up.

Dynamizing Your Overall Delivery

You have now read about some of the components that make up an effective delivery. Primarily, you have looked at the importance of your voice, your body, and your face. All must work together if you wish to dynamize your verbal message.

If you pay attention to the best speakers, you

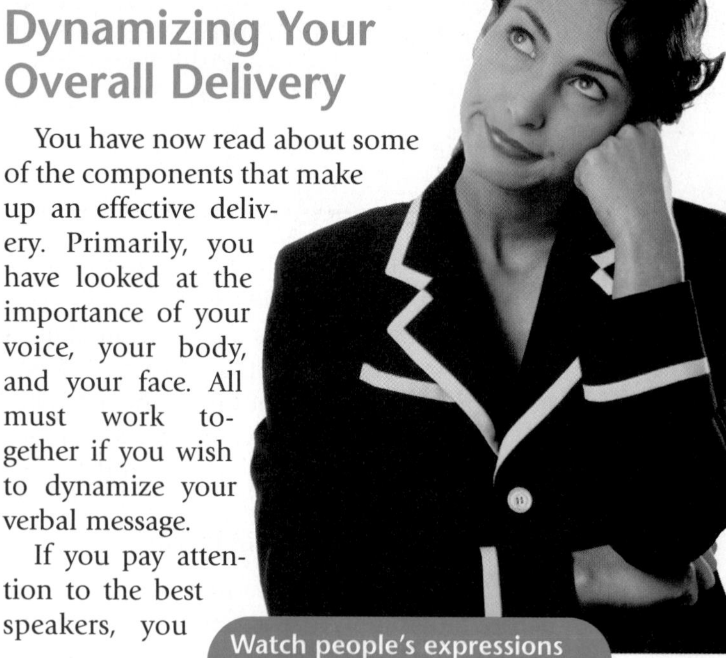

Watch people's expressions for feedback on how to adjust your delivery.

will notice that the parts of the body and the voice often go together, creating a satisfying blend of all of the individual elements. Notice that when a good speaker starts to speak, her movement, her gestures, and her words work together harmoniously. Such speakers may make it all look smooth and easy, but it's not. Getting there is a consequence of paying attention to and practicing the parts that make up the whole.

If you are saying, "But I simply can't deliver a speech, and I can't get any better," remember this story: It has been said that you can't make a silk purse out of a sow's ear. In other words, you can't make something beautiful from something supposedly ugly. Did you know that a scientist did? He purchased a sow's ear from the stockyards and ground it down to a gelatinous state. He then devised a method to produce a form of thread from this matter. With the thread, he created two beautiful, elegant purses. One of them is currently on display at the Smithsonian Institute in Washington, D.C. He did it to prove that nothing is impossible if people put their minds to the task.

The great ones never give up!

Apply this lesson to your speech delivery. Whether it be in music, athletics, academics—or speaking—don't ever give up. The great ones never do.

SECTION 4 REVIEW

Recalling the Facts ...

1. Define the term "sustained eye contact."
2. List three eye-contact strategies (as given in the section) that can help you communicate nonverbally with your audience.
3. Define "audience feedback." Why does a good speaker always have to be aware of audience feedback?

Thinking Critically ....

1. Studies have shown that a speaker's body language and facial expressions often have more impact than a speaker's words. In other words, delivery is more important than content. If this is true, evaluate whether or not this is a positive trait for the American public. What does it say about our heroes? Our political elections? When you are interviewing for a job, do you think that the results of the studies still hold true? Analyze what jobs or occupations might value your speaking content more than your delivery.

Taking Charge ...

1. Read the two selections that follow as if you were a news commentator seated behind a desk. Even though these selections were not delivered as speeches, each allows for a variety of facial expressions. Discover how you would deliver each. Remember the value of variety.

   a. The first selection is from *The American Crisis* by Thomas Paine. Paine's first pamphlet, *Common Sense,* appeared in January 1776, at a time when most Americans were hoping that the conflict with England could be resolved.

(Review continued on next page)

However, Paine pointed out the necessity for a break from England and the need for "an open and determined Declaration for Independence." Shortly afterward, this selection was written.

These are the times that try men's souls; The summer soldier and the sunshine patriot will in this crisis, shrink from the service of his country; but he that stands now, deserves the love and thanks of man and woman. Tyranny, like hell, is not easily conquered; yet we have this consolation with us, that the harder the conflict, the more glorious the triumph. What we obtain too cheap, we esteem too lightly. . . . It would be strange indeed, if so celestial an article as FREEDOM should not be highly rated. Britain, with an army to enforce her tyranny, has declared that she has a right not only to TAX but "to BIND us in ALL CASES WHATSOEVER," and if being bound in that manner is not slavery, then there is not such a thing as slavery upon earth.

. . . If there must be trouble, let it be in my day, that my child may have peace!

b. The next selection shows a very different style of writing with a completely different tone. It is an excerpt from a book by Andy Rooney, of the television program *60 Minutes*, called *And More by Andy Rooney*. The chapter is entitled "Memory."

What does AWACS stand for again, do you remember? Advance Warning something. Advance Warning American Command Ship? That's not it. I'll have to ask someone or look it up. And who was Lyndon Johnson's Vice President? You ought to remember a simple thing like that and I ought to myself, but I don't. There are times when I'm overwhelmed by my vast lack of memory. The other day I forgot my home phone number, and we've had it for thirty years.

I remember reading that we all start losing brain cells that make up the memory when we reach about age twenty, but this doesn't seem to have much to do with my problem. I couldn't remember anything when I was eighteen, either.

Being tall and being able to remember things are probably the two most desirable human characteristics I don't have. Because I am neither tall nor able to remember things, I look for ways to diminish the importance of height and memory.

The trouble with people with good memories is that they keep wanting to show it off to you by remembering things you don't want to hear. Everything reminds them of something they've done before. . . . I'd rather wait until I'm all through living and then review my life and times. Right now, I'm busy with today.

If you delivered these two selections with basically the same facial expressions, then you are not using your face properly. What did you notice that your eyes were doing at different points? Your eyebrows? Your mouth? Your neck and shoulders? Be prepared to read one or both of the selections to another student, a group, or the entire class.

STUDENT WORK

"Who's Playing the Drum?" *By Joseph M. Wycoff*

Joseph M. Wycoff, from Chesterton High School in Indiana, is one of the most successful high school speakers in the history of the National Forensic League's national tournament—a five-time national finalist and two-time national champion. This is an excerpt from a national championship oration Joseph delivered in 1987, when he was a junior in high school. As you read this speech, try to imagine all of the delivery elements and how they could work together for effect.

You know, there's a real science and precision to speaking, and I've taken it upon myself to analyze some of the specialized components that go into the making of a successful speech. I've noticed that one of the most important factors is that you have to have something different to set yourself apart from the crowd. Now, I'm sure that the burning question in all of your minds is, "Why is he standing at the far right side of the microphone?" Well, that's simple. [Pointing] Everyone else stood over there in the center. I'm different. Another thing. Everyone likes to come up to the front and establish eye contact, get a good rapport with the audience—face to face. [Considers, and then turns his back to the audience] How's this for memorable? *Now,* I'm an individual!

I would like to apologize for standing at the far right and turning my back on you, but you do have to admit that I did come across as being an individual. I had *style!* No purpose, but a lot of style. Ironically, being an "individual" contradicted the very thing that I was trying to accomplish: to communicate effectively. But if I had done what everyone else does, it might have been seen as unoriginal and weak . . . and that's exactly my point. It seems that in America today, it's no longer noble to follow, to conform, or to be a part of the group.

Let's face it, followers have a bad name. It's not hard to understand why the problem exists. General Custer did not give followers a good name. Jim Jones at Guyana gave followers the appearance of mindless fanatics. Then, of course, there was General John Sedgewick. He, at the Battle of Spotsylvania in 1864, stood proudly before his men and stated, "Men, don't worry. They couldn't hit an elephant at this dist. . . " I think we have all known the feeling of being led by someone who is not totally on the ball. It's frustrating! We could do it better than he or she could. And so, like the Scylla and Charybdis of Homer's *Odyssey,* we find ourselves faced with a similar dilemma. Either (a) we will follow *no one,* or (b) we will follow *anyone.*

I am reminded of a sign on an Indianapolis lawn which seems to proclaim our modern attitude: "Set of encyclopedias for sale. Never been used. Teenage son knows everything!" We "know it all" appears to be our motto. Evidently, Jane Fonda thinks so. Author Ralph Schoenstein states that recently . . . when he interviewed a group of third graders and asked them to name some of their heroes, one child responded with Michael Jackson, Spiderman, and God. But nearly half responded with "Me." Well, we can hardly blame the children. Maybe they are just a reflection of what they have been taught. In our schools, we now have Gifted and Talented programs and advanced learning courses, all for the purpose of "molding tomorrow's *leaders.*" Who would ever think of teaching them to follow?

We're a society that wants to do it on our own. Why? Maybe it's because of our ambition, lack of trust, or maybe the blow to our egos when we see incompetence and Teflon-tongued con artists rise to the top. Nevertheless, Joseph Epstein of Northwestern University points out that the modern individual seeks to rise above the group as opposed to working with it, and, in the process, helps to destroy our sense of community and commitment to others.

Did you ever wonder why our government at times seems to be so confused? Well, it turns out that it is not just the quality of some leaders, but the quantity as well. Veteran military reporter Arthur T.

Hadley in his book *The Straw Giant* states that part of the problem, at least with our military, is a case of "too many chiefs and not enough Indians." He comments that there has never been a totally successful operational test of the Minuteman missile. The reason is that we have plenty of people who know how to give the orders, but not enough trained personnel who know how to carry them out.

What's wrong with wanting to lead? Nothing. However, there is something wrong when *so many people* want to direct . . . that few or none are left to actually go in that direction. We end up with a case of "divided we stand," or, as in our second area, "united we fall," when we will follow anyone.

It looks as though we are losing the skill of how to be conscientious conformists. We forget a lesson that my father tried to teach me very early. "Before you march to the beat of a different drummer, look back and see *who's playing the drum!*" It's odd to think that a recent survey tells us that at least one-third of all college students firmly believe in ghosts, Atlantis, flying saucers, and Bigfoot. On a college quiz, answers like these were given for general knowledge questions: The Great Gatsby was a magician in the 1930s; Socrates was an American Indian chieftain; Christ was born in the sixteenth century; and who will ever forget that great Roman emperor, Sid Caesar?

Our lack of knowledge, as well as our decision sometimes not to open our eyes to the obvious, may very well be . . . the reason why a group of conscientious individuals at a soccer game can become a violent mob in Europe and kill 56 people . . . or at home become a mob at a Who concert and kill 11. It seems that oftentimes we lose our sense of personal judgment when we are in a group. Yet, both Aleksandr Solzhenitsyn and Albert Einstein have pointed out that we must *stop* seeing the group this way and start seeing it as a combining of personal strengths . . . for our own survival.

How many students are really impressed by the classmate who always has to make an extra comment, appropriate or not, while the teacher is talking, or the classmate who just doesn't have the common sense to sit down and shut up? For teachers, how about administrators who come up with brilliant projects and programs, but don't inform anyone how those programs are supposed to work, and are, therefore, faced with ridicule and chaos? When was the last time that you or anyone else you know volunteered for anything?

What it can basically come down to is . . . for whom or what are we willing to sacrifice?

"Feel free if a relationship becomes dull or sluggish to move out, and don't feel guilty because in our generation lasting relationships between any two people are no longer practical." This is a quote from psychiatrist David Viscott in his book *Feel Free.*

Have we gotten to the point where the simple group of two can no longer function together? How sad if he's right.

But that's also where our hope lies. Some people do believe as David Viscott, but I hope that I am not far off in the assumption that most of us do not. We find commitment in relationships important and necessary. There *are* heroes out there for the follower. In 1982, when a 737 crashed into the icy waters of the Potomac River, *one man* kept other passengers afloat and even passed his lifeline, saving many, before he himself drowned—a commitment to humankind.

In the final analysis, we are all followers. We are students following teachers, employees following bosses, children following parents. We shouldn't have to apologize for those roles. We need to realize that there is no shame in following. First, we are important. The brain may control the heart, but without the heart the brain dies. Second, because we are so important, we have to start becoming conscientious conformists, not blind . . . just lemmings at the cliff's edge.

To whom are you willing to say with pride, "I will follow you"? There are plenty of people out there: at home, at work, at school. People who are willing to show that the conformists, the followers, the team players are noble, humble, and essential . . . if we will all be willing to stop . . . and listen for the drum beat.

Looking Back

Listed below are the major ideas discussed in this chapter.

- Your speaking delivery is the way you "sell" your words, or the verbal and nonverbal manner in which you present your material.
- There are four types of delivery: manuscript, memorized, extemporaneous, and impromptu.
- The extemporaneous method is the method most often recommended.
- The voice is the instrument that carries your words, and your diaphragm is the main power source for effective speaking.
- The air that you need for speaking provides you with the power needed for adequate speaking volume, or the loudness or softness of your voice.
- Simply having the air to speak isn't enough. You must speak at a comfortable rate, or speed, with a pleasant pitch range, or range of notes.
- Good speakers vary their pitch and rate often to avoid speaking in a monotone.
- Good speakers also know when to use emphasis. Emphasis is the stress that you give certain words that you wish to accentuate.
- You must also be sure not to slur your words. You must articulate clearly.
- It is essential that you know how to pronounce all the words that you are going to use.
- Another key element in developing an effective delivery is the use of your body. Even though using your body is nonverbal, it definitely communicates a message to your audience.
- Platform movement involves actually taking steps while speaking. The number of steps depends on the size of the room, the size of the audience, and your emotional intent at the time of your movement.
- You should always keep in mind the distance between you and your audience. This knowledge can keep you from making audience members feel uncomfortable.
- Hand gestures concern speakers the most. "What do I do with my hands while speaking?" is a common question.
- Hand and arm gestures should be kept, for the most part, in your gesture zone. This is an area the size of a small television screen that extends from your waist to your upper chest.
- Facial expression may be the most important part of your oral communication. When you nonverbally involve your face in your delivery, audience members can see how you really feel about your material.
- The eyes are crucial for an effective delivery. You must sustain eye contact with each audience member long enough to make him or her feel a part of your speech.
- Effective eye contact also makes your audience trust you and what you say.
- The best speakers use all aspects of the voice, the body, and the face.

Speech Vocabulary

1. Divide the list into two fairly even sections. For each word in one list, give the definition as given in the chapter. Use the dictionary or the glossary for additional information. Also write an original sentence using the word correctly.
2. For the second list, provide the definition as given in the chapter. Then, instead of writing individual sentences, write a story or a series of paragraphs using the words. The topic of your story is up to you. Make sure it makes sense.

delivery
manuscript method
memorized method
extemporaneous method
impromptu method
vocalized pause
power source
vocal process
phonation
oral cavity
rate
pitch
monotone
inflection
volume
articulation
pronunciation
platform movement
proxemics
posture

General Vocabulary

For the general vocabulary terms, use the dictionary to find the definitions. Make flash cards. Write the word along with a sentence that you've composed on one side, and write the definition on the other side.

regurgitating
methodically
syllable
alienated
superficial

To Remember

Answer the following questions based on your reading of the chapter.

1. The speed at which you speak is known as your speaking ______________.
2. The highs and lows, the notes, that your voice hits while you speak are known as your speaking ______________.
3. Political figures and elected officials often use the ______________ method of delivery to make sure that they don't make an error in their content.
4. The method of speaking that is referred to as "not rehearsed" is ______________.
5. What specific parts of the body are used in the gesture zone?
6. When you look at someone in the audience while you are speaking, it is a good idea to use ______________ eye contact.
7. When you actually take steps in a speech presentation, you are using ______________ movement.
8. The crispness and distinctness of your words show that you have good ______________.
9. Proxemics involves a sense of how much ______________ there is between you and your audience.

Match the number on the left with the letter on the right.

1. Type of delivery that combines the use of notes with the ability to use words and ideas.
2. Not using emphasis or varying pitch and rate.
3. French king with a high-pitched voice.
4. Wrote *The American Crisis.*
5. Loudness or softness of the voice.

a. Charlemagne
b. extemporaneous
c. impromptu
d. rate
e. monotone
f. articulation
g. volume
h. Paine
i. Rooney
j. pitch

To Do

1. Write a paragraph on a topic about which you feel strongly. Now give it orally. Make a voice chart or graph. Plot on the chart or graph where your voice moves. Does your pitch go up? Does

it go down? Is there variety? Are you using all of your pitch range? If not, you are not totally delivering your message to your audience. A tape recorder is an excellent aid for this exercise.

2. Make an educational video of students walking and talking in the hallway, at a dance, or at some other type of gathering. Take note of how their voices and body movements work together as they talk to each other. Pay attention to their nonverbal communication. What did you learn? List your top five observations.

To Talk About

1. How does the spoken message differ from the written message? What are the advantages and disadvantages of each? What is the advantage that verbal emphasis gives to the speaker? What about eye contact? Is it possible for your words to be saying one thing while your eyes say something else? Talk about instances when this might be the case.
2. You have probably heard the phrase "the thrill of victory and the agony of defeat," popularized on television sports programs. Defeat often occurs because some athlete couldn't "deliver" under pressure. In athletics or any other area, why do some people often allow pressure to get to them and keep them from delivering their best efforts? What might be on their minds? How does this specifically relate to delivering a speech? What's your constructive advice?
3. Why do you think that, with the public, a good speaker with an excellent delivery has an advantage over a brilliant thinker who has trouble speaking? Give examples of this phenomenon from the news, your school, history, or your community. Does this advantage always exist?
4. Robert Frost once said, "Half the world is composed of people who have something to say and can't, and the other half who have nothing to say, and keep on saying it." What does this quotation mean? How does it fit politicians? Media figures? Businesses? Educators? Other students? Parents? You?

To Write About

1. Research has shown that a jury, in deciding how believable someone's testimony is, will value nonverbal communication more than verbal communication. Why might this be true? Give three ways in which your body can show others that you are not telling the whole truth. In what situations might you do these things?
2. When you effectively deliver, you get the job done. Select one character from literature who, despite the odds, delivered and achieved his or her objective. What individual elements helped him or her succeed?
3. Why is impromptu speaking so valuable? Describe two situations in which you might be able to use your impromptu ability. How would your voice, your body, and your face have to work with your words? Write at least one paragraph on this topic.

Related Speech Topics

Cooperative education or team teaching
The United Nations
Adoption or foster children
Day-care for working mothers
Any championship sports team
A well-known orchestra
The human brain: networking
The Japanese educational system
The Olympics
The Special Olympics
Improving your job skills: going back to school

Presentations

UNIT CONTENTS

CHAPTER 13

SPEECHES TO INFORM

> "Obviously, a man's judgment cannot be better than the information on which he has based it."
>
> —Arthur Hays Sulzberger, publisher, *New York Times*

Learning Objectives

After completing this chapter, you will be able to do the following.

- Identify the major types of informative speeches.
- Find a good subject for an informative speech, narrow that subject to a manageable topic, and compose a sharply focused thesis.
- Develop interesting material for your speech through the use of anecdotes, quotes, and definitions.
- Integrate audio and visual aids into your speech.
- Give a multimedia presentation using appropriate technology and proven strategies.

Chapter Outline

Following are the main sections in this chapter.

1. Speeches That Instruct, Inform, and Clarify
2. Turning a Subject into a Speech
3. Audio and Visual Aids
4. Creating Multimedia Presentations

New Speech Terms

In this chapter, you will learn the meanings of the speech terms listed below.

public lecture
status report
briefing
fireside chat
chalk talk
advance organizer
cultural literacy
narrowing
thesis
anecdote
quotation
definition
map
diagram
graph
handout
overhead projector
model
cutaway
multimedia presentation
download
scanner

General Vocabulary

Expanding your general vocabulary will help you become a more effective communicator. Listed below are some words appearing in this chapter that you should make part of your everyday vocabulary.

concise
concrete
distinction
ambiguous
intuition
demographics
trivia
senile
etymology
infographic
spontaneity

Looking AHEAD

Providing information, a task we perform hundreds of times each day, is one of the most common and important forms of communication. Yet the techniques for providing information efficiently, gracefully, and in a way that will interest the listener are not well known.

In this chapter, you will discover how to better understand your audience's wants and needs, how to find a subject listeners will want to learn about, and how to narrow that subject so that you can make meaningful and well-informed comments about it. You will also discover methods for illustrating your information, both verbally (through examples, descriptions, and definitions) and visually (through photographs, slides, maps, and diagrams). While any informative speech you give must be accurate, you never escape the responsibility of being interesting.

Introduction

A lot of talking goes on in the world, and a large part of it is done to give instructions, provide facts, or clarify ideas. You give someone directions to study hall and you tell classmates what went on when they missed a day of school. You explain how to do something, what something is, how it works, or how it is used. In short, you provide information to others every day in a hundred different ways.

The complexity of this task may range from giving simple directions (Where's the library?) to explaining a complicated process (What is photosynthesis?). It may be as basic as merely announcing facts (the plans for the next school dance) or as complex as giving an oral report based on research (the causes of the war in Kosovo). In each instance, however, your emphasis is on statements of fact. Your goal is to make the listener understand.

Deep down, we are all curious. It's this curiosity that makes informative speeches such favorites with audiences. Telling people something new is great fun. You will also learn that being knowledgeable about a subject gives you confidence when you speak. Many students find that giving informative speeches is closer to real life than any other speech assignment.

You can turn your scientific knowledge into powerful informative speeches.

SECTION 1 Speeches That Instruct, Inform, and Clarify

We frequently give casual informative speeches to strangers needing directions, classmates making up missed assignments, and so on. In addition, we sometimes find ourselves in more formal situations where we must provide information. Before long, your teacher will probably ask you to give an informative speech to the class. The assignment may ask you to describe an object ("give a speech on the brain"), to explain a process ("give a speech on how to use a digital camera"), or clarify a concept ("give a speech examining the idea of nonviolent resistance").

Types of Informative Speeches

In the world outside your school, speakers find a variety of opportunities for giving informative talks. They include the following.

1. The **public lecture.** As a result of a person's special interest or expertise, he or she may be invited to give a public lecture to a community group or club. If you take a trip to a national student council convention, for example, you may be invited to give an account of your trip to the local Kiwanis Club; and the Garden Club might be interested in your research on the super tomato.
2. The **status report.** Every business and social group must keep up to date on its various projects. Periodically, the group will ask a knowledgeable person to give a status report indicating what has been accomplished so far and what plans exist for the future. Suppose you are a committee chair for a volunteer organization that works with senior citizens. If your committee is planning a senior prom, you may be asked to give a status report on prom plans to the group as a whole.
3. The **briefing.** The briefing is a very common informative speech used to tell members of a group about changes in policy or procedure. You may need to tell the members of your swim team about how to order team T-shirts, or perhaps you may want to tell the yearbook staff about a new layout plan.
4. The **fireside chat.** Named for a famous series of radio broadcasts given by President Franklin Roosevelt, fireside chats usually feature a group leader addressing the concerns, worries, and issues of the moment. Your principal may schedule fireside chats with parents to review school goals and policies.
5. The **chalk talk.** The speaker giving a chalk talk relies on a visual aid (the chalkboard). We can easily imagine a coach showing the team how to arrange its defense or a director outlining plans to present a stage play by using this technique.

President Franklin Roosevelt kept the nation informed with his fireside chats.

Many informative speeches are followed by a question-and-answer period, which gives the audience a chance to participate.

The Six Cs of Informative Speaking

As an informative speaker, your goal is to shed light on a subject by sharing facts that you have learned through experience, observation, listening, and reading. You can explain, for example, how to bake a cake or describe the drugs being used to fight AIDS or discuss how rock musicians rehearse a stage show. As you do so, you introduce facts that are new, show old facts in a new way, and clear up misunderstandings. Your main responsibility is to be accurate, but you must also strive to be clear. The response you want from your listeners is basically, "I understand what you said."

An informative speech should be developed using the six Cs.

More specifically, we can break down the goals of informative speaking into six Cs, the better to remember them. Ask yourself the following questions as you prepare a speech:

1. Is my speech so *clear* that everyone will understand?
2. Is my speech so *concise* that no one's time will be wasted?
3. Is my speech *complete?*
4. Am I confident that my information is absolutely *correct?*
5. Have I provided *concrete* examples so that the audience can see my point?
6. Can I *connect* my speech with what I know about my audience?

Let's take a closer look at each of these goals to explore just how they can best be accomplished.

1. Be Clear ... Surprising as it may seem, being clear is neither easy nor simple (try explaining how to design a web page to someone). How can you be sure your listeners will understand what you mean?

Many speakers make a special effort at the beginning of a speech to help listeners by defining a few important words and phrases. These definitions can be as short as a single word or, in a few special cases, as long as the entire speech. This might be the case, for example, in a speech entitled "The HIV Virus."

The purpose of a definition is to create some common ground between speaker and listener. In particular, plan to explain any technical terms that may be new to your audience. But keep these terms to a minimum—you can baffle listeners with too many terms that make them scratch their heads.

Another part of being clear is making *distinctions.* We make distinctions by saying what something is and, especially, what it is not. Negative definitions clear your listeners' path of obstacles. You could make a distinction, for example, between the space shuttle's liquid fuel engines, which can be turned off, and its solid fuel booster rockets, which can't. Anticipate situations where your listeners might find your remarks *ambiguous.* Ask yourself as you prepare a speech, "Could this point be taken more than one way?"

You can make distinctions using the technique of compare and contrast. A comparison explains how two things are similar. A contrast explains the differences. If you wrote a speech about the movies based on Stephen King's books, for example, you might compare them with horror films of the past such as *The Phantom of the Opera* and *Dracula.* You might contrast them with science fiction films like *Aliens* or *Star Wars.* Be sure, however, that what you use for a comparison is familiar to your listeners. If you compare Stephen King to Jules Verne, most high school students will probably follow your comparison. But if you compare King to H. P. Lovecraft, a less well known author, your audience may be lost.

In the final analysis, the value of being clear must be balanced with other, competing values—the value of being concise, for example. If you spend too much time and effort striving for clarity, you may lose your listeners' interest. Audiences often find long explanations boring. Further, if you are too obvious, you lose the element of surprise. A good speaker learns to balance a variety of desirable qualities without emphasizing one at the expense of another.

2. Be Concise ... Many government officials these days seem to work for the Department of Redundancy Department. Too often, official proclamations seem to make 50 words do the work of 10. Expressions like "Please repeat that again," or "These two are both alike," say the same thing twice. Be conscious of your own language use. Notice whether you say things like "These pens are identically the same," or "She arrived at 8 A.M. this morning." We are all guilty of being too wordy from time to time, but it's a habit that can be broken.

The secret of being concise is to make each word count, and the best way to do that is to use precise and specific language (see Chapter 11 for further details). Using precise language means choosing the word that best fits your meaning. For example, don't say tree if you mean oak, and don't say temporarily reassigned if you mean fired. To become more precise, you may need to enlarge your vocabulary. Take advantage whenever possible of lessons designed to increase your word power.

3. Be Complete ... No speech can be complete in the sense of covering all the possible material. You can, however, create a sense of completion in the minds of the audience by raising certain expectations and then satisfying them. Tell the audience you have three major points. When you say "first," they know you are beginning, and when you say "third," they know you've reached the end. They won't expect a fourth or fifth point even though they realize you haven't covered the subject as thoroughly as possible.

Statements that forecast what the audience can expect are called **advance organizers.** If you say to your audience, for example, "I'm now going to present the three reasons local officials have tried to censor rap music," the audience is set to listen for three different chunks of information. If you introduce each reason with a reinforcing statement, such as "Now let's take a look at the first reason," the audience is reminded of the structure of your speech. When audience members perceive that your speech has a plan and can begin to recognize pieces of that plan, they will feel more satisfied when you finish speaking.

Working from a plan forces you to put your information in order. Clearly, some information is more important than other information. If you fail to distinguish major points from minor ones, the listener must try to remember everything and hope

You may find that visual aids such as a flip chart will help you be concise and organized.

COMMUNICATION Breakthrough

Surgeon General's Report on Smoking

Few government reports have had the drama or impact of the one that was delivered on January 11, 1964, in the auditorium of the Old State Department Building in Washington, D.C.

On that Saturday morning, a day carefully chosen to make headlines in all the big Sunday newspapers, Surgeon General Luther Terry told the nation that "cigarette smoking is a health hazard of sufficient importance . . . to warrant appropriate remedial action." In other words, it was time to do something about smoking.

Although the basic facts about smoking and health had been known for some time, the federal government kept shying away from the issue. Not until 1962 did President Kennedy decide that the government should study the problem. Kennedy asked Terry, the nation's chief health officer, to select an expert committee that would decide, simply, "Is smoking bad?"

Terry and ten people chosen from leading universities worked like prairie dogs, burrowing into stacks of research five stories underground in the basement of the National Library of Medicine at Bethesda, Maryland. After 14 months of study, the committee issued a 150,000-word report that made the following points.

- Cigarette smoking "contributes substantially to mortality"—that is, smoking can kill you.
- Cigarette smokers have a death rate almost 11 times higher than nonsmokers. The sharpest risk from smoking is lung cancer.
- It helps to quit smoking.

As a result of Terry's report, the major TV networks decided to reexamine their advertising policies. Within a few years, smoking ads disappeared from the nation's television screens. Later, the government required cigarette makers to carry warning messages on their ads and packages. The number of smokers in the United States began to decline. But it would have been very difficult to change attitudes without the surgeon general's dramatic announcement.

Questions

1. How effective have efforts been to educate students on the dangers of smoking?
2. Can public speakers help change people's behavior?

to sort things out later. Since no one can do this, a great deal of the information will be forgotten.

This is one of the reasons so many students have trouble taking notes. They assume that everything a teacher says is equally important. As a result, their notes look like a hodgepodge of large concepts and tiny details. In contrast, when listeners have a sense of what to expect, that pattern helps them to separate more important ideas from less important ones. As a result, not only do they remember more, but also they remember what the speaker believes is most important.

Accuracy counts!

4. Be Correct ... There is no substitute for being accurate. Checking and double-checking the accuracy of the information you present goes right to the heart of your credibility. One of the best ways to convince an audience that your information deserves attention is to tell where you found it. As in any communication, when you use ideas that are not your own, you should indicate the source of your material. Writers can do this with footnotes, but speakers need a more subtle technique.

Normally, you identify your sources briefly at the end of the information itself. For example, you might say, "The verdict in the subway shooting trial was an outrage to justice, according to an editorial writer in this morning's paper." For variety, you can occasionally put the identification first: "In an article in the February 27 issue of *U.S. News and World Report,* we read that cheating on standardized tests is widespread."

You don't need to use all the information that would appear in a bibliographical citation. In fact, it would be a poor idea to do so. Usually, the name of an author or the name of a magazine, newspaper, television show, or movie is sufficient. An inquisitive listener can catch you after the speech to obtain a complete rundown of your sources.

5. Be Concrete ... Another valuable technique for making an informative speech effective is to be concrete. Focus on the immediate and the actual. Instead of talking in abstractions, talk in terms of people, places, and things. Individual cases are far more interesting than generalities.

Don't talk about candy if you can talk about Reese's Pieces. Plan your speech on women's soccer around a particular person, perhaps Mia Hamm. Focus your speech on filmmakers by concentrating on one, like Spike Lee.

Spike Lee and Mia Hamm could provide focus for speeches on filmmakers and women's soccer.

A concrete example helps listeners get a mental picture of what you mean. Let's suppose that you have decided to make a general point like this: "Most accidents happen at home." So far, so good, but at this point the audience has only a vague idea of what you mean. The careful speaker immediately supports every general statement with an example: "Kerry Shea, a 14-year-old, said she 'just lost control' of her toothbrush and swallowed it. 'I was brushing the back of my tongue,' she added, 'because I saw on TV that it helps to get a lot of sugar that way, when the toothbrush slipped and I swallowed it.'"

Concrete examples contain physical details. If you were doing a speech on teen crime and needed a concrete example, you could use the case of the New York City transit system. Kids there were caught stealing subway tokens by sucking them out of turnstile slots. According to one official, some kids were making $50 to $100 a day. This example has great details—subway tokens, turnstiles, and teens performing weird physical stunts.

Connect with your audience by imagining how they may feel about your topic.

BEING BRIEF

INSTANT IMPACT

Brevity, Shakespeare told us, is the soul of wit. Unfortunately, we don't always take his advice to heart. Audiences appreciate speakers who get to the point quickly. Don't be like the speaker who told his listeners, "I've been asked to speak for 30 minutes. I don't have enough material to fill that time so I'll talk for 10 minutes and make it seem like 30."

One of the most popular informative speeches given on a regular basis is the president's inaugural address. On a January day following each election, the nation's leader outlines a vision for the future. The shortest inaugural address in history was the first—George Washington spoke just a few minutes, and his speech was a bare 135 words. The longest address was a fatal one. William Henry Harrison delivered a two-hour, 9,000-word speech in 1841, straight into the teeth of a freezing wind. Harrison came down with a cold the following day and died a month later of pneumonia. Take the hint.

Sometimes you may find that a series of short examples works best to support your main point. At other times, a long storylike example may be what you need. In any event, you should never let a general statement stand alone without a supporting example.

6. Connect . . . The last C, connect, requires you to analyze the people who will be in your audience. This may be difficult because most of us tend to see the world from a single point of view—our own. Without ever meaning to, we become prisoners of our own perspective; we have little awareness of what another person is thinking or feeling. With a little extra effort, however, we can learn to imagine how the world looks to someone else. The more we can predict how an audience will interpret what we say, the better we will be able to communicate.

If you are speaking to classmates, you already have a number of insights into their backgrounds and attitudes. Think how you would react if you heard your speech for the first time—would it strike you as interesting, informative, and up to date? Or dull and old hat? Your own *intuition* can help guide you as you prepare a speech for a group of peers.

You can probably make a good guess, for example, about what your classmates know and don't know. Such guesses will help you avoid the mistake of delivering a speech on how to water ski to a classroom full of experts on the subject. If the audience knows quite a bit about your subject, find a way to highlight some less well known aspect of it.

Of course, you sometimes need to prepare a speech for a general audience—an audience of parents, community members, or other adults—that you don't know well. You can probably learn some things about the audience by asking the person who invited you to speak. But for the most part, you must depend on educated guesses to predict what kind of people are in the audience and what they have in common.

You can make some assumptions about an audience by studying their *demographics,* that is, their social, economic, and cultural characteristics. Will the members of the audience, for example, tend to come from the same neighborhood, be about the same age, or have similar political opinions? You may wish to consider the following checklist when you think about the audience you will be facing:

1. How many people will be present? What will be the ages of most of the people in the audience? Will the audience be mostly male, female, or mixed?
2. What are their interests, attitudes, and beliefs?
3. What do they know about the subject?
4. What is their attitude toward it?

Generally speaking, you may assume that adult audiences have what is called cultural literacy. **Cultural literacy** describes the information that an average American citizen can be expected to know. The average listener should know that Columbus sailed in 1492 and that Columbus is the capital of Ohio, for example, but not that *Goodbye, Columbus* is a book by Philip Roth. You won't need to explain a reference to the Supreme Court or the Supremes, but you will have to explain the term supremacist.

Simply put, sensitivity to the audience is one of the keys to successful communication. While you can't choose your audience, you can choose a speech to fit a particular audience. Knowledge of the audience can help you fine-tune your speech as you make changes, both large and small, to suit a specific group of listeners. For more information on audience analysis, see Chapter 14 on persuasive speeches.

SECTION 1 REVIEW

Recalling the Facts ...

1. List five kinds of occasions where you might give an informative speech.

Thinking Critically ...

1. Explain how your approach would change if you were to give a speech on the effects of cigarette smoking to five different audiences: classmates, parents, people between the ages of 20 and 25, retired people, and elementary school children.
2. Using the same five audiences as above, suggest three topics best suited to each.
3. Neil Postman wrote a book about how we all need to develop a better sense of what is garbage. He meant that we need to be alert to what we hear. Some of the information we hear is misleading, based on weak evidence, or is just plain wrong. What are some of the ways we can improve our ability to sort out useful and accurate information from all the rest?

Taking Charge ...

1. Develop a survey to measure attitudes toward a variety of possible speech topics (the media, government, the entertainment industry), and give the survey to several classes in your school. Tabulate and analyze the results. Discuss what these results tell you about potential listeners.

SECTION 2 Turning a Subject into a Speech

Almost without exception, students' biggest gripe about giving speeches is "I don't know what to talk about." Finding an interesting and appropriate subject is always a challenge, but never more so than with an informative speech.

Find a Subject

Knowledge is the stuff from which new ideas are made. But knowledge alone won't write your speech. Anyone can compile a list of facts, but it takes an alert mind to connect those facts.

Suppose you decide to do some research for a speech on national holidays. You gather a number of facts, but they seem to have nothing to do with each other. Now think of those facts as dots in a dot-to-dot puzzle. Unfortunately, no one has numbered the dots. You have to do that for yourself. "Discovery," noted the Nobel Prize–winning physician Albert Szent-Gyorgyi, "consists of looking at the same thing as everyone else and thinking something different."

The key to inventing good speech topics is having a creative mind. What matters is not so much what knowledge you have (though that's important, of course) but what you do with what you know. Being creative with knowledge means using crazy, foolish, and impractical ideas as stepping stones toward more realistic ones. It means breaking the rules occasionally and looking for ideas in unusual places. It means changing your point of view to look at the subject in a new way.

Creative thinking frees us from dull routine. When we stay on our old thought paths, we probably won't find fresh ways of looking at something. We tend not to ask new questions about old ideas. But if we take a creative approach and write "outside the box," we are much more likely to "think differently." And thinking differently is part of inventing good speech topics.

Where, then, can we look for topics, assuming we have the right attitude?

Personal Experience ... You already have a lifetime of experience, and it can be a major source of information. No matter what the topic, first-hand knowledge contributes unique and original information. Even if your own knowledge is incomplete, it provides a good starting point for further research.

Whether your subject is national holidays or Leonardo da Vinci, be creative.

You are almost certainly an expert on something—whether it's changing the points and plugs on a car or baking chocolate chip cookies. Think small. Find an area of interest where you have considerable experience—something you collect, for example. Perhaps you have a ferret for a pet, perform as a magician for birthday parties, or volunteer at the local hospital. Anything you do often and do well is a likely topic for an informative speech because you can speak from experience. That gives you instant credibility.

Observations . . . Another place to look for speech topics is your immediate environment. Whenever you find a scrap of unusual information, file it. You might read, for example, that a newspaper carrier delivering the *Los Angeles Times* heaved a copy of the Sunday paper toward the front lawn of a Hollywood mansion. The paper hit a pet dog, dozing on the porch, and killed it. A subsequent report by the newspaper industry noted that, at an average of 2.3 pounds per day, the *Times* is the heaviest newspaper in the world. Such an item could make a nice lead-in for a speech on the mass media and its ability to overwhelm us.

You might also take the opportunity to be a "participant observer." We all attend meetings, sports events, and public performances. What you see and hear during these events may prove to be just what you need for an interesting speech.

Suppose, for example, that the local auditorium is sponsoring a cat show. Perhaps you could attend and do research for a speech on strange hobbies. What would possess a person to spend hours every day grooming a cat? A branch bank may hold an open house. What better chance to get the lowdown on checking accounts for teens? You can turn almost anything that happens in your neighborhood into an effective, informative speech, given the right frame of mind.

Surveys . . . Thanks to our consumer-driven economy, we have become survey-happy. Almost everyone, it seems, wants your opinion. Were you happy with the mechanic who changed your oil? Have you tried the new cereal with nuts, raisins, and tree bark? Did the plumber communicate effectively when he fixed the leak in your sink? Surveys—whether by phone or in person—are used increasingly by businesses and political groups. Luckily, all these surveys provide new sources of information and new ideas for speech topics.

According to a poll sponsored by the Corporation for Public Broadcasting, for example, we now have a good idea of what teens have on their minds. America's school-aged kids, we learn,

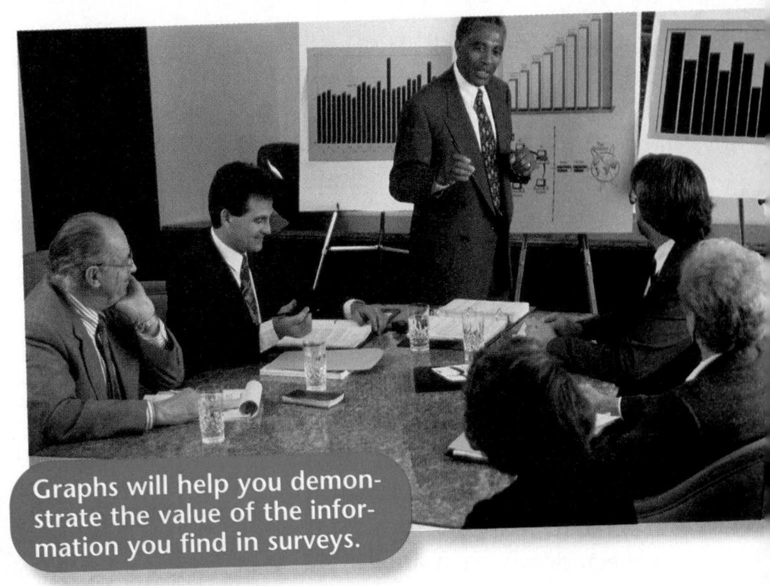

Graphs will help you demonstrate the value of the information you find in surveys.

are more worried about pollution than about getting into college. Their single greatest worry (58 percent, according to the poll) is about making money as adults. Other big worries include pollution and the environment (56 percent), getting AIDS (48 percent), not being successful (47 percent), not getting into college (46 percent), and having to fight in a war (44 percent).

Thus, another way to find a good speech topic is to consider your listeners' interests and concerns. You can discover those through polls and surveys, of course, but you can also find out by less scientific means. Listen to the subjects that come up again and again in your conversations. Be alert to news events, trends in movies and television, prominent personalities, and interesting ideas that crop up in your classes. Browse chat rooms on the Internet to read what topics are hot. Clever speeches grow from the smallest of insights—sometimes a little-known scientific fact or discovery will lead to a fascinating speech.

Narrow Your Subject

Finding a subject is only half the battle in creating an effective informative speech. A subject is a broad area of knowledge, such as romantic literature, astronomy, or soccer. A topic is one particular aspect of a subject. Once you have chosen a general area, you must cut your subject down to size, **narrowing** it to manageable proportions. You can't expect to cover every aspect of your subject in a ten-minute speech, so you have to make some choices about what to include.

Suppose, for example, that you decide to speak about America's westward expansion. You can whittle that enormous subject down by confining it within certain boundaries. You could start by limiting your topic geographically, to a certain area of the West, say, California. Then you could limit your subject to a particular time, perhaps 1849, when the gold rush took place.

The following guidelines may help you narrow your subject down to manageable size:

1. Limit your subject in time. A speech on the high cost of presidential elections could be limited to just one month of the 2000 campaign.
2. Limit your subject in space. In a speech on recycling efforts, avoid state or national statistics and concentrate on efforts in your own community.
3. Limit your subject in extent. Instead of describing all the elements of a well-balanced diet, tackle just one. Speak about how eating fiber affects health, for example.
4. Limit your subject using the principle of divide and conquer. Just when you think you have a manageable topic, try dividing it in half. Let's say you have narrowed your original idea—the world's most famous fictional detectives—to the career of Sherlock Holmes. Now narrow that topic down again: Focus only on Holmes's uncanny sense of smell.

The California gold rush could be a starting point that could lead your speech to Sutter's Mill.

The process of limiting your subject is helpful in several ways. First, it forces you to say more about less; second, it helps you focus your research; and third, it helps you decide what belongs in your speech and what does not. Every speaker can find many tempting pieces of material—funny stories, clever quotes, odd bits of history—but the problem of choosing what to keep is critical, especially when you may be limited to a five-minute speech or less. Sometimes even the most interesting material must be left out to keep your speech focused and on track.

State Your Thesis

Once you have a manageable topic—the California gold rush, for the sake of discussion—you've made great progress, but you're not out of the woods. The next step in turning an idea into a speech requires that you make a positive statement about your topic, a statement often called a **thesis** or sometimes a "statement of purpose."

In your research on the California gold rush, for example, you learn that the employee of a pioneer named John Sutter discovered large nuggets of gold near Sutter's Mill. As news of the discovery spread, thousands of adventurers rushed to the area to stake their claims. These "forty-niners" helped boost California's population from about 15,000 to more than 100,000 in less than a year, and their free spending turned San Francisco into a flourishing city.

This research leads you to develop a thesis for your speech: "The California gold rush sparked the development of the city of San Francisco." Now you've got something you can hang your hat on. A thesis should take the form of a declarative sentence with a subject and a verb, and it should convey in clear language the most important message of your speech. Remember that the more you sweat working out a sensible thesis in advance, the less you'll have to sweat once you begin to speak.

Some sample topics and thesis statements might include:

Topics	Thesis
Teenagers and fads	The slang teenagers use often comes from the latest popular movies.
Healthy lifestyles	Eating five servings of fruits and vegetables each day can dramatically reduce your chances of getting cancer.
Famous musicians	Beethoven's hearing loss may actually have helped him compose music.

Support Your Thesis

Once you have a topic and a thesis, you can turn to the matter of developing your support. For the sake of argument, we will assume that you have already completed your research. The problem at hand is how to use material that you have uncovered to support your thesis. "I am rather like a mosquito in a summer camp," said one writer. "I know what I ought to do, but I don't know where to begin." Let's look first at the kinds of material your research has turned up and then at how you can use that material to bring your speech to life.

Facts ... "Just the facts, ma'am," says Sergeant Joe Friday, a policeman on the old television show *Dragnet,* and that's the attitude many of your listeners may take. Information is built on a network of facts—those small statements about people, events, and other phenomena that make games like Trivial Pursuit possible.

William Shakespeare, for example, had been dead seven years before his plays were published. That statement is a fact; you can look it up. At his death, Shakespeare left just one thing to his wife: his second-best bed, a decision that has intrigued historians ever since. Neither of these statements may throw much light on Shakespeare's life or career, but they are both facts because they can be verified. Their accuracy can be determined by anyone with access to the right documents.

LIBRARY BACKLOG

INSTANT IMPACT

You may doubt whether anyone has a bigger mess than you do in your bedroom, but whatever clutter you've got pales in comparison with the world's largest library. At last count, the Library of Congress had 36 million items—maps, manuscripts, motion pictures, photographs, music scores, sound recordings, and books—in storage, waiting for the day sometime in the distant future when they will be made available to the public.

Most of the material is stored in a huge warehouse in Landover, Maryland, a 30-minute drive from Washington, D.C., and all of it awaits inspection and classification so that the public can find it. Meanwhile, four million new items pour into the library every year.

Library backlogs are "a common condition in the age of the information explosion," says Michael Shelley of the library staff. "We've focused a great deal of attention on this."

Congress has ordered the library to cut the mountain of backlogged material to 8 million items by the year 2000, but only time will tell if the nation can clean out its attic sooner than you can clean up your room.

All facts are true; actual facts, real facts, and true facts are redundant phrases. If a thing is not true, it is not a fact. Facts are the basic building blocks of a speech—they support everything you say. Without them, an informative speech is just a house of cards, ready to topple at the slightest breeze. But some facts are more important than others. The fact that the juice of one lemon, if diluted thinly enough, could cover the state of Oregon is both true and meaningless. The world is full of facts. The challenge is to make facts count for more than mere *trivia.*

Facts should be used to support ideas. Suppose you wish to prepare a speech on the life of Marie Curie, one of the world's greatest scientists. The thesis of your speech is that Curie overcame many disadvantages and achieved success at great personal sacrifice. To convince the audience that your thesis is sound, you present the following facts:

- As a young student at the University of Paris, Curie lived on 60 cents a day.
- She could afford to buy only two sacks of coal for the winter and spent many nights shivering under towels, pillow cases, extra clothing, and any other scraps she could find.
- The science community doubted her discovery of a new element, radium, and challenged her to prove her claim.
- After four years of struggle, she and her husband produced one decigram of radium (about half the size of a small pea) by boiling down and refining eight tons of ore.
- Despite an opportunity to patent a radiation treatment for cancer, Curie refused to accept any money for her discovery. "It would be contrary to the scientific spirit," she said.

Taken together, these facts help convince the audience that you know what you're talking about.

Statistics are a special kind of fact—a fact expressed in numbers—and they can be particularly difficult for listeners to grasp. "It is now proved beyond doubt," noted the author Fletcher Knebel, "that smoking is one of the leading causes of statistics." If you use numbers, round off or approximate wherever possible. Avoid saying "two hundred and ninety-six point five," for example, if you can accomplish your purpose by saying "about three hundred."

Everyone Loves a Story ... Although facts are the backbone of an informative speech, they are not the only kind of material you can use. Another form of information, and one of the most appealing, is the **anecdote.** An anecdote is simply a short story that illustrates a point. Although people often think of anecdotes as humorous, they can also be sad or touching.

Anecdotes can be easily located in a variety of resources, including *The Little, Brown Book of Anecdotes* (edited by Clifton Fadiman). In this volume, you will find stories like these:

- Hank Aaron, baseball's greatest home-run hitter, came to the plate in the 1957 World Series. The catcher, Yogi Berra, noticed that Aaron's bat was turned the wrong way. "Turn it around," Yogi said, "so you can see the trademark." Aaron never moved his gaze from the pitcher, but said without a moment's hesitation: "Didn't come up here to read. Came up here to hit."
- Johnny Carson, long-time host of television's *Tonight Show,* was asked by a reporter once what he would like his epitaph to be. "I'll be right back," was Carson's reply.
- Sophocles, the Greek dramatist, was brought before a court of law at the age of 89 by his son. The son, who wanted to have his father declared *senile,* was afraid that Sophocles would leave him out of his will. To prove his soundness of mind, the aging playwright

How could the Aaron anecdote described in text be used to illustrate a point in a speech about commitment?

DILBERT reprinted by permission of United Feature Syndicate, Inc.

recited passages from his new play, which had not yet been performed. The judges dismissed the case.

Anecdotes spice up a speech. The Aaron anecdote could be used to illustrate a speech on concentration, the Carson anecdote to illustrate how television has changed our daily habits, and the Sophocles anecdote to illustrate how we treat senior citizens. People love to hear stories because stories dramatize ideas and situations. Stories are also far more memorable than any other kind of information. Carefully chosen, one or two anecdotes can give your speech the pizzazz it needs, but use caution. Keep in mind that anecdotes can also distract listeners from your main point and entertain more than they inform.

Quotable Quotes ... Another form of information that you can use to develop your speech is the **quotation.** Again, resources are relatively easy to find. *Bartlett's Book of Quotations* is undoubtedly the most famous, but there are other, more lighthearted books that might help. One such book is *Morrow's Contemporary Quotations,* where you can find gems like these:

- "The first problem for all of us, men and women, is not to learn, but to unlearn."—Gloria Steinem, feminist
- Awopbopaloobopalopbamboom!"—Little Richard, rock star
- "I love Mickey Mouse more than any woman I've ever known."—Walt Disney, animator

Walt Disney's quote about Mickey Mouse could provide some comic relief for your next speech.

You can also search the Internet to find a wealth of interesting and unusual quotations. You might try, for example, Creative Quotations, a site that can be searched by theme, keyword, or by a particular author. You could also try Marsh's Unfamiliar Quotations, a site based on the idea that ordinary people say extraordinary things all the time. Other sites are organized by themes such as vegetarianism or animal rights.

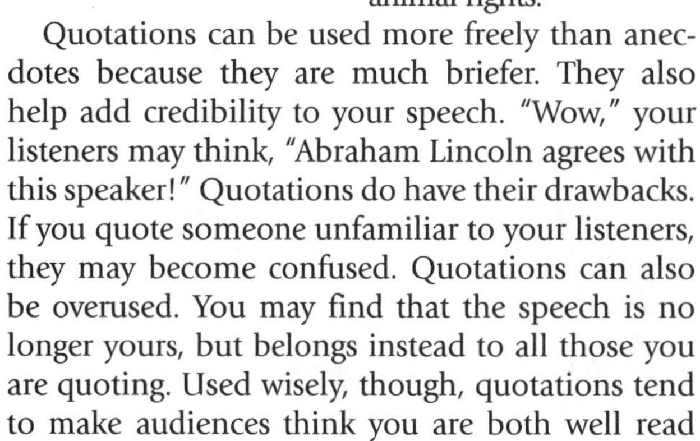

Quotations can be used more freely than anecdotes because they are much briefer. They also help add credibility to your speech. "Wow," your listeners may think, "Abraham Lincoln agrees with this speaker!" Quotations do have their drawbacks. If you quote someone unfamiliar to your listeners, they may become confused. Quotations can also be overused. You may find that the speech is no longer yours, but belongs instead to all those you are quoting. Used wisely, though, quotations tend to make audiences think you are both well read and believable.

COMMUNICATION Breakdown

When Information Isn't Enough

Sometimes information isn't enough to solve a problem. When Judge Clarence Thomas was nominated to the Supreme Court by President Bush in 1991, he couldn't have known that his confirmation hearings would cause a national debate over how men and women treat each other in the workplace.

During the hearings, Anita Hill, an Oklahoma University law professor who had once worked for Thomas, came forward to state that Thomas had sexually harassed her. Hill said that Thomas had repeatedly asked her out for dates and had made suggestive remarks.

Thomas denied the allegations and insisted that he was sensitive to how any person, regardless of race or gender, was treated on the job.

The result of this disagreement became a high-stakes tug of war with both Hill and Thomas trying to convince millions of American TV viewers and 100 U.S. senators that they had been greatly victimized.

One television expert, S. Robert Lichter, said that in the camera's eye, Thomas and Hill were equally believable. "In trials by media, we've gotten used to clear winners and losers," Lichter said. "I'm not seeing that here. I'm seeing both sides doing a good job."

Thomas, who spoke first, was forceful and eloquent, casting himself as the victim of a witch-hunt. Hill, whose voice trembled but whose poise never cracked, seemed equally convincing when she gave a detailed account of the offenses she said Thomas had committed.

In the end, the Senate narrowly approved Thomas's nomination to the Supreme Court (a lifetime job), never directly answering the question of who was telling the truth.

Source: Lichter was quoted in the *Los Angeles Times.*

Question

1. In case of conflicting stories, how can we determine whether one set of facts is more accurate than another?
2. Can you think of other highly publicized political or legal situations in which a great deal of information was presented without obtaining a satisfactory resolution? Be specific in describing this event.

Defining Your Terms ... A fourth kind of information to use in developing your speech is the **definition.** Sometimes simply defining a term is the best way to get an audience headed in the right direction. You may, for example, wish to use a familiar word in a special way. "I am using the word *dog* not in the sense of a pet," you might explain, "but in the sense of a 'hip buddy,' as in 'What's up, dog?'"

You may also wish to trace the history of a word for your listeners. This tactic might help them understand why your choice of a particular word is apropos. Etymological information (*etymology* means the origins of words) can sometimes help correct mistaken ideas. Cinderella's glass slipper, for example, is not glass at all in the original version. In the French version of the story, Cinderella wears a *pantoufle en vair* ("a slipper of fur"), but a translator apparently confused *en vair* with *en verre* (meaning "of glass"). Now all English-speaking people think Cinderella wore a glass slipper (rather uncomfortable, don't you think?).

Is this a crocodile or an alligator? How can you tell?

Descriptions ... The final form of information we will discuss here is descriptions, images that stimulate the audience's imagination. Suppose you want to tell an audience about the difference between an alligator and a crocodile. You could explain their physical features, of course, but why not try a fresh twist? Consider this "personalized" description:

> Alligators have rounded snouts and crocodiles have pointed ones, though if your leg is caught in either, you probably won't appreciate the difference. If the jaws are completely closed around your leg, you might look on either side of the snout to see whether a lower tooth is jutting outside the upper lip. If it is, the creature is a croc.

Descriptions can help you emphasize certain aspects of your topic. They can bring to life an interesting character or create a vivid impression of a particular place. Practice writing descriptions and then try including them in your speeches.

SECTION 2 REVIEW

Recalling the Facts ...

1. How can personal experience be used as a source to find a subject to speak about?
2. List four ways to narrow your subject.

Thinking Critically ...

1. Narrow the following subjects into speech topics. Then write a reasonable thesis for each:
   - rain forest
   - indoor sports
   - heroes and heroines
   - scientific discoveries
   - household chores
2. In what areas do high school students need more information? Do teens know what they need to know about voting, how to get a job, or how to get into college? How do teens get their information on these subjects, and what role does public speaking play in presenting such information?

Taking Charge ...

1. Find an anecdote related to a famous person of your choice.
2. Take a technical subject, like how a pager works, and define five terms related to that topic.

SECTION 3

Audio and Visual Aids

"You can't really appreciate the thrilling beauty of these South American aardvarks unless you can see and hear them in their natural surroundings." Surprisingly, the speaker of these words is stuck in a classroom in Billings, Montana, nowhere near the Amazon jungle. Is there a way this speaker can bring his audience nearer the subject? "Luckily," the speaker continues, "I have brought with me some slides I took in Brazil, and I've also brought some on-the-spot recordings of the noises the aardvarks make."

When you can't bring the real thing to your audience (in other words, nearly all the time), you can arrange the next best thing. In the aardvark example, a speaker brought both pictures and sound to an audience. Such material is referred to as visual and audio aids. Visual aids include anything the audience can see—photographs, cartoons, color slides, videotapes, posters, transparencies, or chalk drawings. Audio aids include anything the audience can hear—music, sound effects, or recorded conversations. The use of these devices can sometimes spell the difference between a ho-hum and a humdinger of a speech.

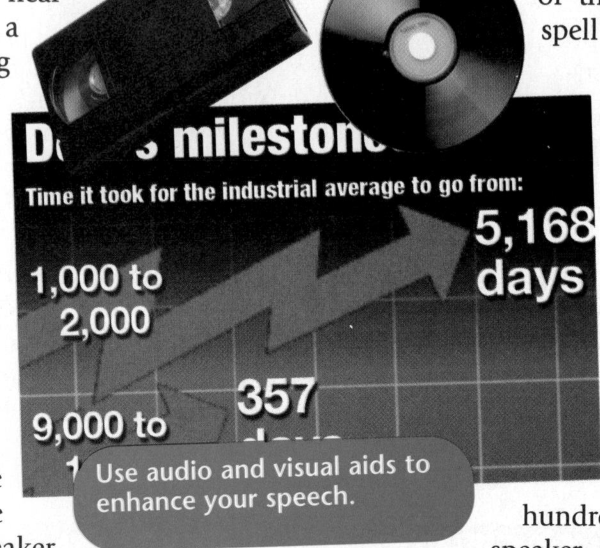

Use audio and visual aids to enhance your speech.

Visual aids, especially, can help a speaker make a point because vision is our most dominant sense. Research tells us that we pay 25 times as much attention to visual information as we do to audio information. "One seeing," says an old Japanese proverb, "is better than a hundred times telling." Still, every speaker should remember that no matter how powerful or striking her visual aids may be, they are meant to enhance and not replace a well-constructed speech.

Two-Dimensional Visual Aids

Illustrations that can be represented on a flat surface are called two-dimensional aids. They include charts, diagrams, maps, drawings, and photographs. These visuals can be displayed on a classroom chalkboard (either drawn there or held up with tape) or on a flipchart (a large pad of paper mounted on an easel). They can be projected on a screen or held up by hand for the audience to see. If the speaker can show the visual without having to hold it, he will be free to use a pointer to describe particular features.

Photographs, Drawings, and Cartoons ... If a picture is worth a thousand words, then using one in your speech can mean a big savings. Furthermore, with a photo you can make people see things that you can't easily explain. Using photographs in a speech, however, can be a tricky business. Make sure that you mount them on heavy construction paper or art boards so that they are easy to handle. Photos should be at least 8 by 10 inches (preferably larger), so that the audience can see them easily. As with other visual aids, you should hide or cover the photos until you are ready to use them and then put them out of sight again when you are done.

Drawings are popular visual aids because they are easy to prepare. If you can use a compass and a straightedge, you can draw well enough for most speeches. If the drawing you need is too complicated for you to draw, find an art student who can help. Cartoons, a special kind of drawing, use humor or satire to make a point. The editorial page of a newspaper can be a good place to get ideas for your own cartoons.

Graphic Representations ... Maps, **diagrams**, and **graphs** are among the many other two-dimensional visual aids that speakers, particularly in the business world, use with success. Maps are certainly the best way to show a geographical relationship. If you want to show the route of the

INSTANT IMPACT

COVERING KOSOVO

Gathering information is never easy, but when bombs are falling and bullets are whizzing around your head, that job becomes even tougher. Journalists used to say that your story would run on page 6 and your obituary on page 12. In 1999 war correspondents were saying the same thing about covering Kosovo.

To cover the conflict, journalists had to take numerous risks, often confronting gunfire without the benefit of armored vehicles or flak vests. But correspondents also found new ways to cover the conflict—the two warring factions posted official statements on their World Wide Web sites. Kosovo, in effect, became the first major conflict to be fought on the Internet.

In Kosovo, policymakers who used to brush off journalists with "no comment" now said "check my web site." One of the most interesting voices in the war came from a holy man toiling in a 600-year-old Serbian monastery, the Rev. Sava Janjic.

During the heaviest fighting in May 1998, Janjic started bombarding the Internet with e-mails to journalists, politicians, and diplomats. Rising at 1 A.M. to take advantage of the best Internet connections, the 33-year-old monk prayed and then surfed the Net.

"It's nice to live in a medieval setting as we monks do, but that doesn't mean we are prepared to accept a medieval mentality," Janjic said. "The Internet enables me to speak from the pulpit of my keyboard."

Source: *American Journalism Review.*

Appalachian Trail from Georgia to Maine, a map is a necessity.

Diagrams are useful when you want to explain a process. If you want to show how an internal combustion engine works, for example, a diagram might save you time and help your audience achieve a better understanding. Graphs are useful for showing relationships among statistical data, such as the crime rate or the increasing price of comic books. It's hard to wring emotion out of numbers, but you can sometimes give them appeal by turning them into graphic images.

Although too old-fashioned for some, the chalkboard can be the ideal visual aid for certain presentations.

One of the problems you may face with aids like these is the time-consuming process of making them in the first place. Business speakers often have a design staff that can spend days preparing a sales chart. Since you don't have that luxury, you must decide whether the time you need to prepare an exciting visual will take too much of the time you need to construct the speech itself. However effective a visual aid might be, it will not hide a weakly written speech.

Fortunately, modern computer graphic arts programs are now available in most schools. You can use programs like Freehand or Adobe Illustrator (to name just a few) to create imaginative and interesting illustrations. Journalists refer to these as *infographics* (*information + graphics*), and examples of them can be found in most newspapers and magazines.

Chalkboard Aids ... One of the easiest visual aids to use is a chalkboard. The chief advantage of using a chalkboard is that you can put information up as you need it and erase material that is no longer needed. Luckily, no one expects blackboard work to be beautiful, so long as the drawing or writing is large and clear. Chalk gives you more flexibility and *spontaneity* than any other kind of visual aid.

Many teachers discourage the use of chalkboards, however, for one important reason: How can you use a chalkboard without turning your back to the audience? Once a speaker turns her back on the audience, more than eye contact is lost. If ever there were an opportunity for the listener's mind to wander, this is it.

With a little forethought, you can overcome this problem. Write out most of what you think you need ahead of time and cover it. Stick to very short messages. If you do write while talking, stand to the side so that the audience will focus its attention on the words as they appear. And consider a handy alternative to the chalkboard—the overhead projector, which we will cover shortly.

Handouts ... **Handouts** include any flyers, brochures, or information sheets that you prepare ahead of time and duplicate so that each member of the audience can have a copy. On the plus side, handouts look professional, and people can take them home after your speech. On the negative side, they can create distractions. It takes time and trouble to distribute handouts, and your audience may study them instead of making eye contact with you. An experienced speaker usually passes out handouts at the end so as not to interrupt the speech itself.

WORDS FROM THE WORKPLACE

David Farabee
State Representative

Q: *How does good communication play a role in your day-to-day activities, Mr. Farabee?*

A: Government, like any service-oriented entity, relies on effective communication skills. Whether you are trying to enact legislation that will affect millions of people, or just pointing people in the right direction through proper government channels, you must relay the appropriate information to ensure accountable and accurate results.

Q: *What tips can you give students about the importance of communication skills in the world of government?*

A: Communication starts with research and knowing the idea or message that one wants to convey. To me, effective communication is nothing more than identifying an idea, learning about it, and then breaking up your knowledge into coherent pieces designed to make your point. After that, communicating the idea to your intended audience is explaining the idea or message (Tell 'em what you're gonna tell 'em), going into understandable detail about the idea or message (Tell 'em), and wrapping up the idea or message in easily understandable language (Tell 'em what you told 'em). While this strategy of communication works for me, it is not the only way to get your point across. Acquiring good communication skills takes practice and research, but if you do the work and acquire the skills, there is nothing that you cannot accomplish!

Projections

Speakers can use a variety of devices to project a visual aid on a blank wall or screen. These devices include an **overhead projector** (a simple device that projects and magnifies material from a transparent sheet of plastic) and a slide projector. The overhead projector can be effective even if some lights are left on, while a slide projector requires that the room be completely dark. Other projection devices include a VCR and a motion picture projector.

Overhead Projector ... A variation on the chalkboard approach is the use of an overhead projector. One advantage of using an overhead is that you can prepare transparencies ahead of time and then lay them on the overhead for viewing. Be sure you become familiar with the projector well before your speech, paying special attention to how to straighten and focus the image.

If you wish to keep some of the image covered, use a large piece of cardboard that is thick enough to cover the image and heavy enough to stay in place. Try to avoid reading the transparency to your audience. Instead, point out the highlights. Above all, stand out of the way so that the image can be easily seen.

Slides ... Color slides are a popular way to illustrate an informative speech because they have a size and vividness unmatched by almost any other visual. Great care must be taken, however, to select only slides that really illustrate the point you wish to make. Many speakers make the mistake of using too many slides and risk boring their listeners. Be sure that the slides you use are sharply focused and have good contrast. A slide that is hard to see is not worth showing.

As valuable as they are, slides have been overused and can easily lull an audience to sleep. Because they have to be used in a darkened room, the slides themselves become the focal point of your speech. Listeners turn their attention from you to the slides, and it may be difficult to get their attention back.

Videotape ... The rapid development of easy-to-use camcorders means that you can now create your own videotape to illustrate a speech. A speech on the fundamentals of pole vaulting, for example, could be improved with video clips of someone actually vaulting. If your school has a VCR that enables you to use special techniques like freeze frame and slow motion, so much the better.

You could create a videotape for your speech if you have access to the equipment.

You might also wish to use material that you have recorded from national or local television programs. Pay close attention to copyright laws to be sure that you do not make illegal use of anything. Often, sponsors permit limited educational use of their programs. Copyright laws do change from time to time, and your teacher will have current information to help you.

Three-Dimensional Visual Aids

Sometimes an actual object—something with height, width, and depth—can make a greater impression than a picture or projection. If you were to give a speech on porcelain dolls, for example, showing the audience actual dolls would have much greater appeal than simply using pictures or slides. In some cases, especially with smaller groups, it may even be possible to let the audience handle the objects. If you decide, however, to pass an object among the members of the audience, be aware that you will lose the attention of each listener in turn as he or she examines the object.

Models ... Occasionally, an object is too large to bring to a speech. You would have a tough time, for example, wheeling in the space shuttle *Discovery* for a talk on space research. But you could use a scale **model.** A plastic model of the space shuttle, scaled down to perhaps one-twentieth of the actual size, would enable you to show the features of the vehicle in an informative way. Similarly, you could make an inexpensive but useful model of a camera with a large box (to represent the body of the camera) and a piece of tinfoil over an opening in the box (to show how the lens and shutter work).

Cutaways ... A variation of the model idea is an object called a **cutaway,** which is essentially a model sliced in two. Your model of the space shuttle, for example, may have a removable side panel that would allow the audience to look inside, the better to examine the flight deck or the crew's quarters. A rather gross form of this idea toured a number of state fairs some years ago. It seems a cow with stomach problems had been fitted with a plastic window in its side, enabling fairgoers to watch the cow's digestive system in action.

Both models and cutaways need to follow the same rules we have discussed for other visual aids. They must be large enough to be seen and clearly relevant to the point under discussion. In addition,

Be sure your visual aids are large enough for everyone to see easily.

the speaker must be sure to practice handling the objects so that he or she won't drop or fumble them at a crucial moment.

Sound Recordings

Audiotapes and records, the main forms of audio aids, have much in common with videotape, especially in terms of how you use them in a speech. You might wish to use an audiotape in a speech on animal communication, for example, to demonstrate the sounds whales make. An audiotape of informal conversation might be helpful in a speech on regional dialects.

If you use an audiotape, be sure that the recording is clear and can be played loud enough for all to hear. Practice using the audiotape and make sure, before speaking, that the tape is cued to the correct position.

Guidelines for Using Aids

Now that we have discussed a variety of audio and visual aids, we want to give you a few guidelines for their use. Whatever visual image you use must be large enough for the audience to see. The larger the audience, the larger the visual aid must be. For an audience of classmates, you can probably use images that fit on a sheet of 8½-by-11-inch paper. Even with an audience the size of a normal class, however, the larger the image you can provide, the more likely it is to be meaningful.

You should master the mechanics of any equipment you plan to use. Take the time needed to become familiar with devices like overhead projectors and VCRs. Set up any equipment you need early so that you are not adjusting it or fiddling with it while delivering your speech. Make sure you have chalk available if you're using the chalkboard and markers if you're using an overhead. Have any handouts you need available and have a plan for distributing them quickly and efficiently.

Remember, too, that the visual aid is *not* the audience. Rookies tend to speak to the aid as if it could hear. If you need to look at the visual aid, get plenty of practice so that you are thoroughly familiar with the procedure you're going to follow.

Television weathercasters appear to be pointing at features on a weather map, but in fact the weathercaster's image

Weather forecasters, like good speakers, have to know their facts before making their presentations.

has been superimposed over a map located in another part of the studio. These speakers have learned how to point to something without looking at it. You can do the same. Learn to use charts and maps with no more than a sidelong glance.

The following summarizes our advice for the use of audio and visual aids.

- Be sure the aid is large enough to be seen or loud enough to be heard.
- Be sure the aid contributes to the idea being presented. If you can get along without it, don't use it. It takes time away from the rest of your presentation.
- Don't stand in front of the aid.
- Talk to your listeners, not to the visual aid.
- Keep any visual aid out of sight until you are ready to use it, and then put it away again when you have finished.
- Don't overdo a good thing. A long succession of slides or charts can become boring.
- Remember Murphy's Law—if something can go wrong, it will. Have a backup plan in case your equipment fails.
- Practice, practice, practice.

Finally, remember that visual or audio aids are only a means to an end. If these aids overwhelm the speech or draw undue attention away from you as the speaker, you would be wise not to use them. Don't forget that you yourself are a visual aid. Consider whether the clothing you plan to wear will contribute or detract from your message. Can you give a serious speech in a clown costume or a humorous speech in your best dress?

A clown costume would be inappropriate for a serious speech.

SECTION 3 REVIEW

Recalling the Facts ...

1. When is the best time during a speech to distribute handouts to the audience?

Thinking Critically ...

1. How can a high school speaker develop greater credibility when speaking to an adult audience? How can an adult speaker hold the interest of a high school audience?

Taking Charge ...

1. Create a graph or chart comparing the means your classmates use to get to school.
2. Create three overhead transparencies for a speech on horror films.

SECTION 4 Creating Multimedia Presentations

By some measures, cell phones and e-mail represent great advances in communication, but by other measures they're still rather basic. The new frontier in communication technology probably lies in multimedia presentations.

What a Multimedia Presentation Includes

A **multimedia presentation** is a speech supplemented with special computer software. This software enables the speaker to combine several kinds of visual and/or audio aids (including charts and graphs, slides and photographs, even animations, video clips, and sound) into one presentation. Popular presentation software includes PowerPoint, Astound, Hyper Studio, and several others.

Depending on the resources available at your school, you may be able to give multimedia presentations in your classes. Such presentations provide good training for speeches you may give outside the classroom—especially in business settings, where multimedia resources are used every day.

Although each multimedia presentation program operates a bit differently, all allow you to use a wide range of material. Suppose, for example, that you are talking about the Lewis and Clark expedition and you want to show your audience a painting of Lewis and Clark's famous guide, Sacajawea.

If the image can be found on the Internet, you can **download** (transfer data from one computer's memory to the memory of another, usually smaller, computer) it directly to your computer. Remember to check whether the image is in the public domain, and thus available at no charge, or is protected by copyright. If the image is from a book or magazine, you can transfer it to disk with a piece of equipment called a **scanner.** Once the digitized image is in your computer, you can then manipulate it to suit your own purposes.

Suppose you want to explain how special effects are used in movies such as *Star Wars.* You can download video clips from the movies—including sound—for presentation in your speech. You can also program your photographs, slides, animations, and other visuals to appear automatically at pre-set times—leaving you free to concentrate on connecting with your audience.

Multimedia presentations can include charts and graphs as well as sound and video.

During the speech, you use a computer to control the order, content, and timing of your presentation. The computer is usually hooked up to a television monitor, a large-screen video projector, or an LCD (liquid crystal display) panel. Some systems have a wireless mouse or remote control that lets you move through your presentation with a minimum of fuss.

Advantages of Using Computer Presentation Programs . . . In a multimedia presentation, you coordinate various media (music, text, illustrations, and so on) to enhance your message. The advantage of using a combination of media is that you can appeal to more than one of your audience's senses. Some of us are visual learners; others need to hear; some need a hands-on approach. No matter what their learning styles may be, your audience will be more stimulated with a multimedia presentation, and therefore more interested in what you have to say.

Computer presentation programs offer a number of important advantages. The slide program you create, for example, serves as an outline for both you and your audience. Rather than looking at your notes, you can glance at the screen along with the audience to check your place in the script. These presentation programs also give your materials a professional appearance. Text and graphics look well designed, not like the hand-drawn or handwritten style of traditional overhead presentations.

In addition, computer presentation programs offer a number of special features. They allow you to make quick insertions of new data (tables, for instance, or charts). You can also easily update or change presentations, unlike more permanent media such as flip charts.

A high school group working on a science project, for example, might use multimedia to improve the effectiveness of its presentation. To make the idea of a black hole more vivid, the group might use a clip from a video such as *A Brief History of Time.* In addition, they might use some futuristic background music to help establish a mood of mystery and awe as they explain their subject.

Even churches, synagogues, and mosques are getting into the act. Several presentation companies are now working with religious groups to make worship services multimedia experiences. For example, some groups are projecting the words for hymns on a wall. Others present missionary reports or news of "blessed events" such as births, weddings, bar mitzvahs, and anniversaries in a multimedia format. The religious leader can even press a button to project a key sermon point on a screen as he speaks.

Effective Graphics

Choosing the right type of graphic or visual aid can make presentations more interesting and can help you present complex information more clearly.

You might use, for example, a

- **Table**—if you want to organize a lot of words, ideas, or numbers.
- **Bar graph**—if you want to show differences in size or quantity.
- **Line graph**—if you want to show a trend.
- **Pie chart**—if you want to show the various parts of a whole.
- **Photograph**—when words aren't adequate.
- **Diagram or flowchart**—if you want to explain a complicated procedure (the parts of a machine, for example, or the way an organization works).

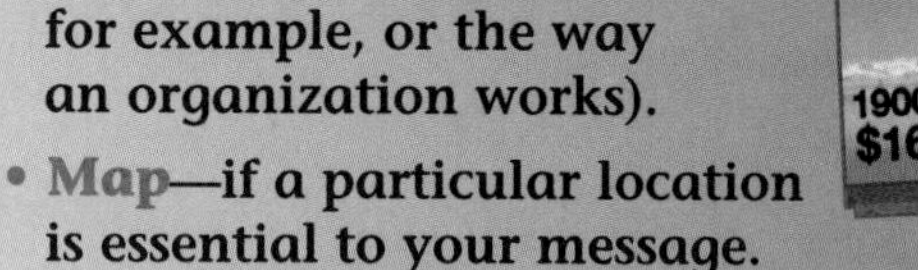

- **Map**—if a particular location is essential to your message.

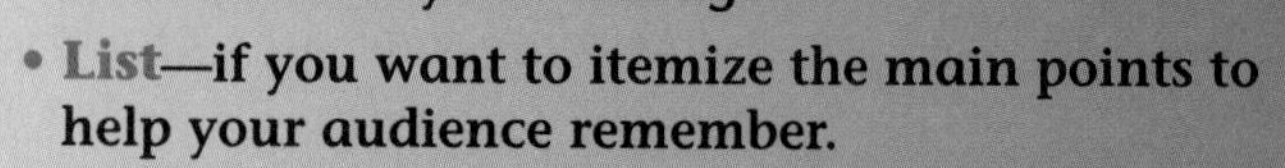

- **List**—if you want to itemize the main points to help your audience remember.

Possible Disadvantages ... Today's high-tech audiences not only want to hear your ideas, they expect to be entertained at the same time. But because modern audiences are "information saturated," it takes powerful tools to get your message across. The new computer programs enable you, for example, to turn important words and phrases into animated action statements that fly across the screen.

But multimedia presentations do have drawbacks—not the least of which is the high cost of the equipment required to show them. Another disadvantage is that it takes a great deal of time to learn how to use the software, to design graphs and charts, to edit sound and video clips (several hours would not be unusual for a 30-second clip), and to organize and rehearse a presentation. If you plan to give a multimedia presentation, be sure to give yourself plenty of time to make sure it comes off just right.

Multimedia presentations require high-cost equipment, time to learn software, and extensive editing to be effective.

Preparing a Presentation ...

Multimedia presentations certainly take time to prepare, but the results may be well worth the effort. A group of researchers at 3M found that speakers who used audio/visual aids were generally more convincing than those who only spoke. Audiences described the visual presentations as clearer, more professional, and more interesting.

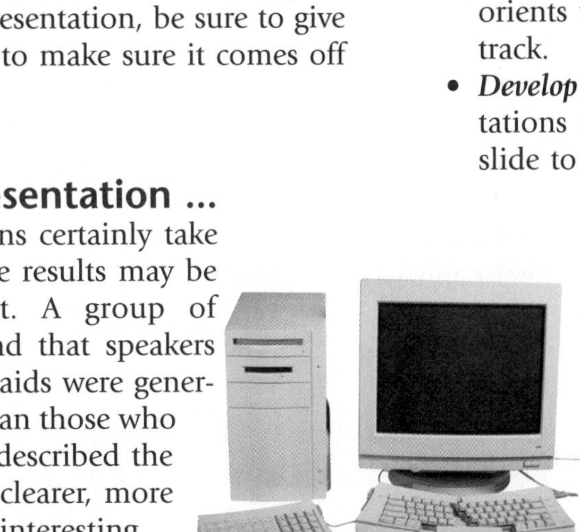

Perhaps most telling of all, the study revealed that those who saw the visual presentation needed less meeting time later (by 24 percent) to finish their business. The underlying conclusion of this study—that visuals can significantly enhance our persuasiveness—takes on new meaning in an era when virtually every presenter has access to communications technology.

Keep these guidelines in mind as you prepare a multimedia program:

- ***Know what you are presenting.*** Have a good research base; knowing the material well can give you a healthy dose of confidence.
- ***Know your audience.*** Find out who they are, as well as their level of interest, knowledge, and experience. Anticipate their questions and build the answers into your presentation.
- ***Use an outline.*** Prepare your script in advance (with an opening, body, and closing). Break down the major subject into supporting topics. An outline presented on a slide orients the audience and helps keep you on track.
- ***Develop a format.*** The most effective presentations use a format that is consistent from slide to slide. Typeface, type alignment, size, and graphic elements should all be part of an overall plan. Once you have the format designed, all you have to do is change the text from one slide to the next, allowing plenty of room for charts or illustrations.
- ***Make it easy to read.*** Limit each slide to a maximum of seven lines of text. The more you ask the audience to read, the less attentive they'll be to what you're saying. Use large type

and set off each of your points with a bullet or number. Make sure you proofread the text carefully to catch typographical errors, punctuation problems, and misspellings.

- *Rehearse.* This is a step that's easy to overlook, so discipline yourself to set up the presentation and go through it just as if an audience were there.
- *Arrive early.* On presentation day, come early and test everything. Review the room setup, making sure that everyone can see the screen. Find the light switches and the drapery pulls.

Strategies for Success ... Presentations may seem as if they run themselves, but it's not quite that simple. You need to think just as much about your people skills as you do about your technical skills. No matter how many high-tech special effects you throw at your listeners, the effort will be wasted if you can't relate to them, person to person. Here are a few strategic ideas to consider as you develop your presentation:

- Analyze how the size and seating arrangement of the room may affect your presentation.
- Get off to a good start and end with a big finish.
- Connect with your audience. Relate to their needs and draw them into your message.
- Use humor, anecdotes, and personal stories to highlight points you want to drive home.
- Never go in without a backup plan. What will you do if the computer program fails to start up? Always carry a backup disk of your presentation just in case. Take a printout of your script as well.
- Be prepared to give your speech even if all the multimedia equipment were to fail. It may not be as dazzling as the speech you had planned, but it will be much better than no speech at all.

SECTION  REVIEW

Recalling the Facts ...

1. What are some of the advantages of using a multimedia presentation?
2. Why is putting your outline on a slide a good idea?

Thinking Critically ...

1. Discuss with your classmates how you might use a multimedia presentation in each of these situations:
   - You've been chosen to deliver some disappointing news at the company meeting, and you expect to encounter some hostility from the crowd.
   - Your last presentation was dry and not very memorable. You're wondering what you could do to improve your next report—a report on intramural participation.
   - You've just begun speaking when a member of the audience asks you a loaded question that catches you off guard.
2. What kind of graphic would you use to illustrate each of the following?
   - The per-person rate for one night at five hotels in town is $107, $172, $62, $97, and $67.
   - Tourism has increased steadily over the last ten years.
   - Some hotels are located in the downtown area, while several others are in nearby suburbs.
   - A view of what one of the hotel rooms looks like.
   - Where the swimming pool and restaurant are in relation to the hotel lobby.

Taking Charge ...

1. Create ten imaginary slides you might use in a multimedia presentation about your school that you plan to give to foreign exchange students.

STUDENT WORK

"Chill Out" *By Lisa Kargo*

Everyone talks about the weather, but no one does anything about it. At least that's the way it used to be, as high school speech champ Lisa Kargo explains in this informative speech on the beneficial effects of cold. Notice how skillfully and entertainingly she blends many facts and theories together. Notice, too, how she gives credit to her sources.

It was the kind of incident that made you say "only in New York City." A man suddenly stops on a busy sidewalk and begins to take off his clothes. In a flash he is stripped all the way down to his . . . shirt and slacks.

I know, you're disappointed that he didn't grin and bare it. But before we accuse our New York friend of wrong-undoing, consider that the temperature outside that day was two degrees below zero—the kind of day when even the icicles are frozen stiff. But if the New York weather was cold, why did our friend attempt sudden exposure? You'll have to wait a few major ideas and some subpoints for the answer.

According to scholar Joseph Campbell, myths and legends about the cold abound in Western culture. But lately, scientific research has uncovered new dimensions about the cold and freezing. At the University of Minnesota this past year, a dedicated group of doctors spent a million-dollar endowment studying the effects of freezing on humans, animals, food, and even tools.

Most people hate the cold, and with reason. In the Midwest we have four kinds of winter—cold, colder, coldest, and use an icepick to take off your clothes. Cold weather causes illness and thousands of injuries and deaths. But the very same cold that brings misery and death can potentially be one of man's most benevolent friends.

In order to melt our perceptions of the cold, I will discuss the following three areas: initially, cold effects, then icy miracles, and finally, frozen medical wonders.

Dr. Cameron C. Bangs, an expert on cold weather injuries, notes that it doesn't require below-zero temperatures before the body begins to react to the cold. Mild cold causes a process known as *vasoconstriction.* The process begins when the brain senses that inner organs are losing their warmth.

In vasoconstriction, the body's blood vessels narrow to reduce blood flow to the surface of the skin. This process minimizes heat loss and keeps warm blood flowing to the heart, lungs, brain, and spinal cord. For this reason people who are stranded in blizzards can survive with skin temperatures as low as 40 degrees because the significant organs inside the body are still warm.

Some weather is just too cold for the normal body process—you know, the kind of weather that makes Midwesterners go to Alaska for the winter. Exposed to this kind of cold, the body will shut off the blood flow to the brain and lungs, leaving only warm blood for the spinal cord and heart. People who have been this cold sometimes hallucinate for hours even after warming up.

After the body performs vasoconstriction, it tries to warm itself by an alternative method—shivering. Shivering occurs when all the muscles contract simultaneously—even the muscles in your jaw—which is why your teeth chatter.

Every once in a while, the body will quickly open up and let blood flow all over for a short period of time. According to Shawna Vogel, in the February 1988 edition of *Discover* magazine, this is why the man in New York, and thousands of others like him, feel extreme warmth and strip off their clothes. Some get so carried away they strip down only to their beads of perspiration.

Our bodies have specific, programmed reactions to the effects of cold. And these reactions bring about icy miracles.

On a frozen December day in 1984, four-year-old Jimmy Tontlewicz went outside to play. He wandered too far out on the ice in Lake Michigan

and crashed through the thin barrier to the frigid water below. He remained there for 20 minutes yet doctors revived him.

We've all heard of cases like Jimmy's—people who crash through a frozen lake or pond, stay under for long periods of time, and then miraculously recover. These people are alive today because of a genetic response to the cold called the *mammalian dive reflex.*

Seals, another mammal, stop breathing when they dive underwater. Their pulse decreases, which reduces stress on the heart. Vasoconstriction occurs at rapid speed, and blood flows only to the heart and brain.

Seals can control their dive reflex, but for humans, it only works in times of intense cold and shocking, life-threatening trauma. An accident victim's pulse is very faint, and they may even experience some paralysis because blood is shut off to the spinal cord. But rescuers now know that the cold keeps the body alive. In fact, they say that no one is dead until they are WARM and dead.

But don't go out and start skating on thin ice. The older you get, the less likely that the mammalian dive reflex will save you. Another advantage of youth.

The cold brings about icy miracles, and modern medicine is beginning to recognize the potential of the cold in enacting frozen medical wonders. In the future, the cold and freezing may cure many a malady.

For example, what can you do for a headache? Take aspirin? Put on a hot pack? The January 1987 issue of *Health* magazine reports that ice packs can actually cure the common headache. Dr. Seymour Diamond states that a headache is caused by swelling in the brain's blood vessels. The cold will constrict the blood vessels, therefore curing the headache. I wish I had the ice concession at school right before final exams.

Other medical uses for the cold have surfaced in just the past five years.

The July 11, 1987, issue of *Science News* reports that liver tumors can now be frozen as an alternative to surgery. After such procedures, a majority of patients show no evidence of the tumor.

The same issue of *Science News* reports on cryosurgery, or the freezing of cancer cells. Cancer cells contain water, and exposing them to extreme cold freezes the water and thus kills the cells. Cryosurgery also freezes the surrounding blood vessels to prevent any recurrence.

You have to admit that having your dead body frozen and revived years later sounds like science fiction, but Avi Ben Abraham, chairman of the American Cryonics Society, states that "we're fighting the most significant struggle in history, the struggle of life against death."

The Trans Time Company of Oakland, California, is one of several companies around the country practicing cryonics, or the freezing of bodies. Many people with inoperative diseases have had their bodies frozen after death, hoping to be revived in an age when their disease can be cured. Others opt for freezing in hope of finding a time when man has cured the most deadly of diseases—death itself. The same cold that makes your nose run may be giving others the gift of the ancient gods—immortality.

The cold may be a source of discomfort, but we are slowly discovering that it can be one of the most benevolent of nature's gifts. People stripping off clothes because of the cold doesn't only happen in New York City. But rumors are circulating that New Yorkers have a sure cure for cold and freezing. They call it July.

CHAPTER 13 Review and Enrichment...

Looking Back

Listed below are the major ideas discussed in this chapter.

- Much of our daily communication is designed to give instructions, provide facts, or clarify ideas.
- Speakers who hope to inform should be sure to be clear, concise, complete, and correct. They should also use concrete examples and connect with listeners.
- One reason we sometimes have difficulty imagining what our listeners are thinking is that most of us are wrapped up in our own points of view.
- Asking some basic questions about your listeners can help you prepare an effective speech.
- Finding a subject to speak on can come from surveys, newspaper articles, conversations, the Internet, and other classes.
- Create a manageable topic by limiting the subject in time, space, and scope.
- A clearly focused thesis will help you decide what material belongs in your speech and what does not.
- Develop your speech through the use of appropriate facts, anecdotes, quotations, definitions, and descriptions.
- Audio and visual aids can reinforce your message and enhance your presentation.
- Visual aids must be large enough to be seen and significant enough to be worthwhile.
- Audio and visual aids are valuable if used confidently but can detract from your speech if presented in a distracting way.
- Presentations that include visual aids are more likely to be remembered better.
- A multimedia presentation can include video clips and animated text.
- A speaker should always be prepared to deliver a speech without any visual aids, in the event that the equipment fails.

Speech Vocabulary

Fill in each blank with the correct word from the list below. No word can be used more than once. Not all words will be used.

briefing	fireside chat	cultural literacy
advance organizer	definition	anecdote
narrowing	thesis	graph
quotation	diagram	model
handout	overhead projector	map
cutaway	status report	multimedia presentation
public lecture	chalk talk	download scanner

1. You would be wise to depend on what you know of history, science, and literature, your ______________, when you suspect someone has made a mistake.
2. Three useful visual aids include a ______________, which tells you where places are; a ______________, which shows you how something works; and a ______________, which shows relationships among numbers.
3. An ______________ can show an audience cartoons, drawings, and other materials on a screen without darkening the room.

4. After choosing a subject, you can limit it by ______________ and then condense your major point into a ______________.
5. To bring appealing material to your speech, you can use a short story—called an ______________—or a statement from a famous person—a ______________.
6. Some of your teachers may be fond of giving a ______________, while a sports coach is more likely to give a ______________.
7. The president's press secretary gives reporters a ______________. The president may give a more personal talk called a ______________.
8. Organizations often hear a ______________ from one of their committees.
9. A statement such as "I will first describe the best breeds for show animals and then look at poodles in particular" helps preview a speech and is called an ______________.
10. A small-scale version of the Globe Theater is called a ______________. If part of it can be removed so people can see inside, that portion is referred to as a ______________.
11. One kind of visual aid, that can be distributed to the audience is called a ______________.
12. To prepare a ______________, the speaker first decided to ______________ an image from the Internet and use a ______________ to digitize a picture from her photo album.

General Vocabulary

Use a dictionary to find the definitions. Match each of the terms on the left with its definition on the right.

1. concise
2. concrete
3. distinction
4. ambiguous
5. intuition
6. demographics
7. trivia
8. senile
9. etymology
10. infographic
11. spontaneity

a. a difference, something unlike another
b. brief, to the point
c. capable of having two or more meanings
d. characteristics of human populations
e. diminished capacity due to old age
f. facts presented in a visual way
g. impulsive, unpredictable behavior
h. insignificant information
i. real, perceptible
j. special insight or a "sixth sense"
k. the origin and development of a word

To Remember

Answer the following questions based on the information in the chapter.

1. What are some ways in which we provide information every day to others?
2. Name the five major kinds of informative speeches.
3. What are some of the ways a speaker can support general statements?
4. Define the term cultural literacy.
5. What are some of the questions you might use to learn more about your audience?
6. List several good methods for finding a subject for a speech.
7. How can a potential subject be narrowed to a manageable topic?
8. What are the characteristics of a thesis?
9. What can a speaker do if the audience's attention appears to wander?

10. What should you keep in mind if you decide to use a chalkboard during your speech?
11. Why shouldn't you fill your allotted speech time with visuals?
12. In what three ways can multimedia visual aids enhance an oral presentation?
13. When creating a multimedia slide, how much text is enough and how much is too much?

To Do

1. Attend a school or public meeting. Community organizations include the city council, the school board, clubs, and support groups. As you listen, sort out the comments people make according to what is genuine information and what is simply opinion. Determine a rough ratio of information to opinion and report back to the class.
2. Practice giving directions to classmates. Tell them how to get to your house from school or how to drive to various locations around town.
3. Write to a government agency or your congressperson for information on a subject of interest.
4. Create a graph or chart comparing the shoe sizes of your classmates.

To Talk About

1. Consider whether the explosion of new information over the past few years has been a blessing or a curse. Are high school students, for example, better informed than their peers of 10 or 20 years ago?
2. What techniques might a speaker use to keep audience interest at a high level?
3. To what extent would a rock concert qualify as a multimedia presentation? How is a concert like and unlike a business presentation?

To Write About

1. Write a letter to the editor of your local newspaper regarding the public image of high school students. Teenagers perform much of the volunteer work and convenience labor that keep a community going, but often face negative stereotypes. Use facts, quotations, and anecdotes to support your position.
2. Gather a group of five anecdotes and five quotations to use in a speech about the "typical" day of a high school student.

Related Speech Topics

Contemporary American musicians (or writers, artists, and so on)
The future of cable television
New medical frontiers
Tanning: healthy glow or risky choice?
Tattoos: a bizarre fashion statement
How safe is bungee jumping?
What is a laser beam?
The causes of smog
Jazz—America's music
What makes a good driver?
The Peace Corps

CHAPTER 14

SPEECHES TO PERSUADE

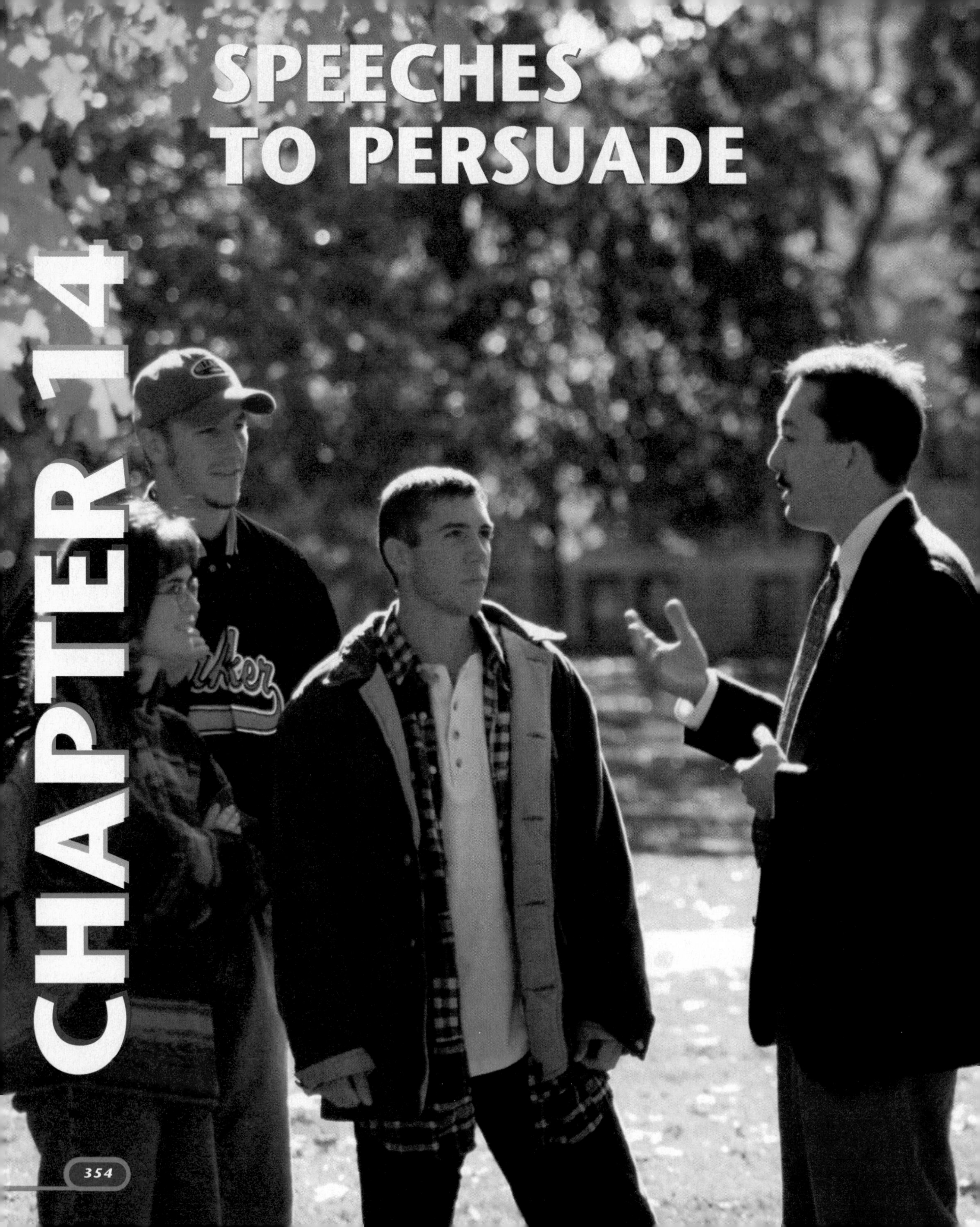

"Character is the most effective means of persuasion."

—Aristotle

Learning Objectives

After completing this chapter, you will be able to do the following.

- Recognize the specific features of the persuasive speech.
- Apply what you have learned about effective persuasive speaking to both your dealings with others and your own life.
- Analyze the type of audience to whom you are speaking.
- Adapt your persuasive approach to match the makeup of your audience.
- Understand and implement logical, emotional, and personal appeals.

Chapter Outline

Following are the main sections in this chapter.

1. What Is Persuasive Speaking?
2. Analyzing Your Audience
3. Appealing to Your Audience

New Speech Terms

In this chapter, you will learn the meanings of the speech terms listed below.

persuasive speaking
supportive audience
uncommitted audience
unbiased
indifferent audience
captive audience
opposed audience
compromise
disclaimer
logos
proof
pathos
ethos
goodwill
integrity
reputation
sincerity
competency
credentials
composure

General Vocabulary

Expanding your general vocabulary will help you become a more effective communicator. Listed below are some words appearing in this chapter that you should make part of your everyday vocabulary.

temperament
cognizant
burgeoning
analytical
palatable
assert
instinctively

Looking AHEAD

In this chapter, you will learn about persuasive speaking. You'll learn effective techniques to enable you to convince others to "buy" what you are "selling," whether it be a product, a belief, an attitude, or an idea. Next, you will analyze the various types of audiences that you might have to persuade and the specific methods of persuasive speaking most likely to be effective for each of these audiences. Finally, you will see how the understanding and implementation of Aristotle's three appeals can add both depth and impact to your persuasive speaking.

Introduction

Would you like to talk to your parents about having some friends over for a party this weekend? Would you like to have a later curfew? Would you like to convince your science teacher that it would be a good idea to work in groups for the next major project? Would you like to make a little more money per hour when you baby-sit for the neighbors? If you answered yes to any of these questions, then you had better know how to speak persuasively.

Attempting to teach her students about the persuasive speech and about how it differs from the other types of speeches, a teacher gave the following explanation to her class: "Remember, if you show us how to put a car engine together, that's a demonstration speech. If you explain to us how the car engine works, that's an informative speech. If you then convince us to buy the car, that's a persuasive speech!"

Parents and children use persuasive speech with each other every day.

SECTION 1 What Is Persuasive Speaking?

A persuasive speech asks your audience to "buy" something that you are selling. It can be a product, but it can also be a belief, an attitude, or an idea. While the informative speech primarily supplies important information to increase understanding, the persuasive speech goes one step further and asks the audience to *do* something based on the information presented.

It doesn't matter whether you are speaking in a court of law, influencing some sort of public policy, or simply convincing your friends to see a particular movie, **persuasive speaking** demands that you effectively (1) induce your audience to believe as you do and (2) influence your audience in order to cause some sort of directed action to take place.

Consider the following situations:

- You wish to convince your parents that you should be able to attend a local concert.
- You want to convince your teacher that more time is needed to complete a class project.
- You wish to show your friends that drinking and driving is not an intelligent way to have a good time.

In each of these situations, you would need to be a persuasive speaker. First of all, you would have to awaken a belief on the part of your listeners that what you are proposing is a good idea. Next, you would have to show them that you have a well thought out plan of action available. Finally, you should

Persuasive speaking skills come into play whenever you influence your friends to do something.

be able to convince your audience that your plan of action is realistic and the right thing to do. People act and react on the basis of what they want, how they think, and how they feel. Consequently, it is your job to "push the right buttons," whether logical or emotional, so that your audience agrees with what you are promoting.

Scholars say that the greatest Roman orator was Marcus Tullius Cicero. In his work *On Oratory,* Cicero said that the skilled speaker is a person of learning and insight. The most important insight that a speaker must have is knowledge of his or her audience. As a skilled persuasive speaker, your first task is to evaluate accurately and perceptively how your audience feels about you and your message. This evaluation, called *audience analysis,* is an invaluable element in the persuasive speaking process. You have to realize that giving a "canned speech"—a planned speech that you deliver the same way to every group—is not always going to work. Each audience is unique. You must be ready to make the needed adjustments so that your spoken words are appropriate and get (or keep) the audience on your side. Next, we'll take a look at the different types of audiences that you might have to persuade.

Daniel Webster, shown in this etching, is considered to have been one of America's finest orators.

SECTION 1 REVIEW

Recalling the Facts ...

1. Persuasive speaking demands that you are effective at doing what two things?
2. Why is audience analysis important?

Thinking Critically ...

1. It has been said that the most difficult audience you will ever have to persuade is yourself. Why might this statement be true? Do you see yourself as a threatening audience? Why?

Taking Charge ...

1. Make two lists. In the first, list products that you might have to persuade people to buy. In the second, list ideas that you might have to promote. Before you make your lists, think of specific instances in school, in your community, on the job, or with your friends that would involve a persuasive approach on your part. Be ready to discuss your lists with other students.

SECTION 2 Analyzing Your Audience

A sign in a high school locker room says:

Get Ready to Play!

Below the sign is a photo of the next opponent. Beneath the picture are key statistics about that team, information on each team member, and a team analysis sheet that projects what the individual players and the team will do in specific game situations. Studying the picture and statistics for several days will help prepare the team for the upcoming game.

Just as good athletes must be aware of the strengths and weaknesses of their opponents, good persuasive speakers must be aware of the attitudes and beliefs of their audiences. These speakers might post a sign that says:

Get Ready to Speak!

As Chapter 2 told you, your audience should never be perceived as the enemy. However, your audience deserves to be well scouted, or analyzed. You cannot prepare the most effective, persuasive speech if you have not taken the time to get to know the people who will be listening to you. How old are they? What is their economic status? Will most of them be male or female? What about their political or religious views? How many will be in attendance? How many are in favor of your position? Against it?

Suppose you were speaking to these groups:

- a parent group about chaperoning a school dance,
- a group of community business owners about sponsoring a school money-making project,
- your neighborhood about an extensive local clean-up campaign, or
- your teachers on the need for them to teach an extra class each day.

Wouldn't the mood or *temperament* of your audience be different in each situation? Wouldn't the mood vary depending on what you were asking the group to "buy"? Most likely, the range would be from very positive to very negative. You owe it to your audience to be *cognizant* of the speaking climate and to present your message accordingly.

Authorities generally agree that most audiences can be classified into one of four categories: supportive, uncommitted, indifferent, and opposed. Often, your audience will be a mixture of these four types. Keep in mind that regardless of the type of audience you are addressing, *your main purpose is to gain the most number of supporters possible.* Use all of the tools at your disposal. An effective introduction and conclusion, convincing arguments,

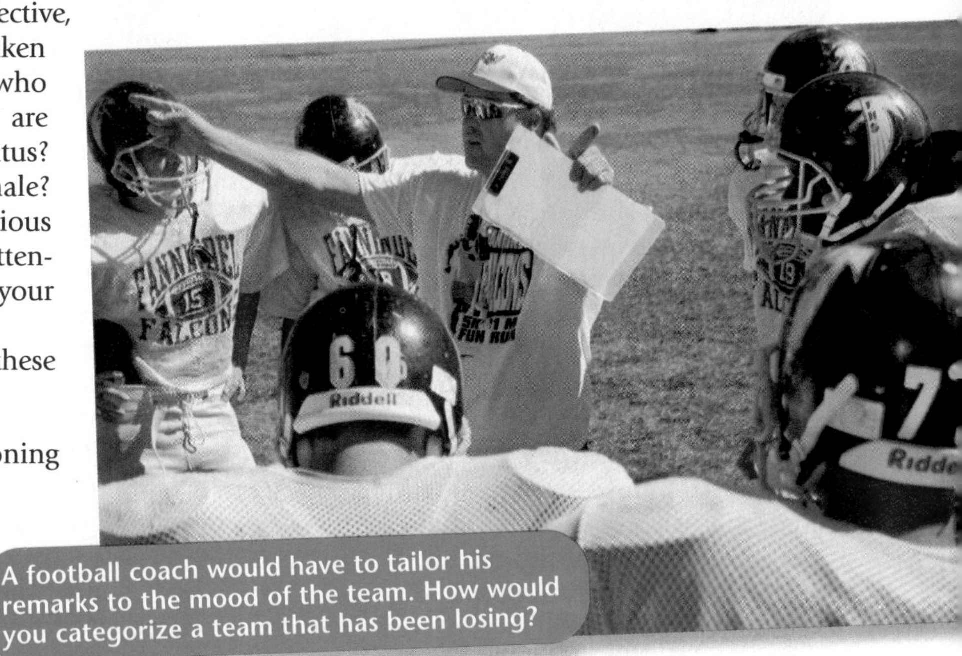

A football coach would have to tailor his remarks to the mood of the team. How would you categorize a team that has been losing?

congeniality, a sharp appearance, and a sense of humor can help you persuade your audience.

The Supportive Audience

Every speaker would like to have a supportive audience. The **supportive audience** is friendly. Its members like you and what you have to say. This is the easiest audience to address because the members are ready to support and promote your ideas. Laughter, hugs, and handshakes come easily with this group. A political candidate asking his staff for its continued efforts after a big win would be addressing a supportive audience. A school team asking the student body at a pep rally for continued support would probably be met with enthusiastic cheers. Your main objective with listeners in this type of audience is to reinforce what they already accept. You want to strengthen your ties with them.

Audiences can be supportive or uncommitted.

Generally, the supportive audience doesn't need a great deal of information. Sometimes, though, the supportive audience has "bought" you as a person but doesn't know much about what you are "selling." In such a case, you need to take the time to present your material thoroughly. For instance, students might strongly support you for a class office because you are well known, well liked, and well respected. If, however, you propose a new homeroom concept as part of your platform, you had better be ready to offer persuasive, well thought out details to support your idea. If you don't, your supportive audience might begin looking for another candidate.

The supportive audience is a speaker's dream. Don't take these listeners for granted, though. Your key to persuasive success is to keep them enthused about you and your objectives.

The Uncommitted Audience

You have a good chance of persuading the **uncommitted audience** because it is neutral. This type of audience isn't for you or against you; its members simply need information to make up their minds. The prevalent attitude among the members of the uncommitted audience is usually, "OK, let's hear what you have to say. Convince me!" It is then your job to be convincing.

When you are interviewing for a job, the employer will usually be impartial. The employer isn't taking sides; she wants the best person for the job, whoever it might be. Similarly, a scholarship committee or a representative from a college you wish to attend will most likely be **unbiased,** or objective. These interviewers want the best applicants to be rewarded and accepted; they have no reason to favor one student over another. With these audiences, you have the task of selling yourself, your talents, and your potential. Specific information such as your past working experience, your current grade point average, your participation in extracurricular activities, and your community involvement might provide the substance needed to bring your listeners over to your side.

Examples of uncommitted audiences can be found every day in courts of law. It's the defense lawyer's job to persuade the jury that the client is not guilty. The jury is, of course, uncommitted until all of the evidence is in and fairly weighed.

Only then can a rational, just decision be reached. Similarly, you face a type of jury every time you speak in front of an uncommitted audience. You can often win your case if you present your position clearly and persuasively and support it with solid information.

The Indifferent Audience

With the **indifferent audience,** your job as a persuasive speaker gets a little tougher. This type of audience is difficult to adapt to because its members are apathetic toward you. While they aren't opposed to you, they can appear openly bored. Part of the problem is that the indifferent audience is often a **captive audience,** an audience that is being forced to be in attendance. Often, the listeners don't believe that what you are saying is relevant to their personal situations.

Your job might be to jar the members of this type of audience into paying attention to what you have to say, by offering a different approach. It is also your job to show them how your message is applicable to their lives. Information is important, but information alone is not enough.

For instance, a teacher was working with a group of students whose academic performance was less than noteworthy. The students kept telling him that their main objective was to get out of school, get a job, make some money, and buy a car. He couldn't persuade them to improve academically until he tried a new approach. The teacher brought in three business owners from the community who told the students what it took to get hired in the current job market. The teacher also had a car salesman come to the class. The salesman went through an itemized analysis of how much money per week each student would have to make to buy a car and to pay for gas, insurance, and repairs. The students then understood that without basic academic skills, they couldn't get a job that would pay

EUSTRESSING OUT

INSTANT IMPACT

More and more corporations are being persuaded that they need more laughter in the workplace. Humor consultants have convinced employers that fun and games can be healing for their employees. For example, Gary Krane, author of *Simple Fun for Busy People,* suggests that employees might want to spend five minutes of each workday "cackling like chickens, or meowing like kittens, or pairing off into thumb-hat wrestling matches, using those office coffee sugar packets." Krane also recommends having a secret handshake for your office, and bringing in a boom box to lift morale by playing Afro-Haitian music or a few polkas.

Syndicated columnist John Leo says that these humor advisers have evolved their own technical terms, including "eustress" (good stress), "psychoneuroimmunology," "humor quotients," and the peril of "TS" (terminal seriousness).

Like all *burgeoning* fields, Leo points out, the humor biz has also evolved trends and a number of statistics.

Loretta Laroche, a humor consultant who has appeared on PBS-TV, once said that healthy people laugh some 100 to 400 times a day. Leo did the math on what this would mean. Yukking it up at this recommended peak capacity for 17 minutes a day would be awesome—24 times an hour, 384 times a day, 2,688 times a week, 139,776 times a year. Are you laughing *with* these humor consultants or *at* them?

WORDS FROM THE WORKPLACE

Peggy Arriola Jasso
Vice President, Retail Banking

Q: *How does communication play a role in your day-to-day work activities?*

A: The way I communicate in my workplace is probably the single most important aspect of my job. I have worked since I was 16 years old and have always been able to maintain an excellent rapport with my fellow workers. Over the years, I have developed a way of communicating that has gained me respect as a manager and the friendship of many people. I always make a point to speak to everyone. I listen and allow my employees to verbalize their feelings before I make decisions.

Q: *What are some communication skills that help you to be successful in your job?*

A: I communicate daily in person, on the telephone, by e-mail, or by letter. It is usually my responsibility to handle the irate or difficult customers. I listen and tell them that I understand their frustration and assure them that I will do everything in my power to correct the problem. Most of the time I am successful using these tactics, and what was once a very difficult situation is turned into a pleasant experience.

Another skill is to never raise my voice if someone is upset. Instead, speak in lower tones. It is not always what you say, it is how you say it.

Over the years, I have had the unpleasant task to terminate many employees. There is one lady who, several years after being terminated by me, called me to thank me for her termination because she realized that I had done the right thing. She has remained a friend for the last 15 years. This is only because of my communication skills.

Q: *What suggestions can you give students to show them the importance of communication skills?*

A: The one thing I tell students is that they cannot go into the work world thinking "I've got a degree, therefore, everyone has to respect me." Respect is something you earn! It can be earned through good communication skills, patience, and time. The skill of communication is something that must be learned through practice. Learn it, and there is no end to where you can go.

enough for them to buy what they were after. Things now made more sense to them. They saw a reason to try.

This particular approach won't work in every situation. You must put forth the effort to find an approach that will get the attention of the apathetic audience. Be dynamic in your approach, and show your listeners that what you are selling is important to them and has a direct bearing on their personal well-being.

The Opposed Audience

Be ready to handle a potential confrontation with the **opposed audience.** The members are hostile to you, to what you are promoting, or to both. Unlike the supportive audience, this type of audience feels no warmth for you and is in no way sympathetic to your feelings or your cause.

With the opposed audience, your objective should simply be to get a fair hearing. Try your best to determine specifically what your audience is hostile about: You? Your cause? A specific statement that you made previously?

When you have reached a conclusion, work with the audience to put out that specific fire. It is often wise when addressing a hostile audience to show that you are willing to **compromise,** or make some concessions of your own. Let these listeners know that you see merit in some of their arguments and that you aren't perfect.

A student government representative was to address the student body of a rival school. When she was introduced, many of the students booed. However, her first words were:

> I'm not surprised at your reaction. May I share with you that I am currently scared to death! Even though we might be adversaries on the basketball court, could we be friends at this assembly and meet each other halfway? Could we forget our differences and work together today? I respect so many things about your school. Today, I trust that we can share with each other about how our respective schools operate. I also trust that one of you will catch me if I faint!

The audience laughed. The students were also courteous throughout the remainder of her speech. The speaker had endeared herself to her audience through her personality and her sense of fair play.

Another way to gain favor with the hostile audience is to use a disclaimer. A **disclaimer** tells listeners what you are *not* saying or lets them know that you don't consider yourself the expert. This reduces the tendency the audience might have to overgeneralize your views. For example, if speaking to school officials about needing a skateboard area, you could say:

> Now I'm *not* saying that every time students have a concern the school should bow down and passively agree. I'm also *not* saying that I am the person who has all of the answers. However, I would appreciate it if you would listen . . .

You stand your best chance of getting a fair hearing from the members of an opposed audience if you can do the following things:

- Convince them that you know how they feel and you believe that their position has worth.
- Avoid needless confrontation.
- Create a situation where there aren't winners and losers.

You have now read about the four types of audiences that you might face in a persuasive speaking situation. You have also been given advice on how to adapt to each. However, analyzing your audience is only the first part of your speaking task. Next we'll take a look at how to be an appealing persuasive speaker.

SECTION  REVIEW

Recalling the Facts ...

1. Briefly describe the four different types of audiences.
2. No matter what type of audience you face, what is your primary purpose?

Thinking Critically ...

1. List one real-life example in which you might have to adapt to (1) a supportive audience, (2) an uncommitted audience, (3) an indifferent audience, and (4) an opposed audience. Remember, an audience might be as small as one person. Now analyze the differences between audiences in real life.

Taking Charge ...

1. Talk to five different people—another student, a teacher, a parent, an administrator, and a neighbor or community member—and have each give his or her own personal definition of what persuasive speaking means. Ask these people to give you specific examples of how their definitions have worked for them in the past.

SECTION 3 Appealing to Your Audience

The saying "Love is blind" means that a couple in love tend to overlook each other's faults or weaknesses. The saying also suggests that people are attracted to others for a variety of reasons. Some of the reasons can be logically explained, and some can't. Often, we are unable to articulate why we are drawn to certain individuals or things—that is, why they appeal to us.

What exactly does the word appeal mean? Let's scrutinize the word a little more closely. Appeal has two different meanings. It can mean an urgent request. It can also refer to what is attractive or interesting about someone or something. Everyone finds certain people, books, movies, automobiles, or music personally appealing. What about persuasive speakers? Must they too have appeal?

A persuasive speaker can often be successful by appealing to the sense of logic of her audience.

If your job is to convince others, it makes sense that you must present an appealing image and message. A persuasive speaker without appeal is like a race car driver without a car; both lack the vehicle needed to bring about success. How can you develop appeal as a speaker? How can you arouse a favorable response when addressing your audience?

In Chapter 1, you read about Aristotle and the art of persuasion. Aristotle, in his work *Rhetoric,* stated that the persuasive powers of a speaker depend on his reasoning, the emotions that he is able to stir in his listeners, and his character. In other words, a speaker's success is the result of his logical appeal, his emotional appeal, and his personal appeal. Each of these deserves a closer look.

Logical Appeal

Someone once said that each person's mind has its own logic, but that it does not often let others in on that logic. As a persuasive speaker, you must definitely let others in on how your thoughts connect. Nothing can turn off listeners more quickly than a speech that has them scratching their heads in bewilderment.

With a logical appeal, you appeal to the intellect of your audience by offering a clearly defined speech that contains solid reasoning and valid evidence. The logical appeal is also known by the Greek word **logos.** It satisfies the *analytical* side of your audience and says to your listeners, "I want this to make sense to you!" and "Do you see how all of this logically fits together?" You can promote your logical appeal by being organized and by offering proof to your audience.

Be Organized ... One way to enhance your logical appeal is by presenting a well-organized speech (the topic of Chapter 9). A student speaker was talking to a women's club about America's preoccupation with entertainment. She said:

> The way to the top these days lies with "putting on a show." However, in our quest for "ultimate entertainment," we've forgotten to look beyond the sizzle to see if what lies behind is truly worth supporting. As we examine this situation, three major areas seem apparent: (1) the

entertainment industry, (2) our political system, and (3) education. Let's look at these areas individually . . .

Not only is the beginning of this speech well organized, but it is also easy to understand. It told the audience specifically what the speaker's thesis was and what her three major areas of analysis would be.

A commentator on a television station was alarmed at the number of young adults who, because of financial hardships, were being forced to return home and live with their parents. The commentator said that over 50 percent of adults between the ages of 18 and 24 were living with their parents. She then gave three reasons why this might be occurring:

- problems with the availability of jobs,
- problems with job layoffs, and
- problems college students had in paying back student loans.

Her reasons were clearly stated and logically *palatable* to the audience. However, you can't merely *assert* that what you are saying is true. Audiences need proof.

Offer Proof . . . Providing proof is another means of appealing to logic. As you read in Chapter 10, **proof** is specific evidence; proof is that which establishes the truth of something. Furthermore, it is part of the supporting materials and details discussed in Chapter 9.

For instance, suppose you were having a discussion with a group of friends about art. Someone says that too much of what is considered art today is nothing but trash. That person objects to the National Endowment for the Arts giving "all of its money" to art that is considered obscene.

You could object by saying, "Oh, yeah, what do you know?" or "I suppose you could do better!" Neither response would persuade your friend to come over to your way of thinking, though. If, instead, you told him that even though some of what he says might have merit, he should consider that over the past 25 years, nearly 100,000 grants have been awarded by the NEA. Of those 100,000 grants, fewer than 20 have been considered controversial.

Do you see how these facts provide proof? Providing proof shows your listeners that you have intelligence, and intelligence is appealing.

Working to improve your logical appeal is a smart thing to do. However, logic by itself isn't always enough. You can also appeal to others emotionally.

Emotional Appeal

What do the following topics have in common?

- the homeless
- cruelty to animals
- nuclear power
- abused children
- the elderly
- sex education in schools
- gun control
- victims of crime

Of course, it would be easy to find volumes of information on each and present numerous facts. However, all of these topics cause many people to

A speech either for or against the use of nuclear power will probably have some elements of emotional appeal.

INSTANT IMPACT

GOOD NEWS ABOUT BAD HABITS

Do you know anyone who has a bad habit? Maybe it's putting things off, avoiding chores around the house, not being on time, or saying "ya know" all the time. Now, there is hope for helping people to break bad habits. Researchers have discovered that if you are trying to persuade someone to break a bad habit, you might have to make from five to seven attempts before the advice sinks in and starts to work. The experts also say to vary your persuasive approach for quicker results. What's the message? Don't give up! Persistent persuasion just might pay off.

react *instinctively* in an emotional manner and let their feelings show. As Aristotle reminds us, emotional appeal is a major consideration in persuasive speaking. Indeed, it often has a stronger impact on an audience than logic or reason. People would like to think that they make decisions based on reason. The truth is, however, that most people rely on their feelings at least as much as on their reasoning. An individual knows that the car that gets 35 miles per gallon is the smart buy, but he may go with the sportier model with the sun roof and the CD player instead.

If it is true that logical appeal aims for the brain, then emotional appeal aims for the heart. Emotional appeal, or **pathos,** involves appealing to people's feelings of love, anger, disgust, fear, compassion, patriotism, or the like. Notice, for example, the intensity of William Barrett Travis as he tried to "light a fire" under the people of Texas and all Americans while he was defending the Alamo against Mexican forces in 1836:

> Fellow citizens and compatriots: I am besieged by a thousand or more of the Mexicans under Santa Anna. I have sustained a continual bombardment and cannonade for 24 hours and have not lost a man. The enemy has demanded a surrender at discretion; otherwise the garrison are to be put to the sword if the fort is taken. I have answered the demand with a cannon shot, and our flag still waves proudly from the walls. *I shall never surrender nor retreat.* I call on you in the name of liberty, or patriotism, and everything dear to the American character, to come to our aid with all dispatch.

His words got the attention of the entire country, and even though the conflict turned into a mas-

Why was the phrase "Remember the Alamo" an appeal to our ancestors' emotions and not to their sense of logic?

sacre, the phrase "Remember the Alamo!" became a national battle cry. The words hit an emotional nerve and inspired people's patriotic spirit. Would logic have worked as well? Probably not.

The late prime minister of Britain, Sir Winston Churchill, once said that "the human story does not always unfold like a mathematical calculation on the principle that two and two make four. Sometimes in life they make five or minus three." He was saying that life is not always logical. Often, it is the emotional, intangible world of our feelings that charts the real course of life.

All people have potential laughter, remorse, hopes, and dreams, and your ability to move them depends on stirring their emotions. Few people enjoy listening to uninterrupted evidence, long lists of facts, and cold, sterile statistics. They may enjoy listening, though, if that evidence is presented in a manner that excites or moves them. Read how a high school student, Kate Eifrig, used evidence, but primarily emotional appeal, to persuade her audience. In regard to the Persian Gulf War, she asks:

> What could be more significant than thousands of human lives? Evidently, fast production was of monumental worth to the military leaders in the Persian Gulf. Did you know that a recent independent Pentagon study announced that many of the military repair parts used in the Persian Gulf War were defective? Some were termed inoperable. Some of these parts were bolts for fighter planes' electrical systems and missile compartments.
>
> How could the government buy these parts without checking them first? Is rapid and careless repair worth sacrificing lives?

Three Appeals in Persuasive Speech

Logical Appeal

The speaker offers an organized, clearly defined speech containing solid reasoning and valid evidence.

Emotional Appeal

The speaker's words arouse feelings in the audience, like anger, disgust, and compassion.

Personal Appeal

The speaker wins the audience's trust through honesty, competency, and credibility.

Do you see her evidence? More importantly, do you feel her message? Do you see why her audience would be shocked and alarmed by this portion of her speech? Kate was saying to her audience, "Let's take action and demand that our government value people more than fast production!" She used evidence to help set the emotional tone that she was after.

Your tone refers to your vocal quality, but it also reflects your overall manner of nonverbal expression. Your attitude about your words as you deliver them contributes to your tone. The tone could be angry, considerate, hopeful, or optimistic, for example. The tone with which you deliver your words can have astounding impact. In 1938, Orson Welles's radio production "War of the

Worlds" caused a nationwide panic by dramatizing a supposed invasion from Mars and presenting it in the form of a newscast. His tone of urgency was so real that many Americans believed him and thought that space creatures had landed.

Orson Welles shocked an entire nation with one radio program.

Even though the emotional appeal is aimed at stirring the emotions in your audience, keep in mind that your audience's reaction is often based on your emotional telegraphing. Telegraphing, which was mentioned in Chapter 12, means leading the way and showing your audience the emotion you wish them to feel by feeling it yourself. How is an audience supposed to feel sympathy or outrage if you aren't supplying an emotional example for them?

Let's examine a real-life story. It involves one woman's fight to have a stoplight erected at a busy intersection. The town board of her midwestern community was initially opposed to supplying money for the stoplight. At a meeting of the board, town "experts" provided numerous facts and figures to show that the stoplight was not needed. Even though they agreed that cars traveled at high rates of speed through the area and that accidents had occurred, they also argued that few of the accidents were serious and that there had been only one fatality over a two-year period.

Then the woman spoke. She provided facts about the number of speeding tickets issued at the intersection by the police each month and about the number of people from a nearby subdivision who had to cross the intersection each day to get to a local shopping mall. However, she concluded her presentation by holding up a picture of a small child about eight years old. In a compassionate speech, she told her listeners that the child in the picture was that one traffic victim.

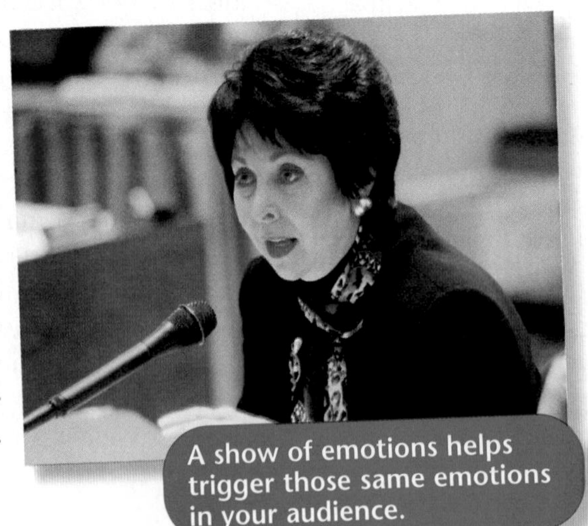
A show of emotions helps trigger those same emotions in your audience.

The woman was not the child's mother, but a friend of the family. She said that she didn't want the members of the board or any other members of the audience to experience the pain of losing a child. A stoplight, she pleaded, could help prevent that pain from becoming a reality.

The town board voted unanimously to erect the stoplight. Her emotional involvement set the tone for her persuasive message and helped turn the town board around. She turned foes into friends in part by using a logical appeal but even more by establishing a strong emotional bond between her and her audience. She cared about the stoplight, yes, but she also showed others that she cared about them and their welfare. Showing the audience that you have their interests in mind is a key component of Aristotle's final appeal, the personal appeal.

Personal Appeal

A famous Hollywood producer once said that he didn't know exactly what talent was but he knew it when he saw it. Personal appeal is much like talent in that people know when someone has it, and they know when someone doesn't have it. Having personal appeal, or **ethos,** means that your listeners will buy what you are selling because they trust in you and your credibility—your believability. Donald Queener, a nationally recognized speech and debate educator who has coached scores of interpretation and oratory champions, says that of all the appeals, personal appeal is the most desirable and the most effective because it can be immediate. It can work with an audience instantaneously.

If you have personal appeal, your listeners trust you. You come across as having their best interests at heart, and your **goodwill** proves that you care about them and about worthwhile issues. Even though being well liked is important for the effective speaker, congeniality is *not* what Aristotle was stressing in his use of the term personal appeal. Each day, the news is full of stories about smiling, friendly swindlers who dupe unsuspecting victims. Instead, Aristotle focused on two essential elements, which he believed formed the backbone of personal appeal: honesty and competency.

Honesty ... People are attracted to honesty. If you are honest, you tell the truth and exhibit personal **integrity**, or a strong sense of right and wrong. Your audience believes what you have to say because your **reputation**—how you are known by others—proves that you are a person of your word and therefore someone to be taken seriously. Honesty has appeal for two reasons. It shows others that you will be an example of what you say—that you will "practice what you preach." It also reveals that you are a person of **sincerity**, of genuineness, and that you mean what you say and speak from your heart.

Michael J. Fox uses his personal appeal to talk to students about drugs and alcohol and to promote research for Parkinson's Disease.

Don't think that appealing to an audience through honesty is limited to interpersonal communication or large audiences. Sometimes you can be your own audience. Chapter 1 used the term intrapersonal communication for these situations. Intrapersonal communication involves the talks that you have with yourself. Often, you can persuade yourself to take a particular course of action based on your own honesty and your personal character. You might make a crucial decision on the basis of believing that honesty is the best policy and feel good about your decision. In other words, honesty can direct your decision making and actually encourage you to appeal to yourself.

There is a group of more than four hundred actors, writers, and agents who want to change the world. Known as Young Artists United and using the motto "It's Cool to Care," they speak at high schools on the dangers of drugs and alcohol. They also spend some of their time painting orphanages and funding teen runaway centers. The actor Michael J. Fox said that he is involved in the group because he wants to give something back to a world that has given him so much. When Fox, a film and television star, spoke at one Los Angeles school, a student responded this way:

> I really listened to what this guy said today, and it made me think about what I'm doing with my life. I hear that he does this kind of stuff for kids all the time. He acts as if he really cares, you know, really wants the best for us. I paid attention because he was being straight with us, being honest. I believed him.

In the example above, Michael J. Fox, representing many others who feel the same way, used his personal appeal—his reputation and his honesty—to appeal to students to do what's right. He told them: "If you don't do drugs, continue to stay away from them," and "If you are involved with drugs, take action and change the course of your life before it is too late!" This is a good example for all of us to follow. Clearly, honesty can do more than make us appealing speakers; it can also help us contribute to changing people's lives.

Competency ... The second essential element of Aristotle's personal appeal is competency. **Competency** means capability. If you are a competent person, you can get the job done. You probably have a solid work ethic, and you value being prepared.

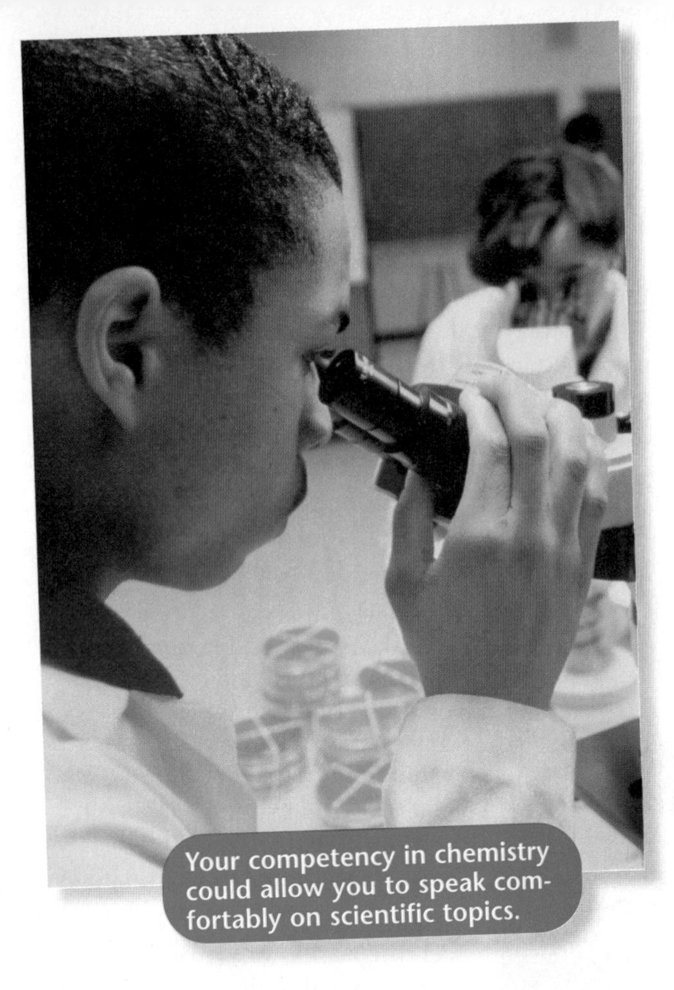
Your competency in chemistry could allow you to speak comfortably on scientific topics.

People who are known to be competent often have impressive **credentials,** or qualifications. These might include an extensive education, a number of outstanding achievements, or a long list of successes in a particular field. Indeed, most people equate competency with hard work and expertise in some particular field. They are impressed by the person who can offer a clear, focused stance on a topic because of expertise of this kind. Special expertise gives such a person the ability to speak with confidence and composure.

A somewhat different kind of expertise is the knack of dealing with people. Have you ever heard someone called a "people person"—someone who just naturally gets along with everyone? If you are a "people person," you stand an excellent chance of convincing your listeners to agree with you because you, too, present your message with confidence and composure.

Speaking with **composure**—speaking in a calm, controlled manner—telegraphs to your audience that you are in charge of the situation. The competent speaker adheres to the saying, "Never let 'em see you sweat!" After all, few listeners will be willing to count on a person who "rattles" easily or "chokes" when the pressure is on. Remember, if those to whom you are speaking don't believe that they can count on you, then they probably won't be persuaded by you, either.

Thomas Jefferson

Providing clear examples for Aristotle's personal appeal is difficult, because much of the persuasive power of this appeal comes from a form of internal energy that doesn't translate well to the printed page. However, one particular example might illustrate this quality. Read out loud the words of Thomas Jefferson, delivered on March 4, 1801, at the first presidential inaugural address in Washington, D.C. Notice the tone that he establishes and how he attempts to persuade the people of a young nation to aid and to support him during his presidency:

> I shall often go wrong through defect of judgment. When right, I shall often be thought wrong by those whose positions will not command a view of the whole ground. I ask your indulgence for my own errors, which will never be intentional. . . . Relying, then, on the patronage of your good will, I advance with obedience to the work.

Jefferson's words exemplify how honesty and competency can work hand in hand to produce a feeling of confidence. "We're all in this together," he seems to say. "We can work as a team to achieve success."

You might be saying, "This isn't the era of Aristotle, and the year 1801 was a long time ago. How do I actually apply all of this to my own life and to today's world?" Maybe the following example will help.

United Approach

A group of students from Apple Valley High School in Minnesota, under the direction of award-winning speech coach, debate coach, and teacher Pamela Cady, was asked this question: "If you had just gotten your driver's license, what would you say to your parents to persuade them to allow you to drive the family's brand-new car?"

At first, the students responded with short, one-sentence answers, including, "I'd cry, stomp my feet, and scream, 'Please!'" However, after they had studied this chapter, they compiled a much more thorough list, utilizing all three of Aristotle's appeals. What do you think of these persuasive ideas?

The following represent logical appeals.

- "Wouldn't my driving be more convenient than your having to drive me everywhere?"
- "I could help you with the errands!"
- "There would be less chaos at home with people rushing to drive everyone everywhere."
- "I could learn how to follow directions."
- "I have done well in Driver's Education. The school and state believe that I am a good driver."
- "I have checked it out, and the insurance would not go up much."
- "The new car would be less likely to have engine problems."
- "I'll pay for my own gas and insurance, plus I will keep the car clean."
- "I'll be sure to call you when I get where I am going."

The following represent emotional appeals.

- "When you were a kid, didn't you want to be given some responsibility, too?"
- "Will you consider my driving if I only ask on special occasions? You know how special some things can be, don't you?"
- "If I'm driving, you don't have to worry about my being in a car where the driver has been drinking."
- "I would feel so proud for others to see me in our new car!"
- "I would never ask if I thought you didn't trust me."
- "How would you feel always having to bum a ride with people?"
- "I would love the responsibility!"
- "I know that you worry about me, so out of respect for you two, I would be extra careful."
- "I would love you guys so much!"
- "This would really enhance my self-esteem."
- "Think what this could do for our communication. We would talk more and understand each other better!"

The following represent personal appeals.

- "I promise to always tell you the truth about where I am going."
- "I don't feel that it is right that my friends always have to drive."
- "Since my sister was allowed to drive a nice car when she first got her license, I think that this would be the fair thing to do, don't you?"
- "Please don't judge me before I have had a chance to prove to you that I can handle this."
- "Have I ever let you down? (I mean when it really counts!)"
- "I would like to show you that I can be as disciplined with a car as I have been with my life."

If you want your parents to buy you a car, you should use all three appeals—logical, emotional, and personal.

COMMUNICATION

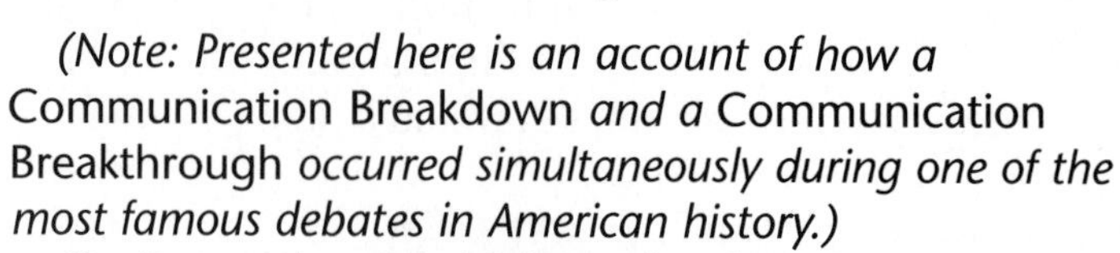

The Nixon-Kennedy Debate of 1960

(Note: Presented here is an account of how a Communication Breakdown *and a* Communication Breakthrough *occurred simultaneously during one of the most famous debates in American history.)*

On September 26, 1960, technology brought to the American public the first of four televised debates between the Republican presidential nominee, Richard M. Nixon, and the Democratic presidential nominee, John F. Kennedy. Nixon and Kennedy would come together, face to face, to be evaluated by more than 70 million viewers. Each candidate was trying to persuade the nation that he was the person to lead the country. Before the first debate, Nixon was the front-runner in the polls; Kennedy was a distant second. However, after the first debate, Kennedy made a significant breakthrough through an amazing appeal, an almost immediate bond that he formed with television viewers. Nixon lost ground.

John F. Kennedy came to Chicago, the site of the first debate, organized and prepared. He was aware of pertinent information regarding domestic policy and well prepared. When Kennedy arrived at the studio before the airing of the live debate, he wore a dark gray suit and a white shirt. However, he noticed that the lights caused a type of glare off the white shirt. Consequently, he had a staff member dash back to his hotel room and get a blue shirt.

Nixon, on the other hand, had been ill; thus, his complexion was white and pasty looking, and he had deep eye shadows. Arriving with just a little time to spare, he wasn't aware of how his light-colored suit and his white shirt meekly faded into the background when hit by the studio lights. To make matters worse, even though Nixon wore makeup to cover his "five o'clock shadow," it didn't prevent the camera from picking up the sweat as it ran down his face.

What was the result? Kennedy came across as having more appeal. Even though Richard M. Nixon was a skilled debater and handled himself admirably in addressing the issues (radio listeners called it a draw), he failed to persuade the voters who watched that he was the more capable presidential candidate. He had lost the "impact of images" battle. When Kennedy spoke, he was calm, controlled, and energetic; he spoke to America as a man with a vision. When Nixon spoke, he appeared tense, almost frightened; and instead of speaking to America, he spoke to Kennedy. Nixon was in the midst of a communication breakdown. He appeared to lack the power and the imagination of his political counterpart.

As one observer said, "Every time that the two men were close together for the nation to see, Kennedy would win a little and Nixon would lose a little." The outcome: Kennedy defeated Nixon for the presidency in one of the closest elections in the history of the country.

Questions

1. Which of the appeals do you think Kennedy used most effectively?
2. Where do you think Nixon made his mistake(s)?

- "I give you my word that I will be a good and responsible driver."

Some of the statements could fit into more than one category, couldn't they? The sophomore students, after discussing their ideas, decided that using a united approach—using two or three of the appeals—would give them a better chance for success than a one-dimensional approach. One student noted that her mother and father would require different approaches. She decided that her mother would need to be approached with logic, while her father would probably relate better to the emotional argument. Does this sound familiar? As you can see, you can persuade more effectively when you intelligently use Aristotle's three appeals.

Persuasive speaking is not easy to explain. So many human factors go into what makes a person convincing that it is difficult to offer a real-world prescription for success. Often, you will have to develop the ability to read your audience and to use in the same persuasive speech all that this chapter has presented. This won't be an easy task.

However, don't believe that good persuasive speakers are simply born with talent or that "either you have it or you don't." There is a step that you can take that will enable you to move closer to being the convincing speaker that you wish to be. What is that step?

The saying goes that the world is made up of three groups: those who watch things happen, those who make things happen, and those who wonder, "What just happened?" Be a person who makes things happen. Join the movers and shakers of the oral communication world. Work to understand what persuasive speaking is, who your audience is, and how Aristotle's appeals can work to your advantage. Then you will have an excellent opportunity to convince others to accept your ideas, motivate others to act, and—yes, as the teacher explained at the beginning of the chapter—persuade someone to buy the car!

SECTION 3 REVIEW

Recalling the Facts ...

1. According to Aristotle, what are the three forms of appeal? Briefly explain.
2. Which two elements form the backbone of personal appeal? Why?

Thinking Critically ...

1. Here is your dilemma: You are running for a class office against a very popular student. You are not the most beautiful or the most handsome person in your class, but you are a hard worker, and you care about excellence. One of your biggest obstacles is that you are brand new to the school, having only been in class for one month. At your previous school, you made good grades and were well liked and respected by students and the faculty. Prepare an extensive list, like the sophomores' list of arguments to drive the family car, giving all the logical, emotional, and personal arguments that you could use to appeal to the student body to vote for you.

Taking Charge ...

1. Keep a journal for at least one day. In it, write down all the times that you had to use persuasive speaking. You might, for example, ask someone out on a date. You might plead with your younger brother or sister to do one of your chores at home. Keep close track of when persuasive speaking is a part of your communication life, regardless of how small that part is. Next, note which appeal or appeals seemed to work best for you—logical, emotional, or personal—and explain why you think this was the case.

TEN CHARACTERISTICS OF PROFESSIONAL PERSUADERS

In analyzing people who are most successful at persuading, convincing, or selling others on their ideas, products, or services, ten characteristics appear to be common among them. Read through this list of ten and see how many apply to you now. Tom Hopkins, a sales trainer and bestselling author, suggests that if you don't find these characteristics in your current bag of traits, consider adopting them to hear more "yeses" in your life.

1 You have a burning desire to prove something to someone.

You have a strong reason for wanting to succeed. Tom Hopkins's reason was to prove himself to his parents. He quit college after 90 days, knowing that formal education wasn't for him. His parents had high hopes for him and were quite disappointed. Hopkins's father told him, "Your mother and I will always love you, even though you'll never amount to anything." According to Hopkins, that was his first motivational talk, and it kindled his desire to become the best.

2 You are an interested introvert, rather than an interesting extrovert.

You are truly interested in other people and in making those people's lives better for knowing you. You have learned how to draw others out, making them feel important and getting to know them well enough to determine how you can help.

3 You radiate confidence and strength in your walk, talk, and overall presence.

You have good posture. You wear your clothing well. You use positive body language cues to let others read your competence level.

4 You balance ego drive and the need for success with warm and sincere sympathy for the people you serve.

Your sincere interest in the happiness of the people you come in contact with creates bonds of trust and openness that allow you to serve not only your prospects well but also the friends, relatives, and acquaintances who are referred to you.

5 You are highly goal-oriented.

Your goals are set and in writing. You know exactly what you're striving for and when you expect to accomplish it. Knowing how your future will look helps keep you focused on doing what is productive today.

6 You put into writing what you plan to do daily.

Having set goals allows you to plan your time most effectively to take steps toward achieving those goals. You rely on proven systems for planning your time and have learned effective time management strategies.

7 You live in the present moment and keep your enthusiasm through crises.

You know the past can't be changed and the future can't be controlled, so you live for today, doing the best you can to make each day a time of accomplishment and fulfillment.

8 You keep yourself in a positive shell and avoid jealousy, gossip, anger, or negative thinking.

You do not allow negativity to steal your energy or tempt you to stray from your chosen course.

9 You love people and use money, instead of loving money and using people.

You understand the old adages that you have to spend money to make money and that persuasion is a people business. You invest wisely in things for the good of the people you serve.

10 You invest monthly in the greatest investment on earth—your mind.

You set a goal of being a life-long learner. You'll never have a dull moment, and you'll achieve tremendous success in whatever you set your mind to studying.

STUDENT WORK

"In a Moment of Silence" *By Rani Waterman*

In this student speech, Rani Waterman attempts to persuade her classmates about the power of silence. Note the use of examples. Do you find them convincing?

"In a moment of stillness/In a moment of semblance/In a moment of silence."

These moments are captured in David Drake's haunting vignette "A Thousand Points of Light" in which Drake sets the stage at a candlelight vigil on the streets of New York. The vigil is for his friends who were victims of AIDS. With a moment of stillness, a moment of semblance, and a moment of silence, Drake mourns all those who died from this terrible disease. Certainly, all of us can understand the role of silence at a vigil. After all, the need for silence is pervasive in our lives. Whether it is berating the people babbling in front of us at the movies, "Be quiet! I vant to hear Arnold shpeak." Or perhaps when you whisper to your high school sweetheart, "Shut up and kiss me, you fool." Or maybe you understood this need when you watched the summer Olympics and listened to John Tesh, commentator/pretty boy, commit gymnasticus interruptus. In other words, ladies and gentlemen, although freedom of speech is one of our most cherished and important rights, we, as Americans, need to rediscover what is missing from so many of our lives: silence. We begin to understand the power of silence as we experience these moments. First, let us share a moment of stillness. Or should I say, the lack thereof.

In my seventh grade geometry class we called him Richie the Rowdy. And frankly, in geometry we never knew the shortest distance between two points because Richie just didn't know when to shut up. My poor teacher tried her hardest to stop her geometry class from going around in circles, but Richie never kept still. Unfortunately, Mrs. Doyle's trouble with Richie is not an isolated incident in American education. A recent article in *Phi Delta Kappa* magazine stated that "The 5 percent of students who noisily disrupt class keep the other 95 percent of the students from working up to their potential." And think about this for a moment: some of those kids, like Richie, who cannot be civilized never grow up but they do get married. Perhaps one reason why there is so much divorce is because men and women never learn how to communicate constructively. As Americans we think that it is our cherished democratic prerogative to utter whatever crosses our minds, whenever we wish, telling it like it is. Or like we want you to think it is. Most couples are not comfortable with what's left unsaid.

According to John Gray, Ph.D., author of *Men Are from Mars, Women Are from Venus,* in a marriage you must "learn to communicate in a way that respects each other's differences and needs." Gray also insists that "when misunderstandings arise, remember that men and women speak different languages; take the time necessary to translate what your partner really means or wants to say. . . . " In short, there must be moments of stillness when you listen and reflect on the innate differences between people. Yet, what Dr. Gray never discusses in this book is that sometimes things are better left unsaid. In relationships our most memorable moments usually involve no words at all. Words are what we often use for lies, false promises, and gossip. As author Tad Friend argues, "Language is a sadly clumsy trowel for digging up buried grief. . . . " We babble with strangers; with intimates we can be silent. In love we are speechless; in awe, we say, words fail us.

In a moment of stillness/In a moment of semblance. . . .

As we all know, semblance suggests a willfully deceptive appearance. We deceive ourselves into believing more is somehow less. Silence gives way to SportsCenter, CNN, WFAN, MTV-H1-life to live, Surround Sound Entertainment, the fax unrolling, the pager chirping, the phone in the car, the phone in the plane, the phone in the bedroom, the phone in the . . . toilet. Ours is the age of distraction. In the

1990s we are constantly assaulted by a barrage of noises from the world around us. No household or personal appliance, no vehicle functions noiselessly, because noise equals power. Recently a manufacturer tried to market a silent vacuum cleaner, but market research indicated it would never sell. Members of the focus group thought if it didn't make noise it wasn't working properly. However, noise is more than a mere annoyance, it's a total body stressor. Paul Lambert, M.D., professor at the University of Virginia Medical Center, has proven that "noise can trigger asthma, high blood pressure, headaches, ulcers, and colitis." Also, in noisy environments, levels of agitation, impatience, and irritability escalate. And if you don't believe me, just ask my mother when I crank up my CD collection. Ya know, that's the same face my mother makes. Rebecca Penneys, professor of piano at the Eastman School of Music in Rochester, New York, suggests, "It's important to take a moment and to find a place where you're not disturbed by the noise of life, where you can get in contact with deep feelings, where you can have a moment of silence." *In a moment of stillness/In a moment of semblance/In a moment of silence . . .*

By now many of you are probably thinking—all right, silence has physical, psychological, and spiritual benefits . . . so what? I understand, after all, as a high school orator I'm anything but. However, we must remember the truth in the ancient aphorism, "Speech is silver. Silence is golden." And the value of silence must never be forgotten.

There is no silence more haunting that what confronts a visitor to the Holocaust Museum as he enters the tiny room piled high with the shoes of the dead. There's an eerie quiet that mere words could never explain. Arthur Fine, director of Jewish family services at Temple Albert and a recent visitor to the Holocaust Museum, believed that "To visit the museum is to visit hell. To see the pictures of our ancestors being tortured is to be tortured as well. The moment I entered the building no one spoke; there was no need to."

Mr. Fine's observation reminded me of a recent trip I took with my father to the Vietnam Memorial. My father is a veteran of Vietnam. He stood staring at the names etched gray in the shiny black marble until he located one name. Lieutenant Peter Hessberg. My father pressed his fingertips to the name and remembered the terrible sounds of a violent jungle firefight. He recalled the horrifying noise of rifle bullets coming too close, artillery shells exploding, the screaming of the wounded men. And the loudest sound of all, the dull thwack as a bullet went through Peter's chest. As my father relived these moments from years gone by, he stood in silence. A silence that honored Peter's memory.

As we walked away from the memorial, my father told me what he had been thinking. With his words echoing in my ears, I recalled the events of last summer, the evening of August 18. I received a phone call from my best friend: she had only five words to tell me, "Beth Brown died last night." And then, there was silence. For those of you who did not know Beth, she was a teammate of mine who graduated last year. . . . But, more importantly, she was my friend. That same evening we went to Beth's home to pay our respects to her family. As I entered the door to her house, her father was there to welcome me. I knew that no words from me could ever end his pain. Our eyes met and without speaking we shared the emptiness, the absence of Beth. *In a moment of stillness/In a moment of semblance/In a moment of . . .*

••••••••••••••••••••••••

Looking Back

Listed below are the major ideas discussed in this chapter.

- Persuasive speaking involves your ability to convince your audience to believe as you do.
- Persuasive speaking means that you are trying to "sell" a product, an idea, or an attitude.
- To become an effective persuasive speaker, you must keep in mind that people react on the basis of what they want, how they think, and how they feel.
- Audience analysis occurs before you speak and is your estimation of how your audience feels about you and your verbal message.
- Audiences are often divided into supportive, uncommitted, indifferent, and opposed.
- The supportive audience likes you and what you are saying.
- The uncommitted audience hasn't made up its mind about you or your message.
- The indifferent audience can take you or leave you; you need to persuade this group that what you are saying has relevance and practical application.
- The opposed audience doesn't like you or what you have to say.
- Audiences are often combinations of these four categories. You must make the necessary adjustments to deal with each type.
- For the persuasive speaker, the word appeal refers to what makes someone attractive or interesting to an audience.
- Persuasive powers depend on logical appeal, emotional appeal, and personal appeal.
- Logical appeal (logos) attracts an audience with an analytical, reason-based approach.
- Emotional appeal (pathos) hits the heart of the audience and stirs feelings of love, anger, compassion, patriotism, family, or the like.
- Personal appeal (ethos) links the speaker with the audience because of the speaker's honesty and competency.
- The best persuasive speaking is often the result of combining the various appeals as appropriate for the makeup of the audience.

Speech Vocabulary

1. For each speech vocabulary word, find the definition as given in the text, along with the page number where you found the information. Write an original sentence for each word to show the word in action. Select five speech vocabulary words that are most important to you. Explain why you made these choices and how these words can assist you as a persuasive speaker.
2. Prepare a quiz. On the left side list 15 of the speech vocabulary words (number them 1–15). Leave out a few letters from each word. For example, you might write "per—si-e s-eaki-g" for *persuasive speaking*. The person taking your quiz must fill in the missing letters to spell each word. Next, on the right side of your paper, list (in mixed order) the definitions for your 15 words and letter them from *a* through *o*. The person taking the quiz must place the letter of the correct definition beside each speech vocabulary word. Prepare an answer key ahead of time.

persuasive speaking
supportive audience
uncommitted audience
unbiased
indifferent audience
captive audience
opposed audience
compromise
disclaimer
logos
proof
pathos
ethos
goodwill
integrity
reputation
sincerity
competency
credentials
composure

General Vocabulary

1. Use the dictionary to define each of the general vocabulary words. Dictate each word to a classmate to work on the spelling. Next, read the definition of each general vocabulary word out loud, and have your classmate tell you the word that matches the definition.
2. Write an original one-page story titled "The Day I Made My First Sale!" Decide what you are selling. Are you going to sell a product? Are you going to try to convince someone that your idea is a good one? Use at least five of the general vocabulary words (underline them) in your story.

temperament
cognizant
burgeoning
analytical
palatable
assert
instinctively

To Remember

Answer the following based on your reading of the chapter.

1. In a persuasive speech, what are some of the things you might be selling?
2. What are the characteristics of a skilled speaker according to the Roman orator Cicero?
3. A jury is an example of what kind of audience?
4. If an audience opposes your ideas, what might you do?
5. Why is proof so important in persuasion?

To Do

1. Go to the library and find additional material about the Kennedy-Nixon debates. What are some specific things that were said in the first debate? In the other three debates? Prepare a report detailing your findings. You may be able to find recordings of the debates. If you can, listen to the persuasive techniques. List the pros and cons of the persuasive speaking of each.
2. Interview someone in sales and find out how he or she "reads" an audience and how he or she deals with an opposed audience. Finally, find out what the salesperson thinks about the three appeals—logical, emotional, and personal. Which works best for the salesperson? Do the three often work together? Get specific, detailed answers and examples.
3. Make a chart describing the appeals used in at least six commercials that you see on television (you might also include radio advertisements or billboards). In one column, list the name of the product being advertised. In the second column, name the type of appeal (or combination of appeals) being used—logical, emotional, and/or personal. Finally, give a quote (exact words) from the commercial or advertisement that proves your point. At the bottom, state which appeal you think is the most persuasive and why.

CHAPTER 14 Review and Enrichment...

To Talk About

1. The writer Johann Goethe said, "He who wishes to exert a useful influence must be careful to insult nothing." What do you think he meant? Should Goethe's advice always be followed? Can you think of an exception?
2. A national survey of more than 270,000 high school students was conducted. The survey concluded that student boredom is the result of (1) unvarying routine in the school day, (2) uninspiring subject matter, (3) unimaginative teaching, and (4) failure to make a connection between what students are expected to learn and real life. Which of these four would you put first? Explain. Are the teachers the only ones to be blamed? How can students, parents, the community, teachers, and school administrators all use aspects of persuasive speaking to help remedy the negative perceptions? Remember to consider intrapersonal as well as interpersonal communication skills.

To Write About

1. One important ingredient of personal appeal is reputation, or how you are known to others and what they think of you. Why do you think that your reputation could be an important factor in whether or not you could persuade someone? Write a one-page paper on how a positive reputation could aid your persuasive effectiveness.
2. In speaking, you compromise by finding a workable middle ground that is acceptable to both you and your audience. Write three reasons why compromising is a wise idea for those trying to persuade others. Give specifics to show when compromising could help you to persuade your parents and your friends. Finally, when is compromising the wrong thing to do?

Related Speech Topics

Persuade your audience that

Dogs are better pets than cats (or change pets).
Year-round school is a bad (or good) idea.
A school dress code is a good (or bad) idea.
Students should have a voice (or no voice) in how their school is run.
Classroom tests are helpful (or not helpful).
Discipline is needed (or not needed) in your life.
The group is more important than the individual in a society (you can reverse these).
Reputation is more important than accomplishments or awards (you can reverse these).

Now go to the library or get on the Internet and do some research on one or more of the following topics:

Nuclear weapons
The homeless
Scientific experimentation on animals
Capital punishment
The prison system
Smoking
Drunk drivers
Instant replay in sports
Women's rights
Censorship

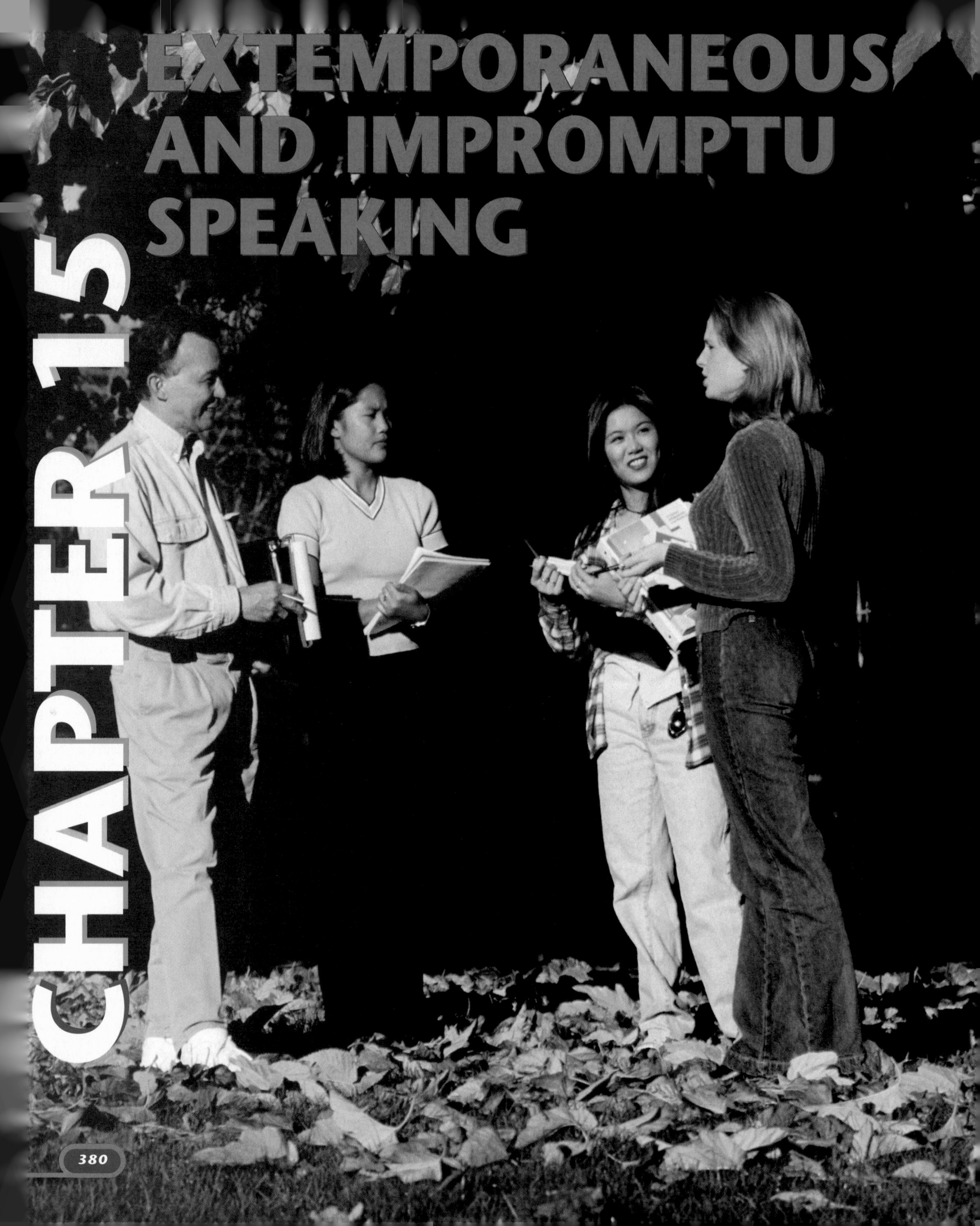

CHAPTER 15
EXTEMPORANEOUS AND IMPROMPTU SPEAKING

"Extemp is life."

—Austan Goolsbee, Professor of Economics
University of Chicago

Learning Objectives

After completing this chapter, you will be able to do the following.

- Define both extemporaneous and impromptu speaking.
- Describe the differences between extemporaneous speaking and impromptu speaking.
- Deliver an extemporaneous speech.
- Deliver an impromptu speech.

Chapter Outline

Following are the main sections in this chapter.

New Speech Terms

In this chapter, you will learn the meanings of the speech terms listed below.

impromptu
extemporaneous
conversational quality
foreshadowing
justification
compelling insight
topic specific
label
analysis
zinger

General Vocabulary

Expanding your general vocabulary will help you become a more effective communicator. Listed below are some words appearing in this chapter that you should make part of your everyday vocabulary.

faltering
fiasco
prescriptive
emulated
qualm
erudite
insinuated

Looking AHEAD

The ability to speak well is becoming more and more important as the United States continues to make a transition from an industry-based economy to a service-based economy. If you want to succeed in an service-based economy, you must be able to communicate effectively. Economist Dr. Joseph J. Penbera points out, "As the need for unskilled labor diminishes in many industries, there will be greater demand for those with . . . the ability to communicate through writing and public speaking." This chapter will introduce some of the skills needed for you to be in demand.

Introduction

You may find yourself chuckling as you listen to a friend mumble and stumble through an oral presentation in class. You don't want to hurt his feelings, but in the immortal words of Homer Simpson: "It's funny because it isn't happening to me." Then comes your turn to speak. Oops! In this chapter you will learn more about taking your turn with the two most common forms of speaking: extemporaneous and impromptu. Mastering these two common forms will help you feel more comfortable thinking and speaking on your feet. Furthermore, you will be better able to say what you mean.

Do you think the same way Homer Simpson does? Do you think something is funny as long as it's not happening to you?

SECTION 1 Extemporaneous Speaking

Although some people believe that extemporaneous speaking is the same as impromptu speaking, there are differences. An **impromptu** speech is generally defined as talking with little or no preparation. Speaking with minimal preparation is sometimes described as "talking off-the-cuff." An **extemporaneous** speech, by contrast, is a presentation that is carefully prepared and practiced in advance. When delivering a speech extemporaneously, you rely on notes or on an outline. Your notes should contain key words or phrases to remind you of the important ideas. Using an outline has two advantages: (1) it will jog your memory and remind you of where you are in the speech, and (2) it allows you to adjust the length of your speech because you can add or drop information as you adapt to an audience's reaction.

Furthermore, you can make last-minute notes on your outline if you become aware of the needs of a particular audience. This flexibility allows you to use essentially the same speech for different audiences. Additionally, an outline can save preparation time and provide better organization than is possible in an impromptu speech. Finally, you will have more control over your thoughts and your use of language.

Political campaigners must be ready to speak extemporaneously on almost any subject.

Developing a Natural Style

The key to effective extemporaneous speaking is to develop a conversational quality. When you speak with a **conversational quality** you sound spontaneous to the audience. You don't want to sound overrehearsed, as if you are reciting from rote memory. Sounding as if you are reciting rather than sounding conversational makes you seem mechanical or stiff. Worst of all, mechanical recitation becomes boring. You need, instead, to develop a conversational style of speaking. And you need to establish the strong eye contact that can only come from not being tied to your notes. In short, to look natural you must practice looking as if you haven't been practicing. After all, the most accomplished actors never appear to be "acting." They seem natural, spontaneous, real. And so should you.

Preparing for Competition

Now that you know the basics of extemporaneous speaking, you may want to "take your act on the road." Many students polish their skills by participating in interscholastic competition. Your teacher can explain how you can become involved in these contests. Not only will you learn, but you will have a lot of fun as well.

"Extemp," as it is known, requires that you analyze a current topic and prepare a speech on that topic within 30 minutes. Usually your speech is then to be delivered in fewer than 7 minutes. Generally, you draw three topics from an envelope and choose one for your speech. Typical topics, ordinarily in question form, include such issues as:

- How can we win the war on drugs?
- What is the future of Eastern Europe?
- Should we have school vouchers?

Once you have selected a topic, you refer to files of collected newspaper and magazine articles that you have brought to the tournament. During your speech, you quote from those articles to help support your answer to the question. The challenge is to organize your thoughts and present them in a clear and meaningful way in only five to seven minutes. Some tournaments allow you to use one notecard; others do not. Judges are instructed to evaluate your performance on how well you answer the question you have chosen.

PERSISTENCE PAYS

INSTANT IMPACT

Too many students lose confidence after *faltering* in their first attempt at public speaking. Even practicing over and over may not be enough. The key to successful presentations of any kind is experience. This lesson was learned by a young man from Exeter, New Hampshire. Asked to address his schoolmates, each of his attempts was a *fiasco.*

He admitted, "I could not speak before the school. Many a piece did I commit to memory, and recite and rehearse in my own room, over and over again, and yet, when the day came, when my name was called, and all eyes turned to my seat, I could not raise myself from it. When the occasion was over, I went home and wept bitter tears . . ."

Later this young man determined that he would conquer his fear, if he died in the attempt. That he succeeded admirably is indicated in the mere fact of his identity. He was Daniel Webster, often still acclaimed as the greatest orator America has ever produced.

Source: Adapted from *A Funny Thing Happened on the Way to the Podium* by Herbert V. Prochnow, Prima Publishing, Rocklin, Calif., 1998, p. 240.

What follows on the next three pages is a sample extemporaneous speech by Jeremy Mallory on the topic "Should Prozac be Banned?" This is a transcript of the speech he delivered to win first place in the final round of the Catholic Forensic League Grand National Tournament. Study this example to learn one possible way you can organize a contest speech. Remember, though, that the opinions expressed are those of the speaker. The speech is not intended to be an endorsement for Prozac or any other drug.

Extemporaneous Contests

Five Tips from a Former National Champion . . . Austan Goolsbee, one of the most successful high school extempers ever (with three national championships), offers advice to aspiring competitors.

- Keep your old speeches. You can use them to practice before a tournament. Also it's fun to look back on speeches from the previous year to see how much you have improved.
- Advanced extempers should choose *prescriptive* topics when possible. A prescriptive topic might be "What should Congress do to reduce drinking and driving?" These topics are the most difficult because they require the speaker to "prescribe" specific policy suggestions. Although it is the most challenging type of question, the answer to the prescriptive topic is the more likely to impress the judge.
- Avoid "canned" introductions. Speakers who use the same introduction round after round not only lose the respect of fellow competitors, they never learn to think creatively.
- Do practice speeches with a limited and specific purpose. In other words, use one practice session just to work on **foreshadowing.** Next, work on the wording of the **justification** step, then work on gestures.
- Enjoy every speech. When you choose your topic, think to yourself, "That's just what I wanted." Right before you enter the room to speak, say to yourself, "It's gonna be a party!"

ANALYSIS SPEECH

A **compelling insight** introduction tells the listeners something they don't know and something they are likely to find interesting. Please note how the discussion of "risk" introduces the idea of evaluating the risks of Prozac later. When you directly connect your introduction to the remainder of the speech, it is said to be **topic specific.**

In an article entitled "Boo! You're Dead!" several Harvard professors tried to figure out what it would take to raise your chance of death by one-millionth: smoking 1.4 cigarettes, drinking a half liter of wine, staying in a coal mine for three hours, spending six minutes in a canoe, drinking Miami tap water for one year, or staying in New York for two days.

The justification step explains the importance of the topic you are discussing. You need to justify for the audience why they should care. Furthermore, you should make a smooth transition from the introduction to the statement of the question to be answered.

Some amount of risk accompanies anything we do, but that doesn't stop us from trying to avoid the big ones. We try to weigh the benefits against the risks to see if that two-day stint in New York city is really worth it. Recently, a drug called Prozac hit the market, then hit the magazine stands on the cover of Newsweek, a feat rarely accomplished by a pharmaceutical. People were excited because it was billed as one of the likely cures for depression. Others dismissed it as a modern snake oil. Still others found dangerous side effects.

Make certain that you state the question exactly. It is your responsibility to answer this question accurately and completely.

Now we need to figure out whether Prozac is a miracle drug or medical disaster, and ask ourselves the question: "Should Prozac be banned?"

The answer to the question is the equivalent of the thesis in an essay. As you remember, the thesis is the central idea or message in either an essay or a speech. You answer the question immediately so that your arguments will follow directly from that answer.

The answer to that question is that Prozac should not be banned.

This is the foreshadowing step. Foreshadowing simply means that you are providing a map to the rest of the speech. This listing of what is to come in the body of the speech is sometimes called partitioning, forecasting, signposting, or mapping.

On one hand, the risks are small, and on the other hand, the possible benefits outweigh the risks.

At this point, you need to return to the first issue that you foreshadowed. Avoid saying tired phrases like, "Now let's go back to the first issue." You also indicate how many subpoints will be discussed under this issue.

So what do Prozac's critics think the drug can do to you? What risks do you take by using the drug? Most critics agree on three potential harms.

Continued on following page

ANALYSIS SPEECH

"Schizophrenia" is the label for the first subpoint under the first major issue. The **label** is the brief explanation of what you are about to discuss. Labels should be short and memorable...

The first potential harm is schizophrenia. Studies documented in the *New York Times* show that 12 out of 1,000 patients using Prozac develop schizophrenia. Given the number of people talking to the walls in the prep room for this event, this seems like a small risk indeed.

The information from the *New York Times* is evidence that supports your argument. The "talking to the walls" comment is an inside joke about the way that students prepare for competition.

The second potential harm is that Prozac does not help everyone. Some who take Prozac may expect the drug to work and have their hopes dashed when it doesn't, which may worsen their depression. But, as the *Christian Science Monitor* points out, "no drug is a panacea except chicken soup, of course." No drug works for everyone. And the easiest cure for high expectations is to lower them—then people won't be disappointed if Prozac fails for them.

This is the second subpoint under the first major issue. Note that following the label "no effect at all," the speaker offers more evidence. The discussion of how "no drug works for everyone" is **analysis.** Analysis is a detailed examination of the information at hand.

The third, and perhaps the most frightening, potential harm is addiction. Whether or not the drug works, people might come to depend on Prozac for their happiness, and since the pills are relatively expensive, that could be a costly prospect. The *Wall Street Journal* argues, however, that any drug can become addictive. The *Wall Street Journal* explains that true addiction, actual physical need, is fairly rare and that physicians can stop prescribing Prozac for patients who merely have a psychological need for it.

The third subpoint begins here. Again, the speaker provides a label, analysis, and evidence to support his thesis.

The risks, then, all things considered, are really quite low.

This is a summary statement that refers back to the entire first major issue.

But what about the benefits? Even a small risk is not worth taking if no benefit can come from it. I'm sure none of us would cross the street in New York unless there was some very good reason to do so. In the case of Prozac, there are two important benefits.

The transition into the second major issue mentions what went before and foreshadows what is coming next.

ANALYSIS SPEECH

Here is the beginning of the first subpoint of the second major issue. Again, you will find a label, analysis, and evidence.

The first, and most obvious, is that it can cure depression. The *Washington Post* estimates that about 20 percent of the people who take Prozac are cured of their depression. For somebody suffering from this incapacitating mental disorder, this is a significant benefit worth considering.

The second subpoint also features a label, analysis, and evidence. Since this is the last subpoint it should be your strongest argument. Save the best for last.

The second major benefit is the so-called placebo effect. Even if the drug has no actual physiological effect, the *New York Times* reports a high number of people who pull out of depression anyway. Some cases of depression, especially those caused by a lack of confidence, can cure themselves if the people believe they should be cured.

Quoting Shakespeare in this context shows the speaker's ability to make connections. Hamlet's observation about the nature of perception could be applied to many topics. General Hamlet, for example, might argue that it is difficult to win a war without the people's perception that the conflict is justified. Professor Hamlet might argue that people must "think" that teacher pay raises are necessary for those raises to happen.

Doctor Hamlet would agree: "There is nothing either good or bad but thinking makes it so." The *Times* even notes cases of people who were actually taking sugar pills and who were cured, literally, by the name of the drug. This may not say much for the honesty of Prozac's manufacturers, but if the depression is lifted, even if it be the name that lifts it, Prozac has proven its benefits to outweigh the risks.

This transition leads into the conclusion of the speech. Avoid saying "In conclusion" or other such obvious statements. If you say "final analysis," it implies that you actually had analysis earlier. Be sure to restate the question and your answer. Also, summarize the major issues briefly as the speaker does.

So in the final analysis, when we ask ourselves the question, "Should Prozac be banned?", the answer is no, it shouldn't be banned. The small risks of harm are outweighed by the significant potential benefits. Whether or not you want to subject yourself to this particular risk, like that six-minute canoe trip, it must be your decision. You must weigh the risk of harm against each potential benefit each time.

This is the **zinger.** A zinger is a concluding statement that is a powerful reminder of the rightness of your position. The audience will remember best what you say last.

If you do not, you may come to understand the words of philosopher Bertrand Russell all too well: "Some people would die sooner than think. In fact, they do."

WORDS FROM THE WORKPLACE

Rodolfo Martinez, Jr.

Financial Consultant

Q: *How does communication play a role in your day-to-day work activities?*

A: Possessing good communication skills is my most important asset. I could not begin to be successful in my business if I were unable to talk with customers. Talking with customers helps me figure out what they think their needs are, as well as helping them understand the services I can provide to meet their needs.

Q: *What suggestions can you give students to show them the importance of communication skills?*

A: Always express your ideas honestly and courteously. Above all, be positive. In my business, it is necessary for me to study, to stay current with new products, and to talk constantly to people about their needs. Another tip is to be a good listener and to show a genuine interest in what people have to say.

Q: *Do you have any personal experiences that might illustrate how good communication skills helped you be successful in a business situation?*

A: Good communication means using words that the listener understands. Many of my clients do not believe that they can find money in their budgets to add regularly to a savings account or to purchase insurance. An example I often use to help people identify where they might be able to save money is the trip to McDonald's. If they would pass up one family trip a week, about $10, they could start a plan that could greatly impact their future lives. People can relate to this, and many will use this as a starting point to start saving.

SECTION  REVIEW

Recalling the Facts ...

1. What are the rules for extemporaneous speaking?
2. Why do you want to develop a conversational style of delivery?

Thinking Critically ...

1. Many speakers begin their presentations with a joke. Why do you think a compelling insight introduction might be a safer strategy than a humorous introduction?

Taking Charge ...

1. Find the text of a speech from a source such as *Vital Speeches.* Outline a brief section of the speech. Working from this outline, deliver the ideas extemporaneously in your own words. Ad-lib as much as possible. Tape-record your best practice speeches for review and critique.

COMMUNICATION Breakthrough

Mallspeak

"I was like, y'know, whatever" just won't cut it anymore. In the world beyond school, students must speak effectively. Employers expect competence and confidence in the people they hire. The imprecise and inarticulate speech of teenagers, sometimes called Mallspeak, has caused concern in both the academic and business communities. Therefore, colleges are now creating special courses to provide training in public speaking.

Smith College, for example, has launched its "speaking across the curriculum" program, featuring "speaking-intensive" first-year seminars with special emphasis on oral presentations. Other colleges have followed suit. M.I.T., Holy Cross, and Wesleyan College have already begun focusing on speaking skills. Mount Holyoke has established a Speaking Center. Mount Holyoke College President Joanne V. Creighton predicts that her school's effort will be widely *emulated.*

At Mount Holyoke, biology professor Rachel Fink had *qualms* about trading some of her students' lab time to accommodate the speaking curriculum. Fink incorporated the curriculum by planning a mock scientific convention, titled "Out of the Lab and Into Your Life," where students distributed research papers and presented extemporaneously their latest findings to their distinguished colleagues. It was a trade-off—because of the time involved, "they didn't get to do fly embryos or chick embryos"—and Fink had her doubts.

But when the day of the convention arrived, Fink was blown away. One team reported on environmental estrogens, hormones that are believed to be reducing fertility levels in many species. The presentation lived up to its catchy title.

"Those students are going to remember 'Impotent Alligators' forever," Fink said.

Still, the Mallspeak issue sizzles. Smith College President Ruth Simmons commented that the way students speak drives her crazy. "Where," anguished Simmons, "will we be in another 30 years?"

In retaliation, an editorial in the Smith student newspaper confidently replied: "Like, running the world, you know?"

Source: Adapted from a *Los Angeles Times* article.

Questions

1. Try to predict the future. What do you think Mallspeak will have evolved into in 30 years?
2. If you could design a course in public speaking, what would you include?

SECTION 2 Impromptu Speaking

Although you frequently may be asked—often to your surprise and dismay—to speak impromptu on almost any occasion, you have actually been preparing for these situations all of your life. You may not be as prepared as you would like, but you have a lifetime of experience from which to draw. The effective speaker selects appropriate supporting materials from memory, organizes them into an easy-to-follow pattern, and delivers them confidently. In other words, you learn how to think on your feet.

Business and civic meetings will test your ability to properly organize your impromptu speeches.

Keep It Simple

Since impromptu speeches are generally brief, simplicity is essential. You should establish a single point of view, choose one or two clear examples or illustrations, and conclude with a short summary and restatement of your main idea. If you have more than a few minutes for your impromptu presentation, you should subdivide the body of your speech into two or three issues and develop each one with supporting materials. Like all speeches, your impromptu presentation should have a definite beginning, middle, and end.

A typical organizational pattern for a brief impromptu speech might include the following:

1. Statement of the main point of your presentation. A short introduction to the main idea can be effective if you have the time (and an idea).
2. Support of the main idea with appropriate reasons, examples, illustrations, statistics, and testimony. Ordinarily, you should rely on your first thoughts, because if you struggle to generate more information, you may forget your initial ideas.
3. Conclusion with a summary and a restatement of the main idea. Be brief—needless repetition is boring and reduces your credibility as a speaker.

If you are called on in a business meeting and have nothing to say, the worst thing you can do is to apologize. Rather than admitting you're unprepared, take a deep breath, and say something like, "I will look into this issue and get back to you."

COMMUNICATION

Break*down*

A Country of Strangers

Before you speak, you must always consider the wants and needs of your audience. In our multicultural society, choosing the right words in impromptu speaking can be extremely difficult. This challenge is made painfully clear in the story of Barbara Wyche, a noted sociologist. She found that speaking well can intrude deeply into personal and family relationships. According to Wyche, as a young black, her black peers never accepted her. Because of her image as a smart child, she said, "nobody would ask me to dance. You see what I'm saying? They wouldn't even think I knew how to dance. I had an inferiority complex, because I really wanted people to like me, and I really loved people and I wanted to fit, and I couldn't fit."

Her father had three years of college and wanted his daughter to attend college as well. He "wanted me to talk, like, very fine, like, 'Thank you.' " And here she put on an *erudite,* quasi-British accent. "My mother let me know that if I came back talking and acting like some of the people that were teaching, I would not be her child," Wyche recalled. "That was again picking up those attitudes that we call 'white.'"

And so the racial imagery *insinuated* itself into the fiber of her family, setting up tensions over class, education, language, and identity that were played out against conflicts between her parents, whose marriage ended when she was ten. "I am a product of class warfare in my own family," Wyche said.

"I would come home from Johns Hopkins University," Wyche went on, "and, you know, you pick up this way of talking to each other. I was good at it . . . So I remember I went home one year, and I told my mother, I said, 'Mama,' I kept talking and talking and talking, and my mother said, 'I'm glad you learned how to talk at school' . . . and I was just talking, talking, talking, and my mama said, 'Speak English or don't talk at all.' I was using GRE and SAT vocabulary. I had made the transition, so my mother didn't know what I was talking about."

Source: Adapted from *A Country of Strangers* by David K. Shipler, Vintage Books, New York, 1997, pp. 309–10.

Questions

1. Do you believe that your friends and relatives judge you by your speech, including your choice of words? Why or why not?
2. How can more effective communication tear down the barriers that separate people?

Don't Panic

Similarly, the worst mistake you can make in an impromptu speech is to panic. Panic usually results in uneasy silence or unnecessary rambling. As a prospective impromptu speaker, you should minimize your concerns by reading widely and by being a good observer and listener. Remember, too, that your audience is aware that you're speaking off-the-cuff and will adjust its expectations accordingly. Most audience members will respond positively if they sense you're trying to incorporate your knowledge into a clear and meaningful presentation.

Getting Ready to Compete

As with extemporaneous speaking, you can polish your impromptu skills through competition. The rules for impromptu speaking, though, vary greatly from contest to contest. The National Forensic League, for example, allows each student five minutes for preparation and then another five minutes to present the speech. At the college level, the American Forensic Association allows a total of seven minutes for both preparation and speaking; the speaker may choose how to divide those minutes.

Generally there are three types of impromptu topics. These are: (1) *words,* such as orange, love, greed, and happiness; (2) *quotations,* such as "We have nothing to fear but fear itself," or "A bird in the hand is worth two in the bush"; (3) *people/places/events,* such as Nelson Mandela or the Vietnam War Memorial or the New Millennium.

Remember, though, that the key is to practice. Only through practice can you begin to feel comfortable with the pressure of such limited time to prepare. Also, through practice you will become more skilled at connecting what you know to the precise wording of the topic. Of course, increasing what you know by reading more and discussing more would be advisable as well.

To help you with your first contest impromptu speech, here is a student example on the topic "elephants." Study the comments that accompany the text on the following pages to learn one effective way that you can organize an impromptu speech.

Nelson Mandela would be an ideal choice for a *people/places/events* impromptu presentation.

INSTANT IMPACT

BE A CABBAGE

A speaker at a luncheon gave a tremendous talk and received a standing ovation. The president of the club was so impressed that he said to the speaker, "Everyone here is so enthused. Won't you please say a few more words since we have ten minutes left of our regular time?"

The request challenged the speaker to draw on all of her impromptu skills. How would you have responded to this difficult situation? This speaker thought for a moment and said, "Once there was a little baby cabbage who said to his mother, 'Mommy, I'm worried about something. As I sit in this row of cabbages and grow and grow day after day, how will I know when to stop growing?' 'The rule to follow,' said the Momma cabbage, 'is to quit when you're a head'."

Good advice for all of us.

ANALYSIS SPEECH

Because you have a limited time to come up with an introduction, you must search your memory for appropriate stories, examples, or illustrations. Your first thought should be to brainstorm everything you can think of that has some connection to elephants or whatever the topic happens to be. This brainstorming will not only generate an idea for an introduction but can also give you supporting material for the rest of the speech.

There is a story about six blind men touching an elephant. One man feels the tail and says, "Oh, it's a rope." One comes in contact with a leg and thinks it's a tree. Another man grasps the ear and speculates that it's a fan or a leaf. Still another man walks along the side of the elephant and concludes that it's a mountain. But none of these men realizes that it's an elephant.

This transition connects the opening illustration with the thesis, or main idea of the speech.

Although this story illustrates how we must see the whole of anything in order to understand it, it is also true that most of us, in fact, do not recognize the whole importance of the elephant.

This thesis statement is made more memorable because of the play on words using "mammoth."

I believe that we should not overlook the "mammoth" accomplishment of these pachyderms.

Here the speaker explains what will be discussed in the rest of the speech. This is the "tell 'em what you're gonna tell 'em" step.

Let us consider their contribution in two areas: the elephants, themselves, and what the elephants can teach us about ourselves.

The first issue starts with a joke, but note that the speaker then turns her attention to more serious concerns. Raising the possibility of extinction gives importance to discussing this particular topic.

Each elephant makes a signifiicant sacrifice for our benefit. Did you know that every time you munch a peanut butter sandwich, you are grabbing goobers out of the mouths of baby elephants?

On a more serious note, in California many people are beginning to boycott the use of ivory in products. These people are concerned that elephants are hunted down and destroyed just for their tusks. Furthermore, they express the fear that elephants may become extinct some day as a result of man's greed.

Continued on following page

ANALYSIS SPEECH

Here the speaker moves to the second issue. She begins the discussion of this issue by referring to a familiar children's story. If you can, you, too, should try to incorporate supporting material that has universal appeal.

The selfish slaughter is even more depressing when we consider what elephants can teach us about ourselves. In one of Dr. Seuss's best-loved stories, Horton the Elephant promises, "I meant what I said and I said what I meant, an elephant's faithful one-hundred percent." This faith, this commitment, is an important lesson for all of us.

This second lesson we can learn from elephants simply adds further proof to her argument. But it also reminds the audience that you can learn interesting things by listening in class.

But perhaps the elephant is most familiar to us as the symbol of the Republican Party. We learned in history class that the elephant as a symbol for Republicans came from the imagination of nineteenth-century cartoonist Thomas Nast. The teacher told us that the elephant was chosen because it is clever but not easily controlled.

This brief conclusion refers back to the thesis and then ends with a strong last thought. You want the audience to "never forget" you either.

So we should be clever enough to remember the accomplishments of these powerful pachyderms, for as we all know, the elephant never forgets.

SECTION 2 REVIEW

Recalling the Facts ...

1. Name the three steps in a typical organization pattern for an impromptu speech.

Thinking Critically ...

1. In *Silent Messages,* Albert Mehrabian argues that facial and body language account for more than 50 percent of a listener's emotional response. Some 40 percent of the response is triggered by nonverbal vocal qualities. The words themselves only account for 10 percent or less of the response. Why do you think that words matter so little?

Taking Charge ...

1. Everyone in class is to write three to five impromptu topics on individual slips of paper. Draw three topics each, giving yourself a minute to gather your thoughts. Deliver your impromptu speech in approximately two minutes.

   Evaluate each student speech to determine if it followed the three steps for impromptu speaking outlined in this section.

STUDENT WORK

"Tourists and Terrorists" *By Austan Goolsbee*

If you travel for business or pleasure, you are often reminded of the safety measures taken to prevent acts of terrorism. You are required in airports, for example, to pass through metal detectors. Austan Goolsbee won the National Championship in extemporaneous speaking with this speech that answered the question: "Do the Middle East hostage takers have the NATO nations locked in a no-win stranglehold?"

When we talk about the problem of international terrorism in the world today, we are talking about the ability of one man to hold an entire nation in fear. And the hostage takers in the Middle East have found out the most effective way to exploit the Western media. They now take someone alive. It is more effective to have a hostage scream in front of a camera than it is to snipe someone from a building. But there is no more poignant question or issue facing us today. After all, just this morning it was reported in the *Cincinnati Enquirer* that an American journalist was taken hostage and beaten by Lebanese hostage takers. So we need to ask a very important question: "Do the Middle East hostage takers have the NATO nations locked in a no-win stranglehold?

If we look first at the technical inexperience we have in dealing with hostage takers and, second, at the political headlock we've gotten ourselves in, we can see that the horrifying answer to this question is yes. But let me explain.

Initially, what we must understand is that we are technically unprepared and here there are four key factors to consider. And the first is information. Quite simply we don't have enough, we don't exchange what we do have, and we don't know where to get more. According to the *Wall Street Journal* this morning, finally the Eastern European nations are beginning to come to our aid and they have pledged to exchange information with us. Unfortunately, what the *Wall Street Journal* does not point out is that this information can't be recalled on the floppy disc of a computer. It is names, it is places, it is times, things that most people, even the experts, don't understand. We have tried this exchange in the past and it doesn't work. Without the information we are in a no-win situation because we don't know what to do.

The second important factor is our infiltration techniques. Because experts on global terrorism say that Western Europeans don't mix well when they are trying to portray people from the Middle East. This severe problem in infiltrating has resulted in only an estimated .02% of Middle East terrorist groups being compromised. So what we have to understand is that without infiltration we won't get access to any more information, more of a no-win situation. In other words, we don't know where they're going to strike next.

The third more important factor is how we choose to retaliate. Or the way we behave. Because there is a distinct difference between rescue and military operations. And we are used to the latter. In fact, *World Press Review* in March points out that the inexperience we have is based on our Western European traditions. We are often faced with IRA bombings and snipers and we have experience with that kind of terrorism. What we don't know is how to deal with someone holding a live hostage. We don't want to endanger the lives of these hostages. This helplessness only exacerbates our no-win situation.

This leads us to our fourth and final factor. We don't have any practice. When it comes right down to it, we can't play games with human lives. And because hostage situations are so rare, we don't have the opportunity to develop the technical experience to avoid these no-win situations.

Unfortunately, technical inexperience is only part of the problem. To understand the true magnitude of the situation, we must realize that we have a stranglehold on ourselves and are quickly running

out of breath. Here there are three important factors we need to consider.

The first is our inability to address the causes of international terrorism. *World Press Review* in May stated that terrorism is usually caused by radical Mideastern groups like Iran's Islamic group or radical PLO members who want drastic changes in the international balance of power. However, NATO alliances can't change the balance of power because of significant domestic opposition. For example, the United States can't stop terrorism tomorrow by saying we are now opposed to the Israeli nation. Margaret Thatcher can't suddenly say that the Ayatollah Khomeini is now my best friend. She would be humiliated before her own people. Another no-win situation.

A second consideration is that we face retaliation. *Newsweek* reminds us that we can't predict what terrorists are going to do when we attack them. Of course, *Newsweek* can't summarize the terror caused by the actions of NATO alliances. In fact, when the United States bombs Libya, Libya decides to take British citizens hostage. And so what happens is these NATO nations, who all have different strategies for dealing with terrorism, are then confronted with a no-win stranglehold because politically we are riding off in all directions at once.

But the final, most important, factor is that we end up negotiating with irrational people because that is the only alternative. And it doesn't work. In the book *Getting To Yes,* William Ury argues that in evaluating your negotiation option, you have to look at what your best alternative is. And in the case of Middle East terrorists, your best alternative is to let the hostages die. And so, too often our negotiations result in the very deaths we were trying to prevent.

So in the final analysis, in answering the question: "Do Middle East hostage takers have NATO nations in a no-win stranglehold?"—if we look first at the technical inexperience we have and second, at the political headlock we have ourselves in, we'll see that the answer is simply yes. After all, if we think back to the man who was kidnapped just last night, we can see that terrorism is a fundamental threat to freedom. And that threat limits our freedom to go where we want. And we become haunted by the idea that in the Middle East everyone has the right to go anywhere he wants . . . once.

• •

CHAPTER 15 Review and Enrichment...

Looking Back

Listed below are the major ideas discussed in this chapter.

- An impromptu speech is generally delivered off-the-cuff while an extemporaneous speech is prepared and practiced in advance.
- The key to effective extemporaneous delivery is to develop a conversational quality.
- Extemporaneous speaking contests require that you analyze a current event topic and then prepare a speech on that topic within 30 minutes.
- An impromptu speech should establish a single point of view, choose one or two examples or illustrations, and conclude with a short summary and restatement of your main idea.
- The worst mistake you can make in an impromptu speech is to panic.

Speech Vocabulary

Using the following list, make flash cards. On one side of each card, print each new speech term. On the other side, write the definition. Keep track of the words that give you problems and eliminate the words you can handle.

impromptu
extemporaneous
conversational quality
foreshadowing
justification
compelling insight
topic specific
label
analysis
zinger

General Vocabulary

Write a definition for each of the terms listed below and then use each in a sentence.

faltering
fiasco
erudite
insinuated
emulated
qualm
prescriptive

CHAPTER 15 Review and Enrichment...

To Remember

Answer the following based on your reading of the chapter.

1. What is the purpose of the justification step in an extemporaneous speech?
2. What makes a zinger important?
3. What are the advantages of a speech outline?
4. A typical impromptu speech would follow what organizational pattern?

To Do

1. Prepare an outline for your next speech. Read your outline aloud to check whether it works when spoken. Are the main points clear? Is it interesting? Is it persuasive? Is it too long? Revise your speech as needed.
2. Watch *Headline News* on CNN. After two minutes, turn off the television set. Repeat what you heard, combining the wording of the professional announcer with your own. Repeating this exercise every day will increase your working vocabulary, build your fluency, and enhance your knowledge of current affairs.

To Talk About

1. You can learn a great deal from the mistakes of others. Have the class discuss instances where they observed problems in someone's presentations. How do you apply what you have observed?
2. Discuss some of the benefits of participating in extemporaneous speaking competitions. Consider the advantage of being able to organize your thoughts quickly during a timed essay exam. What other skills might you gain from extemporaneous speaking?

To Write About

1. Pick a current event in which you are interested. Now write an essay about this topic in the form that you have always used for English class. Next write an essay on the same topic using the form of the model extemporaneous speech in this chapter. Which is the better essay? Why?
2. Pick an impromptu topic from the list below in Related Speech Topics. Write out an impromptu speech, trying to follow the form of the model impromptu in this chapter. Take only a few minutes to prepare and then begin writing. Were you able to think of enough examples and illustrations?

Related Speech Topics

Extemporaneous
How should Congress reform welfare?
Is there a cure for health care?
What are the long-term effects of Internet shopping?
What is ahead for the stock market?

Impromptu
Scandals
Censorship
War
Work
Astrology

CHAPTER 16

INTERPRETATION

"Above all, the art of reading aloud should be cultivated."

—Alfred Lord Whitehead, discussing the aims of education

Learning Objectives

After completing this chapter, you will be able to do the following.

- Define oral interpretation.
- Choose material to use for reading.
- Analyze the meaning and feeling of a selection.
- Practice the delivery of a selection.
- Discuss the elements of Reader's Theater.

Chapter Outline

Following are the main sections in this chapter.

1. What Is Oral Interpretation?
2. Choosing Your Material
3. Interpreting Your Material
4. Presenting Your Material

New Speech Terms

In this chapter, you will learn the meanings of the speech terms listed below.

oral interpretation
rhapsode
anthology
theme
mood
persona
first person
third person
second person
dramatic monologue
interior monologue
omniscient
meter
rhythm
rhyme
auditory
scene setting
offstage focus
aural

General Vocabulary

Expanding your general vocabulary will help you become a more effective communicator. Listed below are some words appearing in this chapter that you should make part of your everyday vocabulary.

enhanced
mimic
minstrel
recitation
spellbound
paraphernalia
compelling
tedium
apoplectic
introspective
nectar
motif

Looking AHEAD

In this chapter, you will learn about the remarkable history of oral interpretation and how the long tradition of sharing literature orally continues today. You will discover that this experience of sharing can benefit you and others. As you become a better oral interpreter, your understanding of literature will be *enhanced* because you will become a more careful reader. Careful reading will lead you to new insights about the meaning of the literature as well as make you more sensitive to the beauty of language. The audience, too, will share in this intellectual and emotional experience, for you will not only entertain audience members with your performance, you will bring literature alive for them.

Introduction

When Dr. Seuss died, an entire nation mourned. Appearing on the television program *Saturday Night Live,* the Reverend Jesse Jackson read from Dr. Seuss's beloved story *Green Eggs and Ham.* It was a fitting tribute: Millions of children, after all, have grown up in a world peopled by Hunches in Bunches and Brown Barba-Loots. In fact, your first experience with oral interpretation might have been when one of your parents interpreted Dr. Seuss for you: "I do not like green eggs and ham. I do not like them, Sam-I-am."

Whether you realize it or not, oral interpretation is still an important part of your life. When you read aloud in class from an essay you've written, you're interpreting your words for your classmates. When you listen to the news on radio or television, the reporters are practicing the art of oral interpretation for you. Storytelling, a form of oral interpretation, has become an important tool for persuasion in the boardrooms of America. Moreover, oral interpretation can be great fun. In a memorable episode of the television show *The Simpsons,* Marge (the mother) flashes back to her high school days and her participation on the speech team. In one scene, Marge, an academic standout, performs her interpretation of the play *Butterflies Are Free* and wins the heart of the classic bad boy Homer (the father).

Dr. Seuss stories, read aloud to you as a child, were probably one of your first experiences with oral interpretation.

SECTION 1 What Is Oral Interpretation?

If you can accurately *mimic* the voice of your favorite celebrity or cartoon character, you are gifted in the skill of impression. You should not, however, confuse this ability with the art of oral interpretation. In oral interpretation, you do not impersonate a familiar voice—be it Eddie Murphy or Bugs Bunny. Rather, you try to create an appropriate and original voice to give life to words on a page. After analyzing the meaning and feeling behind those words, you use your voice and body to share the words with others. **Oral interpretation,** then, is the art of communicating works of literature by reading aloud well.

The history of oral interpretation as a distinct art—apart from public speaking and theater—is difficult to define. The formal study of oral interpretation as a separate activity didn't begin until early in the nineteenth century. In 1806, Harvard College offered courses that included "the interpretive approach to literary materials."

However, oral interpretation is one of the oldest of human social activities. Until paper replaced memory, people needed to communicate ideas orally. Literature was passed down from generation to generation in oral form. Professional storytellers made their livings by traveling through the countryside and entertaining people. Recently, storytelling has experienced a rebirth in the United States. The business world now realizes that storytelling can be an effective tool to persuade a potential client of the quality of a product, or to convince employees of a policy change.

Everyone enjoys having someone read to them. You can entertain and enlighten your friends by interpreting your favorite literature passages.

WELL...THAT'S MY ADDRESS...WHAT DO YOU THINK?
Brooke

IT'S AMAZING...EVERY TIME YOU SAY WORDS WITH M OR F SOUNDS, THE TIP OF YOUR NOSE PALES AND WIGGLES UP AND DOWN.
e-mail: NineCWL@aol.com
http://www.chickweed.com

THIS IS THE FIRST TIME I EVER HEARD ANYONE DELIVER A SPEECH ON METAPHASIC CHROMOSOME FORMATION THROUGH CLENCHED TEETH.

BEING PREPARED

INSTANT IMPACT

Speakers who can interpret words with passion and power can inspire people to change the world. Nelson Mandela mastered this art of oral interpretation. Born the son of a Tembu tribal chieftain in 1918 in South Africa, he renounced his right to succeed his father and, instead, chose a political career. He became a lawyer and an honorable member of the African National Congress (ANC). In 1962, he was arrested by the South African security police for his bold opposition to the white government and its apartheid policies of racial, political, and economic discrimination against the nonwhite majority. In 1964, more charges were brought against Mandela, including high treason, sabotage, and conspiracy. On the foggy morning of April 20, 1964, while standing on a crowded dock, he delivered his famous "I am prepared to die" speech. He said, "During my lifetime I have dedicated myself to this struggle of the African people. I have fought against white domination, and I have fought against black domination. I have cherished the ideal of a democratic and free society in opportunities. It is an ideal which I hope to live for and to achieve. But if needs be, it is an ideal for which I am prepared to die." His words inspired many that day to continue to fight for freedom. One such man was Alan Paton, famous for his impassioned speeches and writings that brought notice to the suffering black man under apartheid. So, like Nelson Mandela and Alan Paton, remember that nothing you write or say will ever be as passionate or powerful as the truth.

The "poet's corner" in London's Hyde Park offers daily exposure to oral interpretations.

Even though the oral tradition has been with us as long as human interaction, historians point to ancient Greece as the birthplace for the art of interpretation. Wandering *minstrels* known as **rhapsodes** would assemble to read their works in public competition. The recitations were often accompanied by music from a lyre or other primitive instrument.

Poetry reading was popular during the Augustan Age (27 B.C.–A.D. 14) in Rome. It is said that the Emperor Nero would allow no one to leave a reading in which he was competing until he himself had finished reading. Dr. Paul Hunsinger, a professor of speech, characterized Nero as a "ruthless contestant" who paid five thousand young men to applaud him at one competition. After losing to the poet Lucan, Nero ordered him never to read again. Nero went so far as to destroy the statues and busts of other poetry readers.

Recitation contests continued throughout the Middle Ages among minstrels, who competed for prizes provided by the nobility. In Margaret Bahn's book *A History of Oral Interpretation,* you can learn about Anglo-Saxon, Celtic, and Norse oral literatures. Any study of the oral tradition should also include a review of the literary works of India, China, Africa, and the Middle East.

Reading aloud has played an important role in the cultural history of our country as well. Before radio and television, many families would read aloud in the evenings. Young children, *spellbound* by the great works of literature, would spend hours in shared adventure. Much as musicians give concerts today, oral interpreters around the turn of the century would go on tour. These tours brought entertainment and culture to even the most remote regions of our country.

Today, as writers attempt to reach a wider audience, "performance poetry" is gaining popularity, sometimes in the form of "poetry slams" in coffeehouses or bookstores. Larry Goodell, a poet and practitioner of the art, explores the creative possibilities of oral interpretation. Costumed in an old robe and makeup, Goodell dances and chants. He has been known to read poem fragments written on cardboard dog biscuits as a musician accompanies him on an electronic saxophone. Although few poets perform oral interpretation with such *paraphernalia,* most writers now recognize the need for students to hear the range and diversity of contemporary works—works that enrich and expand our enjoyment of literature and each other.

Nero was a skilled, but ruthless poetry reading competitor during the Augustan Age.

SECTION 1 REVIEW

Recalling the Facts ...

1. Why is impersonating a familiar voice not interpretation?
2. How might businesses use the art of storytelling?

Thinking Critically ...

1. At current rates, some 90 percent of the world's languages will vanish during the next century. As these languages face extinction, what can be done to preserve the stories and memories that will be lost in the disappearing words?

Taking Charge ...

1. Performance poets like Larry Goodell are dedicated to "oral poetry." These artists use things other than the words—such as costumes, props, and music—to help the audience appreciate the power and magic of language. Goodell explains: "Things I make extend from the words, sometimes cradle them like a mouth cradles the words you say, before they are said."

   Now it's your turn. Choose a short poem to read. As you interpret the poem for the class, incorporate things that will extend the meaning of the words. You could, for example, perform dribbling tricks with a basketball as you interpret John Updike's poem "Ex-Basketball Player."

SECTION 2 Choosing Your Material

When you are assigned to give an oral interpretation in class, you have a problem: where to look for material to perform. Although you have a seemingly unlimited range of material available to you, how do you find it? Many interpreters have found anthologies to be useful, because they include a wide selection of materials in a single volume. **Anthologies** are books that include literary works by subject matter, such as love, war, or nature. Other anthologies are collections of poetry or different types of prose, such as short stories, essays, or humorous pieces. If you are interested in contemporary music, for example, you could turn to the anthology *The Poetry of Rock,* edited by Richard Goldstein. If you are interested, on the other hand, in interpreting poems on the subject of loneliness, several excellent selections appear in the anthology *Pictures That Storm Inside My Head,* edited by Richard Peck.

Another way to find material for oral interpretation is to ask your teachers to provide suggestions. They have a wealth of reading experience that they can share. Your school librarians can recommend literature that they believe might be suitable for reading aloud.

Consider the works of Ogden Nash if you'd like to present a poetry interpretation.

Your most important consideration, though, should be your own tastes in literature. You are more likely to devote time and energy to the performance of material that you care about. When forced to read material that you find boring or confusing, your performance will suffer.

The key, then, is to choose a work that you enjoy reading. Think back over the poems and stories you have read. Which ones moved you the most? Which ones made you stop and think? Chances are that the selections you remember as favorites will be good choices for your first oral interpretation.

As you select material to read aloud, you will also want to consider the quality of the literature. Why? Because literature that has worth or merit gives you, the reader, something to interpret. True, a grocery list is writing that matters, but how many different interpretations can you give to a gallon of milk and a loaf of bread? If, however, you read Henry David Thoreau's observation that "the mass of men lead lives of quiet desperation," then you have layers of meaning to interpret. What did Thoreau mean by "quiet desperation"? How does that desperation affect people's lives? For you as an interpreter, Thoreau provides much food for thought.

Look for writings that are valued both for their beauty and for their permanence or universal interest. These writings give you material for oral interpretation and you can also learn much from them. Literature of high quality offers insights into life, inner truths that teach lasting lessons. When T. S. Eliot, in his poem "The Love Song of J. Alfred Prufrock," has the speaker admit that he has measured out his life "in coffee spoons," you are introduced to a *compelling* symbol. The spoons represent the *tedium* of a life lived from one cup of coffee to the next. Your challenge as a reader is to present the speaker's struggle against this tedium so that the listeners share in his frustration.

In choosing material, you should also consider the occasion and the desires of your audience. If you are given three minutes to share a work of literature in class, you may want to avoid long, complex stories. Your material should be suitable and meet the audience's expectations.

Choosing Material for Oral Interpretation

T. S. Eliot

Alex Haley

William Shakespeare

Amy Tan

Emily Dickinson

Maya Angelou

When selecting material for an oral interpretation, you should consider your personal tastes in literature and the occasion for the interpretation. The writers shown here will appeal to different speakers and be appropriate for different occasions.

SECTION 2 REVIEW

Recalling the Facts ...

1. Name three things you should consider in selecting material for an interpretative reading.
2. What are the literary works called that collect material by subject matter?

Thinking Critically ...

1. Some 57 percent of American children aged three to five are read to by a family member every day of the week. What might be done to bring reading aloud into the lives of the other children?

Taking Charge ...

1. Make a list of five selections that you might use for an oral interpretation in class. Remember to consider these four factors: your personal tastes, the quality of the literature, the occasion, and the desires of the audience.

SECTION 3

Interpreting Your Material

To interpret a selection well, you must first understand it. You reach this understanding by considering both the meaning and the feeling of the selection. Once you have determined the meaning and feeling of a particular work, you must adapt your interpretation to the requirements of the form: prose, poetry, or drama.

Director Alan Pakula and author Harper Lee watch the filming of her Pulitzer prize–winning novel *To Kill a Mockingbird.*

Meaning

The meaning of any selection includes all the ideas that are communicated by the work. You analyze those ideas as a means to an end—the performance. An important part of the process of analysis is to know what each word means (and how each word relates to every other word) so that you can share that understanding with the audience. For example, if you are reading from Harper Lee's novel *To Kill a Mockingbird* and you don't know that *apoplectic* can describe a person in a fit of rage, then you may not correctly understand how to interpret that passage.

You must, of course, determine the denotation of words like apoplectic—that is, the dictionary definition or explicit meaning. You should also determine the connotations—the implied meanings. The connotations are especially important to an interpreter because they suggest associations that go beyond the dictionary definition. If you were to ask your classmates to define love, you would have as many different definitions as you have classmates. The same is true for poets writing of love; some will say love is affection, some, an affliction.

To make sure you understand the meaning of a selection, try paraphrasing it. If you can put the ideas of the work into your own words, then you are off to a good start in understanding what the author is trying to say to you. These "author messages" or central ideas in a literary work are the **themes** that you must make clear in your interpretation. In *To Kill a Mockingbird,* for example, an important theme is that to understand a person you must climb in that person's skin and walk around in it. Knowing this theme helps you to make choices in interpreting the denotative and the connotative meanings of all the words.

Feeling

Dylan Thomas

After you have analyzed the connotative meanings of the words in your selection, you will begin to understand not only the themes of the work but also the feelings the author is trying to arouse. A particular feeling in a work is often described as the **mood.** The mood is the emotional tone created by the work.

Just as your moods change throughout the day, however, so does the emotional tone of any work of literature. Consider the Dylan Thomas poem "Do not go gentle into that good night":

COMMUNICATION **Break down**

Public Clutterance . . .

Peggy Noonan, a speechwriter for former President Ronald Reagan, explains the importance of oral interpretation in delivering any public speech:

The irony of modern speeches is that as our ability to disseminate them has exploded (an American president can speak live not only to America but to Europe, to most of the world), their quality has declined.

Why? Lots of reasons, including that we as a nation no longer learn the rhythms of public utterance from Shakespeare and the Bible. When young Lincoln was sprawled in front of the fireplace reading *Julius Caesar*—"Th' abuse of greatness is, when it disjoins remorse from power"—he was, unconsciously, learning to be a poet. You say, "That was Lincoln, not the common man." But the common man was flocking to the docks to get the latest installment of Dickens off the ship from England.

Source: Excerpted from *What I Saw at the Revolution* by Peggy Noonan (New York: Random House, 1990).

Questions

1. Do you agree with Peggy Noonan that the quality of "public utterance" has declined in this country?
2. Should students be required to read aloud from Shakespeare, the Bible, and Dickens to learn the rhythms of language?

Do not go gentle into that good night,
Old age should burn and rave at close of day;
Rage, rage against the dying of the light.

Though wise men at their end know dark is right,
Because their words had forked no lightning they
Do not go gentle into that good night.

Good men, the last wave by, crying how bright
Their frail deeds might have danced in a green
bay,
Rage, rage against the dying of the light.

Wild men who caught and sang the sun in flight,
And learn, too late, they grieved it on its way,
Do not go gentle into that good night.

Grave men, near death, who see the blinding
sight
Blind eyes could blaze like meteors and be gay,
Rage, rage against the dying of the light.

And you, my father, there on the sad height,
Curse, bless, me now with your fierce tears, I
pray.
Do not go gentle into that good night.
Rage, rage against the dying of the light.

What is the general mood of the Thomas poem? If you knew that Thomas was angry that his father had given up the will to live, do you think it would make a difference in your interpretation? Do you think Thomas admires the "wild men" who are described in the poem? If you do, then you must use your voice to show the mood changing from anger to admiration and back to anger again.

Interpreting Prose

When you tell a personal story, you are the narrator of the events that you relate. In interpreting a work of prose, however, you need to analyze the form of the written narration to determine who is the narrator. The form of the narration tells you who is telling the story, whom that person is telling the story to, what relationship that person has to the events described, and how much knowledge that person has of those events.

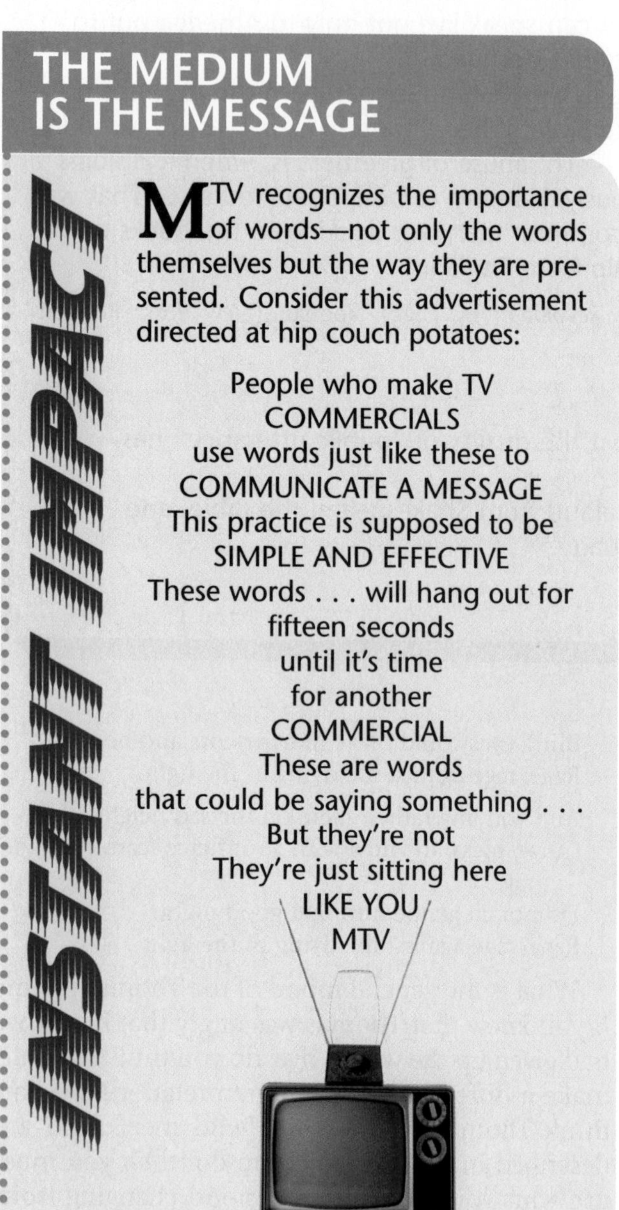

THE MEDIUM IS THE MESSAGE

INSTANT IMPACT

MTV recognizes the importance of words—not only the words themselves but the way they are presented. Consider this advertisement directed at hip couch potatoes:

People who make TV
COMMERCIALS
use words just like these to
COMMUNICATE A MESSAGE
This practice is supposed to be
SIMPLE AND EFFECTIVE
These words . . . will hang out for
fifteen seconds
until it's time
for another
COMMERCIAL
These are words
that could be saying something . . .
But they're not
They're just sitting here
LIKE YOU
MTV

Once you have determined who is the fictional speaker (the **persona**), you use your imagination to fill in the details—such as vocal characteristics and facial expressions—necessary to re-create that speaker, that "voice," in the minds of the listeners.

The outlook from which the events in a novel or short story are related, called the point of view, varies from story to story and within stories. Many authors write in the **first person,** using *I* to identify the narrator. Others prefer the **third person,** describing characters as *he* or *she.* Occasionally, you will find a work written in the **second person,** in which the author addresses *you* (for example, this sentence and this textbook). Let's look at each of these more closely.

Author Toni Morrison's writing could provide you with excellent material for interpreting prose.

First-Person Narrations ...

In a first-person narration—a story whose narrator is *I*—the author may be using a variety of approaches. One popular form of first-person narration is the **dramatic monologue.** A dramatic monologue presents a single character speaking. Although you may associate this approach with the theater, authors of prose use the technique when they want you to overhear somebody speaking aloud to another person. Another form of first-person narration is the **interior monologue.** Here, the author has the narrator speaking to himself or herself. We hear the narrator's thoughts. Consider this passage from Tom McAfee's short story "This Is My Living Room."

> My Living Room
>
> It ain't big but big enough for me and my family—my wife Rosie setting over there reading recipes in the *Birmingham News* and my two girls Ellen Jean and Martha Kay watching the TV. I am sitting here holding *Life* magazine in my lap. I get *Life,* the *News,* and *Christian Living.* I read a lot, the newspaper everyday from cover to cover. I don't just look at the pictures in *Life.* I read what's under them and the stories.

Does this image look like "My Living Room" to you? Why or why not?

Actor Robin Williams gives voice to a multitude of characters.

Read the McAfee selection again, and ask yourself these questions: What does the narrator look like? How is he dressed? Where does he live? What kind of accent might he have? How old is he? How does the narrator feel about his wife and children? Is he "happy" with his life? Answering these kinds of questions will help you decide how to portray this narrator in your interpretation.

Third-Person Narrations ... In a third-person narration, the narrator is not *I*—the person to whom the story is happening—but an observer of the action. Third person can allow the narrator to tell the story through the eyes of more than one character. Typically, the narrator is all-knowing—or **omniscient**—and moves freely into and out of the minds of various characters. As an example, consider this passage from Flannery O'Connor's short story "A Good Man Is Hard to Find":

> The grandmother didn't want to go to Florida. She wanted to visit some of her connections in east Tennessee and she was seizing at every chance to change Bailey's mind. "Now look here, Bailey," she said, "see here, read this . . . Here this fellow that calls himself The Misfit is aloose from the Federal Pen and headed toward Florida and you read here what it says he did to these people. Just you read it."

Read this selection again, asking yourself the same kinds of questions that you answered for the McAfee passage. Note that a significant difference exists between the McAfee and O'Connor stories. As you interpret the McAfee story, you must portray one character: the "I." In the O'Connor story, however, you have two characters: the author's omniscient narrator's "voice" and the grandmother's "voice." The challenge for you as an interpreter is to create two unique voices for these characters. The grandmother must talk like this specific grandmother would talk. Furthermore, the narrator must sound different from the grandmother.

Interpreting Poetry

As you interpret prose or poetry, you need to be especially sensitive to the author's intent. Determining the author's intent is crucial, because you must always respect the integrity of the words in the work. Understanding some technical terms—*meter, rhythm, rhyme, imagery*—will help you determine the author's intent in poetry.

Meter ... When you hear the word **meter,** you probably think of a unit of measurement. Meter, in poetry, is also a way of measuring. Instead of measuring distance, though, meter measures the rhythm in a line of poetry. The pattern of this rhythm is determined by what syllables you stress in the words that make up the line.

You place stress on particular syllables based on your knowledge of proper pronunciation and on your interpretation of the poem. You can look up proper pronunciation in any dictionary, but your understanding of the poem is up to you. You should never sacrifice meaning as you vocalize the meter, but you should also never lose sight of the pattern provided by the poet. As an interpreter, you must balance these two factors, meaning and pattern.

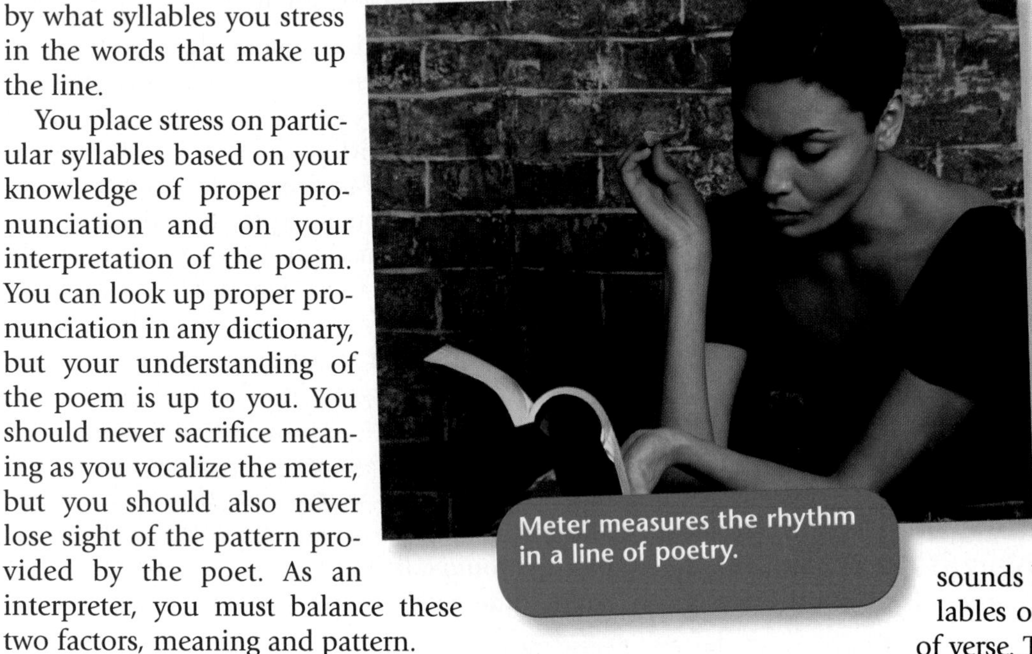

Meter measures the rhythm in a line of poetry.

Remember that the choices you make about meter do make a difference. For example, rapid, regular recurrence of stress often suggests increased tension, and a slower repetition of stress suggests a more *introspective* mood.

Rhythm ... In poetry, **rhythm** is defined as the flow of stressed and unstressed syllables. The effect of rhythm on meaning should be your primary concern as a reader. Listeners can only concentrate on a given idea for a brief period of time. Therefore, you must pace your reading to allow the listener to relax occasionally and reflect on what has been said.

The poet may use pauses within a line to establish a rhythm that is like a melody. Note the breaks created by Shakespeare's use of commas in the lines that follow. Shakespeare was a master of pauses, those "sounds of silence."

It was a lover and his lass,
With a hey, and a ho, and a hey nonino,
That o'er the green corn-field did pass
In the spring time, the only pretty ring time,
When birds do sing, hey ding a ding, ding;
Sweet lovers love the spring.

Read the poem again as if there were no commas in the middles of lines 2, 4, and 5. Do not pause at all as you read these lines. Do you hear how the poem's rhythm has been lost? As an oral interpreter, you must always be aware of the rhythm of any literature that you perform.

Rhyme ... In a poem **rhyme** is a repetition of sounds between words or syllables or the endings of lines of verse. This repetition pleases the ear; author M. H. Abrams described the effect as the "delight given by the expected but variable end chime." You, as an oral interpreter, must be careful not to change this "delight" into a singsong pattern of delivery that distracts from the effectiveness of your reading. To ensure that the rhyme scheme doesn't overwhelm the listeners, experienced interpreters often pause in unexpected places and emphasize words that are not at the ends of lines. In analyzing different poems, you have to decide in each case how to maintain control over the rhyme of the work, as well as the

WORDS FROM THE WORKPLACE

Melissa Hendrix
TV News Co-Anchor

Q: *As a news anchor, how important are communication skills?*

A: Extremely, especially in the newsroom, where you are not only presenting the story to the viewing public, but also communicating with reporters, interviewees, the camera crew, and other staff. Communication is also very important among the staff to ensure that the facts of the story are correct, and that the presentation of those facts is not misleading or contradictory.

Q: *On an average day, how many news items come into the newsroom?*

A: A few hundred stories come into the newsroom each day. We prioritize the stories by local news, state news, national news, and international news. We choose the stories to be presented according to the number of people who will be affected by the news item.

Q: *How are you able to condense news items down to a given time frame for presentation?*

A: A typical news story gets about 25 to 30 seconds of air time. We condense the story to include "Who, What, Why, and Where," without overloading the viewer with too much information, which can confuse them. We must present the facts as succinctly as possible, without losing the importance of the story. If we need more time for a story, we generally give it to a reporter who will package the item in a one- to two-minute segment.

Q: *How do your communication skills help when interpreting and presenting some of the harder stories?*

A: I believe that viewers appreciate sincerity when the news is reported. There is a great difference between just reading the news to the viewers, and presenting the story in a sincere manner. As an anchor, you should truly care about each story you present!

rhythm and meter, to avoid a mechanical or predictable pattern that takes away from the audience's enjoyment of your performance.

Let's consider how to do this by examining the poem "Success Is Counted Sweetest," by Emily Dickinson. The poem describes how those who lose at something understand better what it means to win than those who are the victors. Perhaps you know this truth already.

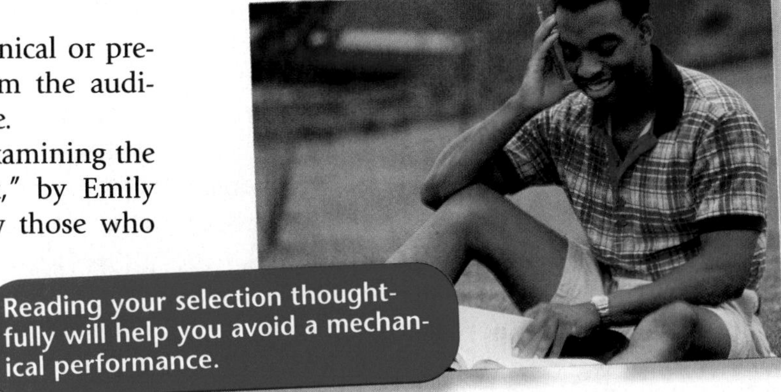

Reading your selection thoughtfully will help you avoid a mechanical performance.

Success is counted sweetest
By those who ne'er succeed.
To comprehend a *nectar*
Requires sorest need.

Not one of all the purple host
Who took the flag today
Can tell the definition,
So clear of victory.

As he, defeated—dying—
On whose forbidden ear
The distant strains of triumph
Burst agonized and clear!

Note how Dickinson rhymes the second and fourth lines in each stanza—for example, *succeed* and *need* in the first stanza. One way that you might avoid a too-strong, singsong pattern in your delivery of the first stanza would be to give special emphasis to the words *ne'er* and *comprehend.* You might also briefly pause before delivering each of these words. In addition, you might try pausing after *requires* rather than *nectar.* A final suggestion: When you read the word *need,* lower your pitch slightly and say the word quietly. By doing so, you will deemphasize the rhyme and also suggest the mood of the poem.

If you study the second stanza, you will find an imperfect rhyme in the second and fourth lines: *today* and *victory.* We think of Dickinson as a "modern" poet, and one of the reasons is her willingness to subordinate rhyme to meaning. As an oral interpreter, you have to be willing to make those same artistic choices.

Imagery ... As you may recall from Chapter 11, the word imagery refers to language that creates mental pictures. These pictures differ in the minds of the reader and the listener. An image creates in each person an association with some real-life experience that is unique to that person. For example, the image of a bicycle in a poem may remind you of your first trip to the grocery store alone. The person sitting next to you may think, instead, of crashing into the neighbor's new car. This recalling of what we have previously experienced gives the poetry (or prose) its emotional power.

As an oral interpreter, you should pay special attention to a writer's use of imagery. In Grace Butcher's poem "On Driving Behind a School Bus for Mentally Retarded Children," the poet compares the children to flowers. This metaphor is used throughout the poem to illustrate the unique challenges faced by the children. In reading this work aloud, you must use your voice creatively to suggest the meaning and feeling of the poet's metaphor.

Full deep green
bloom-fallen spring
here outside,
for us.

They,
like winter-covered
crocuses:
strange bright
beauty
peeping through
snow that never
melts—

(How quietly,
how quietly,
the bus.)

These flowers have no fragrance.
They move to an eerie wind
I cannot feel.

They rise, with petals fully
opened,
from a twisted seed
and neither grow
nor wither.

They will be taught
the colors of their names.

Interpreting Drama

When you see a play performed on stage, the actors attempt to become the characters portrayed. The goal of the actor is to make the performance as close to real life as possible. In contrast, the reader in traditional oral interpretation of drama tries to suggest those characters. For example, a reader, at a dramatic moment in the script, might have tears welling up in his eyes. The actor, to go beyond the mere suggestion of an emotional climax, might have tears streaming down his face.

In contemporary speech competition, "Humorous Interpretation" and "Dramatic Interpretation" are memorized events often described as "acting from the waist up." This description arises from the practice by many competitors of pretending to be the characters in their selections. Some of these performances include extensive use of gestures and actual movement around the room. By taking on the techniques of acting, these speech competitors may no longer be presenting a traditional oral interpretation, but they are creating a powerful union of the two arts.

Recently, "Duo Interpretation" has become a popular competitive event at many tournaments. This event lets two interpreters work as a team, allowing each performer the chance to respond to the genuine emotions and rhythms of another. Rules vary. For example, some tournaments require scripts; others do not.

Regardless of your approach, as an interpreter of drama, you need to help your listeners create a mental image of the characters you are suggesting. You must provide the visual and **auditory** (hearing) clues that will stimulate the imagination of each audience member.

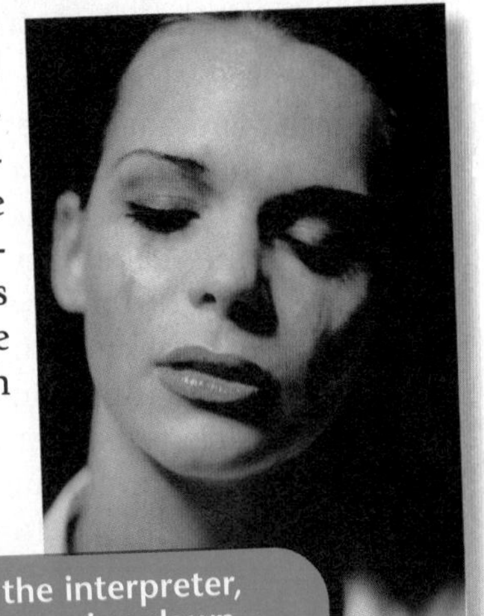

The actor, unlike the interpreter, may have tears streaming down his face.

SECTION 3 REVIEW

Recalling the Facts ...

1. What is the difference between the theme and the tone of a work?
2. Why is imagery important to oral interpretation?

Thinking Critically ...

1. Peggy Noonan argues that the quality of modern speeches has declined because we no longer learn the rhythm of public utterances from Shakespeare and the Bible. If Noonan's assessment is accurate, then what should be done to improve oratory today?

Taking Charge ...

1. Many interpreters read two or more selections built around a theme. This program of reading provides an opportunity to show how different authors approach similar themes. You will find an example of a programmed reading at the end of this chapter. The student chose selections that celebrated the many sounds of poetry that cause the listener to want to "speak like rain" (her theme).

   Now it's your turn. After deciding on a subject—death, friendship, patriotism, or the like—find two to five short poems and formulate a theme that shows the relationships among them.

SECTION 4

Presenting Your Material

Choosing and analyzing material for oral interpretation is only part of your preparation. Next, you have to prepare and practice for the actual performance. Some of the keys to unlocking the mystery of effective presentation involve introducing material, cutting material, developing material, and practicing material.

What type of introduction do you think is appropriate for this scene from *Romeo and Juliet?*

Introducing Your Material

You will need to prepare an introduction for your interpretation. The principles you learned in earlier chapters about writing a good speech introduction still apply here. Some distinctions, though, should be noted.

First, you are responsible for giving your listeners the information they need to understand the selection. Characters need to be identified, relationships explained, and important plot points outlined. You don't want to spoil the story by "giving away the ending," but you don't want your listeners confused either.

A second requirement for an effective introduction is to establish a mood that is consistent with the mood of the selection itself. For example, if you were reading from *Romeo and Juliet,* a Shakespearean tragedy, you probably wouldn't begin by cracking jokes. A humorous introduction, however, might be appropriate for *Romeo and Juliet* if you were going to perform only the scenes with speeches by Juliet's nosy nurse, who provides comic relief in the play.

Finally, keep your introductions brief. If you are allowed five minutes for your entire performance, you shouldn't spend most of that time explaining what you're going to do. Most introductions can be kept to around a minute (or less). Remember, you need only include the information necessary for the audience to share the meaning and feeling of your selection. (For an example, see the student speech at the end of the chapter.)

Cutting Your Material

You may need to cut, or condense, your selection. This may be necessary for several reasons: You may have too much material for the time allowed, certain parts of your selection may be inappropriate, or a particular episode may lessen the overall effect you are seeking. If you are working with a longer short story or a novel, you will usually choose a climactic scene and present only that scene. In that case, when writing the introduction, you will tell the audience what they need to know to understand the scene. Other guidelines that may prove useful include the following:

- Always cut in, not out. In other words, build your cutting around your favorite lines and those lines that you feel are the most important to understanding the selection. If you tried to cut *Gone with the Wind* down to a five-minute presentation by taking out—one by one—the lines you didn't need, you would quickly lose your interest in the project (and your youth). What you should do is pick your favorite scene and highlight those lines you most want to keep (in priority order), as well as those needed to make sense out of the story. As soon as you've highlighted a total of four minutes' worth of lines—stop! Save the extra minute for your introduction.
- Eliminate dialogue tags, the parts of written dialogue that tell us who is speaking. Consider the following example:

  "May I have another chocolate bar?" Jane asked.

  "But you have already had three this morning," Elizabeth replied.

  "Jane asked" and "Elizabeth replied" are dialogue tags. Such tags can usually be cut. However, if it might not be clear who is speaking or if this is the first time a character has spoken in the material you are using, the tags should not be cut.
- In drama, eliminate stage directions (*Elena rises, crosses left*), as well as lines that suggest physical action. For example, suppose in your selection Larry asks Melvin why he is tap-dancing. You have to eliminate that line so that your listeners don't expect you to tap-dance. (Alternatively, you could suggest the movements in some limited way or start taking tap-dancing lessons.)
- Eliminate minor characters that might confuse your listeners.
  - Cut references to events that you do not have time to fully explain.

Eye contact is necessary for effective interpretation.

Developing Your Material

In developing your selection for performance, you need to work on certain skills that will improve your effectiveness as a reader. These delivery skills include eye contact, character placement, characterization, word color, and showmanship.

Eye Contact ... You have already learned about the importance of eye contact. In oral interpretation, how much eye contact is enough? How often should you look up from the script, and when? These questions are a source of great controversy among the teachers of interpretation. Some say that a fifty-fifty balance is appropriate. Others argue for maintaining eye contact with the audience as much as 90 percent of the time. Regardless of your position on this issue, you need to remember two factors: (1) You must look at the script often enough to remind the audience that you are sharing a work of literature. (2) You must not be tied to the script, or the audience will soon tire of staring at the top of your head.

Effective interpreters often use a technique known as **scene setting.** They use their eyes to focus the scene that they are describing on an imaginary stage in front of them. This helps the audience members to see that same scene in their imaginations. When not scene setting, these speakers look into the eyes of individual audience members or at the script.

Character Placement ... If you are portraying various characters, then you must "place" them by looking at a different location for each one. By directing your focus to different locations, you can create the illusion that a number of characters are speaking to each other. Readings of drama require this skill, but prose, too, can necessitate character placement. In prose readings, most interpreters place the narrator directly in front of them, with the rest of the "voices" distributed to the left and to the right. In drama, the most important characters are placed closest to the center, with the minor characters farther to the sides.

Let each characterization reflect the unique qualities of the "voice" for whom you are speaking.

Take care not to place characters too far apart. If the characters are widely separated, the time it will take for you to rotate your head to the proper position will cause you to pause too long between speakers. The effect of these long pauses is similar to what happens in plays when actors do not pick up their lines: The performance drags. It is also important to be consistent in your character placement, or the audience may become confused as to who is speaking.

Characterization ... Look around your classroom. No two of your classmates sound or act the same. Similarly, each character you portray in a selection must be distinct. Each should be characterized by a unique voice, facial expression, and body position.

To create distinctions in voice, some interpreters experiment with a variety of pitch patterns. Some vary the pacing, making the characters speak at different rates of speed. Others try to re-create dialects, the pronunciation that is used in a particular area. Whether or not you use a dialect should depend on your ability to make it convincing. An annoying or distracting characterization damages the integrity of the selection and makes for a disappointing performance.

You should also avoid using a stereotypical voice that lessens the believability of a character. Stereotypical voices usually turn into nothing more than caricatures, comic exaggerations that lack uniqueness. Not everyone from the South talks with a drawl, and not every football lineman plays without a helmet.

Along with vocal distinctions, you should respond with your face and the rest of your body to each word spoken by a character. If a character is happy, the audience should not only hear that happiness in the warmth of your voice but see it in a smiling face and relaxed body as well. Each character and each moment in the script require subtle changes in facial expressiveness and posture. The audience must see you suggest the individual characteristics of each person in the selection in order

Word color and showmanship help you give a convincing interpretation.

to get caught up in the magic of the illusion that these people are real.

Word Color ... You must give each word in your selection its due. Your responsibility is to change written symbols into sound symbols by "coloring" them with your voice. You would not, for example, say "I want to kiss you" and "Please pass the butter" in the same way. You must suggest the denotative and connotative meanings with vocal variety. But how? Experienced interpreters use, in combination or alone, some of the following techniques: pauses of varying lengths before key words, changes in pitch, holding vowels, hitting consonants, manipulating tempo, and unusual or unexpected emphasis.

To see how these techniques can make a significant difference in an interpretation, experiment with them on any literary work included in this chapter. You can change the entire meaning of a particular work by varying your voice in these ways.

Showmanship ... The sense of professionalism that you must have when performing is called showmanship. From the moment you leave your seat until you have returned to your place, you should make it clear that you enjoy the act of sharing literature with an audience. If you mumble misgivings under your breath or seem hesitant at any point, the experience of your listeners is lessened. Care about your material. Care about the people in your audience. Show them.

Practicing Your Material

You need to practice your material by reading it aloud. Silent rehearsal does not allow you to experiment with a variety of vocal approaches. Furthermore, you should try to practice the material exactly as you plan to present it. In the early stages, however, you might want to break the performance down by practicing a few lines at a time. By polishing shorter sections, you won't fall into the trap of simply running through the material to get the practice session over. Memorized material should never sound as if you are merely reciting

Practice reading aloud with a parent or friend.

COMMUNICATION Breakthrough

Against Forgetting

Oral interpretation expresses the unexpressible in terms of the unforgettable. Take Sonia Schreiber Weitz, a Polish survivor of five concentration camps, and author of the book *I Promised I Would Tell,* for example. Sonia travels around the country speaking about her experiences through her poetry. One of the most difficult things for her to talk about is sneaking into her father's barracks to see him one last time before he was taken away on a transport. Audiences are able to understand the emotions she felt, and to never forget them, as she reads her poem "Victory":

Victory

I danced with you that one time only.
How sad you were, how tired, lonely . . .
You knew that they would "take" you soon . . .
So when your bunkmate played a tune
You whispered: "little one, let us dance,
We may not have another chance."

To grasp this moment . . . sense the mood;
Your arms about me felt so good . . .
The ugly barracks disappeared
There was no hunger . . . and no fear.
Oh what a sight, just you and I,
My lovely father (once big and strong)
And me, a child . . . condemned to die.

I thought how long
Before the song
Must end

There are no tools
To measure love
And only fools

Would fail
To scale
Your victory

In 1945, while Weitz was in Auschwitz, Poland, the Nazis began evacuating the camps. Weitz was among the walking dead who participated in the final march. She composed the following poem in her head while marching.

Death March

A night . . . A storm . . .
Their blood still warm,
Soaking into the snow.
Their bodies recoil
Upon frozen soil,
Of pain, that whips.
Their lifeless lips belie this final hell.
At the break of dawn
They barely moan,
A silent: "Sh'mah-Israel"

Source: *Facing History and Ourselves: I Promised I Would Tell,* Sonia Schreiber Weitz (National Foundation, 1993). Reprinted with the permission of the publisher.

Questions

1. Do you ever find it easier to write about something than to talk about it?
2. How might the reading of poems make the telling of horrifying experiences more "unforgettable"?

the words from rote memory. You must make the material seem fresh, as if you were performing it for the first time. You must seem to be thinking as the character you are portraying. This quality is necessary for a believable reading.

Try tape-recording your practice and listening to it several times to check word color, articulation, pronunciation, pacing, and use of pauses and emphasis. It is important that you have absolutely crisp, clear vocalization. Some interpreters find it helpful to mark manuscripts as a reminder of when to pause and which words to emphasize. Whether you mark your manuscript or not, you should spend the time necessary to become completely familiar with your material. In other words, you should look down at your manuscript because you choose to, not because you have to. Avoid looking down on words: The up-and-down movement of your head should come between words so as not to create motion that will distract from giving each word its full worth.

These students are portraying Orville and Wilbur Wright in a Reader's Theater performance. Do they appear to be enhancing the story?

In using a manuscript, be careful not to wave it around as you gesture. The manuscript should remain still at all times. Furthermore, do not hold it too low. If you hold it too low, you will have the tendency to drop your head too far as you struggle to see the words on the page. A final suggestion: Rather than reading from a book, most interpreters photocopy or type up their material. They then cut and paste the sections they are going to read onto sheets of paper and place them in a binder.

Reader's Theater

Group reading of literature offers the participants the opportunity to create "theater of the mind." In group reading, most of the action takes place in the imaginations of audience members. Typically, the readers "suggest" movement rather than actually move as actors do. Group reading sometimes takes the form of Reader's Theater. Although definitions vary, Reader's Theater generally involves two or more interpreters sharing an oral reading with an audience.

The sharing process in Reader's Theater includes vocal and physical suggestion as well as the elements of staging. Staging is usually minimal, but scenery, lighting, costuming, and makeup have been successfully used in some productions. The emphasis in staging choices should be determined by whether the meaning of the literature is made clearer or not. Staging should always enhance the literature.

Other common characteristics of Reader's Theater include the following:

- A narrator who introduces the different portions of the program and provides transitions between them
- **Offstage focus**—a technique by which the readers use scripts and envision the scene out in the audience

Remember, the primary concern in Reader's Theater is intensifying the **aural** appeal of the performance—that is, its appeal to the sense of hearing.

SECTION 4 REVIEW

Recalling the Facts ...

1. Explain the five guidelines for cutting material.
2. Why is showmanship important?
3. What is offstage focus?

Thinking Critically ...

1. A "duo interp" team from Florida performed an excerpt from the taped conversation of Monica Lewinsky and Linda Tripp. The team consisted of two boys parodying these women in highly unflattering ways. Are there limits to how real people should be portrayed? What are those limits?

Taking Charge ...

1. A successful oral interpreter creates an environment for understanding the selection shared. This introduction to the reading not only should be appropriate but also should demonstrate the imagination of the performer.

   If you look in a mirror and raise one hand, which hand are you really raising in your mirror image? Joyce Carol Oates poses this question in her poem "Love Letter, with Static Interference from Einstein's Brain." Perhaps Oates borrowed this mirror *motif* from a story about Lewis Carroll reported in the London *Times* on January 22, 1932. According to this story, Carroll asked his cousin Alice Raikes in which hand she held an orange. Alice replied, "The right." So Carroll asked the young girl to stand before a mirror and tell him in which hand she now held the orange. And Alice replied, "The left." For you see, in a mirror all asymmetrical objects go the other way. So let us go the other way . . . through the looking glass . . . that is poetry. We begin our journey with an excerpt from Ishmael Reed's "beware: do not read this poem."

   tonite, thriller was
   abt an ol woman, so vain she
   surrounded herself w/ many mirrors

   it got so bad that finally she
   locked herself indoors & her
   whole life became the mirrors
   one day the villagers broke
   into her house, but she was too
   swift for them, she disappeared into a
   mirror . . .
   the hunger of this poem is legendary
   it has taken in many victims
   back off from this poem
   it has drawn in yr feet
   back off from this poem
   it has drawn in yr legs . . .

   it is a greedy mirror
   you are into this poem . from the waist
   down

   nobody can hear you can they?
   this poem has had you up to here belch
   this poem ain't got no manners
   you cant call out from this poem . . .
   do not resist this poem . . .
   relax now & go w/this poem
   this poem is the reader & the
   reader this poem

   statistic: the us bureau of missing persons
   reports
   that in 1968 over 100,000 people
   disappeared
   leaving no solid clues
   nor trace only
   a space in the lives of their friends

   Now it's your turn. Choose a short poem and write an imaginative introduction for it. Share both your introduction and the poem in a performance for the class.

STUDENT WORK

Speak Like Rain *by Sharahn McClung*

Sharahn McClung was the 1991 Catholic Forensic League high school national champion in oral interpretation of prose and poetry. Her poetry program consisted of five poems unified by the theme "speak like rain."

Good morning, daddy!
Ain't you heard
The boogie-woogie rumble
Of a dream deferred?

Listen closely:
You'll hear their feet
Beating out and beating out a—

You think
It's a happy beat?

Listen to it closely:
Ain't you heard
something underneath
like a—

What did I say?

Sure,
I'm happy!
Take it away!

Hey, pop!
Re-bob!
Mop!

Y-e-a-h!

For Langston Hughes, the "yeah" in his poem "Dream Boogie" is an affirmation of life. The knowing that no matter how many dreams may be deferred, there is still the possibility, the hope for a happy beat. And we hear this happy beat from the playgrounds in Harlem to the plantations of East Africa.

Isak Dinesen, who spent part of her life on a plantation in Kenya, once observed how Kikuyu tribesfolk reacted to their first hearing of rhymed verse. Although they had a strong sense of rhythm, they knew nothing of verse. That is, until they were sent to missionary schools. "On Reading Poems to a Senior Class at South High," by D. C. Berry:

Before
I opened my mouth
I noticed them sitting there
as orderly as frozen fish
in a package.

Slowly water began to fill the room
though I did not notice it
till it reached my ears

and then I heard the sounds
of fish in an aquarium

and I knew that though I had
tried to drown them
with my words
that they had only opened up
like gills for them
and let me in.

Together we swam around the room
like thirty tails whacking words
till the bell rang
puncturing
a hole in the door
where we all leaked out

They went to another class
I suppose and I home
where Queen Elizabeth
my cat met me
and licked my fins
till they were hands again.

To amuse herself one evening, Isak Dinesen spoke to the tribesfolk in Swahili verse. "Ngumbe na-pende chumbe, Malaya-mbaya. Wakamba na-kula mamba." The meaning of the poetry was of no consequence to the tribesman . . . only the sounds. "Jabberwocky" by Lewis Carroll:

'Twas brillig, and the slithy toves
  Did gyre and gimble in the wabe;

All mimsy were the borogoves,
And the mome raths outgrabe.

"Beware the Jabberwock, my son!
The jaws that bite, the claws that catch!
Beware the Jubjub bird, and shun
The frumious Bandersnatch!"

He took his vorpal sword in hand;
Long time the manxome foe he sought—
So rested he by the Tumtum tree,
And stood awhile in thought.

And, as in uffish thought he stood,
The Jabberwock, with eyes of flame,
Came whiffling through the tulgey wood,
And burbled as it came!

One, two! One, two! And through and through
The vorbal blade went snicker-snack!
He left it dead, and with its head
He went galumphing back.

Isak Dinesen discovered that the tribesfolk would wait for the rhyme and laugh at it when it came. When she tried to get them to finish a poem she had begun, they would not. They turned their heads away. "Cracked Record Blues" by Kenneth Fearing:

If you watch it long enough you can see the clock move,
If you try hard enough you can hold a little water in the palm of your hand,
If you listen once or twice you know it's not the needle, or the tune, but a crack in the record when sometimes a phonograph falters and repeats, and repeats, and repeats, and repeats—

And if you think about it long enough, long enough, long enough, long enough then everything is simple and you can understand the times,
You can see for yourself that the Hudson still flows, that the seasons change as ever, that love is always love,
Words still have a meaning, still clear and still the same;
You can count upon your fingers that two plus two still equals, still equals, still equals, still equals—

There is nothing in this world that should bother the mind.

Because the mind is a common sense affair filled with common sense answers to common sense facts,
It can add up, can add up, can add up, can add up earthquakes and subtract them from fires,
It can bisect an atom or analyze the planets—
All it has to do is to, do is to, do is to, do is to start at the beginning and continue to the end.

Dinesen recalled that as the tribesfolk became used to the idea of poetry, they begged: "Speak again. Speak like rain." Although Dinesen did not know why they thought verse to be like rain, she believed it to be an expression of applause. For, in Africa, rain was always longed for and welcomed. "Jazz Fantasia" by Carl Sandburg:

Drum on your drums, batter on your banjoes, sob on the long cool winding saxophones.
Go to it, O jazzmen.
Sling your knuckles on the bottoms of the happy tin pans, let your trombones ooze, and go husha-husha-hush with the slippery sand-paper.

Moan like an autumn wind high in the lonesome treetops, moan soft like you wanted somebody terrible, cry like a racing car slipping away from a motorcycle cop, bang-bang! you jazzmen, bang altogether drums, traps, banjoes, horns, tin cans—make two people fight on the top of a stairway and scratch each other's eyes in a clinch tumbling down the stairs.

Can the rough stuff . . . now a Mississippi steamboat pushes up the night river with a hoo-hoo-hoo-oo . . . and the green lanterns calling to the high soft stars . . . a red moon rides on the humps of the low river hills . . . go to it, O jazzmen.

So let us always give this gift to each other, to speak like rain.

CHAPTER 16 Review and Enrichment...

Looking Back

Listed below are the major ideas discussed in this chapter.

- The oral tradition is as old as human interaction.
- Ancient Greece is the birthplace of the art of interpretation.
- When selecting material to read, you should consider the quality of the literature, the occasion, and the desires of the audience.
- To interpret a selection, you must analyze the meaning and feeling of the material.
- As an interpreter of prose, you must analyze the narration to determine the point of view.
- In interpreting poetry, you must control the meter, rhythm, rhyme, and imagery in the work.
- When interpreting drama, you must help the listeners create a mental image of the characters you are suggesting.
- Your introduction should give the listeners the information they need to understand the selection.
- You may need to cut your selection when you have too much material, when certain sections are inappropriate, or when a particular episode lessens the overall effect.
- Effective presentation requires mastery of these techniques: eye contact, character placement, characterization, word color, and showmanship.
- Tape-recording your practice sessions can help you evaluate your progress as you prepare for a performance.
- Reader's Theater offers the participants the opportunity to create "theater of the mind."

Speech Vocabulary

Match the speech term on the left with the appropriate description on the right.

1. rhapsodes
2. persona
3. anthologies
4. mood
5. rhythm
6. meter
7. aural
8. scene setting
9. omniscient

a. narrator
b. measures rhythm
c. wandering minstrel
d. all-knowing
e. using an imaginary stage
f. books that include literary works by subject matter
g. related to sense of hearing
h. flow of stressed and unstressed syllables
i. emotional tone

CHAPTER 16 Review and Enrichment...

General Vocabulary

Use a dictionary to define the following terms and then use each in a sentence.

enhanced
mimic
minstrel
recitation
spellbound
paraphernalia
faltering
compelling
tedium
apoplectic
introspective
nectar
motif

To Remember

Answer the following based on your reading of the chapter.

1. Impersonating a familiar voice is not interpretation but ______________.
2. Poetry reading was popular during the ______________ Age in Rome.
3. Name three things you should consider in selecting material for oral interpretation.
4. The ______________ is the emotional tone that predominates in a selection.
5. A story in which the narrator uses "I" is written in ______________ person.
6. When an author moves freely into and out of the minds of the characters, the story is probably written in ______________ person.
7. Rhyme is a repetition of ______________.
8. When readers use their eyes to place what they are describing on an imaginary stage, they are using a technique known as ______________.
9. ______________ refers to the sense of professionalism you have when performing.
10. Name three guidelines that you should use in cutting, or condensing, material.

To Do

1. Young children are a responsive audience with immediate and honest feedback. Arrange to visit an elementary school to read to the children. After reading an appropriate selection, ask the children to critique your effort.
2. Record yourself reading a brief poem. Evaluate your interpretation for word color, pacing, articulation, pronunciation, and use of pauses and emphasis.

To Talk About

1. When a news anchor reads a story about the damage caused by an earthquake, is that oral interpretation? Why or why not?
2. What is suitable material for oral interpretation? The list of ingredients on a cereal box? The telephone book? Instruction manuals? Explain.
3. If you were going to read a Dr. Seuss book to children, which one would you choose? Why?

To Write About

1. Write a poem consisting of nonsense words that suggest meaning by the sounds they create. For inspiration, you might refer to "Jabberwocky" by Lewis Carroll beginning on page 423.
2. Write a one-page essay discussing why parents should be skilled at oral interpretation.
3. Choose a country in which you are interested. Research and write a brief description of the oral tradition in that nation.

Related Speech Topics

Professional storytellers
Learning dialects
Norse oral literature
Celtic oral literature
The history of Reader's Theater
Your favorite poet

CHAPTER 17

SPEECHES FOR SPECIAL OCCASIONS

"I am the most spontaneous speaker in the world because every word, every gesture, and every retort has been carefully rehearsed."

–George Bernard Shaw

Learning Objectives

After completing this chapter, you will be able to do the following.

- Define the specific purposes of several special occasion speeches.
- Discuss the characteristics of these speeches.
- Describe some of the more popular contest speeches.

Chapter Outline

Following are the main sections in this chapter.

1. Courtesy Speeches
2. Ceremonial Speeches
3. Contest Speeches

New Speech Terms

In this chapter, you will learn the meanings of the speech terms listed below.

speech of presentation
speech of acceptance
after-dinner speech
commencement address
commemorative speech
testimonial speech
eulogy
original oratory
dramatic interpretation
humorous interpretation

General Vocabulary

Expanding your general vocabulary will help you become a more effective communicator. Listed below are some words appearing in this chapter that you should make part of your everyday vocabulary.

reiterate
eloquent
transformation
miffed
procession
hoke
dignitary
converse
evoking
suffice
combustion
refrain

Looking AHEAD

Although the primary purpose of most special occasion speeches is not to inform or persuade, they do require the same fundamentals of public speaking, the same analyzing of purpose. In this chapter, you will learn to present three general types of special occasion speeches: courtesy, ceremonial, and contest speeches.

Introduction

When *Sesame Street*'s Kermit the Frog won an honorary degree from Southampton College, Samantha Chie, a marine biology major, said, "Now we have a sock talking at our commencement. It's kind of upsetting." Clearly, Chie was not impressed by Kermit's "doctorate of amphibious letters."

Although you may never upset people as a commencement speaker, you will be called upon someday to speak at a public or business gathering. Special occasion speeches are part of our everyday lives. These speeches are special because they focus on particular situations: an address given at a school assembly, a testimonial speech offered at an awards banquet, a eulogy spoken by a friend at a funeral. What follows will help you learn how not to upset people.

Commencement speeches are just one type of special occasion speeches.

SECTION 1 Courtesy Speeches

You present a courtesy speech to fulfill certain social customs. If you need to say "thank you," for example, you may find yourself preparing a speech of acceptance. Typical courtesy speeches include introduction, presentation, acceptance, and after-dinner speeches.

Introductions

If you have had the uncomfortable experience of being the new kid in school, then you know the need for successful introductions. Waiting to make friends can be one of the loneliest periods in a person's life. You find yourself wondering if you will be accepted. You worry about what they think of you, what they might be saying.

Although more formal than making friends in a new school, speeches of introduction matter in the same way because they break down the barriers between people. Introductory speeches serve two functions: to make the audience want to hear the speaker and to make the speaker want to address the audience. You need to achieve these goals in only a minute or two.

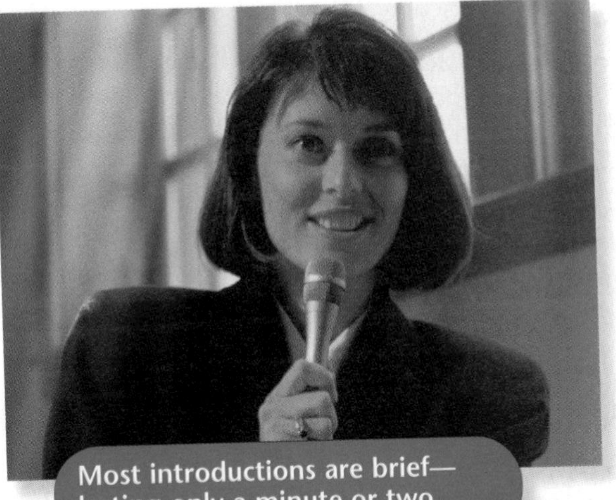

Most introductions are brief—lasting only a minute or two.

Because most speeches of introduction are brief, they must be well planned. You should plan to do some or all of the following in your speech:

- Refer to the occasion that has brought the audience together.
- Name the speaker (mention the name again at the end of the introduction).
- Build enthusiasm by relating information about the qualifications of the speaker.
- Share information about the subject to heighten interest, if the speaker wishes you to.
- Explain why this speaker is to give this talk to this audience at this time.
- Conclude by welcoming the speaker to the microphone or the podium.

Successful writers of introductions are usually fans of Mark Twain. Why? Twain understood one factor that contributes to a memorable speech—humor. If you can combine humor with a meaningful message, then your chances for writing an effective introduction are greatly increased. Consider the following excerpt from one of Twain's many humorous speeches of introduction.

> I see I am advertised to introduce the speaker of the evening. . . . As a pure citizen, I respect him; as a personal friend for years, I have the warmest regard for him; as a neighbor whose vegetable garden adjoins mine, why—why, I watch him. That's nothing; we all do that with any neighbor.
>
> General Hawley keeps his promises not only in private but in public. . . . He is broad-souled, generous, noble, liberal, alive to his moral and religious responsibilities. Whenever the contribution box was passed, I never knew him to take out a cent. He is a square, true, honest man in politics, and I must say he occupies a mighty lonesome position. . . . He is an American of Americans. Would we had more such men! So broad, so bountiful is his character that he never turned a tramp empty handed from his door, but always gave him a letter of introduction to me. . . .

COMMUNICATION **Break***through*

Working for Peanuts

Charles Schulz, who created the beloved cartoon strip "Peanuts," was once invited to give a speech to a group of 400 exceptional high school students. This special occasion provided Schulz an opportunity to offer advice that might be useful to these young people. He has said that he had great difficulty in coming up with an appropriate subject. After much soul-searching, he decided against discussing the need for dedication and hard work. He chose, instead, to break away from what he considered the trite recommendations he suspected the students had heard so many times before.

In his book *You Don't Look 35, Charlie Brown!,* Schulz shared what he said in this special occasion speech.

"I am not one to give advice," he said, "and always hesitated to do so with my own children, but tonight I am going to give you some advice that is very important. . . ." He then told them to go home and begin asking questions of their parents, to stop saying things to their parents, and instead begin asking things about their parents' pasts that demonstrate a real interest, and pursue the questioning. "Don't stop until you have learned something about your father's first job or your mother's early dreams. It will take energy, but it will be infinitely worthwhile, and it must be done now. It must be done before it is too late."

Source: Charles M. Schulz, *You Don't Look 35, Charlie Brown!* (New York: Henry Holt and Company, 1997).

Questions

1. Do you believe that this advice from Charles Schulz is still very important?
2. What would you say if you had the opportunity to speak to a group of high school students on a subject of your choosing?

Pure, honest, incorruptible, that is Joe Hawley. Such a man in politics is like a bottle of perfumery in a glue factory—it may modify the stench if it doesn't destroy it. And now, in speaking thus highly of the speaker of the evening, I haven't said any more of him than I would say of myself. Ladies and Gentlemen, this is General Hawley.

Source: Albert Bigelow Paine, *Mark Twain: A Biography,* Harper and Brothers: 1940, Dora L. Paine

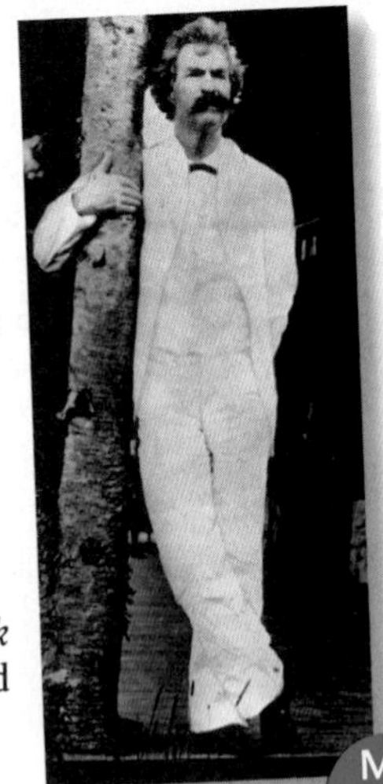

Mark Twain was a brilliant satirist.

Twain's introduction takes a few satirical swipes at General Hawley, which is fine, but you must be careful not to embarrass the person you are introducing. Hawley was a public figure and a personal friend; therefore, Twain could take certain liberties in this particular case. Good judgment is always a must.

Here are a few reminders for making a successful introductory speech: Check the pronunciation of all words, including the speaker's name; verify the accuracy of all biographical and other information; analyze the audience's expectations.

Reprinted with special permission of King Features Syndicate.

Speeches of Presentation

When a person receives a gift or award, a **speech of presentation** is needed. The presentation speech is usually brief. Of course, the length depends on the formality of the occasion. Typically, when you give a speech of presentation, you are speaking on behalf of some group, and you should reflect the shared feelings of that group. You can focus those feelings by choosing words that give deeper meaning to the circumstances that surround this special occasion. For example, the audience's expectations at a retirement party vary significantly from those at the annual Motion Picture Academy Awards (Oscar) ceremony. Certain guidelines, however, generally apply.

Does this girl look like she could be the "Most Valuable Player" described in the text?

1. State the person's name early in the presentation (unless building suspense is appropriate).
2. Explain the award's significance as a symbol of the group's esteem.
3. Explain how the person was selected for the award.
4. Highlight what makes this person unique. Use anecdotal information and a brief list of achievements.
5. Hand the award to the recipient.

Here is an example of a typical speech of presentation. The speech was given by a student to honor her teammate who was about to receive the Most Valuable Player award on their high school golf team.

No one is more deserving of Most Valuable Player recognition than Alysen. True, she is only a sophomore, but she led the team as if she were our most experienced golfer. If you've ever played a round of golf with her, you know what I mean by "led." In any foursome, she always seemed to be ten paces in front of everyone else, and you felt like you had to run to keep up.

And this year, no one was able to keep up with her or with her success. As a district medalist and a top ten finisher in the state championship, Alysen capped what was a remarkable year in competition. But speaking on behalf of her teammates, we are most proud of Alysen for the character she demonstrated both in victory and defeat. We voted her this honor because of that character. If she made a birdie or if she missed a three-foot putt, there was always a smile for everyone, a joy in the simple playing of the game.

As Will Rogers once observed, "It is great to be great, but it is greater to be human." So this Most Valuable Player award is presented to Alysen—a great human being.

Speeches of Acceptance

Jack Benny, on accepting an award, once ad-libbed, "I don't deserve this, but then, I have arthritis and I don't deserve that either." Even though recipients of awards or gifts usually have some advance notice, a **speech of acceptance** is most often, at least in part, impromptu (impromptu speaking was discussed in Chapters 12 and 15). Even if you are able to prepare your acceptance speech, part of it will need to be impromptu because you will need to tailor your remarks to what was said by the presenter. The remarks that you make serve a double purpose: to thank the people who are presenting the award or gift and to give credit to those people who helped you earn this recognition. The formality of the situation should guide you in preparation, but generally you should consider the following:

Andre Braugher was brief, sincere, and direct when thanking presenter Halle Berry and others as he received his "Outstanding Lead Actor" Emmy award.

1. Be brief, sincere, and direct.
2. Thank the group for the award.
3. Discuss the importance of the award to you.
4. Thank others who helped you win the award—minimize your worth, praise the contributions of your supporters.
5. *Reiterate* your appreciation.

If you have ever been a member of a team that lost the big game, then you can appreciate Adlai Stevenson's famous concession speech—a speech in which he accepts not an award but defeat. In that speech, he compares himself to a boy who has stubbed his toe in the dark—"too old to cry, but it hurts too much to laugh."

Stevenson was one of the most *eloquent* politicians of the twentieth century. Consider this excerpt from his speech accepting the nomination as Democratic candidate for president on July 26, 1952.

> I accept your nomination—and your program.
>
> I should have preferred to hear those words uttered by a stronger, a wiser, a better man than myself. But after listening to the president's [Harry Truman's] speech, I feel even better about myself.
>
> None of you, my friends, can wholly appreciate what is in my heart. I can only hope that you understand my words. They will be few. . . .
>
> And, my friends, even more important than winning the election is governing the nation. That is the test of a political party—the acid, final test. When the tumult and the shouting die, when the bands are gone and the lights are dimmed, there is the stark reality of responsibility in an hour of history haunted with those gaunt, grim specters of strife, dissension, and ruthless, inscrutable, and hostile power abroad. . . .
>
> Let's face it. Let's talk sense to the American people. Let's tell them the truth, that there are no gains without pains, that we are on the eve of great decisions, not easy decisions, like resistance when you're attacked, but a long, patient, costly struggle which alone can assure triumph over the great enemies of man—war, poverty, and tyranny—and the assaults upon human dignity which are the most grievous consequences of each.

An analysis of an exeptional impromptu speech given by pro golfer Justin Leonard following his 1998 British Open win follows on the next page.

How Pro Golfer *Justin Leonard* Said All the Right Things

Following is Justin Leonard's impromptu acceptance speech following his 1998 British Open win. In it, Leonard had foresight enough to ask for names of the most important people to thank, and then delivered his speech with humor, gratitude, and emotion.

It is correct to make more of the award than the acts that led to receiving it.

Humor keeps the audience on the side of the speaker.

Humility after a victory is a sure winner.

It is important to thank two or three very important people by name in the acceptance, then thank the rest personally later.

Flattery for the host and others involved is always a crowd pleaser.

Pause for emotion rather than try to talk through it.

Humor is a good transition from emotions back to comments.

Final comments usually are best given with a little humor to help close with a bang.

Accepting the award, Leonard steps up to the microphone and says:

"I made a few notes. [Laughter]

"It's been a great week. It hasn't hit me yet, so if it hits me during the speech, I'll go ahead and apologize.

"There are a few people I'd like to thank from the championship committee; . . . I thought the course was just fabulous this week. I think all of the players would agree with that. I don't know if you have control of the weather, but if you do, nice job. [Laughter]

"Mr. Bonallack, thank you for all your preparations and for allowing me to come over here and get a chance to play. I came over the last two years to qualify, was fortunate enough to qualify for the championship. Hopefully I won't have to again, but if I do, I'll come. [Laughter]

"I'd also like to thank my playing partners all week long, especially the last two days. Darren Clarke on Saturday. Darren and I actually met during the qualifying for the championship at St. Andrews. He's a great guy. He's a great player, and he had a great week. It was nice. We had a nice, relaxing round.

"Today I felt real fortunate to be paired with Fred Couples. You know, I call him a friend of mine. He's just great. We laughed our way around. He's always very relaxed. And he's really one of my favorite players. So, it was a real honor to play with him and to be able to play well. [Applause]

"I'd like to congratulate [low amateur] Barclay Howard. I had opposite tee times with you Thursday and Friday, so I got to watch quite a bit of your play. Outstanding. I think the American side in the upcoming Walker Cup Matches is going to have a tough time with you. [Applause]

"I'd also like to congratulate Jesper [Parvenik] and Darren. They're both wonderful players. They both deserve to win this tournament. I think it just happened to be my week. But I'm sure that both these players will win many more tournaments and many more majors. I just feel fortunate to be able to do what I did against two great players. [Applause]

"I just want you to know that I'm here alone this week. Just myself and my caddie, Bob Reifke. [Applause as Leonard sniffles and holds back tears]

"Moment, please. [Applause/cheers]

"I think it just hit me. [Laughter]

"But to everybody: my family, all my friends in Dallas, Randy Smith my instructor, I know they're kicking themselves, but this isn't some place you can just, you know, catch a 5 o'clock flight.

"I'm looking forward to getting home. I know they're having a really fun time right now. [Laughter] So, I'll make sure I get some Advil on the way through the airport for them. It's a shame they couldn't be here, but at the same time, maybe that helped me focus a little bit. So, anyway, I know they're here with me in spirit, and that's really all that matters. Thank you." [Applause]

ROBOT REDFORD REFLECTS

INSTANT IMPACT

Commencement speakers generally feel a bit nervous but pleased to have been asked. But at Maryland's Anne Arundel Community College, one not-entirely-welcome commencement speaker felt nothing, because he was an *it:* a 5-ft.-2-in.-tall, 175-lb. mobile machine loaded with a computer named, by its California manufacturer, Robot Redford.

Surprisingly, the invitation originated with the dean, Anthony Pappas, who wanted to dramatize the high-tech *transformation* of the working world. Said Pappas: "This will call attention to the college's new unit in computer sciences and technology." Some among the 551-member class were *miffed.* "I don't like the idea," said Kimberly Roy, the student-government president. "It is not a human being like we are. We deserve more."

Robot Redford, remotely controlled and made of fiberglass and aluminum, marched in the academic *procession,* but was not dressed in gown and mortarboard. "We don't want to *hoke* it up," said Sara Gilbert, a spokesperson for the college. The address was delivered from the wings to the robot's speaker by its creator Bill Bakaleinkoff. He said of his creation: "As soon as he gets ten minutes into his speech, they'll forget that he's a robot. Afterward they'll probably take him to the local malt shop and buy him new batteries."

Source: Adapted from *Time* magazine.

After-Dinner Speeches

As hard as it may be to swallow at the time, many banquets or meals are followed by someone presenting what is known as an **after-dinner speech.** The traditional after-dinner speech is expected to be entertaining. Remember, though, that you can be entertaining without being funny.

The key is to enjoy yourself, and then the audience is more likely to enjoy your presentation. On these occasions, most audiences want a message of some sort presented in a lighter, if not humorous, way. Be likable. Share your message in a relaxed and uncritical manner, and adapt to the mood of the audience. If the audience is not responding to your humorous stories, then you should shift the focus of your speech away from jokes to avoid bombing.

The casual style that you need requires careful preparation. You should organize your presentation around a theme. All of your supporting material—illustrations, statistics, examples, narrations, anecdotes—should relate to that theme. The following excerpts are from a Nebraska student's state championship after-dinner speech. Note how all of the supporting material reinforces his theme of "too many intellectuals."

> A dim chamber.
> Velvety dust creeping across the floor.
> The scent of dead books.

After-dinner speeches are generally expected to be entertaining, but you will still need to focus on your message.

Blue haze falls from the pipes as a dreary voice flows from a shadow in the corner. Seven enchanted bibliophiles cluster around a worn, scarred table, performing the ancient rites. These members of the Duluth Directory on Deductive Discussion carry the illness.

Another scene. The depths of a dirty, empty library hold the bodyless mind of one Aristotle P. Chaucer, Jr. Pen choked by hand, it struggles across the paper, attempting to write that crucial document for which so many wait. The Fred Friendly Fan Club Constitution is in the hand of one afflicted by that same disease.

Still another scene. A hand attached to some distant brain guides a stub of chalk on an enormous gray slate. Chalk dust settles to the floor as the long-sought formula for the chemical composition of armadillo saliva is revealed. The same malaise affects this being.

Yes, a plague creeps through our society. While some euphemistically refer to the illness as knowledge, we now recognize it for what it really is: the cancerous growth of intellectualism.

While the illness receives very little attention—the telethon never made it on the air—millions of Americans are afflicted with this awful disease. It is entirely possible that someone in this room is an intellectual.

I perceive your sudden nervousness as you wonder if the person next to you is a carrier. Don't worry. While it is true that "a little knowledge is a dangerous thing," small doses encountered by most people present an insignificant health hazard—our lack of logical thinking provides natural immunity. . . .

When we realize, however, how firmly entrenched in our society intellectualism is, we begin asking ourselves more and more: "*Gee whiz,* what can we do?" Well, the first step in halting the spread of intellectualism is the realization that you—yes, you—may suffer from some latent form of this syndrome. It is important, then, that you examine yourself weekly for these symptoms of intellectualism.

1. Sitting in the park, staring at pigeons, and thinking of hunchbacks and Dylan Thomas.
2. Talking to yourself and (here's the important part) not understanding a word you say.
3. Knowing that Norman Mailer doesn't work at the post office.
4. Taking your phone off the hook to watch *Firing Line.*
5. Wearing a corduroy smoking jacket with leather elbow patches.
6. Laughing at the thought of what H. L. Mencken would have said if he met Gertrude Stein.
7. Worrying about being hit by space junk.

SECTION 1 REVIEW

Recalling the Facts ...

1. What are the guidelines for a speech of presentation?
2. How should you organize an after-dinner speech?

Thinking Critically ...

1. Imagine that you are the speech writer for Robot Redford, the computerized robot that gave a graduation address. What would you say about the "high-tech transformation of the world"?

Taking Charge ...

1. Now it's your turn. Try your hand at preparing a courtesy speech. Write and deliver a brief speech of introduction for one of the following:

   a. a friend running for the student council,

   b. a teacher recognized for excellence in the classroom, or

   c. a college financial officer addressing the senior class about scholarship opportunities.

SECTION 2 Ceremonial Speeches

The addresses known as ceremonial speeches are usually part of a formal activity. They often help the audience tie the past, present, and future together. The most common types of ceremonial speeches are commencement addresses and commemorative speeches, which include testimonials and eulogies.

Commencement Addresses

Some high schools select a member or members of each graduating class to present a valedictory, or farewell, speech. Another common practice is to invite a *dignitary* to address the graduating class. In either case, the speaker is giving a **commencement address,** or graduation speech. A commencement address should both acknowledge the importance of the ceremony and honor the graduates. The challenge for the speaker is to keep the attention of restless students and relatives who are already looking past the ceremony and toward the future. Therefore, most commencement addresses pay respect to the past but focus on the future of the graduates. If you are chosen to speak at a graduation ceremony, you should choose examples and illustrations that celebrate the collective experiences of the audience members. Humor, if appropriate, can ease the tension and make the ceremony more enjoyable for everyone. Successful commencement speakers are positive and uplifting.

New Jersey governor Christine Todd Whitman delivers a commencement address at Colgate University.

The graduation speech excerpts that follow come from a speech written by Sara Martin for her graduation from Columbine High School in 1999.

> During World War II the people of Cambridge, England, set out to preserve the exquisite stained glass windows of Kings College Chapel. The people took apart the windows and numbered each piece. Then, families took the fragments and hid them in sugar bowls and sock drawers.
>
> The chapel made it through the war unharmed and the people brought back the pieces and reconstructed the windows. The lines where the pieces were broken are still visible. Maybe the beauty now revealed is that an entire community came together and restored the vision. Though flawed, it was made stronger than ever.
>
> In a way, each of us is a piece of a Columbine community stained glass through which the sun shines bright and against which the wind blows cold. The piece we carry is made up of elements given to us by the literature that we read, the teachers we learn from, and the models we observe. It is a vision within us of which the totality is unknown until we die.
>
> . . . Our piece of the greater window is a stained window made of pieces from our own experiences, . . . made of pieces of glass given to us. It is our responsibility to accept those pieces. If we cherish them, we begin to recreate the pictures of our own window and determine the colors and their hue.
>
> . . . Our own window can be vibrant in color and spirit—a collection of the gifts given to us by the people who surround us. Or, our window can be blurred and colorless. We must recognize the pieces and create the window within us.
>
> Because of what occurred on April 20, I am beginning to see what my window must reflect in order to fit into the larger window. I must live life with a concentrated purpose and a dedication to each moment. I must remember our friends who lost their lives. . . . I must recognize what I have learned: to love deeply and to appreciate every word and every gesture of every person I love or will love.
>
> So, now, we are being called upon to take our pieces and rebuild the window of our community. And though we have faced disasters of our own

Hackneyed Themes We Know and Love

The Reverend J. Pittman McGehee, commencement speaker at The Kincaid School in Houston, began his speech by listing the Top 10 Worst Commencement Address Themes in the history of high school graduations.

10. **You are the future of America.**
9. **Your future is ahead of you.**
8. **When the going gets tough, the tough get going.**
7. **The higher you climb, the better the view.**
6. **When you're not the lead dog, the view is always the same.**
5. **Tomorrow is the first day of the rest of your life.**
4. **It's a cold, cruel world out there.**
3. **It's a wide wonderful world out there.**
2. **Ten top tips for tip-top graduates.**
1. **You're good enough, you're smart enough, and doggone it, people like you.**

and our window may appear to have been shattered, we can achieve a greater beauty as we put the pieces back together again. Let the light shine through the stained glass, colored by these last four years, these last four weeks. Let us recognize what is worthy to be saved, to be restored, and in unity rebuild the Columbine window from which others may draw their inspiration.

Commemorative Speeches

You have heard the expression, "a picture is worth a thousand words." Some commemorative speakers in our country's history demonstrate that the *converse* is true: the right words are worth a thousand pictures. A **commemorative speech** is an inspiring address that recalls heroic events or people. John F. Kennedy's inaugural address, Douglas MacArthur's "Old Soldiers Never Die," and Ronald Reagan's speech following the *Challenger* space shuttle disaster are commemorative speeches that succeeded in capturing our collective imagination, in inspiring us to reaffirm ideals, in taking snapshots of history.

Another example is President Franklin Roosevelt's first inaugural address, delivered on March 4, 1933. That address contains one of the most memorable lines in speech-making history: "The only thing we have to fear is fear itself." According to speechwriter and columnist William Safire, that phrase was added at the last moment to avoid the negativity in an earlier draft: "This is no occasion for soft speaking or for the raising of false hopes." The lesson for you is that careful revision can strengthen not only a commemorative speech but any writing that you do. Let's look more closely at Roosevelt's revised draft in the following excerpt.

> This is preeminently the time to speak the truth, the whole truth, frankly and boldly. Nor need we shrink from honestly facing conditions in our country today. This great nation will endure as it has endured, will revive and will prosper.
>
> So, first of all, let me assert my firm belief, that the only thing we have to fear is fear itself—nameless, unreasoning, unjustified terror which paralyzes needed efforts to convert retreat into advance.

Roosevelt's inaugural address recalls a special event. Other commemorative speeches are given to honor individuals—the testimonial speech and the eulogy.

General Douglas MacArthur's "Old Soldiers Never Die" is a classic commemorative speech.

Testimonials ... You have witnessed countless testimonials by simply watching television ads. When Michael Jordan hawks a particular brand of athletic shoes or you are told that "nine out of ten doctors agree," the advertisers are hoping that the prestige of their spokespersons will persuade you to purchase their product.

Cashing in on the name and prestige of someone else, though, is not the only form of testimonial. A **testimonial speech** is an address of praise or celebration honoring a living person. The purpose of these presentations is to pay tribute to a special person—to generate appreciation, admiration, or respect. These speeches are often given at celebrity roasts or as toasts at retirement dinners or wedding celebrations. You may

COMMUNICATION

Break*down*

Mashing the Potato Circuit

In this excerpt from his book, Great Political Wit, *Bob Dole relates some of his not-so-special occasion speeches.*

Anything that keeps a politician humble is good for democracy. Back in 1961, when I was a young congressman visiting Indiana on the mashed potato circuit, the name Bob Dole had little marquee value. So the local dinner chairman resorted to drastic measures in hopes of hyping the box office. On arriving in town, I was whisked off to the local radio station, where the announcer gave a more or less accurate rendition of my résumé.

"The guest at this evening's dinner," he began, "will be congressman Bob Doyle [sic]. He will speak at the American Legion Hall. Tickets have been slashed from three dollars to one dollar. A color television set will be given away. You must be present to win, and we're not going to draw until Congressman Doyle gets through talking. Doyle was born in Kansas, raised in Kansas, educated at the University of Kansas. Prior to World War II he was a premedical student. He fought in Italy, where he suffered a serious head injury. Then he went into politics."

By the time I was nominated for Vice President in 1976, most people managed to at least spell my name right. Everything happened so fast at the convention—only a few hours separated President Ford's invitation to join the ticket from my introduction to a national television audience. Nevertheless, I got off a few decent one-liners at the expense of the opposition. Or so I thought. By the time I finished, the adrenaline was really pumping. Returning to the holding room just off the convention floor, I ran into my mother.

"How did I do?" I asked her.

"You usually do better," she said.

Although my oratorical skills have never been confused with those of a Lincoln or a Churchill, I've at least avoided the fate of Warren G. Harding, the Ohio politician who invented the word "bloviate" to describe his unique platform style—a lumpish mix of spread-eagle patriotism, numbing alliteration, sentences that didn't parse, and phrases that didn't soar. Harding's contemporary H. L. Mencken feasted on what he called Gamaliell. To him, a typical Harding speech was reminiscent of "a string of wet sponges . . . tattered washing on line . . . of stale bean soup, of college yells, of dogs barking idiotically through endless nights. It is so bad that a sort of grandeur creeps into it . . . it is a rumble and bumble, flap and doodle, balder and dash."

Questions

1. Dole had his mother to keep things in perspective. How do you keep things in perspective when everything goes wrong?
2. How do you think H. L. Mencken would have described your public speaking? Try to choose vivid language.

hear a testimonial speech at a farewell banquet for a favorite teacher. The length of these speeches varies, but generally they last no more than a few minutes.

How can you make your testimonial speech successful? First, research carefully the person honored. If you can offer insights into what makes the person so deserving, your speech will be more successful. Language choice is crucial; the level of formality should fit the occasion. The tone of your speech should be warm and caring. A creative approach with appropriate humor that makes this special event memorable is desirable. Remember, audience members are there to pay tribute as well. Honor their feelings by *evoking* a strong sense of celebration.

During a heartfelt tribute delivered to him on February 16, 1992, at the Forum in Los Angeles, Earvin "Magic" Johnson watched and listened as Kareem Abdul-Jabbar expressed what must have been in the minds of everyone who loves the game of basketball. The special occasion was the retiring of Johnson's team number, 32.

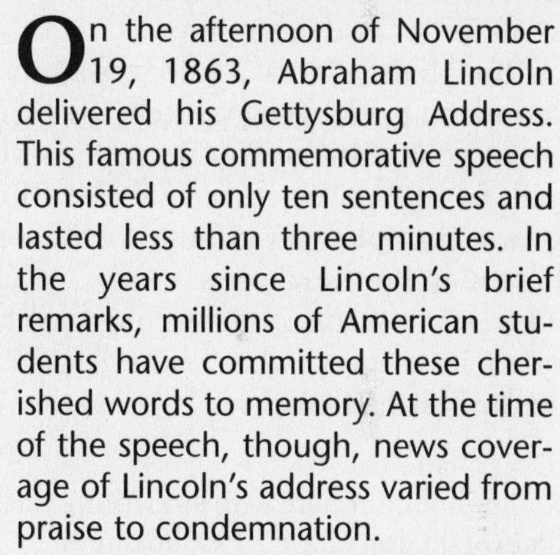

Magic Johnson's number—32—was retired in 1992 as a tribute to his basketball skills.

> Ladies and gentlemen, here we are again, and it's a whole lot of emotion in this moment. You know it's gonna be awful hard for me to do this, but I'm gonna do the best I can. It was a long time ago when we first welcomed this young man out here on this court. And in the interim, he's taught us a whole lot. He's taught us a lot about him. He's taught us about ourselves. He's taught us about the game of basketball. He's taught us about winning. He's taught us about perseverance. And all of our lives are enriched by him.
>
> I think the most important thing for me was that Earvin made me realize that I was having a good time. It's difficult sometimes, you know? You get caught up in the difficult part of your job, and you don't realize what it is you're doing, and what it is you're sharing with everybody, the whole basketball-loving public in America, and all the great Laker fans we have here.
>
> And I want to say personally . . . I just got back from Boston last week and you wouldn't believe it, I know you wouldn't believe it, but the people there, they miss us. And that came as a big shock to me. But walking down the streets of Boston and hearing people saying how much they wish we were still out there going at it again, so they could have some enjoyment.
>
> Thank you, Earvin. Thank you very much. I just want to say in those times when we'd be driving through the outskirts of Detroit on a cold winter's night, and you'd have me smilin', thank you, Earvin. We love you. I love you. Good luck.

MORE THAN FOURSCORE AND SEVEN YEARS AGO . . .

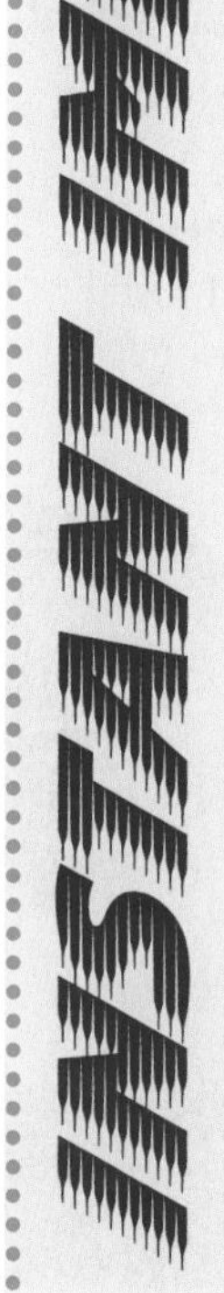

On the afternoon of November 19, 1863, Abraham Lincoln delivered his Gettysburg Address. This famous commemorative speech consisted of only ten sentences and lasted less than three minutes. In the years since Lincoln's brief remarks, millions of American students have committed these cherished words to memory. At the time of the speech, though, news coverage of Lincoln's address varied from praise to condemnation.

- *Chicago Times*—"Mr. Lincoln did most foully traduce [slander] the motives of the men who were slain at Gettysburg."
- *Chicago Tribune*—"The dedicatory remarks of President Lincoln will live among the annals of man."
- *London Times*—"The ceremony was rendered ludicrous by some of the sallies [lively remarks] of that poor President Lincoln. . . . Anything more dull and commonplace it would not be easy to produce."

Eulogies . . . A **eulogy** is generally thought of as a speech given to praise or honor someone who has died. The speaker, therefore, should try to relate to the audience the significant meaning in that person's life. Because eulogies are usually delivered at funerals or memorial services, the speaker must respect the religious beliefs of members of the family as well as the deceased.

In preparing a eulogy, you should decide whether you want to choose a biographical or a topical approach. As you attempt to chronicle a person's entire life, you will discover that the biographical speech often contains so many details that you lose the significance of the moment. In the topical approach, however, you can focus on personal qualities or specific achievements from which the audience can gain inspiration or understanding.

Although the tone of a eulogy is almost always solemn and the language sincere, you can be creative in your choices. You must, however, select details with great sensitivity and care. The following two examples pay tribute to the deceased in different and unusual ways.

Sportscaster Bob Costas carefully chose details to include in his eulogy of baseball star Mickey Mantle.

One ninth-grade student eulogized her grandmother in a speech that reminds us that we all have "unfinished business."

Dear Grandma,

I'm not quite sure why I'm writing this letter. I know you don't have a P.O. box up there. I just want a chance to tell you how much I miss, need, love, and thank you.

Unfinished business. We each have our own unfinished business. My math homework was due Tuesday, and I'm only on problem 3; I can't spend the night at Jenny's because I haven't finished vacuuming the den; and I won't receive my allowance until all the leaves are raked and bagged. Oh, we all have our own incomplete chores, but I'm referring to another kind of unfinished business—the kind between my grandmother and me.

So often loved ones are taken away, and inevitably we grieve, but too many times our lasting sorrow overwhelms us because we fail to tell others how much we love them in the living years. I deeply regret not telling my grandmother her importance in my life. If only, if only I'd said goodbye, eye to eye, heart to heart. If only we all told our loved ones how much we need, love, and thank them before it's too late. If only we finished our business.

Grandma, I need you. I need the crumpled Kleenex always waiting in your pocket to wipe away my tears, and I need your bedtime fairy tales that taught me morals and made me smile. But most of all I need your good advice.

Today, in our independent society, we seldom feel the need to verbally accept others' spiritual gifts. Psychiatrist and author Gerald G. Jampolsky writes, "giving means that all of one's love is extended with no expectations." If only we would accept that gift of extended love and then express our appreciation.

I love your comforting arms that swallow my troubles with every hug. I love your shiny white locks. With every curl lies a bit of wisdom. I love your presence.

Playwright Thornton Wilder states, "There is a land of the living and a land of the dead, and the bridge is love, the only survival, the only meaning." If only we could communicate our love in the land of the living, it could form the bridge to the land of the dead.

Grandma, I thank you for your lessons in life: you taught me to plant pansies and make apple pies, but you also taught me through love that all things are possible.

Thanks that are so often felt but so seldom expressed. It doesn't go without saying. In the book of Job, chapter 1, verse 21, we learn, "The Lord giveth and the Lord taketh away." So before he takes what he's given, let us tell those special individuals what they've given to us. Let us finish our business.

Following the death of the newsman Harry Reasoner, his longtime friend Andy Rooney eulogized him on the television program *60 Minutes.*

His friends here at *60 Minutes* have lived with Harry's death for five days now. It's not a good thing to have to do. People keep asking how we feel. How does anyone feel when one of their best friends dies? Reporters ask a lot of dumb questions. "How do you think he'd like to be remembered?" "What one thing do you remember most about Harry Reasoner?" After 25 years of working with him, traveling with him, eating and drinking with him, what one thing do I remember most? Ridiculous.

Harry was an infinitely complex person. It's hard to believe that great brain with everything that was in it is gone. He wasn't like anyone I ever knew. If you think you know what he was like because you saw him so often here on *60 Minutes,* you're wrong. No matter what you thought he was like, I can promise he wasn't like that. [Highlights from Reasoner's illustrious career followed, with voice-overs by Rooney.]

I talked with Harry about death—his and mine—as recently as six weeks ago and I know he had no intention of dying. Harry was the smartest correspondent there has ever been on television, but he did more dumb things than most of them, too. He would not have died at age 68 if this were not true. How does the smartest man I have ever known lose a lung to cancer and continue smoking two packs of cigarettes a day? I'm sad but I'm angry, too, because Harry was so careless with our affection for him.

SECTION 2 REVIEW

Recalling the Facts ...

1. What is the purpose of a testimonial speech?
2. What two things should a commencement address do?

Thinking Critically ...

1. Should eulogies be given only for persons who are praiseworthy? Does every human being have some essential worth? Explain your answer.

Taking Charge ...

1. Now it's your turn. Prepare a brief eulogy to honor someone who recently died. You might choose to write about someone you knew, a celebrity, or another public figure. Refer to the examples that you just read for inspiration and ideas.

SECTION 3

Contest Speeches

Each year, thousands of students participate in interscholastic speech competitions. A tournament hosted by a high school or college takes place somewhere in the United States almost every weekend of the school year. If you would like to benefit from this valuable activity, you should discuss the opportunities available at your school with your speech teacher.

The rules that govern speech contests vary from state to state and between the national organizations—the Catholic Forensic League and the National Forensic League—that offer competitive events. With a few exceptions, the speech events generally fall into two categories: public speaking and interpretation. Some of the more popular events include original oratory, extemporaneous speaking, and dramatic and humorous interpretation.

Interscholastic speech contests generally have two categories: public speaking and interpretation.

Original Oratory

The speech contest event in which you write on a topic of your own choosing is known as **original oratory.** Most states require that you memorize your speech and limit it to ten minutes in length. The key to oratory is to remember that it is a persuasive speech. To be convincing, therefore, you should pick a topic you feel strongly about. Typical topics include everything from the importance of community to neglect of the elderly.

Oratory demands careful and complete preparation. The successful orator "lives" with her speech over a period of weeks or months. Painstaking revision and updating of the materials are therefore necessary to keep it fresh.

In preparing the speech, use the organizational principles outlined in Chapter 9, and choose language for grace and precision. Keep in mind that the rules often limit the number of quoted words you can have in your speech. The National Forensic League, for example, allows no more than 150. You have the responsibility to cite the sources from which you obtained ideas. A rehash of a *Time* or *Sierra* magazine article is insufficient and, if extensively paraphrased, unethical. Furthermore, do not expect your speech coach to write your oration for you. The event is called "original" oratory for a reason.

Extemporaneous Speaking

As you will recall from your study of Chapter 15, in extemporaneous contest speaking, participants pick one topic from a choice of three and then prepare a 5- to 7-minute speech on that topic. The topics are based on current issues and are usually presented in question form. Usually there are two divisions within extemporaneous, national and international topics. For example, a contestant might be asked to choose between the following for national topics:

- Do politicians have a right to privacy?
- How can we win the war on drugs?

- How can we better provide for the elderly in our nation?

Contestants are allowed 30 minutes to prepare their speeches. In preparing the speech, a contestant is allowed to access only those documents or background information that he or she has brought to the contest. In some tournaments, especially those that are held earlier in the competing schedule, extemporaneous speakers may bring a single notecard to guide them through the speech. Evaluation is based on several factors, but content, how well you answer the question or discuss the topic, is the major factor in the judge's evaluation.

TYPES OF SPECIAL OCCASION SPEECHES

Courtesy speeches, including introductions, presentation and acceptance speeches, and after-dinner speeches.

Ceremonial speeches, including commencement addresses, commemorative speeches, and eulogies.

Contest speeches, including original oratories, extemporaneous speeches, and dramatic and humorous interpretations.

Impromptu speeches.

Dramatic and Humorous Interpretation

The interpretation events allow you to choose the material you want to perform. Do you have a favorite role in a play that your theater department is not going to produce? Have you ever wanted to be more than one of the characters in a play? **Dramatic interpretation** and **humorous interpretation**—sometimes separate categories and sometimes combined—give you the opportunity to share your acting talents. To paraphrase Whoopi Goldberg, you are the show.

The fine line between acting and interpretation is discussed in Chapter 16. *Suffice* it to say that in the memorized interpretation events, the competitors are generally "acting from the waist up," while in the scripted events the reader is expected to suggest rather than become a character.

The rules for interpretation events vary greatly from state to state. For example, some states permit extensive movement, and some do not; some permit singing, and some do not. Each judge, too, seems to have a different philosophy about what is preferable and what is acceptable.

How, then, do you know what to do? The skills you need to become an "interper" are treated at length in Chapter 16. In general, study the rules for each tournament carefully, and try to make artistic decisions that honor the integrity of your selection. Do not rewrite Shakespeare because you can't understand *whence* and *whilst* and *woo.* If you perform "The Belle of Amherst," do not give Emily Dickinson a southern accent. Do not scream or cry as a way to win favor from the judge when it is clear that the character you are playing would not.

Give much thought to the kind of material that is suitable for you. Try to choose a selection that fits your personality and stretches you as a performer but is not beyond your grasp. For example, a male who cannot play female characters should avoid portraying Joan of Arc. Some selections require a number of characters—you should be certain that you can make them all unique and believable. Character differentiation that is mechanical or distracting is undesirable. In tournament competition, your goal is to make the performance so affecting, so real, that the judge forgets it is a contest.

Other Contests

If you are seeking scholarships for higher education, some clubs and organizations sponsor speech contests for cash prizes—in many cases, for thousands of dollars. The contests offered vary from community to community but include the following.

1. The American Legion Oratorical Contest. You must write, memorize, and deliver an eight- to ten-minute oration on some aspect of the United States Constitution. The contest also requires that you speak extemporaneously for three to five minutes on one of four of the Constitution's articles or amendments.
2. The Veterans of Foreign Wars' "Voice of Democracy" Contest. You must write and tape-record on cassette a three- to five-minute speech on a theme that changes yearly. You enter the cassette into the competition, and it is evaluated for content and delivery.
3. The Optimist Club Oratorical Contest. You write and deliver a four- to five-minute speech on a yearly theme. The competition is for students under 16, and it provides an excellent opportunity for younger students. The text of a winning oration is included in this chapter.

THE SPEECH COLLECTOR

INSTANT IMPACT

"Curse of a Malignant Tongue," "Not Just a Farmer," and "Before the Diet of Worms" are just a few of the many "world famous orations and speeches" included in Roberta Sutton's *Speech Index,* an index to collections of speeches. Other speech indexes provide more recent works. These references include responses to toasts, responses to speeches of blame, speeches concerning commencement, speeches concerning *combustion*—usually not at the same time—and many others. The date and place of presentations are given, along with the anthology in which they appear.

Reading and studying some of the most powerful speeches ever delivered will help you improve your own speech writing, which will, in turn, make your next speaking engagement a success.

But What If You Don't Win?

Most students who compete in speech soon tire of hearing this familiar *refrain* at every award ceremony: "There are no losers today. You are all winners simply by participating." Since speech contests are competitive, it is only natural that you will want to win. Unfortunately, the ranking of contestants is a subjective undertaking. Judges will disagree. One judge may compliment you on your creative approach to a topic; another may say that same approach is overused.

If you are to find satisfaction in speech competition, then you should set your own standards. Strive for excellence as you define it, and settle for no less. Certainly, you need to adapt to the audience—your judges—but not if that means compromising your integrity. In the final analysis, your success in any competitive activity depends on the goals you have for yourself. Satisfy your own high standards of performance, and the reward will always be there. If the only goal you have is to win, you have already lost.

WORDS FROM THE WORKPLACE

W. M. Luce
Educational Consultant

Q: *How does communication play a role in the day-to-day activities of your work?*

A: My job is all about communication! To motivate, to inspire, to inform, to persuade, and to entertain are my goals every time I get in front of an audience. My audiences expect to gain something of value from me. If my content is not what they want or need, then the line of communication is closed.

All kinds of communication are involved with my job, including body language. I communicate with my hands, my face, my total body movement, and variations in voice. I must constantly assess my audience for signs that assure me that communication is happening. If they are not absorbing it, there is no communication.

Q: *What tips can you give to students about the importance of communication skills?*

A: Be aware of your audience. Are they engaged with you and what you're doing? I always like to tell jokes at appropriate moments. This helps to entertain, but it also gives me some feedback about how well they are listening. I like to be "fired up" when I speak. The emotion I give off can become infectious. The positive feedback I receive from the audience helps me to sustain my own genuine enthusiasm. Look for lots of eye contact. I really like to look into the eyes of people and see how they are responding.

There is a great deal of work that goes on before the "show." Getting the correct information together in a format that I can deliver, with a specific audience in mind is very important. Every time I am asked to give a speech, workshop, or lecture, I find a certain sense of anxiety comes over me. Nothing I can do prior to a presentation is more calming than the practice sessions.

SECTION  REVIEW

Recalling the Facts ...

1. What is the key to writing an original oratory?
2. Name three speech contests that give monetary awards to the winners.

Thinking Critically ...

1. Most students write oratories on topics of their choosing, because they feel strongly about the subject. Some students are given topics by their coaches. Do you think a student should try to persuade an audience about a topic he, himself, doesn't care about? Explain your answer.

Taking Charge ...

1. A popular speech event at some tournaments is original prose and poetry. In this event, the student competitor writes and performs his or her own literary effort. Now it's your turn. Write a poem or a short piece of prose (two to three minutes long) and perform it for the class. Include a brief introduction to help the audience understand and enjoy your performance.

STUDENT WORK

"Optimism in My Life" *By Diana Marianetti*

Diana Marianetti, a tenth-grade student from New Mexico, won $1,500 in the Optimist Club Oratorical Contest. Note how she develops the theme "Optimism in My Life." Also, enjoy her self-effacing sense of humor.

When you see me, I know what you're probably thinking . . . you're probably thinking of one of those dumb blonde jokes. I understand. It is, after all, a burden to be tall and leggy with long, flaxen hair. OK—I am not really that tall and I'm not really that blonde, but, in my defense, I am pretty darn dumb. It all started in my childhood . . . when we were putting up the wallpaper in my bedroom. My father, the do-it-yourselfer, asked me to go get a yardstick. I marched out to the backyard and picked up, you guessed it, the nearest stick. My school experience hasn't been a whole lot better. In math and science, the slowest child in Luxembourg can kick my butt.

Is it any wonder that it is difficult to have optimism in my life? After all, ladies and gentlemen, we have moved beyond the dumbing down of America to the numbing down of America. Quite simply, America has stopped caring.

To understand the effects of numbing on our optimism, we must recognize first that we are living in an age of distraction, and second, that all of this new information moves us toward compassion fatigue.

So what does it mean to live in the age of distraction? Let me explain.

When I was 10 years old, my best friend Nina and I were inseparable. She lived at my house on the weekends and we both lived in her pool during the summer. But, after a while, she stopped coming over. *90210, The Simpsons,* and *Days of Our Lives* were more important to her. Meanwhile, the days of our lives were passing us by, and we rarely saw each other. Award-winning journalist Linda Ellerbee explains this phenomenon. When she was 8 years old, she and her best friend Lucy spent the majority of their time trying to fly from the swings in Linda's backyard. However, when Lucy's parents bought a television, Linda no longer had someone to fly with. The flickering box in her living room had become Lucy's entertainment, her friend. Linda Ellerbee remembers, "I never had another first best friend. I never learned to fly either. What's more, I was right all along: television [ate my best friend]."

And so I am a little bit numb and a little less optimistic because we are being led inexorably toward compassion fatigue. Boston *Phoenix* writer Mark Leibovich explains that when we are constantly bombarded with tragic information like AIDS, homelessness, and drug addiction, we become immune to their horror. We don't *want* to lose our optimism, so we become numb to it. Day after day, we listen to the news informing us of the latest murders, kidnappings, and accidental deaths. We begin to live by the words of Russian dictator Joseph Stalin, who said, "One death is a tragedy; a million, just statistics." . . .

In a way, compassion fatigue all started with an optimistic advertising campaign. Remember the ad "Save the Children"? With just 26 cents a day, you can save this child. The first time you see the ad, you are struck with guilt. The second time you see it, you linger over the photograph, and then turn the page. The third time you see it, you turn the page without hesitation. And the fourth time you see it you acknowledge with cynicism how the ad is crafted to manipulate us with guilt. In short, we have given up on optimism, we have given up on hope.

But what can we do? Well, most importantly, we must continue to humanize our challenge. For when we think about our problems as people—as men, as women, and especially as children—the answer is not compassion fatigue. It is compassion.

Now, I admit, selflessness is a hard sell. Self-sacrifice is never easy, and having optimism in my life is sometimes a challenge. But, hey, I'm . . . dumb enough to believe we ought to try.

CHAPTER 17 Review and Enrichment...

Looking Back

Listed below are the major ideas discussed in this chapter.

- Introductory speeches serve two functions: to make the audience want to hear the speaker and to make the speaker want to address the audience.
- Introductory speeches refer to the occasion, name the speaker, build enthusiasm, share information, and explain why this speaker is giving this talk to this audience at this time.
- Presentation speeches should reflect the feelings of the group. These speeches usually state the name of the person receiving the award, explain the award's significance, describe how the recipient was selected, and highlight what makes this person unique.
- Speeches of acceptance are usually brief and impromptu but generally thank the group for the recognition, discuss the importance of the award, and thank supporters.
- The traditional after-dinner speech is entertaining, with all humor used relating to a specific theme.
- Commencement speeches should both acknowledge the importance of the ceremony and honor the graduates.
- Commemorative speeches recall special events or pay tribute to individuals.
- The testimonial speech honors a living person; a eulogy honors the dead.
- The original oration is a persuasive speech the contestant writes on a topic of his or her own choosing.
- In extemporaneous contest speaking, the speaker draws a topic on a current event and prepares a speech in 30 minutes.
- Dramatic and humorous interpretation are contest events for students who want to perform works of literature.

Speech Vocabulary

In each of the following sentences, fill in the blank with the missing term.

speech of presentation
speech of acceptance
after-dinner speech
commencement address
commemorative speech
testimonial speech
eulogy
original oratory
dramatic interpretation
humorous interpretation

1. Audiences expect an ______________ to present a message in a lighter, if not humorous, way.
2. A ______________ acknowledges the importance of the ceremony and honors the graduates.
3. Testimonials and eulogies are two types of ______________.
4. When Michael Jordan hawks a particular brand of tennis shoe, that is a form of ______________.
5. A ______________ is generally thought of as a speech given to praise or honor someone who has died.

6. An ______________ is a speech you write on a topic of your own choosing.
7. In the memorized ______________ event, the competitors are usually "acting from the waist up."
8. If a classmate is receiving a gift, you would prepare a ______________.

General Vocabulary

Use a dictionary to define each of the following words and then use each in a sentence.

reiterate	dignitary	miffed	hoke	evoking	suffice
eloquent	transformation	procession	converse	combustion	refrain

To Remember

Answer the following based on your reading of the chapter.

1. List five guidelines to follow in a speech of introduction.
2. Speeches of acceptance serve a double purpose: to ______________ and to ______________.
3. In his concession speech, ______________ compared himself to a boy who has stubbed his toe in the dark: "too old to cry, but it hurts too much to laugh."
4. Ronald Reagan's speech following the *Challenger* disaster is an inspiring example of a ______________ speech.
5. Kareem Abdul-Jabbar's tribute to Earvin Johnson is a form of the ______________ speech.
6. If you wanted to find a particular oration in a collection of speeches, to which reference work in the library would you turn?
7. List five guidelines that you might follow in a speech of presentation.
8. ______________ is a contest speech event that requires you to draw a topic and prepare a speech in thirty minutes.
9. In the scripted interpretation events, the reader is expected to ______________ rather than "become" the characters.
10. List five guidelines to follow in a speech of acceptance.

To Do

1. Question your parents about their pasts. Choose one incident from those discussions and prepare a short speech on the topic "A Turning Point."
2. Attend a speech tournament. After watching a few rounds of competition, be prepared to discuss the differences between what the speech competitors did and what you do in class.
3. Experienced speakers know that libraries contain reference works that are collections of humorous anecdotes. These anecdotes can be used to "spice up" an occasional speech. To learn how to use these valuable resources, find three humorous anecdotes on a general topic of your choosing—fashion, sports, education, health, or the like.

CHAPTER 17 Review and Enrichment...

To Talk About

1. Some schools—perhaps yours—select students to speak at the graduation ceremony. How should these speakers be chosen? Grades? Talent? Popularity? Who should select these speakers? Administrators? Teachers? Committees of teachers and students?
2. Most audiences expect after-dinner speeches to be entertaining. What are some topics you would find worthwhile and enjoyable? Why?
3. Lanny Naegelin, former coordinator for five high school speech and theater programs in San Antonio, Texas, believed that students involved in competitive sports received more public recognition than students involved in speech activities. Is that fair? What, if anything, can be done to educate the community about the value of speech?
4. Judging speech tournaments involves subjective evaluation. For example, you have to choose one humorous interpretation over another. This process is analogous to deciding who is funnier, Eddie Murphy or Bill Cosby. How can we more fairly judge artistic endeavors?
5. Your best friend has been invited to be the after-dinner speaker at a banquet honoring a basketball coach whose team had a losing record. What advice might you give your friend?

To Write About

1. You are invited to be a guest speaker at a banquet honoring students who have volunteered their time to community service. Write a speech of introduction for yourself.
2. Imagine you have been asked to come back to speak at your 20-year high school class reunion. Write a brief speech in which you look back on how the world has changed.
3. Write an introduction for one of your classmates that could be used during the next series of assigned speeches in your class.

Related Speech Topics

Pay tribute to a personal hero.
Present an award or gift.
Accept an award or gift.
Introduce someone famous to the class.
Celebrity roasts
Toasts that butter up

The "occasional speaking" of (choose one):
- Jesse Jackson
- John F. Kennedy
- Martin Luther King, Jr.
- Mark Twain
- Madeleine Albright
- Cesar Chávez
- Sally Ride

Problem Solving and Conflict Management

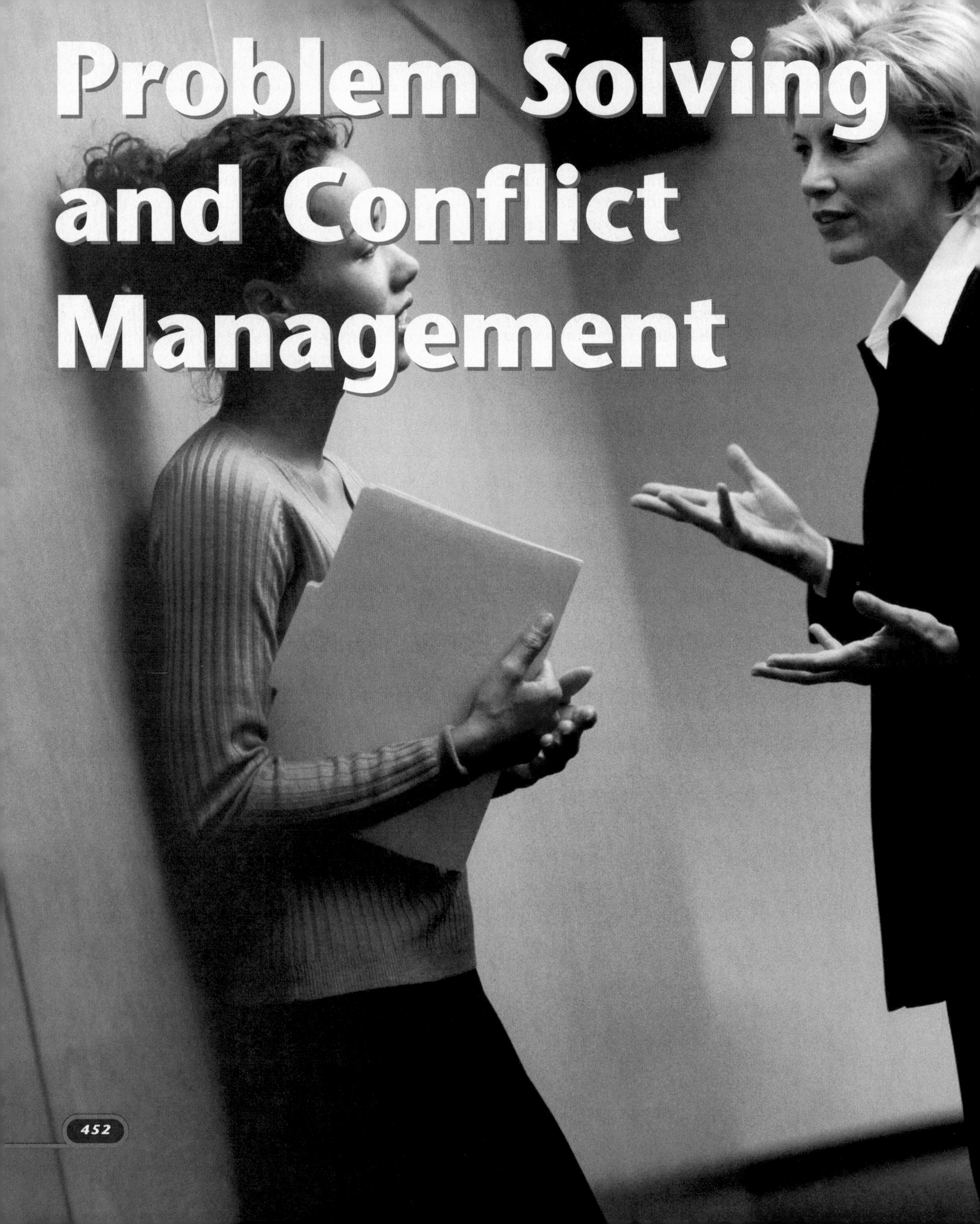

UNIT CONTENTS

CHAPTER 18

SUPPORTING YOUR VIEWS

> "There is no polish without friction."
>
> –Frederick Douglass

Learning Objectives

After completing this chapter, you will be able to do the following.

- List the five common strategies for resolving conflicts.
- Practice the four techniques for negotiation.
- Give examples of the ways in which people participate in informal debate.
- Define basic debate terms.
- Prepare for and participate in an informal debate.

Chapter Outline

Following are the main sections in this chapter.

1. The Art of Negotiation
2. Informal Debate
3. The Advantages of Debate
4. Debate Terminology
5. The Debate Process

New Speech Terms

In this chapter, you will learn the meanings of the speech terms listed below.

negotiation
debate
I-message
avoidance
accommodation
competition
compromise
collaboration
integrity
informal debate
proposition
resolution
affirmative
negative
status quo
burden of proof
argument
case
brief
constructive
refute
rebuttal
format
flowsheet

General Vocabulary

Expanding your general vocabulary will help you become a more effective communicator. Listed below are some words appearing in this chapter that you should make part of your everyday vocabulary.

barter
alienate
equitable
innuendo
intimidation
vouchers
deficit

Looking AHEAD

In this chapter, you are going to learn about a new kind of communication—debate. You'll learn what debate is, its different forms, and its special terminology. You'll also learn how studying and practicing debate can help you achieve your goals. But first, you will learn some important principles of negotiation. Both debate and negotiation will be invaluable as you support your views throughout your life.

Introduction

We do not live in a perfect world. You will not always agree with everyone you meet in life. You can probably think of plenty of examples: the bully who won't leave you alone, the parent who won't let you stay out late enough, the boss who won't give you a raise, and on and on.

Each of these situations creates a problem for you. Often you will be able to reach a solution through the process of negotiation. **Negotiation,** at its best, is a cooperative relationship in which both sides want to reach an agreement. Sometimes, though, negotiation is less than cooperative. Therefore, you need a more formal method of solving problems. **Debate,** from a Latin word meaning "to battle," is an important method of solving problems in a democracy.

In fact, the founding fathers of our country were highly skilled debaters. By the 1650s, most colonial colleges required debate as a means of training young scholars. For example, when Thomas Jefferson was a student at the College of William and Mary, he participated in debates. Jefferson was taught by George Wythe, the same "debate coach" who tutored such famous orators as Henry Clay and John Marshall. At the time, debate was considered to be the best way to develop the character and skills required of citizens in our young nation.

The challenge of learning to negotiate and to debate awaits you in this chapter. True, hard work lies ahead, but the rewards are significant. You will improve your ability to research and develop arguments, to organize your thoughts, and to speak extemporaneously. Moreover, you will be able to support your views.

George Wythe (left) coached both Thomas Jefferson and Henry Clay (pictured above) in the art of debate.

SECTION 1 The Art of Negotiation

You may think negotiation is not very important to you. But just wait until you find yourself haggling over the price of your first car. You'd better believe that the used-car salesperson trying to sell you the latest lemon on the lot knows how to negotiate. You should know what he or she knows, if only to protect yourself. But saving a buck is not the only reason to learn the principles of negotiation.

Why Negotiate?

Negotiation is not always about money. Certainly, learning negotiation skills can help you get pay raises, sell your home for more, even *barter* to borrow your neighbor's lawn mower. More important, though, is the opportunity to improve your personal relationships. You, too, can win friends and influence people.

Suppose your best friend wants to borrow money from you. The amount he wants to borrow is more than you can afford and your friend gets angry when you refuse to help him. Suppose your father insists you wash the car every Saturday, but your older brother has no chores. Suppose your curfew is an hour earlier than for any of your friends. Clearly, for each of these situations, you need to develop ways to resolve a conflict. Conflict expert Dr. Kenneth Thomas has developed strategies for resolving conflicts, as outlined in the chart on page 458. It explains the strengths and weaknesses of various options for dealing with conflict.

Techniques of Negotiation

There is more to negotiation than getting your own way. You might want to avoid the strategy of Scott Adams (creator of the comic strip "Dilbert") of making the final suggestion in any meeting. This maneuver involves waiting until near the end of the allotted meeting time, when "patience is thin and bladders are full." At this point, Adam says to offer your suggestion. Explain that your suggestion is based on all of the good thoughts that have been presented at the meeting, "no matter how ridiculous they might be."

Perhaps more useful than the "Dilbert" maneuver are these four techniques for effective negotiation:

1. **Be Positive**
   Negative words can close the door to negotiations. These words turn people off to your message. These words limit because they suggest refusal and denial. Think, for example,

Negotiating can sometimes lower prices on big-ticket purchases such as automobiles.

how much you dislike it when someone tells you "no." Jack Griffin, author of *How to Say It at Work,* has a list of 50 such words that you should avoid:

I
mine
you
yours
afraid
bad luck
blame
cannot
cheated
circumstances
cornered
crisis
delay
delinquent
demand
disaster
excuse
experiment
fail
fault
fear
final
forgot
frustrating
guess
hopeless
impossible
impractical
inadequate
insist
loser
loss
lost
make do
must
nervous
no
nonnegotiable
one-time offer
overloaded
panic
relax
slipped
sorry
stupid
tired
unaware
unfair
unreasonable
wasted

Source: Adapted from Jack Griffin's *How to Say It at Work,* Prentice-Hall Press, Paramus, N.J., 1998, pp. 15–17.

2. Use Three-Part Messages

Most of us rely heavily on **I-messages,** statements that emphasize what we want. These

FIVE COMMON STRATEGIES FOR RESOLVING CONFLICTS

1 **Avoidance** is a strategy in which an individual tries to resolve a conflict by withdrawing or by denying that a problem exists. This strategy is a lose-lose approach because we attempt to satisfy neither our concerns nor the concerns of the other party. In other words, our position is not to take a position. Frustration and anger usually result from this approach.

2 **Accommodation** is a strategy in which differences are minimized, smoothed over, or suppressed. This strategy is a lose-win approach because one individual accommodates, goes along with, whatever the other individual thinks is best. The accommodating person may be cooperative, but he is unassertive. This approach generally leads to a feeling of powerlessness and frustration for the person giving in.

3 **Competition** is a strategy that focuses on defeating or outshining another person rather than resolving the problem. This strategy is a win-lose approach because each person is intent upon satisfying only his or her concerns, and in the end one person wins and the other loses. Competing is the direct opposite of accommodating. Remember, though, that competition can be good. Constructive conflict, where we encourage people to disagree and play devil's advocate, is different from competing to win at all costs.

4 **Compromise** is a strategy in which each individual gives up something in order to meet in the middle. This strategy is a win/lose-win/lose approach because we make trade-offs to arrive at satisfactory outcomes and to save time. This type of negotiated settlement, based on mutual concessions, can reduce conflict without actually resolving it. We both compromise; we split the difference.

5 **Collaboration** is a strategy that focuses on resolving conflict. This strategy is a win-win approach because the experience, expertise, and perceptions of both parties are recognized and valued. You work together. Collaborating is the most ideal position and the one that takes the most patience and commitment to achieve. Collaborating satisfies the concerns of all parties. Collaboration builds consensus (agreement).

(Adapted from *Office Politics for the Utterly Confused,* by William A. Salmon & Rosemary T. Salmon, McGraw-Hill, N.Y., N.Y., 1999, pp. 133–136.)

kinds of messages can *alienate* people, and therefore can be counterproductive in negotiation. For example, saying, "Stop talking so I can get a word in edgewise!" will not bring you closer to a satisfactory resolution. If you were to attend a business seminar on negotiation, you would learn that two-part messages are more effective: "When you keep talking, it hurts my feelings." Even better, though, is the three-part message advocated by Dr. Thomas Gordon, a leader in effectiveness training.

1	2	3
When you (X)	I feel (Y)	because (Z)

Using this pattern, a teacher might say: "When you don't do your homework, I feel disappointed, because you don't learn what you need to know." The three-part message is an important tool in negotiation because both sides are forced to clarify the key issues.

3. Be Prepared

Aristotle once observed that "the way to achieve success is first to have a definite, clear, practical ideal." Today, Aristotle might have said that you need an "ideal deal." In other words, you have to define what it is you want. You shouldn't ask the boss for a pay raise without having an amount in mind. Therefore, you must have the reasons for a raise carefully researched and documented. Do your homework. Know the facts before you open your mouth. Talking "from the seat of

I-messages seldom bring satisfactory resolutions. In fact, they alienate others.

COMMUNICATION

Breakdown

A Cultural Crash Course

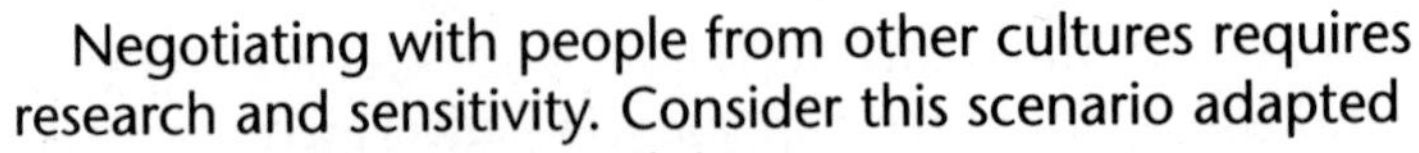

Negotiating with people from other cultures requires research and sensitivity. Consider this scenario adapted from the book *BusinessSpeak* by Suzette Haden Elgin.

Chet Filmer and Leslie O'Connor were well aware that making a presentation to a group of seven Japanese executives would be a bit different. They'd been thoroughly briefed, and their boss had seen to it that they each got a long list of tips on doing business with the Japanese. They thought they were ready.

Chet and Leslie had designed a script that went with their slides. For each slide, they did three things: they carefully and courteously explained the theme of a painting, said a few words about the artist, and explained why the work was a perfect expression of one or more principles dear to the three Japanese firms represented. It took a while, but they were willing to give it all the time and care necessary. And then Chet took the last few slides—the ones that set out the necessary information about expenses, tax benefits, and other financial details—and wound up the session.

"There you have it, gentlemen!" he said in conclusion. "And now my associate and I would be happy to answer any questions that you might have."

He waited through a long silence. The body language he was observing in his audience gave him no clues to their reactions; he couldn't interpret it at all. "No questions?" he asked uneasily.

Chet was sure something was wrong. The first time he was able to get close enough to Leslie to check with her, he whispered, "What do you think?"

"I'm not sure," she said softly, the smile on her face never wavering, "but I don't have the feeling we were a smash hit."

Leslie was on to something. In fact, the Japanese businessmen were offended. The Japanese executives in this scenario did not perceive the careful and explicit details in Chet and Leslie's presentation as courtesy but as evidence that the two Americans found them lacking in both intelligence and sophistication. The Japanese expect adults to rely heavily on presupposed information when communicating with other adults. The emphasis on details made them feel as if they were being treated like children.

The lesson: Always be aware of cultural differences so that you don't offend others.

Questions

1. Do both negotiating sides have a responsibility to adapt to cultural differences?
2. How would you research such differences?

your pants" or "off the top of your head" rarely impresses anyone.

It is wise to have alternatives in mind. You may not get exactly what you want in any negotiation. Be able to justify your best alternative. Suppose you make a case for being paid $10 each time you wash the car. If your father says you have to continue washing the car and he still refuses to pay you, you might want to offer an alternative. Perhaps your older sister could wash the car every other week. If not profitable, at least you could suggest that it's *equitable* (a fair distribution of work).

Finally, you should know as much as possible about the position of the other party. Try to understand the "why" of his or her position. Perhaps your parents won't extend your curfew because your grades are low. Or maybe it's because they don't trust your friends. Without knowing the "why," you will find it difficult to prepare satisfactory responses to their concerns.

Whether negotiating with your parents or others, be prepared.

4. Tell the Truth

Your reputation is built on your integrity. To have **integrity** means that you are true to yourself. You should never sacrifice your values or standards to achieve your negotiation goals. You gain the respect of others by doing what is right. Never make promises you can't keep. Never put others in a position where they have to compromise their integrity. Peter Scotese, the retired CEO of Spring Industries, once said that "Integrity is not a 90 percent thing, not a 95 percent thing; either you have it or you don't."

SECTION 1 REVIEW

Recalling the Facts ...

1. Name the three parts of the three-part message.
2. What does integrity mean?
3. What are the strategies for resolving conflicts?

Thinking Critically ...

1. Suppose that your school has decided to require uniforms. The administration, however, is going to let the students choose the type of uniform that everyone must wear. In this section, you learned that it is easier to work with people than to work against them. And yet not all high school students get along with or even like each other. What are some of the things you could do to convince people who dislike each other to collaborate?

Taking Charge ...

1. Attend the next meeting of the student council or any other school organization. Which of the five approaches to negotiation did you see employed? How did the approaches used affect what was accomplished?
2. To learn how negative words can affect your message, write a brief speech trying to persuade the audience to take action on a particular issue. For example, ask them to donate blood. Incorporate as many of the 50 negative words from this section as you can.

SECTION 2 Informal Debate

We have defined debate as a battle between ideas. That means when people disagree, and each puts forward an idea in an attempt to show that this idea is superior to another, a debate is going on. The process of negotiation is a kind of informal debate. **Informal debate** is any debate conducted without specific rules. It's an unstructured, open-ended discussion of opposing ideas.

Before we begin our study of formal debate, let's take a quick look at some different types of informal debate. You may be surprised at how much you already know about debate and how many debates in which you have already participated.

Personal Debate

You could say that people debate themselves all the time. This is the intrapersonal communication discussed in Chapter 1. When you have a personal problem, you consider alternatives as you try to solve the problem. Maybe you can't decide whether to go out for the basketball team or the marching band. You like both, but the schedules conflict. There's no way you can do both. In such a case, you might make a list of the pros and cons of both options. You might sit in your room and think to yourself, "If I went out for basketball, I'd get to hang out with all my hoop buddies, but I'd also have to put in a lot of hours of hard work—all that running every night. But if I joined the band . . ." In cases like these, your mind is a battleground for a clash between opposing ideas. In other words, a silent debate is going on inside your head. Eventually, one side's ideas will overpower the other's, and there will be a winner. You engage in this kind of internal debate several times a week as you solve life's everyday problems.

Disagreements and Arguments

You probably don't need to be told what an argument is. Very few people go through life without getting into at least an occasional argument. Of course, there are all kinds of arguments—friendly ones, heated ones, serious ones, amusing ones. All of these arguments are, in a sense, debates. They are battles between opposing ideas.

Your brother claims it's your turn to mow the yard, but you say it's his turn. You give your reasons and try to show your mother why his reasons don't make sense. He does the same. In this case, there is a clash of ideas in which a parent acts as a judge to determine

Personal debate might find you debating yourself over whether to go out for basketball or marching band.

Developing your debate skills could help you present your side of an issue the next time you and your parents disagree.

whose reasons are better. Your skills as a debater may determine whether you lounge coolly in front of the computer surfing the Internet or strain and sweat behind the lawn mower. Later those same skills might help you persuade a boss to accept your proposal for a new project.

Group Discussion

Often, members of a group disagree about a course of action. In these cases, an informal debate occurs. Here's an example. It's a hot summer day, and you and several friends have decided to go swimming. The problem is that some of your friends want to go to the community pool, but some of them want to go to the lake outside of town.

How do you solve the problem? If only one person has a car and a driver's license and that person is bigger and stronger than everyone else and always likes to get his or her way, the problem is solved. If, however, everyone has an equal say, the group will probably solve the problem by listening to the reasons different people give for going to the lake or the pool.

- The pool is closer.
- The lake is prettier.
- The pool water is cleaner.
- The lake water doesn't have chlorine in it.
- There will be more boys (or girls) at the pool.
- They've got a great water slide at the lake.

This battle of ideas would go on for a while, and during the conversation more people would begin to favor either the pool or the lake. The reasons for picking one solution would tend to outweigh those for picking the other. Some members of the group would argue more persuasively than others. Eventually, several people would swing over to one side, and the problem would be solved. The group as a whole would have acted like a jury in deciding the outcome of this informal debate.

Sometimes group discussions are determined by consensus (agreement), but other times by the most "powerful" member.

Organizations and Meetings

You probably belong to at least one organization that has meetings from time to time: your school class, Girl Scouts, a church committee, the athletic letter–winner club, Future Farmers of America, or the yearbook committee. Your meetings may be very informal, perhaps not much different from a discussion among a group of friends. In a larger organization, your meetings might be conducted according to the rules of parliamentary procedure (see Chapter 20). In either case, informal debate will occur as you and the other organization members discuss ways to solve problems.

Let's say, for example, that your sophomore class needs to raise a great deal of money to finance next year's

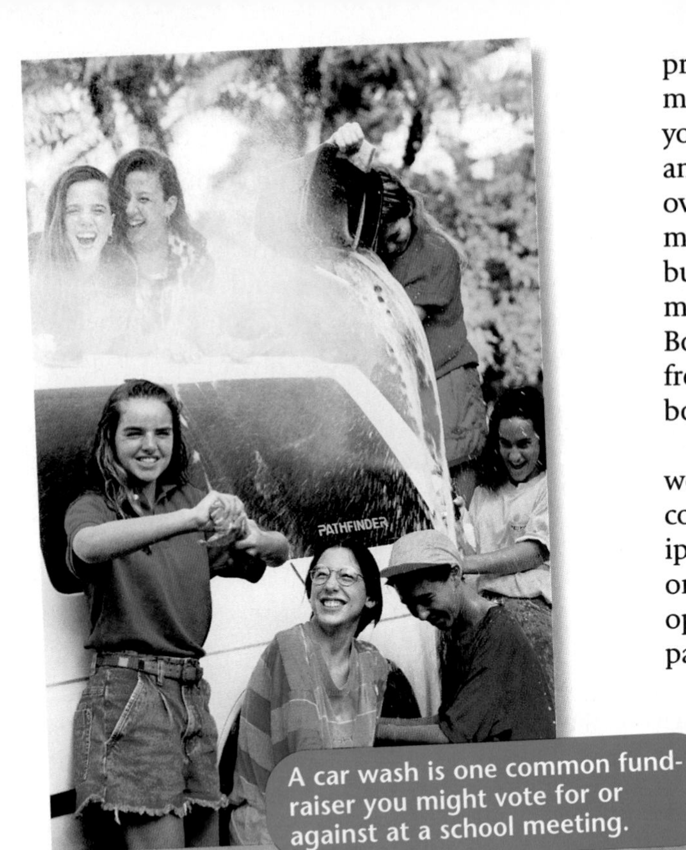

A car wash is one common fund-raiser you might vote for or against at a school meeting.

prom. You've got several ongoing projects to raise money, but you're looking for one big project for your sophomore year. One person has suggested an elaborate series of car washes every weekend over a six-month period, while another has recommended "selling" the members of the class to local businesses. The businesses would then contribute money to your class based on the students' work. Both ideas would require a lot of volunteer time from class members, so it's not practical to do both. One idea must be chosen. A debate begins.

If you have a strong opinion as to which method would be more fun and interesting—and, of course, would raise more money—you may participate in the debate by giving reasons for or against one of the alternatives. Even if you don't express an opinion in front of the group, you will probably participate in the debate as a judge, since the class will finally vote. Whether you speak or not, you will be participating in an informal debate.

SECTION 2 REVIEW

Recalling the Facts ...

1. Debate is a battle between ___________.
2. When you debate without specific rules, the process is described as ___________.

Thinking Critically ...

1. Working in pairs, observe each of your school's clubs and organizations. Contact the officers of each group to find out when the organization will have its next meeting and whether it would be all right for members of your class to attend as observers. The observers should report back to the class how much and what types of debate took place in these meetings. Discuss and evaluate what advantages, if any, would result from the use of formal debate procedures and skills.

Taking Charge ...

1. Make a list of the ideas you've debated with yourself over the past several days. Compare your list with your classmates' lists. If any ideas appear on more than one list, discuss whether or not the debates led to the same conclusion.
2. Role-play an argument between siblings. First, brainstorm as a class to generate a list of common topics over which siblings disagree. Then role-play the situations, which could involve from two to four siblings. Evaluate each situation to see if there were winners. If so, discuss which arguments or tactics proved most effective for the winners.

SECTION 3 The Advantages of Debate

There are many ways in which you can benefit from studying and practicing debate. Becoming an accomplished debater will help you immediately and in the future as well. Here are just a few of the advantages of becoming a better debater and a better evaluator of debates.

Career

In many of the careers you might pursue after leaving school, you will encounter situations in which you may or may not be chosen to move up to a position of higher responsibility and pay. In those careers, your success will often depend on your ability to persuade people. Most of the workplace situations in which you'll need to impress and persuade other people will involve some degree of debating skill. Managers and coworkers will challenge your opinions the way a debater is challenged. You'll have to think quickly and improvise rather than rely solely on prepared remarks. All of these skills are skills that you can begin developing as a debater.

Managers and coworkers help each other by examining and analyzing issues at work.

Helping Others

We all feel better when we can help other people. Think back to the class meeting example you read about earlier, when the class was deciding how to raise money for the prom. In that situation, the person who understands debate will be able to assist everyone in the class. How? By helping the class members focus on the key issues, by presenting the arguments for and against each alternative clearly and logically, and by helping the class evaluate those issues fairly.

In debate, you learn to narrow the issues so that they can be examined and analyzed, one at a time. You also learn how to present logical, well-supported arguments and how to find and point out errors in other arguments. All of this helps everyone move closer to the truth and to the best solution for the problem. In so doing, you help everyone involved.

As a Voter

As you learn about debate, you will become a more effective evaluator of arguments. You will become a more analytical listener. If you listen to two candidates debate, you'll be better able to tell which candidate is the better prepared, the more logical, and the quicker thinker—all qualities that would help that person perform her duties successfully if elected. You would also become more knowledgeable and able to make a more informed

COMMUNICATION

Breakthrough

International Debate

Tim Averill's original idea was to take his championship Manchester, Massachusetts, high school debate team to London to celebrate its twentieth anniversary. As Averill organized the trip, his London contacts kept suggesting that Manchester represent the U.S. in the World School Debating Championships. Manchester accepted the invitation and joined 12 other countries.

Some topics were sent to the debaters several months before the competition, and the remainder of the topics were announced with one-and-a-half hours' notice and prepared by the teams with no assistance from their coaches. For the debates, the U.S. team from Manchester was assigned the following topics:

- This House believes that nuclear energy is worth the risk.
- This House believes that today's heroes are hollow.
- This House would abolish all monarchies.

Manchester was also assigned the following topics, for which they had 90 minutes' preparation time:

- Resolved: that this House welcomes the fall of Communism.
- Resolved: that this House would close down Hollywood.
- Resolved: that this House believes that the war against discrimination has been fought badly.

"The emphasis is upon 'public persuasion,'" said Averill, "and the careful use of a relatively small amount of evidence." Each team is encouraged to have an advocacy position, but it is the ethos of the individual speakers that determines the outcome—humor and wit are required and rewarded. Unlike policy debates in America, the international debates focus more on the speaker's own knowledge than on documentation.

Members of the Manchester team were impressed by the quality of argument and delivery of the international champions (New Zealand). They learned much about style and technique from this memorable competition. Averill adds, "More importantly, we had the opportunity to get to know students from all over the world, to share ideas and opinions, and to assess our educational system by comparison."

Questions

1. Do you think the ethos of individual debaters should determine the outcome of debates? Why or why not?
2. One of the topics debated was "Resolved: that this House would close down Hollywood." What arguments might you have presented on this topic?

Do you feel strongly enough about an issue at school to seek election to your student council?

choice for the candidate you felt had the "right" ideas. As Thomas Jefferson argued, an informed electorate is necessary for a democracy to work.

As a Citizen

What are some of the "hot topics" at your school or in your community right now? Do you have strong feelings about any of these issues? If so, wouldn't you enjoy standing up at a school board meeting or a city council meeting and clearly and logically pointing out to everyone there why your solution was preferable to the other solutions being offered? If challenged or attacked, wouldn't you gain satisfaction from being able to respond to the challenge with several well-supported counter-attacks? Even more important than your personal satisfaction would be the community service that would result from your informal debate efforts. When you feel strongly about an issue, you can help the members of your community by helping them choose the best solution to their problem.

SEE IT AGAIN

INSTANT IMPACT

In March 1954, Edward R. Murrow, a prominent news commentator, used his television series *See It Now* to debate Joseph McCarthy, the Wisconsin senator and Communist hunter. Pointing out contradictions in McCarthy's statements and challenging his "facts," Murrow invited McCarthy to respond.

On April 6, McCarthy responded on *See It Now* that Murrow was "the leader and the cleverest of the jackal pack which is always found at the throat of anyone who dares to expose individual Communists and traitors." Throughout the broadcast, McCarthy used the very tactics—*innuendo, intimidation,* and falsehood—that Murrow had accused him of using. This second broadcast defined the characters of the two debaters. Wanting to be precise, Murrow read from a prepared text, while McCarthy made personal attacks on Murrow. McCarthy resorted to exaggeration; Murrow documented claims carefully.

Kathleen Hall Jamieson and David S. Birdsell, in *Presidential Debates,* conclude that: "Had McCarthy not engaged Murrow in debate before a common audience, and in the process confirmed the charges he was attempting to dispatch, the damage to McCarthy's credibility would have been less severe."

By the end of 1954, McCarthy was condemned by other members of the Senate. His public support eroded, and McCarthy died in 1957 from health problems.

WORDS FROM THE WORKPLACE

Priscilla Patiño Riette

Supervisor, Training and Technology

Q: *How does communication play a role in your day-to-day work activity?*

A: Communication plays a significant role in my daily activities. My position requires constant contact with people in the corporate and field offices. This liaison role is important because I am generally the first person the user contacts with technology-related problems or questions. Without good communication skills, I would not feel as competent in achieving the good rapport I have with the user community.

Q: *What specific communication skills do you use in your job?*

A: If a user is reporting a problem, I will generally take notes during the conversation. Once the problem is reported, I repeat the "symptoms" just to be sure I have understood the situation. In most cases my suggestion will be the fix to the problem. If I am unable to fix it, however, I have gained enough information to direct the user to the person or department able to help. Without these communication skills (listen/repeat/resolve or conclude), I am certain I would not be as successful as I have been in my work all these years.

Q: *What suggestions can you give to students to show the importance of good communication skills in the world of work?*

A: For the younger generation entering the work force today, I would definitely suggest they be prepared to meet situations with open minds and hearts. Do not expect a perfect world. Using basic communication skills such as the ones I have listed above are the keys to success. Do not assume knowledge before getting all the facts. It is okay to ask questions or to say, "Let me see if I understand what you are saying." I let people have their time before I respond. This technique helps them to feel we have the same level of understanding. We are equal. These are the keys to win-win relationships.

SECTION 3 REVIEW

Recalling the Facts ...

1. Describe three benefits of debate.
2. Explain how learning about debate will make you a better citizen

Thinking Critically ...

1. Do you believe that debate can change the minds of people? Select a recent presidential campaign and research the debates between the candidates. If possible, obtain transcript or a video of one of the actual debates. Re-create that debate for the class. Have class members vote for a candidate before the debate, and have them vote again after the debate. If opinions shifted, to what do you attribute those changes?

Taking Charge ...

1. Attend a school debate competition. Afterward, give a brief speech on "What Excites Me about Debate" or "What Frightens Me about Debate."

SECTION 4 Debate Terminology

Debate terms may seem hard at first—just like chemistry terms.

Part of what confuses many students as they begin to learn about debate is the terminology. Debate has a language all its own. Many of the terms are not used anywhere except in debate, which means you've never seen most of the terms before, and so you must learn many new words in a hurry. It's like trying to read Shakespeare for the first time, or learning chemistry. Of course, the terminology that is offered here is just an introduction to the world of debate. If you are interested in learning more, you should consider participating in interscholastic debate. Talk to the school sponsor for more information.

Once you learn the meanings of the new terms, though, you can proceed to the more fun and exciting parts of debate. Let's take some time to study the terminology of debate so that we can then move on to actual debating.

Proposition

One of the most important debate terms is **proposition.** Proposition is really just another word for statement. It is the statement of the point to be debated. It states a fact, a belief, or a recommendation to do something. Another way of explaining proposition is to say that it's a formal way of stating an opinion. Here are some examples:

- The minimum age for drinking alcohol should be raised to 25. (a proposition of policy)
- Christopher Columbus discovered America. (a proposition of fact)
- Honesty is more important than friendship. (a proposition of value)

Debaters are very careful about the way they word their propositions. The reason for their concern is that each word in the proposition can have a major influence on what happens during the debate. You will learn more about good and bad wording for propositions later in this chapter.

Resolution

Resolved is a formal word used to introduce a proposition. It doesn't affect the meaning of the proposition; it just introduces it formally. It does imply that some careful thought went into stating the proposition in those exact words.

In a practice debate, these students are resolving that penalties for convicted drunk drivers be more severe. To strengthen their argument, they are holding photos of teens killed by drunk drivers.

A proposition that begins with the word resolved is often called a **resolution.** A resolution is a formal statement of opinion. Here are some examples of resolutions. Note that they are the same as the propositions used previously. Nothing has changed in their meaning; they are just more formally stated.

- Resolved: that the minimum age for drinking alcohol should be raised to 25.
- Resolved: that Christopher Columbus discovered America.
- Resolved: that honesty is more important than friendship.

Affirmative and Negative

Affirmative and **negative** are two words that you probably already know. Affirmative means yes, or true; negative means no, or false.

These terms are important in formal debate because every proposition is worded so that you must either agree or disagree with it. You say either "Yes, that is true" or "No, that is false." During a formal debate, one side, called the affirmative side, tries to prove that the statement is true. The other side, called the negative side, tries to prove that it's false. For example, in a debate of the proposition that the minimum drinking age should be raised to age 25, the affirmative side would argue that, yes, it should be raised. The negative side would argue that, no, it should not be raised.

Status Quo

Status quo sounds much more complicated than it really is. It is a Latin phrase that simply means *the way things are now*—the existing conditions. The opposite of status quo is *change.* If every year for the last ten years your school has had a total enrollment of about 1,200 students, then an enrollment of 1,200 is the status quo. If next year the enrollment suddenly jumped to 2,000, that would be a change from the status quo. In formal debate, the negative side usually defends the status quo, arguing that there's no need to change—that whatever exists now is what should continue to exist.

Burden of Proof

Burden of proof is a term used both in formal debate and in law to refer to the duty or responsibility to prove something. In a criminal trial, for example, the prosecution has the burden of proof. It's the prosecuting attorney's job to prove that the accused person is guilty.

There is no burden of proof on the defense attorney. The defense attorney doesn't have to prove that the accused person is innocent. According to our system of laws, the accused person is "innocent until proven guilty."

In formal debate, the burden of proof is on the debater arguing for the affirmative. He or she must prove that there is a problem with the status quo and that it should change. Just as the jury assumes the accused to be innocent until proven guilty, the debate judge assumes the status quo to be the best solution until proven otherwise.

Argument

You know what an argument is—you've probably had your share. In debate the word argument has a meaning a little different from the one you're used to. Debaters use the word **argument** to refer to a reason for favoring their side

Lawyers must be skilled debaters.

of the proposition. The argument also includes the facts that support that reason. Each debater goes into a debate with several arguments that he or she will try to use to win the debate.

Evidence

You also know the word evidence. As Chapter 10 pointed out, it refers to information that helps prove something. Fingerprints and eyewitness accounts are evidence in trials. Facts, statements, reports, and quotes from experts are examples of evidence used in debates. Each side tries to find as much evidence as possible to prove its side of the proposition.

Case

If you watch courtroom dramas on television, you've probably heard the lawyers talk about "winning the case" or how they have "a great case." These lawyers are using the word **case** much as formal debaters use it, to mean the total group of arguments. The case is the combination of all the debater's ideas and evidence organized and arranged to be as convincing as possible. Knowing that lawyers carry their written arguments in a brief*case* may help you remember the meaning of this debate term.

Brief

Briefcase may also help you remember another term. Again, like lawyers, debaters talk about their briefs. A **brief** is what you might expect—something less than total, something that's not complete. In debate, a brief is an outline of both the affirmative and negative cases. Debaters use the brief as a guide and summary before and during the debate. It allows them to see all the relevant issues of the debate at a glance.

Constructive

The word **constructive** has a special meaning in formal debate. You can see in this unfamiliar adjective a clue to its meaning. The clue is the familiar verb construct, which means to build something. In debate, constructive describes specific speeches that debaters make during the debate. The constructive speeches are those that put forward an argument, that build an argument for one side or the other. When debaters give constructive speeches, they are building or presenting their arguments.

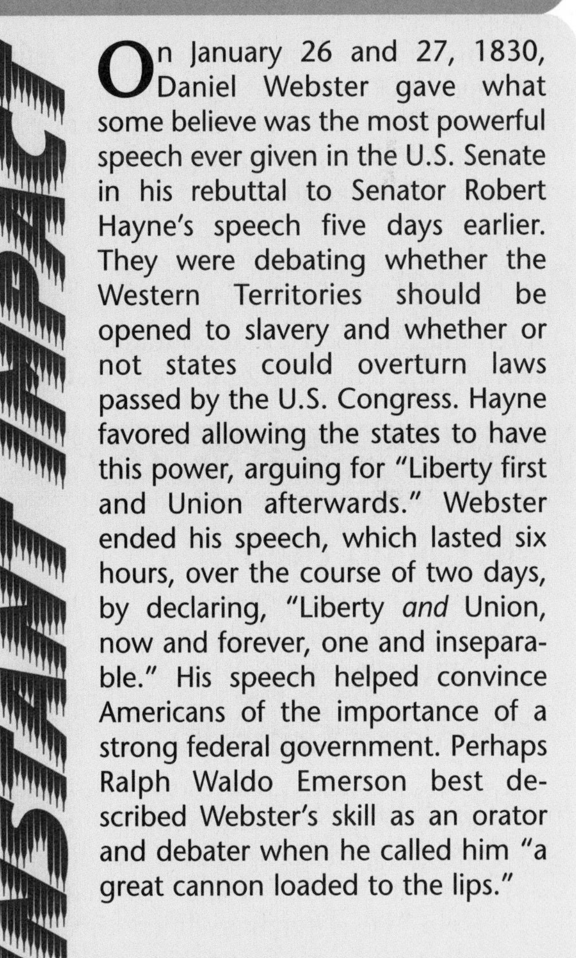

INSTANT IMPACT

A CANNON LOADED TO THE LIPS

On January 26 and 27, 1830, Daniel Webster gave what some believe was the most powerful speech ever given in the U.S. Senate in his rebuttal to Senator Robert Hayne's speech five days earlier. They were debating whether the Western Territories should be opened to slavery and whether or not states could overturn laws passed by the U.S. Congress. Hayne favored allowing the states to have this power, arguing for "Liberty first and Union afterwards." Webster ended his speech, which lasted six hours, over the course of two days, by declaring, "Liberty *and* Union, now and forever, one and inseparable." His speech helped convince Americans of the importance of a strong federal government. Perhaps Ralph Waldo Emerson best described Webster's skill as an orator and debater when he called him "a great cannon loaded to the lips."

Refute

To **refute** something means to show that it is wrong—to prove that something someone said is false. If someone said that your grandmother wears no footwear other than army boots, you could refute this by producing a picture of your grandmother in her house slippers. If your teacher said you hadn't handed in your homework, but then you found it in her stack of homework papers, you would be refuting her statement.

Photos could provide a way to refute another's argument.

An important part of formal debate is refuting your opponent's arguments. You do this by offering evidence to show why your opponent's statements are false. When you refute an argument, you are offering a refutation.

Rebuttal

A **rebuttal** is a speech that contradicts an earlier statement. The rebuttal tries to show that the earlier statement is wrong or false. The term sounds somewhat like the term you just learned—refute—and it should, because their meanings are very similar. In formal debate, there is an important difference, however. Refutation is the act of attacking your opponent's argument. Rebuttal is the act of countering your opponent's attacks on your arguments so that you can rebuild your argument. Consider this example:

- You present an argument in your constructive speech:
  "25-year-olds are more mature than 21-year-olds, so there would be fewer accidents if we raised the drinking age."
- Your opponent refutes your argument:

"There is no evidence to support the statement that 25-year-olds are more mature than 21-year-olds."

- You rebut your opponent's refutation:

"In a study conducted by the psychology department at Harvard, 25-year-olds were shown to score significantly higher on maturation scales than 21-year-olds."

SECTION 4 REVIEW

Recalling the Facts ...

1. What is the opposite of status quo?
2. What do you call the outline of both the affirmative and negative cases?

Thinking Critically ...

1. Debaters take great care in defining the terms in a debate. Suppose you were debating the proposition "Resolved: that honesty is more important than friendship." Does it make a difference how each debater defines friendship? Why?

Taking Charge ...

1. Write ten propositions dealing with issues you'd like to see debated. Following each, tell whom you would like to see debate the issue. For example, you might want to see a national high school debate champion and your mother debate the proposition "Resolved: that adults will no longer be allowed to limit the time their children spend watching television." Be sure to begin each proposition with the word resolved. Make sure that each proposition is a yes-no statement.

SECTION 5

The Debate Process

Let's now look briefly at how a debate works. We'll outline the basic process so that you'll have enough knowledge to conduct a debate in your classroom. Remember that if you want to participate in interscholastic competition, you should talk to the debate sponsor in your school. The sponsor will explain the two types of formal debate practiced in high school contests—Lincoln-Douglas debate and policy debate.

Working with a friend may help you get started on your first debate.

Getting Started

Of course, every debate begins with a topic. You need a problem, and you need a proposed solution to that problem (the proposition). While there are countless problems that could be debated, people often pick the more controversial issues. These are the topics about which many people on both sides of the issue feel strongly. Here are some broad issues that could serve as topics for debate:

- Changing driving age to 18 years old
- Uniforms in public schools
- *Vouchers* for public education
- The federal *deficit*
- Health care legislation
- Penalties for driving while intoxicated
- Public employees' right to strike
- Censorship of rock music
- Term limits for legislators

It's not enough, however, to pick an issue. You can't just choose one of the issues above and say, "Let's debate." To make the issue debatable, you must write a proposition in its proper yes-no form. The proposition also needs to focus on one part of

Reprinted with special permission of King Features Syndicate.

the issue, and it must be clearly worded so that there's no confusion about what's being debated.

The careful wording of a proposition is a key difference between debate and the heated discussions people sometimes get into. In those discussions, the argument isn't clearly focused on one definite part of the issue. Instead, everybody offers his or her own propositions, and people rarely take the time to define terms. That is why little progress is made in clarifying the issues or solving the problem in such arguments.

Here are some examples of poorly worded propositions:

- Resolved: that uniforms are bad.

The language is vague (what does "bad" mean?) and it is not clear what is being proposed.

- Resolved: that the federal deficit should be reduced by raising taxes and cutting military spending.

There are two different propositions, and you can't debate two at once

- Resolved: that the penalties for drunk driving are necessary.

No change is proposed, the proposition must clearly state a proposed change from the status quo.

As soon as you have your proposition, you are ready to divide into teams. You need a team for the affirmative, a team for the negative, and a judge. It's up to the affirmative team to prove the proposition. The negative team defends the status quo and tries to discredit the proposition.

Formats

Several different formats are used for formal debate. **Format** refers to the procedure that will be employed to conduct a particular debate. The format specifies the order in which the debaters will speak and the amount of time allowed for each speech. The main purpose of establishing a format is to give both sides an equal opportunity to make their cases. Since the affirmative side is proposing change (arguing for the proposition), it goes first and usually speaks last as well. For a classroom debate, you can devise whatever format you like, as long as the rules are clear ahead of time and fair to both sides.

Strategy

Following are a few general suggestions for preparing and arguing your case. Basically, you want to gather as much evidence as possible to support your case and to refute your opponent's case.

- *Work hard.* Many debates are won or lost before they begin. Everyone on the team must work to gather evidence.
- *Anticipate.* In your research, you'll come across evidence that will support your opponent's arguments. Don't overlook this information. Use it to anticipate your opponent's arguments and then plan how you will respond.

Plan your strategy carefully.

- *Build a sound case.* Pick the three or four strongest reasons for your side of the proposition and support those reasons as best you can with strong evidence. Organize your case logically (refer to Chapter 10).
- *Listen.* Listen closely to what your opponent says. You want to find weaknesses in your opponent's evidence and arguments. Remember to listen to what the evidence actually says, not what your opponent claims it says. For example, your opponent may make an illogical assumption based on his or her evidence. The fact that 10,000 17-year-olds were killed in car accidents doesn't by itself prove that the driving age should be raised to 18.
- *Take notes.* As the debate goes on, you will need to take careful notes to keep track of both your statements and your opponent's. Formal debaters call their notes a **flowsheet.**
- *Speak clearly and logically.* Organize your thoughts before you speak so that you are sure to make your points. It's important not to get too excited or rushed in your eagerness to refute your opponent's arguments.

Take careful notes while listening to the opposition.

SECTION 5 REVIEW

Recalling the Facts ...

1. What is the key difference between a formal debate and a heated discussion?
2. Give two examples of poorly worded propositions and explain why they create problems.

Thinking Critically ...

1. Students who participate in policy debate competitions learn that if the judge believes that the debate is a tie, she will vote for the negative team. Does this practice seem fair to you? Why?

Taking Charge ...

1. As a class, pick the two or three most interesting topics from the list on page 473 and debate them in class.
2. As you prepare for the debates, keep in mind that the best debaters are able to anticipate arguments from the opposing team. Take some time to think of opposing arguments and what your response will be.

STUDENT WORK

"The Play's the Thing" *by Jasmine Barnsley*

Students and parents often find themselves informally debating the value of competition. Jasmine Barnsley argues in excerpts from her speech that "the play's the thing."

It was a moment made for heroes: the 90,185 fans, the eerie stillness, and the final penalty kick to clinch a storybook series. When United States defender Brandi Chastain blasted the ball into the goal to win the women's World Cup, the crowd erupted into celebration. And at home my nine-year-old cousin Bekah leapt off the couch, placed her hands on her hips and proclaimed, "I'm gonna be a professional soccer player when I grow up! You see now that we won the World Cup all of the girls will be famous and Nike will give them all sorts of money to be on TV and did you see when that girl just took her shirt off? That's what I want."

And in our family, Bekah gets what Bekah wants. My aunt drives her to every soccer-related function. And Bekah is not only driven, she is "driven." But she is not alone. How many of us have forgotten what Shakespeare once suggested, albeit in another context: "the play's the thing." We have become so concerned with what time the exercise class is, when the credit card bill is due, where the shorts that go with the uniform are, how we can get one kid to the ice arena and then the other across town in five minutes, or in my case in Economics class, why everyone keeps laughing at that curve, that we simply don't have time to revel in each moment.

Bekah, along with too many kids today, has forgotten what it means to play. The thing to them is winning, the thing to them is to be the next Brandi Chastain, the next Tiger Woods. Now I am not saying that we shouldn't have dreams. But too many of us, in focusing on one dream, miss out on the joy that is present in each moment. Too many of us have forgotten how to play, and too many of us believe that when our dream doesn't come true that F. Scott Fitzgerald was right: there are no second acts in America. But Fitzgerald was wrong . . .

We can all learn from the man who was dying from Lou Gehrig's disease in the book *Tuesdays with Morrie.* His friend asks Morrie if he could wave a magic wand and be given 24 hours to do whatever he wanted, what would his perfect day be. Morrie answers: "I would have a lovely breakfast, then I would go for a great swim, then I would have a simple lunch with my friends, and we would walk in the park and talk about how much we meant to each other. Then I would have a dinner at a place with great pasta and I would dance with my wife until I was exhausted."

Mitch is taken aback by this response and says, "seems pretty simple." You see, what Morrie has figured out is that the best things in life are the simple everyday pleasures that we so often take for granted. These are the shining moments, and whenever I think of my own shining moments, I am always reminded of my grandma.

Grandma's was not an easy life. She grew up in a small adobe "casita" near an irrigation ditch in Tularosa, New Mexico, among pomegranates, quince trees, and five brothers and sisters. Each day from the moment she got home from school until she finally got her siblings into bed, she worked her hands raw. And yet, she became her high school's first Hispanic valedictorian and with that honor came a full college scholarship.

Unfortunately, though, her father became deathly ill and her family needed her more than ever. My grandma faced a difficult choice: to stay at home or to leave. So she made a promise to her father, a promise I was reminded of as I read the words of the poet Jimmy Santiago Baca, "Te prometi a ti y a todas las cosas vivas, que nunca te abandonaria." I promised you and all living things, I would never abandon you.

You see, whether Bekah becomes the next Brandi Chastain or not, is not important. For the play, the show must go on. It is what Bekah takes from each moment during soccer practice, at the games, or even the countless hours in the car with her mother. These will become Bekah's shining moments, and that is a lesson I learned from my grandma, mi abuela, nunca te abandonaria.

CHAPTER 18 Review and Enrichment...

Looking Back

Listed below are the major ideas discussed in this chapter.

- Negotiation can be a cooperative relationship.
- The five common strategies for conflict resolution are avoidance, accommodation, competition, compromise, and collaboration.
- Four techniques for effective negotiation are be positive, use three-part messages, be prepared, and tell the truth.
- Debate is a method used to solve problems.
- You can help your career, help others, and help as a voter and citizen by becoming a better debater and a better evaluator of debates.
- Debatable issues must be stated in proper form to allow for a successful debate. A proposition must be worded so that it can be answered yes or no; it must focus on one part of an issue; it must be clearly worded; and it must not favor one side or the other.
- Several different formats are used to structure debates. The affirmative side usually speaks first and last.
- To be successful at debate, you must work hard, anticipate your opponent's arguments, build a strong case, listen closely to your opponent's arguments, take notes, and speak clearly and logically.

Speech Vocabulary

Match the speech term on the left with the definition on the right.

1. argument
2. status quo
3. case
4. proposition
5. negative
6. refute
7. debate
8. negotiation
9. affirmative
10. rebuttal

a. Existing conditions
b. A method used to solve problems
c. Yes
d. Statement of a point to be debated
e. Total group of arguments
f. Reason for favoring a particular side of a proposition
g. Show how something is wrong
h. A speech countering your opponent's attacks on your arguments
i. A way of reaching a cooperative relationship
j. No

General Vocabulary

Write a definition for each of the terms listed below and then use each in a sentence.

barter	equitable	deficit	intimidation
alienate	voucher	innuendo	

CHAPTER 18 Review and Enrichment...

To Remember

Answer the following based on your reading of the chapter.

1. What is the difference between negotiation and debate?
2. Name four broad areas that can be helped by a person's learning about debate.
3. What word is used to introduce a formal debate's proposition?
4. What are the two sides called in a formal debate?
5. Find a word that means the opposite of *status quo.*
6. Is the negative side in a debate more like the prosecution or the defense in a court trial?
7. Does a debater's case include his or her evidence, or does the evidence include the case?
8. Which comes first, a constructive speech or a rebuttal speech?
9. How many parts of an issue can be included in a properly worded debate proposition?
10. What is the main purpose of establishing a debate format?

To Do

1. If your television receives cable broadcasts of either local or national political proceedings (for example, on C-SPAN), tape a debate. Bring the tape to your class. After watching the video, analyze the strengths and weaknesses of the debaters involved.
2. Debates usually deal with the most serious, emotionally charged issues. Brainstorm with the class to create a list of the most trivial, unimportant issues possible. Then choose three or four of the least important issues to debate. Divide the class up into two sides for each of those issues and debate the propositions.
3. Survey the school population to find out what issues in your school and community concern students. Pick the three or four issues that most concern students, and schedule debates for each of those topics periodically throughout the school year. Assign different members of the class to alternating sides of the various issues, and then stage the debates at a scheduled school assembly. Have the student body vote for the winner in each debate. You may want to experiment with various formats. For example, in some debates, members of the student body could ask specific questions of each debate team.

To Talk About

1. Some people seem to enjoy arguments and have a flair for them. Are you one of those people? If so, why do you think you enjoy arguments? If you are not one of those people, why do you dislike arguments?
2. Have you ever held back in an informal debate during a meeting, even though you felt you had something important to say? Why

did you hold back? What effect do you think your comments would have had on the course of the discussion and the results?
3. Recall debates you have seen on television or at debate contests. What speeches or qualities of the debaters impressed you the most?
4. When you are engaged in an argument with friends, do you usually get your way? If so, what strategies do you use to convince your friends that your suggestion is the best? If you often lose arguments, what strategies have you observed being used by your friends who usually win the arguments?

To Write About

1. Write a short story of two to four pages. Write it in the third person, with the main character being someone at a school or group meeting. This character has something to say but is afraid to speak up. What happens?
2. Opportunities for arguments present themselves constantly. As a rule, most of us either respond to the issue and debate it, as long as the other person is willing, or shy away from the confrontation. Write an essay explaining which course of action you believe to be better. If you think that whether you should debate the issue depends on the issue and its importance, give specific examples as to which issues are worth debating and which aren't.
3. Over the next few days, be aware of debates that you have with yourself. Write out the arguments that each side of you is presenting. Use two different names for yourself, and write the debate as a back-and-forth discussion between the two characters.

Related Speech Topics

The following list contains several potential topics for debates.

The voting age should be lowered from 18 to 12.

Potential voters should be required to pass, with a score of 70 or above, a test covering the prominent issues in a given election year.

Failure to vote in an election should result in a 5 percent increase in a qualified voter's personal income tax for the 4 years following that election.

Loyalty to parents is more important than loyalty to peers.

The experience gained from a part-time job is more valuable than the money earned in that job.

CHAPTER 19

LINCOLN–DOUGLAS DEBATE

"It is better to debate a question without settling it, than to settle a question without debating it."

—Joseph Joubert

Learning Objectives

After completing this chapter, you will be able to do the following.

- Discuss what values are, what importance values have, and how questions of value are different from other questions.
- Analyze questions in terms of value judgments.
- Write cases that argue for and against value propositions.
- Debate a complete round in the Lincoln–Douglas format using your organizational, cross-examination, and rebuttal skills.

Chapter Outline

Following are the main sections in this chapter.

1. A Question of Values
2. Preparing for Battle: Writing Cases
3. Structuring Your Speeches

New Speech Terms

In this chapter, you will learn the meanings of the speech terms listed below.

Lincoln–Douglas debate
factual proposition
policy proposition
value proposition
value
ought
signposting
value premise
value criteria
first affirmative constructive (1AC)
first negative constructive (1NC)
cross-examination
first affirmative rebuttal (1AR)
negative rebuttal (NR)
second affirmative rebuttal (2AR)
prep time

General Vocabulary

Expanding your general vocabulary will help you become a more effective communicator. Listed below are some words appearing in this chapter that you should make part of your everyday vocabulary.

renowned
sanctity
covert
affluent
surrogacy
evasive
dire

Looking AHEAD

In this chapter, you are going to learn about a particular kind of formal debate—Lincoln–Douglas debate. If formal debate is new to you, you may at first get the impression that formal debaters speak a foreign language. The unfamiliar vocabulary and new concepts may seem very challenging.

Do not be discouraged. Learning formal debate is like learning any activity. If you make a serious effort and are persistent, you will soon master the rules of Lincoln–Douglas. And the effort will be well worth it, since Lincoln–Douglas debate is an attempt to resolve value conflicts, a process that lies at the heart of our democratic process. This means that as you study this chapter, you will be developing skills that will make you a more effective citizen.

Introduction

Should police officers be allowed to stop and search your car randomly as a part of the effort to win the war on drugs? Should high school administrators be able to censor student newspapers? Is it fair for the government to tax the poor to fund new public highways? Politicians too often try to answer these difficult questions with snappy sound bites, like "Just say no" and "Read my lips." Most people would agree, though, that questions such as these require thorough discussion and much thought.

Indeed, these questions can lead to even more difficult underlying questions:

- Should we value privacy more than we value stopping crime?
- Should students' rights be different from those of their parents?
- Does each citizen have special obligations to every other citizen?

While these broad questions may seem abstract and confusing, they are important questions—questions that need to be answered clearly and intelligently.

How does one even begin to tackle such complex questions? One way is to learn about and then participate in **Lincoln–Douglas debate** (or *L–D* for short). L–D is a competitive type of formal debate practiced at high schools across the nation. Even if you never compete in a tournament, though, understanding the process of Lincoln–Douglas debate is of great value. It teaches you to argue logically and persuasively about ethical issues. It also helps you learn to persuade others when confronted with issues that involve ethical decision making. You will learn to analyze and to speak about questions of public policy and personal moral choice by attempting to resolve ethical dilemmas. Such ethical dilemmas occur when choices have to be made between alternatives that are equally desirable or undesirable.

In the previous chapter, you learned about propositions. The first section of this chapter discusses the specific kind of proposition used in Lincoln–Douglas debates.

Abraham Lincoln won the famed Lincoln-Douglas debates with intellect, strategy, and speaking ability.

COMMUNICATION

Breakthrough

The Lincoln–Douglas Debates

In 1857, the black slave Dred Scott sued his "master" for his freedom on the basis of his five-year stay in the free territories of Illinois and Wisconsin. The Supreme Court denied Scott a trial. It ruled that Scott was a slave, not a citizen. As a slave, he was less than a person—mere property. Therefore, said the Court, slaves could be taken to any state, free or not, and still could not sue for their freedom. Furthermore, the Court proclaimed that no state could rightly force slaveholders to give up their slaves, because to do so would deprive citizens of their property. The *Dred Scott* decision deeply divided the nation and once again thrust the slavery issue into the forefront of political debate.

One year later, Abraham Lincoln, Republican nominee for an Illinois Senate seat, challenged Democratic nominee Stephen Douglas to a series of debates. After Dred Scott, the focus of the debates was fated to be the slavery issue. Lincoln depicted Douglas as pro-slavery and a defender of the *Dred Scott* decision. Lincoln opposed slavery, although he was forced to adopt the conservative position that he would not force the states to surrender their rights.

Many initially thought that Lincoln, with his unsightly mole, high-pitched voice, lanky stature, baggy clothes, and unshined shoes, had virtually no chance against the polished, confident "Little Giant" Douglas. With his *renowned* oratorical skills, Douglas was considered the foremost debater of his day. Yet Lincoln managed to trap Douglas in a dilemma: He asked Douglas, what if the people in a state decided to vote to free the slaves? After all, it was Douglas who supported the right of the states to choose.

Douglas was forced to admit that if the people wanted to, they could free the slaves, regardless of the *Dred Scott* decision. In making this admission, Douglas split his party, many of whom were counting on him to defend slavery to the last. Even more importantly, Lincoln captured the nation's attention and, in the words of the Stanford University historian David Kennedy, "won a clear moral victory."

The Lincoln–Douglas debate competitions of today take more than their name from these historical confrontations. Although the formats of the debates are significantly different, the emphasis on intellect, strategy, and speaking ability remain crucial to the success of the debater. Furthermore, the competitors, like Lincoln before them, try to convince those people sitting in judgment that they have won clear moral victories.

Source: David Kennedy and Thomas Bailey, *The American Pageant,* D.C. Heath and Co., 1987.

Questions

1. Given Lincoln's unsightly appearance, do you think that the outcome of the debates would have been different had television coverage been possible at that time in history?
2. How important is it that a victory be moral?

SECTION 1 A Question of Values

You may have found yourself debating with friends about who is the best rock 'n' roll artist. Most artists, as you know, are popular only for a short time. In a poll of 600 musicians and songwriters, the Beatles were selected as the greatest rock 'n' roll artists of the twentieth century. Not everyone agrees with that choice, of course. Over 700,000 fans make the pilgrimage to Graceland—the home of Elvis Presley—each year. Many of these fans are teenagers. So, Elvis or the Beatles? How are such questions decided in formal debate? In other words, what kind of proposition do these questions involve?

Debate Propositions: Which Type?

At the end of the Beatles' song "Strawberry Fields Forever," does John Lennon say "I buried Paul," or does he say "cranberry sauce"? This question is a factual proposition. **Factual propositions** are either true or false. To determine whether John says, "I buried Paul" or not, you need only play back a tape of this song until you arrive at a conclusion.

Contrast the "I buried Paul" versus "cranberry sauce" question with the following proposition: "Should the United States government conduct scientific studies to determine whether Elvis is alive?" This type of proposition, a **policy proposition,** focuses on the desirability of a particular course of action. To evaluate the action, we could create a plan to find Elvis and then debate the advantages and disadvantages of the proposed plan. By weighing the advantages and disadvantages as well as the workability of our plan, we would be able to answer the question.[1]

The **value proposition,** however, cannot be answered by knowing the facts or by predicting the effects of a plan. Value propositions—such as "Is listening to the Beatles better than listening to Elvis?"—are the basis for Lincoln-Douglas debate. The value proposition debated is generally called the resolution. (Recall from Chapter 18 that in formal debate, propositions are stated as resolutions.) Typically, these resolutions involve philosophical judgments and thus are more difficult to answer than questions of fact or policy. Why? Because there is no right or wrong answer. For example, to answer the Beatles-Elvis question, you must somehow compare the worth of listening to the Liverpool lads with the worth of kicking back with the King. How do you decide which has greater "worth"? The answer is by applying values.

What Are Values?

What is a value? A **value** is simply a standard we apply to judge something right or wrong, good or bad. You have a set of values. You may value the loyalty of a friend or the privacy of being left alone in your room. As the novelist James Michener explains, "Values are the emotional rules by which a nation governs itself. Values summarize the accumulated folk wisdom by which a society organizes and disciplines itself. And values are the precious

1. Policy propositions are also used in another type of competitive debate: policy debate. In a policy debate, a team of two debaters affirm and a team of two debaters negate a question of social policy. The question of social policy is the resolution. During the 2000–2001 school year, for example, most policy debate students researched and debated the following resolution: "Resolved: that the United States federal government should significantly increase protection of privacy in one or more of the following areas: employment, medical records, consumer information, search and seizure." The complexities of policy debate would require another book to explain. If you would like to participate in this worthwhile form of competitive debate, talk to your teacher about the opportunities available at your school.

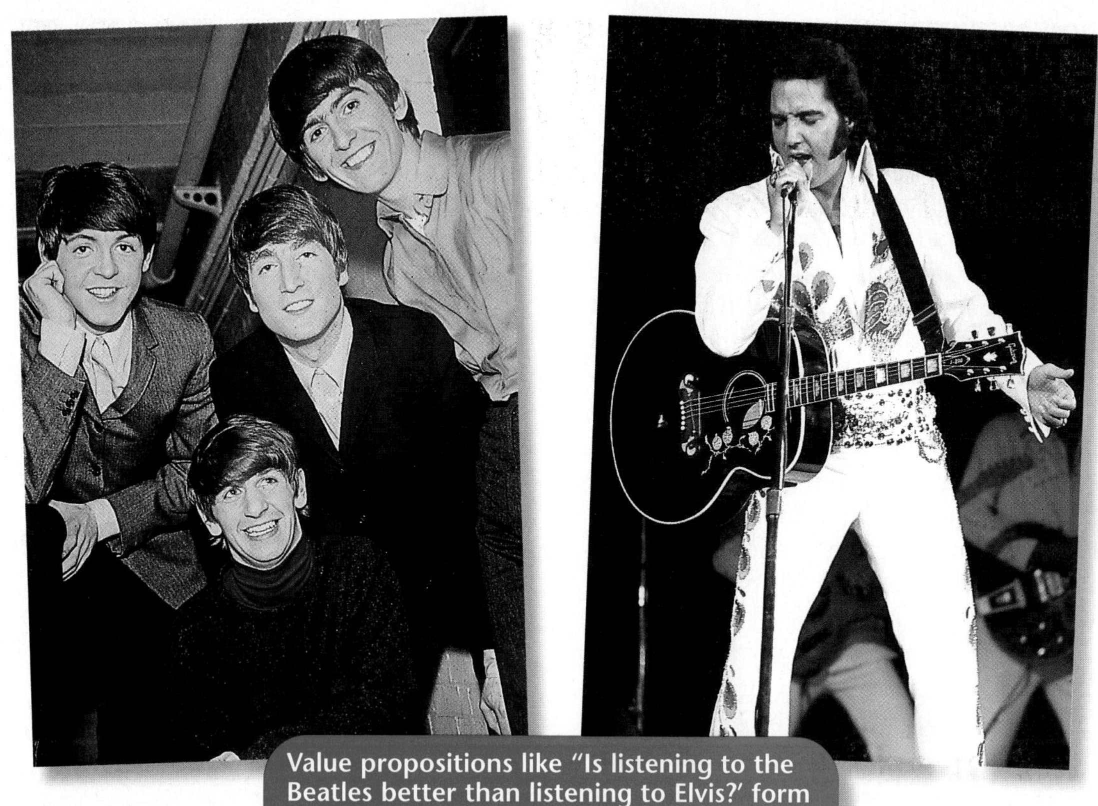

Value propositions like "Is listening to the Beatles better than listening to Elvis?' form the basis for Lincoln–Douglas debate.

reminders that individuals obey to bring order and meaning into their lives."

These standards are of different types. They may be moral values: Is something just or unjust, fair or unfair? They may be aesthetic values: Is something beautiful or ugly, artistic or inartistic? They may be political values: Is something democratic or tyrannical, helpful to freedom or harmful to it? To resolve the Beatles–Elvis question, you might apply the value of musical importance. In that case, you would make a choice based on the standard of who played a more important role in the history of rock 'n' roll. If you applied a different value—say an aesthetic one based on the quality of lyrics—you might come to a different conclusion.

The choices we make as a society reflect the values that we as individuals hold most dear. Consider the question of whether the death penalty ought to be legal. If you believe the *sanctity* of human life is the highest value, then, by that standard, you would oppose the death penalty. Suppose you are debating the question of whether the government ought to place restrictions on certain types of handguns. If you wished to uphold the value of public safety, you might answer yes, handguns should be restricted to protect the general public. If, on the other hand, you wished to uphold the value of personal freedom, you might answer no, handguns should not be restricted, because any limitation would make people less free.

The Rules of the Game: Value Analysis

So you know what values are, and you know that Lincoln–Douglas debate is concerned with questions of value. The responsibility of the L–D debater is to find the values within a resolution, to apply those values, and then to prove or disprove the resolution. Consider, for example, the following resolution: "Resolved: that the United States ought to value global concerns above its own national concerns." In order to learn how to "find" values in such statements, you must first understand more about the nature of values. Furthermore, analyzing and applying values involves certain rules. You need to know some of these rules.

Perhaps the best way to understand how value analysis works is to imagine that you wake up one morning and you rule the world. You can do virtually anything you want (within the laws of nature—in your fantasy, you still can't fly, nor can you leap tall buildings in a single bound). Given your great power, you may decide to allow abortion on demand, or you may decide to make abortion illegal. You may choose to force students to perform community service. Maybe not. It's your choice. Whatever you think is right. But before you make your decisions, you have much thinking to do: Why should you prefer one question to another? What is important to you? In short, the ultimate question you must ask yourself is "How *ought* things be?"

Ought refers to your idea of the ideal. When you are discussing what "ought" to be, your are describing how you think things should be, regardless of how they actually are now. Although some debaters use the terms should and ought interchangeably, there is a difference. *Should* simply suggests doing what is appropriate or fitting. *Ought* refers to a moral obligation based on a sense of duty. Furthermore, how things ought to be and how things actually are involve two different issues. Many people make the mistake of assuming that things are supposed to be the way they are.

As you learned in Chapter 10, on logic and reasoning, it is an error in reasoning to state that just because something is, it also ought to be. To understand why, consider the following examples: There is homelessness. Does that mean there ought to be homelessness? People are suffering. Does that mean people ought to suffer? People ought not starve to death in the wealthiest nation in the world, but they do. People ought not to steal, but they do. Lincoln–Douglas debate explores the world of *ought,* not the world of *is.* L–D leaves the world of *is* to economists, scientists, and historians.

Three American debaters on the left take on a team from Scotland at the World Schools Debating championships.

Facts and Values: Establishing Valid Arguments

Our explanation of what ought to be may seem to imply that facts have no place in Lincoln–Douglas debate. Not true. Facts and other forms of evidence are a crucial part of debate, just as they are crucial in any discussion. For example, if you were debating whether or not limitations on firearms sales are justified, you would want to provide statistics indicating the number of deaths caused by handguns each year.

Facts alone cannot establish the validity of a value statement, but facts combined with the right values can. If your best friend is drowning, for example, the fact that you can swim does not necessarily mean you ought to save her. Suppose you agree, though, that all people who can help others in trouble ought to do so (a value judgment). You then point out that you can swim and that your friend is drowning. You have proven that you ought to help your friend. Of course, if it can be shown that both of you would drown in the attempt, then that value judgment can be challenged.

Now suppose you are arguing that the government ought not legalize drugs. You may list various harmful effects of drugs: antisocial behavior, increased crime rates, cost to society, and so on. These harmful effects, by themselves, do not prove that drugs should be illegal. You must also make the value judgment that allowing people to harm themselves is wrong. When you make this judgment, the argument is complete: (1) harming oneself and others is wrong, (2) drugs harm people in numerous ways, (3) therefore, the government ought not legalize drugs.

Some Values Commonly Used in Lincoln–Douglas Debate

Some of the values most commonly used in Lincoln–Douglas debate include the following:

1. Liberty. People and governments ought to act so that each individual has the greatest possible freedom (without harming others). *Possible applications:* arguing for free speech, against compulsory national service, for legalizing drugs.
2. Equality of opportunity. Government policies should give all citizens fair access to jobs and services. *Possible applications:* arguing for affirmative action programs to remedy past discrimination, against dividing high schools into vocational and college preparatory programs.
3. Democracy. The people ought to have the maximum possible role in determining questions of right and wrong. Major policy decisions should be put to public debate or vote. *Possible applications:* arguing in favor of making sensitive government information available to the public, against allowing the government to take *covert* actions.
4. Justice. This is usually seen as a value that protects other values, such as liberty and fairness. Plato's classic definition of justice is "giving equal amounts to equals and unequal amounts to unequals." Examples of what may be given include wealth, political

privilege, and punishment. *Possible applications:* arguing that the *affluent* nations of the world ought to feed the poorer nations or that the right to a fair trail justifies limiting press coverage.

Knowledge of these values—liberty, equality of opportunity, democracy, and justice—will help you to analyze most L–D debate resolutions. Many other values are argued in L–D debate, however.

Remember, a value is a concept, not a particular document or court ruling. Some debaters, for example, try to use the United States Constitution as a value. The Constitution as a document is not, in itself, a value. There are, however, values embodied within the Constitution. These values include freedom of speech, the right to a fair trial, and individual liberty.

SECTION 1 REVIEW

Recalling the Facts ...

1. What are the three types of debate propositions? How do they differ?
2. Name some of the values most commonly used in Lincoln–Douglas debate.

Thinking Critically ...

1. As a class, agree on a topic that is important and controversial in your school. Try to determine what values are at stake in the conflict. If students are not allowed to leave campus, for example, two values in conflict might be freedom and safety. How can such values—freedom and safety—be compared in making decisions? Do you think the potential for lawsuits is an important factor in most school decisions?

Taking Charge ...

1. Ethical issues are debated and discussed by people in all walks of life. Interview someone, and report on the moral complexities that arise for that person in the workplace. Possible interviewees include the following:
   - A local politician or judge. Judges sometimes must make decisions that conform to the law but that conflict with their personal beliefs. Politicians often pass laws that sacrifice some people's interests. How do they justify these compromises?
   - A reporter. Journalists often have their "journalistic integrity" challenged in cases where they have to decide what to print and what to withhold. What are some of the guidelines they use in making these judgments?
   - A teacher. Should a teacher reward a student with a passing grade for exceptional effort even though the student's test scores earn a failing mark? How can a teacher fairly measure and reward subjective areas like class participation?

SECTION 2 Preparing for Battle: Writing Cases

Armed with your knowledge of values, you are ready to learn how to write cases. Remember from the previous chapter that your case is your total group of arguments—your basic position on the resolution. It is made up of all the arguments that you choose to present. Most L–D debaters use a format that includes four steps: (1) introduction, (2) definitions and analysis of the resolution, (3) establishing the values, and (4) arguments.

A general rule about writing cases: You should always tell the judge and your opponent when you are moving from section to section in your case. For example:

- "First, we should examine the key terms in the resolution (give your definitions)."
- "Now, I will present my value for the round (give your value)."
- "At this point, I will offer criteria (give your criteria)."
- "Next, I will present the first argument (state the argument)."

This technique of telling people when you are moving from section to section of your case is called **sign-posting.**

The Introduction

In the introduction, you always state your position in the debate—whether you are arguing the negative or the affirmative. In addition, you would like to start with a compelling statement to support your position. Many debaters choose to begin their speeches with a quotation. The quotation should lead smoothly into the specific resolution and should support your side. For example, suppose that you're on the affirmative side, and the resolution is "Resolved: that paid *surrogacy* ought to be legal." You are arguing that the government should allow contracts for surrogate mothers—women who are paid to have babies for others. You might begin like this:

> In *Maher v. Roe,* the Supreme Court ruled, "the right of procreation without state interference has long been recognized as one of the basic civil rights of man . . . fundamental to the very existence and survival of the race." Because I agree with the Court's ruling that couples must be allowed to establish families without government interference, I affirm the resolution: that paid surrogacy ought to be legal.

If you represent the negative side, on the other hand, you might begin this way:

> The journalist Ellen Goodman recently wrote in the *Boston Globe:* "It is fair to ask about the moral

The first step in preparing your case could be to consult your coach.

> limits of commerce. . . . We impose limits on our medical commerce . . . we cannot sell a kidney. We should not be able to sell a pregnancy." Because I agree with Ms. Goodman that it is morally unacceptable to place pregnancy on the market, I negate the resolution and stand resolved that paid surrogacy ought not be legal.

Of course, picking an appropriate quotation is not the only way to begin your debate case. Try experimenting with the various methods of introducing speeches that were discussed earlier in the book.

Definitions and Analysis of the Resolution

You will need to offer definitions for key terms in the resolution. Otherwise, there is no common ground for debate. Take, for example, the resolution "Resolved: that honesty is more important than loyalty." What do honesty and loyalty mean? Since different people have different meanings for these terms, it's important to agree on meanings.

In defining such terms, you should try to be reasonable—not too broad nor too restrictive. A definition that is too broad is vague and gives us no starting place for discussion. "Honesty is being faithful" is an example of a too-broad definition. In contrast, definitions can be too restrictive: "Honesty is telling the truth when your mother asks where you were last Saturday night." Such restrictive definitions limit the discussion too much.

Some debaters may try to "define you out of the round" by presenting completely unreasonable interpretations—for example, "Honesty is telling the truth specifically to hurt someone's feelings" and "Loyalty is performing noble acts to demonstrate faithfulness." These unreasonable definitions make fair debate impossible. Skilled debaters point out unfair interpretations to the judge.

In addition to defining key terms, you will need to analyze other aspects of the resolution. Look again at the sample resolution, "Resolved: that honesty is more important than loyalty." If you are observant, you noticed that the resolution does not contain the word *ought.* The resolution says *is.* Does this particular wording mean the resolution is one of fact, not values? No. All Lincoln–Douglas debate resolutions are propositions of value. What the resolution really asks is, "Ought loyalty be valued above honesty?"

Furthermore, in order for the debate to be meaningful, there must be a conflict. That is, you must come down on one side or the other. It is pointless to agree that you can be both honest and loyal—so neither loyalty nor honesty is more important. If you do not discuss those times when you had to choose between honesty and loyalty, then why debate at all? Consider this conflict scenario. You are in a grocery store with your best friend. Your friend shoplifts a candy bar but is seen by the store manager. You friend flees as you are detained by the security guard. The guard knows you are innocent but insists that you name the shoplifter. Honesty or loyalty—which is more important?

Clearly, conflict is necessary for debate. The conflict must be real, however. If you can watch *60 Minutes* on Sunday and also go to a movie on Saturday, you do not have to decide which entertainment choice should be more highly valued. But if the movie and the TV show are at the same time on the same day, you have a conflict.

Establishing Values

An important step in developing your case is to establish a **value premise.** The value premise establishes a standard by which one can evaluate whether or not the resolution is true. A value premise provides a starting point for an argument by summarizing the value you are using as the basis for the argument. In giving the value premise, you are asking the judge to accept it as the standard for deciding the debate. In other words, you are telling the judge that whichever speaker better upholds your value premise should win the debate.

Consider the following example. You are debating the resolution "Resolved: that limitations on

This high school senior, president of a city-wide student council, speaks in support of public education. She is stating her value criteria.

the right to bear arms in the United States are justified." If you are on the affirmative side, you want to choose a value that will support the resolution, so you select the value "public safety." By using this as your value premise, you are saying to the judge, in effect, that the decision in the debate should be based on which position better protects or preserves public safety—yours or your opponent's. You will argue that limiting handguns (the affirmative position) would better uphold public safety and that you should therefore win.

Suppose that you are on the negative side of the resolution "Resolved: that searching through student property in an effort to maintain discipline in school is justified." As the negative speaker, you are arguing that random searches through students' property by teachers and other school officials are not justified. Therefore, you might want to choose the value of privacy as your value premise and assert that the side whose arguments allow for greater privacy should win. You will argue that the affirmative speaker favors violating privacy by permitting searches through student property. You, the negative speaker, support a position that better upholds privacy and, by that standard, should win.

Both the negative and affirmative speakers may state **value criteria.** Value criteria provide further standards of judgment for evaluating whether or not the value premise has been realized. If a student upholds the value premise of justice, the student may argue that the value criterion should be based on which position better preserves and protects justice. Preservation and protection of justice become, then, the value criteria (standards of judgment) for deciding who wins.

Arguments

After offering definitions, a value premise, and value criteria, you're ready to present your arguments—the reasons for favoring your side of the resolution. Here are two important points to remember.

1. Always Make Your Arguments Refer Back to Your Value Premise ... Your value premise is the core of your case. Consider again the resolution "Resolved: that limitations on the right to bear arms in the United States are justified." You are the affirmative speaker and have presented the value premise of public safety. Each of your arguments, then, must mention public safety. For example, in your first argument, you might give statistics indicating that unlimited handgun sales present a high risk to human life. Then you could state that the risk to human life also risks public safety. Therefore, you would conclude, limitations are justified. We could represent the reasoning as follows: (1) Public safety is the most important value. (2) Guns threaten public safety. (3) Limitations on guns are justified to protect public safety.

Suppose, though, that you are debating the resolution "Resolved: that burning the American flag is morally acceptable." As the affirmative speaker, you present the value premise of free speech and state that all political speech is morally acceptable. Your first argument asserts that flag burning is a type of political speech. Because political speech must be protected, flag burning is morally acceptable. In other words: (1) Free speech is the most important value, so all political speech should be protected. (2) Flag burning is a type of political speech. (3) Flag burning is morally acceptable, since it upholds free speech.

2. Always Relate Your Evidence to Your Value Premise ... Remember that evidence only supports your case if you relate it to your value premise. Suppose you're debating the resolution "Resolved: that protection of the environment ought to be valued above the development of natural resources." The affirmative speaker may present evidence that proves the environment is being destroyed in various ways. This evidence, however, does not help the affirmative case unless the affirmative speaker has also presented a value premise that suggests that the environment ought to be protected.

Two Michigan legislators seem ready to present their arguments.

One type of evidence that L–D debaters commonly use is quotations from famous philosophers. Make certain when you use such quotations that they actually apply to your arguments and aren't just thrown in to impress the judge. Consider the "Flag burning is morally acceptable" resolution. It would be appropriate to use the following quotation from former Supreme Court Justice William Brennan: "We do not venerate the flag by prohibiting its desecration, for in so doing, we dilute the freedom that this cherished emblem represents." If, on the other hand, you quote the French philosopher Descartes's saying, "I think, therefore, I am," you are not thinking, nor are you debating the specific resolution.

Debate Skills

A good round of debate will include two features: clash and crystallization.

Clash . . . Clashing means making your arguments directly conflict with your opponent's. Although clashing may be something you try to avoid in your day-to-day communication, it is a desirable goal in L–D debate. Debate rounds without clash are sometimes described as being like two ships passing in the night.

You clash with your opponent's arguments by refuting them—by showing how they are flawed. To refute is not merely to repeat what you have said in earlier speeches.

In refuting your opponent's arguments, you should address them in order. You might, for example, say: "In John's first argument, he claims that all political speech should be protected. I have two responses. First, some types of political speech clearly ought not receive protection. John, you cannot express your dissatisfaction with the president by bombing the White House. Second . . ."

Note that in giving your refutation, you follow a pattern:

1. You briefly state your opponent's argument.
2. You say how many responses you have.
3. You make the responses, numbering each one as you go.

This pattern will help keep your speeches organized and clear.

Let's look at some common techniques of refutation: counterexamples, analogies, and contradictions.

Counterexamples. Suppose that your opponent offers an example in an attempt to support a general principle. For instance, suppose you are debating whether or not homeless people who beg are invading pedestrians' privacy. Your opponent points out that some beggars are alcoholics just trying to support their addiction. You could respond with the counterexample of families forced to beg in order to survive on the streets.

Analogies. Analogies can be useful in refuting arguments that are not supported by evidence. Suppose you're the negative speaker debating the resolution "Resolved: that the United States ought to value global concerns about its own national concerns." Your opponent makes the following points:

MODEL UNITED NATIONS

INSTANT IMPACT

Have you ever wondered what it would be like to serve in the United Nations? What if you were a delegate representing Denmark? Or Madagascar?

Competitive debate takes many forms, and one popular debate activity for students is sponsored by the Model United Nations Association. This international curriculum belongs to a long tradition of international education through simulation. Model United Nations at the college level traces its beginnings to a national Model League of Nations. In 1974, the sponsors of the National Collegiate Model United Nations decided to develop a program for high school students.

The first National High School Model United Nations conference held in the spring of 1975 was an immediate success. The difficulties of administering two national conferences, one immediately after the other, prompted the sponsors to create the International Model United Nations Association to supervise the high school conference.

The International Model United Nations Association has developed an innovative set of projects in addition to the conferences. An educational video, *Simulating the United Nations: Classroom to Conference,* is designed to help schools new to Model United Nations establish their programs and develop United Nations–based curricula for the classroom. The video is aimed at maximizing participation by new and old delegates alike—the key to getting the most out of Model UN on any level.

(1) The United States is a world leader with the capability of helping other nations. (2) All leaders capable of helping others in need ought to. (3) Therefore, the United States should value global concerns above its own national concerns. You can attempt to refute this argument with an analogy: Just because you are the best student in your biology class does not mean that you have a study session at your house every night to bring up the grades of the other students. This analogy exposes the fallacious assumption in the argument of the affirmative speaker.

Consider another example. Suppose you are the affirmative speaker, and you're defending global concerns. The negative speaker states: (1) The United States must take care of national concerns before addressing global concerns. As the philosopher Hans Morganthau once wrote, "A foreign policy guided by universal moral principles . . . relegating the national interest to the background is . . . a policy of national suicide." (2) Therefore, national concerns ought to be valued above global concerns.

The negative speaker's reasoning is flawed, because valuing something "before" something else is not the same as valuing it "above" that other thing. You can illustrate the flaw to the judge by analogy. Cocoa beans may come before chocolate, but that doesn't make them more valuable than chocolate. Algebra comes before calculus, but that doesn't make algebra more valuable than calculus. You may ride the bus before you go to school, but that doesn't mean you value the bus more than school. Analogies can be a concise and compelling strategy in debate—as long as they apply to the argument.

Contradictions. Sometimes, speakers present values that contradict their arguments. Suppose that you are debating the resolution "Resolved: that communities in the United States ought to have the right to suppress pornography." If the affirmative speaker defends free speech, you should point out to the judge that suppressing pornography will make speech less free—a contradictory position taken by the affirmative.

Crystallization . . . Crystallizing means choosing the most important arguments and linking them back to the values presented in the

"That's an excellent prescreened question, but before I give you my stock answer I'd like to try to disarm everyone with a carefully rehearsed joke."

round. Numerous issues will be introduced in any debate. It is your responsibility to focus on the key issues that the judge should weigh in reaching a decision. When you crystallize, you tell the judge the major issues that have been presented and why your value is superior. Finally, you give impact to the process of crystallization by explaining to the judge why you are winning each of the key issues.

SECTION 2 REVIEW

Recalling the Facts ...

1. In writing cases, most L–D debaters use a format that includes four steps. What are they?
2. What is a value premise? Explain the purpose of the value premise in judging a round of competition.

Thinking Critically ...

1. Lincoln–Douglas debate tournaments require that you debate on both the affirmative side and the negative side of a topic. You may have very strong feelings about issues such as abortion and capital punishment. Are there any topics concerning which you would find it impossible to argue for the side that disagreed with your beliefs? Do you think it's valuable to understand all sides of an issue? Why?

Taking Charge ...

1. Think of one compelling argument you could use to affirm the following Lincoln–Douglas debate topics. Then think of one argument that you would use to counter that argument for the negative side. Now find one piece of evidence to support each of your arguments.
   - Resolved: that no war is ever morally justified.
   - Resolved: that speech training is more beneficial than participation in sports.
   - Resolved: that domestic assistance programs should be valued more than international assistance programs.

SECTION 3 Structuring Your Speeches

Because Lincoln–Douglas debate is practiced nationwide, the National Forensic League has endorsed a special format for all L–D debaters to use:

1. First affirmative constructive (1AC): six minutes
2. Negative cross-examines affirmative: three minutes
3. First negative constructive (1NC): seven minutes
4. Affirmative cross-examines negative: three minutes
5. First affirmative rebuttal (1AR): four minutes
6. Negative rebuttal (NR): six minutes
7. Second affirmative rebuttal (2AR): three minutes

All of these speeches taken together make up one round of Lincoln–Douglas debate. Note that for both the affirmative and the negative, the total speaking time is thirteen minutes (with three minutes apiece for cross-examination). Each debater is usually given three minutes of total preparation time to be used throughout the debate.

Let's look at each part of this format in detail to see how each is structured.

The Constructives

Recall from Chapter 18 that constructives are the speeches that put forward your arguments. In L–D debate, the affirmative and the negative speakers have one chance each to present constructives.

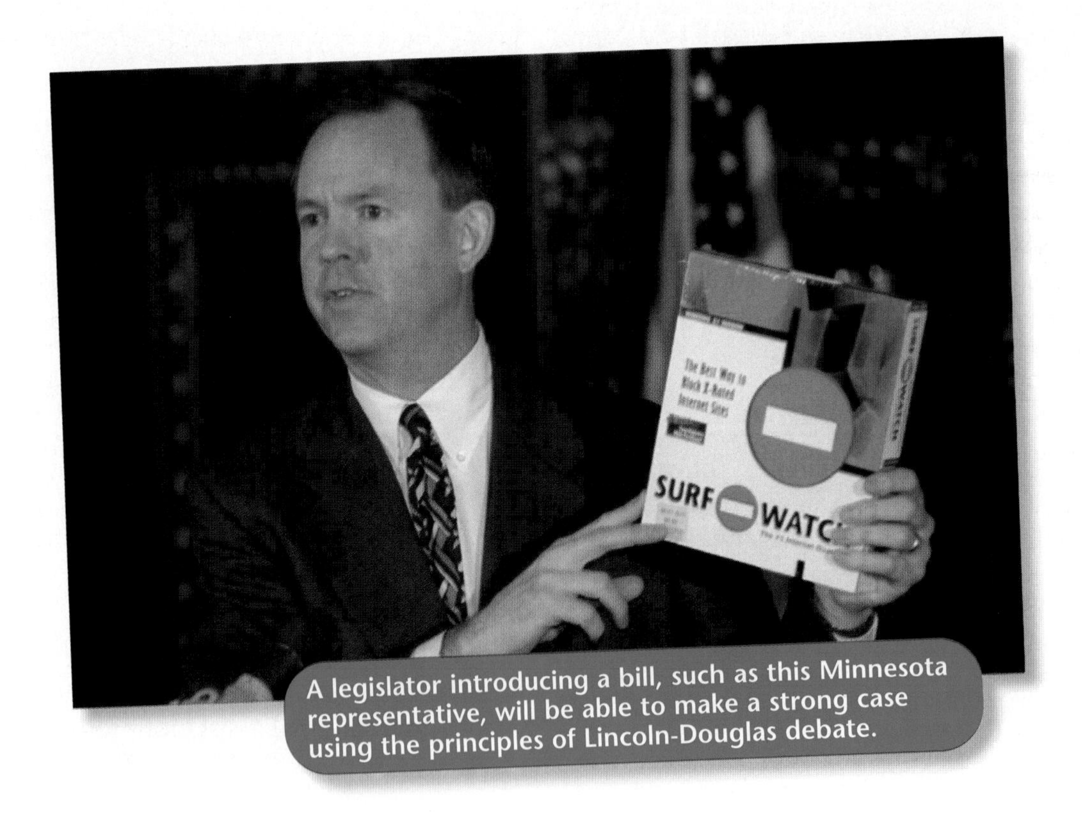

A legislator introducing a bill, such as this Minnesota representative, will be able to make a strong case using the principles of Lincoln-Douglas debate.

First Affirmative Constructive (1AC) —Six Minutes ... The **first affirmative constructive (1AC)** is the one speech that is prepared entirely before the round. If you are taking the affirmative position, you begin the debate by reading your affirmative case, and then you wait to be cross-examined by your opponent.

The elements of the 1AC were described earlier, when we discussed writing cases: the introduction, definitions, value premise, value criteria, and arguments. In addition, you should include a brief conclusion that summarizes your position. In terms of time allocation, your introduction should be about one-half minute long; your definitions, value premise, and value criteria, about one minute; your arguments, about four minutes; and your conclusion, about one-half minute.

A cross-examination period follows each of the constructives. The same strategies apply to both, so we will consider them together later.

First Negative Constructive (1NC) —Seven Minutes ... In the **first negative constructive (1NC),** most speakers also begin with their prepared constructive presentation (lasting three to four minutes). The remainder of the speech is devoted to refuting the affirmative constructive. The negative constructive speech, then, should do two sets of things: First, it should include an introduction; a value premise and possibly value criteria; counterdefinitions, if necessary; and the negative arguments. Second, it should clash with and refute the affirmative value and arguments.

Suppose that you and Karen are debating the resolution "that communities in the United States ought to be able to decide whether or not flag burning will be legal." Karen is on the affirmative side, and she chooses to defend the value of democracy. In the following exchange, you gamble with a why question.

You: Karen, you offer us the value of democracy.

Karen: Right.

You: What is the justification for democracy—why is democracy better than tyranny?

Karen: Er . . . because we ought to always allow the majority to decide what is right and wrong.

You: Hmmm . . . the majority, eh? Aren't there certain issues that the majority ought not be able to decide?

Karen: Er . . . no, I don't think so.

You: What if the majority in this country decided that all people born in 1970 will be executed tomorrow? Would that be OK?

Karen: No, I don't think so . . . (Karen has just contradicted herself).

In this exchange, you have established that some things ought to be outside the influence of majority opinion. All you have to do now is show that flag burning is one of those things.

Responding to Questions

Finally, let's consider some guidelines for responding to questions during **cross-examination.** During cross-examination, which follows each speaker's constructive, the speaker who has just spoken is questioned.

- Never let them see you sweat.
- Respond to each question thoughtfully and confidently. If you appear *evasive,* then the judge may wonder what else you are trying to hide.
- Know your case thoroughly and plan responses to anticipated questions.
- Avoid making speeches. Stick to the question asked; don't offer long, rambling explanations.
- Prepare carefully. Preparation will help you avoid falling into cross-examination traps.

The Rebuttals

As you learned in Chapter 18, rebuttal is the act of countering your opponent's attacks on your arguments so that you can rebuild your arguments. The rebuttal speeches come after the constructives. Before learning about the specific strategies for each rebuttal, you should know some of the general principles.

1. The purpose of a rebuttal speech is to bring the round into focus in such a way that you

The National Forensic League endorses a format for Lincoln–Douglas debate that consists of seven speeches, totalling 13 minutes. These speeches, taken together, make up one round of Lincoln–Douglas debate.

are able to defeat your opponent's arguments. You "sign the ballot for the judge" by giving the judge clear and specific reasons to vote for you.

2. You may extend (provide new responses to) arguments introduced in the constructives, but you should not initiate whole new arguments. Bringing up new arguments in rebuttals is described by some as "sliming." Sliming is a term that is also used to describe other debate tactics considered questionable or unethical—for example, distorting your opponent's position or asserting that an argument was dropped when, in fact, that is not the case.
3. When you run short on time and still have several arguments to answer, then you must attempt to find a common fault in the arguments. This technique of attacking the common flaw is known as grouping. For example, you and Farzana are debating the resolution "that communities in the United States ought to have the right to suppress pornography." You are the affirmative speaker, and in the first rebuttal you find yourself with only thirty seconds to respond to two more arguments. The arguments are that pornography is a legitimate form of political speech and that communities ought not have the right to censor political speech. All is not lost, because you can refute both these arguments by proving that pornography is not a form of political speech (much evidence exists to support this position). Here's how you might structure the few remaining seconds of your time:

Farzana has two more arguments. First, she says that pornography is a form of political speech. Second, she says that communities ought to have the right to censor political speech. Realize, however, that both of these arguments assume that pornography is political speech. This assumption is incorrect because . . .

4. Point out dropped arguments to the judge. Dropped arguments are simply arguments

that a debater failed to respond to. The significance of any argument dropped by your opponent should be explained and weighed in the context of the resolution.

5. Fallacious assumptions and glaring contradictions should be highlighted at the beginning of the rebuttal to provide a showcase for these potentially devastating attacks.
6. Most debaters begin their rebuttals by refuting their opponent's analysis, and then they return to their own case. If you end the speech with your own arguments, you focus the judge's attention on the resolution from your perspective. In short, you place the round in your ballpark—a technique known as ballparking.
7. You should always crystallize, as described earlier. You may be winning some arguments and losing some arguments—clarify why the ones you are winning outweigh the others. Tell the judge why the arguments that you are winning matter in the round. Explain to the judge what is important and what isn't. Finally, link the crucial arguments back to your value. After all, the value is the standard you provided for deciding the round.

Representative J.C. Watts from Oklahoma was chosen to be the first respondent to a "State of the Union" address.

First Affirmative Rebuttal (1AR)—Four Minutes ... The **first affirmative rebuttal (1AR)** is generally considered to be the most challenging speech in L–D. You have only four minutes to answer the seven minutes of negative constructive. Beginning debaters, victimized by poor time allocation, often lose rounds because they unwisely drop arguments. To avoid such *dire* consequences, consider this approach:

1. Spend from thirty to forty-five seconds highlighting the value clash. Emphasize why your value position is superior.
2. Use approximately one and a half minutes refuting the negative argumentation. Group arguments when necessary, but at least mention each position advanced by your opponent. Clash with any unreasonable counter-definitions (definitions different from yours) that might undermine your entire case.
3. Use the remaining time to reestablish the strength of your case. Give impact to any arguments dropped by your opponent. Incorporate damaging admissions from cross-examination. Extend your original positions with evidence when appropriate (to respond to challenges for additional support). Link all of your arguments back to your value, and sign the ballot for the judge.

Negative Rebuttal (NR)—Six Minutes ... The **negative rebuttal (NR)** is the negative speaker's last chance to speak. You will have no opportunity to respond to the final affirmative rebuttal, so you must "shut down" those

SOMETHING OF VALUE

INSTANT IMPACT

"I fell off the stage, ripped my skirt, and cut my hand," remembers Mary Ambrose, the first national champion in high school Lincoln–Douglas debate competition. Ambrose took her tumble in June of 1980 immediately following the final round of the National Forensic League tournament in Huntsville, Alabama.

The topic in that first national competition focused on whether social security financing mechanisms should be preserved. Ambrose believes she won the final round because her argumentation was more "values-centered." She offered "self-sufficiency of the system" as her value position. Her opponent presented no competing value, Ambrose recalls.

Today, Ambrose is a trial lawyer and teaches law at Loyola University in Chicago. She credits her Lincoln–Douglas debate experience for giving her the ability to argue in front of a jury. "I learned that there has to be a theme and persuasiveness, not just the presenting of evidence," Ambrose says. "Lincoln–Douglas gave me added sophistication and it taught me that you need a kernel value."

arguments that you anticipate will be raised in that rebuttal. Shutting down arguments means preempting responses that the affirmative debater could offer that could sway the judge to vote for the resolution. You should emphasize the arguments that you think can win the round for you and minimize the arguments that you believe have the potential to defeat you.

The first part of the NR (about four to four-and-a-half minutes) is structured like the 1AR—you begin with the value clash, refute the affirmative case, and return to defending your own case. The last one-and-a-half to two minutes, though, should be spent crystallizing your arguments. Pick the two or three most important issues in the round from your perspective, and state why you are winning them. This crystallization will force the affirmative speaker to address the issues of your choosing and to appear to be somewhat on the defensive. Do not get sidetracked by trivial technicalities or dropped arguments that have no significance. Select, instead, the issues that stake out fundamental disagreements.

Second Affirmative Rebuttal (2AR)—Three Minutes ... Although your time is limited for the **second affirmative rebuttal (2AR),** you no longer need to be so concerned with coverage. You can focus on three or four issues of crucial importance (one should always be the value clash). You can avoid getting "ballparked" by the negative if you emphasize the value clash first and then examine the negative crystallization from the perspective of the affirmative case. Link all arguments to the value clash, and conclude by signing the ballot for the judge.

Using Prep Time

In most rounds, you will be given three minutes of preparation time, or **prep time.** Affirmative speakers try to allocate two minutes before the 1AR and one minute before the 2AR. More time is needed before the 1AR because of the difficulty of organizing responses to the negative constructive.

COMMUNICATION

Breakdown

Political Pinocchios

The purpose of debate is to determine the truth. But how can we tell if those politicians engaging in televised debates are being honest? Technology offers a new way to determine who is lying and who isn't.

A recently developed computer system can detect the little movements that a person's facial muscles make when the person is displaying emotion. Smiling makes crow's feet form around the eyes, for example, while frowning involves movements in forehead muscles. The system imposes a grid over a baseline black-and-white photograph of the subject's face when it is free from all expression. Any change in expression, even one that is very small or very fast, is recognized as a departure from baseline.

By analyzing the person's facial expressions, we can tell how that person truly feels, because facial expressions are hard to fake, even for experienced liars. Suppose a candidate is angered by a certain statement but wishes not to show that anger. According to a leading researcher, no matter how fast the candidate covers an angry frown with a smile, the computer system will detect the changing expression.

What about the lie detector, or polygraph? Isn't it just as effective? We might have trouble convincing politicians to agree to be hooked up to polygraphs during TV debates. But even if we could, we might not want to rely too heavily on the results.

Polygraphs use sensors to record changes in a person's respiration, heart rate, blood pressure, and skin conductance (how much sweat is being produced). The general idea is that a person who is lying will experience emotional stress. Emotional stress will produce certain bodily responses, such as increased heart rate and sweating.

This principle doesn't always hold up. Experienced liars may feel no emotional stress when they lie. Clever liars may be able to manipulate the test in various ways (for example, by taking a tranquilizer before testing). In either case, these people's bodily responses may indicate that they are not lying, even though they are. Also, people who are not lying may be experiencing a great deal of emotional stress during the test. They may be upset because they have been wrongfully accused. The bodily responses of these people may suggest that they are lying even though they aren't.

The new computer system for detecting facial expressions may be harder to fool than the polygraph. As suggested earlier, the muscle movements involved in facial expressions are very difficult to control. Although a flash of anger or embarrassment may pass so quickly that the human eye cannot detect it, the computer will pick it up. So perhaps we can finally tell if those politicians are being honest—or just playing Pinocchio.

Questions

1. How might political campaigns change if the voters always knew when a candidate was lying?
2. Can you think of times when a politician should mislead voters?

Prepare well in advance of your debate.

Most negative speakers split their prep time, using half before the 1NC and half before the NR. You should try to avoid using prep time before cross-examination. Instead, prepare some questions ahead, and generate additional ones during your opponent's constructive.

SECTION 3 REVIEW

Recalling the Facts ...

1. What is the format for Lincoln–Douglas debate?
2. What should you try to achieve during the rebuttal speeches? What are some strategies you might use?

Thinking Critically ...

1. You will note that the affirmative speaker has three speeches while the negative speaker has only two. Although both sides have the same amount of time to speak, the affirmative speaker has the advantage of presenting her side both first and last. Why do you think this format was chosen? Can you think of a format that would be fairer to both sides?

Taking Charge ...

1. The national debate topic for high school students in 1931 was, "Resolved: that chain stores are detrimental to the best interests of the public." That topic might generate some heated debate even today. According to the *Utne Reader*, when 34,300 mall shoppers across the country were interviewed, 75 percent said that they weren't shopping for a specific item. Shopping, it seems, has become a national pastime.

   After reviewing the guidelines for wording a debate resolution in Chapter 18, write your own. Try to choose a topic area in which you are interested, such as minimum educational standards, required community service, or student rights.

   Note that the wording of the debate resolution from 1931 is more suited to Lincoln–Douglas competition than to policy debate today. The question of what is "detrimental" calls for a value judgment rather than a change in policy.

STUDENT WORK

"Supporting Your Views," by Colleen Melia

Colleen Melia, a student at Manchester High School (Manchester, Massachusetts), prepared this first affirmative constructive speech for a competition in Lincoln–Douglas debate. If you were debating on the negative against Colleen, what would you argue? Would you, for example, refute her position on the moral judgment of our representatives? Are these representatives any more moral than their constituents? What do you think of her use of such words as spineless and petty? Remember, if you are interested in finding out more about debate, you should visit with your school's debate sponsor.

"Government includes the art of formulating a policy and using the political technique . . . to receive general support; persuading, leading, sacrificing, teaching always because the greatest duty of the statesman is to educate."

As Franklin Delano Roosevelt wrote, the primary duty of a politician is leadership. Because I feel that Congress ought to display this leadership and value the national interest above the desires of his constituents when the two values conflict, I stand affirmatively resolved: That members of the United States Congress ought to value the national interest above constituent's interest when the two are in conflict.

The value position I will uphold is "leadership." I would argue that our Congressional representatives ought to display leadership and prioritize the nation instead of buckling under and spinelessly acceding to the individual interests of constituents when the conflict occurs. My criterion is a just society.

Before proceeding to my three lines of analysis, I find it important to clarify a few terms:

to value—to honor
national interest—concerns affecting the nation as a whole
constituent's interests—concerns affecting an individual voter in a district

This leads me to my first line of analysis: *The Congressional Representative Does Not Have a Supreme Obligation to a Constituent's Interests.*

In analyzing the representative's relationship to his constituency, there are two dimensions to be explored. The first is the selfish nature of the constituents. When their concerns conflict with those of the nation, they are always going to demand, without assessing the conflict, without considering whether the concern is justified, that their desires take priority. When in conflict with the nation, the constituents will refuse to rationally examine this problem, and instead, will demand the advancement of their own will, even at the cost of the nation. The Federalist Papers conclude:

> ". . . the mild voice of reason, pleading the cause of an enlarged and permanent interest, is but too often drowned, before public bodies as well as individuals, by the clamors of an impatient avidity for immediate and immoderate gains."

The innate ignorance of constituents and their overriding selfishness demonstrate the illegitimacy of valuing their demands over the nation's interest. The second, and key part of the relationship between representative and represented is consent. What we have to realize is that the resolution asks us to look at the conflict as it is perceived by Congress. Constituents can't really assess the national interest, as their perception is blurred by their own interests. The representative is in a much better position than constituents to evaluate the conflict. As David Callahan and Bruce Jennings write:

> "The representative has an almost unlimited license to make legislative decisions based on his or her own moral judgment of the best interests of the represented and the common good of the political community as a whole."

Because under democracy, citizens give their authority to elected representatives through con-

sent, they should realize that although the representative will value their opinions, ultimately, she may be compelled to make decisions which run contrary to their concerns, should they conflict with the national interest.

Due to the illegitimacy of acting solely on constituent desires, we see that their concerns cannot subjugate the national interest.

This point is further developed by my second line of analysis: *Members of Congress Are Uniquely Obligated to the National Interest.*

As one of the key parts of the American system of government, members of Congress have a unique responsibility to support the national interest. For example, Congress is the only part of our government empowered to spend money. Because they possess this power, they are obligated to use it and their other privileges in support of the national interest.

Furthermore, we see that supporting the national interest over constituent will is generally a much more beneficial position. While constituents within our society do have individual rights, they do not possess these rights to the point that they can indulge their own petty and selfish whims at the cost of everyone else in America. We see that in the interest of leadership, representatives are uniquely obligated to preserve the national interest. We cannot make the exception to the rule here and value selfish wants over the nation's interest.

This point is further developed by my third and final line of analysis: *Leadership Obligates Members of Congress to Prioritize the National Interest.*

In justifying a prioritization of national interest, we must analyze the obligations of the representative. What we have to realize here is that a constituent's interests are highly individualized and selfish concerns. We are not even looking at a general interest of a constituency.

When returning to the value of leadership, we realize that a lack of leadership is one of the flaws within our current government. Representatives concede too often to their constituents, becoming mere puppets for those they represent, instead of trying to LEAD our nation—their primary obligation as members of Congress. Congress's refusal to balance the budget is just one of countless examples of the lack of Congressional leadership. It is very poor leadership to simply and only follow what constituents want rather than to strive to understand the national interest, explain it to constituents, and educate the represented as to why their interests cannot always be paramount. The representative's job is not to do things which would be contrary to his conscience, such as allowing pushy pressure groups within his constituency the ability to override the whole nation, just as the representative would not expect constituents to act in a manner contrary to their consciences.

So clearly, we have to realize that the selfishness and ignorance of constituents, as well as consent under democracy, justify prioritizing the national interest to promote leadership.

•••••••••••••••••••••••••

Looking Back

Listed below are the major ideas discussed in this chapter.

- Debate propositions are of three kinds: factual, policy, and value.
- A value is something we apply to judge something right or wrong, good or bad.
- *Ought* refers to your idea of the ideal.
- Commonly used values in L–D debate include liberty, equality of opportunity, democracy, and justice.
- Common techniques of refutation are counterexamples, analogies, and contradictions.
- Most L–D debaters write first affirmative constructive speeches that have four parts: (1) introduction, (2) definitions and analysis, (3) establishing of values, and (4) arguments.
- The negative constructive should (1) present a value premise, counterdefinitions (if necessary), and the negative arguments and (2) clash with and refute the affirmative value and arguments.
- The purpose of rebuttals in L–D is to place the round into focus by crystallizing the most important issues and by providing a comparison of the two value positions.

Speech Vocabulary

Match the speech vocabulary term on the left with the correct definition on the right.

1. ought
2. 2AR
3. NR
4. value
5. value premise
6. policy proposition
7. 1NC
8. 1AC
9. cross-examination
10. factual proposition
11. signposting
12. value criteria

a. The first speech in a debate round
b. The period for asking and answering questions
c. Final affirmative speech
d. Refers to your idea of the ideal
e. A standard we apply to judge something right or wrong
f. A statement that is either true or false
g. Focuses on the desirability of some course of action
h. A standard in L–D to evaluate whether the resolution is true
i. The first time the affirmative constructive is refuted
j. The final negative speech in L–D
k. Additional standards for evaluation values
l. Tells people when you are moving from one section to another

General Vocabulary

Define the following terms and use each in a sentence.

renowned
sanctity
covert
affluent
surrogacy
evasive
dire

To Remember

1. The ____________ is considered the most difficult speech in Lincoln–Douglas debate.
2. "Resolved: that the United States government should conduct scientific research to determine whether Elvis still lives" is an example of a ____________ proposition.
3. Bringing up new arguments in a rebuttal is commonly referred to as ____________.
4. Your ____________ is the value that you will be defending in the round.
5. In the original Lincoln–Douglas debates, ____________ represented the side of states' rights.
6. If you are running out of time in a speech, you can ____________ your opponent's arguments and answer them all at once.
7. Lincoln–Douglas debates consider propositions of ____________.
8. The side that supports the resolution is called the ____________, while the side that opposes it is called the ____________.

To Do

1. Browsing in the current periodical section of the library, find five magazine articles relevant to the resolution you're debating. Find five more relevant articles by using the *Reader's Guide to Periodical Literature.*
2. Using the subject guide to *Books in Print,* find five books published in the last two years relevant to your debate resolution. Talk to your librarian about obtaining one or two of them on interlibrary loan if your library does not own the books, or try to find them in a university library.
3. Research the original Lincoln–Douglas debates in the library. Examine the arguments and strategies used by both sides. Do you think Lincoln or Douglas was more persuasive?

To Talk About

1. What benefits come from studying and debating both sides of an issue, even when you may strongly disagree with one side? Does it compromise your personal sense of ethics to uphold a point of view with which you disagree?
2. Attend a local debate tournament. Discuss how what you observed differs from the fundamentals you learned in this chapter.
3. Four values were mentioned in this chapter: liberty, equality of opportunity, democracy, and justice. What are some other values that you could defend in a Lincoln–Douglas debate?

To Write About

1. Some people advocate a "two-track" system for education in which some students receive preparation for college and some students receive vocational training. Those who support the two-track system argue that it will increase the quality of American education. Opponents object that a two-track system is unfair and would deprive many qualified students of the chance for a college education. Write either an affirmative or a negative case for the resolution "Resolved: that a two-track system of education is justified."
2. Write an essay describing the benefits you might receive from debate. Can it help you in real life? In other classes? Will it help you in the future? How?
3. Although we know today that slavery is morally wrong, there was a time in this country when slavery was acceptable to most people. Write a brief essay about another value that has changed over time.

Related Speech Topics

The following list contains several potential topics for debates.

Competition versus cooperation: Which ought we value more?
Ought we allow mandatory prayer in schools?
Flag burning: Is it morally acceptable?
Should schools teach values, or is that the role of parents?
The values of Martin Luther King, Jr.
Political debates
Congressional debate
National security versus the people's right to know: Ought the government keep sensitive information away from the public?

CHAPTER 20

PARLIAMENTARY PROCEDURE

"*The job of a citizen is to keep his mouth open.*"

–Günter Grass, novelist

Learning Objectives

After completing this chapter, you will be able to do the following.

- Explain how parliamentary procedure supports the democratic process.
- Organize the first meeting of a new club.
- Participate in a group meeting by making, seconding, and amending motions.
- Lead a meeting in the role of the presiding officer.
- List the most commonly used motions in ranked order.

Chapter Outline

Following are the main sections in this chapter.

1. Learning the Rules
2. Getting Down to Business
3. A Member's Responsibilities
4. The Order of Precedence

New Speech Terms

In this chapter, you will learn the meanings of the speech terms listed below.

parliamentary procedure
chair
house
bylaws
orders of the day
old business
new business
adjourn
minutes
quorum
executive session
main motion
reconsider
order of precedence
subsidiary motion
privileged motion
incidental motion
table a motion
call for the question
amend

General Vocabulary

Expanding your general vocabulary will help you become a more effective communicator. Listed below are some words appearing in this chapter that you should make part of your everyday vocabulary.

Parliament
innumerable
clique
railroad
painstakingly
agenda
restate
germane
preamble
suspend

Looking Ahead

The best meetings are often noisy, exciting affairs with people bouncing ideas off one another. But beneath the noise and commotion is an orderly system, a system of rules that ensures the right of each person to be heard.

This system, called parliamentary procedure, empowers the members of the meeting to take action through a majority vote. By learning the system and especially by frequent practice, you will become a more effective participant in meetings and hence, a better citizen.

Introduction

> Each player takes the colored token nearest to him on the board, and uses it throughout the game. The player having the red token, Miss Scarlet, rolls the die and moves first.

The description above, in case you haven't guessed, is taken from the rules of the popular board game Clue. In that game, players try to discover the identity of a murderer. To do so, however, they must follow a strict set of rules. A player could cheat, of course, by ignoring one of the rules (for instance, sneaking a peek at another player's clue cards), but by so doing that player would defeat the purpose of the rules: namely, to give each player an even chance to win.

We play many games throughout our lives. Some are more serious than others, but in each we agree to play by the rules. Our ability to play well often depends on whether we understand the rules and how well we can use them to our advantage.

Democracy is much more than a game, of course, but it, too, has its rules. Our ability to act as effective citizens in a democracy depends to a great extent on our knowing the rules and learning how to play by them. Let's look more closely at why we need rules in a democracy. Then we'll begin to examine the rules themselves.

Parliamentary procedure allows for smooth-running meetings the same way rules allow for smooth-running board games.

SECTION 1 Learning the Rules

We use several different sets of rules in our democracy. The Constitution, for example, is the basis of our legal system, and the Bill of Rights defines our individual freedoms. When we meet in groups, however, we follow a system of rules called **parliamentary procedure.** We use these rules whether we are meeting with the student council, a school club, or any other organization. These rules also apply to the meetings of all our governing bodies, from the town council to the U.S. Congress.

The rules of parliamentary procedure used in many contemporary legislative bodies have evolved from the model created by the British Parliament hundreds of years ago.

The rules of parliamentary procedure provide the fair and balanced system we need to work together. The rules are called parliamentary because they follow ideas originally developed by the British *Parliament.* In fact, these rules represent more than five hundred years of human history. Over the past centuries, people have written and rewritten the rules as they learned how to make them better. As a result, the rules have come to reflect the experience and wisdom of hundreds of organizations and *innumerable* individuals.

The British rules of government were brought to North America by the early colonists and introduced at the first New England town meetings. When Thomas Jefferson became president of the United States in 1801, he published the first American book on parliamentary procedure. "I have begun a sketch," Jefferson wrote, "which those who come after will successfully correct and fill up, till a code of rules shall be formed." Jefferson's book became the basis for the rules adopted by Congress and was the foremost authority on American parliamentary procedure for many years.

Robert and His Rules

As time passed, it became necessary to adapt Jefferson's rules to meet the needs of day-to-day life. General Henry Robert, an Army engineer, took on the task after a frustrating personal experience. Robert belonged to many church and civic groups and was asked once, quite without warning, to lead a meeting. "My embarrassment was supreme," Robert later recalled. "I plunged in, trusting to Providence that the assembly would behave itself, but with the plunge went the determination that I would never attend another meeting until I knew something of parliamentary law."

This Texas Legislature parliamentarian (seated) is responsible for keeping track of all the legislature's procedures.

Robert studied the rules of the British Parliament and the American Congress. Eventually he blended the best of both into *Robert's Rules of Order*, a handbook that he published in 1876. Robert hoped to create a system of etiquette that could guide people through their meetings. He wanted to show group members how to resist overbearing leaders and ruthless *cliques*. He also wanted to give group members the know-how they needed to combat those seeking to railroad their way to power. (*Railroad* means to push something through in great haste.)

Even foreign ministers follow *Robert's Rules of Order*. The "rules" are used internationally.

Robert's book was an instant hit and has remained popular ever since. In 1970, a team of experts brought out a modern, updated version, *Robert's Rules of Order Newly Revised* (updated again in 1981 and 1990), which serves today as the parliamentary handbook for most organizations. Thus, Robert's famous book has become our foremost guide to democratic action. Thoughtful study and a few days of practice will help you master the democratic procedures he so *painstakingly* described.

"The careful reading and use of *Robert's Rules* can help guarantee orderliness and fair play in the conduct of a variety of our everyday activities," said Floyd Riddick, parliamentarian of the U.S. Senate.

As you begin to learn parliamentary procedure, you may feel intimidated by the complexity of the system. These feelings will soon disappear, though, with a little patience and perhaps a handy reference or crib sheet nearby. Learning parliamentary procedure is important because it gives us a chance to put democracy into practice.

Failure to learn these rules will lead to the frustration of attending meetings where you don't understand what is going on. Worse, it may lead to your suffering defeat because your opponents know more than you about parliamentary procedure.

Fundamental Principles of Parliamentary Procedure

A good place to start learning the rules of parliamentary procedure is with a few basic principles. These principles will enable you to reason out the answers to most parliamentary questions. The principles may seem simple and familiar, but you should be careful not to underestimate their importance. The basic principles of parliamentary procedure are as follows.

1. Do One Thing at a Time ... The principle "one thing at a time" emphasizes the importance of order. Group members may consider, for example, only one motion at a time. By keeping everyone's attention focused on just one thing, the group leader can keep a meeting on track. This makes it more likely that difficult issues will be resolved in a reasonable amount of time.

2. The Majority Decides ... A primary purpose of parliamentary procedure is to see that the wishes of the majority are carried out. Majority simply means more than half of the votes cast. (This is also called a simple majority.)

When you join a group, you voluntarily agree to accept what the majority decides. Until the vote on a question is taken, every member has the right to speak for or against a proposal and to persuade others to share that opinion. Once the votes are in, however, the decision of the majority becomes everyone's decision.

3. The Rights of the Minority Are Protected ... Truly democratic organizations make arrangements to protect those who are in the minority—that is, on the side with less than half the votes. These members are entitled to the same consideration and respect as those who are in the majority. You may be in the majority today but in the minority tomorrow. That means that everyone has a stake in protecting these rights.

One specific way that parliamentary procedure protects minority rights is the two-thirds vote. Several motions, including any that limit the right to speak or debate, require a two-thirds vote to pass. Thus, a simple majority of members cannot close off discussion if others still wish to be heard.

4. Conduct a Full and Free Discussion ... All members of the group have the right to express their opinion fully and freely without interruption or interference, provided they stay within the rules. Members also have the right to know the meaning of the question under discussion and what its effect will be. Members can always request information on any motion that they do not understand so that they can vote intelligently.

5. Act with Fairness and Good Faith ... Trickery, delaying tactics, and railroading can destroy the fairness of any meeting.

NO PLACE TO GO, NOTHING TO DO

INSTANT IMPACT

The life of General Henry M. Robert reminds us of the saying that "what a man amounts to is what he does with his time when he has nothing to do." Robert, a U.S. Army engineer, had helped build the defenses of Washington, D.C., and Philadelphia during the Civil War. After the war, he found himself stationed at a lonely fort during a harsh winter. With nothing to do and no place to go, Robert decided to make the most of his leisure time—by writing a handbook to help people run meetings.

At the end of the winter, Robert had a 15-page manuscript ready for printing. Surprisingly, publishing houses turned it down, saying there was little demand for such a book. Robert decided to pay for its publication himself, a decision that would turn out to be a blessing in disguise. Since Robert was paying the bills, he could revise and add to the book as he pleased.

When sales of Robert's book reached a half-million copies, he published an enlarged edition called *Rules of Order Revised.* He also wrote two other books on the subject—one for those who wanted an advanced version, *Parliamentary Law*, and one for beginners, *Parliamentary Practice*.

COMMUNICATION

"I . . . Looked Down into My Open Grave"

In a lonely grave lies the man who saved a president, the man who performed what one historian has called "the most heroic act in American history." Yet he is a man whose name few if any of us remember: Edmund G. Ross.

In 1866, when Ross was elected to the U.S. Senate from Kansas, President Andrew Johnson and the Congress were locked in a ferocious battle over how the South should be treated after the Civil War. The president vetoed bill after bill because he thought that Congress wanted to treat the former Confederate states too harshly. Johnson himself was a Southerner. Finally, in complete frustration, the senators decided to get the president out of office. If two-thirds of the senators would vote to impeach Johnson, he would be forced to leave.

Senators who opposed the president hoped that Ross would join their side because he had a long history of opposing slavery. At the age of 28, Ross had helped rescue a fugitive slave. Later, he had quit his newspaper job to enlist in the Union Army.

On March 5, 1868, the impeachment trial began. Observers soon realized that matters of law were not important to the senators: they wanted Johnson out; any reason would do. As the trial neared its conclusion, it became clear that only one more vote was needed to impeach Johnson. The one senator who had not yet announced how he would vote was Edmund Ross. Most people were sure Ross would vote to impeach. "I did not think," said Senator Sumner of Massachusetts, "that a Kansas man could quibble against his country." Yet Ross remained silent, vowing that Johnson should have a fair trial.

As a result of his silence, Ross was pestered, spied on, and subjected to every kind of pressure, including threats of violence. He was the target of every eye, his name was on every tongue, and his intentions were discussed in every newspaper.

At last the fateful day arrived. Ross described it this way: "The galleries were packed. Tickets of admission were at an enormous premium." Every senator was in his seat, including one who was desperately ill and had to be carried in. When it came time for Ross to vote, the Senate chamber fell silent.

"How say you?" said the Chief Justice. "Is Andrew Johnson guilty or not?"

"I almost literally looked down into my open grave," Ross said later. "Friendships, position, fortune, everything that makes life desirable to an ambitious man were about to be swept away by the breath of my mouth, perhaps forever."

Ross spoke so quietly that he was asked to repeat his answer. And then in a voice that everyone could hear, he said, "Not guilty." The president was saved.

Question

1. Why do you think an impeachment requires a two-thirds vote rather than a simple majority vote?

Parliamentary principles grant equal rights to both supporters and opponents of proposals.

Members can ethically use parliamentary principles to support or defeat a proposal. When they use these principles to intimidate opponents or deny the rights of others, their tactics are destructive and contrary to the spirit of fair play.

These five principles show that parliamentary procedure is founded on common sense, which makes them easy to learn and remember. After a little practice, you will feel at home with the vocabulary, patterns, and rhythm of parliamentary procedure. Before long, you will feel confident in presenting and defending your ideas in a group. As you gain knowledge of parliamentary procedure, you will help the groups you belong to become more effective, and you will also take a big step toward assuming a leadership position yourself.

SECTION 1 REVIEW

Recalling the Facts ...

1. Briefly describe the roles Thomas Jefferson and Henry Robert played in the development of parliamentary procedure in the United States.
2. What are the five basic principles of parliamentary procedure?

Thinking Critically ...

1. Discuss some of the sets of rules that govern our lives. Examples might include the rules your parents set at home, school rules, local and state laws, and perhaps some unstated rules, like the ones that define what is socially acceptable in a given group or setting. Consider how these rules have come into being, how they can be changed, and how they are enforced.
2. Explain the importance of principle 2 and principle 3 listed on page 513 in the American democratic system. Think of (or research) recent law cases that demonstrate these two principles.

Taking Charge ...

1. Invite a representative of a local governing body—the town council, the state legislature, or a county board—to visit your class and talk about how parliamentary procedure works. Ask the speaker how the meetings of the governing body to which he or she belongs would be different if they weren't conducted according to parliamentary procedure.
2. Make a list of every school and community group you can think of that conducts its meetings according to parliamentary procedure. Can you think of some that don't? Why don't they?

SECTION 2 Getting Down to Business

Let us suppose that you and a group of friends have decided to start a new school club. It seems that all of you are upset about having to dissect a fetal pig in biology class, and you wish to start an animal rights group. As far as you know, the school has never had such a club before. For the purpose of our discussion here, we won't worry about how to get the school to officially recognize your club. We'll focus our attention strictly on how you organize a new club and hold a meeting.

Your first step is to arrange a time and place for the meeting. Let's say that several people who share your interest in animal rights agree to meet after school on Tuesday in a science classroom. On that Tuesday, you call the meeting to order (acting as the unofficial group leader). This is a signal to the people present that from this moment forward, they should conduct themselves according to the rules of parliamentary procedure.

You next announce the first order of business—in other words, the first item on the meeting's *agenda*. This task is to elect a president and secretary. In our case, your three best friends—the only other people attending this meeting—elect you president.

Now that you are legitimately the person in charge of the meeting (called the **chair** in parliamentary procedure), the group can really get down to business. The group, by the way, is referred to as the **house** during its meetings. You will probably start by discussing the purpose and goals of your group, but you will also want to agree on a few special rules called **bylaws.** A rule that sets a time and place for regular meetings is a bylaw.

When the gavel comes down, the meeting begins.

What Officers Do

An important part of any group's bylaws is a description of the officers the group needs. Let's take a look at these positions and their responsibilities.

The President ... As the new Animal Rights Club president, what are you supposed to do? In the simplest sense, you conduct the meetings. Your responsibility is to see that the group handles its business in a fair and efficient manner. Specifically, you must balance two competing claims: the right of the majority to prevail and the right of the minority to be heard. As Thomas Jefferson, the author of the Declaration of Independence, once said, "Let us hear both sides of the question."

Your first task is to call the meeting to order, which basically means that members stop talking among themselves and give you their full attention. Tap the gavel (no chair should be without one) to signal that the meeting is going to begin, and then state in your firmest voice: "The regular meeting of the Animal Rights Club is now open." Having accomplished that, you work your way, step by step, through an agenda that has been prepared ahead of time—a list of topics and items of business that are to be discussed.

The correct parliamentary name for the agenda is **orders of the day.** In most organizations, the orders of the day begin with the reading and approval of the minutes of the preceding meeting, followed by officer reports, committee reports, unfinished business (sometimes called **old business**), **new business** (subjects brought up for the first time), and announcements. The final action of the group is to **adjourn**—in other words, close the meeting.

One of your most difficult jobs as chair will be to keep the members' minds on the business before them. Discussions have a tendency to get out of hand—one stray comment can lead to another, and soon the group is talking about last night's party instead of a committee report. As chair, you must make sure the discussion stays focused.

- **Insist on a motion.** One way you can keep people focused is to ban any discussion unless there is a motion before the group. Members can't actually take any action until a motion has been made. Therefore, discussion without a motion before the house is pointless.

  After a member has made a motion, another member must second the motion (in other words, endorse what the first member said). To assist the maker of the motion, the chair should *restate* it before debate is allowed. Restating the motion helps clarify it for the members and it also transfers ownership: The motion now belongs to the group, not to the maker.
- **Open the floor for discussion.** As chair, you, and only you, decide who "gets the floor." Normally, you call on the person who made the motion to speak first, though it is not necessary to do so. After that person has spoken (and under the rules, no one may speak for more than ten minutes), you call on others who wish to speak.

GUESS WHAT.. OUR CLASS HAD A MEETING, AND I'VE BEEN MADE PROGRAM CHAIRMAN..

I GET TO SPEND ALL DAY WATCHING PROGRAMS..

THE PROGRAM CHAIRMAN HAS TO ORGANIZE ALL THE ACTIVITIES AND ENTERTAINMENT FOR EVERY MEETING
© 1995 United Feature Syndicate, Inc.
4/20

If possible, choose a speaker in favor of the motion, then one opposed, then one in favor, and so on. You should let everyone who wishes to speak do so before you allow anyone to speak a second time. Ordinarily, no one may speak more than twice on any particular motion.

- **Call the question.** After you feel the discussion is over, say, "Are you ready for the question?" This asks the members if they are ready to vote. If no one objects, you put the question to a vote. If someone does object, discussion continues unless two-thirds of the members vote to close debate.

To conduct a vote, you say, "The question is on the adoption of the motion to donate $25 to the animal shelter. All those in favor of the motion say 'aye.' " Those members who are in favor will now say "aye." After you have heard the response, you say, "Those opposed say 'no.' " Next, you announce the result with the words, "The ayes have it; the motion is carried" or "The motion is defeated."

If anyone doubts whether you have correctly interpreted the voice vote, that person may call for a "division of the house." In that case, another vote will be taken. The second time a vote is taken, the chair normally asks members to raise their hands to vote and counts the votes. Then, if a division of the house is called again, the chair may call for a standing vote. Those in favor stand up—the better to be counted—and then those opposed stand up. If the majority wishes, a secret, written ballot may be used.

- **Make rulings.** As chair, you have a number of other, more technical duties. You are required, for example, to determine whether something is *germane,* or pertinent, to the discussion. For example, on a motion to meet with the school's science teachers to discuss their dissection policies, one member begins to speak about how her little brother once put his pet hamster in the microwave. Another member objects, saying that the fate of the hamster is not germane to the motion at hand. You rule that the hamster is indeed out of order and ask the hamster owner's big sister to confine her remarks to the subject before the group. Anyone bringing up a topic that is not germane may be ruled "out of order" by the presiding officer.

The Vice President ... Ideally, the vice president (and all the officers) should have poise, a clear, strong voice, and a thorough understanding of parliamentary rules. The vice president's most important responsibility is to take the place of the president when he or she must be absent. Occasionally, the vice president may be assigned additional special duties.

The Treasurer ... The treasurer acts as the group's banker. He collects and spends money on the group's behalf. Normally, the treasurer gives a report on the group's financial status at each meeting, as well as an annual written report.

The Secretary ... The secretary keeps written records of the organization's activities. These records are called **minutes** and become the official history of the organization. Members can refer

Raise your hand, then wait for recognition from the chair before speaking.

to the minutes of past meetings to find out what they have said about a particular issue before. At the beginning of each meeting, the secretary reads the minutes of the previous meeting to check their accuracy and to remind the group of what it did at the last meeting.

The secretary's minutes should include the following:

1. The date, place, and time of the meeting.
2. The names of the officers and guests present and, if the group is small, of the members.
3. Whether the minutes of the previous meeting were read and approved.
4. A summary of officer and committee reports.
5. All main motions, including the name of the member who made the motion.
6. Major points of discussion and whether main motions were passed or defeated.
7. Announcements and the time of adjournment.

The secretary is also responsible for keeping a roll of all members and for calling the roll when requested. From time to time, the president may ask the secretary to read a motion back to the group, especially when the motion has been changed or reworded.

Additional Officers in Large Organizations ... Large organizations may need additional officers. These positions might include a corresponding secretary, who has the job of writing letters on the organization's behalf; a sergeant-at-arms, who helps maintain order and acts as a doorkeeper; and a parliamentarian. The parliamentarian assists the chair by referring to the relevant section of the bylaws or *Robert's Rules* to settle an argument. The chair may ask the parliamentarian for her opinion, but only the chair can actually make a ruling on what the group should do.

The treasurer must keep track of all accounts.

Quorum and Executive Session

You can play video games by yourself, but you can't hold a meeting alone. No meeting can officially take place without a **quorum** (pronounced *kwor'um*), which is the minimum number of members who must be

present for the group's decisions to take effect. Normally, a quorum means a majority of the members. Congress, for example, can make no law unless a majority of its members are present. Although a majority works well as a quorum for most groups, some very large organizations have set their quorum at one-fourth of the membership, one-tenth, or even less if low attendance is common.

Quorum refers only to the number of members present, not the number who are voting. Suppose, for example, that an organization has 50 members and its bylaws state that one-half of the members must be present to constitute a quorum. If 30 members show up for a meeting, a quorum has been reached. Suppose, however, that only 20 of those attending actually vote. The results will still be official.

Groups decide issues based on having a quorum present at the time of voting.

If there are not enough members present to make a quorum, the group can do nothing more than adjourn. If, during the course of a meeting, the chair notices that a quorum has been lost (members have begun leaving, say, to watch the Super Bowl on television), the chair should stop the meeting.

On some occasions, a group may wish to close its meeting to outsiders. Imagine, for example, that a reporter from the school paper is attending an Animal Rights Club meeting when a matter of an extremely personal nature comes up. At this point, a member can request that the group go into **executive session.** An executive session is a special kind of meeting or a special portion of a meeting that is open only to members. Such sessions are called to discuss the conduct and possible discipline of group members. In our case, for example, the group has learned that one of its members recently shot a deer on a hunting trip. Members are honor-bound not to divulge to outsiders what has been discussed during executive session.

SECTION 2 REVIEW

Recalling the Facts ...

1. What are the major responsibilities of a chair before, during, and after a meeting?
2. What are some of the ways groups become bogged down in meetings? How can a good presiding officer rescue the meeting from total collapse at those points?

Thinking Critically ...

1. Have a class discussion on the qualities of a good committe chair or class officer. Who do you feel are the best elected officers, at school and on the local, state, national, and international levels and why? What leadership qualities does each possess? What mistakes might an elected officer make to alienate his or her followers?
2. Practice analyzing a set of minutes. Obtain the minutes of a recent meeting from a school or local organization and analyze what happened during the meeting. Can you determine what decisions the group made and what actions the group took? Discuss with classmates what the most important decision of the meeting was and why.

Taking Charge ...

1. Pretend for a day that your class schedule is really a series of meetings. Observe what each teacher does to call the class to order. Discuss with classmates which techniques seem most effective. What is the cost of wasting time at the beginning of a class?

SECTION 3 A Member's Responsibilities

Members of organizations, too, have their duties and responsibilities. Even if you are not an officer, you should, for example, attend the meetings with reasonable regularity. During a meeting, you should pay attention to the business at hand and to the speaker who holds the floor. You should not talk, move about, or stand unless you want to be recognized by the chair.

Feel free to express your opinion while a subject is being discussed. But once the question is settled, support the outcome. Withhold any criticism you might have of either the action or those who supported it. This is one of the most important principles of parliamentary procedure, one that allows us to live in an atmosphere of mutual respect and regard no matter how much we may disagree with one another.

We can summarize the responsibilities of a member like this:

1. Arrive promptly at meetings.
2. Address the chair as Miss President, Madame President, or Mr. President.
3. Wait to be recognized by the chair before speaking.
4. When you are recognized, stand, speak clearly, and then sit down.
5. Make a motion by saying, "I move that . . ." Do not say, "I make a motion."
6. Address all remarks to the chair. Make no personal comments toward another member.
7. Ask questions if you don't understand the question on the floor.
8. Call for a vote if you feel debate has gone far enough.
9. Call out "Division" if you doubt the result of the vote as announced by the chair.
10. Respect the right of the majority to decide.

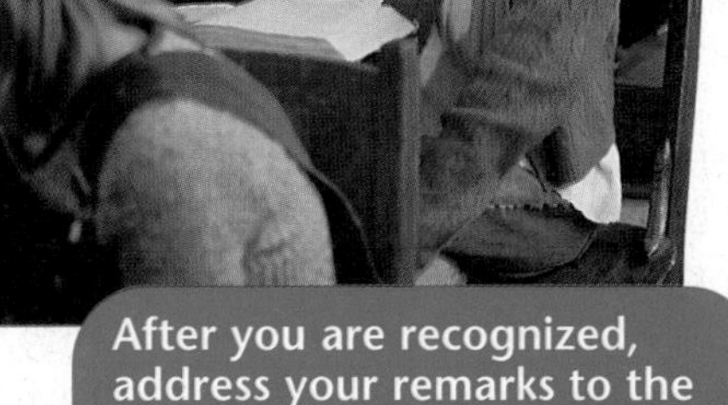

After you are recognized, address your remarks to the chair, not the group.

One of the most important things a member can do is to make a motion. Most games begin with a throw of the dice, a flick of the spinner, or a card drawn from the deck. In parliamentary procedure, the real action begins when someone makes a motion.

Any member has the right to present a motion. To do so, he or she rises, addresses the chair, and waits for recognition. The chair recognizes a member by calling the member's name, at which time the member has the floor and is thus entitled to speak.

The Main Motion

Motions that ask the group to take action are called **main motions.** (Several other kinds of motions will be discussed later.) Main motions should be stated in a positive form if possible, because most of us find positive statements ("let's do this") easier to grasp than negative ones ("let's not do that").

If a member happens to offer a motion in the negative, the chair can suggest changing it. Suppose a member of the Animal Rights Club says, "I move that we don't eat meat at school." Club members may be confused about exactly what the motion means. The chair might ask the person who made the motion to rephrase it like this: "I move that we boycott meals in the cafeteria until the school agrees to provide a vegetarian alternative."

Anyone who proposes a long or complicated motion should prepare a written copy ahead of time and give it to the secretary. (By the way, the chair can request that all motions be submitted in writing.)

Members of the Animal Rights Club might, for example, make the following main motions:

- "I move that we ask the school board to ban fur; leather belts, shoes, and watchbands; and any other types of clothing made from animals from the school building."

CURFEW IN PARADISE

INSTANT IMPACT

A curfew bill created by a group of Honolulu high school students was signed into state law by Governor John Waihee of Hawaii. Although the original bill, drafted by students at Kaimuki High School, was altered by state legislators, its goal of keeping teenagers off the city's streets late at night remained intact. The curfew prohibits anyone under age 16 from being in public areas between 10 P.M. and 4 A.M. unless accompanied by an adult.

The law recommends that violators of the curfew and their parents or guardians participate in family counseling or community service.

"As far as we know," said a spokesperson for the Hawaii Department of Education, "this is the first time Hawaiian students have submitted and lobbied [for] a bill in the state government."

Prepare ahead of time if you intend to present a long or complicated proposal.

- "I move that the Student Council make an annual donation to the local Humane Society."
- "I move that we change our school mascot from the Tigers to the Silicon Chips."

Generally, four things can happen to a main motion. It can be passed, postponed, sent to a committee for study, or defeated. Remember that if a motion is defeated, it cannot be brought up again at the same meeting. Parliamentary procedure stresses the principle that a motion may have only one hearing per meeting, but it does allow one exception. A member may move to **reconsider** a main motion that has already been passed or defeated. Only a member who voted on the winning side may move to reconsider.

Resolutions ... Special occasions sometimes call for a special kind of main motion called a resolution. A resolution traditionally begins with an explanation of why the motion should be passed. This *preamble* includes a list of reasons, each in a paragraph beginning with "Whereas." Following the preamble, the main motion is stated, usually with this formula: "Now therefore be it resolved,"

WORDS FROM THE WORKPLACE

Ed Archangel
Corporate Training Facilitator and Consultant

Q: *How does communication play a role in the day-to-day activities in your work?*

A: Communication is the *central tool* to everything I do. In arranging training sessions, I must deal with many people to make sure the class is worthwhile for everyone in attendance. I must deal with administrators who are responsible for soliciting and reserving the space for each attendee. I do this by e-mail and other written forms, so there is no eye contact or tone of voice involved. This means that my written words are critical. There is also the need to communicate with other facilitators to arrange room space, overhead projectors, meeting dates, and various other necessities. During the meeting, because of cultural differences, I must make participants feel that communication is viable, so being open and honest is imperative. I must help the audience understand the concept "message sent–message received." Everything I do is done to encourage people to participate in a positive learning experience.

Q: *What advice can you give to students to show them the importance of communication?*

A: I would tell them not to make assumptions. You cannot afford to make the mistake of thinking you know what people are feeling or thinking. You must listen to them. I can't stress that enough. Use active listening skills to understand what is being communicated. Don't be afraid to ask follow-up questions to check for understanding. But the key, as I said, is to listen.

Body language is also very important. Your tone of voice, hand gestures, and eye contact—all are important. If you pay attention to body language, you will hear not just with one part of your sense, but with your eyes and heart.

or simply, "Resolved, that . . ." A complete resolution might look something like this:

> WHEREAS Mr. Bob Olson has served our school well as a sensitive counselor, and
>
> WHEREAS his concern for animals has led to his decision to turn his own home into a shelter for stray cats and dogs, and
>
> WHEREAS Mr. Olson has worked as a volunteer for a week at the Humane Society,
>
> NOW THEREFORE BE IT RESOLVED that the Animal Rights Club does hereby congratulate Mr. Olson on his contributions to a better life for small animals and, in recognition thereof, awards Mr. Olson the club's Good Citizen of the Year Award.

Like main motions, resolutions can be passed or defeated.

Seconding a Motion ... After someone has made a motion, another member must second the motion (this can be done without being recognized by the chair). A motion is seconded to show that more than one person favors the proposal. The major purpose of requiring a second is to prevent groups from wasting time on something that only one person wants to talk about.

If a motion is not seconded immediately, the chair says, "Is the motion seconded?" or "Is there a second?" If no one seconds the motion, the motion is dead. Some routine motions, such as approving the minutes, are frequently put to a vote without a second. (If any member objects to the lack of a second, however, the chair must call for one.) In addition, a few special kinds of motions do not need a second. We will discuss these motions later.

Debate and Discussion

"Democracy is that form of government," wrote James Dale Davidson, executive director of the National Taxpayers Union, "where everybody gets what the majority deserves." Finding out what the majority deserves—or at least what it wants—is why we have debate. But no matter how free-wheeling the debate may be, it must follow certain rules: Speakers are limited to ten minutes at a time, their comments must be germane, they must address their remarks to the chair, and they must at all times keep their remarks courteous.

If you wish to be successful in debate, you must be well informed, sure of your convictions, and fearless in the face of opposition. At the same time, successful debate depends to some extent on good manners. In debating a motion, you should avoid making comments about someone else's personality and should never question another person's motives. If you feel another speaker is mistaken, do not call him a liar. Instead, simply say, "I think the last speaker was misinformed." A member's name should not be mentioned, either, though a speaker can refer to "the last person who spoke."

A parliamentary discussion should help members reach a better understanding of the proposal before them. If the discussion is carried on in the proper spirit, members will leave their differences at the meeting and not let grudges keep them from remaining friends.

SECTION  REVIEW

Recalling the Facts ...

1. What is one of the most important things a member can do?
2. What four things can happen to a main motion?

Thinking Critically ...

1. Parliamentary procedure stresses the idea that a motion should only be considered once during a meeting. There is, however, one exception. What is that exception and why is it permitted in the rules?

Taking Charge ...

1. Write motions that could be presented at meetings for each of the following groups: an athletic booster club, a snow-skiing club, an international club, and a student council. Try to create three motions for each group.
2. Write short arguments for and against each of the following motions:
   - "I move that we oppose the city's new curfew law, which requires all teenagers to be off the street by 10 P.M. each night."
   - "I move that we support the school board's decision to ban any clothing, like bandannas or pro-football jackets, that might show membership in a gang."
3. Find out what constitutes a quorum for several of the governing bodies in your community. Do your school clubs have official quorums? Why or why not?

SECTION 4 The Order of Precedence

Parliamentary procedure becomes complicated at times because people are complicated. Our thinking process is not as simple as yes, no, and maybe. We may feel, for example, that we don't have enough information to make a sound decision, that the room is too hot or too cold, or that the meeting has been going on too long and we need a break. Parliamentary procedure makes room for these concerns and many others through a system of minor motions, all of which are governed by the order of precedence.

Try to attend a session of your state legislature, where you will see parliamentary procedure used to its full extent.

Some Motions Have Higher Rank than Others

In a large, formal meeting where people are experienced in parliamentary procedure, the action can seem furious. "Motions seem to dart in and out like bees around a beehive," as one expert puts it. Before one motion can be settled, another takes its place before the house, and then another and another. Sessions of the U.S. Congress, shown on CNN, offer ample illustration of such activity.

All this commotion may be confusing at first, but once the chair sorts things out, this much is clear: Parliamentary procedure requires that some kinds of motions be considered before others.

The concept that underlies the relationship of motions to each other is called the **order of precedence.** You might think of it as a ranking system, with the most important motion at the top (where it has priority over all the others) and the least important at the bottom. (See the chart on page 527 for a detailed description.) When a motion of greater priority is raised, it moves any other business to the back burner. This motion may then be resolved or may itself be pushed out of the way by another, higher-ranking motion.

The order of precedence enables the chair to determine with precision what issue should be discussed. It also tells the chair when a particular motion is out of order and must therefore be ignored for the time being, and in what order votes should be taken on pending motions. Any motion before the house that has not been settled is said to be "pending."

Let's see how the order of precedence actually works. Suppose someone says, "I move that we stage a demonstration in front of Pets R Us to

Parliamentary procedure allows no heated argument even when a question is referred to a committee.

protest the sale of parrots, an endangered species." The motion is seconded and debate begins. Before long, someone makes a motion to amend the main motion. "I move that we amend the motion by striking 'Pets R Us' and inserting 'all three pet stores in town.' " The motion to amend is in order at this point because it ranks higher than the main motion. Before the motion to amend is seconded, however, someone else gains the floor and says, "I move that we refer this question to a committee. I don't know if parrots are really endangered or not." The motion to refer ranks higher than the motion to amend. Thus, this motion is now in order and must be considered before the other two.

Handling parliamentary motions is a little like making a stack of blocks. As you work your way up (by making motions), you place one block on top of another. As you work your way down (by voting), the top block is taken off first. When a group does not observe the order of precedence and tries to pull the bottom block out first, the whole structure collapses.

Three Kinds of Minor Motions

Motions other than main motions can be divided into three categories: subsidiary, privileged, and incidental. Each type of motion has its own role to play in bringing problems to a reasonable, democratic solution.

- **Subsidiary motions** help to settle the main motion. Sometimes called a parliamentary "tool kit," they give members the means to tinker with main motions until they are in just the right form.
- **Privileged motions** deal with problems aside from the main motion that need urgent attention. You might move, for example, to take a short recess until "the fire goes out and the smoke has cleared." This motion has higher status than a subsidiary motion because what it calls for is of immediate importance.
- **Incidental motions** deal more with the process than with the actual content of any motion. An example of an incidental motion is a request for a roll call vote. Each type of minor motion includes several specific subtypes, as described in the following sections.

Subsidiary Motions ... While a main motion is pending, members may wish to change it, postpone it, or set it aside. The motion to amend the main motion is a subsidiary motion. Other subsidiary motions include limiting, extending, or cutting off debate.

Let's take a closer look at each of the seven subsidiary motions.

To table a question The purpose of the motion to table a question is to set the topic aside temporarily so that the house can turn to something else. (The term "lay on the table" grew out of an old parliamentary custom of laying a written motion on the clerk's table.)

Suppose a particular subject is being discussed. You want to speak on the subject but must leave the meeting for a few minutes. In such situations, you may say, "I move to lay the question on the table," or simply, "I move to **table the motion.**" If you are successful, the issue will be set aside. The idea is not to kill a motion but to delay its discussion. Whenever you are ready to get back to the motion, you can move to "take the motion off the table."

To call for the question When people continue to discuss a subject beyond your patience or endurance, you may **"call for the question."** That simply means to stop talking and vote. The chair then calls for a second and, on receiving it, takes a vote on whether or not to close the discussion. Note that members vote on the motion to call for the question before voting on the main motion. In more informal groups, members may call out, "Question!" and the chair, if it seems there is no objection, may simply go to a vote on the motion itself.

To modify debate If time is short, you may wish to limit debate on a particular subject. Although normal procedure permits each person to speak twice for ten minutes, you may decide it would be better to limit each person to one five-minute comment. If so, you "move that debate be limited." If, on the other hand, the issue needs more discussion than usual, you may move to extend debate.

To postpone definitely When it seems best to delay the discussion of a question (perhaps because a member who has vital information on the subject is not present), you should use the motion to postpone definitely. In doing so, you must specify the particular date or time the motion will be reconsidered. If, for example, you believe a motion should receive further study, you might say, "I move to postpone until the next meeting." If you think another issue should be decided first, you might say, "I move we postpone considering dues until we have first taken action on our budget."

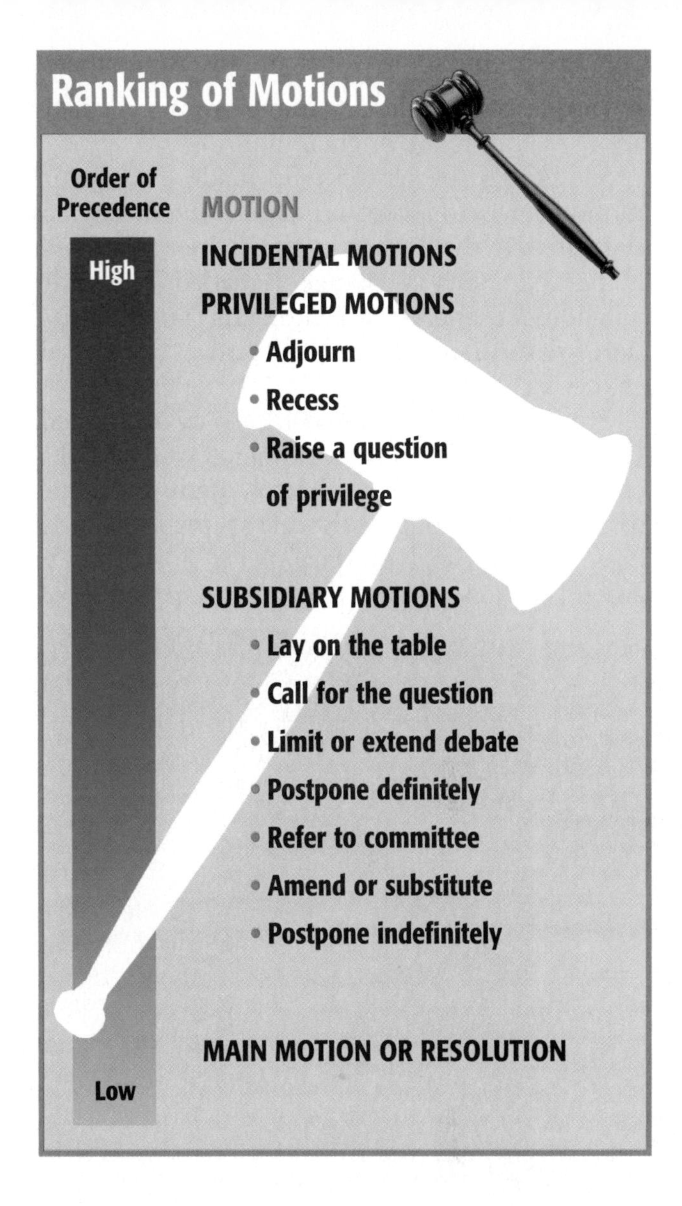

Ranking of Motions
Order of Precedence
MOTION
High
INCIDENTAL MOTIONS
PRIVILEGED MOTIONS
• Adjourn
• Recess
• Raise a question of privilege
SUBSIDIARY MOTIONS
• Lay on the table
• Call for the question
• Limit or extend debate
• Postpone definitely
• Refer to committee
• Amend or substitute
• Postpone indefinitely
MAIN MOTION OR RESOLUTION
Low

To refer to a committee Sometimes it may be necessary to send a motion to a committee for fine-tuning. A committee is a small, representative group of members, usually no more than 12, who give careful attention to a particular topic.

To amend A main motion sometimes needs a few changes before it will be acceptable to a majority of the members. In such cases, you may wish to **amend** the main motion. An amendment to a motion can be made in one of three ways:

1. By inserting, or adding, words,
2. By striking words (that is, removing them), or

3. By striking some words and inserting others.

In simplest terms, the amending process is chiefly a way of editing the original motion.

Sometimes the person who made the original motion agrees to accept a change someone else has suggested. In that case, no vote on the amendment is needed. Such a change is called a friendly amendment. Friendly amendments can often save time, particularly when they reflect only small changes.

Amendments themselves can be amended. During debate on an amendment, you may discover that no one is completely happy with the wording even though everyone seems to favor its basic idea. If so, you may make a motion to amend the amendment, a procedure called a secondary amendment. Fortunately, there is no such thing as a third-degree amendment—or meetings might never end.

A motion to ban junk food from school can be killed if the motion is postponed indefinitely.

To postpone indefinitely Despite how it sounds, the motion to postpone indefinitely is designed to kill and not postpone. Normally, opponents of a motion try to defeat it by a vote, but once in a while they prefer to avoid voting entirely. For example, suppose a motion comes before the school board to ban junk food from school premises. After some discussion, the board members come to realize that banning junk food might hurt the speech team. (The team sells candy bars to help pay for trips to tournaments.) Still, the board does not want to vote in favor of junk food. So the members decide to postpone the motion indefinitely. In this way, they can kill the motion without ever actually voting on it.

Privileged Motions ... Privileged motions have to do with mistakes or problems that must be corrected immediately. Because of their urgency, they are given high priority. Privileged motions include requests to stop the meeting or to set a meeting time for another day. Let's take a closer look at some of the most commonly used privileged motions.

Adjourn Adjourn is the term to use for ending a meeting. A member may move that the meeting be adjourned. More often, the chair just announces that, if there are no objections, the meeting is adjourned. When all the business before the house has been completed, the chair typically says, "Since there is no further business, the meeting is adjourned."

Recess A recess is just a short intermission. Most organizations use a recess to give members a break, usually lasting no more than a few minutes. Following a recess, members take up the business of the house at the point where they left off.

Raise a question of privilege A motion to raise a question of privilege makes an urgent request touching on the welfare of the group as a whole. You may ask, for example, that "the group help catch the gerbil I let loose by mistake." Or you could request, through the same procedure, that the house go into executive session to discuss a sensitive personal matter.

Motion	Requires Second	Debatable	Amendable	Vote Required
Incidental Motions				
Appeal decision of the chair	Yes	Yes	No	Majority
Point of information	No	No	No	None
Point of order	No	No	No	None
Suspend the rules	Yes	No	No	Two-thirds
Privileged Motions				
Adjourn	Yes	No	No	Majority
Recess	Yes	No	Yes	Majority
Raise a question of privilege	Yes	No	No	Majority
Subsidiary Motions				
Lay on the table	Yes	No	No	Majority
Call for the question	Yes	No	No	Two-thirds
Limit or extend debate	Yes	No	Yes	Two-thirds
Postpone definitely	Yes	Yes	Yes	Majority
Refer to committee	Yes	Yes	Yes	Majority
Amend the amendment	Yes	Yes	No	Majority
Amend	Yes	Yes	Yes	Majority
Postpone indefinitely	Yes	Yes	No	Majority
Main Motions				
Main motion or resolution	Yes	Yes	Yes	Majority
Reconsider	Yes	Yes	No	Majority
Take from table	Yes	No	No	Majority

Incidental Motions ... The final category of minor motions is a broad group called incidental motions. Like privileged motions, these motions usually apply to something other than the business at hand. Since they arise only incidentally—that is, from time to time—and must be decided as soon as they are raised, they have the highest priority of any motion.

Appeal the decision of the chair If you disagree with the chair's decision, you may appeal and ask that the house decide the question instead. The purpose of this appeal is to protect members against unjust rulings or technical errors. You should not hesitate to appeal if you disagree with the chair's ruling, but you should use good judgment, too. Unjustified or excessive appeals may damage the chair's credibility and thereby weaken the whole organization.

Point of information A point of information is usually a request for a simple explanation. For

COMMUNICATION

Breakdown

A Filibuster Stalls the Civil Rights Act

Your parents may think you talk a long time on the phone, but no matter how long-winded you are, you probably can't hold a candle to a United States senator in the middle of a filibuster.

The filibuster has been used as a parliamentary tactic since Roman times, but it is most often associated with the U.S. Senate. A filibuster is simply an attempt to delay a meeting so long that those in the majority will give up whatever motion it is that they wish to pass. Sometimes a tiny minority of members may try a filibuster to block the passage of some motion they have no hope of defeating in a vote. The tactic is especially effective at the end of a congressional session when senators are pressed for time to pass other major bills.

At times filibusters are quite comical. Some senators have been known to read from the telephone directory just to waste time. Others have resorted to reading the *World Almanac,* baseball statistics, and Aesop's fables.

Senator Strom Thurmond of South Carolina established the one-man endurance record of 24 hours and 18 minutes when filibustering against the 1957 Civil Rights Act, but he had the benefit of friendly interruptions, such as frequent quorum calls. Senator Wayne Morse of Oregon spoke alone and without interruption for 22 hours and 26 minutes, fighting an oil bill in 1953.

Filibusters can be used to stop a group from taking action, even when the majority view is clear. The most notorious filibuster was organized by Russell Long of Louisiana, who led 18 southern senators in a battle against the Civil Rights Act of 1964. Each of the senators spoke about 4 hours at a time and was interrupted by lengthy questions from sympathetic colleagues. Only after 74 days of this delay were enough senators willing to vote for cloture (a move to end debate requiring a three-fifths vote) and finally pass the bill.

The major argument for the filibuster centers on the protection it offers for minority rights. Senator Everett Dirksen of Illinois called it "the only weapon which the minority has to protect itself." On the other hand, parliamentary procedure must also ensure majority rights. Massachusetts Senator Henry Cabot Lodge summarized this view by saying to "vote without debating is perilous, but to debate and never vote is imbecilic."

Questions

1. At one time the Senate had no limit on debate. Should governmental bodies set limits on debate and, if so, what should those limits be?
2. Can you find any information on filibusters in your state legislature?

example, you might rise and say, "Point of information. Is there enough money in our account to cover the cost of the dance?"

Point of order The purpose of a point of order is to enforce the rules. A member can even interrupt another speaker to make a point of order. The chair, for example, may have given the floor to the wrong person. You could rise and say, "Point of order. This speaker has already been given two opportunities to speak." Once a point of order has been raised, the chair must make an immediate ruling.

Providing information in advance so all members can examine it before voting may avoid excessive "point of information" requests.

Suspend the rules A group can *suspend* any of its rules if they get in the way of the group's progress. The Animal Rights Club may have a rule, for example, that says all meetings must adjourn by 4:30. If a discussion is still going strong at 4:25, you may move to suspend the rule about adjournment to allow the discussion to continue past 4:30.

SECTION 4 REVIEW

Recalling the Facts ...

1. Explain how to apply the order of precedence during a meeting.
2. Briefly explain how incidental motions, privileged motions, and subsidiary motions differ from each other.

Thinking Critically ...

1. Discuss the ranking of motions. What are some reasons why one motion might be ranked above another? Why is the main motion the lowest-ranking motion? Why is a motion to adjourn the highest-ranking motion?
2. Can small, informal groups adapt the rules of parliamentary procedure to keep their meetings from becoming too technical? What modifications of the basic rules could they use? What shortcuts could they take? What rules should never be altered, no matter how small the group?

Taking Charge ...

1. Practice the rules of parliamentary procedure by holding a mock meeting in class to debate the morality of animal rights. Name a chairperson, and appoint someone to be the parliamentarian. The specific issue you might debate could be a ban on all medical research on animals that results in their death. After the meeting, ask the parliamentarian to evaluate how well the students conducted the meeting. Did they consistently follow parliamentary procedure?

STUDENT WORK

"Student Council Minutes"

The following minutes come from a student council meeting devoted to plans for the fall Homecoming dance and a district convention. In what ways do these minutes conform to the usual standards of parliamentary procedure? In what ways do they not?

Student Council Minutes

September 23, 2000

President Annie Hernandez called the meeting to order at 7 a.m.

All members were present.

Adam opened the meeting by suggesting that the council create a package deal for the sale of T-shirts, Homecoming tickets, and Knightcards since there was a lot of money involved. Because the council had already started selling them separately, however, we decided to do the package deal next year, but keep selling them separately this year.

Cindy reported that 10 pizzas had been donated by Domino's and two from Godfather's for the Homecoming dance. PTO said that they would arrange for the parent volunteers to sell the pizza. Each slice will be sold for $1. Cindy did say that they needed wax papers to put the pizza on and will speak to the lunch ladies.

Annie said that in order to decorate the gym, everyone would be excused at 12:55 on Friday.

Marc added that the decoration committee still needed tin foil for the walls. Walker said that he would call Sam's Club to see if they have it in bulk amounts.

Annie reminded everyone that the council will meet at 10 a.m. Saturday to clean up the gym. She also said that tomorrow would be devoted to District Convention. Each team is assigned to a task:

Team 1 = Registration, mailings, maps
Team 2 = Mini-sessions or alternatives
Team 3 = Speakers
Team 4 = Miscellaneous
Team 5 = Food
Team 6 = Homecoming

Walker announced that he has decided to run for a district office.

Mr. Toalson reminded the council to sell as many T-shirts as possible.

The meeting was adjourned at 7:40 a.m.

Suzanne Schaffer, Secretary

Looking Back

Listed below are the major ideas discussed in this chapter.

- The rules we use to make group decisions are called parliamentary procedure.
- The goal of parliamentary procedure is to help people conduct their business in an orderly and effective way. The rules are designed to make sure that the will of the majority prevails but also that the minority has an opportunity to speak and be heard.
- The system we call parliamentary procedure evolved from the rules of the British Parliament. An American, Henry Robert, developed a version that ordinary groups could use in their meetings. This version is contained in a guidebook called *Robert's Rules of Order Newly Revised.*
- The basic principles of parliamentary procedure are based on common sense. They include do one thing at a time, the majority decides, the minority must be protected, conduct a full and free discussion, and act with fairness and good faith.
- The chair, or presiding officer, runs each meeting. He or she decides who gets to speak and keeps the group on task. The chair also makes rulings from time to time.
- Typically, small organizations have a vice president, a treasurer, and a secretary in addition to a president. Large organizations may have several additional officers.
- Groups must have a quorum present at a meeting to conduct business. If a group wishes to close its meeting to outsiders, it may go into executive session.
- Members ask their groups to take action or make decisions through main motions. A main motion must be seconded by another member. It can be passed, postponed, sent to committee for study, or defeated.
- Members use subsidiary motions to fine-tune main motions. They use privileged motions to interrupt current business for something of great urgency, and they use incidental motions to make requests concerning the way the meeting is being run.

Speech Vocabulary

Match these speech terms with the definitions on top of page 534.

1. parliamentary procedure
2. chair
3. bylaws
4. orders of the day
5. new business
6. adjourn
7. amend
8. minutes
9. reconsider
10. quorum
11. executive session
12. order of precedence
13. privileged motion
14. call for the question

a. the person in charge of a meeting
b. business discussed for the first time
c. motion to close a meeting
d. system for ranking motions
e. minor motion to correct an urgent problem
f. official written record of a meeting
g. kind of meeting closed to outsiders
h. motion to take a vote
i. the agenda for a meeting
j. minimum number of members needed
k. to change or modify a motion
l. set of rules based on British example
m. motion to look again at a motion
n. the rules a group agrees to abide by

General Vocabulary

Use a dictionary to find the definition of each term. Then match the term on the left with the correct explanation on the right.

1. Parliament
2. innumerable
3. clique
4. railroad
5. painstakingly
6. agenda
7. restate
8. germane
9. suspend
10. preamble

a. an exclusive group
b. being extremely careful
c. list of things to be done
d. national legislative body
e. repeat in a new form
f. related or pertinent
g. to interrupt or stop
h. to push through
i. too many to be counted
j. introduction to a formal document

To Remember

Answer the following based on your reading of the chapter.

1. Parliamentary procedure protects two vital democratic rights: the right of the majority to ____________ and the right of the minority to ____________.
2. The most important guidebook for parliamentary procedure is called ____________.
3. The first principle of parliamentary procedure, ____________, helps groups stay on task.
4. Issues left over from a previous meeting are called ____________. Issues that come up for the first time during a meeting are called ____________.
5. The secretary keeps records of each meeting. These records are called ____________.
6. How many members must be present at a meeting for there to be a quorum?
7. A special kind of main motion, usually written with a preamble, is called a ____________.
8. Why must a motion be seconded?
9. The highest-ranking privileged motion is ____________.

CHAPTER 20 Review and Enrichment...

To Do

1. Contact your state legislature and inquire about its own specialized rules—its bylaws. What are some of these rules and what is the purpose of each?
2. Watch newspapers and magazines for stories about people who have broken the rules (whether official or cultural/ethical). Clip these articles out, bring them to class, and discuss them with your classmates.
3. Find out what it takes to start a new club at your school.

To Talk About

1. Discuss whether the rules of parliamentary procedure work for everyday use or are better suited for large, formal gatherings like those of state legislatures and the U.S. Congress.
2. What danger exists if one person in a meeting knows the rules of parliamentary procedure better than everyone else?
3. What power does knowledge of the rules of parliamentary procedure give a person?

To Write About

1. Write an essay about rules that apply in a democratic society. Consider the legal system, the unwritten "social system" that tells us how we should treat each other in public, codes of ethics, and value systems. To what extent do these systems protect us from our own worst instincts?
2. Obtain a copy of the minutes of a recent meeting of any organization. Reconstruct the meeting in the form of a dramatic play.

Related Speech Topics

British Parliament
Thomas Jefferson and the Declaration of Independence
Qualities of a good leader
Henry Robert, author of *Robert's Rules of Order*
The presidential nominating process
Election campaigns
Election reform

The Person Revisited

UNIT CONTENTS

CHAPTER 21

BUILDING LEADERSHIP

"The very essence of leadership is that you have to have a vision."

–Theodore Hesburgh

Learning Objectives

After completing this chapter, you will be able to do the following.

- Define the terms leadership and leader and then effectively apply these terms to intrapersonal and interpersonal communication.
- List the specific components of leadership.
- Understand the correlation between leadership skills and self-confidence.
- Realize the importance of effective speaking in leadership.
- Implement leadership skills in your daily life.

Chapter Outline

Following are the main sections in this chapter.

1. Leadership and Learning Styles
2. The Planks of Leadership

New Speech Terms

In this chapter, you will learn the meanings of the speech terms listed below.

leader
leadership
learning styles
vision
conflict management

General Vocabulary

Expanding your general vocabulary will help you become a more effective communicator. Listed below are some words appearing in this chapter that you should make part of your everyday vocabulary.

culmination
entrepreneur
facilitate
harmoniously
forfeiting
simulated

Looking AHEAD

The late comedian John Belushi once said, "Everyone is in some way a leader. Large or small, we all have an influence on somebody. The leaders gain the glory," he noted, "but they also feel the pain." The purpose of this chapter is to offer you some tips on what it takes to make Belushi's leadership "glory" a real-world possibility.

The following pages should make you more aware of what it takes to come out on top, and what steps should be taken if you wish to bypass leadership problems.

The first step is to examine leadership and learning styles—and to find out what it takes to understand not only those who lead but also those who are led. The next step is to analyze the planks of leadership and examine what qualities must be studied and then practiced by the effective communicator who wishes to lead and direct others.

You are all leaders. You might lead in some classes, with certain friends, in certain clubs or organizations, or in your family. What is your style? It is important that you realize that just as it takes hard work and planning to construct a house, it takes dedication and thought to lead others. Let's put your words to work!

Introduction

What do the words leader and leadership mean to you? Is a leader the person who is the "boss"? The authority figure? The biggest? The loudest? Generally speaking, a **leader** is the person who directs or who is in charge of others—while **leadership** focuses on the talents, qualities, and skills that the leader uses to influence people. But all leaders aren't the same.

Psychologist Dean Keith Simonton noted that many historical leaders have been very different. Beethoven's musical genius and leadership came with a price: he was rude to friends and to his servants. George Washington was a military mastermind, but he was a poor public speaker.

Beethoven's rude and tyrannical treatment of others made him an unpopular leader.

Simonton adds that one characteristic of leadership is undeniable: a genuine passion for the task at hand.

Speech and leadership work hand in hand. At some time in your life, by choice or otherwise, you will find yourself in a position where leadership is demanded. Your spoken words and the way you use them become your credibility.

The nationally recognized Hugh O'Brien Leadership Conference explains that some people are natural leaders with charisma and magnetic personalities. The conference believes also that leadership is most often the *culmination,* or the result, of a number of individual qualities that should be examined and then put into practice.

The first two chapters of this book compared the building of a good speaker to the building of a well-made house. Now, in the final chapter, we come to the roof. The roof is the top of the house and is the last part of the construction. Isn't the roof an extension of the construction below it? In a similar manner, leadership is the "extension" that often results when you add a constructive, confident attitude to a solid sense of personal integrity. And the "Planks of Leadership" make up the "roof," or the final step—in completing our "House of Effective Oral Communication."

SECTION 1 Leadership and Learning Styles

A line from the popular musical *The Music Man* declares that when it comes to selling, "Ya gotta know the territory." In other words, you need to know the makeup of your target people and what makes them tick if you want to sell your product. Every leader is, in a sense, a salesperson. He or she is selling an idea or a course of action—and asking others to buy in and follow. But what style works? Is there a sure-fire approach that will be effective in any territory? The answer, unfortunately, is no—for when it comes to leadership, unlike some clothes that you can buy, one size does *not* fit all. Different people are often swayed or influenced by different leadership approaches. Let's now take a look at three leadership styles, as suggested by Patricia Pitcher in her book *The Drama of Leadership:* the technocrat, the artist, and the craftsman. After reading, decide what leadership style is attractive to you, consider the positives or negatives of each, and choose one you might be tempted to follow.

Technocrats are no-nonsense leaders often more interested in numbers than in people.

Leadership Styles

The Technocrat. The technocrat leads by having a strong sense of the bottom line and often spends more time figuring out numbers and strategy than figuring out people. This leadership style, says author Pitcher, is no nonsense. It is a "my way or the highway" approach to motivating others. The only voice that the technocrat wishes to hear is his or her own, and people often follow because they are afraid not to do so. The technocrat prioritizes logic over emotion. The technocrat is intense, detail oriented, and hard headed, refusing to compromise. The main objective for the technocrat is to get the job done, and he or she is only focused on that goal.

THE WIZARD OF ID — **Brant parker and Johnny hart**

RESPECT AND RECOGNITION FOR LATINO LEADERS

INSTANT IMPACT

Writing for the July 1999 edition of *Newsweek,* Christy Haubegger, president and publisher of *Latina* magazine, sings the praises of her Hispanic people. She reminds us that Spanish was the first European language spoken on this continent and that the Latino population is becoming more and more influential in our society and growing seven times faster than the general public.

She also makes a serious point about leadership and role models. Americans too often know Latinos only as athletes and entertainers, but very soon, "all American children can dream of growing up to be writers like Sandra Cisneros, astronauts like Ellen Ochoa, or judges like José Cabranes of the Second Circuit Court of Appeals."

She looks forward to the day when *all* children will be required to know at least two languages, when living with one's extended family will become "hip" again, and when "American men finally know how to dance—specifically with a partner!" And even though the country is *loca* for singer Ricky Martin, Christy Haubegger wants the rest of the Latino population to receive the respect and recognition it deserves. "After all," she reminds us, "don't forget that Latinos are 11 percent of the country!" Thirty million Hispanics in America would certainly agree.

The Artist. The artist leads by imagination and intuition. Even though he or she doesn't know how all of the pieces fit together, the artist has a distinct vision of the "big picture." This leadership style actively invites others to share ideas and isn't afraid to show emotion and laughter. The artist, though sometimes unpredictable, is a daring *entrepreneur,* or one who goes after new ideas and sees things from a different perspective. The artist can be found in any social or professional location where originality and creativity are important. Sometimes we are fascinated with the artist and go along with him or her—just to be a part of the unique possibilities that might result from this type of leadership.

The artist can be found in any profession but is most often associated with performers.

The Craftsman. The craftsman (male or female) leads by common sense and integrity. A person who can be trusted, the craftsman is well balanced and an excellent listener. This leadership style draws followers because the craftsman is a caring, logical person who values getting the job done, but refuses to sacrifice people and their views and feelings in the process. The craftsman is liked because he or she is predictable and seems to "have it all together." This leadership style isn't afraid to venture into creative thinking, but is always aware

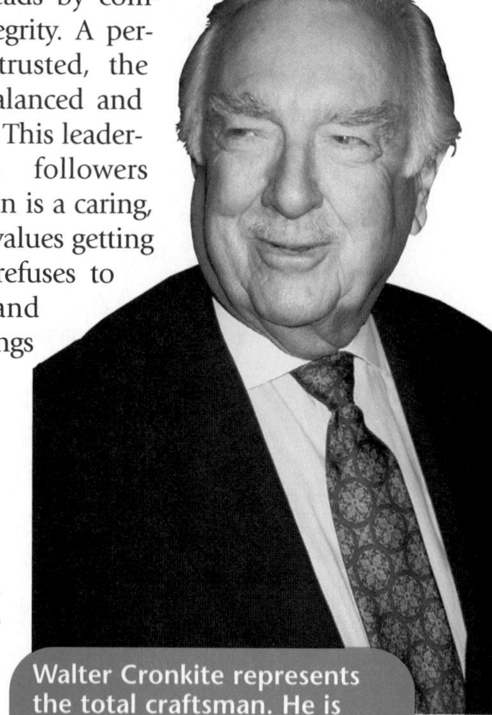

Walter Cronkite represents the total craftsman. He is considered one of the 20th century's finest newsmen.

LEADERSHIP

What qualities make these people leaders?

Colin Powell

Eileen Collins

Cesar Chávez

Madeleine Albright

George W. Bush

Oprah Winfrey

of the real world and what is reasonable. The craftsman is skilled at decision making and strategically avoids making others feel like winners and losers.

The Answer Is in the "Blending" ...

These are three leadership profiles that you may have encountered somewhere in your life. Which style is the best? Author Pitcher states that there are times when the technocrat is needed, and the tough, "just give me the facts" approach is smart. When Thomas Buckley first ran for auditor of Massachusetts in 1941, his speech consisted of only seven words:

"I am an auditor . . . not an orator!"

He continued to run (and win!) for years after, each time campaigning with these same seven words. Needless to say, Buckley was all business. However, Pitcher says that her research shows that the technocrat leadership style is on the way out. More and more, those in charge are realizing that people *need* people—and that social and professional success sometimes depends more on effective communication that builds teamwork and collective problem solving than it does on a dictatorial approach based on intimidation that stresses everyone out.

The answer to the best leadership style, she concludes, is a blending of the artist and the craftsman: a leadership style that combines creativity and genuine enthusiasm with levelheadedness, compassion, and collaboration.

Learning Styles

A good leader knows that before there can be effective motivation, there must be effective communication. Obviously, if you know how people learn best, you have a better chance of getting and keeping their attention.

Teachers acknowledge different learning styles within their classrooms.

Perhaps when you read the sentence "A leader knows that people learn differently," you think it is referring only to classroom teachers. Not so. All leaders are teachers in some way. They teach specific strategies and lessons. They teach and promote certain attitudes. They teach about people and life.

The best speakers, teachers, and leaders are those people who can use their words to communicate with the greatest number of people. To do that, you need to be familiar with people's **learning styles**—the ways that they learn most effectively. We examine four learning styles here: discussion, logic, design, and emotion.

Learning Style 1: Discussion ... Some people learn best through meaningful discussion. They want to be actively involved in the oral communication process, with lots of dialogue and feedback. They appreciate face-to-face communication. Getting everyone's opinion is important to them, and they love to brainstorm, or throw many ideas out onto the table. They enjoy discussing each item before making a decision. They are alert and involved when they have the opportunity for verbal interaction.

Learning Style 2: Logic ... Others learn best when things are presented logically, with a "just the facts" approach. Discussed in Chapter 10, logic stresses analysis, organization, and an approach focusing on "good sense." Some members of this group, not impressed by a lot of talk, are genuinely interested when they hear a direct, logical, to-the-point plan of action.

Learning Style 3: Design ... Some people learn best when they can see and hear how the "big picture" fits together. People in this category might include engineers and other builders and designers. They are encouraged when the leader presents a clear picture of relationships and shows how the different parts are all going to work together as a smooth-running unit.

A factual approach will appeal to those with a logical learning style.

Learning Style 4: Emotion ...

For many people, the best communication is a hands-on approach, one in which the leader is energetic and fired up. As you have probably heard before, enthusiasm is contagious. Often, a leader who shows the group that he or she is emotionally involved with a specific project or idea will quickly attract highly involved and committed followers.

Do any of these methods sound familiar? Which would work best for you? Knowing about learning styles can help a leader communicate with others. There are other ways of categorizing learning styles, but keeping these four types in mind should help when you are thinking about using your words to reach everyone. If you know how people learn—what approach excites them—you have a much better chance of communicating effectively with them.

Hands-on leaders like these fix-up volunteers will likely appeal to your emotions.

SECTION 1 REVIEW

Recalling the Facts ...

1. List the three leadership styles as given in the section. Which one sometimes puts numbers ahead of people and their feelings?
2. Which leadership style depends on imagination and intuition?
3. What do you call it when you "combine" leadership styles to get the best overall approach to leadership?
4. List the four different learning styles as given in the section. Which one stresses a knowledge of the "big picture"? Which one involves enthusiasm and a fired-up presentation?

Thinking Critically ...

1. One leadership style is that of the technocrat. It is said that this type of leader is on the way out, because the future will call for a great deal more team building and consensus building. However, think about class projects, work that has to be done on the job, or even balancing a checkbook. When might some qualities of the technocrat be useful? Unfortunately, the technocrat can go too far in his or her leadership approach. Give some examples of how this leadership style might turn some followers off.

Taking Charge ...

1. Analyze and evaluate leadership styles by using the media. What television shows depict people who "lead" differently? What about your favorite characters in current movies? How about people in the news? Make a list of the three different leadership styles. After each, list the individuals who might fall in each category. You should have at least *two* for each category. Be prepared to explain your reasoning, based on the definition for each leadership style as given in the chapter.

SECTION 2 The Planks of Leadership

Based on a study that was done by management specialist Thomas Peters, everyone who has made history—from Martin Luther King, Jr., to Thomas Jefferson—has had these "top 10" things in common:

1. committed
2. focused
3. passionate
4. risk-taker
5. creative, or peculiar
6. honest
7. not perfect
8. tuned into followers' needs and aspirations
9. good at what they did
10. didn't care if they made some people angry

Obviously, leaders are people who aren't afraid to give power and authority to others and who, in addition, have the power and the drive to "make things happen."

As you read the following discussion, pay attention to the specific communication strategy at the end of each plank. Each will show you how to demonstrate the qualities of leadership by using appropriate verbal, nonverbal, and listening strategies to promote both individual and group communication effectiveness.

Plank 1: A Leader Has a Sense of Vision

On July 20, 1999, America celebrated the 30th anniversary of the first man to walk on the moon. When scientists proposed the idea of a human being in space, let alone a person walking on the moon, few thought it was possible. But a sense of vision, as well as follow-through, turned this goal into a reality. Such a sense of vision is one key trait of a leader.

Vision drove Apollo 11 astronauts Neal Armstrong, Buzz Aldrin, and Eugene Cernan to train for and successfully complete the first U.S. moonwalk.

Simply put, **vision,** as it applies to leadership, means the ability to see more than just the obvious. Leaders with a sense of vision can often "solve the puzzle" because they have the ability to see the scope of a situation in its entirety and then focus on what really matters. Often, vision enables a leader to spot a need that must be met, to create a product or program that has tremendous possibilities, or to see how the pieces in the "big picture" could better fit together within a plan or an organization.

There's a difference, however, between making random predictions and being able to display a true sense of vision. Consider these predictions that were made in the 1960s by people who thought they had a sense for what would occur at the turn of the millennium. According the *New*

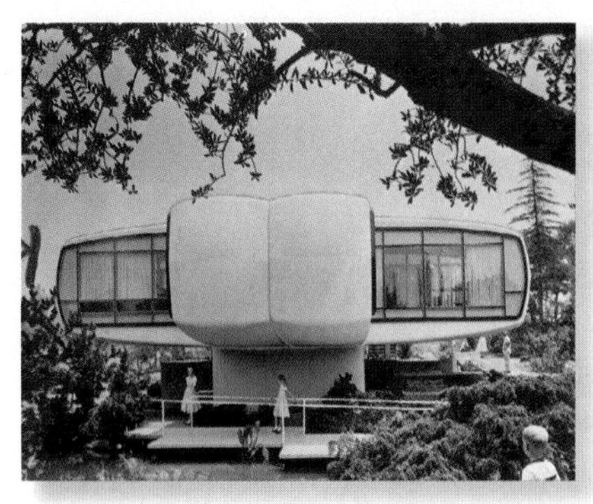

These illustrations represent some of the scientific predictions made for the late twentieth century. Have any of them come true?

York Times, in 1966, Arthur C. Clarke predicted that by the year 2001, inventors would make construction materials stronger than steel but lighter than aluminum. Because of this, houses would be able to fly. As he said, "Whole communities may migrate south in the winter." In 1967, *Science Digest* predicted that by the turn of the century, "Discarded rayon underwear will be bought by chemical factories and converted into candy." Obviously, these predictions failed to come true, and their "vision" was, to say the least, a little clouded. But these rather humorous failures shouldn't stop the rest of us from trying to discover what true vision is.

To truly develop a sense of vision, a leader must have insight, look at the long-term perspective, and ponder the "big picture." As Anil Nanji, a successful California businessman, points out, vision is not only a picture of the way things should be, but also a guiding light that helps one channel the decisions and actions that accompany that vision.

Sinclair Lewis spoke little, but wrote volumes. He exemplifies the *doer.*

Specific Communication Strategy: As a leader, practice creative thinking skills, but also seek out the ideas of others so that you can truly grasp the "big picture." Look at a situation, and then take a step back and consider another perspective. Use your intrapersonal and interpersonal communication skills. Ask yourself and others: What are the parts and how do they fit together to form the whole? What do we want to accomplish? What are our goals? What do we dare to dream? How can we best actualize our vision? When a leader shares plans with others and opens the door to dialogue, it often results in more effective long-range planning. A good leader recognizes the importance of gathering and using accurate and complete information as the basis for making communication decisions.

Plank 2: A Leader Is Willing to Act

Novelist Sinclair Lewis was invited to give a lecture to aspiring authors. He began his lecture by asking, "How many of you really intend to be writers?" Everyone in the room raised their hands. "In that case," responded Lewis, "my advice to you is to go home and write." With that, he left the room.

Now, Lewis may have been overly blunt in his approach, but his point was clear. Leaders are doers. They take action. They believe in getting the job done and getting it done well. After all the talking, analyzing, and pondering, it is the leader who says to the rest of the group, "OK, let's get started. Let's do something *now*!"

While speaking at a leadership seminar, a university professor said that it was time for students to

WORDS FROM THE WORKPLACE

Natasha Swan
Director of Services

Q. *How does good communication play a role in your day-to-day activities, Ms. Swan?*

A. Effective communication skills are essential to the daily routine of my job. As Director of Services, I deal with member conflicts and concerns daily. I also deal with members on a one-on-one basis during consultations and personal training sessions. I have to make sure that things are presented properly, and I listen very carefully to each person. One of the most important things that I have learned here is that communication isn't only speaking, but is listening and body language as well. Communication is a very big part of the service we render because we generate revenue through sales. In order to sell your service, you must know how to communicate very effectively; therefore, we work on it daily.

Q. *Do you have any stories that might illustrate how good communication skills helped in a business situation or, for that matter, how poor communication skills hurt a situation by losing a customer or sale for the company?*

A. My communication skills are tested daily with member concerns, and resolving member conflicts. I constantly watch my posture, my eye contact, and the tone of my voice. My most memorable communication experience was when a woman about 65 years old, weighing 300 pounds, told me that one of my 22-year-old personal trainers had a crush on her, and she wanted me to let him know that she was married. When situations like this occur, it is very important that I listen attentively and paraphrase what the member is saying to make sure that I have a clear understanding of what the person is telling me. In this case my communication through voice tone, eye contact, and actual language let her know that I was listening and it satisfied her concern. Everyone wants to be treated with respect and made to feel you are concerned about their problems. It is not always easy to do this, but you must make every attempt to do so.

quit thinking and talking about success and to start acting. Unlike Sinclair Lewis, he offered more detailed advice. He suggested that the students map out a specific plan of action and then start working to actualize their goals. The seminar, which was titled "Now Is the Time to Start Thinking and Growing Rich," dealt with both personal and material success. It stressed that personal leadership begins with a philosophy of action. Here's an example of what happens when an individual is determined to take positive action to achieve success.

L. Strauss was the last of his brothers to leave Bavaria (now part of Germany) for the United States. The year was 1847, and he was only 18 years old. Quick to learn English and an excellent salesman, Strauss reached California during the gold rush. His brothers, who owned a dry goods business, quickly put him to work. On one specific venture, he was told to fill his backpack with goods and not to return until everything in the pack had been sold. Soon everything was sold except for a few rolls of canvas. He approached an old miner and offered him the canvas for his tent. The miner responded that he didn't need material for a tent; instead, he needed pants that wouldn't wear out.

Strauss took the canvas to a tailor, who stitched together a pair of sturdy, waist-high overalls. The miner bought the jeans, and soon the word spread.

What was the man's name? Levi Strauss. His pants were known simply as Levi's. Soon after, Levi started to make shirts, jackets, and other clothing. Why? He saw a need, he saw a market, he saw an opportunity. *Levi* is a household name today around the globe because Levi Strauss had the nerve to act back in 1847. Levi Strauss was a leader! You can learn a valuable lesson from this story. Allow your vision to work for you, and then get in there and get your hands dirty. While luck might sometimes *facilitate* positive results, it is most often leadership that will make those results happen.

Levi Strauss invented the pants that wouldn't wear out.

Specific Communication Strategy: When leadership is needed, take charge. Make statements to the group such as these: "Here's what we now need to do." "Let's now make a specific list of who's responsible for what. We'll report back tomorrow on our progress." "It's time that we quit talking and start doing!" Let your spoken words show that you are not afraid of a challenge and that you will act on getting the task completed.

Plank 3: A Leader Makes Good Decisions

Nothing will kill the credibility of a leader more quickly than to be perceived by others as indecisive when the time comes for decision making. However, there is a world of difference between simply making a decision and making the right decision. Your decisions should show intelligence, but they should do more. They should reflect ethical communication—and show that you feel a sense of social or professional responsibility for those who are your followers. Let's look at three specific questions that a good leader might answer before making a final decision.

Decisiveness increases a leader's credibility and appeal.

Question 1: Am I knowledgeable about the issues and the people involved? ... A good leader does homework and is informed about the facts that might affect his or her decision on a particular issue. Once again, it is important to gather accurate and complete information. Are important statistics about the issue needed? What about past history? What does the current literature say about this concern? Knowing all you can about the issues involved can provide you with the scope necessary to make a good decision and can add credibility to your position as a solid decision maker.

Indecision lessens a leader's credibility.

In addition to being knowledgeable about issues, you need to know about people. How will the group react to this decision? Do you have the group's best interest in mind? Are you considering what they will think, as well as how they will feel? What will be the long-range effect on everyone involved? A good leader remembers that people are the most important part of any decision made!

Question 2: Am I making decisions in the correct order? … A good leader has to know how to prioritize and to put what is most important first. A school committee that spends hours on getting a big-name band to entertain the hundreds of people who will be attending an end-of-the-year dance—before it decides on a location large enough to accommodate all of those people—might run into problems later. A good leader decides on the larger issues first and then moves down the list, realistically considering needs versus wants before prioritizing. Are you working with something that is essential or something that would be a luxury? How will one decision affect another? Making a correct decision is a big job; making the decision when it should be made is equally important.

Good leaders are able to prioritize and keep things in balance.

Question 3: Am I aware of the risks involved? … While a good leader should be informed and able to prioritize, she or he must also be willing to consider taking a chance sometimes if the situation is right. You can't always act according to what has been done before. Sometimes risk taking shows creativity, insight, and progress.

In taking risks, however, a good leader is never caught off-guard. You must know ahead of time the potential consequences of your decision. Is the risk a smart one? Might the risk be too costly? It would be foolish for the pilot of a commercial aircraft to suddenly disregard the instructions of the air traffic controller and strike out on his own. He would be putting the lives of everyone on the plane in jeopardy. As an effective leader and decision maker, you must sometimes use your instincts, but you must also use your common sense and sound judgment when the well-being of others is at stake.

If you consider each of the three questions in this section when making important decisions in your personal, professional, school, community, and family life, then you may find stepping to the front and leading others less fearful and more productive.

Specific Communication Strategy: When sharing your final decision with others, try to focus your communication on three terms: what, why, and how. If others clearly understand what your decision is, why you made it, and how you believe it can be carried out, then they are more apt to respect the decision. Even if they disagree with the final determination, they will respect the time, energy, and thoroughness that went into the decision-making process. And if you include how you plan to implement the decision, others will gain a sense of confidence in the workability of your plan of action. Also, remember to tell the members of the group that you appreciate their input and that this input was seriously considered before making the final decision. Decisions are often met with more approval when people understand rather than assume why a decision was made.

Air traffic controllers must be acutely aware of risks, using their specialized training to keep airspaces safe.

Plank 4: A Leader Can Handle Conflict

Of all the qualities of a leader, none ranks higher than being able to work *harmoniously* with people and make them feel good both about themselves and about the group's objectives. A fact of life for anyone in charge of a group, however, is that not everything always runs smoothly. Problems arise and personalities clash. This is why a leader must work diligently to solve problems, manage conflicts, and build consensus among the group.

How should a problem situation be handled? First of all, good leaders know that intense arguing and emotional outbursts won't help. All that happens when emotions are allowed to run wild is that communication takes a back seat to confrontation, which gets in the way of what both the leader and the group are after. Cool heads must prevail. An awareness of the principles of conflict management can help. **Conflict management** is the ability to turn a potentially negative situation into a positive one.

A good leader like NFL coach Tony Dungy is a cool head in the midst of conflict.

A speech consultant who was working with a group of business supervisors and executives on improved communication and better public speaking offered the following plan for conflict management. The plan, which had worked for him and countless others, includes four steps:

Shut up!
Look up!
Hook up!
Chill down!

1. ***Shut up!*** A good leader doesn't always have to be the one doing the talking. If you are having a problem with a person, keep quiet and listen to what that person is saying. Don't interrupt! Allow the other person to finish speaking before you talk.
2. ***Look up!*** Establish eye contact with the person. Don't look off to the side or down at the floor. Let the person know that you are genuinely involved with what he or she is saying by looking at him or her, showing an understanding, responsive attitude.
3. ***Hook up!*** It is important to "hook up" emotionally with the other person to try to understand her or his point of view. You may need to see the situation from another perspective and understand why someone else might not feel as you do.
4. ***Chill down!*** When you do verbally respond to the other person, make your comments rational, sensitive, and constructive. Don't permit your temper or the heat of the moment to control a situation and allow it to escalate into an even larger problem.

Try this four-point plan in your dealings with other people. Your conflict management skills may not only improve the situation but also increase your confidence in how you communicate with others on a daily basis. It's worth a try!

Closely associated with conflict management is a leader's willingness to get along with others. Even though getting along often takes hard work, it's worth the effort. After all, you can't make it all alone—but a leader who won't make an effort to create a harmonious working environment might find that he or she is having to do all of the work alone.

One way to create a harmonious working environment is to praise people's efforts. Studies have shown that people like to be told when they are doing things right. It establishes a group rapport and also increases productivity. In complimenting people, vary the words that you use.

COMMUNICATION

Break through

The Special Olympics

Eunice Kennedy Shriver, the sister of John F. Kennedy, had a sister, Rosemary, who was developmentally disabled. After visiting many hospitals for the disabled, Shriver was appalled at the crowding and understaffing she saw. She was also appalled that the patients never had to engage in any type of exercise and, thus, were in poor physical condition. Told that running, jumping, and playing could injure the children, Shriver took matters into her own hands. She started an exercise class and constructed a playing field for the mentally handicapped in her own backyard! Her involvement grew until, in 1968, what is known as the Special Olympics was officially started.

The Special Olympics trains developmentally disabled children and adults for athletic competition. Events include basketball, bowling, diving, floor hockey, gymnastics, ice skating, soccer, track and field, volleyball, wheelchair events, and several others. Currently, over 10,000 communities around the world offer Special Olympics programs, with over a million athlete-participants in the United States alone.

The Special Olympics has two major objectives: 1) to promote physical and emotional growth through friendship and family support and 2) to offer opportunities for achievement and courage through athletics. Eunice Kennedy Shriver is a leader because she saw a need and then acted. What is the result? The Special Olympics has become a symbol that communicates to the entire world that people really do care about each other.

All of the work for the Special Olympics is done by volunteers. Over 100,000 volunteers worldwide are involved. One of the most rewarding jobs as a volunteer is to be one of the "huggers." It is their job to grab and hug the competitors as they cross the finish line. Every contestant has a "hugger."

Says one volunteer mother, "Everyone involved with the Special Olympics is a leader because when all of the voices are heard laughing and cheering together, we all feel inspired and understand that each of us is depending on the other person. That makes me feel good inside!"

Questions

1. What does the volunteer mother mean by this last statement? Why could it be true that "Everyone involved with the Special Olympics is a leader"?
2. Why is it noteworthy that all of the work done in the Special Olympics is done by volunteers?

Words lose their impact if they are used insincerely or are repeated over and over. For instance, here are some words you could use to compliment and encourage others: great, wonderful, outstanding, excellent, perfect. Also, try to verbalize praiseworthy traits such as hard-working, dedicated, detail-oriented, trustworthy, responsible, caring, considerate, loyal, dependable, honest, friendly. What terms can you add to either list?

Specific Communication Strategy: In a tactful manner, summarize for others what they have said to you so that they know that you were paying attention to them. Also, pay careful attention to how you say something. You can add to your effectiveness as a good leader if you will pay close attention to the tone of your voice and the nonverbal signals that you are giving. Body language speaks just as loudly as words, so convey through body language a message that shows people, "I take seriously what you have to say and I am really listening!"

Babe Ruth was never afraid to fail!

Plank 5: A Leader Works to Avoid Pitfalls

You have probably heard the saying, "Forewarned is forearmed." It means that being conscious of a potential problem ahead of time might help you "cut it off at the pass"—stop it before it gets started. With this in mind, be alert to the following four pitfalls of leadership and work to avoid them.

Pitfall 1: Being Afraid to Fail ...

Leaders don't like to make mistakes. A good leader tries to be conscientious and show the group that she or he can be counted on to do things correctly. However, a leader should not always play it safe. If, as a leader, your attitude is "I'd like to try that but I'm afraid that I'll fail," then you might be *forfeiting* some of the creativity and personal vision that the group counts on you to provide.

Don't be afraid of what your instincts and personal intuition might be telling you to do. Of course, you have to make sure that you are not being reckless in your judgment, but you should also keep in mind that many great leaders failed at one time or another. The baseball great Babe Ruth was a home-run king, but he also led the major leagues in strikeouts. The explorer Christopher Columbus left Europe to find the East Indies; he failed to find them, but he found America. The inventor and genius Thomas Edison had an interesting philosophy about failure. He said that when his work produced 99 failures in a row, he then knew 99 ways that didn't work and was closing in

A VOICE SPEAKS OUT FOR WALDEN WOODS

INSTANT IMPACT

Don Henley, the musician who brought "The End of the Innocence," "All She Wants to Do Is Dance," and "The Boys of Summer" to the music charts, is now leading the way to preserve Walden Woods in Concord, Massachusetts. Walden Woods is a famous landmark because it was the birthplace for the ideas of Henry David Thoreau, the great American thinker, writer, and philosopher.

When Henley learned that developers were planning to construct condos and office buildings, he founded the Walden Woods Project, aimed at purchasing a part of Walden Woods, saving it, and preserving it for history. Henley estimates that the project will cost about $10 million.

In an interview, Henley urged students to get involved and start fundraisers. Leadership, he says, means that you don't wait for somebody else to "get the ball rolling"—you take the initiative yourself. He believes that the efforts to save Walden Woods can work because "people—the media stars, the politicians, the average citizen, the young people of the country—working together can make a difference."

One of Don Henley's favorite quotes by Thoreau is: "I went to the woods because I wished to live deliberately . . . to see if I could learn what it had to teach, and not, when I came to die, discover that I had not lived." Thanks to Henley's speaking out, future generations will still be able to study the woods that inspired these words.

Source: *Scholastic Scope.*

on finding the solution. Abraham Lincoln lost five political elections before he eventually became president.

As a good leader, don't live with a fear of failure. If your group knows that you have its best interests at heart, it will most likely support your efforts. Go for it!

Pitfall 2: Not Paying Attention to Details ... Of course, a good leader should focus on the "big picture," but he or she should also pay attention to the small things. A good leader is aware that paying attention to details early will help make the big picture much clearer and better defined later.

Details matter! If handled correctly, they can make you appear organized and competent to your group. If handled incorrectly, they can make you appear foolish and inept. In 1987, for example, the Nobel Prize Committee for Science and Economics notified Donald O. Cram that he had won the Nobel Prize in chemistry. The problem was that Donald O. Cram is a California rug-shampooer. The award was really meant for Donald J. Cram.

Ignoring details or dismissing them as being "too trivial" often results in projects that don't work or organizations that fall apart. It was a detail—the seemingly insignificant O-ring—on the space shuttle *Challenger* that ultimately caused the loss of seven lives and a huge setback for the space program.

The space shuttle *Challenger* explodes shortly after liftoff.

COMMUNICATION

Breakdown

The Call That Wasn't Made

It was a day like any other day on the campus of Valparaiso University, a small educational institution in the heart of the Midwest. Then it happened—an explosion. Suddenly the serene campus setting turned into mass hysteria. The explosion had occurred in an advanced chemistry class, and nearly 40 students and a professor had been seriously injured. Some of the victims wandered around in shock, while others simply stared ahead, numb and disbelieving.

Within a matter of minutes, calls had been made to police, firefighters, hazardous material specialists, and medical personnel. Almost immediately, all were on the scene. However, in the midst of the confusion and rush, one phone call was *not* immediately made: a phone call to the hospital emergency room alerting its staff that a large number of people injured by a chemical explosion would be on their way.

Don't be alarmed. The situation just described is a *simulated* disaster, part of the community's Disaster Drill Alert. In a newspaper article, the drill coordinator, Gregory L. Eckhardt, said of the failure to call the emergency room: "It's communication. We've got to get everyone on the same frequency." He noted that everything else in the drill worked well that day and the cooperation was tremendous.

A hospital spokesperson said it best. She said that the bad news was that people in a leadership position forgot to make the call. However, the good news was that it happened when everything was pretend. "When lives are on the line," she said, "the job will get done because now everyone has learned."

Exerpted from the *Gary Post-Tribune.*

Questions

1. Why are details important to leaders?
2. Why is it important for leaders to have followers whom they can count on to get jobs done?
3. The Valparaiso University example is a type of directed practice experience. Why is a trial run-through often a good idea for those in charge?

Pitfall 3: Forgetting People and the Original Objectives ... A major pitfall for any leader is to forget the human factor in the decision-making process or to lose sight of what it was that the group was originally after. As a conscientious leader, you need to ask yourself these questions: "What exactly is it that we were trying to accomplish?" "Who were the people who played key roles and worked hard right from the start?" It is often easy for those in charge to get sidetracked or detoured. Stay on track. Furthermore, reward group members who deserve special consideration for being there when times were tough.

Pitfall 4: Not Listening to Others ... It is important to listen to others, for a variety of reasons. Not only is it a nice thing to do, but it is also smart. By listening to others you can gain new insights, stimulate new ideas, and build on the input of others. Seeing other perspectives and synthesizing different viewpoints enables leaders to have a better understanding of a situation. As the owner of Motivation Media, a broad-ranging corporate communications company, explains, "In some ways, I think I never have my own idea. What I have is an ability to synthesize the thinking and contributions of others." The company credits its success to its ability to listen to customers, and then to incorporate the findings so that service is always top notch.

People also appreciate the opportunity to be heard. This does not mean that every idea has equal merit or will be acted on immediately, but it does mean that leaders gain respect and support from others by establishing a rapport that is open to input. This may take the form of brainstorming or evaluating, or it may involve expressing feelings or simply venting concerns. If handled in an atmosphere of mutual respect, this will lead to a happier, more comfortable, more successful group of people.

Specific Communication Strategy: This is a good time to make use of your intrapersonal communication skills and remind yourself of some important points. Give yourself a good talking-to and consider all of your options. What are the risks? Have you thought through all of the details? What was the primary issue and who were the people there from the start? Did I listen to others before making a decision? Answer these questions to yourself. Hopefully this activity will eliminate a few of the pitfalls that signal "Beware: Danger Ahead!"

Plank 6: A Leader Knows How to Motivate

When the USA Women's Soccer Team won the World Cup in 1999, its victory over the top-rated team from China rocked the sporting world. Certainly, there was little doubt that its accomplishment was a result of great skill, but it was also coupled with a tremendous desire to win, to beat the odds, to reach new heights of success. Whether it was star goalkeeper Brianna Scurry or Brandi Chastain, who scored the winning kick, the team was filled with leaders who were motivated to excel.

Leaders must know how to motivate. This young man seeking an at-large position on a city council obviously has the support of his peers.

Recall from Chapter 1 that to motivate means to inspire either yourself or others (or both) to act. Motivation is the consequence of all that this chapter has discussed. Therefore, it was left near the end for a reason. This is because motivation may be created by any number of factors.

- The honesty and integrity that you show
- The strong work ethic that you exhibit
- The discussion that you promote
- The logic and intelligence that you put forward
- The "master plan" of action that you offer
- The emotion that you share
- The creativity that you lend
- The confidence and decisiveness that you exhibit

Motivation is a very personal thing. What motivates some won't motivate others. Thus, the job of a good leader is to know his or her group well enough to know what will work with whom. There is no textbook that can specifically prescribe how every leader can motivate every group member. The truth of the matter is that in the end, motivation occurs as a result of the people in your group trusting you enough to follow your advice.

Specific Communication Strategy: Read the advice given for Planks 1–5. Work on making both your verbal and your nonverbal communication clear and meaningful. At the same time, leave room for the creativity and spontaneity that often come when the leader and the group are functioning cooperatively as a productive unit.

Wanted: Leader

Must be able to see the "big picture"; solve problems through analysis and discussion, followed by action; teach people according to different learning styles (discussion, logic, design, and emotion); make good decisions based on knowledge, priorities, and awareness of risks; handle conflict; avoid pitfalls like being afraid to fail, not paying attention to details, and forgetting original objectives; and motivate self and others.

So there you have the six planks of leadership. To be a good speaker and a good leader, you must work from the inside out and establish a strong value system that will anchor your words and give them substance.

True leaders, contrary to what some might believe, are everywhere. They are both female and male, young and old, rich and poor, and they represent various ethnic groups. It is our job to recognize the tremendous leadership potential that people have. In the tragic shooting that took place at Columbine High School (Colorado) in April 1999, one girl, who was trapped in a small, hot band room with scores of other students, told how three or four "geeks," the "not-real-popular kids," took charge and articulated a well-organized plan of escape through the overhead heating and cooling ductwork. Their leadership saved lives.

Everyone has leadership potential. Your ideas might not be great when it comes to literature and writing plays, but what about your thoughts on writing music? About a trade such as carpentry? About cars? About kids and teaching? Share your ideas. Listen to the ideas of others. You just might uncover some real eye-opening solutions and discoveries.

Being a good leader is tough, but those who use their communication skills to inspire others, to promote smart problem solving, and to help all of us get along better with each other are certainly building a bright future and are destined to end up—like the roof on our house of communication—at the top!

These Columbine High School students performed a tribute to their twelve slain fellow students at a professional baseball game.

SECTION 2 REVIEW

Recalling the Facts ...

1. One of the planks of leadership said that "a leader can handle conflict." List the four steps that a speech consultant gave to businesspeople that also might work for you.
2. Which one of the planks was based on the idea that "leaders are doers"? What person from history whose name appears on a popular brand of jeans was definitely a "doer"?
3. Which plank is often a result of all of the others and was saved until last?
4. In an Instant Impact, singer Don Henley "got involved" to help save Walden Woods from developers. What famous person lived a while in Walden Woods and was a philosophical leader in his own day?

Thinking Critically ...

1. The book *21-Day Countdown to Success* by Chris Witting talks about some examples of people who didn't give up when faced with initial failure. For instance, a newspaper once fired a young cartoonist because he didn't "have any good ideas." It was Walt Disney. Basketball icon Michael Jordan was cut from his junior high school basketball team. News personality Katie Couric flopped in her first TV job because she had a "squeaky voice." Yet, none of these three gave up.

   Why is it important that leaders be able to bounce back from adversity? Think of a person (or people) from history or from current events (news, sports, business) who wasn't afraid to fail and who achieved personal or professional success. What qualities did she or he exhibit that you might want to apply to your own life?

Taking Charge ...

1. Several leadership pitfalls are listed in this chapter. What are your own leadership problems? List two pitfalls that you find difficult to overcome when attempting to lead. Try not to use the ones listed in the book; think of your own. Katie Couric, when told that her voice was a problem on the air, took voice lessons. What can you list as some possible solutions or action steps that you might use to solve your leadership problems? Jot them down—and then be prepared to discuss your observations with the class. Be ready for a small group discussion or an informal oral presentation.

STUDENT WORK

"The Last American Hero" *By Diane Matesic*

The author Gertrude Stein wrote the famous line, "A rose is a rose is a rose." In the spirit of this line, we might also say, "A good speech is a good speech is a good speech." In other words, regardless of when it was written, a good speech presents truths that can apply to our lives. The following speech, which was briefly referred to in Chapter 1, is offered here in its entirety. Its message, written and delivered in 1977 by Indiana student Diane Matesic, still rings true today. Keep leadership in mind as you read.

I'm going to give you three pairs of men. For each category, choose the one best personifying the quality of leadership. In the area of sports, Babe Ruth or Hank Aaron; national leaders, Winston Churchill or Gerald Ford; and as statesmen, Patrick Henry or Henry Kissinger. If you picked the first man in each category, congratulations, for you are part of the 82 percent of Americans who felt likewise, as indicated by a recent Stanford University poll. But why? What seems to separate the heroic figures of the past from the leaders of today, who seek a parallel admiration?

The hero of the past was the primal "man of action"—the man of adventure whose courage or sense of duty led to his great achievements. Looking back, we can see a long line of legendary heroes. We stand in awe at the determination of Caesar and Napoleon's absolute power of conquest. And Joan of Arc, Daniel Boone, Abraham Lincoln, and Thomas Edison all show off heroic stature. In more recent times, we have seen Charles Lindbergh become "The Legend of the Lone Eagle," while other figures such as Oliver Hazard Perry, Sergeant York, and General MacArthur capture the popular imagination of Americans. But where are the heroes of today? A nation hungry for heroes who ignite people's imaginations is finding no successors to "Lucky Lindy" or "Honest Abe."

Joan Valdez, in her book *The Media Works,* has stated that the last traditional American heroes were the television cowboys of the 1950s. And so, as Roy Rogers and the Lone Ranger rode off into the sunset, unfortunately, so did an American myth! Today, we can no longer tell tales of noble men because we don't believe that noble men exist. And we really can't be blamed, can we? In the last 20 years, we have seen President Kennedy assassinated; 50,000 deaths in Vietnam; and a president and a vice president denounce, defend, deny, diminish, and then die before our very eyes. We have seen politicians unwilling to stand for anything, sports become big business, and technology perfect the "three-year car." In short, one of the reasons why the hero has become an endangered species is that no one trusts anyone anymore. Naturally, the more self-conscious we become, the more intolerant. We don't believe in solutions or solution makers.

For much of this, we can blame the media. It has done such a masterful job of "telling it like it is" that almost everyone knows everything about everybody. And any figure threatening to rise above the masses is systematically dissected with surgeonlike precision. The media no longer builds heroes, it unmasks them. Gone are the days where we read of Babe Ruth pointing to center field before clouting a home run. Today the media zooms in on Johnny Bench crying after his divorce, Gerald Ford falling on the ski slopes, and Jimmy Carter lusting after women in *Playboy* magazine. More and more, the average citizen knows that the men in the spotlight, just like everyone else, put on and take off their trousers one leg at a time—often in places where they shouldn't!

However, it's not as if we aren't trying. Mick Jagger, Farrah Fawcett, and Robert Redford are all idolized by many. Unfortunately, though, we're getting to the point where, as Andy Warhol predicted, soon everyone will be the hero of his or her choice for 15 minutes. Now, instead of seeing John Wayne struggling in the sands of Iwo Jima, we see something very different.

The van went down the road in Woodstock, Illinois, at about 60 miles per hour. Seeing the lights from an oncoming car, it was time for the

game to begin. The boys, holding 10- to 15-pound rocks in their hands, waited for the right instant. Then they threw! David Claus was the driver coming the other way. The first rock merely shattered the windshield. The second tore off the top of his head. Three days later, five young men were arrested and taken to the police station. When they arrived, admirers yelled and cheered. For what?

You see, the harm of losing our authentic heroes goes much, much deeper and is far more significant than merely voiding our bubble-gum card fantasies. One harm is that we have allowed ourselves to pay homage to those certainly less than virtuous. Isn't Alice Cooper a hero to the thousands who go wild when, at the end of his performance, he tears off the limbs of a baby doll? And in the film version of *Bonnie and Clyde*, who were you eventually rooting for?

Still reeling from the leaders who have let us down and bored with the present, we see ourselves moving toward a condition of stoicism, which is symptomatic of our problem. We no longer strive for excellence or originality. Thus, harm number two ushers in the Age of Mediocrity, for if there is no one to inspire us to do great and noble things—quite frankly, we don't! At Cornell University, an Arts and Science student can now receive a Bachelor of Arts degree without ever having to read a single line of Plato, the Bible, Shakespeare, or Einstein. A prominent attitude is that if Johnny isn't "turned on" to Plato, or if Shakespeare isn't "his thing," then, well, to each his own. And what about the pride we have in our language? A newspaper recently came out with an interesting article. In it, companies handling health insurance reported some revealing word concoctions. Among them were people with "falls teeth," "very coarse veins," "high pretention," and one woman who had had a "misconception."

This may seem humorous or surprising to some, but others won't believe it; and that wouldn't be surprising either—for our third harm, although less obvious, is perhaps the most damaging. It involves our attitude. We've become a nation of ready-made cynics, skeptics, and critics, where mockery is fashionable and "to score" on someone is "the thing."

Solving these problems isn't easy. It's hard to find the man or woman who can lead us out of controversy and into the light when controversy is all that we see. In 1977, there are no more black or white issues. The answer, I think, is one of perspective. In classical times, heroes were God-men. In the Middle Ages, they were God's men. In the Renaissance, they were universal men. In the nineteenth century, they were self-made men. Now, we must look to the common man, for it is with the common man that the future of heroism and national spirit lies.

I feel that we have two obligations. One is to recognize an act of nobility as being heroic in itself. The second is to realize that the common man actually does have heroic potential. Your mission (should you decide to accept it) is to make a stand for democracy by voting in elections at all levels, for the family by turning off the television set, and for people by telling someone that not all Polish jokes are funny.

Contemporary theologian Paul Tillich stated in his book *The Courage to Be* that religion is anything that you take seriously. Acts of nobility needn't be based solely on issues of earth-shattering proportion, but more on quiet, personal ones which we take very, very seriously.

Earlier, you were given some choices. You now have another. You can take seriously what I've mentioned, or you can forget me and all that I've said. If you again choose the former, you can help actualize the idea that the only person who can ever be termed "The Last American Hero"—will be the last American! Then, with a Walter Mitty smile playing about our lips, a cloud of dust, and a mighty "high-oo Silver," each of us can walk off triumphantly . . . into the sunset.

•••••••••••••••••••••••••

Looking Back

Listed below are the major ideas discussed in this chapter.

- Leadership involves your ability to motivate yourself and others.
- A leader is a person who puts leadership skills into action.
- Leadership styles vary. There is the technocrat, the artist, and the craftsman.
- The best leaders often blend styles to reach a broader audience.
- The planks of leadership provide a framework for leadership.
- A good leader has a sense of vision and sees how the "big picture" fits together.
- A good leader is a doer who will take charge of a situation and get things done.
- A good leader is aware that people learn differently and adjusts his or her leadership style to meet the demands of the group.
- A good leader knows not only how to make decisions but also the order in which decisions should be made.
- A good leader knows conflict management skills.
- A good leader is aware of body language and the impact of nonverbal communication.
- A good leader is aware of pitfalls to avoid.
- A good leader can effectively do whatever it takes to motivate others.
- The spoken word should always be used constructively.

Speech Vocabulary

leader
leadership
learning styles
vision
conflict management

1. Write the definition as given in the chapter, and list the page number for each word. Write an original sentence showing the speech term "in action."
2. Prepare a quiz. On the left-hand side of your paper, list the new speech terms, leaving out some of the letters of each word. (Example: —e—der—hi— for *leadership*.) On the right-hand side of your paper, list the definitions of the terms in a different order. Have a classmate take your quiz by matching each term with the correct definition. Be sure to have an answer key.

General Vocabulary

1. Define each general vocabulary term and use it in an original sentence.

culmination
entrepreneur
facilitate
harmoniouslyp
forfeiting
simulated

2. Write a story titled "The Day I Had to Take Over the Class and Become the Leader." Select at least three new speech terms and at least three general vocabulary terms and use them effectively in the story. Be sure that your story is at least one page long and makes sense when read aloud.

To Remember

Answer the following questions based on your reading of the chapter.

1. A leader who has a sense of ____________ can see a situation in its entirety and keep both details and the "big picture" in perspective.
2. A leader must be willing to ____________ if anything is ever going to get done!
3. Because people have different ____________ ____________, leaders should use a variety of strategies to "connect" with followers.
4. If you are able to handle a stressful situation and turn a potentially negative situation into a positive one, then you have excellent ____________ ____________ skills.
5. Often, your nonverbal communication, or your ____________ ____________, will convey more to people than the words that you speak.
6. List the four leadership pitfalls.
7. As discussed in the Communication Breakthrough, people who ____________, that is, who donate their time and efforts, can accomplish great things for humanity.
8. The planks of leadership illustrate six characteristics of a good leader. List the first five.
9. A tragedy took place at Columbine High School. Based on what you read, who were the students who took charge and led others to safety?

To Do

1. Construct a chart on a large sheet of paper. On one side of the chart, make a heading that says, "What a Leader Does." On the other side of the chart, make a heading that says, "What a Leader Doesn't Do." Now fill in the chart. Be sure to make your work colorful and attractive, and be sure that you include some original ideas on leadership in addition to what the chapter taught.
2. Interview a leader. The person can be in your school, your community, or your family. Find out that person's views on (a) why leadership is important, (b) where leadership is most needed in our society, (c) why some people are afraid to lead, and (d) how best to motivate others. Be ready to present your findings to the class. Also, note why you selected the person and why you consider her or him a noteworthy leader.
3. Make a collage—"an artistic composition of materials pasted over a surface, often with a unifying theme." The theme is "Leadership around the World." Cut out pictures, words, and phrases that you can use to portray this theme. Your collage should have many words and pictures if you are going to create the impact that you want. With your teacher's permission, you might be able to work in teams of two. Be neat and complete in your work.
4. According to a recent leadership styles study by Korn and Ferry, "A combination of so-called feminine and masculine traits is needed for leadership in the 21st century." Those surveyed perceived men as risk taking, self-confident, and very competitive. They perceived women as stronger at listening, building relationships, and being able to share power and information. Survey the other students in your class. See if they agree with the findings of this study. Ask for them to give examples to validate their reasoning. Write the responses, and be ready to make a class presentation.

CHAPTER 21 Review and Enrichment...

To Talk About

1. Why in today's world are people often skeptical about many of their leaders? Why don't they trust some of them? Use newspapers, magazines, radio, and television to give some specific examples of what you mean. What lessons can you learn about your own leadership from what you see some other leaders doing?
2. A leader often sees a need and then takes the initiative to fill that need. In Japan, productivity and efficiency are primary concerns. This has created grueling work schedules, reducing the time workers have to spend with their families. Now, a company called Japan Efficiency has made it possible for busy workers to "rent" people to take their places in family visits. It sounds silly, but it's true. Sons and daughters who don't have the time to visit the family anymore can hire professional actors or actresses (at $1,150 for three hours) as substitutes. Says one Japanese reporter, "The parents are aware of what's going on, but they just want to hold a child or give advice to the younger generation." What is your reaction to this whole situation? What do you think of this company, Japan Efficiency? What do you think of what the children are doing? What about the elderly?
3. The quality of leadership is often dependent on the quality of "followership." Why are followers important? What are some important responsibilities that followers should have, and why is "followership" a vital element in a democracy?

To Write About

1. An Illinois girl wishes to be on the all-male wrestling team. Does she have the right? What problems might she encounter? What might be something positive that could come out of her wrestling? Write your responses to these questions in complete sentences. Be sure to make your reasoning clear.
2. Why is it important to get along with others? In an essay at least one page long, give your own three- or four-point plan for conflict management, and the steps that you would take to handle a stressful situation. Give examples, if possible, and explain your reasoning.

Related Speech Topics

How I can be a leader in the classroom, at work, in my home, and in the community
Why America needs the volunteer
Why getting along with people matters in leadership
The person in the news that I most admire as a leader
Why parents must be leaders at home
Why a leader must sometimes be a follower
How nonverbal communication can make or break a leader
Why self-discipline is important to a leader
The elements of leadership that most people forget
Why everyone is a leader at one time or another
Media stars as leaders: do they shine or not?

Glossary

A

abstract word—a word that names an intangible, such as quality, attribute, and concept
accommodation—a negotiation strategy in which differences are minimized, smoothed over, or suppressed (lose-win approach)
acronym—a word formed from the initial letter of each of the major parts of a compound term
active listening—a listening role in which the listener participates and shares in the communication process by guiding the speaker toward common interests
adjourn—the final action of the group—to close the meeting
advance organizer—introductory statements that forecast what the audience may expect
affirmative—yes or true
affluent—having a generously sufficient and typically increasing supply of material possessions
after-dinner speech—an entertaining speech that follows a banquet or meal
agenda—orders of the day; a list of things to be done
aggressive tone—a pushy or brash way of communicating, which considers only one point of view, with little or no room for compromise or discussion
alienate—to make hostile, unfriendly
allegory—the use of symbolic, fictional figures and actions (such as in a story or painting) to express generalizations about human existence
alliteration—the repetition of the sounds at the beginnings of two or more words that are close together
allusion—a reference to a well-known person, place, thing, or idea
ambiguous—capable of being understood in more than one way
amend—a proposal to change a motion
analogy—an illustration in which the characteristics of a familiar object or event are used to explain or describe the characteristics of an unfamiliar object or event. The extended use of a metaphor or simile, often in the form of a story
analysis—a separation of a thing into the parts or elements of which it is composed; an examination of a thing to determine its parts or elements—also a statement showing the results of such an examination
analytical—marked by the ability to separate a thing into the parts or elements of which it is composed, or to examine a thing to determine its parts or elements
anecdote—a short story used by a speaker to illustrate a point
anthology—a collection of passages from literature
anthropologist—a scientist who studies human beings, including their physical characteristics and environmental, social, and cultural relations
antithesis—a contrasting of ideas by means of parallel arrangement of words, phrases, etc; the opposite
apathetic—having little or no interest or concern (indifferent); having or showing little or no feeling or emotion
apoplectic—affected with, inclined to, or showing symptoms of stroke
appreciative listening—a listening style used to enjoy and savor pleasurable sounds such as music or nature
appropriateness—being especially suitable or compatible
argument—a reason for favoring one side of a proposition and the facts that support that reason
articulation—the crispness and distinctness of a speaker.
assert—to state or declare positively and often forcefully and aggressively
assertion—a positive declaration
assertive tone—a direct, yet tactful, communication approach
assonance—the repetition of vowel sounds
attribution—the act of crediting a work (such as literature or art) to a particular author or artist
audience analysis—the process by which a speaker considers the needs and expectations of the audience that will be listening to the speech
auditory—relating to or experienced through hearing
aural—relating to the sense of hearing
author card—a card cataloging a book that is organized by author's last name
avarice—excessive desire for wealth or gain; greediness
avoidance—a negotiation strategy in which an individual tries to resolve a conflict by withdrawing or by denying that a problem exists (lose-lose approach)

B

barter—to trade by exchange of goods
begging the question—an argument that assumes whatever is trying to be proven is already true
bias—an often prejudiced outlook
body—the part of the speech that provides the content and analysis that prove the thesis statements
body language—the way one uses his or her body to send messages

bombard—to assail (attack violently with blows or words) persistently
braille—a system of writing for the blind that uses characters made up of raised dots
brainstorming—a process in which group members offer their ideas—as many as possible, as quickly as possible—as a way to encourage creative thought and solutions
brash—lacking restrainment and discernment; tactless
bridge—a transition from one answer to another
brief—an outline that summarizes specific case arguments
briefing—a speech informing members of a group of changes in policy or procedure.
burden of proof—a term used in formal debate and in law to refer to the duty or responsibility to prove something
burgeoning—growing and expanding rapidly
bylaws—a set of special rules agreed upon by the members of a group

C

cadence—the measure or beat of a rhythmical flow
call the question—a proposal to take an immediate vote on a motion.
canned—prepared in advance in standardized form for nonspecific use or wide distribution; lacking originality or individuality
captive audience—an audience that has been forced to be in attendance
card catalog—a catalog that tells what books a library has and where they can be found
case—the debater's ideas and evidence organized and arranged into a position supporting one side of a resolution
case study—the analysis of a "typical" example in great detail, in order to draw general conclusions
causality—a claim that one event is the result of another event
cause-effect pattern—a pattern of organization that arranges elements of an argument in a "because this happened, this resulted" sequence
chair—the meeting's chairperson
chalk talk—a speech in which the speaker uses a visual aid—a chalkboard—to convey information
chauffeur—a person employed to drive an automobile
chronological pattern—a pattern of organization that arranges the elements in time sequence, or in the order in which they happened
circumstantial evidence—the evidence at hand. It may suggest a conclusion, but it does not prove it.
climactic pattern—a pattern of organization that arranges the elements in order of importance
clique—a narrow exclusive circle or group of persons, especially one held together by common interests, views, or purposes
cognizant—having a knowledge of something through personal experience; mindful, aware
cohesion—a quality of group discussion in which members have respect for each other, share similar values and rely on one another for support
collaboration—a negotiation strategy that focuses on resolving the conflict; the experience, expertise, and perceptions of both parties are recognized and valued (win-win approach)
combustion—an act or instance of burning; a slow oxidation; a violent agitation
commemorative speech—an inspiring speech recalling heroic events or persons
commencement address—a speech given during a graduation ceremony
common ground—a sense of a shared goal or interest
communication—the process of sending and receiving messages
communication barrier—any obstacle (may be attitudinal, social, educational, cultural, or environmental) that gets in the way of effective communication
comparative—considered as if in comparison to something else
compelling—forceful; demanding attention
compelling insight—an understanding, or seeing into, a situation (insight) that is forceful or demands attention (compelling)
compendium—a brief summary of a larger work or a field of knowledge
competency—an ability to get something done
competition—a negotiation strategy that focuses on defeating or outshining another person rather than resolving the problem (win-lose approach)
competitive—an atmosphere that can foster divisiveness among members because they contend with each other as rivals; also the burden of a negative counter-plan to show that both the affirmative and negative proposals should not be adopted
composure—a calm, controlled manner
compression—the act of reducing size or volume by squeezing or pressing together (usually to achieve simplicity)
compromise—a negotiation strategy in which each individual gives up something to meet in the middle (trade-offs) (win-lose win-lose approach)
concise—expressing much in few words
concrete—a real or actual thing or class of things; not abstract or theoretical
concrete word—a word that names a thing that is perceived through the senses
confidence—a feeling of belief in oneself and one's ability to control a specific situation
conflict management—the ability to turn a potentially negative situation into a positive one
connotation—the meanings and feelings associated with a word by an individual, based on personal experience
conscience—the sense of the moral goodness or blameworthiness of one's own conduct, intentions, or character

together with a feeling of obligation to do right or be good
consensus—a nearly unanimous agreement among group members about a particular solution
consonance—the repetition of consonant sounds
constructive—from construct—to build something; in debate, a speech in which arguments are initially advanced and defended
constructive conflict—a situation in which group members use their differences to discover the best ideas
content—the information or topics presented and their substance, meaning, and significance
conversational quality—speech distinguished by sounding spontaneous
converse—something reversed in order, relation, or action
covert—not openly shown or engaged in; covered over
conviction—a strong belief in one's message and a determination to convey that message to the audience
cooperative—an atmosphere that encourages members to work together toward a common end or goal
correlation—a claim that two or more events are related in some way
courtesy—politeness, manners, and respectful consideration for others
credentials—qualifications
credibility—a person's ability to inspire belief
criteria—a set of standards that a solution must meet
critical listening—a listening style used to evaluate and analyze a message for logic and value
criticism—an evaluation or judgment—usually negative
crooned—sang in a soft, gentle, and intimate manner
cross-examination—a period following each speaker's constructive during which the speaker who has just spoken is questioned
crystallize—to cause to become a definite form
culmination—climax or fulfillment
cultural literacy—the information that an average American citizen can be expected to know
cutaway—a model that shows the inner workings of an object

D

database—a collection of related information
debate—a method to solve problems; a formal contest of skill in reasoned argument
dedication—a willing desire to practice and be committed to one's speech
deduction—a form of reasoning in which one argues from generalizations to a specific instance
deficit—a deficiency in amount, especially an excess of expenditures over revenue
definition—an explanation of a term; it reflects the speaker's intended meaning or specialized use in the context of a speech
degraded—reduced from a higher to a lower rank or degree
delivery—the mode or manner that a speaker uses to transmit words to an audience
demeaning—degrading, debasing: lowering in status, esteem, quality, or character
demographics—the statistical characteristics of human populations
denotation—the basic and generally understood meaning of a word found in the dictionary
diagram—a visual aid used by a speaker to explain a process
dialogue—conversations between actors, two persons, or groups
dignitary—a person of high position or honor
dire—warning of disaster; desperately urgent
disclaimer—a speaker's attempt to explain what is not to be inferred by the speech, or an acknowledgment of incomplete expertise on the subject
disconcerting—confusing, upsetting
discriminative listening—a listening style used to single out one particular sound from a noisy environment
discussion—a cooperative exchange of information, opinions, and ideas
disintegration—the act of breaking apart or decomposing; loss of unity
disruptive conflict—a conflict that divides members into competing sides, which refuse to compromise to the point that no group discussion decision can be achieved
distal—apart from the point of attachment
distinction—the difference between words, objects, ideas, etc., explained by saying what something is and, especially, what it is not
distortion—a twisting out of the true meaning; a false or unnatural appearance
diverse—varied, differing from one another, unlike
download—to transfer data from one computer's memory to the memory of another, usually smaller, computer
dramatic interpretation—a speech contest event in which a speaker memorizes and performs a work of literature of a more serious nature
dramatic monologue—a first-person narration in which a single character speaks

E

eloquent—having or showing clear and forceful expression; vividly or movingly expressing or revealing
emancipation—the act of freeing from restraint, control, or the power of another
embalm—to treat (a corpse) so as to protect from decay
emotional appeal—a persuasive technique that involves "striking an emotional chord"; the speaker uses issues and values such as patriotism, family, and honor to win the audience's favor
empathic listening—a style of listening encouraging people to talk freely without fear of embarrassment
empathy—a sincere understanding of the feelings,

thoughts and motives of others
emulated—strived to equal or excel; imitated
enhanced—added or contributed to, improved
enthusiasm—the energy, both intellectual and physical, a speaker transmits to inspire an audience
entrepreneur—one who organizes, manages, and assumes the risks of a business or enterprise
epitomize—to serve as the typical or ideal example of
equilibrium—a state of balance between opposing elements; a state of intellectual or emotional balance: poise
equitable—a fair distribution
erudite—marked by extensive learning or scholarship
ethical (personal) appeal—a persuasive quality based on the speaker's natural honesty, sincerity, and commitment to what is right and good
ethics—a person's sense of right and wrong
ethnicity—the condition of belonging to a particular race or people
ethos—the Greek word for character; the term is associated with Aristotle's personal (ethical) appeal
etiquette—the forms (conduct or procedure) prescribed by custom or authority to be observed in social, official, or professional life: decorum
etymology—the history of words as shown by tracing their development and relationships
eulogy—a speech praising or honoring someone who has died
euphemism—a word or group of words substituted for a word that is offensive or distasteful
evasive—tending or intended to elude or avoid, usually by dexterity or stratagem
evidence—anything that establishes a fact or gives cause to believe something
evoking—calling forth or up; to bring to mind or recollection
exaggerate—to enlarge (as a statement) beyond normal, beyond bounds or the truth
excursion—digression (the act of turning aside from the main subject of attention); a pleasure trip
expedient—adapted for achieving a particular end; governed by self interest
extemporaneous—not planned or rehearsed beforehand
extemporaneous method—a delivery method in which the speaker refers only to notes or a brief outline
eye contact—a device speakers use whereby they look directly into their listener's eyes in order to emphasize a point or to show how strongly they feel about something

F

facilitate—to make easier
factual proposition—a proposition that is either true or false
fallacy—an error in reasoning or a mistaken belief
false analogy—a comparison of two things that are not really the same
false comparison—a comparison of unlike things
false premise—an erroneous assertion; a premise that is faulty and will lead to an error in deduction
faltering—hesitating in speech, purpose, or action
fear—a biological process that activates our emergency energy system so that we can cope with danger; unpleasant, often strong, emotion caused by anticipation or awareness of danger
feedback—a reaction that the receiver gives to a message offered by the sender
fiasco—a complete failure
filter—to use emotional barriers (based on background and personality) to absorb information selectively
fireside chat—a speech in which a leader informally addresses the concerns, worries, and issues of the group
first affirmative constructive (1AC)—a speech that is prepared before the round in which the affirmative speaker presents the affirmative case
first affirmative rebuttal (1AR)—in Lincoln-Douglas debate, the speech made by the affirmative speaker that responds to the negative case and rebuilds the affirmative case; in policy debate, this speech responds to the negative block and extends the argument that the second affirmative rebuttal will need to win the debate
first negative constructive (1NC)—in Lincoln-Douglas debate, the speech in which the negative speaker presents the negative case and refutes the affirmative constructive; in policy debate, the first negative speaker presents the negative position in the debate
first person—referring to the person speaking (I, me, we, us)
flippant—lacking proper respect or seriousness
flowsheet—a record of the words or arguments written down during the debate
follow-up question—a question that helps the interviewer pursue topics that come up unexpectedly in the course of the interview
foreshadowing—giving a hint or suggestion of beforehand
forfeiting—losing, or losing the right to, by some error, offense, or crime
format—(1) a programming style or specialization (2) the general organization established for the conduct of the debate. It specifies the amount of time and the order in which each debater is allowed to speak.
forum—a post-panel discussion in which panel members invite questions and comments from the audience
friendliness—a warm, congenial attitude

G

germane—pertinent, applicable
ghostwriter—a person who writes for, and in the name of, another person
gigantic—exceeding the usual or expected (as in size or force); enormous

gluttony—excess in eating or drinking
good will—a genuine interest or concern
graph—a visual aid used by a speaker to demonstrate a statistical relationship
groupthink—a desire to go along with the group even at the possible cost of abandoning one's personal beliefs
grovel—literally, to creep with the face to the ground to show subservience; to abase (humble or degrade) oneself

H

handout—written material (fliers, brochures, or information sheets) prepared and duplicated before a speech and supplied to the audience as reference material
haphazardly—marked by lack of any plan, order, or direction
harmoniously—in agreement; marked by accord in sentiment or action
hasty generalization—a faulty argument based on incomplete or unrepresentative information
haven—a place of safety, or a place offering favorable opportunities or conditions
hoke—(used with "up") to make corny; phony
house—(1) a term used to refer to the group during its meetings (2) the area in which the audience sits
humorous interpretation—a speech contest in which a speaker memorizes and performs a work of literature of a lighter nature
hyperbole—a method of saying more that what is true, or exaggerating, for the sake of emphasis

I

ignoring the question—a speaker's attempt to divert the attention of the audience from the matter at hand
imagery—language that creates pictures in the mind and excites the senses
I-message—a statement that emphasizes what one wants
impression—how the audience perceives the speaker based on the way he presents himself and his ideas
impromptu—made or done as if on the spur of the moment; having little or no preparation
impromptu method—a delivery method that is completely unrehearsed; the speaker uses no notes and relies on his or her ability to offer an immediate verbal response
incidental motion—any proposal to change how the meeting is being run
incorrigible—incapable of being corrected, amended, or reformed
indented—set in from a margin (in an outline, subordinate or supporting ideas are indented)
index—an alphabetical list found in the back of the book that tells the reader the exact page on which one can find particular information
indifferent audience—an audience that is apathetic or disinterested in the speaker and his topic. This audience does not find the topic relevant to their personal situation.
induction—a form of reasoning in which specific cases are used to prove a general truth
inflection—the altering of a speaker's tone or pitch to create emphasis
infographic—an illustration created by a computer graphic arts program, such as Freehand or Adobe Illustrator
informal debate—any debate conducted without specific rules
inhibition—an inner check on free activity, expression, or functioning
innovation—a new idea, method, or device
innuendo—hint, insinuation, especially a veiled reflection on character or reputation
innumerable—too many to be numbered
insinuated—introduced gradually or in a subtle, indirect, or artful way; implied in a subtle or devious way
instinctively—knowing or acting below the conscious level; arising spontaneously and being independent of judgment or will; a natural, inherent attitude, impulse, or capacity
integrate—to form, coordinate, or blend into a functioning whole
integrity—a strong sense of right and wrong; adherence to a code of values
intensification—the act of making more acute or sharpened; an enhancement
interior monologue—a first-person narration in which the narrator is speaking to himself or herself
interlibrary loan—a cooperative system by which libraries lend specific books to one another
internship—a position as an unpaid volunteer working to gain experience
interpersonal communication—communication that takes place any time messages are transmitted between two or more people
interviewer—the person who asks the questions in an interview
intimacy—close association, contact, or familiarity
intimate distance—the distance used primarily for confidential exchanges (within eighteen inches), almost always reserved for close friends
intimidation—the act of making timid or fearful, to frighten; to compel or deter by or as if by threats
intrapersonal communication—an inner dialogue conducted with oneself to assess one's thoughts, feelings, and reactions
introduction—the beginning of a speech; it contains the attention-getter, the link statement, the thesis statement, and frequently a preview statement
introspective—reflectively looking inward, examining one's own thoughts or feelings
intuition—quick and ready insight; the power or faculty of knowing things without conscious reasoning
irony—a figure of speech using words that imply the opposite of what they seem to say on the surface

irrational—not governed by reason; lacking normal mental understanding or coherence

J

jargon—the specialized vocabulary of people in the same profession or similar group
jeopardy—exposure to loss; peril, hazard, risk
jump on the bandwagon—persuasive technique based on the need to conform
justification—the act of proving to be just, right, or reasonable

L

label—a descriptive or identifying word or phrase
leader—a person who effectively uses leadership skills
leadership—an ability to motivate and unite others to work together to accomplish a specific task
leading question—a question that "puts words" in the subject's mouth.
learning styles—the different ways in which people learn most effectively
Lincoln-Douglas debate—a competitive type of formal debate, addressing propositions of value, practiced at high schools across the nation
link—(1) an explanation by the negative team demonstrating that the affirmative plan has a direct link to its disadvantage (2) the statement in an introduction that comes between the attention-getter and the thesis statement and logically connects the two
listening spare time—thinking time created by the ability to listen faster than people can speak
logic—the science of reasoning which uses a system of rules to help one think correctly
logical appeal—the use of sequence, analysis, organization, and evidence to prove a point and persuade
logos—a Greek word for logic and reason; the term is associated with Aristotle's logical appeal

M

main heading—one of the major divisions, areas, or arguments of the speaker's purpose statement
main motion—a proposal that asks the group to take action
manipulate—to influence, especially with intent to deceive; to manage or use skillfully
manipulating—influencing, especially with intent to deceive
mannequin—a lifeless form representing the human figure
manuscript method—a delivery method in which the speaker writes out and subsequently reads the speech, word for word
map—a visual aid used by a speaker to demonstrate a geographical relationship
mediation—an intervention between conflicting parties to promote reconciliation, settlement, or compromise
memorized method—a delivery method in which the speaker memorizes and then gives the speech word for word without the use of notes
mesmerized—hypnotized, held spellbound, or fascinated
message—that which is sent or said
metaphor—a figure of speech that compares two unlike things without using the words *like* or *as*
meter—a measure of the rhythm in a line of poetry
methodically—in an orderly arrangement
microcosm—a little world, community, or unit that is a typical or ideal example of a larger one
miffed—in a state of ill humor (as from a trivial quarrel)
mimic—to imitate closely
minstrel—one of those known as "rhapsodes" in ancient Greece, these wanderers read their works (often accompanied by music) in public competitions
minutes—the written records of an organization's meetings
model—a miniature representation of something
moderator—the person in a group who leads the discussion (gets the discussion started, keeps it on track, and brings it to a close)
monopolize—assume complete possession or control of
monotone—a tone in which words are delivered at the same rate and pitch without variation
mood—the emotional tone created or expressed in a work
motif—a dominant idea or central theme
motivation—an inner drive, need, or impulse that causes a person to act
multimedia presentation—a speech supplemented with special computer software, which allows the speaker to combine several kinds of visual and/or audio aids

N

name calling—to give someone a negative label without any evidence
narrative—the telling of a story
narrowing—to limit and more closely define a topic
nectar—the drink of the Greek and Roman gods; any delicious drink; a sweet plant secretion that is the raw material of honey
negative—no or false
negative rebuttal (NR)—in Lincoln-Douglas debate, the final speech made by the negative speaker that summarizes the debate and attempts to "shut down" the arguments that can be anticipated in the affirmative speaker's rebuttal
negotiation—the act of conferring with another (or others) so as to arrive at the settlement of some matter
new business—subjects brought up for the first time in a meeting

newness—an original or unique approach to a topic
nonassertive tone—a communication approach that lacks action and energy, and appears disinterested and uninvolved
nonverbal communication—facial expressions or body movements used to express attitudes or moods about a person, situation, or idea
nonverbal message—facial expressions and body language used to convey messages not spoken
notes—a listing of ideas in brief, outlined form
nuclear family—a family group that consists only of mother, father, and children

O

offstage focus—a technique used in Reader's Theater in which readers use scripts and envision the scene out in the audience
old business—business not completed in a previous meeting
omniscient—a type of narration (third-person) in which the narrator is all-knowing and moves freely in and out of the minds of the various characters
online—a service that provides rapid access to many computer databases
open-ended question—a question that allows the subject to decide how best to answer. It encourages a comprehensive, in-depth response and discourages a yes-no or true-false response.
opposed audience—an audience that is hostile to the speaker or the speaker's topic
oral cavity—the mouth
oral interpretation—the art of communicating works of literature by reading aloud well
oral, or verbal, communication—communication that is primarily spoken
orator—a person who delivers oratory and uses words effectively
oratory/rhetoric—the art or study of public speaking
order of precedence—the relationship of motions to each other
orders of the day—an agenda or list of topics to be discussed during a meeting
organization—a system of structure and form that enables the audience to follow along easily in a speech
original oratory—a speech contest in which contestants write on a topic of their choice
ought—a person's idea or concept of the ideal—a moral obligation based on a sense of duty
outline—a logical, organized framework for a speech; it shows how the speech will progress
overhead projector—a visual aid used by a speaker to project transparencies (often charts and graphs) onto a blank wall or screen
oxymoron—a literary device that places words that are in opposition directly beside one another, such as *cruel kindness*

P

painstakingly—marked by expending or showing diligent care or effort
palatable—agreeable or acceptable to the mind (or to the palate or taste)
panacea—a remedy for all difficulties or ills
panel—an informal discussion that takes place before an audience
parallelism—the use of the same grammatical form to express ideas that should, logically, be treated equally. This often involves the repeating of words or phrases.
paraphernalia—articles of equipment, accessory items, personal belongings
paraphrase—to repeat in one's own words
paraphrasing—rewording an original passage
Parliament—an assembly that constitutes the supreme legislative body of the United Kingdom
parliamentary procedure—a system of rules followed in group meetings based on ideas developed in the British Parliament
passive listening—a listening role in which the listener does not share in the responsibility, nor involve himself in the communication process
pathos—the Greek word for feelings and emotions; the term is associated with Aristotle's emotional appeal
pause—a lull in the conversation. It often provides a good opportunity for the interviewer (unprompted) to convey more information.
people skills—the ability to work well with others by using polite communication procedures
perception—how one sees things
performance anxiety—a specific stage fright, often associated with musicians, actors and other entertainers
peripheral—outside our direct field of vision and hearing; the outward bounds: border area
persona—the fictional speaker of the work to be interpreted
personal distance—the distance comfortable for conversation between friends (a foot and a half to four feet)
personal space—a comfort zone each person maintains around himself or herself where intrusions would be unwelcome
personification—giving human characteristics to nonhuman things
persuasive speaking—speaking that influences others to believe or think something, or to take action
pervasiveness—the act of becoming diffused (spread out) through every part of
phobia—a persistent, irrational fear that causes a person to avoid specific situations
phonation—voice production

picturesque—resembling a picture; bringing about mental images
pitch—the vocal notes (highs and lows) that a speaker reaches while speaking
plagiarism—copying or imitating the language, ideas, or thoughts of another and passing them off as one's original work
platform movement—walking or stepping in a directed manner from one spot to another while speaking
polarizing—dividing group members into competing sides that refuse to compromise
policy proposition—a proposition that focuses on the desirability of a particular course of action
pollster—one who questions people to obtain information or opinions to be analyzed
portfolio—a portable case containing a sample of a job candidate's best school assignments or examples of other work done
posture—the position of the body when it is still
power source—the origin of the energy needed to make things go
preamble—an introductory statement, specifically the introductory part of a constitution or statute that usually states the reasons for and intent of the law
premise—an assertion that serves as the basis for argument
prep time—the preparation time allotted during rounds for organizing responses and preparing questions
prerequisite—something that is necessary to an end or to the carrying out of a function
prescriptive—that which is laid down as a guide or rule of action. (In a speech, a *prescriptive topic* requires the speaker to "prescribe"—lay down as a guide or rule—specific policy suggestions.)
preview statement—the statement at the end of the introduction that presents an overview of the major areas that will be discussed in the body of the speech
prioritizing—arranging in order of importance
privileged motion—a proposal to resolve an urgent problem other than the main motion
problem-solution pattern—a pattern of organization that presents a problem and then provides possible solutions
procession—a group of individuals moving along in an orderly often ceremonial way
professional communication—the communication that takes place on the job or is related to a career
pronunciation—the production of correct sound and syllable stresses when speaking
proof—specific evidence that establishes the truth of something
propaganda—material designed to distort the truth or deceive the audience
proposition—a statement of the point to be debated
prospective—relating to or effective in the future; likely to come about
proxemics—the study of spatial communication; in oral communication, refers specifically to the distance between the speaker and the audience
proximal—next to or nearest the point of attachment
proxy—one who acts as a substitute for another
public distance—the distance maintained between strangers. At this distance people barely acknowledge each other's presence (twelve feet and beyond).
public lecture—a lecture delivered to a community or school group
puff ball—an easy, open-ended question
purpose statement—a statement that presents the selected speech topic and the speaker's specific purpose in speaking

Q

qualm—a sudden feeling of doubt, fear, or uneasiness
questions of evaluation—questions that ask group members to agree or disagree on possible solutions and to make a value judgment
questions of fact—questions that ask group members to recall information that pertains to the questions at hand
questions of interpretation—questions that ask group members to give their opinions on what the information means
quorum—the minimum number of members that must be present in order for the group's decisions to take effect
quotation—a statement which repeats the exact words that someone else has said

R

railroad—to put through (as a law) too hastily
rapport—a feeling of trust and cooperation
rate—the speed at which a person speaks
reasoning—the process of thinking, understanding, and drawing conclusions about some evidence
rebuffed—rejected or criticized sharply
rebuttal—the act of countering an opponent's attacks to one's argument and thereby rebuilding the argument
receiver—a person who intercepts a message and then decodes it
reciprocal—a mutual corresponding or communicating
recitation—delivery before an audience, usually of something memorized
reconsider—a move to reexamine a main motion that has already been passed or defeated
refrain—a regularly recurring phrase or verse
refute—to prove that something is wrong or false (using evidence)
regurgitating—throwing out, back, or up
reiterate—to state or do over again or repeatedly
renowned—widely acclaimed and honored; celebrated, famous
repetition—the act or process of repeating

reprimanded—reproved (scolded or corrected) sharply, usually from a position of authority
reputation—the way that a person is known to others
resolution—(1) a formal statement of opinion (2) a special type of main motion that begins with an explanation of why the motion should be passed
responsible—answerable and accountable for one's actions
restate—to state (say) again or in another way
retention—an ability to retain (or remember) things in mind that makes recall and recognition possible
rhapsodes—wandering minstrels in ancient Greece that would assemble to read their works in public competition
rhetorical—relating to or concerned with the art of speaking or writing effectively. (A *rhetorical question* is one that is stated for effect and does not require an answer; *rhetorical devices* are tricks of language such as testimonials, false comparisons, and "jump on the bandwagon" suggestions.)
rhetorical questions—queries (questions) that don't really demand a verbal response; a question that is stated for effect, not requiring an answer
rhyme—the repetition of sound between words or syllables or the endings of lines of verse
rhythm—the flow of stressed and unstressed syllables in a poem
rife—widespread, prevalent, abounding
rigorous—that which is harsh, severe, or strict; scrupulously accurate or precise
round table—a special panel discussion in which a small group of participants talk about a topic of common concern while sitting around a table, or in an open circle

S

sanctity—the quality or state of being holy or sacred; holiness of life and character
scanner—a device enabling the transfer of a computer image to disk
scenario—a sequence of events, especially when imagined; an account or synopsis of a possible or projected course of action or events
scene setting—focusing the scene described on an imaginary stage in front of the reader
second affirmative rebuttal (2AR)—in policy debate, this speech summarizes the affirmative position and gives a clear presentation explaining why the major issues in the debate have gone affirmative
second person—referring to the person spoken to (you)
segregation—a cutting off from others, especially a separation by race, class, or ethnic group
self-esteem—the person value that one feels for oneself, often realized through self-discovery
sender—a person who transmits a message
senile—old, aged; especially exhibiting a loss of mental ability associated with old age
sequential—following in sequence, making a continuous or connected series; following in a chronological order
serendipity—making a pleasant discovery by accident
sign—a type of inductive reasoning in which one draws conclusions about a situation based on physical evidence
signposting—a preview of arguments to be made later in a speech
simile—a figure of speech that compares two unlike things using the words *like* or *as*
simulated—created or given the effect or appearance of; faked
sincerity—the quality of being honest or genuine
slang—nonstandard words associated with certain groups
sloth—laziness
social communication—the communication that occurs in your personal and your community life
social distance—the distance generally maintained between people in most social and business exchanges (four to twelve feet)
sound bite—short cuttings from interviews heard on television and radio broadcasts
sounding board—a person or group on whom one tries out an idea or opinion as a means of evaluating it
sparkler—information given in the course of a response that makes the point come alive. Analogies, stores, anecdotes, and quotes all make great sparklers.
spatial pattern—a pattern of organization that arranges the elements on the basis of space or situational relationships
speech of acceptance—a brief speech given by a person who receives a gift or an award
speech of presentation—a brief speech presenting a person with an award or gift
spellbound—held by or as if by a spell: fascinated
spontaneity—the quality or state of being spontaneous—doing or producing freely and naturally; impulsive, instinctive
stack the deck—to present unbalanced evidence that only presents one side
stage fright—the nervousness felt by a speaker or performer in front of an audience
status quo—the existing conditions or the way things are at the present moment
status report—a report summarizing a group's past achievements and future goals
stereotyping—labeling every person in a group based on a preconceived idea as to what that group represents
stoic—not affected by passion or feeling, especially showing indifference to pain; impassive, apathetic
subject—the person who answers the questions in an interview
subject card—a card cataloguing a book that is organized by subject
subordination—ranking in terms of importance
subsidiary motion—a proposal to adjust or fine-tune a main motion

suffice—to meet or satisfy a need; be sufficient
summarize—to cover the main points in a compact manner without wasted words (to "sum up")
superficial—of or relating to the surface or appearance only; shallow
supporting materials—information that supports and reinforces the main headings of a speech. Supporting materials are not to be confused with details, which are more specific.
supportive audience—an audience that likes the speaker and what the speaker has to say. This audience is willing to support and promote a speaker's ideas.
suppress—to restrain from the usual course of action; to keep from expressing
surrogacy—the act of taking the place of another, or the substitution of one for another
suspend—to stop temporarily, make inactive for a time
syllable—a unit of spoken language consisting of an uninterrupted utterance; a commonly recognized division of a word
syllogism—a form of deductive reasoning made up of two premises and a conclusion
symbol—anything that stands for an idea and is used for communication
sympathetic—capacity to enter into and share feelings or interests of another; expressing sorrow for another's loss or misfortune
symposium—a formal discussion in which several experts present a variety of points of view in the form of short speeches; an open discussion between experts and audience may follow the speeches
synonymous—alike in meaning or significance
systematic—having a regular method or order

T

table a motion—to set aside a motion for the time being
table of contents—an outline of the general plan or organization of a book. Generally found at the beginning of the book, it is a list of the book's main sections and chapters.
tact—diplomacy in dealing with others
tangible—perceptible (that which we are aware of through the senses), especially touch
tedium—boredom
temperament—characteristic or habitual (force of habit) inclination or mode of emotional response
testimonial—a celebrity or expert endorsement of a message
testimonial speech—a speech of praise or celebration honoring a living person
theme—the central idea of a literary work
thesis—a statement defining or expressing the purpose of a speech
thesis statement—the statement that presents the overall purpose of the speech
third person—referring to the person spoken of (he, him, her, she, it, they, them)
timbre—distinctive tone
title card—a card cataloguing a book that is organized by title
tone—a combination of the pitch and timbre of a person's voice, one's pauses, rhythm, and unique pronunciation. It is often a reliable clue to a speaker's feelings.
tone of voice—the pitch and timbre (distinctive tone) of a person's voice
topic specific—a speech is "topic specific" when the introduction is directly connected to the rest of the speech
town hall meeting—a discussion in which a group of citizens meets in a public place to discuss community problems and vote on possible solutions
transformation—the process, act, or instance of changing in composition or structure, outward form or appearance
transition—a word or phrase in a speech that connects one part of a speech to the next
trivia—unimportant matters

U

ubiquitous—existing or being everywhere at the same time; widespread
unbiased—objective
uncommitted audience—an audience that is neutral (or has not made up its mind) about the speaker's topic
understatement—the use of "reverse exaggeration" to draw attention to an absurdity for the sake of emphasis
unobtrusive—not bold or aggressive; inconspicuous

V

value—a standard applied to judge whether something is right or wrong
value criteria—concepts that provide further standards of judgment for evaluating whether or not the value premise has been realized
value premise—a supposition that provides a standard of judgment to evaluate whether or not a resolution is true
value proposition—a type of proposition, involving philosophical judgements, for which there is no right or wrong answer
verbatim—word for word account of an interview
vested—fully and unconditionally guaranteed (as a right, benefit, or privilege). (A vested interest is one in which the holder has a strong commitment.)
vicariously—sharing someone else's experience by using imagination or sympathetic feelings
vision—the ability to see more than the obvious; to look beyond and ahead for answers and possibilities
vocal process—the system that produces sound
vocalized pause—a meaningless saying such as "you know," "uh," "and a," used to fill moments when the speaker is not sure what to say next

volume—the loudness or softness of a speaker's voice
vouchers—(as in *school vouchers*) a form or check indicating a credit against future purchases or expenditures
vulnerable—susceptible; having little resistance to; open to attack or damage

W

written communication—any communication that must be read

Y

yes-no question—a question that may be answered with a simple "yes" or "no" and allows the subject to answer the question without elaborating

Z

zinger—(in a speech) a concluding statement that is a powerful reminder of the rightness of your position

Glosario

A

abstract word—abstracto palabra una palabra que describe un intangible, tal como una cualidad, atributo y concepto.
accommodation—acomodo estrategia de negociación en la que las diferencias se minimizan, se atenúan o se suprimen (enfoque pierde-gana).
acronym—sigla palabra formada por la letra inicial de cada una de las partes principales de un término compuesto.
active listening—escuchar activamente una forma de escuchar en la cual el que escucha participa y comparte en el proceso de comunicación al dirigir a la persona que habla hacia intereses comunes.
adjourn—clausurar la acción final del grupo—levantar la sesión.
advance organizer—resumen inicial discurso de introducción que da una idea de lo que puede esperar la audiencia.
affirmative—afirmativo sí o verdadero.
affluent—acaudalado que tiene mucho más que suficiente y típicamente, disponibilidad creciente de posesiones materiales.
after-dinner speech—discurso de sobremesa un discurso entretenido que sigue a un banquete o comida.
agenda—agenda órdenes del día, lista de cosas a realizarse.
aggressive tone—tono agresivo forma prepotente o insolente de comunicarse, que considera un solo punto de vista, y no deja nada o casi nada de espacio para discutir o llegar a un arreglo.
alienate—enajenar tornarse hostil, poco amistoso.
allegory—alegoría uso de figuras de ficción o acciones simbólicas (como en un cuento o cuadro) para expresar generalizaciones sobre la existencia humana.
alliteration—aliteración la repetición de sonidos al comienzo de dos palabras que están cerca una de la otra.
allusion—alusión una referencia a una persona, lugar, objeto o idea bien conocida.
ambiguous—ambiguo capaz de ser entendido en más de una forma.
amend—enmendar una propuesta para modificar una moción.
analogy—analogía una ilustración en la cual las características de un objeto o evento familiar se utilizan para explicar o describir las características de un objeto o evento desconocido. El uso extendido de una metáfora o símil, a menudo en la forma de una historia.
analysis—análisis separación de un todo en las partes o elementos que lo componen; examen de un todo para determinar sus partes o elementos—también el informe que muestra los resultados de tal examen.
analytical—analítico marcado por la habilidad de separar un todo en las partes o elementos que lo componen, o el examen de un todo para determinar sus partes o elementos.
anthology—antología una colección de pasajes de la literatura.
anthropologist—antropólogo científico que estudia a los seres humanos, incluyendo sus características físicas y sus relaciones ambientales, sociales y culturales.
antithesis—antítesis un contraste de ideas mediante el uso paralelo de palabras, frases, etc.; lo opuesto.
apathetic—apático que no tiene ningún interés o preocupación (indiferente), que tiene o demuestra muy escaso o ningún sentimiento o emoción.
apoplectic—apoplético afectado por, con tendencia a, o que muestra síntomas de una apoplejía.
appreciative listening—escuchar apreciativamente un estilo de escuchar que se utiliza para gozar y saborear sonidos placenteros tales como la música o la naturaleza.
appropriateness—apropiado ser especialmente apto o compatible.
argument—argumento una razón para favorecer una parte de una propuesta y los hechos que respaldan dicha razón.
articulation—articulación la claridad y precisión de un orador.
assert—aseverar afirmar o declarar positivamente y a menudo en forma enérgica y agresiva.
assertion—aseveración enunciación positiva.
assertive tone—tono asertivo comunicar los planteamientos en forma directa, pero con tacto.
assonance—asonancia la repetición de sonidos vocales.
attribution—atribución acto de reconocer una obra (como ser, de arte o literaria) a un artista o autor determinado.
audience analysis—análisis de la audiencia el proceso mediante el cual un orador considera las necesidades y expectativas de la audiencia que estará escuchando el discurso.
auditory—auditivo relacionado o experimentado a través del oído.
aural—auditivo relacionado con el sentido del oído.
author card—tarjeta de autor un sistema de catálogo de libros mediante tarjetas organizadas de acuerdo con el apellido del autor.
avarice—avaricia deseo excesivo por la riqueza, o las ganancias; codicia.
avoidance—evasión estrategia de negociación en la cual un individuo trata de resolver un conflicto retirando o negando la existencia de un problema (enfoque pierde—pierde).

B

barter—trueque comerciar mediante el intercambio de bienes.
begging the question—dar por sentado lo que queda por probar un argumento que asume que lo que sea que está tratando de probar ya es cierto.
bias—sesgado punto de vista a menudo prejuiciado.
body—cuerpo la parte del discurso que proporciona el contenido y análisis que prueba las afirmaciones de tesis.
body language—lenguaje corporal la forma en que uno usa su cuerpo para enviar mensajes.
bombard—bombardeo asalto (ataque violento de palabras o golpes) persistente.
Braille—Braille sistema de escritura para los ciegos que utiliza caracteres formados por puntos sobresalientes.
brainstorming—lanzar ideas proceso en el cual un grupo de miembros expone sus ideas, lo más rápido y variado posible para estimular el pensamiento creativo y las soluciones.
brash—descarado que carece de restricción y discernimiento, sin tacto.
bridge—puente la transición de una respuesta a otra.
brief—escrito una reseña que resume los argumentos específicos del caso.
burden of proof—peso de la prueba un término utilizado en un debate formal y en el derecho para referirse al deber o responsabilidad de probar algo.
burgeoning—floreciente que crece y se expande rápidamente.
bylaws—estatutos un conjunto de reglas especiales acordadas entre los miembros de un grupo.

C

cadence—cadencia medida o compás de un fluido rítmico.
call the question—llamar a voto una propuesta para tomar un voto inmediato sobre una moción.
canned—envasado preparado de antemano en forma estandarizada para uso no específico o amplia distribución, carente de originalidad o individualidad.
captive audience—público cautivo un público que ha sido forzado a asistir.
card catalog—tarjetero un catálogo que indica los libros que tiene una biblioteca y dónde se pueden encontrar.
case—caso las ideas y evidencias de la persona que participa en el debate, organizadas en una postura que apoya un lado de una resolución.
case study—estudio de casos el análisis en gran detalle de un ejemplo "típico," con el propósito de obtener conclusiones generales.
causality—causalidad la declaración de que un evento es el resultado de otro evento.
cause-event pattern—patrón causa efecto un patrón de organización que ordena los elementos de un argumento en una secuencia de "debido a que esto sucedió, esto resultó."
circumstantial evidence—evidencia circunstancial la evidencia a la mano. Podría sugerir una conclusión, pero no la prueba.
climactic pattern—patrón culminante un patrón de organización que ordena los elementos en orden de importancia.
clique—camarilla exclusivo círculo cerrado o grupo de personas, especialmente aquéllas que se mantienen unidas por intereses, puntos de vista o propósitos comunes.
cognizant—conocedor que tiene conocimiento de algo por experiencia personal, atento, informado.
cohesion—cohesión cualidad de una discusión de grupo en la cual sus miembros se respetan mutuamente, comparten valores similares y cuentan con apoyo mutuo.
collaboration—colaboración estrategia de negociación que se centra en resolver el conflicto; la experiencia, pericia, y percepciones de ambas partes son reconocidas y valoradas (enfoque gana—gana).
combustion—combustión acto o instancia de quemarse, oxidación lenta, agitación violenta.
commemorative speech—discurso conmemorativo un discurso emotivo que recuerda eventos o personas históricas.
commencement address—discurso de graduación un discurso que se da durante una ceremonia de graduación.
common ground—interés mutuo un sentido de una meta o interés compartido.
communication—comunicación el proceso de enviar y recibir mensajes.
communication barrier—barrera a la comunicación cualquier obstáculo (ya sea de actitud, social, educacional, cultural o del medio ambiente) que se entromete en una comunicación efectiva.
comparative—comparativo considerado como si estuviera comparado a otra cosa.
compelling—apremiante fuerte, que demanda atención.
compelling insight—percepción apremiante comprensión o percepción, situación (percepción) muy fuerte que demanda atención (apremiante).
compendium—compendio breve resumen de una obra más extensa o de un campo del conocimiento.
competency—habilidad la habilidad de lograr algo.
competition—competencia estrategia de negociación que se centra en derrotar u opacar a la otra persona más bien que en resolver el problema (enfoque gana—pierde).
competitive—competitivo una atmósfera que propicia la división entre sus miembros ya que compiten entre sí como rivales. También, la carga de un plan alternativo negativo, para demostrar que tanto las proposiciones afirmativas o negativas no se deben adoptar.
composure—compostura un comportamiento calmo, controlado.
compression—compresión acto de reducir el tamaño o volumen comprimiendo o apretando (normalmente para lograr simplicidad).
compromise—transar una estrategia de negociación en la cual cada individuo sacrifica algo para llegar a un acuerdo (trade-offs— intercambios) (enfoque ganar—perder).
concise—conciso expresar mucho en pocas palabras.

concrete—concreto cosa real o efectiva, o categorías de cosas; no abstractas o teóricas.
concrete word—palabra concreta una palabra que nombra algo que se percibe a través de la frase.
confidence—confianza un sentimiento de creer en un mismo y en su habilidad para controlar una situación específica.
conflict management—manejo de conflictos la habilidad de convertir una situación potencialmente negativa en una positiva.
connotation –connotación el significado y sentimientos asociado a una palabra por una persona, basado en experiencia personal.
conscience—conciencia sentido de corrección moral, o de merecimiento de culpa por la propia conducta, intenciones o carácter unida a un sentimiento de obligación de hacer lo correcto o de ser bueno.
consensus—consenso acuerdo casi unánime entre los miembros de un grupo sobre una solución en particular.
consonance—consonancia la repetición de sonidos consonantes.
constructive—constructivo un discurso en el cual los argumentos se presentan y defienden desde el inicio.
constructive conflict—conflicto constructivo situación en la que un grupo de miembros usa sus diferencias para descubrir las mejores ideas.
content—contenido información o tópicos presentados y su esencia, significado e importancia.
conversational quality—calidad coloquial discurso que se destaca por aparentar ser espontáneo.
converse—inverso algo que tiene el orden, relación o acción invertida.
conviction—convicción un fuerte convencimiento respecto de nuestro mensaje y la determinación de comunicar dicho mensaje a la audiencia.
cooperative—cooperación atmósfera que alienta a sus miembros a trabajar unidos para lograr un fin o meta común.
correlation —correlación dos o más eventos relacionados en alguna forma.
courtesy—cortesía urbanidad, buenos modales y respetuosa consideración hacia los demás.
covert—solapado que no se muestra abiertamente, intereses ocultos, encubierto.
credentials—antecedentes calificaciones.
credibility—credibilidad la habilidad de una persona de inspirar que las personas lo crean.
criteria—criterio conjunto de normas que se deben tomar en cuenta para llegar a una solución.
critical listening—escuchar críticamente una forma de escuchar utilizada para evaluar y analizar un mensaje buscando su lógica y su valor.
criticism—crítica evaluación o juicio—generalmente negativo.
crooned—canturreo cantar en forma suave, dulce e íntima.
cross examination—contrainterrogatorio el período que sigue a la intervención de cada orador en el cual se interroga al orador.
crystallize—cristalizar hacer que tome una forma definitiva.
culmination—culminación clímax o realización.
cultural literacy—alfabetismo cultural la información que se puede esperar que el ciudadano americano promedio conozca.
cutaway—recortado un modelo que muestra la composición interior de un objeto.

CH

chair—presidente la persona a cargo de la reunión.
chalk talk—presentación ilustrada un discurso en el cual el orador utiliza ayuda visual—una pizarra—para transmitir información.
chauffeur—chofer persona empleada para conducir un automóvil.
chronological pattern—patrón cronológico un patrón de organización que ordena los elementos en una secuencia de tiempo o en el orden en que estos sucedieron.

D

database—base de datos una colección de información relacionada.
debate—debate un método para solucionar problemas; una competencia formal de habilidades en un argumento razonado.
dedication—dedicación el deseo de practicar y comprometerse con su propio discurso.
deduction—deducción una manera de razonar en la cual uno argumenta desde generalizaciones hasta una instancia específica.
deficit—déficit deficiencia en cantidad, especialmente por excesos de gastos en relación con los ingresos.
definition—definición la explicación de un término; refleja el significado deseado por el orador o el uso especializado en el contexto de un discurso.
degraded—degradar rebajar de un rango o grado más alto a uno más bajo.
delivery—presentación el modo o manera que un orador utiliza para transmitir palabras a una audiencia.
demeaning—rebajar degradar, desvalorizar; bajar la condición, aprecio, calidad o carácter.
demographics—demografía características estadísticas de las poblaciones humanas.
denotation—denotación el significado básico y generalmente conocido de una palabra contenida en un diccionario.
diagram—diagrama una ayuda visual utilizada por un orador para explicar un proceso.
dialogue—diálogo conversación entre actores; dos personas o grupos.
dignitary—dignatario persona con un cargo honorífico o de muy alto rango.
dire—de mal agüero advertencia de desastre, sumamente urgente.

disclaimer—aclaración el intento del orador de explicar lo que no se infiere por el discurso o el reconocimiento de una falta de experiencia en la materia.
disconcerting—desconcertante desorientante, perturbador.
discriminative listening—escuchar en forma discriminada un estilo de escuchar utilizado para aislar un sonido en particular de un entorno ruidoso.
discussion—debate intercambio cooperativo de información, opiniones e ideas.
disintegration—desintegración acto de romper o descomponer, pérdida de la unidad.
disruptive conflict—conflicto disociador conflicto que divide a sus miembros en dos bandos en pugna, los que se niegan a hacer concesiones hasta el punto en que no se puede alcanzar una decisión de grupo.
distal—distante del centro lejos del punto de unión.
distinction—distinción diferencia entre palabras, objetos, ideas, etc. que explica diciendo lo que es una cosa y, más especialmente, lo que no es.
distortion—distorsión deformación del verdadero significado, apariencia falsa o anormal.
diverse—diverso variado diferente de otra, distinto.
door opener—invitación una frase utilizada por la persona que escucha para invitar e instar a que la persona que habla continúe.
dossier—historial inventario personal de vida, incluyendo información laboral.
download—descargar transferir datos de la memora de una computadora a la memoria de otra computadora, normalmente más pequeña.
dramatic interpretation—interpretación dramática un evento competitivo de discursos en el cual el orador memoriza y representa una pieza de la literatura de una naturaleza más seria.
dramatic monologue—monólogo dramático un relato en la primera persona en la cual un solo personaje habla.

E

eloquent—elocuente que posee o muestra una expresión clara y vigorosa, expresándose o revelando los hechos en forma vívida y conmovedora.
emancipation—emancipación acto de liberarse de las restricciones, control o poder impuesto por un tercero.
embalm—embalsamar tratar (un cadáver) para protegerlo de la descomposición.
emotional appeal—apelación emocional una técnica de persuasión que involucra "tocar un punto emocional"; el orador utiliza temas y valores tan variados como el patriotismo, la familia y el honor para ganarse el favor de la audiencia.
empathic listening—interlocutor enfático estilo de escuchar alentando a las personas a hablar libremente sin temor o vergüenza.
empathy—empatía una sincera comprensión de los sentimientos, ideas y motivaciones de los demás.
emulated—emulación esforzarse por igualar o superar, imitación.
enhanced—intensificar agregar o contribuir a, mejorar.
enthusiasm—entusiasmo la energía, tanto intelectual como física, que transmite el orador para inspirar a su audiencia.
entrepreneur—empresario alguien que organiza, administra y asume los riesgos de un negocio o empresa.
epitomize—epitomar servir como el ejemplo típico o ideal de algo.
equilibrium—equilibrio estado de balance entre elementos opuestos, estado de equilibrio intelectual o emocional: serenidad.
equitable—equitativo distribución justa.
erudite—erudito marcado por un amplio conocimiento o ilustración.
ethical (personal) appeal—apelación ética (personal) una cualidad persuasiva basada en la honestidad, sinceridad y compromiso natural del orador a lo que es correcto y bueno.
ethics—ética el sentido de lo correcto y de lo incorrecto en una persona.
ethnicity—étnica condición de pertenecer a una raza o pueblo en particular.
ethos—ethos palabra griega para el carácter; el término es asociado con el atractivo personal (ético) de Aristóteles.
etiquette—etiqueta formas (de conducta o proceder) determinadas por la costumbre o la autoridad que se deben observar en la vida social, oficial o profesional: decoro.
etymology—etimología historia de las palabras que se muestra siguiendo su desarrollo y relaciones.
eulogy—elogio un discurso alabando u honrando a alguien que a muerto.
euphemism—eufemismo una palabra o grupo de palabras utilizadas para sustituir una palabra que es ofensiva o de mal gusto.
evasive—evasivo con tendencia o intención de eludir o evitar, usualmente por medio de habilidad o estratagema.
evidence—evidencia cualquier cosa que establece un hecho o da causa a creer en algo.
evoking—evocación recuerdo, llamado; traer a la mente, rememorar.
exaggerate—exageración agrandar (una aseveración) fuera de lo normal, que sobrepasa límites y vá más allá de la verdad.
excursion—desviación digresión (acto de alejarse del principal sujeto de atención), viaje de agrado.
expedient—conveniente adaptado para lograr un fin en particular; gobernado por el propio interés.
extemporaneous—improvisado sin planificar ni ensayado con antelación.
extemporaneous method—método extemporáneo un método de presentación en la cual el orador se refiere solo a apuntes o a una breve reseña.
eye contact—contacto visual una característica utilizada por los oradores mediante la cual miran directamente a los ojos del que lo escucha a fin de enfatizar un punto o demostrar lo serio que ellos consideran este asunto.

F

facilitate—facilitar hacer más fácil.
false analogy—falsa analogía una comparación de dos cosas que no son realmente iguales.
false comparison—comparación errónea una comparación entre dos cosas diferentes.
false premise—premisa falsa una declaración errónea; una premisa que es fallida y que resultará en un error de deducción.
faltering—vacilar titubear en el discurso, propósito o acción.
factual proposition—propuesta objetiva una propuesta que es verdadera o falsa.
fallacy—falacia un error de razonamiento o una convicción equivocada.
fear—temor proceso biológico que activa nuestro sistema energético de emergencias de modo que podamos manejar el peligro; emoción desagradable, a menudo fuerte, causada por la sensación o conciencia de peligro.
feedback—retroalimentación la reacción que el receptor entrega a un mensaje ofrecido por el transmisor.
fiasco—fiasco fracaso completo.
filter—filtrar usar barreras emocionales (basadas en antecedentes y personalidad) para absorber selectivamente la información.
fireside chat—conversación junto al hogar un discurso en el cual e líder se dirige al grupo de manera informal respecto de las preocupaciones, temores y problemas del grupo.
first affirmative constructive—(IAC)—primera afirmación constructiva discurso que se prepara antes de una ronda en la cual el orador afirmativo presenta un caso positivo.
first affirmative rebuttal—(1AR)—primera refutación afirmativa en el debate Lincoln—Douglas, el discurso pronunciado por el primer orador afirmativo que responde al caso negativo y vuelve a construir el caso afirmativo; en un debate sobre políticas, este discurso responde al bloque negativo y amplía el argumento que la segunda refutación afirmativa necesitará para ganar el debate.
first person—primera persona refiérese a la persona que habla (yo, nosotros).
first negative constructive—(INC)—primera negación constructiva en el debate Lincoln—Douglas, el discurso mediante el cual el orador negativo presenta el caso negativo y refuta la aserción constructiva; en un debate sobre políticas, el primer orador negativo presenta la posición negativa del debate.
flippant—impertinente que carece de un adecuado respeto o seriedad.
flowsheet—hoja de flujo un registro escrito de las palabras o argumentos presentados durante un debate.
follow-up question—pregunta complementaria una pregunta que ayuda al entrevistador a perseguir temas que surgen en forma inesperada durante el curso de una entrevista.
foreshadowing—presagiar dar una pista o sugerencia con antelación.
forfeiting—enajenar pérdida o pérdida de derechos, por algún error, ofensa o crimen.
format—formato (1) un estilo de programación o especialización. (2) la organización general establecida para la conducción de un debate. Especifica la cantidad de tiempo y el orden en el cual se permitirá hablar a cada participante.
forum—foro debate que viene a continuación de un panel en el cual los panelistas participantes invitan a la audiencia a formular preguntas y hacer comentarios.
friendliness—amigable una actitud cálida, agradable.

G

germane—pertinente relativo, aplicable.
ghostwriter—colaborador anónimo una persona que escribe para y en nombre de otra persona.
gigantic—gigantesco que excede lo usual o esperado (como en tamaño o fuerza); enorme.
gluttony—gula exceso en la comida o bebida.
good will—buena disposición un interés o preocupación genuino.
graph—gráfico una ayuda visual utilizada por un orador para demostrar una relación estadística.
group think—pensamiento de grupo deseo de continuar con el grupo aún a costa de tener que renunciar a sus propios principios.
grovel—arrastrarse literalmente, arrastrarse con la cabeza en el suelo para demostrar sumisión; rebajarse (humillarse o degradarse) a sí mismo.

H

handout—volante material escrito (volantes, folletos u hojas informativas) preparadas y duplicadas con antelación a un discurso y proporcionadas a la audiencia como material de referencia.
haphazardly—al azar marcado por la falta de planificación, orden o dirección.
harmoniously—armoniosamente de acuerdo; marcado por una concordancia en sentimiento o acción.
hasty generalization—generalización apresurada un argumento fallido basado en información incompleta o poco representativa.
haven—asilo lugar seguro o un lugar que ofrece oportunidades o condiciones favorables.
hoke—falsificar (utilizado con "up") trillar, imitar.
house—sala (1) un término utilizado para referirse al grupo durante sus reuniones. (2) el área en el cual la audiencia toma asiento.
humorous interpretation—interpretación humorística un concurso de hablar en público en el cual un orador memoriza y representa una obra literaria de naturaleza ligera.
hyperbole—hipérbole un método de decir más de la verdad o de exagerar a modo de énfasis.

I

I—message—mensaje yo enunciado que enfatiza lo que una persona desea.
ignoring the question—ignorar la pregunta el intento

por parte del orador de desviar la atención de la audiencia del asunto en discusión.
imagery—imaginería lenguaje que crea imágenes en la mente y excita los sentidos.
impression—impresión cómo percibe la audiencia al orador basado en la forma en que se presenta a sí mismo y a sus ideas.
impromptu—impremeditado elaborado o hecho en ese momento, con muy poca o ninguna preparación.
impromptu method—método improvisado un método de entrega sin ensayo previo; el orador no utiliza apuntes y se apoya en su habilidad para ofrecer una respuesta verbal inmediata.
incidental motion—moción incidental una propuesta para cambiar la forma en que se está conduciendo una reunión.
incorrigible—incorregible incapaz de ser corregido, enmendado o reformado.
indented—sangría dispuesto con un espacio desde el margen (en un resumen las ideas subordinadas o de apoyo llevan sangría).
index—índice una lista en orden alfabético ubicada al final de un libro que informa al lector la página exacta en la cual puede encontrar información en particular.
indifferent audience—audiencia indiferente una audiencia apática o no interesada en el orador y en su tema. Esta audiencia no encuentra que el tema es relevante para su situación personal.
induction—inducción una forma de razonamiento en la cual se utilizan casos específicos para probar una verdad general.
inflection—modulación el cambio en el tono o volumen de voz por parte del orador con el objeto de crear énfasis.
infographic—gráfico informativo ilustración creada por un programa de arte gráfico de una computadora como ser el "Freehand" o el "Adobe Illustrator."
informal debate—debate casual cualquier debate realizado sin reglas específicas.
inhibition—inhibición freno interno impuesto a la libertad de acción, expresión o funcionamiento.
innovation—innovación una nueva idea, método o dispositivo.
innuendo—indirecta sugerencia, insinuación, especialmente una reflexión velada sobre el carácter o la reputación.
innumerable—innumerables demasiados para ser contados.
insinuated—insinuado introducido en forma gradual o de modo sutil, indirecto o astuto implícito en forma insidiosa o tortuosa.
instinctively—instintivamente conocer o actuar bajo el nivel consciente, que surge en forma espontánea e independientemente del juicio o voluntad; una actitud, impulso o capacidad natural e inherente.
integrate—integrar formar, coordinar o mezclar en un todo funcional.
integrity—integridad el fuerte sentido de lo que es correcto e incorrecto en una persona.
integrity—integridad fuerte sentimiento de bien y de mal; adhesión a una escala de valores.
intensification—intensificar acto de hacer más agudo o intenso; un realce
interior monologue—monólogo interior una narración en primera persona en la cual el narrador se está hablando a sí mismo.
interlibrary loan—préstamo interbiblioteca un sistema de cooperación mediante el cual las bibliotecas se prestan libros entre sí.
internship—práctica puesto de voluntario sin sueldo que trabaja para adquirir experiencia.
interpersonal communication—comunicación interpersonal comunicación que se lleva a cabo en cualquier momento en que se transmiten mensajes entre dos o más personas.
interviewer—entrevistador la persona que hace las preguntas durante una entrevista.
intimacy—intimidad relación estrecha, contacto o familiaridad.
intimate distance—distancia íntima la distancia que se utiliza principalmente para intercambios confidenciales, casi siempre reservada para amigos cercanos (una dieciocho pulgadas).
intimidation—intimidación el acto de volver tímido o temeroso, asustar, forzar o disuadir por medio de amenazas reales o aparentes.
introduction—presentación el inicio de un discurso; contiene el llamado de atención, la declaración de vínculo, la declaración de la tesis y frecuentemente, una declaración de antecedentes.
introspective—introspectivo reflexionar mirando hacia adentro, examinar sus propios pensamientos o sentimientos.
intuition—intuición percepción rápida y espontánea; el poder o facultad de saber las cosas sin raciocinio consciente.
irony—ironía una expresión que utiliza palabras que sugieren lo opuesto de lo que parecen decir en la superficie.
irrational—irracional no gobernado por la razón; carente de comprensión o coherencia mental normal.

J

jargon—jerga el vocabulario especializado de personas en la misma profesión o en un mismo grupo.
jeopardy—riesgo expuesto a pérdidas; peligro, albur, riesgo.
jump on the bandwagon—hacer suya una causa triunfante técnica persuasiva basada en la necesidad a pertenecer.
justification—justificación acción que prueba la justicia, corrección o racionalidad.

L

label—rótulo palabra o frase descriptiva o de identificación.
leader—líder una persona que utiliza las habilidades de liderazgo con efectividad.
leadership—liderazgo la habilidad de motivar y unir a

otros para que trabajen unidos para lograr una tarea específica.
leading question—pregunta capciosa una pregunta que "pone palabras" en la boca del sujeto.
learning style—estilo de aprendizaje las diferentes maneras en que las personas aprenden con eficacia.
Lincoln-Douglas debate—debate Lincoln-Douglas tipo competitivo de debate formal, que se ocupa de proposiciones de valores y se practica en las escuelas secundarias del todo el país.
link—vínculo (1) una explicación por parte del equipo negativo que demuestra que el plan afirmativo tiene un vínculo directo con su desventaja. (2) la declaración en una introducción que viene entre el llamado de atención y la declaración de la tesis y que conecta a los dos de una forma lógica.
listening spare time—tiempo de sobra para escuchar tiempo para pensar creado por la habilidad para escuchar más rápido de lo que la gente puede hablar.
logic—lógica la ciencia de razonar que utiliza un sistema de reglas para ayudar a la persona a pensar correctamente.
logical appeal—apelación lógica el uso de la secuencia, el análisis, la organización y la evidencia para probar un punto y persuadir.
logos—logos una palabra griega que significa lógica y razón; el término se asocia a la apelación lógica de Aristóteles.

M

main heading—encabezado principal una de las principales divisiones, áreas o argumentos de la declaración de propósito del orador.
main motion—moción principal una propuesta que pide al grupo que tome acción.
manipulate—manipular influenciar, especialmente con la intención de engañar, manejar o utilizar hábilmente.
manipulating—manipulando influenciando, especialmente con la intención de engañar.
mannequin—maniquí forma sin vida que representa a la figura humana.
manuscript method—método de manuscrito un método de entrega en la cual el orador escribe y posteriormente lee el discurso palabra por palabra.
map—mapa una ayuda visual utilizada por el orador para demostrar una relación geográfica.
mediation—mediación intervención entre partes en conflicto para promover una reconciliación, un acuerdo o un compromiso.
memorized method—método de memoria un método de entrega en la cual el orador memoriza y luego presenta el discurso palabra por palabra sin el uso de apuntes.
mesmerized—hipnotizado hipnosis, mantener embelesado o fascinado.
message—mensaje aquello que se envía o dice.
metaphor—metáfora una expresión que compara dos cosas distintas sin el uso de las palabras igual a o como.
meter—metro medida del ritmo en una línea de poesía.
methodically—metódicamente con una disposición ordenada.
microcosm—microcosmo mundo pequeño, comunidad o unidad que constituye un ejemplo típico o ideal de uno más grande.
miffed—irritable en un estado de mal humor (como resultado de una pelea sin importancia).
mimic—mimo imitar fielmente.
minstrel—trovador uno, de los que en la Grecia antigua eran denominados "rapsodas," estos itinerantes leían sus trabajos (frecuentemente con acompañamiento musical) en competencias públicas.
minutes—acta el registro escrito de las reuniones de una organización.
model—modelo una representación en miniatura de algo.
moderator—moderador miembro de un grupo que dirige un debate (inicia el debate, lo mantiene dentro del tema y cierra el debate).
monopolize—monopolizar asumir el control o posesión total.
monotone—monótono un tono en el cual las palabras se entregan a la misma velocidad y entonación sin variación.
mood—ambiente el tono emocional creado o expresado en una obra.
motif—motivo idea dominante o tema central.
motivation—motivación una fuerza, necesidad o impulso interior que causa que la persona actúe.
multimedia presentation—presentación con medios múltiples discurso complementado con programas software de computación, que permite al orador combinar varias clases de medios auxiliares visuales y/o auditivos.

N

name calling—insultar dar a alguien una etiqueta negativa sin tener evidencia.
narrative—narración contar una historia.
narrowing—enfocarse limitarse y definir un tema de manera más precisa.
nectar—néctar el brebaje de los dioses griegos y romanos; cualquier bebida deliciosa, secreción dulce de una planta que constituye la materia prima de la miel.
negative—negativo no o falso.
negative rebuttal—(NR)—refutación negativa en un debate Lincoln - Douglas, el discurso final pronunciado por el orador negativo que hace un resumen del debate y trata de "callar" los argumentos que se pueden prever de la refutación hecha por el orador afirmativo.
negotiation—negociación el acto de conferenciar con otro (u otros) para llegar a un arreglo sobre alguna materia.
new business—nuevo asunto asuntos presentados por primera vez en una reunión.
newness—novedoso un enfoque original o único hacia un tema.
nonassertive tone—tono no asertivo forma de comunicación que carece de acción y energía y aparece como carente de interés e indiferente.

nonverbal communication—comunicación no verbal las expresiones faciales o movimientos corporales utilizados para expresar actitudes o sentimientos respecto de una persona, situación o idea.
nonverbal messages—mensajes no verbales las expresiones faciales o movimientos corporales utilizados para transmitir mensajes no hablados.
notes—apuntes un listado de ideas escritas en forma breve y ordenada.
nuclear family—núcleo familiar grupo familiar consistente solamente en un padre, una madre y sus hijos.

O

offstage focus—enfoque hacia fuera del escenario técnica utilizada en reader's theater en el cual lectores utilizan libretos y se imaginan la escena afuera, entre la audiencia.
old business—asuntos pendientes asuntos que no fueron concluidos en reuniones anteriores.
omniscient—omnisciente un tipo de narrativa (en tercera persona) en la cual el narrador lo sabe todo y se desplaza con libertad dentro y fuera de las mentes de los distintos personajes.
online—en línea un servicio que proporciona acceso rápido a muchas bases de datos computacionales.
open-ended question—pregunta abierta una pregunta que permite que el sujeto decida cuál es la mejor manera de responder. Fomenta una respuesta integral y profunda y trata de evitar una respuesta sí o no, verdadero o falso.
opposed audience—audiencia opositora una audiencia que es hostil hacia el orador o al tema de su presentación.
oral cavity—cavidad oral la boca.
oral interpretation—interpretación oral el arte de comunicar obras de la literatura mediante una lectura adecuada en voz alta.
oral or verbal communication—comunicación oral o verbal comunicación que es principalmente hablada.
orator—orador una persona que presenta oratoria y que utiliza las palabras eficazmente.
oratory or rhetoric—oratoria o retórica el arte o el estudio de hablar en público.
order of precedence—orden de prioridad la relación de las mociones entre sí.
orders of the day—orden del día una agenda o lista de temas que se discutirán durante la reunión.
organization—organización un sistema de estructura y forma que permite que la audiencia pueda seguir un discurso en forma fácil.
ought—deber idea o concepto que tiene una persona de un ideal—obligación moral basada en un sentimiento de deber.
outline—reseña un marco lógico y organizado para un discurso; indica la forma en que progresará el discurso.
overhead projector—proyector de transparencias una ayuda visual utilizada por un orador para proyectar transparencias (frecuentemente cuadros y gráficos) hacia una pared o telón.
oxymoron—oxímoron un dispositivo literario que une palabras que están en directa oposición, tal como "bondad cruel."

P

painstakingly—esmeradamente caracterizada por dedicar o mostrar un esmerado cuidado o esfuerzo.
palatable—apetitoso agradable o aceptable a la mente (o al paladar o al gusto).
panacea—panacea remedio para todas las dificultades o enfermedades.
panel—panel de expertos discusión informal que tiene lugar ante una audiencia.
parallelism—estructura paralela o paralelismo el uso de la misma forma gramatical para expresar ideas que debieran, lógicamente, ser tratadas con igualdad. Esto frecuentemente involucra la repetición de palabras o frases.
paraphernalia—pertrechos equipo, accesorios, bienes personales.
paraphrase—paráfrasis repetir en sus propias palabras.
paraphrasing—parafrasear expresar un segmento original con palabras diferentes.
parliament—parlamento asamblea que constituye el cuerpo legislativo supremo en el reino unido.
parliamentary procedure—procedimiento parlamentario un sistema de normas observado en reuniones grupales basado en ideas desarrolladas en el parlamento británico.
passive listening—escuchar pasivamente una forma de escuchar en la cual la persona que escucha no comparte la responsabilidad ni se involucra con el proceso de comunicación.
pathos—pathos la palabra griega para sentimientos y emociones; el término se asocia a la apelación emocional de Aristóteles.
pause—pausa una brecha en la conversación. Frecuentemente proporciona una buena oportunidad para que el entrevistado (sin ser inducido) ofrezca mayor información.
people skills—habilidad con la gente habilidad para trabajar bien con otras personas por medio de una cortés comunicación.
perception—percepción cómo uno ve las cosas.
performance anxiety—ansiedad ante el público una forma de miedo al escenario, a menudo asociado a músicos, actores y otros artistas.
peripheral—periférico fuera de nuestro campo directo de visión y audición; los límites externos, área límite.
persona—persona el relator ficticio de la obra que será interpretada.
personal distance—distancia personal la distancia cómoda para una conversación entre amigos (entre un pie y medio a cuatro pies).
personal space—espacio personal una zona de comodidad que cada persona mantiene a su alrededor y en la cual una intrusión no sería bienvenida.
personification—personificación asignar características humanas a objetos no humanos.

persuasive speaking—oratoria persuasiva oratoria que influencia a otros a creer o pensar en algo o a tomar acción.
pervasiveness—capacidad de penetración la acción de difundirse (esparcirse) por todas partes.
phobia—fobia un miedo persistente e irracional que hace que una persona evite situaciones específicas.
phonation—fonación la producción de la voz.
picturesque—pintoresco semejante a un cuadro, que produce imágenes mentales.
pitch—tono las notas vocales (agudas o graves) que el orador alcanza cuando habla.
plagiarism—plagio copiar o imitar el lenguaje, ideas o pensamientos de otro o pasarlos como el trabajo original de uno.
platform movement—movimiento escénico caminar o desplazarse de manera dirigida desde un punto a otro mientras se habla.
polarizing—polarización división de los miembros de un grupo en dos bandos rivales que rehusan hacer concesiones.
policy proposition—propuesta de políticas propuesta que se enfoca hacia la conveniencia de un plan de acción determinado.
pollster—encuestador persona que hace preguntas a la gente para obtener información u opiniones para análisis.
portfolio—carpeta archivador portátil que contiene una muestra o ejemplo de los mejores trabajos escolares ejecutados por un candidato a un puesto de trabajo.
posture—postura la posición del cuerpo cuando está quieto.
power source—fuente de poder el origen de la energía necesaria para que las cosas funcionen.
preamble—preámbulo declaración introductoria, específicamente la parte introductoria de una constitución o estatuto que normalmente formula las razones y la intención de la ley.
premise—premisa una aserción que sirve como la base para un argumento.
prep time—tiempo preparatorio el tiempo preparatorio permitido en cada ronda para organizar las respuestas y preparar las preguntas.
prerequisite—prerequisito algo que es necesario para un fin o para llevar a cabo una función.
prescriptive—prescripción lo que se establece como guía o norma de ación (en un discurso, un tópico de prescripción requiere que el orador "prescriba"—establezca como guía o norma—indicaciones de políticas específicas).
preview statement—declaración previa la declaración al final de la introducción que presenta una vista general de las principales áreas que se discutirán en el cuerpo del discurso.
prioritizing—prioridad arreglar en orden de importancia.
privileged motion—moción privilegiada una propuesta para resolver un problema urgente distinto a la moción principal.
problem-solution pattern—patrón de solución de problemas un patrón de organización que presenta un problema y luego ofrece posibles soluciones.
procession—procesión grupo de individuos que se mueven en un orden determinado, a menudo en forma ceremonial.
professional communication—comunicación profesional la comunicación que tiene lugar durante el trabajo o que está relacionada a una carrera.
pronunciation—pronunciación la producción de los sonidos y entonación correcta de las sílabas al hablar.
proof—prueba evidencia específica que establece la verdad de algo.
propaganda—propaganda material diseñado para deformar la verdad o engañar a la audiencia.
proposition—proposición una declaración del punto a ser discutido.
prospective—perspectivas relativo a o efectiva en el futuro, probable de acontecer.
proxemics—proxémica el estudio de la comunicación espacial; en la comunicación oral, se refiere específicamente a la distancia entre los oradores y la audiencia.
proximal—próximo más cercano al punto de unión.
proxy—apoderado alguien que actúa como substituto de otro.
public distance—distancia pública la distancia que se mantiene entre extraños. A esta distancia las personas apenas si reconocen la presencia del otro (doce pies de distancia o mayor).
public lecture—conferencia pública una conferencia realizada a la comunidad o a un grupo académico.
purpose statement—declaración de propósito una declaración que presenta temas selectos del discurso y el propósito específico del orador al hacer la presentación.
puff ball—pregunta suave una pregunta abierta fácil de contestar.

Q

qualm—desasosiego sentimiento súbito de duda, temor o intranquilidad.
questions of evaluation—preguntas de evaluación preguntas que se formulan a los miembros de un grupo solicitando su opinión negativa o positiva con respecto a posibles soluciones y la emisión de un juicio de valores.
questions of fact—preguntas pertinentes preguntas formuladas por los miembros de un grupo que guardan relación con los hechos en discusión.
questions of interpretation—preguntas de interpretación preguntas que solicitan a los miembros de un grupo que den sus opiniones sobre el significado de la información.
quorum—quórum el número mínimo de miembros que deben estar presentes a fin de que se aprueben las medidas del grupo.
quotation—cita una declaración que repite las palabras exactas que otra persona dijo.

R

railroad—apresurar aprobar (una ley) muy precipitadamente.
rapport—afinidad sensación de confianza y cooperación.

rate—ritmo la velocidad a la cual habla una persona.
reasoning—razonamiento el proceso de pensar, comprender y sacar conclusiones respecto de alguna evidencia.
rebuffed—denegar agudo rechazo o crítica.
rebuttal—refutación el acto de contrarrestar el ataque de un oponente al argumento de uno y de esa manera reconstruir el argumento.
receiver—receptor una persona que intercepta un mensaje y luego lo decodifica.
reciprocal—recíproco correspondencia o comunicación mutua.
recitation—declamación recitación ante una audiencia, generalmente de algo memorizado.
reconsider—reconsiderar una moción para reexaminar la moción principal que ya ha sido aprobada o rechazada.
refrain—refrán frase o verso que se repite regularmente.
refute—refutar probar que algo es equivocado o falso (utilizando evidencia).
regurgitating—regurgitar devolver hacia fuera, atrás o hacia arriba.
reiterate—reiterar decir o hacer otra vez una cosa, o en forma repetida.
renowned—renombre aclamado y honrado universalmente; célebre, famoso.
repetition—repetición el acto o proceso de repetir.
reprimanded—reprimenda reprobar (regañar o corregir) severamente, generalmente desde una posición de autoridad.
reputation—reputación la forma en que una persona es conocida por los demás.
resolution—resolución (1) una declaración formal de opinión. (2) un tipo especial de moción principal que comienza con una explicación de porque la moción debe ser aprobada.
responsible—responsable responsabilidad y reconocimiento de las consecuencias de sus acciones.
restate—volver a exponer volver a exponer (decir) lo mismo o en otra forma.
retention—memorizar habilidad para retener (o recordar) asuntos en la mente que hacen posible el reconocer y el recordar.
rhapsodes—rapsoda trovadores itinerantes de la antigua Grecia que se reunían para leer sus obras en competencia pública.
rhetorical—retórico relativo o concerniente al arte de la oratoria o de escribir en forma efectiva. (Una *pregunta retórica* es aquella que se formula para crear un efecto y no requiere de respuesta; los *dispositivos retóricos* son tretas del lenguaje como los testimonios, las falsas comparaciones y las sugerencias de "subirse al carro de la victoria.")
rhetorical questions—preguntas retóricas interrogaciones (preguntas) que no necesitan de una respuesta oral; una pregunta formulada para causar un efecto, que no necesitan de respuesta.
rhyme—rima la repetición del sonido entre palabras o sílabas a al final de las estrofas de un verso.
rhythm—ritmo el flujo de sílabas acentuadas y no acentuadas en un poema.
rife—corriente difundido, frecuente, abundante.
rigorous—riguroso aquello que es duro, severo o estricto, escrupulosamente exacto o preciso.
round table—mesa redonda debate especial de panelistas en el cual un pequeño grupo de participantes conversa sobre un tópico de interés común sentados alrededor de una mesa o en un semi círculo.

S

sanctity—santidad la cualidad o estado de ser santo o sagrado: santidad de vida y carácter.
scanner—explorador dispositivo que permite la transferencia de una imagen computacional a un disco.
scenario—escenario secuencia de eventos, especialmente cuando son imaginarios; un relato o resumen del curso proyectado o posible de eventos o acciones.
scene/setting—escena/situación concentrar la escena descrita en un escenario imaginario frente al lector.
second affirmative rebuttal—(2AR)—segunda refutación afirmativa en un debate de políticas, este discurso resume la posición afirmativa y hace una presentación clara explicando por qué los principales puntos del debate se han tornado afirmativos.
second person—segunda persona refiérese a la persona a la cual se le habla (usted, tú).
segregation—segregación separación del resto, especialmente una separación debido a la raza, clase o grupo étnico.
self-esteem—autoestima el valor personal que uno siente por sí mismo, a menudo logrado a través del auto descubrimiento.
sender—transmisor la persona que envía un mensaje.
senile—senil anciano, de edad avanzada, especialmente cuando demuestra una pérdida de la habilidad mental a causa de la vejez.
sequential—secuencial seguir una secuencia, hacer una sucesión continua o relacionada; seguir un orden cronológico.
serendipity—buena suerte descubrir algo agradable por casualidad.
sign—signo un tipo de razonamiento inductivo en el cual uno saca conclusiones sobre una situación basado en la evidencia física.
signposting—ideas clave revisión previa de los argumentos que se van a desarrollar con posterioridad en un discurso.
simile—símil una expresión que compara dos cosas distintas utilizando las palabras "igual" o "como."
simulated—simulado creado o dado el efecto o apariencia de, falsificado.
sincerity—sinceridad la cualidad de ser honesto o genuino.
slang—jerga palabras no convencionales asociadas a ciertos grupos.
sloth—holgazanería pereza
social communication—comunicación social la comunicación que tiene lugar en la vida personal y comunitaria.
social distance—distancia social la distancia que generalmente se mantiene entre las personas en la mayoría de los intercambios sociales y comerciales (entre cuatro y

doce pies de distancia).
sound bite—"mordida de sonido" pequeños trozos de entrevistas que se transmiten por televisión y transmisiones de radio.
sounding board—"junta de resonancia" persona o grupo de personas en las cuales se prueba una idea u opinión como medio de evaluación.
sparkler—chispa información que se entrega durante el curso de una respuesta que hace que el punto tome vida. Las analogías, historias, anécdotas y citas todas ellas dan mucha chispa.
spatial pattern—patrón espacial un patrón de organización que ordena los elementos sobre la base de relaciones de espacio o de situación.
speech of acceptance—discurso de agradecimiento breve discurso dado por una persona que recibe un regalo o un premio.
speech of presentation—discurso de premiación un breve discurso para entregar un premio o un regalo a una persona.
spellbound—hechizado atrapado por o como por un hechizo; fascinado.
spontaneity—espontaneidad la cualidad o estado de ser espontáneo—hacer o producir libre y naturalmente, impulsivo, instintivo.
stack the deck—asegurar el resultado para presentar evidencia no equilibrada que solo presenta un lado de las cosas.
stage fright—miedo al público el nerviosismo que siente un orador o artista frente a una audiencia.
status quo—status quo las condiciones existentes o la forma en que están las cosas en este momento.
status report—informe de situación un informe que resume los anteriores logros de un grupo y sus metas futuras.
stereotyping—asignar estereotipos considerar a todas las personas en un grupo de acuerdo a las ideas preconcebidas de lo que ese grupo representa.
stoic—estoico no afectado por la pasión o los sentimientos, especialmente la demostración de indiferencia ante el dolor, impasible, apático.
subject—sujeto la persona que responde a las preguntas del entrevistador.
subject card—tarjeta de contenido un sistema de catalogar mediante tarjetas que están organizadas de acuerdo al contenido.
subordination—subordinación catalogar de acuerdo a la importancia.
subsidiary motion—moción auxiliar una moción para ajustar o mejorar una moción principal.
suffice—suficiente que cumple o satisface una necesidad; adecuado.
summarize—resumir que cubre los puntos principales en forma compacta sin derroche de palabras ("compendiar").
superficial—superficial de o relativo a la superficie o solamente a la apariencia, trivial.
supporting material—material de apoyo información que apoya y refuerza el encabezado de un discurso. El material de apoyo no debe confundirse con los detalles, que son más específicos.
supportive audience—audiencia sustentadora una audiencia a la cual le agrada el orador y lo que éste tiene que decir. Esta audiencia está dispuesta a apoyar y promover las ideas del orador.
suppress—suprimir restringir el curso normal de acción; evitar la expresión.
surrogacy—subrogancia el acto de tomar el lugar de otro, o la sustitución de uno por otro.
suspend—suspender parar temporalmente, mantener inactivo por un tiempo.
syllable—sílaba unidad de lenguaje hablado consistente en una sola pronunciación, división comúnmente aceptada de una palabra.
syllogism—silogismo una forma de razonamiento deductivo compuesto de dos premisas y una conclusión.
symbol—símbolo cualquier cosa que represente una idea y que se utilice en la comunicación.
sympathetic—simpatía capacidad de entender y compartir los sentimientos o intereses de un tercero, de expresar dolor por la pérdida o desgracia de otra persona.
symposium—simposio debate formal en el cual varios expertos presentan un conjunto de puntos de vista mediante discursos breves; los discursos pueden dar lugar a un debate entre los expertos y la audiencia.
synonymous—sinónimo similar en sentido y significado.
systematic—sistemático tener un método u orden regular.

T

table a motion—archivar una moción una propuesta para postergar momentáneamente una moción.
table of contents—tabla de contenido un esbozo del plan general u organización de un libro. Generalmente se encuentra al inicio del libro, es una lista de las principales secciones y capítulos del libro.
tact—tacto diplomacia en el trato con terceros.
tangible—tangible perceptible (aquello que podemos percibir a través de los sentidos) especialmente por medio del tacto.
tedious—tedioso cansador a causa de lo largo o aburrido.
tedium—tedio aburrimiento
temperament—temperamento característica o inclinación habitual (fuerza de hábito), o forma emocional de respuesta.
testimonial—testimonio el patrocinio de un mensaje por parte de una celebridad o experto.
testimonial speech—discurso testimonial un discurso de elogio o celebración en honor de una persona en vida.
theme—tema la idea central de una obra literaria.
thesis—tesis una declaración que presenta o expresa el propósito general de un discurso.
thesis statement—declaración de tesis la declaración que presenta el propósito general de un discurso.
third person—tercera persona refiérese a la persona sobre la cual se habla (él, ella, eso, ellos).
timbre—timbre tono distintivo.
title card—tarjeta de título un sistema de catalogar libros mediante el uso de tarjetas organizadas por título.

tone—tono la combinación del volumen y el timbre de la voz, pausas, ritmo y pronunciación única de una persona. Frecuentemente es un indicio seguro de los sentimientos del orador.
tone of voice—tono de voz el diapasón y timbre (tono distintivo) de la voz de una persona.
topic specific—tópico específico un discurso tiene un "tópico específico" cuando su introducción está directamente conectada al resto del discurso.
town hall meeting—reunión de alcaldía debate en que un grupo de ciudadanos se reúne en un lugar público para discutir sobre problemas de la comunidad y votar sobre posibles soluciones.
transformation—transformación el proceso, acto o instancia de cambiar la composición, estructura, configuración externa o apariencia.
transition—transición una palabra o frase en un discurso que une una parte del discurso con la siguiente.
trivia—trivialidades asuntos sin importancia.

U

ubiquitous—ubicuo existir o estar en todas partes al mismo tiempo; diseminado.
unbiased—imparcial objetivo.
uncommitted audience—audiencia no comprometida una audiencia que es neutral (o que aún no se ha decidido) hacia el tema del orador.
understatement—declaración exageradamente modesta el uso de "exageración al revés" para llamar la atención a un absurdo con el propósito de dar énfasis.
unobtrusive—discreto que no es osado o agresivo; indiscernible.

V

value—valores normas aplicadas al juicio para juzgar si algo está bien o mal.
value criteria—criterio valórico conceptos que proporcionan normas adicionales de juicio para evaluar si se ha efectuado una premisa valórica.
value premise—premisa valórica suposición que proporciona normas de juicio para evaluar si una decisión es cierta o no.
value proposition—propuesta de valores tipo de propuesta que involucra juicios filosóficos para las cuales no existen respuestas correctas o incorrectas.
verbatim—verbatim el recuento de una entrevista palabra por palabra.
vested—establecido completa e incondicionalmente garantizados (como un derecho, beneficio o privilegio). (Un interés adquirido es aquel en el cual el tenedor tiene un fuerte compromiso.)
vicariously—indirectamente compartir la experiencia de otro usando la imaginación o sentimientos de simpatía.
vision—visión la habilidad de ver más allá de lo obvio; buscar más allá y al futuro para encontrar las respuestas y posibilidades.
vocal process—proceso vocal el sistema que produce sonidos.
vocalized—muleta pausa, palabras sin significado tales como "tú sabes," "ha," y "este" utilizadas para llenar los vacíos cuando el orador no está seguro de lo que dirá a continuación.
volume—volumen el nivel de la voz del orador.
voucher—recibo (como en el caso de los recibos escolares) un formulario o cheque que indica un crédito contra futuras compras o gastos.
vulnerable—vulnerable susceptible; que tiene poca resistencia; expuesto a un ataque o a daños.

W

written communication—comunicación escrita cualquier comunicación que deber ser leída.

Y

yes-no question—pregunta sí o no una pregunta que puede ser respondida con un simple "sí" o "no" y que permite que el sujeto responda ala pregunta sin elaborar.

Z

zinger—(en un discurso) una aseveración final que constituye un poderoso recordatorio de la rectitud de su posición

Index

A

B

C

D

E

F

J

K

N

O

P

T

U

Y

Photo Credits

1 Associated Press; 2 Myrleen Cate/Index Stock; 4 Frank Siteman/Index Stock; 6 Ken Weingart/Index Stock; 7 © PhotoDisc; 8 © Wally McNamee/CORBIS; 9 Randy Taylor/Index Stock; 10 (top) CORBIS; (center) Paul Seligman/Sygma; (bottom) Gary Hershom, CORBIS/Reuters Newsmedia Inc.; 11 Peter Beck/The Stock Market; 12 (left) CORBIS/Lynn Goldsmith; (right) AP Photo/Charles Bennett; 13 Gary Bogdon/Sygma; 14 © Bettmann/CORBIS; 15 © Ted Spiegel/CORBIS; 16 (top) Zephyr Pictures/Index Stock; (bottom) Zefa-Motions Emotions/Index Stock; 17 (top) Stewart Cohen/Index Stock; (bottom) CORBIS/AFP; 18 Keith Meyers/CORBIS; 24 PhotoDisc; 26 AP Photo/Soile Kallio, Lehtikuva; 27 AP Photo/Kevork Djansezian; 28 AP Photo/Lauren McFalls; 29 CORBIS/Hulton-Deutsch Collection; 30 © Gianni Dagli Orti/CORBIS; 31 (left) Novastock/Index Stock; (right) AP Photo/Emile Wamsteker; 33 (top) © Don Milici; (bottom) © Wally McNamee/CORBIS; 34 Stan Felleman/Index Stock; 35 (left) Rudi Von Briel/Index Stock; (right) Bruce McAllister/Index Stock; 36 © Bettmann/CORBIS; 37 Eric Sanford/Index Stock; 38 AP Photo/Bob Child; 39 (left) © Don Milici; (right) AP Photo/CBS, Alan Singer; 41 David Davis/Index Stock; 42 Barry Winiker/Index Stock; 43 (top) © Bettmann/ CORBIS; (bottom) Mug Shots/The Stock Market; 44 © Bettmann/CORBIS; 50 © Tony Stone Images; 52 © 1998–99 Tony Stone Images; 54 Craig Witkowski/Index Stock; 57 (left) Chuck Savage/The Stock Market; (right) © Bettmann/CORBIS; 59 © PhotoDisc; 61 CORBIS/Kevin Fleming; 62 CORBIS/Owen Franken; 64 (top) Peggy Koyle/Index Stock; (bottom) © PhotoDisc; 65 Barbara Haynor/Index Stock; 66 Stewart Cohen/Index Stock; 67 © PhotoDisc; 68 © Bettmann/CORBIS; 69 Jon Riley, © 1998–99 Tony Stone Images; 70 SW Productions/Index Stock; 72 Kindra Clineff/Index Stock; 76 Mitch Diamond/Index Stock; 78 © 1998 Tony Stone Images; 79 Jeff Greenberg/Index Stock; 80 © PhotoDisc; 82 AP Photo/Eric Draper; 85 © Don Milici; 86 © PhotoDisc; 87 José L. Pelaez/The Stock Market; 88 SW Productions/Index Stock; 89 (left) Daniel Fort/Index Stock; (right, all 3) Index Stock; 90 © Moshe Shai/CORBIS; 91 (top) Leland Bobbe, © 1998–99 Tony Stone Images; (bottom, first) © Don Milici; (bottom, second) Jeff Greenberg/Index Stock; (bottom, third) Myrleen Cate/Index Stock; (bottom fourth) © Kashi; 92 © PhotoDisc; 93 Zefa-Motions Emotions/Index Stock; 94 Index Stock; 98 Zephyr Pictures/Index Stock; 100 Stock Solution/Index Stock; 101 (top) Jeff Greenberg/Index Stock; (bottom) Bettmann/CORBIS; 102 Mauritius/Index Stock; 103 (left) Greg Smith/Index Stock; (right) AP Photo/Richard Drew; 105 Index Stock; 107 Stewart Cohen, © Tony Stone Images; 108 (left) Paul Barton/The Stock Market; (right) Bob Winsett/Index Stock; 109 Stewart Cohen/Index Stock; 111 Gary Conner/Index Stock; 112 (top) Omni Photo Communications, Inc./Index Stock; (bottom) SW Productions/Index Stock; 113 David Young-Wolff, ©Tony Stone Images; 120 John Coletti/Index Stock; 122 AP Photo/Ray Amati; 123 Robert E. Daemmrich, © 1998–99 Tony Stone Images; 124 AP Photo/Chris Gardner; 125 CORBIS/Neal Preston; 126 AP Photo/Danny Feld; 127 © PhotoEdit; 128 AP Photo/Virginia Sherwood; 130 (left) José Pelaez/The Stock Market; (lower left) Index Stock; (right) Karl Neumann/Index Stock; 131 Ian Shaw, © 1998–99 Tony Stone Images; 132 Associated Press; 134 (top) Matthew Borkoski/Index Stock; (bottom) © Neal Preston/CORBIS; 135 AP Photo/Marion Curtis; 136 Associated Press; 137 Associated Press; 138 AP Photo/Charles Bennett; 139 © Don Milici; 140 © PhotoDisc; 141 CMCD, © 1997–99 PhotoDisc, Inc.; 142 George White, Jr./Index Stock; 143 (top) Bob Winsett/Index Stock; (bottom) Derek Cole/Index Stock; 144 © 1997–99 PhotoDisc, Inc.; 146 © 1997–99 PhotoDisc, Inc.; 150 Robert E. Daemmrich, © 1998–99, Tony Stone Images; 152 © Paul Barton/The Stock Market; 154 AP Photo/Ed Betz; 155 Associated Press; 156 Raeanne Rubenstein/Index Stock; 157 AP Photo/John Gillis; 158 David Young-Wolff, © Tony Stone Images; 160 (top) © Don Milici; (bottom) Culver Pictures; 161 Walter Hodges, © Tony Stone Images; 162 Stewart Cohen, © Tony Stone Images; 163 Chip Henderson/Index Stock; 164 Tom & Dee Ann McCarthy/The Stock Market; 166 © Kashi; 168 Brian Bailey, © 2000 Tony Stone Images; 169 PhotoDisc; 170 Mark Harmel, © 2000 Tony Stone Images; 171 (left) Stewart Cohen/Index Stock; 172 Scott Witte/Index Stock; 178 © 2000 Tony Stone Images; 180 Chip Henderson/Index Stock; 182 Jim McGuire/Index Stock; 183 © Don Milici; 184 AP Photo/Michael Okoniewski; 185 Bill Bachmann/Index Stock; 186 Seth Resnick/Index Stock; 187 (left) Ron Keller/Index Stock; (right) Bill Lai/Index Stock; 188 © Don Milici; 191 Jeff Greenberg/Index Stock; 192 Tom McCarthy/Index Stock; 196 Stewart Cohen/Index Stock; 197 Arnie Sachs/Sygma; 198 Jeff Greenberg/Index Stock; 199 Jean-Francois Podevin/Index Stock; 204 Tom McCarthy/Index Stock; 206 John Riley, © 1998–99 Tony Stone Images; 207 PhotoEdit; 208 CORBIS; 209 AP Photo; 210 Tom & Dee Ann McCarthy/Index Stock; 211 Bob Winsett/Index Stock; 212 (top) © Kelly-Mooney Photography/CORBIS; 213 (left) Rob Bartee/Index Stock; (right) © John Henley/The Stock Market; 214 Charlie Borland/Index Stock; 215 Associated Press AP; 216 OB Productions/The Stock Market; 217 (left) Jim Schwabel/Index Stock; (right) Chuck Carlton/Index Stock; 219 AP Photo; 220 © PhotoDisc; 223 Bettmann/CORBIS; 224 (top) © PhotoDisc; (bottom left) © Joseph Sohm, ChromoSohm, Inc./CORBIS; (bottom right) José Luis Pelaez, Inc./The Stock Market; 226 © Bettmann/CORBIS; 228 Roy Morsch/The Stock Market; 234 Mug Shots/The Stock Market; 236 Zefa-Taste of Europe/Index Stock; 237 (top) AP Photo; (bottom) © PhotoDisc; 238 © Historical Picture Archive/CORBIS; 239 (top) © Bettmann/CORBIS; (bottom) Daniel Fort/Index Stock; 240 (top) © CORBIS; (bottom) © Peter Turnley/CORBIS; 241 © Jacques M. Chenet/CORBIS; 242 Ernest Manewal/Index Stock; 244 (top) Jean-Francois Podevin/Index Stock; (bottom) CORBIS; 245 © Bettmann/CORBIS; 246 Ed Elberfeld/Index Stock; 247 AP Photo; 248 José Pelaez/The Stock Market; 249 © Bettmann/CORBIS; 254 James Darell, © 1998–99 Tony Stone Images; 256 © Bettmann/CORBIS; 257 (top) Aneal Vohra/Index Stock; (bottom) Mike Agliolo/Index Stock; 258 Bill Lai/Index Stock; 259 (top) Canstock Images, Inc./Index Stock; (bottom) MarkGibson/Index Stock; 260 © CORBIS; 262 (left) © Roger Ressmeyer/CORBIS; (right) © Bettmann/CORBIS; 263 (left) Zephyr Pictures/Index Stock; (right) Kevin Fleming/CORBIS; 265 The Stock Market; 267 (top) Frank Primelife/Index Stock; (bottom) AP Photo; 268 Peter Beck/The Stock Market; 269 CORBIS; 270 © CORBIS; 271 Mark Segal/Index Stock; 273 (top) © Bettmann/CORBIS; (bottom) © PhotoDisc; 274 (top) AP Photo; (bottom) CORBIS/Bettmann; 276 (top) IT Stock Int'l./Index Stock; (bottom) John Madere/The Stock Market; 277 Michael Powers/Index Stock; 278 CORBIS/ Bettmann; 284 Doug Menuez/PhotoDisc; 286 © Lynn Goldsmith/CORBIS; 287 (top) © PhotoDisc; (bottom) Patricia Barry Levy/Index Stock; 288 AP Photo; 289 (top) Grantpix/Index Stock; (bottom) Don Milici; 290 Doug Menuez/PhotoDisc; 291 © Dennis Degnan/CORBIS; 293 (top) © Flip Schulke/CORBIS; (bottom) art © Randy Miyake; 294 © CORBIS; 295 Aneal Vohra/Index Stock; 296 © Francesco Venturi, Kea Publishing Services Ltd./CORBIS; 297 CORBIS/Bettmann; 298 Dave Ryan/Index Stock; 300 (top) © PhotoDisc; (bottom, all) © Don Milici; 301 (top) © Reuters Newsmedia Inc./CORBIS; (bottom) © PhotoDisc; 302 © Don Milici; 303 (top) SW Productions, Inc./Index Stock; (bottom) © Ted Streshinsky/CORBIS; 304 AP Photo; 305 (left) Mauritius/Index Stock; (right, all) © Don Milici; 306 Zefa-Taste of Europe/Index Stock; 307 Todd Powell/Index Stock; 308 (left) SW Productions, Inc./Index Stock; (right) Benelux Press/Index Stock; 310 (top) Mark Downey/Index Stock; (bottom) Mauritius/Index Stock; 311 Rob Gracie/Index Stock; 318 © 2000 Tony Stone Images; 320 ©

PhotoDisc; **322** CORBIS; **323** © Oscar White/CORBIS; **324** (top) Don Hutchings/PhotoEdit; (bottom) © Bettmann/CORBIS; **325** Ed Honowitz, © 1998–99 Tony Stone Images; **327** (left) CORBIS; (top right) CORBIS; (bottom right) CORBIS; **328** Omni Photo Communications, Inc./Index Stock; **330** (top) CORBIS; (bottom) © Seth Joel/CORBIS; **331** Richard Shock/Index Stock; **332** (top) CORBIS; **334** © Bettmann/CORBIS; **335** AP Photo/Jerome Delay; **336** CORBIS; **337** CORBIS; **340** CORBIS; **342** CORBIS; **343** AP Photo/Dawn Villella; **344** CORBIS; **345** Fisher/Thatcher, 1998–99 Tony Stone Images; **347** Bill Bachmann/Index Stock; **354** © PhotoDisc; **356** Jon Riley, © 2000 Tony Stone Images; **357** Myrleen Cate/Index Stock; **358** CORBIS; **359** AP Photo/Bill Janscha; **360** (left) Omni Photo Communications, Inc./Index Stock; (right) Alan Klehr, ©1998–99 Tony Stone Images; **361** Steven Begleiter/Index Stock; **364** Mauritius/Index Stock; **365** Firefly Productions/The Stock Market; **366** Bill Lai/Index Stock; **367** (left) Chris Minerva/Index Stock; (right, all) © Don Milici; **368** (top) © Bettmann/CORBIS; (center) Ryan McVay © PhotoDisc; (bottom) Sheryl Maree Reily, © 2000 Tony Stone Images; **369** AP Photo/Joe Marquette; **370** (left) Andy Sacks, © 1998–99 Tony Stone Images; (right) © Bettmann/CORBIS; **371** David Young-Wolff, © 1998–99 Tony Stone Images; **372** © Bettmann/CORBIS; **380** Stewart Cohen/Index Stock; **382** Associated Press/Twentieth Century Fox; **383** AP Photo/Stuart Ramson; **389** © Lawrence Manning/CORBIS; **390** Loren Santow, © 1998–99 Tony Stone Images; **391** © Kelly-Mooney Photography/CORBIS; **392** © CORBIS; **393** Joe Lange/Index Stock; **400** AP Photo/Victoria Arocho; **402** CORBIS/Bettmann; **403** Bob Jacobson/Index Stock; **404** Will & Deni McIntyre, © 1998–99 Tony Stone Images; **405** © Gianni Dagli Orti/CORBIS; **406** CORBIS/Bettmann; **407** (top left) Culver Pictures; (top center) Tony Karody/Sygma; (top right) Culver Pictures; (bottom left) AP Photo; (bottom center) Culver Pictures; (bottom right) AP Photo; **408** (top) AP Photo; (bottom) CORBIS/Hulton-Deutsch Collection; **409** AP Photo/Al Goldis; **410** AP Photo/Hyperion Books for Children, Dwight Carter; **411** (top) Ewing Galloway/Index Stock; (bottom) Vince Bucci, CORBIS/AFP; **412** IT Stock Int'l./Index Stock; **413** Bill Lai/Index Stock; **415** Zefa-Motions Emotions/Index Stock; **416** Jim McGuire/Index Stock; **417** (top) © George Kleiman/CORBIS; (bottom) © Don Milici; **418** Greg Smith/Index Stock; **419** (top) Jim McGuire/Index Stock; (bottom) © PhotoEdit; **420** AP Photo/Michael Caulfield; **421** AP Photo/Rich Pedroncelli; **428** AP Photo/South Bend Tribune, Jim Rider; **430** (left) CORBIS; (right) Terry Wild Studio; **431** AP Photo/NBC Saturday Night Live, Mayella Matthews; **432** (top) AP Photo/United Media, Jeanne Schulz; (bottom) AP Photo; **433** AP Photo; **434** AP Photo/Kevork Djansezian; **435** AP Photo/Ian Stewart; **436** Fisher/Thatcher, © 2000 Tony Stone Images; **438** AP Photo/Michael Okoniewski; **439** © CORBIS; **440** AP Photo/Comedy Central, Al Levine; **441** AP Photo/Pat Sullivan; **442** (top) AP Photo/Ron Heflin; (bottom) Kindra Clineff/Index Stock; **444** © Don Milici; **445** © PhotoDisc; **446** Frank Siteman, © 1998–99 Tony Stone Images; **452** © 2000 Tony Stone Images; **454** © PhotoDisc; **456** (left) Culver Pictures, Inc.; (right) CORBIS/Bettmann; **457** The Stock Market; **459** Tony Stone Images; **460** Bill Melton/Index Stock; **461** © PhotoDisc; **462** (top) Truitt Photographics/Index Stock; (bottom) Skjold; **463** (top) SW Productions, Inc./Index Stock; (bottom) Omni Photo Communications, Inc./Index Stock; **464** Chris Lowe/Index Stock; **465** Dan Peha/Index Stock; **466** © Index Stock; **467** PhotoEdit; **469** (top) Richard Harris/Index Stock; (bottom) AP Photo; **470** Denni MacDonald/PhotoEdit; **471** Image Ideas/Index Stock; **472** Omni Photo Communications, Inc./Index Stock; **473** Tom McCarthy/Index Stock; **474** Chip Henderson/Index Stock; **475** Stewart Cohen/Index Stock; **480** © Digital Stock; **482** Bettmann Archive; **485** Sygma; **486** AP Photo, Steven Adams; **488** AP Photo, Mark Wilson; **489** AP Photo, Jon Adams; **491** AP Photo, Chris Putman; **492** AP Photo, Dale Atkins; **496** AP Photo, Jim Mone; **498** Arroyo Grande High School; **499** AP Photo, Brian Diggs; **500** © PhotoDisc; **502** © PhotoDisc; **508** © Tony Stone Images; **510** Stewart Cohen/Index Stock; **511** (left) Philip de Bay, CORBIS/Historical Picture Archive; (right) CORBIS/Hulton-Deutsch Collection; **512** (top) AP Photo; (bottom) © Robert Maass/CORBIS; **514** © CORBIS; **515** AP Photo; **516** AP Photo; **517** © PhotoDisc; **518** © CORBIS; **519** Chip Henderson/Index Stock; **520** © Philip Gould/CORBIS; **521** © PhotoDisc; **522** © Bob Krist/CORBIS; **525** AP Photo; **526** Bruce Ayres, © 2000 Tony Stone Images; **528** SW Productions/Index Stock; **530** © Laura Dwight/CORBIS; **531** CORBIS; **536** © Digital Stock; **538** Peter Cade, © 2000 Tony Stone Images; **540** CORBIS/Archivo Iconografico, S.A.; **541** John Olson/The Stock Market; **542** (top) John Boykin/Index Stock; (bottom) CORBIS/Mitchell Gerber; **543** (top left) AP Photo/David Guttenfelder; (top center) AP Photo/Peter Cosgrove; (top right) AP Photo/Alan Greth; (bottom left) AP Photo/Louisa Buller; (bottom center) AP Photo/Jim Cole; (bottom right) AP Photo/File; **544** (top) Tom & Dee Ann McCarthy/The Stock Market; (bottom) Gary Conner/Index Stock; **545** SW Productions/Index Stock; **546** (top) © CORBIS, Original image courtesy of NASA/CORBIS; (bottom) © CORBIS; **547** (top left) © Bettmann/CORBIS; (top center) © Bettmann/CORBIS; (top right) © Bettmann/CORBIS; (bottom) CORBIS; **549** (top left) © Carl Corey/CORBIS; (top right) SW Productions/Index Stock; (bottom) Barbara Haynor/Index Stock; **550** (top) John Dominis/Index Stock; (bottom) Mark Gibson/Index Stock; **551** AP Photo/Chris O'Meara; **552** AP Photo/Michael Okoniewski; **553** CORBIS/Bettmann; **554** © CORBIS; **555** Craig Witkowski/Index Stock; **556** AP Photo, Vin Catania; **558** AP Photo/Ed Andrieski